LETTERS

OPENING

O Ind	Indirectness needed
O Dir	Directness needed
O Qual	Quality needs improvement

COVERAGE

C Inc	Incomplete
C Ex	Excessive information
C Exp	Explanation weak
C Id	Identification incomplete

ENDING

E AC	Action needed
E AC S	Action too strong
E AC W	Action too weak
E IT	Individually tailored for the situation
E OS	Off-subject close needed

TECHNIQUE

Adp	Adapt to the reader
Awk	Awkward writing
Bky	Bulky paragraphing
Chop	Choppy sentences
Dl	Dull writing
Emp +	Too much emphasis
Emp −	Too little emphasis
Intp	More interpretation needed
Los	Loose writing
Ord	Order of presentation weak
RS	Rubber stamp expression
Trans	Transition weak

EFFECT

Conv	Not convincing
GW	More goodwill needed
Hur	Hurried treatment
Log	Logical?
Neg	Negative effect
Pers +	Too persuasive
Pers −	Not persuasive enough
Ton	Improve tone of words
YVP	More you-viewpoint needed

REPORTS

TITLE

T 1	Incomplete
T 2	Too long

LETTER OF TRANSMITTAL

LT 1	Opening directness needed
LT 2	Content inadequate
LT 3	Findings not needed
LT 4	Expression of attitude needed
LT 5	Friendlier, more conversational style needed

SYNOPSIS

S 1	Direct beginning assigned
S 2	Indirect beginning assigned
S 3	Coverage is (a) scant or (b) too detailed
S 4	Make more interesting

ORGANIZATION

O 1	Plan not the best
O 2	Illogical order
O 3	Overlapping parts
O 4	More subparts needed
O 5	This subpart does not fit here
O 6	These parts not equal in importance
O 7	Improve talking quality of captions
O 8	Captions not grammatically parallel
O 9	Captions too long
0 10	Monotonous repetition of words

INTRODUCTION

I 1	Inadequate content
I 2	Content is (a) scant or (b) too long
I 3	Vital information omitted
I 4	Findings not needed here

COVERAGE

C 1	(a) Scant or (b) too detailed
C 2	Scant analysis
C 3	Too dependent on graphic aids
C 4	Relate to report goal
C 5	Distinguish fact from opinion
C 6	More factual support needed

WRITING

W 1	More reader adaptation needed
W 2	Overuse of passive voice
W 3	More conciseness needed
W 4	Consistent impersonal style appropriate here
W 5	More personal style needed
W 6	Abrupt shift. Use transitional (a) paragraph or (b) words and sentences
W 7	Questionable paragraphing

GRAPHIC AIDS

GA 1	(a) Not enough or (b) too many
GA 2	(a) Too large or (b) too small
GA 3	Not appropriate
GA 4	Placement could be improved
GA 5	Not best appearance
GA 6	Refer to the graphic aid
GA 7	Make references incidental

LAYOUT AND MECHANICS

LM 1	Too (a) fat, (b) skinny, or (c) unbalanced
LM 2	Neat?
LM 3	Rough margins
LM 4	Improve spacing. (a) Too much, (b) too little
LM 5	Illogical page numbering
LM 6	Page appears (a) choppy or (b) heavy
LM 7	Illogical selection of caption type or position
LM 8	Questionable form

Business
communication
Theory
and application

1984   FIFTH EDITION

Business communication Theory and application

Raymond V. Lesikar, Ph.D.
NORTH TEXAS STATE UNIVERSITY

RICHARD D. IRWIN, INC.
Homewood, Illinois 60430

ISBN 0-256-03157-6

Library of Congress Catalog Card No. 83–81771

Printed in the United States of America

2 3 4 5 6 7 8 9 0 1 0 K 9 8 7 6 5

Preface

Because the previous editions were so well received, this Fifth Edition of *Business Communication: Theory and Application* remains substantially in its original mold. As you would expect, however, I made some content changes. Some of these changes were dictated by movements in the field. Some were mere matters of updating. And some were other changes that I felt would improve the book.

Following the practice set in earlier revisions, I worked again to expand the applications of communication theory to everyday business communication situations. I updated the book throughout, especially by bringing in such topics as computers, word processing, and international communication. Because the area of job applications is undergoing change, I revised this part by including current approaches and style preferences.

As in earlier editions, I prepared new problems throughout—both for letters and reports. They remain the realistic and challenging business cases which I feel are best for applying and emphasizing the textbook principles. Also, I added more examples—especially in the chapters on letters.

The basic plan of the book remains unchanged. It is first to summarize communication theory and then to relate theory to applications in business. This approach is defensible. In fact, research conducted by Maxine Hart of Baylor University supports it.[1] Also, this approach answers much of the criticism the business communication field has received over the years.

The coverage of communication theory is selective. It must be so for reasons of space economy. I have chosen those topics which seem to me most helpful to the student in developing an understanding of organizational communication. As you will see, I have relied heavily on the contributions of general semantics. Very clearly, this subject matter provides a base for understanding the problems and principles of communicating in business.

Perhaps some will feel that I have oversimplified the theory material.

---

[1] Maxine Hart, "An Experimental Study in Teaching Business Communication Using Two Different Approaches: Theory and Application vs. Writing Approach," *The Journal of Business Communication* 17, no. 1 (Fall 1979), pp. 13–25.

Certainly it could have been covered in greater depth and with much greater sophistication. My goal, however, was to overcome the communication barriers which a discussion of "theory" typically raises in the student's mind. Such barriers can be overcome only by clear, simplified explanation. I am confident that I have succeeded in this endeavor.

My coverage of the traditional business communication areas of correspondence, report writing, and oral communication builds from the theory presented. At the appropriate places, the theory is related to application. Because the theory applies to almost every instruction given, the more obvious relations are left to the student. To do otherwise would have a cluttering effect and would be highly repetitious. It was my hope to cover the application areas with sufficient thoroughness to permit the option of building a course primarily around this material and of using the theory parts as supplementary reading.

As in all such works as this, I am indebted to many people for their assistance. Foremost, I am indebted to those scholars who have contributed over the years to the general knowledge in the fields from which I have drawn my information. I must especially acknowledge the contributions of my dear friend and former teacher and colleague, William P. Boyd, now Professor Emeritus at The University of Texas at Austin. The effects of his teachings are liberally scattered throughout this book. Those others from whom I have borrowed directly are acknowledged at specific spots of reference in the book.

As this edition retains inputs made by others in past editions, the contributors from the past continue to deserve recognition. Standing out among these people are Jim Stull, San Jose State University; Berle Haggleblade, California State University; James L. Godell, Northern Michigan University; and John D. Pettit, North Texas State University. I would also like to thank all those who contributed through suggestions made informally at conference meetings. In addition, a very special acknowledgment goes to Douglas Shepard, State University of New York, for his excellent assistance as editor-proofreader. All credit for the improved accuracy of this edition goes to him.

Finally, and most importantly, I acknowledge the contributions of my dear wife. Her patience, love, and understanding through countless hours of my work on writing projects deserve very special recognition.

RAYMOND V. LESIKAR

Contents

Effects of words. Examples of word choice. Overall tone of courtesy: *Singling out your reader. Refraining from preaching. Doing more than is expected. Avoiding anger. Showing sincerity.* Technique of emphasis: *Emphasis by position. Space and emphasis. Mechanical means of emphasis.* Coherence in the letter: *Tie-in sentences. Use of pronouns. Transitional words. A word of caution.* International correspondence: *Effects of culture. Two basic questions.* An approach to letter problems: *Determination of primary objective. Selection of direct or indirect plan. Choice in the middle ground. The plans illustrated.* The structure of the letter: *Selection of the words.* A concluding and forward look.

The routine inquiry: *A question beginning. Adequate explanation. Structured questions. Goodwill in the ending. Routine inquiries illustrated.* Inquiries about people: *Privileged communication. Question content. Examples of personnel inquiries.* Favorable responses: *Situation identification. Good-news beginnings. Construction of answers. Handling negatives. Consideration of "extras." Cordiality in the close. Favorable replies illustrated.* Routine acknowledgments: *Acknowledgment in the beginning. Goodwill talk and resale. A friendly, forward look. Routine acknowledgments illustrated.* Personnel evaluation reports: *Directness in the opening. Systematic presentation of facts. The problem of fair reporting. Natural friendliness in the close. Case examples.* Claim letters: *Directness in spite of negativeness. Need for identifying facts. Forthright statement of what is wrong. Explanation of facts. Choice in handling the error. Doubt-removing friendliness in the close. Claim letters illustrated.* Adjustment grant: *Need to overcome negative impressions. Direct presentation of decision. Avoidance of negatives. Regaining lost confidence. Happiness in the close. Three case illustrations.* Order letters: *Clear and forthright authorization. Specific coverage of the sale. A cordial close. An order illustrated.*

Letter problems—1

Routine inquiries. Favorable replies. Inquiries, prospective employees. Personnel reports. Claims. Adjustment grants. Orders.

Refused request: *Strategy development. Opening contact and setup of the plan. Presentation of the reasoning. Positive handling of the refusal. Off-subject goodwill close. Cases in refusal strategy.* Adjustment refusals: *Determination of basic strategy. Opening setup of the reasoning. Presentation of reasoning. Positive coverage of refusal. Off-subject closing talk. Adjustment refusals illustrated.* Vague and back orders: *Consideration in handling. Variations in opening possibilities. Tact in handling the delayed shipment. A pleasant ending picture. Illustrated handling of delayed order.* Credit refusals: *Strategy and the reason for refusal. The buffer beginning. Justification of the refusal. Tact in the refusal. A closing forward look. Cases in review.*

Appendixes

one

Communication theory

The role of communication in the business organization

IF YOU ARE like most of us, you spend more time communicating than doing anything else. Probably you spend a large part of each day talking and listening. And when you are not talking or listening you are likely to be communicating in other ways—reading, writing, gesturing, drawing. Or perhaps you are just taking in information by seeing, or feeling, or smelling. All of these activities are forms of communication; and certainly you do them throughout most of your conscious moments.

Something we do so much must be important. Probably it is the most important of all our activities. It is easy to see that communication is the activity which has enabled us to develop the civilized society we know today. It is one activity which we human beings clearly do better than the other forms of life on earth; and largely it explains our dominant role. It is the activity which has enabled us to organize—to work in groups. And through organization we have been able to overcome barriers to our existence which individually we would not have been able to overcome. But there is no need to discuss further how communication contributed to the development of us human beings. Its role is obvious to us all. We need only to conclude that communication is extremely vital to our success and well-being in civilized society.

An essential to organized activity

Just as communication is vital to our existence in civilized society, it is vital to the functioning of the organizations[1] which our society has produced. In fact, we could go so far as to say that organizations exist through communication; without communication, there would be no organizations. As Herbert

---

[1] Throughout this work the term *organization* is used to refer to any goal-oriented group of people, such as businesses, churches, labor unions, and government agencies. Because business organizations are of primary concern to us, however, most of the illustrative material used pertains to them.

Simon expressed it, ". . . without communication there can be no organization, for there is no possibility then of the group influencing the behavior of the individual."[2]

If you need proof of the importance of communication to organized activity, you need only apply your good logic to any real-life example. Take, for example, a very simple organization. It is made up of just you and one other person. Assume that this organization has an objective—one that is unfamiliar to each of you. You may even assume that both of you know what this objective is. Now, assume that both of you no longer can communicate. You cannot read; you cannot speak; you cannot write; you cannot gesture; you cannot draw. If the two of you make any progress at all, it is likely to be by individual effort. Strain your imagination as you will, there is simply no likelihood of coordinated effort resulting without communication.

Without question, communication is the ingredient which makes organization possible. It is the vehicle through which the basic management functions are carried out. Managers direct through communication; they coordinate through communication; and they staff, plan, and control through communication. Hardly an action is taken in any organization without communication leading to it.

The high frequency of communication

Just how much communicating a business organization needs depends on a number of factors. The nature of the business certainly is one. Some (such as insurance companies) have much greater need to communicate than do others (such as janitorial services). The organization plan of the company also affects the volume of communication, for much of the information flow is provided by the structure. Also, the people who make up the organization affect the volume of communication. As we shall point out later, every human being is different. Each has different communication needs and abilities. Thus, varying combinations of people will produce varying needs for communication.

Although the communication needs vary by company, people in organizations communicate more than most of us suspect. According to one generally accepted estimate, between 40 and 60 percent of the work time spent in a typical manufacturing plant involves some phase of communication. Of course, these percentages are only averages. Some employees spend much more of their time communicating. In fact, the higher up the organization structure the employee is, the more communicating he or she is likely to do. Typically, top executives spend from 75 to 95 percent of their time communicating. Unskilled laborers, on the other hand, need to communicate little to do their work.

Without question, communication is important to the business organization. Because it is important, it stands to reason that business wants its communication to be well done. But all too rarely is business satisfied with what it gets. Unfortunately, to use the often quoted words of an authority

[2] Herbert Simon, *Administrative Behavior*, 3d ed., Free Press, New York, 1976, p. 154.

in the field, "Of all the things business executives do, they are worst at communicating."

Communication illustrated: Dan's half hour

The role of communication in organized activities is perhaps best explained by illustration of a real situation. By design, our illustration is both detailed and scant. It is detailed because it is made up of illustrations of the minute and specific communication events which occur in business. It is scant because at best it covers only a sample of the almost infinite number of events.

For this review we could select any organization, as communication is vital to every conceivable type. Our choice is the Typical Company, manufacturer of a line of quality whatsits. The Typical Company is moderately large, with scores of departments and hundreds of workers doing a thousand and one tasks. It employs crews of salespeople who sell the manufactured whatsits to wholesalers all over the country. Like most companies in its field, Typical works to help move its products from wholesaler to retailer and from retailer to the final consumer. And it works to keep the consumer happy with the purchase. The Typical Company is indeed typical.

Our review begins with the workday of Dan D. Worker, a clerk in Typical's order department. (We could, of course, have selected any of Typical's employees.) Dan's communication activities begin each day the moment he awakens. But for our purposes we shall pick up Dan's activities as he rides to work in a car pool with three of his co-workers. Of course, Dan and the members of his car pool communicate as they travel. Obviously, communication has a social use, and riding to work is a form of social occasion for Dan and his friends.

Most of their talk is about trivial matters. They talk primarily to entertain and to while away the time. There is a joke or two, some comments about politics, a few words about a coming football game, and some raves about the new woman at the company switchboard. Such talk, of course, is of little direct concern to Typical except perhaps as the talk affects the general happiness and welfare of the company's workers.

In time, the conversation drifts to subjects more pertinent to Typical and its operations. Someone mentions a rumor about a proposed change in promotion policy. Then Dan and the others bring in their own collection of rumors, facts, and opinions on the subject. And in the process they form opinions and work up emotions concerning the Company and its policies. This communication activity has little to do with manufacturing whatsits, nor is it related to Dan's duties at Typical. But it has affected Dan's outlook, and he just might not put out very much work for Typical today or any other day. He might not trust Typical quite so much the next time the union contract problem comes up.

When the four reach the plant, the gate guard receives the message communicated by the green sticker on the windshield and waves the car through. They drive past the most convenient parking spaces, for they receive clearly the message on signs at these sites: "Reserved for the President,"

"Reserved for the Sales Manager," "Reserved for the Production Superinten-dent," and so on. As Dan enters his work area, he files past the time clock, punches his card, and thereby communicates to the payroll department a record of his attendance.

As Dan enters his work area, he engages in more social communication. He exchanges "good mornings" with each of his colleagues, and he makes small talk with two of them as they wait for the Company whistle to communi-cate the message that it is time for work to commence. Although this small talk with associates has little to do with manufacturing whatsits, it helps to create a happy and friendly attitude among Dan and his co-workers. And such an attitude can be conducive to productivity.

When the 9 o'clock whistle blows, Dan begins his work as order clerk. The morning mail, already delivered to his desk, produces first an order from one of Typical's salespeople in the field. Using the computer terminal at his work station, Dan enters the pertinent information: quantities, types, salesperson credited, sales district, purchaser identification, and such. As a part of the Company's data base, this information will become a part of a number of reports programmed to serve the information needs of Typical's employees. Shipping department workers will get the information they need to fill the order. Sales managers will receive summary reports of the activities of their salespeople. Production planners will receive the inventory and prod-uct demand information they need to work out production schedules. And the top executives will get the overall activity reports which give them the performance information they need in guiding Typical's course.

Among those in the shipping department who will receive the order information is Geraldine Peevy, the department secretary. One of Ms. Peevy's duties is to send the shipping details to the customers in specially adapted acknowledgment letters. The Typical Company uses a specially adapted letter rather than a routine form acknowledgment because the firm recognizes the goodwill-building effect of making every communication contact as favora-ble as possible. Obviously, individually composed letters are expensive; so Ms. Peevy cheats a little by selecting from a half dozen basic form letters stored in the memory of her word processor. Of course, the word processor will reproduce the letter and adapt it to the one customer.

Contents of the next envelope Dan opens are not so positive as the first. This one is a note from a Typical salesperson in the field who reports on a difficulty a customer is having with a whatsit. Using his computer terminal, Dan enters the pertinent facts (model number, defect, age, and such) into the Company's data base. There it will become a part of summary reports which may be useful to production control and product design. Then Dan forwards this message through interplant mail to the customer services department. Here Typical's individualized attention will be given to the problem, for Typical knows that it is good business to keep its customers satisfied. Probably someone in customer services will communicate with some of Typical's technical personnel in an effort to find the cause of the difficulty. Then they will pass on their findings to the salesperson in the field, who will personally visit the customer to report the information.

Occasionally, such problems cannot be so easily solved. When a whatsit is defective, for example, customer services will make a fair and speedy adjustment. Or if the defect occurs frequently enough, a full-scale investigation may result. Possibly one or more of the Company's technical specialists will be assigned to the problem, and they will spend days or weeks or even longer periods searching for the answer to the problem. When they find the answer, they will communicate this information through some form of written report.

As Dan opens the third envelope, he recognizes the familiar off-color brown of employee relations stationery. Inside he finds a printed memorandum with an instruction sheet attached. This memorandum, signed by the president, explains the new promotion plan Dan and his friends discussed on the way to work. The instructions tell Dan to post the memorandum on the department bulletin board. As Dan posts the memorandum, he reads the Company's explanation. There is much in it that he had not considered before, and some of the "facts" his friends used in their arguments are strongly refuted. Dan is now somewhat confused, but he begins to feel that the Company may have a point or two.

On the way back to his desk, Dan passes the office of Mary Kapel. Last week, Mary was promoted to chief order clerk—a job Dan had wanted. Dan observes Mary sitting at her large double-pedestal desk (Dan's desk has one pedestal). He sees Mary's name printed on the door, and he observes the carpeting on the floor. These objects clearly communicate to Dan a message of Mary's success. Mary is busily working and does not see Dan go by. "That stupid, puzzled look on her face shows she doesn't know what she's doing," Dan thinks. "She sits at her desk so high and mighty." Mary certainly communicates a lot to Dan, and without saying a word.

Dan passes the water cooler where James Hooker and another worker are standing. Dan does not care much for Hooker. In fact, he has had a few run-ins with the man since Hooker joined Typical three weeks ago. Dan cannot explain exactly what went wrong. At the beginning Hooker appeared to be a pleasant enough chap. He and Dan had lunch together that first day. But soon after that time Hooker started to find fault with some of the work procedures in the department. He even pointed out some things that Dan could do "to improve operations." As Dan saw it, there was little a neophyte like Hooker could tell a man who had been on the job for almost 20 years.

As Dan passes the cooler he waves his hand slightly in a feeble gesture of recognition. Hooker responds halfheartedly with a nod of the head. These simple gestures clearly communicate how these men feel about each other. Dan's thoughts now are even more hostile. He wonders how long it is going to take John Riley, his department head, to notice how much time Hooker spends at the water cooler, in the rest room, and at coffee. Yesterday Dan saw Hooker getting ready to go home for the day a full ten minutes before quitting time. As Dan sees it, Riley must like Hooker. The two talk together a lot, and Riley has accepted a number of Hooker's suggestions. But Riley always has had his favorites, Dan thinks.

Dan returns to his desk; but before he can resume his work, Riley walks up. "Have you given any more thought to that reporting procedure change we talked about yesterday?" Riley asks.

Riley is referring to a change he has had in mind for quite a few years. Last week he asked Hooker to do some research on the possibilities of the procedure. It was then that Hooker talked with Dan about the plan, and it was then that the two had another one of their run-ins.

Riley's words bring Dan's temper to a slow boil. "Riley certainly is sold on that asinine idea of Hooker's," he thinks to himself. "Sure, it will save time now, but it won't give us much information. But you can't fight city hall." Dan forces a smile which belies his inward feeling as he responds: "Yes, I have, Mr. Riley. It's a great idea. We should put it into effect right away."

A few minutes later as Riley walks away, Dan glances at his watch. It is 9:30—half an hour of a typical day.

Reviewing Dan's activities, we find that most of what he does involves communication in one way or another. Some of the forms of communication are easily recognized, such as speaking, listening, reading, and writing. But some are more subtle. Primarily these are the nonverbal types. One form is body motions (kinesics). Another is the communication message made by how far or close people stand when communicating (proxemics). Then there are the communications we make through facial expressions. As we noted above, even objects like desks and carpeting communicate, and so can people just by being seen. In fact, it is impossible for people knowingly in the presence of each other not to communicate.

Clearly, Dan communicated more than first meets the eye. From the moment he left home to the moment he looked at his watch, Dan was giving, receiving, or handling information. Nothing that he did directly involved making whatsits, which, of course, is the Typical Company's main reason for being. Yet there is no question of the importance of his activities to Typical's operations. Obviously, Dan's work assignment more directly involves communication than do many other assignments at Typical. But there are many other communication-oriented assignments in the Company; and every Typical employee's workday is spotted in varying degrees with communication in one form or another. If we were to trace the workdays of each Typical employee and combine our findings, we would come up with an infinitely complex picture of the communication that goes on at Typical. We would see that communication truly plays a major role in Typical's operations.

Main forms of organizational communication

The importance of communication in business becomes even more apparent when we consider the communication activities of an organization from an overall point of view. As we can see from a review of Dan's half hour at

Typical, these activities fall into three broad categories of communication: internal-operational, external-operational, and personal.

Internal-operational communication

Internal-operational communication consists of the structured communication within the organization directly related to achieving the organization's work goals. By "structured" we mean that such communication is built into the organization's plan of operation. By the "organization's work goals" we mean the organization's primary reasons for being—to sell insurance, to manufacture nuts and bolts, to construct buildings, and the like.

The Typical Company, to use a familiar example, has as its major work goals the making and selling of whatsits. In achieving these work goals, it has an established plan of operation, and communication plays a major role in this plan. More specifically, each of Typical's employees has an assignment in the plan. For the plan to work, some communicating must be done. In some of the assignments certain working information is needed. And so that all assignments may be performed as a harmonious and unified effort, certain coordinating information must be communicated. All this information flow is internal-operational communication.

Specifically, internal-operational communication is carried out through any number of structured activities. In the Typical Company, for example, much of the internal-operational information is entered into the Company computer to become a part of the Company's data base. From the data base, programmed reports are developed to give each operations department the information it needs. For example, sales reports and inventory records combine to communicate production needs to the production planning department. Then the production planning department communicates this need to the various production departments through a strategically planned work schedule.

Within each production unit and between production units there is, of course, additional communicating that must go on. Superiors make decisions and transmit them to subordinates. Departments exchange information, and workers communicate working information with each other. Memoranda are written, reports are prepared, conversations are held, all in the process of coordinating efforts and supplying the information needed to achieve the organization's goals. In every division of the company and in every activity, similar internal-operational communication occurs.

External-operational communication

External-operational communication is that part of an organization's structured communication which is concerned with achieving the organization's work goals and which is conducted with people and groups outside the organization. It is the organization's communication with its publics—its suppliers, service companies, customers, and the general public.

Into this category fall all of the organization's efforts at direct selling—

the sales representative's sales spiel, the descriptive brochures, the telephone callbacks, the follow-up service calls, and the like. Included also are all of an organization's advertising efforts. For what is advertising but a deliberate, structured communication with an organization's publics? Radio and television messages, newspaper and magazine space advertising, and point-of-purchase display material obviously play a role in the organization's plan to achieve its work objective. Also falling into this category is all an organization does to enhance its public relations. This includes its planned publicity, the civic-mindedness of its management, the courtesy of its employees, the condition of its physical plant. All these and many more communication efforts combine to make up the organization's external-operational communication.

The extreme importance of an organization's external communications hardly requires supporting comment. Certainly, it is obvious that any business organization is dependent on people and groups outside itself for its success. It is an elementary principle of business that, because a business organization's success is dependent on its ability to satisfy the needs of customers, it must communicate effectively with these customers. It is equally elementary that in today's complex business society, organizations are dependent on each other in the manufacturing and distribution of goods as well as the sale of services. And this interdependence necessarily brings about needs for communication. Just as with international communication, these outside communications are vital to an organization's operation.

Personal communication

Not all the communication that goes on in an organization is operational, however. In fact, much of the communication in an organization is without purpose as far as the organization is concerned. Such communication may be classified as personal.

Personal communication is all that incidental exchange of information and feeling which human beings engage in whenever they come together. Human beings are social animals. They have a need to communicate, and they will communicate even when they have little or nothing to express.

Much of the time friends spend with each other is spent in communication, for it is simply the thing to do when people get together. Even total strangers are likely to communicate when they are placed in a position together, as for instance on a plane trip, in a waiting room, or at a ball game. Such personal communication also takes place in the work situation, and it is a part of the communication activity of any business organization. Although not a part of an organization's plan of operation, personal communication can have a significant effect on the success of this plan. This effect is a result of the influence personal communication can have on the attitudes, opinions, and beliefs of the members of the organization.

Attitudes of the organization members toward the organization, their fellow employees, and their assignments directly affect the members' willingness to do their assigned tasks. And the nature of conversation in a work situation affects attitudes. In a work situation where heated words and flaming tempers often are present, the participants are not likely to make their usual productive effort. Likewise, a rollicking, jovial work situation is likely to have an equally adverse effect on productivity. No doubt somewhere between these extremes the ideal productive attitudes lie.

Also affecting the organization members' work attitudes is the extent of personal communication permitted the members. Absolute denial of the communication privilege could lead to some degree of emotional upset, for people hold dear their right to communicate. On the other hand, excessive personal communication could interfere directly with their work effort. Probably somewhere in the middle-ground area lies the optimum policy toward personal communication.

Personal communication also can help to form attitudes and beliefs, which are stronger and have more lasting effects on the mind than opinions. As was illustrated in the preceding account of Dan's workday at Typical, Dan and his car-pool friends spent some of their conversation time discussing a proposed new policy for Typical. And in talking, each helped to crystallize the opinions of the others. It is in this way that all members of an organization determine much of what they think about their organization, their co-workers, and their work situation in general. What they think can affect their relationships with the organization. And what they think can have a direct influence on productivity.

Communication network of the organization

Looking over all of an organization's communication (internal, external, and personal), we see a most complex mass of information flow. We see an organization literally feeding on a continuous supply of information. More specifically, we see dozens, hundreds, or even thousands of individual members engaging in untold numbers of communication events throughout each working day. The picture of this network of information flow is infinitely complex.

In simplified form, this infinitely complex information flow in a modern-day organization may be likened to the network of arteries and veins in the body. Just as the body has arteries, the organization has well-established channels of information flow. These are the formal and established channels of communication—the main line of the organization's operational communication. Included here are the reports, records, and other forms which supply working information to the various parts of the organization; the orders, instructions and messages which flow up and down the organization's authority structure; and the letters, sales presentations, advertising, and publicity which go to an organization's publics. These main channels do not just happen; they are carefully thought out, or at least they should be. In the modern office, these channels are formed by computer information systems. Information from work stations is put into the company's data base. And from the data base the information can be assembled at the work station needing it.

Our overview also shows us a secondary network of information flow corresponding to the veins of the body. This is the network made up of the thousands upon thousands of personal communications which take place in any organization. Such communications follow no set pattern but rather form an intricate and infinitely complex web of information flow linking all of the members of the organization in one way or another.

The complexity of the network cannot be overemphasized, especially in the larger organizations. Typically it is not a single network at all. Rather, it is a complex relation of smaller networks made up of groups of people. The relationships are made even more complex by the fact that the people in the organization may belong to more than one of these groups, and group memberships and the linking between groups are continually changing. Truly, the network structure in a large organization is so complex as to defy description.

Known as the "grapevine" in management literature, this informal communication system is far more effective than a first impression might indicate. Certainly it consists of much gossip and rumor, for this is the nature of human conversation. And it is as fickle and inaccurate as the human beings who are a part of it. Even so, the grapevine carries far more information than the formal communication system; and on many matters it is more effective in determining the course of an organization. Wise managers recognize the presence of the grapevine. They learn who the talk leaders are; and they communicate to them the information that will do the most good for the organization. That is, they keep in touch with the grapevine, and they turn it into a constructive tool.

Effects of changing technology

From the preceding review it appears that much of the communication that goes on in organizations is written communication—letters, memoranda, reports, and such. Thus, it is vital that we address a question that sometimes is heard. It is the question of the role of written communication in the years ahead. The evidence suggests that we are moving rapidly into the age of automated communication—the age of the paperless office. This will be a time when there will be no letters, no reports, no files. Instead, each work station in an organization will be equipped with a computer terminal, or perhaps a microcomputer. As a result, internal-operational communications (including memoranda and reports) will be done primarily through computers. In the short run, a company's written external-operational communications (mainly letters) will be done through the word-processing capabilities of the computers; and they will be in paper form. But in time, company-to-company computer link-ups will develop; and in more time there will be consumer-to-company link-ups. The result will be that computer-to-computer communication will replace conventional letters.

Although it is impossible to say with certainty what the future holds, it appears reasonable to say that computer technology will bring about revolutionary changes in communication. In fact, revolutionary changes are occurring now; and probably they will continue to occur at an accelerating rate. But we must keep in mind that these changes are primarily in the nature of the transmission—not in the messages communicated. There is no evidence which even remotely suggests that the needs for the messages communicated in letters, reports, and memoranda will decrease. And of even greater importance, there is absolutely no evidence to suggest that these messages can be handled in a way which does not require the basic writing skills. Clearly, business writing is here to stay. In fact, the increasing complexity of the technological world of the future is likely to require more—not less—of it.

A preview to the presentation

The foregoing review merely skims the surface; yet, hopefully, it has given you an appreciation of the importance of communication to yourself and to organizations. It has shown you how extensive communication is, how it permeates every segment of the organization in a most intricate and complex way. And it has shown you that good communication is vital to the successful operation of an organization. These conclusions, combined with the convincing evidence that most organizational communication is not well done, should lead you to yet another conclusion: that communication is an area deserving increased study by those concerned with improving the operations of an organization.

In the following pages such a study is undertaken. Its approach is first to gain an understanding of what communication is—how it works and how it does not work. The material covered here borrows from many disciplines—from psychology, sociology, and linguistics. But primarily it borrows from the relatively new discipline of general semantics. Perhaps the term *general semantics* requires definition, for the generally used meanings of the two words in the term do not apply in this case. In a simplified sense, general semantics concerns the study of reality, of our perception of reality, and of how we relate to our perceptions in words, thoughts, and actions. Its emphasis is on recognizing the true nature of reality. Much of the source material for this review is highly sophisticated, but every effort has been made to simplify it. Perhaps some people will look upon it as being oversimplified.

After establishing a foundation of understanding, our study shifts to applications of this theoretical material to the real-life activities of an organization. For reasons of course design, much of the material concerns written communication. Specifically, we shall emphasize the areas of correspondence and report writing, for these are vital areas in today's business organization. Here our emphasis will be on communication with words and concepts that match reality, which is a primary message from the theory chapters. We shall give some emphasis to other areas, especially oral communication. It should be apparent, however, that this coverage is far from complete. The almost infinite nature of the subject makes it so. Even so, the applications presented should show you the ways to handle the theoretical material in your day-to-day work in business.

Questions & Problems

1. Explain the role of communication in the development of civilized society.
2. Discuss the role of communication in organized activity.
3. Contrast the role of communication in organizations of human beings with communication in organizations of other forms of life (for example, ants).
4. Make a list of the types of external-operational and internal-operational communication that occur at your school.
5. Review Dan's half hour and note the communications that probably were true to fact and those that were not true to fact. Are there any obvious differences in the effect of each on the organization?
6. Select an organization with which you are acquainted and construct a diagram showing its network of communications. Construct its formal communication and informal communication structure. Discuss and explain these structures.
7. Describe the changes in business communication that are likely to occur in the next 20 years.
8. Discuss the effects of the "paperless office" on the need for business writing skills.
9. At the conclusion of a long and bitter strike,

the Timms Manufacturing Company found through a survey that a strong majority of the people in the community sided with the union. Give a probable explanation. What would you suggest the company do to regain the lost goodwill.
10. Mary Cabot is one of 12 workers in Department X. She has strong leadership qualities, and all of her co-workers look up to her. She dominates conversations with them and expresses strong opinions on most matters. Although she is a good worker, her dominant character has caused problems for her superior. As the new supervisor for Department X, today you have directed the workers to change a work procedure. The change is one that has proved to be superior wherever it has been tried. Soon after giving the directive, you notice the workers talking in a group, with Mary the obvious leader. In a few minutes she appears at your office. "We've thought it over," she says. "Your production change won't work." Explain what is happening. How would you handle the situation?
11. Trace the lines of formal communication at your university. Discuss some of the more significant informal communication lines.
12. "One cannot not communicate." Discuss.

A model of the process

2

ACONVENTIONAL ANALYSIS of communication begins with a definition of the term. Many such definitions exist; so we would have no difficulty finding one suitable for our use. But our approach is not conventional. We shall not use words to define words, for, as we shall see, such definitions are dangerous. Instead, we shall use an operational definition. By operational definition we mean one which demonstrates how something works. In the following pages an operational definition is presented in the form of a model.

Specifically, in our presentation of the model we shall attempt to look with scientific diligence into the phenomenon of human communication. We shall take the event of one human being communicating with another. By choice we shall use a face-to-face oral communication event, for this is the communication situation with which we are best acquainted. Later we shall adapt it to written communication. Our plan will be to take this event and place it under the microscope of our minds. We shall try to determine how the process works, and, conversely, how it does not work.

In developing our model, we must lean heavily on the theoretical, for we are not dealing with a subject on which much factual support is available. The theoretical material presented, however, represents authoritative thinking[1] on the subject. Regardless of its factual bases, this presentation will give us a meaningful understanding of communication, and it will provide us with principles which can be applied successfully to real-life communication problems.

A common misconception

Before beginning our analysis of the model, let us dispense with a misconception which many of us have. If you are like most people, you have never

[1] The following discussion of the communication process is adapted from the classic description by Wendell Johnson, "The Fateful Process of Mr. A Talking to Mr. B," *Harvard Business Review*, vol. 31, no. 1 (January–February, 1953), pp. 43–50.

thought much about what communication really is. If you have thought about it, probably you viewed communication as a very normal human activity. This assumption is far from correct.

Human communication, at least the verbal part of it, is far from being a normal function. That is, it is not the sort of thing we would do anyway if left to nature's devices, as is the case with many of our other activities. Our hands, for example, would perform their normal functions of picking up and handling things whether we grew up with wild animals in a jungle or with civilized people. Likewise, our mouths would take in food, and our teeth and jaws would chew it in either event. And so would most of our other body parts function normally without instruction from other human beings. The same cannot be said of the major organs used in communication. Our vocal apparatus would not make words if we were not taught to make them. Neither would our brains know them nor our hands write them without instruction. Clearly, communication is a function which we must learn. It was originated by human beings, and it must be acquired from human beings.

The communication environment

Study of the communication process logically is preceded by an analysis of the environment in which communication occurs. This is the sensory environment in which we find ourselves throughout every waking moment. It is made up of all the signs existing in the world of reality which surrounds each of us. At this moment, your sensory environment is the real world surrounding you as you read these words. It consists of all the signs your senses can detect. More specifically, it is all you can see, taste, smell, hear, or feel in that part of the world which surrounds you.

At this point perhaps some definitions are needed, although the terms will be explained in detail in following chapters. By "world of reality" or "real world" we mean that which actually exists. It contrasts with that world which exists only in the minds of people. Of course, one may argue that what exists in the mind also is real—that, right or wrong, the content of a mind exists in that mind. For our purposes, however, we must allow this inconsistency in our definition. As you will see in following chapters, it is important that we distinguish between what actually is in the world around a communicator and what the communicator says or thinks is. Often the two are not the same.

By "signs" we mean all that from the real world which can act as a stimulus to us. In other words, it is all that which our sensory receptors can detect. It is that which our eyes can see, our ears can hear, our nostrils can smell, our tongues can taste, or our flesh can touch. It may be a word spoken, the sound of objects crashing together, a printed word, the aroma of a flower, the movement of a bird, or the like. Thus, an individual sign is a portion of the real world which can create a response within us.

By deduction from the preceding comment we know the meaning of "sensory receptors." The term refers to those body organs which we use to detect the signs in the real world. Specifically, we refer to our eyes, our noses, our ears, our mouths, and our flesh with its ability to detect surface and temperature differences.

Sign detection

From the infinite number of signs existing in our communication environment, our sensory receptors continuously pick up some. Or stating it another way, the signs around us continuously produce responses within us through our receptors. Perhaps this phenomenon can be explained best by example.

At this very moment you are looking at this printed page. On it there are words (signs) which your eyes are picking up. We hope that these are the primary signs you are receiving, but there are others. Probably you pick up some of them from time to time. Perhaps there are various noises about you—voices from another room, the ticking of a clock, a radio playing in the distance, the movements and sounds made by a roommate. From time to time you may become aware of being hot or cold, or your back may itch, or your sitting position may become uncomfortable. Thus, as you read these pages your sensory receptors continuously pick up signs from all these parts of the reality which surrounds you.

Sensory limitations

How many and what signs we can detect from the real world, however, are limited by our sensory abilities. In short, the human sensory receptors are limited. They are not capable of detecting in the real world all signs which we know exist. For example, our eyes can detect only a small part of the total spectrum of wavelengths, and the ability to detect within these wavelengths varies from person to person. We can see only a fraction of the distance a hawk can see. Our ears can pick up only a narrow band of the whole range of air vibrations, and the abilities of human beings to pick up sounds within these ranges vary. As we all know, dogs and birds can hear much that we cannot hear. Likewise, we can smell only the stronger odors around us. Dogs and most other animals do a much better job of smelling. And so it is for all our senses. Clearly, our senses are limited, and they detect only a small portion of the reality surrounding us.

Selective perception

In addition to being incapable of detecting all that exists in the real world around us, our sensory receptors can pick up some signs and ignore others. Place yourself, for example, in a roomful of talking people, and notice how it is possible to tune in on one conversation and to ignore others. Or notice how you are able to focus your vision on one minute object and then to expand your view to a much broader picture. To varying extents, all of us have this ability, and we can make use of it with all our senses.

Varying alertness and perception

Our detection or nondetection of signs depends also on our receptiveness to signs. There are times when we are keenly alert to our communication environments, and there are times when we are not so alert. Certainly, you have experienced occasions when you were sleepy, in a daze, or just daydreaming. During such times you missed many of the signs in your communication environment. When you are asleep, you detect almost none.

To this point we have shown how each of us lives in an environment of signs and how these signs are with us throughout each day. We have shown also how we vary in our abilities to detect these signs, how we can tune them in or tune them out, and how our alertness to them varies from time to time. With this knowledge of the communication environment as a foundation, we are now ready to describe the communication process.

The communication process

To illustrate our description of the communication process, we shall use two hypothetical characters. Let us call them John and Mary. These two people are somehow in a communication situation. Let us make it a face-to-face, personal situation, for this is the most common form of human communication. Then, after we have traced the process through this basic situation, we can adapt it to other communication situations, such as that between writer and reader.

Our plan is first to describe verbally the communication process as it occurs. We shall begin with John as he exists in his communication environment. We shall trace the development of the communication effort to the formulation of the message and the transmission of it into Mary's environment. Then we shall trace briefly the message as it communicates with Mary. Following our verbal review of the process, we shall summarize with a diagram of the model (Figure 2–1) we have described. By design our description will be short, for the major phases of the process are the subjects of the following chapters.

Reception of signals

Let us begin our illustration as John and Mary are talking to each other; and let us first look into the communication process as it occurs in John. At this moment, as in all of his conscious moments, John's sensory receptors are picking up signs from his communication environment. As we know, his environment is infinitely filled with signs, but John picks up only a few of them. Probably his eyes are picking up Mary's image as well as some of the surrounding real world. His nose may be detecting Mary's perfume. His ears may be picking up various sounds from outside the room. But the dominant signs are likely to be the words which Mary sends into John's environment. Whatever they are, John picks up some signs, and the communication process begins.

The signs picked up now travel as stimulations through the nervous

Figure 2-1

19

Chapter 2
A Model of the
Process

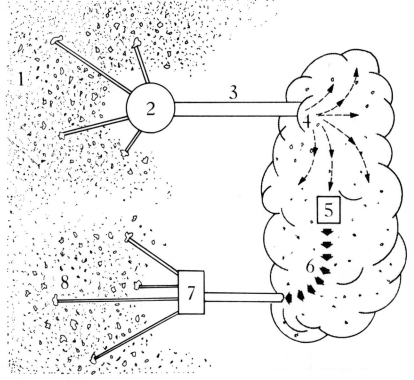

Explanation:
1. This area represents our communication environment. It is all the signs and symbols that exist in the real world that surrounds us.
2. Our sensory receptors pick up some (far from all) of the signs and symbols.
3. Those signs and symbols which are picked up go through our nervous systems and into our mental filters.
4. Our mental filters give the signs and symbols meaning. The meanings received add to the content of the filters.
5. Sometimes the meanings we form trigger communication responses.
6. We form these responses through our mental filters.
7. We send our responses as symbols through speaking, writing, and so on.
8. These symbols become a part of the communication environments of others. Here they may be picked up by the sensory receptors of others, and another cycle begins.

system of John's body and on to his brain. They go out again to the muscles and glands and feed back into the nervous system, where they bring about various reverberations of stimulations. This is the preverbal neurophysiological stage of communication. It is a stage about which we know little that is definite, yet scientists assure us that it does occur in the manner just described.

> Though our factual information is meager as yet, certainly it is sufficient to demonstrate that the nervous system is not merely a hypothetical construct. We can say with practical assurance that stimulation of our sensory end organs is normally followed by the transmission of nerve currents into the central nervous system, with a consequent reverberation effect. . . .[2]

---

[2] *Ibid.*, p. 46.

Flow to the brain

The reverberations John's nervous system develops reach John's brain. They enter as a continuous stream, for as we have noted, the senses continuously pick up signs from the communication environment. From time to time this stream will vary in its speed of flow and in its volume. Sometimes it will run fast and strong, as when his environment is filled with strong signs and John's mind is keenly alert. At other times it will run slowly, as when John is in a stupor and his communication environment has no signs strong enough to break the spell. Most of the time, of course, the stream runs somewhere between these extremes.

Role of the filter

When this stream of stimuli reaches John's brain with all of its resulting reverberation effect, it goes through what we shall call the "filter" of the mind. In this stage John's brain gives meaning to the stimulations received. And the meanings given depend largely on the makeup and current condition of John's filter.

By "filter," we mean all that exists in John's mind which will influence his interpretation of any signs received. The filter is in reality all that John is and all that he has ever been. It is made up of all he knows and all he thinks, and it includes all he thinks he knows. It includes all of his emotional makeup; and it includes all of his opinions, attitudes, and beliefs. It is apparent that John's filter is unique. In fact, of the four-billion filters on earth, no two are identical.

All filters differ because no two people have identical experiences, knowledge, emotional makeups, thought processes, and the like. For this not to be so, two people would have to live side by side every moment of every day. They would have to act alike and think alike. They would have to perceive identical signs from identical sensory environments, and they would have to react in exactly the same way to these perceptions. Obviously, such identical existences do not occur. In fact, the possibilities for differences in filter makeups are so great that differences outnumber similarities.

Since filters are so different, and since meaning is determined by the filter, it is apparent that meanings assigned to a given set of signs will also differ. To illustrate this major truth of the communication process, consider the different meanings John might give to the words "Watson is a union member." First, assume that John comes from an independent and individualistic rural family which has for years been critical of labor. Throughout his life John has heard critical comments about unions and union members. In fact, he has made some such remarks himself. Let us also assume that John is now a ranking officer in the company, with many years of experience in haggling with union officials. Thus, his labor experiences and his knowledge of labor unions and their membership have been quite negative. Now, as the words strain through John's filter, they register a somewhat unpleasant meaning.

On the other hand, had John been born into a family sympathetic to labor, or perhaps if he were a rabid union worker, the meaning given would be different. Instead of going through a negatively biased filter, the symbols would now go through a positively biased filter. The resulting meaning given the symbols in question would be much more favorable.

For another example, assume that John's receptors pick up the symbol "liberal" in a comment about some proposed legislation. If John's filter contains favorable references to this controversial word, a favorable reaction will come about. On the other hand, John's filter could contain quite negative references to the word. His experiences, for example, could have taught him that things liberal are things to be feared and despised. They could have taught him that the true connotation of the symbol lies somewhere between these extremes. Or they could have conditioned him to regard the word with suspicion and confusion. In each of these events, John's response to these symbols would vary.

Similar illustrations may be made with other words. In a given sentence, "house" might have one meaning to a destitute mountaineer, another to a middle-class citizen of a big city, and still another to a rich southern planter. "Capitalist" might stir up all sorts of vile responses in the mind of a dedicated Communist; quite different responses could be expected from a political scientist, an economist, and a zealous American patriot. "Our forefathers" would not get identical responses from an anthropologist and from one whose experiences include hearing traditional Fourth of July orations. Our illustrations could continue through thousands of similar symbols.

The illustrations used thus far have concerned words. We have used words because they are the easiest to use and because they are the most important signs in our study of communication. Words, however, are only one of the sign forms in our communication environment.

Similar filter responses occur with other signs our receptors pick up and pass through our filters. For example, the sight of a grasshopper resting on a leaf or of ants swarming on an anthill might strike the American child as an interesting nature study. Youngsters in a primitive tribe might have experiences which prompt them to see a delicious meal. The sight of a five-foot king snake might strike terror in the mind of one conditioned to fear all snakes; yet a snake fancier would find the reptile to be a friendly and harmless pet. Cool breezes coming off the sea might mean pleasant sleeping to the vacationing tourist, good sailing for the sailboat enthusiast, and a factor to be considered by one going fishing. And so it is for all the signs our receptors pick up.

Some of the signs recorded, of course, do not bring about such clear and distinct reactions as the examples given. In fact, many bring about multiple, mixed, or confused reactions. When such an indefinite response occurs, the content of the filter is equally indefinite. It is easy to see why filters so often hold indefinite information, for little in reality is clear-cut and precise. For example, one's filter might contain hundreds of reactions concerning a certain politician. Some of them might be strongly positive, some strongly negative, and some in between. Any mention of the politician would result in a mixed reaction. So it is with much of what exists in the filter.

Obviously, the differences in filter makeups are infinite, and the foregoing discussion and illustrations barely begin to explain them. Perhaps enough has been given to provide you with a general idea of the vital role of the filter in communication. But because this role is so vital to an understanding of communication and is in fact the heart of all communication problems, it is the subject of detailed discussion in a later chapter (Chapter 4). For the moment we have sufficient information to understand how the stimuli going through the filter are given meanings and how these meanings will differ from filter to filter.

The symbolizing stage

The meanings John's filter gives the stimulations he receives react on John in some way. This reaction may be wholly within the mind, as when John is passively receiving information. In some instances, his reaction may trigger strong physical movements. He may, for example, swing a clenched fist at one who, according to his filter, has insulted him. Or he may quickly jump to avoid danger when his filter gives meaning to a frantic "Watch out!" In most communication situations his response is to communicate his reaction to those with whom he is communicating.

When the reaction to symbols received is a communication response, the symbolizing stage of the communication process begins. This is the stage in which the mind searches for a means of presenting its reaction to those with whom it wishes to communicate. Since most of our communication uses words, which are our most common symbols, this stage is likely to consist of finding the words that will convey the meaning intended. It could, however, concern selecting facial expressions, body movements, hand signals, or any other form of symbol.

As the symbolizing stage involves the innermost workings of the mind, our knowledge of it is limited. There is evidence, however, which indicates that one's competency at this stage is related to mental ability. Especially is one's symbolizing competency (the ability to select words) related to knowledge of language. A knowledge of language gives one an appreciation of the strength and limitations of verbal communication. Also, such a knowledge equips one with a variety of symbol forms; and the greater the number of symbol forms in the mind, the more precise and discriminating can one be in selecting from them.

As we shall see in Chapter 5, symbolizing is a highly imperfect act. In the first place, the symbols we use do not carry perfectly clear meanings. Most have multiple meanings, and many are vague and general. Then there simply is not a sufficient supply of symbols to communicate all one thinks or sees. We have about 700,000 symbols in the English language. But we must use them to communicate about billions upon billions of objects and events in reality. In addition to the inadequacy of symbols, we all have some limitation in using those which are available. It is no easy task to put in symbol form what is in our minds. Even if we have plenty of time available, as when we are writing, we are rarely satisfied with our symbolizing efforts. Our efforts are even more unsatisfactory when we symbolize our reactions in seconds or even split seconds, as when we are carrying on a conversation.

Act of encoding

The symbolizing stage ends when John encodes his response. In this part of the symbolizing stage John sends the symbols he has selected to Mary. Since he and Mary are engaged in face-to-face communication, probably he encodes with vocal sounds (air vibrations made with his vocal cords). That is, he speaks words. But instead of words, or perhaps as a supplement to them, he might encode with body movements, gestures, or facial expressions.

As graphically summarized in Figure 2–1, the encoding of the message ends the first cycle of the communication process. This is the cycle which describes the role of the communicator (John, in this case) in the process. Now we begin another and identical cycle—this time to describe the role of the communicatee (Mary).

The cycle repeated

However they are sent, the symbols encoded by John move into Mary's sensory environment. Here they vie for attention with other signs Mary's receptors are capable of picking up. And just as was the case in a similar situation in the first cycle, Mary will detect only some of the many signs existing in her environment. Those she does pick up go through the nervous system and on to Mary's brain. Here they are processed through Mary's filter. It is at this point that communication is most likely to fail. As is the case with John's filter as well as with every other filter, Mary's filter is unique. No one else has her exact experience and knowledge. No one else has her precise emotional makeup. And no one else has her exact opinions, attitudes, and beliefs. Thus, because each of their filters is unique, the meaning Mary gives to John's words will differ from the meaning John intended. The difference, of course, may be barely discernible, in which case for all practical purposes communication will be successful. Fortunately, most human communication falls in this category. But the difference could be significant. When this is the case, miscommunication is the result.

The meaning Mary's filter gives the symbols received brings about a reaction in Mary. Since she and John are engaged in face-to-face communication, more than likely she will communicate this reaction. Thus, the symbolizing stage begins for Mary. Now Mary's brain searches for the symbols which will convey her reaction. She encodes these symbols and sends them into the sensory environment of John. And then begins a third cycle, which may lead to a fourth, and a fifth, and on and on as long as both feel a need to communicate.

The model and written communication

Although the foregoing description of the communication process applies specifically to a face-to-face situation, it generally fits written communication as well. But some significant differences exist.

Effects of creativity

Perhaps the most significant difference between face-to-face and written communication is that written communication is more likely to be a creative effort of a mind. The fact is that it is more likely to be thought out and less likely to be a spontaneous reaction to signs received by the receptors. More specifically, the message in a written communication is more likely to be a result of stimuli produced by the mind than of outside stimuli picked up by the sensory receptors.

In report-writing situations, for example, before beginning the work, writers have decided to communicate; or perhaps someone has decided for them. Before they begin the task of communicating, they gather the information which will form the basis of the communication. Then, through logical thought processes, they encode the communication which will accomplish the communication objective. Thus, there is not likely to be an interchange of stimuli between communicants, nor is there likely to be any triggering of desires to communicate. The process is a creative and deliberative one.

On the other hand, a letter-writing situation can be an exception, at least to some extent. In a sense, a letter situation can be like a face-to-face situation in slow motion. Stimuli picked up by one person's receptors could produce a reaction which would bring about a communication response—in this case a written letter. This letter could in turn bring about a communication response in its reader's mind. Thus, a reply would be written. This reply could then bring about another reply. And the cycle could be repeated as long as each letter brings about a communication response. Even so, letters represent more deliberate and creative efforts than face-to-face communication.

The lag of time

Most obvious of the differences in face-to-face and written communication processes is the time factor. In face-to-face communication the encoded messages move instantaneously into the sensory environments of the participants. In written communication, however, some delay takes place. Just how long the delay will be is indeterminate. Priority administrative announcements or telegrams may be read minutes after they are written. Routine letters require a day or two to communicate their contents. Research reports may take weeks in communicating their information to the intended readers. And all such written communications may be filed for possible reference in the indefinite future. They may continue to communicate for months or years.

The lag of time also makes a difference in the return information one gets from communicating. Return information, commonly called "feedback," helps greatly in determining when clear meaning is being received. In face-to-face communication, feedback is easy to get. The participants are right there together. They can ask questions. They can observe facial expressions. They can repeat and simplify whenever it appears to be necessary. In written communication, feedback is slow at best. Often it does not appear to occur at all. But even when there is no apparent communication response, feedback can occur. For example, a failure to answer a letter may communicate unconcern, forgetfulness, or even contempt.

Limited numbers of cycles

A third significant difference between face-to-face and written communication is the number of cycles typically occurring in a communication event. As previously noted, face-to-face communication normally involves multiple exchanges of symbols; thus, many cycles take place. Written communication, on the other hand, usually involves a limited number of cycles. In fact, most written communication is one-cycle communication. A message is sent and received, but none is returned. Of course, there are exceptions, such as letters and memorandums which lead to a succession of communication exchanges. But even the most involved of these would hardly match in cycle numbers a routine, face-to-face conversation.

The universal ingredients of human communication

The differences in face-to-face and written communication processes are significant, but the similarities are even more vital to our study of communication. These similarities are vital because they comprise the universal ingredients of all human communication. To know and understand them is to know and understand communication. Thus, they are the basic substance of any meaningful study of the subject.

The communication environment

The first universal of human communication is the communication environment of those engaged in communication. All communication must enter such an environment and must compete for detection by the sensory receptors with the other stimuli which happen to be in the environment at the time.

The filter of the mind

In all forms of human communication the stimuli picked up by the sensory receptors are passed through the filter of the mind. Because the filter is the product of all one's experiences and all one's thinking, sharp differences exist in filter makeups. In fact, of all the differences between people, probably none are greater than the differences in their filters. Yet it is through these sharply different filters that people must attempt to communicate meaning.

The encoding and decoding processes

Encoding and decoding are the third and fourth universal ingredients of the process of human communication. The universal role of these functions should be apparent. All purposeful human communication uses symbols (words, gestures, facial expressions, and so on), for symbols are our primary conveyors of meaning. As we human beings have thousands of symbols at our disposal, there must be the process of selecting the ones which will best carry a given message. And there must be the process of giving meaning to the message. Encoding and decoding are these processes.

Some fundamental truths of communication

A review of the communication process reveals certain fundamental truths which will help us in our understanding of the subject. Three in particular stand out.

Communication is imperfect

First is the obvious truth that communication is imperfect—that it is not the highly precise activity some people think it is. Convincing explanations support this observation. The most obvious explanation lies in the countless variations which exist in human filters. Since meanings are determined through filters, no two of which are precisely alike, meanings any two people give to a set of symbols vary. For the same reason, a message sent by one person never is precisely the message received by another.

The imprecision of the symbols used in communication is the second explanation of communication imperfection. As will be discussed in greater depth in Chapter 5, the symbols we use (mainly words) are crude substitutes for reality. Typically, symbols have multiple and vague meanings, and they are not consistently used.

Yet another explanation of communication imprecision is that people vary in their abilities to encode meanings. Not all people know the same symbols, nor are all people equally proficient at selecting and putting together the symbols to be used in messages. For example, two people with varying encoding abilities trying to communicate the same message would select different symbols and arrangements of symbols. The result would be that the message is changed and different meanings are received.

We communicate about ourselves

A second observation which we may draw from our description of the process is that, when we communicate, we communicate about ourselves. In fact, in the process of symbolizing, we attempt to select symbols which tell what is going on inside us. In effect, when we communicate, we are really saying: "This is how I perceive or react to the stimuli I am receiving."

To illustrate this point, take a situation in which our two characters, John and Mary, are viewing a painting. John remarks, "This is a beautiful painting." But what John really is saying is, "As I view this painting as picked up by my receptors, it is pleasing to me." Viewing the same painting, Mary comments, "What a hideous painting this is!"

In reality, a painting is neither beautiful nor hideous. It is only a composition of matter. The qualities of beauty and hideousness are reactions in the minds of the viewers. Thus, what each is saying in reality is: "As I view this picture as picked up by my receptors and relayed through my nervous system and strained through my filter, the picture appears to be beautiful (or hideous) to me."

A related point worth noting is that our communications are based on limited inputs. As we shall note in the following pages, the stimuli we receive are a small part of those available to us. That is, we perceive only a part of the reality about which we communicate. Thus, our verbal messages are based on abstractions—on selected bits of the whole about which we communicate.

Meaning is in the mind

A third significant observation we may draw from the process is that meaning is in the mind and not in the symbols used. In a sense, this observation is a corollary of the preceding one, but it is so fundamental to an understanding of communication that it deserves our special emphasis. It should be clear from the description of the process that symbols do not have meaning. If they did, there would be no communication problems, for communication would be precise.

Putting it another way, we can say that people have meaning in mind when they use symbols. It is their hope that the symbols they use will be given similar meaning in the minds of those with whom they communicate. The proximity of the meaning given in the minds of those involved in the communication is a measure of the success of the communication effort. As has been noted, precise agreement rarely if ever occurs.

From this observation we can gain one of the major lessons of communication—that in communication our emphasis should be on "What did the speaker mean when he or she used those symbols?" rather than on "What do those symbols mean in my mind?" If all of us understood and practiced this fundamental truth, we would eliminate a major portion of the misunderstanding in the world today.

Questions & Problems

1. What is meant by operational definition?
2. Construct your own definition of communication. Compare it with the operational definition given in the text.
3. Although communication is not a normal function for human beings, it is for ants and bees. Discuss.
4. Explain the meaning of real world, signs, and sensory receptors.
5. Describe the sensory environment in which you are at this moment. Contrast that part with which typically you are aware with that part with which you typically are unaware.
6. Without looking, describe in as much detail as possible some object you have seen many times (a watch, dollar bill, and so on). What part of the operational definition of communication does this illustrate?
7. Following an incident involving a worker and the worker's supervisor, workers who observed the incident were questioned about what had happened. Some reported that the supervisor remained cool throughout the incident and attempted to calm down the worker who was yelling and shaking his fist. Some reported that both people were emotional. And some saw the worker as calm and collected and the supervisor as emotional and upset. All those reporting were honorable people. Explain how this could happen.
8. Margaret Lewis, a very conscientious student, is at the last meeting of a class before a major exam. "Will we cover Chapter 7 on the examination?" she asks the professor. Laughter is heard around the room. "They are laughing because I answered your question the moment before you asked it," the professor says. Explain what happened from a communications viewpoint.

9. "Professor Oliver is really a great teacher," says Emily to her friend Bill. "He's so brilliant as a lecturer. And he's really interested in students." Bill responded with these words "That creep? I had him last semester. He's terrible." Explain from a communications viewpoint.
10. Explain why no two filters are quite the same.
11. From your own experience select an example of miscommunication. Use the model to explain how the miscommunication occurred.
12. The exact conversations of an organization's meeting were transcribed, typewritten, and distributed to the membership. How well does the communications model fit here? Do all the differences between face-to-face communication and written communication apply?
13. Explain each of the universal ingredients of human communication.
14. Sandra and Betty were engaged in an intellectual argument. Said Sandra after listening to Betty's argument, "You've really proved my point—not yours. You used the word 'preponderance,' which means the big majority. So what you really said was that my position has stronger support." Discuss the fundamental truth of communication illustrated here.
15. Relate the following conversation between a supervisor and an employee to the fundamental truths of communication.
    Supervisor: "You stupid or something? I've told you in clear, simple English what to do. I can't tell you no plainer."
    Worker: "I'm sorry, but I don't understand your explanation."

Perception and reality

3

THE PRECEDING REVIEW of the communication process clearly shows us that when we communicate we symbolize (put into words, gestures, and so on) our reaction to the reality we perceive. But just what is reality? And how do we perceive it? The answers to these questions are basic to our understanding of communication.

Reality defined

As we defined it in Chapter 2, "reality," or the "real world," is all that actually exists, contrasted with what exists only in the minds of human beings. Our definition includes all that our senses can perceive—all that we can see, smell, taste, hear, or feel. It includes also much that our senses cannot perceive. Of course, what exists in the mind also is real, for it does exist in the mind. But it is important for our analysis to distinguish between what actually is in the world around us and what we just think is there.

That which has substance

Obviously included in this definition is all that we think of as having substance—that is, all that which has physical shape and composition. Included would be most of what we can see and feel around us: the chair you sit in, the desk before you, this book, your own body. It includes all that we commonly refer to as matter—rocks, soil, water, and plants. In general, it is all that the eye can see or that the sense of touch can detect.

Reality without substance

Reality also includes much which does not have shape or form. The invisible air you breathe is as real as the ground you walk on. Equally real is the existence of space—of nothingness. Nothingness is all about us; in fact, it is in far greater supply than the tangible parts of reality. In addition, vibrations in the air (we detect them as sounds) are certainly a part of reality. So is time. So are the qualities of light and color. And so are thoughts in the mind. None of these parts of reality are tangible so far as our unaided senses are concerned. Yet there is no doubt about their presence.

The reality of events

Included also in our definition of reality are all the events which take place in the real world. By events we mean any changes in the relationships of the parts of reality. A car moving over a road changes its relationship with the other parts of reality which surround it. The same is true of a person slipping on a banana peel, a fist striking a tabletop, a wind moving the leaves in a tree. Obviously, the parts of reality are not static. They move around or in some way change their relationships with the other parts of reality.

Although we know they occur and we communicate about them, events are hard to isolate. We isolate them by giving them beginnings and ends. But in the real world, they do not exist this way. Rather, events are parts of the continuous existence of the things in reality. For example, we may see an event as the striking of a fist against a tabletop. But when we do so, we arbitrarily begin and end the action. The fist (or hand) involved is in continuous existence. Its individual fingers were involved in events as they formed a fist. And again they were involved in events as they moved to open the fist. Obviously, such events flow into one another. Thus, identifying events is somewhat arbitrary.

Position relationships

Even the static position relationships of the elements of reality are a part of reality. Illustrating this point is a tale told by a popular comedian about a man caught in the company of a married woman by the woman's husband. When asked by the husband what he was doing there, the man replied, "Everybody's got to be someplace." Aside from the humor of the anecdote, it presents a basic truth of reality: All of reality must be somewhere. Everything must have spatial relationships with other things. For example, a box may be stacked on another box. It may have objects stored inside it, and these objects are arranged in some way within the box. All such relationships of objects are a part of the reality in which we exist.

However vague our definition may be, we all know that reality does exist. We know it because we perceive some of it. Unfortunately, however, we do not perceive reality precisely. Thus, since communication is the symbolizing of our reactions to our perceptions, imprecise perceptions must result in imprecise communication. As was discussed in Chapter 2, some of the blame for our imprecise perception we may place on the limitations of our sensory organs. The remainder of the blame we may place on our lack of understanding of reality. For this latter reason, we shall next analyze the characteristics of reality and our perceptions of them.

The infinity of reality

A major reason why we human beings err in our perceptions of reality is that there is so much of it. The world of matter and events is all so tremendously involved and complex that for all practical purposes it is infinite in nature. Because of the infinite nature of reality, it is humanly impossible to know even a substantial part of all the facts involved in any one object or event; and it is likely that different people would perceive differently the parts of a given object or event. Thus, when we symbolize our reactions to reality (which is what we do when we communicate), we symbolize our reactions to a small part of the whole, and to parts which others perceive differently from us. More than likely, we are not conscious of these limitations. These concepts are perhaps best explained by illustration.

Infinity in a sheet of paper

To illustrate the concept of the infinite nature of reality, take some familiar object around you—say a single sheet of theme paper. One common variety has a double red stripe down the left margin; and it has some 30-odd blue parallel lines running horizontally across the page. It is a rather simple thing as objects go—at least, that is how it appears to most of us at first glance. But let us take a closer look.

Close inspection with the naked eye shows us that the red lines are not so sharp and clear as they at first appeared. The lines are fuzzy, to say the least, and the intensity of color varies from place to place. The same is true of the blue lines. And the white space is not all white, for here and there are little flecks of dark matter.

These observations alone are enough to prove that countless variations exist on the paper. But our case would be even more convincing were we to give this same page a microscopic inspection. Under such an inspection we would find that each line contains many more irregularities than we are able to detect with the naked eye. We would see many more flecks in the paper; and we would see that each has a shape, color, and size unlike any of the others. We would see that the paper is made up of thousands of compressed fibers, and we would see that each of these fibers is different from any of the others. The edges of the paper would take on a different appearance. Instead of the smooth, straight line we see with the naked eye, we would see a rough and ragged edge of loose fibers.

We could take our inquiry a step further into the submicroscopic world. Here we would find that each little fiber, each fleck, each particle of dye on the lines is made up of atoms. And as we know from our study of physics, the atom is a universe in itself—a whirling mass of electrons with a nucleus composed of protons and neutrons. And there are millions upon millions of atoms in our sheet of paper. Their variations also approach infinity.

The infinite number of characteristics in our simple sheet of paper illustrates the nature of what we would find in any part of reality we would choose to examine. In fact, many parts would present even greater complexity. An automobile, an electronic computer, or a building, for example, each presents much greater complexity in overall makeup. Each consists of hundreds of distinguishable parts; and as with the sheet of paper, each of these parts has its own infinite characteristics. Without question, the world of reality is indeed infinite in its complexity.

Limiting effects on perception

Because of the infinite nature of the real world, we have some difficulty perceiving it. Two of the major explanations of this difficulty deserve our attention. First, our sensory organs are inadequate to cope with this complexity. Second, our perceptions are not uniform.

Inadequacy of sensory organs. From the preceding discussion it should be apparent that our sensory organs can pick up only some of the details in a given object or event. They cannot pick up everything. Our eyes cannot detect all the minute details in reality. Our ears can detect only some of the sounds which occur around us. And so it is with our other senses. There simply are too many details in reality, and our sensory organs are too limited for our perceptions to even approach detailed completeness. Thus, we can never perceive everything about anything. In fact, at best we can perceive only a small part of the whole.

To illustrate the point, imagine that you are watching a football game. The teams line up. The ball is snapped. Then for a few seconds there is bedlam. Players block, run, and fall. The crowd roars, and the officials scurry about. Action is everywhere, and you are perceiving it. Yet how much of the reality of this event do you really perceive? How much do you miss? And when the play is over and you make some comment about it, on how much of all that took place is your comment based? Did you see the guards pull out, the linebackers close the hole, or the offensive tackle hold the opposing player? Did you see each muscle twitch, each facial grimace, each bead of perspiration? There is no question about it; you did not see all that happened. In fact, you missed most of it.

Because you saw so little of all that went on, can you really comment on the event accurately? "That was a well-executed play," you might say, for this may be how your senses perceived it. But is it not quite possible that had you perceived more of the situation, you might find your comment to be wrong? Could it not be that the play worked because one of the opposing players tripped on a shoestring or that an undetected clip took out a key defender? Or that some of the defenders were loafing or made key mistakes? Certainly, all these happenings are possible.

Perception differences. A second explanation of why the infinite nature of reality causes communication difficulty is that, because of its infinite nature, any object or event can be perceived in many different ways. People standing side by side looking at or listening to the same things will not receive the same perception. There are so many complexities and variations in the real world that each of us cannot perceive precisely the same ones.

Our illustration of the football play describes this phenomenon well. So many separate events occur in any one play that two people sitting side by side are likely to perceive different ones. So numerous are the possibilities, in fact, that probably no two spectators in a packed stadium will detect precisely the same ones.

Perhaps even better illustrations can be gathered from the files of almost any law enforcement agency. It is all too common for witnesses to a crime to come up with conflicting accounts of the actions witnessed. Countless cases can be found in which eyewitnesses to a given event sincerely disagree on the parts of the event. One witness may see an accused assailant angrily attacking a victim; another witness may see the accused heroically defending himself or herself from the alleged victim. Or, for another example, a gentleman, in passing a lady on the street, may see only a well-dressed lady in a brown dress; his wife may see a clear picture of the lady and her dress down to such details as her blue eyes and her alligator shoes.

From this analysis comes a question which is basic to our understanding of communication. When people communicate their perceptions of the same objects or events, are they really communicating the same thing? When, for example, in the preceding illustration the lady discusses the dress with her husband, do they have in their minds identical concepts of the dress? Does "that dress" mean the same to the gentleman as "that dress" does to the lady? The answer is an obvious no. And so it is with all other perceptions.

Some applications in communication

From this analysis of the infinite nature of reality come some meaningful applications to communication. First is the need to recognize that you and those with whom you communicate do not detect the same characteristics of what you communicate about. When you write or talk about your perceptions of something, are you and your reader or listener really communicating about the same thing? When, for example, you write in a business letter about an order for a "tennis racquet," do you perceive the same object in reality that your reader perceives? In your mind "tennis racquet" may be just what meets the eye of a casual observer. You may see a metal frame, a leather grip, and string. Your tennis-playing reader, on the other hand, may see an aluminum alloy frame of scientific design, precisely made to meet specifications of flexibility, weight, and balance. Your reader may see the grip as more than just leather, but an intricate design that permits maximum control. And your reader may not see mere strings but a precise quality of gut strung to a precise tension. You should recognize these differences, for they may determine the success of the communication.

Another application of the infinite nature of reality involves any communication situation in which information is presented. In presenting information clearly and correctly, you may need to acknowledge that you have not told all. In writing a report, for example, you present the data you have gathered on a problem. But never can you gather all the data involved. As an objective report writer, you should recognize this limitation. You should make certain also that your reader recognizes it. That is, you should tell the reader of limitations whenever it is appropriate. Specific ways of doing this are described in later chapters on report writing.

Yet another application technique concerning the infinite nature of reality comes from Alfred Korzybski, the founder of general semantics. Korzybski suggested the use of "etc." after all statements. He reasoned that when we communicate about something, always there is more that we could say. We cannot say it all. In the interest of correct communication, he reasoned, we should make this fact clear to our readers. His advice is good. We would be wise to follow it, at least in our thinking.

Uniqueness in everything

A second observation we may make from our inspection of reality is that everything is unique. The sheet of paper we described, for example, is so infinite in its makeup that no other sheet could duplicate it precisely. There never has been one exactly like it, and there never will be one exactly like it. So astronomical is the number of variations in each sheet that exact duplication is beyond the realm of probability.

Uniqueness illustrated

The same observation holds true for any event or object in the world of reality. Every grain of sand on the beach is unlike every other. Every snowflake has its individual characteristics. Every human being now living or who has ever lived is different from every other one. And so it is with every puff of smoke, every hamburger, every apple, every blade of grass, every cat, and every cup of tea. Even carefully matched jewelry, standardized manufactured parts, and the like have differences at the microscopic and submicroscopic levels. Without question, uniqueness is a quality of every object in reality. No two have ever been found to be exactly the same, nor are they likely to be found.

Likewise, no two events can ever be precisely the same. For example, over the years baseball players have hit baseballs millions of times, and each hit has been unique. In the first place, the objects involved in each hit have been different. The balls have been similar, but not precisely the same. The same is true of the bats, the players, the gloves, and the like. In the second place, the continuous change occurring in all objects over time makes exact duplication impossible. A ball hit one moment is not the same ball hit a moment later. In the third place, the movements involved always will differ. Each ball hit will have its unique trajectory and speed. It will land in one unique location. In all such events there will be many very loose similarities, but never exact duplication.

Effects on perception

Some of the differences we speak of are minute, of course. Some are so infinitesimal that we must go to the miscroscopic or submicroscopic level to find them. Because these differences are so small, it is apparent that we cannot detect them without technical aids such as the microscope. Our ears, our eyes, or any of our other sensory organs simply are not capable of detecting such differences.

Because we must go to the microscopic or submicroscopic level to find such differences, you might well ask our reason for mentioning this point. If we must go to such extremes to detect them, can these differences affect our perception of reality? The answer to this question is vital to our understanding of our perception and, conversely, our communication.

Admittedly, the foregoing analysis was presented to prove the point that everything is unique. In many respects it draws an impractical and fine line of distinction. For most practical purposes the insignificant and almost imperceptible differences in reality are of little value to us, and not being able to perceive them does not affect our communication significantly. To consider them every time we communicate would confuse us more than it would help us. But there are communication difficulties which result from the uniqueness of all parts of reality. These we should understand.

These communication difficulties stem primarily from our failure to perceive the uniqueness of the objects and events about which we communicate. More specifically, when we perceive reality, we tend to assume erroneously that similarities rather than differences exist in the real world to which our communication relates. We tend to stress similarities and to ignore differences. Because such practices are contrary to the reality about which we communicate, error in communication results. This cause of miscommunication is discussed in more detail in Chapter 6.

Applications of uniqueness in writing

In the applications chapters of this book the role of uniqueness in communication is emphasized again and again. As the preceding review implies, it is the unique qualities of reality that we communicate about most often. For example, reports typically require that we look for and explain points of uniqueness in a problem. In a problem to determine why store X has a better sales record than store Y, we would emphasize the differences in operations of the two stores. In a scientific study, we would describe the uniqueness of our methodology so precisely that someone else could do the study exactly as we did. In a technical paper, we may need to use words in a special (unique) way. Thus we would need to describe these unique meanings.

Of course, sometimes we emphasize similarities in communication. For example, a report problem may seek a production technique that will give performance identical to a current technique. Or a study may seek to equate certain personal characteristics with success in a given occupation. Or a business may use form letters to cover often recurring situations (a practice that saves time but often does not produce best results). Even so, these examples are exceptions. As a general rule, communication in business emphasizes the uniqueness of a situation.

All in process

A third observation we can make of the real world about us is that it is a world of process. It is continually and forever changing. Nothing remains static. Nothing is now as it was before; and as things are now, they will never be again. Perhaps the foregoing discussion sounds like an overstatement; but it, too, describes reality as it really is. As in our discussion of uniqueness, in the short run the process of reality is perceptible only at the microscopic and submicroscopic levels. It is so apparent in the long run, however, that there can be no doubt about its existence. Again, illustrations best serve to prove this point.

Changes in inanimate things

Take some object around you—say the chair in which you are sitting. As you look at it, probably you see it as being static. It appears very much the way it appeared yesterday and the day before. But if you look closely, you can see evidence that it is not exactly as it once was. Here and there, you may find scratches or nicks, and maybe the color has begun to fade. In all likelihood the glue or screws that hold it together have loosened a bit. Thus, you have evidence that some change has taken place, and you know full well that similar changes will continue to take place. You know that over time the chair will receive additional scratches and its screws and glue will weaken more and more. Someday it will deteriorate to the point that it will be discarded. Perhaps it will decay on a junkpile, or it may be burned. Eventually, it will become dirt or ashes or something far different from what it is today.

Or take the illustration of a visit to a hallowed battlefield of a war fought a century or more ago. Assume that you are listening to the commentary of a guide who describes the events which took place here. "Over there on the knoll General Blain set up his command post from which he directed his battle strategy. Down there by the brook his cavalry assembled, and over there in the wooded area his infantry prepared for the charge across the meadows ahead." And on and on he talks, giving you a vivid picture of the battle fought long ago in this very place. Probably you are moved with emotion. Here you are in the very place where so much history took place.

Now let us look at the place as it really is. Let us look to see how much remains of the scene at the time of battle. The brook is still there, but its path has changed. And the water which flowed through it then is far, far away. How many of the trees that were there at the time of the battle are still alive, and how many of the trees now present were even seedlings then? Much of the soil on which the soldier's feet trod has long since washed away. The grass now in the meadow is a hundred generations removed from the grass the soldiers saw. What, then, remains of the place where the battle was fought? Although it may sound like a play on words, we might conclude that we are at the same place, but the place is not the same.

Such changes, of course, are obvious over long periods of time. Others are more apparent and occur more rapidly. Without refrigeration, a pail of fresh sweet milk, for example, may change to sour milk in a day or two. Sometime later, it will become clabber; and after even more time, it may become cottage cheese. A piece of ice placed on a hot stove will change to water, then to steam, and then seemingly will disappear before your eyes. White, dry flour can change in a matter of minutes to dough, then to bread. And certainly, we all marvel at the wonders of chemistry in transforming petroleum into various forms of plastics. A student of chemistry could continue this discussion through countless examples.

Changes in the living

Just as all matter is in a constant state of change, so does all life change. So obvious a point as this hardly needs discussion, for we have only to trace our own lives back to the time of birth to prove the point. Certainly, we are not now the physical beings we once were. We are bigger and stronger; even our features are different. And we know that this physical change will continue as long as we live—that at every passing moment imperceptible changes take place and that these changes become perceptible over time.

Equally apparent but all too often overlooked are the changes which take place in our minds—in how we think and what we know. From the time of birth this process of change begins, and it continues until death. We are continually receiving new knowledge, having new thoughts, and generally taking different views of the world about us.

This point can be illustrated by a review of your own development. Go back a few years and analyze the you of that time. How different are you now from what you were then? How much more do you know today? Are there any beliefs, opinions, or attitudes which have changed? Are you the same person emotionally? Unless you are a most unusual person or one who does not comprehend this analysis, you will find vast differences. You simply are not the same person you were then. Significant changes have taken place. They are taking place now. They will continue to take place as long as you live.

Error effect on perception

No one will seriously argue that such changes do not take place, for the facts are most obvious. A problem does arise, however, from our failure to consider properly the changing nature of reality when we perceive reality. All too often we see reality as if it were static—as if it has always been the way it is and always will remain that way. And because reality simply does not remain static, such perceptions must lead to some error.

Examples of error resulting from failures to consider the process nature of reality come from all areas of human activity. For example, two business executives once were discussing consulting services they had used. One spoke in glowing terms of the services of a certain consultant. The other responded, "I can't believe that. We used the man once. He almost ruined us!" As it turned out, the second executive had used the consultant many years earlier. This was a time when the consultant was just beginning his practice and before he had developed his current expertise. The consultant had changed; yet, in the mind of one executive, he remained the same.

Even nations are guilty of this form of perception error, as is evident from a review of history. A major reason for war, for example, has been to avenge wrongs done by one nation against another generations earlier. That is, nations have often looked at past relationships with other nations as if they were in the present—as if the people responsible for these relationships still represented their nation. Thus, they have blamed inhabitants of the present for acts of their ancestors. As a result, people have hated and killed and engaged in acts which in time people not yet born may again use as justification for more war. If we look at such situations with clear, objective eyes, we see that the people involved have failed to consider the fact that reality has changed.

Among the better examples of this error are those which involve statistical comparisons. In a heated political campaign a certain candidate for mayor berated his opponent by pointing out that, during his opponent's administration, expenditures exceeded those of three preceding administrations combined. It was a statement of fact. But it failed to consider the most significant fact of all—that the administration criticized covered a period of extraordinary growth which saw population more than double in size. Certainly, this great change justified at least some of the increased expenditure.

A few years ago a sportswriter noted that one of today's superstars in baseball signed a million-dollar contract. In the sportswriter's words, this contract was "a record in anybody's book" and that it "dwarfs the $80,000 received by Babe Ruth in his prime." Even the most elementary student of economics could point out that Ruth's $80,000 was much better than the figure suggests to today's people. In the first place, Ruth's pay was not subject to today's high income tax rates. In the second place, dollars of the 1920s bought far more than today's dollars. A 1925 Ford, for example, sold for $250—hardly a suitable down payment for the models of today. The writer failed to take into account the very significant fact of change.

All too often each of us is guilty of this perception error in referring to our acquaintances. Our perception of a person may be based on what we knew of her or him at one point in time, and we tend to hold this perception. From the moment we register the perception, however, our acquaintance changes, just as everything else changes. In time, our perception may no longer fit; yet we are not likely to alter it. As a result of this tendency, when we communicate about people, erroneous impressions may be sent or received, depending on the time of reference to the individuals concerned.

Changing reality and written communication

The failure to communicate change can be a major cause of error in written communication. To illustrate the point, a business report showing a company's 1935 net profit of $3 million has one meaning, a 1955 net profit of $3 million another, and a 1985 net profit of $3 million yet another. For another example, the writer of a report on a production problem may reject certain production equipment because of a record of bad performance on the 1981 model. The current model may be quite different. For yet another example, a letter evaluating a job applicant covers a definite period—the time the writer observed the subject. As the subject of the letter could be quite different now, the writer should clearly note the time covered by the report. We could use countless similar examples.

Because time can affect communication so vitally, Alfred Korzybski suggested dating all references to people and things with date subscripts (John Smith$_{1937}$, Mary Pitts$_{1984}$, San Francisco$_{1871}$). Although the practice has not caught on, the logic is sound. We would do well to include a date reference whenever place in time will aid the clarity of our writing. And when we read messages, we would do well to keep in mind the place in time of the objects and events reported.

Relative nature of perception

As if the complexities resulting from its infinite, unique, and process nature were not enough, reality becomes even more complex because of variations in our perceptions of it. Some variation in perception results from shortcomings and differences in our sensory organs. As we have discussed these possibilities at some length, we may turn our attention to a second explanation of perception variation. It is that we do not all observe an object or event from the same position. Thus, we perceive the object or event differently.

To illustrate the point, take the words often used to berate someone's intelligence: "He doesn't know which end is up!" The chances are that this is a true statement, and it is equally true of the speaker. Actually, the direction "up" is a relative thing—in this case it is relative to the ground. But the ground is not a flat surface, for our earth is shaped like a round ball. Thus, from any point on the ball the direction up is different from the direction up at any other point. To see the point, imagine that you are looking at the earth from far out in space. Now imagine a person standing on the North Pole pointing up and another person standing on the South Pole pointing up. They are pointing in opposite directions. And if every person on earth were pointing up, would not each be pointing in a direction which coincided with no other?

For another example, take an automobile moving along a highway at 70 miles per hour. Inside the automobile you observe a little fly flitting from the front to the back at a speed of 20 miles per hour. Now, as you look at its movement from your point of reference inside the car, the fly clearly flew at 20 miles per hour from front to back. If, however, your reference is the side of the road, would you not see the little fly move backward at 50 miles per hour? And when its flight is done, would it not resume its sitting speed of 70 miles per hour?

These examples, of course, are the more obvious ones. But to some degree, perception of the same objects or events will vary from one person to another, depending on the points of reference. A stage play from backstage looks altogether different than it does from out front. Fight fans on one side of the ring may see hard, solid punches to the jaw; those on the opposite side may see the same blows roll harmlessly off. The crew of a bomber may see its bombs form interesting puffs of smoke as they hit their targets; people down on the ground see terrible destruction. Football spectators high up in the stands clearly see an act of pass interference committed on the field, but the official on the spot sees a skillfully executed save. Thus, we see that regardless of what reality may really be, we cannot and do not perceive it the same way. Much depends on our position of reference.

Truth and reality

The confusing picture of reality we have unfolded leads us to a question which human beings have been trying to answer throughout history. It is the question of the meaning of "truth." The question was debated by the early philosophers, and it has held the attention of scholars ever since. We are no nearer the truth today, and the foregoing discussion explains why. We have seen that the real world is so complex that it is impossible to know all about anything. And because we cannot know all about anything, is not the likelihood good that usually we do not know enough to be certain? Is there not always some risk involved with incomplete information? Then, also, because each of us sees reality in a slightly different way, there is further confusion on just what the true reality is. Obviously, the answer to our question is as elusive now as it has ever been.

You should keep this point in mind when you write business reports. As you will see, a report seeks truth. Its general goal is to provide the facts of reality a company needs in its operations. Its emphasis is on the facts and of an objective interpretation of the facts. The task of writing such reports is no simple one. It may well be impossible.

Questions & Problems

1. What is the relationship of reality to communication?
2. Explain the nature of reality using the reality which surrounds you at this moment to illustrate your explanation.
3. Select a simple object and explain its infinite makeup.
4. Discuss the reality around you which your senses cannot detect.
5. If uniqueness in some object cannot be detected by our sensory receptors, how can it be

important to our understanding of communication?
6. Explain how an understanding of the process nature of reality helps us to understand communication.
7. Susan Hathaway has bought the same brand of automobile for 37 years. "I once owned another brand," she explained. "And I learned my lesson from that experience." Discuss the reality of this situation.
8. "Sure I know Sam Allen," an executive reported

to a person considering Sam for employment. "He and I were in high school together. He's shiftless and lazy." Discuss the executive's perception.

9. A personnel executive explained that she gave importance to grades when hiring a recent college graduate. In hiring people who have been out of college for some time, however, she gave grades little importance. Discuss the reality involved in her logic.

10. "I'm sorry," a purchasing agent told the salesperson. "We buy only well-known brands. No offense, but I've never heard of your company." Discuss.

11. An ancient philosopher once noted that we cannot step into the same river twice. Discuss.

12. A witness at court balked when taking the oath to "tell the truth, the whole truth, and nothing but the truth." The witness responded that he could not take the oath. Discuss.

13. Give examples (other than those in the book) to illustrate the *(a)* infinite, *(b)* unique, and *(c)* process nature of reality in business writing situations.

4 The filter of the mind

WE HAVE LEARNED from the preceding discussion that reality is infinite, unique, and forever in process. We have learned also that our ability (or perhaps *inability* would be the better word) to perceive causes difficulties in communicating. Our perception limitations, however, do not explain all of our miscommunication problems, or perhaps even a major part of them. Of major significance are our limitations in handling the perceptions we are able to register.

The handling of our perceptions, of course, involves the filter process described in Chapter 2. Specifically, it involves how we give meaning to the reality our sensory receptors pick up and pass through our minds. Thus, it is the nature of the filter to which our analysis of communication now turns.

A storehouse of knowledge

Basic to our analysis of the filter is the role knowledge plays in determining meaning. As we all know, our minds serve as storehouses of knowledge. Just how knowledge is stored (learned) is a most complex subject about which psychologists long have been concerned. In general, they agree ". . . that learning is a process of doing things, finding out and evaluating what has happened, storing the experience, and trying again—using past experience as a jumping off place."[1]

More specifically, learning involves the basic area of classical conditioning (Pavlov and his salivating dog) and of instrumental behavior (trial-and-error, reward-and-punishment learning). It includes the more complex area of skills acquisition. And of greatest significance to human beings, it includes all that which we acquire through the symbolic learning process. It is the area

---

[1] Harold J. Leavitt, *Managerial Psychology*, 4th ed., University of Chicago Press, Chicago, 1978, p. 58.

of symbolic learning about which we are most concerned, for it is through symbols (mainly words) that the more complex forms of knowledge are acquired. Unfortunately, we know very little about symbolic learning.

Although a sophisticated analysis of how knowledge is acquired would be helpful to us in understanding communication, our present needs are served by a simplified, practical review of how knowledge affects our communication. Such a review logically begins with our first learning experiences—experiences which take place in infancy. At an early age we human beings begin to receive information picked up by our sensory receptors, and we give meanings to this information. The meanings received remain with us for varying periods. Much of the information stays with us for very brief moments—mere seconds and perhaps even fractions of seconds. Some of it remains with us for longer periods—days, weeks, months, years. Some stays with us for a lifetime.

To illustrate this point, consider your learning process at this very moment. As you read this information, you are receiving the symbols presented on this page. As you read each sentence, the exact words used are in your mind—at least for a brief moment. Very soon the exact impressions you receive will be forgotten. Later you are likely to remember only the major points presented; and as time goes on, you will forget more and more of these.

Thus, we can see that as our receptors bring in information to our minds, we are continuously adding to our storehouse of knowledge; and at the same time, we are continuously losing some of its content. What is stored is forever changing. Hence, at any given moment of time our minds are equipped with a given storehouse of knowledge. At any other moment the storehouse will be somewhat different.

As our sensory organs pick up perceptions and relay them to our brains, the meanings we give these perceptions are governed by the knowledge stored at the moment. For example, assume that you live in a primitive society. Your sensory receptors have never perceived a radio, or anything resembling it. Thus, your filter contains no knowledge of this device. Now you walk into a room and hear voices and music, and there on the table before you is a little box from which the sounds appear to come. It is a most frightening phenomenon, for your mind contains no knowledge which will explain such sounds coming out of a box.

What is your reaction? Maybe you will hurl your spear through it, for surely this mysterious box is evil. All of the unknown, you have been taught to believe, is evil. And if you are a brave soul, maybe you will stand your distance and cautiously watch. Or if you are a coward, perhaps you will bolt and run away screaming, with your arms flailing about wildly.

On the other hand, assume that you are now yourself. You walk into the room and hear the music. You know that the box is a radio, for you have seen radios many times. You know that radios are sources of enjoyment—not of fear. Thus, when your perception of this radio goes to your brain, the knowledge that radios are enjoyable devices governs your interpretation. Or putting it in more technical language, the stimulus (perception of the radio) triggers a response (pleasure) which similar stimuli have triggered before and have stored in your brain.

Admittedly, this one example was selected to dramatize the role of knowledge in communication. Any bit of knowledge, regardless of its nature, could have done the job. In any event, the principle involved is the same: the knowledge stored in the mind at the time information is received influences the meaning the mind gives the information.

The knowledge stored does not have to be true knowledge, for the effects of true information and misinformation are the same. All that matters is how the mind accepts the information. If, for example, someone's mind has stored the erroneous information that all snakes are dangerous, this person's reaction to a communication about snakes will be influenced by this misinformation. And the effort will be much the same until the filter receives additional information which will alter the knowledge stored. It is the same for all the knowledge stored in any mind, regardless of the degree to which the knowledge resembles reality.

The role of opinions, attitudes, and beliefs

Included also in our mental filters are the viewpoints we hold about the reality in which we live. More especially, we are referring to our attitudes, opinions, and beliefs. They differ from knowledge in that they concern matters on which there is no unanimity. Yet they are not exclusive of knowledge, for they may be well supported by factual matter. Like our storehouses of knowledge, our attitudes, opinions, and beliefs have strong influence on how we interpret the information our receptors pick up and relay through our minds.

What the terms mean

Before we discuss the role our opinions, attitudes, and beliefs play in communication, let us define these three terms as we shall use them. In a sense, all are similar, for all refer to our viewpoints about the reality which surrounds us. They differ, however, in the degree of intensity with which we hold them.[2]

Opinions are the least intense of all and refer to viewpoints concerning those areas of reality which are least critical in our lives. For example, one may have opinions on such matters as the latest fad in ladies' fashion, the merits of an advertising technique, the value of the forward pass in football, the effectiveness of closed-circuit television in teaching, or the desirability of a pending piece of legislation.

Attitudes are our viewpoints on more important matters. As we shall see, these are the intermediate matters in life. They are more vital than

---

[2] Bernard Berelson and Gary A. Steiner, *Human Behavior*, Harcourt, Brace & World, Inc., New York, 1964, p. 558.

the everyday matters of opinions, yet they fall short of the core matters in life upon which beliefs are based. How one thinks on the question of socialized medicine, for example, might well fall in this category. Other likely examples are one's viewpoint on government regulation of business, employment of women, and labor-management relations.

Beliefs are our viewpoints on the most critical values in life. As previously implied, they concern those matters we hold most dear—matters of morality, religion, government, and the like. For example, one may believe in the immortality of the soul, in witchcraft, in academic freedom, in rugged individualism, in respect for law and order.

Obviously, our definitions are not clear-cut for the terms overlap. There are no sharp lines dividing opinions from attitudes from beliefs. What is an opinion to one person may be an attitude to another and a belief to yet another. Nevertheless, these definitions give us a general guide to understanding the makeup of this element in our filtering process.

How viewpoints are formed

Why we think the way we think is a subject about which psychologists have long been concerned. They still have much to learn about it, but they have advanced findings which are of concern to us in our study of communication.

Through objective reasoning. First, we reach some of our viewpoints through rational thought processes. That is, we sometimes gather the evidence involved in a matter, weigh it, and reach a decision through objective thought processes. This is the pattern of thinking wise people have followed since the beginning of civilization. But this objective procedure is not so often practiced as we like to think. As Harold J. Leavitt expressed this point, "Most of us accept or reject new ideas or change our behavior more in response to feelings than to facts."[3] Even when we try to reason objectively, we are likely to be influenced by the more subjective factors described in the following paragraphs.

Perhaps it is alarming to hear that we human beings are not the rational creatures we like to think we are, so let us illustrate the point. Take some strong belief that you have—say something concerning religion or politics. Now think of someone with a strongly different belief. For the purpose of illustration, let us call this person Susan. Next, ask yourself the question, "Would I not have the same belief as Susan if I had lived in her environment?" Before you answer the question, assume that in early infancy you exchanged homes with Susan, and that she has lived your life and you have lived hers. Instead of getting the benefits of your environment, particularly your family's teachings, you got hers and she got yours. Is it not likely that you would have her belief and she yours? And would you not be likely to argue and defend her belief as vigorously as you now defend your own? And so it would be for many of the subjects of your opinions, attitudes, and beliefs.

---

[3] Leavitt, *Managerial Psychology*, p. 127.

Social strata and viewpoints. Our social strata also play a heavy role in determining our viewpoints. By "social strata" we mean the levels or segments of society into which we fall—whether we are rich, poor, or somewhere in between; Jew or Gentile; male or female; white or black; Irish, Polish, English, or Indian; Northerner, Southerner, or Westerner; and so on. To some extent, our social inheritance determines the experiences we have and the pressures society places upon us. They condition us to view reality in a way peculiar to the strata to which we belong. The result is a significant and somewhat lasting effect on our attitudes, opinions, and beliefs.

Five areas of our social structure play a significant role in determining our attitudes, opinions, and beliefs. Three are major; two are relatively minor. The major ones include class, ethnic status, and residence. The minor ones are age and sex.

Although basically determined by economic status, class also is determined by such factors as education and occupation. Family status in the community also may be a determinant. Without question, one's class does determine significantly one's thinking on certain matters. People born into low-income families, for example, are subjected to hardships and deprivations which are likely to influence their viewpoints on many matters. Because they have been poor all their lives, they are likely to favor legislation which will assist their class. Thus, in politics they are likely to be liberal. Because they had little time for exposure to the finer things in life, they are not likely to appreciate the aesthetic. And because they have lived their lives in positions subordinate to others, they are likely to accept authoritarian methods with little question. Their viewpoints would not likely be the same had they been born to another class.

Residence, of course, is the geographic area in which one lives. We all know that people in some areas think differently on some matters than do people in others. One born into a given area is likely to succumb to the existing thinking. Thus, a person from the U.S. South is likely to think differently on the question of states' rights than a person from the Pacific Northwest or New England. Likewise, natives of the Russian province of Georgia are destined to have viewpoints on some matters different from those of people from Siberia or the Ukraine. Similar differences exist in many countries of the world.

Ethnic differences pertain to our national, racial, and religious inheritance. For example, members of minority races are likely to have strong viewpoints on matters stemming from their experiences with prejudice. On the other hand, those from nonpersecuted races enjoy a different social inheritance and may have altogether different viewpoints on such matters. For another example, the clannish living of many nationality groups in our major cities contributes to the formulation of common and different viewpoints. The Irish of New York City, the Poles in Chicago, the Chinese in San Francisco all live in a manner that sets them apart from those around them. As a result, they are likely to hold viewpoints differing from those generally held by other citizens on such matters as respect for elders, morality, recognition of authority, and importance of savings.

Religion serves as a third example of the effect of ethnic inheritance on our viewpoints. Obviously, a religion is a system of beliefs, and the systems in existence differ rather sharply. Typically, we inherit this system of beliefs from our families. We may depart somewhat from these beliefs, but most of us are likely to hold them throughout our lives.

Although minor determinants of the strata which govern at least some of our viewpoints, sex and age nevertheless play a significant role. Viewpoint differences related to sex are readily apparent. In our culture, boys place greater importance on physical powers than do girls. In addition, boys are less emotional in their dealings with each other; they are more active in politics; they are more concerned about the technical areas. Likewise, age helps to form distinguishing viewpoints among us. In youth, we tend to be rebels in our thinking—to be different and to oppose convention and authority. As we grow older, we tend to turn toward more conservative thinking. We tend to become less tolerant, to lose some of the effects of education as we grow older.

Early influence of the family. Just how we form our viewpoints is a most complex subject about which there is not complete agreement. There is general agreement, however, that we acquire much of our thinking from the people in our lives. That is to say, we human beings are not primarily the rational creatures we like to think we are. Rather, we are more like parrots. We tend to accept much of our thinking somewhat blindly from others.

Foremost among those who influence our thoughts are the members of our own family. At an early age we human beings begin to acquire the thinking of our family. Some of this thinking we are taught deliberately, but much of it we acquire through observation. However it is done, the results are the same. Our earliest thinking on such matters as religion, politics, ethics, cultural tastes, and the like is the thinking of our family.

Change effects of groups. Many of the viewpoints acquired from our social strata or our family stay with us for a lifetime. This is certainly true in such areas as religion and politics. It is obvious, however, that as time goes by, we begin to question some of our attitudes, opinions, and beliefs. And occasionally we alter some of them.

As we have mentioned, some of our viewpoint changes result from logical thought processes, for we can on occasion be rational beings. More often, however, our viewpoint changes are influenced by groups to which we belong. Throughout our lives we hold membership in many groups—religious, family, social, and so on. In considering our attitudes, opinions, and beliefs, we refer to these groups, and we are heavily influenced by the thinking within them. Thus, the desire to conform is a major factor in determining our attitudes, opinions, and beliefs.

A high school boy, for example, would be inclined to change a viewpoint to conform with that of his peers on matters he considers important to his membership in the group. He might discard the puritan thinking given him by a straitlaced family for the more permissive standards of his friends. If the group is a street gang, he would be likely to adjust his viewpoints to conform with the gang's opinions on law and order and its attitudes on morality in general.

Similarly, other groups influence the thinking of all of us. If we are members of labor, we are likely to accept the prevailing viewpoint toward management held by other members of labor. If we are part of management, we are likely to assume the traditional viewpoint of management toward labor. Members of the medical profession are generally of one mind on issues such as socialized medicine. College professors are united in their beliefs in academic freedom. And so it is with all groups. Each has some effect on the thinking of its members.

It should be apparent that all of us belong to many groups. We may at the same time be a member of a social set, a church, a profession, a civic organization, a hobby, a club, and a political party. As a member of these groups, we are subject to the pressures to conform to each. Obviously, we cannot always succumb to all pressures, for some must sometimes conflict. As a member of a church group, we may be under the group's pressure to accept a philosophy of charity to all the unfortunate. Our professional peers, on the other hand, may favor a minimum of government help in all areas of activity. Thus, we could submit to only one of the groups' pressures. We would have to make a choice.

Similar pressures exist when we leave one group for another. Members of labor suddenly promoted to the ranks of management find themselves facing new group pressures and leaving old ones. Likewise, beginning teachers find that their new group holds some different viewpoints from those they held while they were members of the student group. In such cases the usual result is a change in viewpoint to conform with that of the new group.

Self-interest as a determinant of viewpoint. Closely related to the influence of groups[4] on our thinking are the effects of self-interest. There is no doubt about it. We hold certain viewpoints simply because it is to our best interests to do so.

For example, an otherwise upstanding citizen who fudges on tax returns might build up opinions and attitudes which support her or his actions. "Everybody does it" might be the justification—or perhaps, "They expect you to work it close." An ambitious business person might support a policy of ruthless business dealings with the attitude that business is a dog-eat-dog activity and that ruthlessness is a necessary ingredient in successful strategy. Similarly, people of means are generally opposed to government programs which take from them and give to others. They reason that such acts discourage initiative and encourage the growth of a welfare class. The poor, on the other hand, generally support such legislation, and they support their stand with such arguments as "It is our just share" or "Don't penalize us for the accident of birth."

How viewpoints affect communication

Once formed, our attitudes, opinions, and beliefs tend to persist. This is not to say that they do not change, for we have shown that pressures for

---

[4] Actually, our submission to the pressures of groups is for reasons of self-interest. We conform to the thinking of the group because we want the acceptance of the group.

change are continually with us and that these pressures bring about changes in viewpoint. But the resistance to changing them is forever present; and the longer we hold a viewpoint, the greater this resistance is likely to be.

Especially is the resistance to change strong on viewpoints concerning matters in which we are emotionally involved or strongly interested. Two people of different religious convictions are not likely to convert each other, regardless of how long they argue or how logically they present their beliefs. Likewise, it is a rare case when a political conservative can change the viewpoint of a political liberal, and vice versa. In such instances each is more interested in presenting his or her own case than in hearing the case of the other. And so it is with all the attitudes, opinions, and beliefs we hold. We sometimes change them, but the change comes slowly. Most of the time we resist successfully.

The facts that our mental filters contain attitudes, opinions, and beliefs and that we resist changing them play a major role in determining the meanings we give to our perceptions. When the incoming information is in accord with our viewpoints, we tend to accept it. When it runs contrary to our viewpoints, we tend to reject it. Accepted information is positively received, for it falls in place with what is already in the filter. On the other hand, information rejected produces a negative reaction. It may be upsetting and may be likely to bring about a negative communication response. Such information is not communicated easily—at least the message received is not the one intended.

The influence of emotions

Another factor in the filtering process is the emotional state of the mind at the time the mind receives the perception. Before we explain this factor, however, let us get a more precise understanding of emotions. Specifically, let us determine what they are and how they are formed. Then we shall explore the manner in which they affect communication.

Emotions may be defined as the sources of energy which make the mind work. Without them, we would be in a continual stupor. Our existence would be somewhat like that of a vegetable. In addition, without emotions, we would not exist long, for the energy of emotions is a vital part of the survival effort of our species. When we perceive danger, we have the emotion of fear, which serves to protect us from that danger. When we are confronted by an antagonist, we become angry, and our anger serves in our defense against our antagonist. We love our children; thus, we protect them, thereby promoting the survival of our kind.

Our emotional energy results from an automatic response to certain of the perceptions which our sensory receptors receive and pass on to the brain. They occur much as do our reflexes. They are inevitable. Certain perceptions trigger certain emotional responses. For example, if someone bumps us, perhaps even accidently, we tend to become angry. When someone shouts contemptuous words to us, we respond with hatred. When an attractive member of the opposite sex smiles at us, we are filled with excitement. Perhaps we are able to control our emotions in such cases, but our emotions are aroused nevertheless. We can no more stop such reactions than we can stop the eye from blinking when an object suddenly moves dangerously toward it.

From the foregoing discussion it should be apparent that the emotions triggered play a part in determining the meanings we give to the perceptions we receive. The emotional energy brought about becomes a part of the filtering process. Thus, it plays a role in determining the meanings given to perceptions which follow. In other words, the emotional state of the mind at the moment a perception is received helps to determine the meaning the mind gives the perception.

To illustrate this point, take the case of a salesperson named Smith who makes her first call on an executive named Jones. As Smith enters Jones's office, she cheerfully says "Good morning." Now, normally, such cheery words would bring about a cheerful response; but this time, let us assume that the situation is not normal. Jones has just arrived at work after an assortment of harrowing experiences. He did not sleep well last night. Breakfast was terrible. He had a fight with his wife. Traffic was unusually bad on his way to work. And now, after arriving at work, he is given a priority assignment which must be completed by noon. It is a five-hour job, so he will have to work hard to meet his deadline. Obviously, Jones is emotionally upset. Everything has gone wrong. He has more work than he has time to do, and here he is approached by a salesperson who wants some of his valuable time. So Jones's filter gives a negative meaning to Smith's "Good morning." "What's good about it?" might well be Jones's thought, if not his response.

For another example, take an opposite situation. This time, let us assume that Jones is in excellent spirits when Smith approaches him with her cheerful "Good morning." Jones's holdings in the stock market have just advanced sharply. His business in general is unusually good. He had a good night's sleep, a most enjoyable breakfast, a pleasant conversation with his wife, and a relaxing drive to the office. His work for the day appears to be manageable. He sees Smith not as an intruder in a busy work schedule but as a friendly salesperson—one who might hold a key to more business profit. Now as the cheerful "Good morning" goes through Jones's filter, it receives the full, happy connotation Smith intended.

The filter, in summary

From the foregoing discussion, we have seen that the filtering process involves principally three factors. The first is the knowledge the mind contains, for new perceptions are given meaning as they relate to what is already in the mind. Second are the viewpoints (specifically attitudes, opinions, and beliefs) which the mind holds. These viewpoints serve as determinants of acceptance for the incoming perceptions, and they play a major role in determining the emotional effect of the perceptions. Third is the emotional state of the mind, which serves as a general conditioner of the incoming perceptions.

All three of these factors are forever changing, and sometimes they behave inconsistently and illogically when we consider the influences of the emotional state of the individual. At any given moment in time the filter has a given makeup of knowledge, viewpoints, and emotional energy. Its makeup at the precise moment it receives a perception determines the meaning we give that perception.

Questions & Problems

1. Select an incident from your experience that illustrates how knowledge affects communication.
2. From your viewpoints select an attitude, an opinion, and a belief. As well as you can, explain why you hold each of these viewpoints.
3. Discuss how your attitudes, opinions, and beliefs influence your communication.
4. Explain and illustrate how viewpoints can change.
5. Discuss the role of viewpoints in communicating.
6. Mary and Clara are intelligent and capable executives for the same company. Each was assigned the task of evaluating the proposed plan for promoting a new product. After long and careful thought, Mary and Clara arrived at opposite conclusions. And each was certain of being right. Each argued that information she gained through experience supported her conclusion. Explain this situation.
7. Members of Department X watched as their new supervisor entered the work area. It was the first time any of them had seen him. "Look at that square," said Mary. "That crew haircut is right out of the 50s. I'll give odds that he's a stickler for detail and a real taskmaster." Her co-workers generally agreed with her. Discuss.
8. For many months the department supervisor had been watching George. The supervisor was pleased with all that he saw and had concluded that George was the person to promote to team leader when old Mr. Koontz retired. The supervisor changed his opinion abruptly when George told him about the new motorcycle he

had bought. Discuss from a communications point of view.
9. Dr. Katherine Wentzel, an economic adviser to the president, was riding home in a taxi after a long day's work. She had spent the day with a committee of high-ranking legislators working on legislation designed to stimulate the economy. As she was pleased with the legislation that her work had helped to produce, she proceeded to tell the cab driver about it. To her surprise the cab driver responded with these words: "That's just more of that big brother government. Why don't they leave the economy alone and let it run without interference?" Discuss.
10. Albert Dodge, a recent college graduate in engineering, is employed as a production engineer by Boone Manufacturing Company. From an article in a technical journal Albert read about a new production technique which had proved to be highly successful when used by companies doing production work similar to that done by Boone. So he decided to try the procedure. After explaining the procedure to Wilburn Latham, the veteran supervisor in charge, Albert got this response: "It won't work. I've been doing this work for 35 years. Started when I was 15. Learned it from the ground up. I know it won't work." Discuss.
11. At the age of 20 Billy Joe left his parents' farm to take a job at a factory in the city. All his life Billy Joe had been a hard worker. "A day's work for a day's pay" was a principle he believed in strongly. Billy Joe worked very hard on his new job. And for the first week he produced

150 units. The shop average was 80. After observing his production record, Billy Joe's boss remarked, "This kid is a real worker. He'll go places." The same day one of Billy Joe's fellow workers commented to another worker, "We'd better get this kid in line. He looks like a troublemaker." Discuss.

12. Professor Smiley conducted the following test among business executives. He wrote a short article advocating some fairly innovative business procedures and gave the article to two very similar groups to read. The article read by one group named a nationally known management consultant as the author. The article read by the second group identified its author as an unknown graduate student. Professor Smiley found that support for the procedure presented in the article was much stronger in the first group than in the second. Discuss.

13. For 30 years William Wills has worked as a machinist. And for most of this time he has worked in an all-male environment. Recently, women workers have joined his ranks. When told that the rejection rate for work done in his shop had reached a record high, he responded: "What do you expect with women doing men's work?" When confronted with data showing that there was little difference in rejection rates of men and women workers, he replied, "That's mainly because the inspectors are women." Discuss.

Words and meaning

5

OF ALL THE SYMBOLS we use in communicating, the most important by far are words. As we have noted, we use many other symbols—facial expressions, hand and body movements, grunts, and the like, but these we use primarily to convey the simple message of our emotions or to supplement our verbal communication. The bulk of our deliberate communicating we do with words. As they are the primary medium of our communication, they deserve special study.

Language and human progress

The important role of words in our communication is even more evident when we look at their influence on human progress. Our language, which is a systems of words, is credited with giving us superiority over the other forms of life.[1] Other species, it may be pointed out, are stronger, more efficient, and better equipped in many ways. But we human beings alone have language,[2] and language has enabled us to combat the problems of life with unusual success.

Through our use of language, we human beings have been able to bind time.[3] By "time binding" we mean that human beings of one generation have been able to communicate with human beings of other generations. From those who have lived before us, we have been able to learn from the records of their knowledge and experience. We are able to communicate our knowledge and experience to those who will live after us. And we are

---

[1] Irving J. Lee, *Language Habits in Human Affairs*, Harper & Row, New York, 1941, pp. 3–5.

[2] This statement is made with the knowledge that dolphins, gibbons, and other relatively intelligent animals make some use of symbols. As interesting as the studies of these animals may be, there has not been uncovered any evidence that these animals have a system of symbols which in any way is comparable to the language of human beings.

[3] Alfred Korzybski, *Science and Sanity, An Introduction to Non-Aristotelian Systems and General Semantics*, 3d ed., Country Life Publishing Corp., Garden City, N.Y., 1948, p. 376.

able to exchange knowledge with those of other times. Thus, because we have language, we human beings are the only life form which has not been limited to knowledge that can be learned from the trial-and-error experiences in a single lifetime. The results have been that we have built a vast storehouse of knowledge. With this knowledge we have managed to achieve our present state of superiority.

The foundation of language

Words, like any other form of symbol, have the objective of conveying our impressions of reality. But as we have seen, reality is infinitely complex. It is made up of billions upon billions of objects, each different from all others and continuously changing. It is comprised of billions upon billions of events, each different from any other event that ever has taken place or will take place. The task of words to convey precisely this complex reality most certainly is a gigantic one.

To convey exactly the meaning of each object and event with words would require that we use new and different words for each object and event. Once used, the words would have to be discarded, for they could never again apply. They would never again apply because the precise event or object they cover would never again occur or exist. Obviously, such a system of symbols would not work. In the first place, it would have to be as complex and involved as reality itself, and this would be an impossibility. In the second place, for language to be effective, some form of meaning of the symbols must be agreed upon by the participants in communication. Our mental limitations make it necessary that we achieve such agreement by repetitious use of somewhat general symbols. Thus, we human beings have been forced to form a simpler-than-reality language—a language that makes single words cover a broad area of reality. And so that some agreement on meaning can be reached, we must use these words again and again.

Classification based on similarity

Although no one really knows how our early ancestors built our language, the finished product gives us evidence that they built it around classifications of their perceptions. Probably they began by reviewing reality, looking for similarities in what they saw. When they found similarities, they built classifications and devised words for them. Then, when viewing these groups, they found that broader similarities were present in some of them, and again they built classifications and selected words for them. Again and again, they combined groups into broader concepts and supplied words. They did this as long as it was practical for them to do so.

This process of classifying perceptions and combining classifications into broader concepts is not so exact as this simplified description might imply. At best, the classifications are fuzzy; they are not clearly separated. There is considerable overlap and duplication of the classification possibilities. Nevertheless, the process gives us a meaningful comprehension of the structure of language and how it relates to reality.

This general process of forming language is referred to in the writings of Alfred Korzybski[4] as the "structural differential" and later was popularized by S. I. Hayakawa[5] as the "abstraction ladder." Hayakawa's words are most appropriate, for they describe the process which has occurred. In each of the steps of classification, human beings have abstracted from reality. From all the characteristics involved, they have selected certain ones as a basis for grouping the objects or events at each stage. That is, they have abstracted similarities and based their words on them.

Illustration: "Fido" and the "economy"

In constructing our language, probably our ancestors began with the more obvious events and objects in life. Perhaps on one occasion members of a tribe of our ancestors perceived a certain little animal that was living around their village. Their perceptions, of course, included only some of the reality in this animal, for there was much that they could not detect. They could not perceive the bones, blood, flesh, and body organs; the cells that made up these parts; the structure of the cells; and the like. But these parts were nevertheless there.

Their perceptions were of individual animals—little four-legged, pointed-nosed, short-haired creatures. Each had its distinctive markings, its unique personality, and a body of its own. Perhaps our ancestors befriended one of these animals and induced it to live in their camp. In time, they found need to communicate about this one animal which they perceived separately from the others. So they selected a word for it. Let us say that the word was "Fido."

Our primitive ancestors had other perceptions of Fido, however. Sometimes they did not perceive him alone, but with other creatures that looked something like him. Our primitive ancestors were aware that some of these creatures were not exactly like their Fido. They had hair of different lengths, and the colors of their coats varied. Some were quite small when compared with Fido, and some were much larger. Also, their noses were of different shapes, and they held their tails in different positions. In spite of these differences, our ancestors perceived some similarities. The creatures they observed all had four legs, two eyes, and a tail. Most of them barked. They wagged their tails when they were happy. So our ancestors overlooked the many differences; and on the basis of the few similarities, they made a classification. They called this group "dogs."

From time to time, our tribe of ancestors had many occasions to communicate about dogs; so they constructed some higher level classifications based on some other characteristics they perceived. When they thought of the dogs that lived with them on a family basis, they linked them together with the cats, birds, and other creatures they owned. These were their "pets,"

---

[4] *Ibid.*, p. 393.

[5] S. I. Hayakawa, *Language in Thought and Action*, Harcourt, Brace & World, Inc., New York, 1949, p. 179.

and they represented a wide assortment of creatures. Their differences were infinite, but they had one thing in common. They all were owned by our ancestors, and they lived with them on a friendly basis.

Sometimes our ancestors looked upon their pets as a part of everything else they owned. They grouped them with their stone axes, their furs, their pottery, and other such items. When they had this thought, they needed another word—a shortcut to listing "pets, stone axes, furs, etc." So they formed a new word—"possessions." More than the preceding illustrations, this word grouped items that were sharply different. These items had one thing in common—they were all of the tangible things our ancestors owned.

In time, there were occasions when our ancestors viewed all of their possessions in terms of how well off they were in comparison with their neighbors. Probably they perceived that some of them had more possessions and some had less. Their references no longer were to items owned but to an idea they attached to these items collectively. They called this concept "wealth."

Still later, perhaps, there came a time when our ancestors looked at how they lived with other human beings. They perceived a system in which they and their neighbors worked to secure their wealth. They noted that they worked to make additional items of wealth and that they stored their wealth. They saw also that they bartered their wealth. All of these activities they perceived as one. They named it "the economy."

Whether language developed in the general manner just described we shall never know. But we know that the process is logical. And we know that the structure described exists in our language.

Illustration: Words about "mosquito"

For another example, take the everyday situation involving a little creature buzzing around your head. As you perceive the creature buzzing, you could say something about it. If it had a name, you might refer to it by name. Since it does not, you refer to it with words such as "that dadburned mosquito."

You might next make some derogatory comment about all of its kind. So you would use the broader classification term "mosquitoes." A step up the classification scheme you could refer to mosquitoes as members of a broader group of creatures, "insects."

At this point your references could depart from the biological classification and shift to a broad reference to the effect of insects on our lives. As you view insects in mass, they are a "nuisance," as are many other creatures and things. Perhaps you would next consider nuisance as a part of the broader category of "unpleasantness," for nuisances are only one of the unpleasantnesses of life. Finally, unpleasantness would be one of the possible subclassifications of "living." Thus, the buzzing of the mosquito, and of all mosquitoes, is a nuisance; and nuisance is a form of unpleasantness, which is a part of living.

From the preceding descriptions of the classification process, we may make two basic observations. First, it is apparent that the classifications we make in arranging word meanings are based on similarities rather than differences. Second is the obvious fact that the higher levels of classification are more difficult to comprehend than the lower forms. Both of these observations explain major problems in communication.

Emphasis on similarities. In the effort to devise a manageable, workable language, human beings had to find some means of simplifying the reality they perceived. As we have observed, the reality to which language must refer is too complex and involved for human beings to have done otherwise. Thus it was that they classified the elements of the real world on the basis of similarities. In doing this, they ignored the big bulk of the differences present.

Any object in the real world will illustrate the point—a dog, a house, a chair, a radio. As was illustrated previously, in arriving at the common term "dog" for all the creatures in a class, early people used a few biological similarities as a base. To be sure, the resulting classification is made up of creatures with many similar characteristics. They all have four legs, a tail, two eyes, five toes. Most, but not all, bark. Most have hair, but there are exceptions. We could name additional similarities. The point which needs to be made, however, is that all the differences in the animals have to be ignored.

Differences in dogs far outnumber similarities. In size, dogs range from the tiny Chihuahua which can stand in the palm of your hand to the 250-pound Saint Bernard. The sounds they make run the range from high-pitched yelps to deep thunderlike barks. Some dogs have floppy ears; others have erect ears; and some have ears that are between these extremes. Their hair runs the gamut from none, as with the Mexican hairless, to the long mane of a Yorkshire terrier; and it may range in coarseness from silky fine to wire-stiff. In color they are black, brown, red, white, plus a variety of combinations. We could go on and on from the more obvious differences to the differences at the microscopic level. Our eventual conclusion would be the obvious one: the differences among dogs outnumber the similarities. As we shall see in Chapter 6, this aspect of our language development is the source of some problems in communication.

Word difficulty and the classification scale. As we move along the classification scale from the object or event to the broadest category, the words take on a progressively increasing difficulty of comprehension. At the bottom of the scale, when the reference is based on our sensory experiences, clarity is more likely to exist. If we make a reference to "that dadburned mosquito," our words would convey a fairly accurate message to anyone around us who would also observe this one creature. As we move up the scale to a comment about the mosquito, there would still be a likelihood of clear understanding, for most of the people with whom we communicate have seen and experienced mosquitoes. When we use the word "mosquito," they are not likely to have difficulty visualizing these creatures collectively.

When we move up the scale to insect, we take a long step, for we cover a broad assortment of creatures. The meaning the word conveys to each person will differ somewhat, depending on each person's experiences and observations of the creatures in this group. Certainly, most people have an idea of what an insect is, but it is at best a vague one. Were we to ask them to draw a picture of the meaning they receive, we would get a confusing assortment of drawings.

Meaning becomes much more diffused when we move up the scale to "nuisance." At this point we can no longer look to reality for a picture. We cannot see a nuisance, nor can we touch it or smell it. In fact, it is not even a part of reality. Instead, it is an evaluation of some of the events in reality. It is a word about other words. Thus, if it exists at all, it exists only in the minds of people. Because minds work in so many different ways, the meaning of the word must vary somewhat from mind to mind. And because the word is not directly related to something in reality, it cannot carry anything but a vague meaning.

Similarly, the next two words in the classification scale are vague in meaning. "Unpleasantness" and "living" have no direct object or event relationship in the real world. They differ from "nuisance" not in the vagueness of their relationship; they differ primarily in the breadth of their coverage. Living encompasses unpleasantness, and unpleasantness encompasses nuisance. The indefiniteness of the meanings of all three is quite comparable.

We could make similar analyses with any classification structure, and we would have no difficulty arriving at the same conclusion. We would not fail to find that the higher in the classification structure a word is, the farther from the objects and events of the real world are its references. Thus the greater is its vagueness. Take words like "democracy," "security," "love," "patriotism," "liberal," "coordination," "equilibrium," and "sin." All of them are near the top of the scale, and all of them have nonspecific meanings. Were we to ask any group of people to define them, we would be likely to get as many definitions as there are people in the group. Because the high-level words do not have clear and precise meanings, communication which uses them cannot be clear and precise.

This observation does not mean that such words should be avoided. They definitely have a place in our communication. Generally, they refer to the more sophisticated concepts, ideas, and relationships which intelligent people have developed. The advancement of knowledge could not proceed without them. The point is, however, that we should be aware of the communication risks we run when we use them. We should be aware that not all people will agree on the meanings of the words. And we should be aware that the higher up the classification structure the word is, the greater is the likelihood of its confusion.

Although the use of higher level words is justified, good communicators will be wary of using them. They will move down to the lower level words as often as it is necessary to achieve understanding. The reasoning for this conclusion should be apparent from the foregoing discussion. The objective of purposeful communication is to form as precise a meaning as possible in the mind of another. We can do this best by using words which make precise references in the mind. These are the words which are at the bottom of the scale—those which relate directly to the reality perceived by human beings. These are the words which bring about images of things and events we human beings have experienced. They are far more precise than those words which have as their references relationships and intangible structures which exist only in the mind.

To illustrate the point, assume that you must communicate with Joe Hill, an employee who has not been doing his job well. You could talk in words of a high level of classification to him, saying, "If you persist in your inefficiency, you will be disciplined." Probably he would get the general idea of your message. You would communicate more clearly, however, with these words: "If you make any more of these handles too small, you will be docked $3 for each one." This latter comment relates directly to Joe's experiences in the real world. As his job consists of making handles, he has lived this experience many times. He knows what size a handle should be, and he knows when one is too small. Likewise, he has seen, held, and spent dollars, and he knows what it is to lose them. The message is a clear one, for it relates directly to Joe Hill's real world.

The question of meaning

The foregoing analysis leads to the overall conclusion that language is structured to fit in the mind. From this conclusion, one may reason further that there must be some relationship between words and meaning. To the uninformed reader, this relationship may appear to be all too obvious. Further inquiry will reveal that it is not so obvious and is in fact a most complex subject.

Location in the mind

Perhaps the most difficult communication principle for the uninformed student to accept is that words in themselves do not have meaning. As was concluded in Chapter 2, meaning lies in the mind, not in the symbols (words are symbols) we use. Words do not naturally convey the meaning of a given object or event. A rose just as appropriately could have been called a cow, or an oak, or a dodo. All that really matters is that the symbol and the real-life object or event it represents be associated in the mind.

If words actually had meaning, our communication problems would be greatly simplified. There would be no word barriers between people. If we were to say "run" or "talk" or any other word, all people would understand us, whether they were Swedes, Germans, Chinese, or Congolese. This is the way it would have to be if meaning were in the word. But it is not. The Swedes, Germans, Chinese, and Congolese all have their own words.

Meaning and dictionaries

That words are used to represent one and only one meaning or that they have one correct meaning is a popular misconception. As we have noted from our analysis of the communication process, meanings are determined by the filters of the mind. Thus, since all filters differ, there cannot be precise uniformity in meaning. Of course, there can be and is some general agreement as to the meanings represented by words. In no way have we intended to say that words represent completely different meanings in each mind. The differences we refer to are minute for the most part.

These general agreements on the words we use are recorded in our dictionaries. As helpful as dictionaries are, their use is distorted. In the minds of many, they are supreme authority. One would think that their makers have superhuman intelligence and are permitted to dictate correct word usage. Their role is far from this.

Actually, dictionaries are made by teams of readers (lexicographers) who cover widely the literature of the day. Primarily, they read the works of the better minds—those who have gained some measure of eminence in their respective fields. As the lexicographers read, they look to see how these people use words, and they record all manner of usages. They compile tens of thousands, perhaps millions, of usage examples. Usages they find in sufficient quantity they keep; others they throw out. The words and uses remaining make up the dictionary. Obviously, it is a dictionary of usage—not of edict.

Living nature of language

Because minds differ, people continually use words in new ways. Sometimes they invent new words. Sometimes they borrow words from another language. Others read or hear these usages, and they follow. In time the new words and usages become accepted, and they find their way into the dictionaries. So it is that language is continually changing. Words begin, they change, they end. The result is a living language.

The living nature of language explains some of its complexity. It explains why we have so many words. To illustrate the point, take a look at the latest *Webster's New International Dictionary*. It contains some 2,600 pages, each filled with fine print. And most of the words listed have many definitions. It is estimated that the 500 most commonly used words in English have a total of 14,000 listed definitions—an average of 28 per word.

The multiplicity of word definition is so great that one can use any page in the dictionary to prove the point. The little word "cat" illustrates well the multiplicity of meaning. The most common cats are the alley types. They are different from the big jungle beasts that perform in circuses. Then there are the spiteful women known as cats. Sailors of today know a cat as the tackle used to hoist anchors, and sailors of the past knew it as a nine-cord whip used to flog them when they required discipline. To some, a cat is a type of fish; to others, it is a game. Workers on a construction job know a cat to be a heavy piece of mechanical equipment. Then there are the various slang uses of the word *cat*. Doubtless there are others.

Good illustrations are plentiful. See what you can do with "ring," "head," "form," "spirit," "fast," "mark," "bag," and "stand." Then work on some verbs such as *sweep, make, do, go, run.* The examples could go on and on. In fact, a quick look at a dictionary page will show you that multiple meanings of words are the rule, not the exception.

The fact that we have so many words and that they have so many definitions explains some of our communication problems. So many words and definitions are available that it is impossible for any two people to have precisely the same knowledge of words and definitions. If precise communication is to occur, all people involved must have a common understanding of the symbols used. Thus, with different assortments of words and definitions in their minds, is there any wonder that people often fail to communicate?

Connotative and denotative meaning

Making the area of word meaning even more confusing is the fact that the meanings we assign to words are not determined by their real-world references alone. To be sure, some of the meanings derived from words are based on references in the real world, but many of them exist only in the mind. Those meanings which are based on references to the real world are called *denotative* meanings. Meanings which exist in the mind rather than in the real world are *connotative* meanings. Most words have both forms of meaning.

The denotative meanings we derive from words are based on the classification process we traced earlier. These are the meanings which relate directly to the real world—the objects or events the words stand for. To illustrate, it is a denotative meaning if one can point directly to the object or event in reality and say, "This is a football," "This is a party," or "This is a dog." The meanings the words bring to mind are clearly the objects or events to which we point. Or putting it another way, these are the meanings which *inform* us of the real-life objects or events about which we communicate.

Connotative meanings, on the other hand, bring in a qualitative judgment. Thus, they add to or detract from the denotative meanings. They are meanings which build inside people. They are based on experiences, biases, emotions, opinions, attitudes, beliefs, and the like rather than on references in the real world. They are the meanings which arouse some personal feeling toward the objects or events of reference.

Reviewing these definitions, we can conclude that denotative meanings are the meanings which *inform;* connotative meanings are the meanings which have some affective results. For example, take some object in reality—say a ragged, unshaven, dirty man walking down a road. We could use a number of words to refer to him. We could call him a tramp, a bum, a vagrant, a hobo, a vagabond, a wanderer, or a knight of the road. All of these words perform the same informative function. They point to this one man.

In the minds of most people, however, the connotations of the words differ to some degree. Not all of us will receive the same connotations from the words, but probably we shall agree on most. We see a tramp as a down-and-out and perhaps immoral fellow; a bum is even lower. "Vagrant" has less of the bad connotations of "tramp" and "bum," but the word lies in the same general category. "Hobo" has a somewhat adventurous meaning in the minds of most of us; and "vagabond" has a little bit more. "Wanderer" has none of the negative moral connotations of the preceding words—in fact, "wanderer" borders on being a favorable reference. "Knight of the road" is even more favorable; in fact, this term has elegance.

Salespeople may intend to convey the same denotative meaning with "Hello," "How are you, sir?" and "Hiya, bud." But the connotative meanings are not the same. A restaurant sign may say "crispy fried fish" or "dead fish boiled in oil" and point to the same object. But the connotations of the two expressions differ sharply. A hard worker may be referred to as aggressive, eager, or enthusiastic. Again, the denotations would be the same, but not the connotations. The same is true of the following groups of words and expressions:

Died, deceased, croaked, kicked the bucket.
Bout, altercation, fight, donnybrook.
Story, fib, falsehood, lie.
Rout, debacle, defeat, moral victory.
Depart, go, leave, get out.
Be silent, hush, be quiet, shut up.
Expectorate, eject from the mouth, spit.
Stout, obese, fat, blubbery.

From the preceding analysis of connotative meanings we can see that words have an emotional quality. Those that give the same information—that is, those that point to the same objects or events—are likely to convey different messages to the mind. For this reason, any attempt to communicate a particular message involves much more than choosing words which point to the objects or events in that message. The words selected, with all their denotative and connotative effects, will determine the message a communicant receives.

A series of differences between a labor union and the management of a certain company serves further to illustrate connotative effects from word choice. In discussing a proposed new contract, both sides argued about every provision. Their arguments brought in some classic examples of word choice for connotative effect. Concerning a provision to change the rate of pay for certain work groups, labor charged "infringement on seniority rights." Management justified the provision with "equal pay for equal work." The matter of an employee welfare fund was referred to by labor as "an example of Christian charity." By management, it was labeled "an inroad of communism." Other points of discussion brought in such emotionally charged words as "arbitrary decision," "freedom of choice," "the American way," "question of integrity," "featherbedding," "a fair deal," and "a matter of honor."

There can be no question about it: connotative differences are real, and they have a major effect on our communication. Skillful communicators know this fact well, and they very carefully choose their words for connotations as well as denotations. So if you are to acquire skill in communication, you must do likewise. Specifically, you must become a student of words. Especially must you study the shades of connotative differences in the meanings of words, and you must learn how these words can enable you to achieve a desired effect.

Context as an aid to meaning

In spite of all the complexities of words and their meanings, we do a reasonably good job of communicating with them. A good part of the credit goes to the role context plays in determining meaning. By "context," we mean the total situation in which a word is used. Specifically, this includes, first, the physical environment in which the communication is made. Second, it includes all the information in that communication, including the words themselves. How these two factors aid in determining meaning is best shown through illustration.

Context of the physical environment. The word *fast* is a word of multiple meanings; thus, on occasion it will give us some problem in determining which of its various meanings to use. The physical context in which the word is used, however, usually tells us the meaning. If we are at a racetrack watching the horses run and hear someone say, "He's a fast one," the odds are that the words refer to the running speed of a horse. The fact that we are at a racetrack, where horses are the center of interest, gives us this meaning. The same words heard at a party would be likely to refer to a person of questionable morals. Again, the physical context gives us the meaning. For similar reasons of context, "fast" communicated in a certain work situation at a textile mill would refer to the permanency of color of the materials. Spoken to a sailor on the job, it could refer to the permanence of a knot. If made in conversation with one who has not eaten for a few days, the word would appropriately refer to an abstinence from food. In each of these cases, physical context provides assistance in determining meaning.

Physical contexts are often so clear that they not only help to determine meaning—they also do the work of words. If at a baseball game we see the hot dog vendor come by, we do not have to say "I want to buy two hot dogs, please." We need to say only "Two," or perhaps we need only to raise two fingers. The context takes care of the rest. In World War II an American general's reply to a German ultimatum to surrender was a terse "Nuts." The context carried his full message much more accurately than a page of words would have done. Or take the case of the boss who found his workers playing cards rather than working on a high-priority job. His abbreviated comment "By tonight, or else" was crystal-clear to all concerned. Either they completed the priority job by that night, or they would be in for trouble.

Context of the surrounding words. Verbal contexts help to determine meaning by supplying some help in defining words. If you were to hear someone say that "George lost his glub yesterday," you would not know what a "glub" is, but you know from the surrounding words that it is something that can be possessed. Next you hear that "George had gone to get some flea powder, and when he got back he found the glub's cage door open." Now the verbal context has told you much more. You know that a glub is some kind of animal, for it is kept in a cage; and if it has fleas, probably it has fur. If the conversation continued long enough, in time you would have a good idea of what a glub is like.

The significance of verbal contexts may also be shown with word omissions. As most politicians will confirm, words or expressions lifted out of the whole message may take on an entirely different meaning. For example, John Smith, a candidate for the office of governor, might quote a very prominent citizen as saying, "Smith would make a good governor." Assume that the quote is correct—that the citizen actually said the words. But what if the words were lifted from the complete statement "Smith would make a good governor if he had the intelligence to match his arrogance." In this case the lifted part is inconsistent with the whole.

As the map fits the territory

In reviewing the preceding discussion, we can see that in a sense we live in two worlds. First, of course, is the world of reality, which we have described as an infinite and complex world. Because it is so infinite and complex, and because our sensory receptors are limited, we can perceive only parts of it.

Second is the world of words in which we live. This is the world of symbols which stand for the reality we perceive. As we have seen, this world is based on perceptions, which, as we know, are limited. It is based on inaccurate substitutes for the real thing. The conclusion from this reasoning should be apparent. The verbal world is different from the real world. To some degree it must be inaccurate. Certainly, it is incomplete, for words cannot cover all the reality in any real-world situation. The extent to which the real world and the verbal world differ is a measure of the miscommunication of a given communication effort.

In looking at the verbal world and the real world, we can see a territory-map relationship. The real world, of course, is the territory. The world of words is a representation of that territory. Just as a good map must fit the territory it represents, so must the words of our communication fit their territory. A map which has reversed the locations of Chicago and Atlanta or New York and Los Angeles or which has omitted a key highway going westward from Cleveland does not represent its territory. Some people will look at such a map, believe it, and try to use it. But they will have problems. Likewise, words which do not represent their territory are likely to cause problems. Like good maps, words must fit the reality to which they refer.

It is important also that we recognize the verbal world for what it is— a world of words and not of reality. Words are not the real world, just as a map is not the territory. As we shall see in the following chapter, we sometimes confuse this relationship. We sometimes act on words which misrepresent reality as if they were reality. We let words take the place of reality. The result is miscommunication.

Questions & Problems

1. Make a list of the types of symbols that we use in communicating. Give examples of each.
2. Discuss the role of language in the development of human progress.
3. Why did language develop around similarities rather than differences?
4. For each of the following objects construct an abstraction ladder of words:
   a. A bird in a tree.
   b. This book.
   c. Your desk.
   d. A pebble on the beach.
5. Are high-level abstractions ever useful and appropriate in communication? Give examples to support your discussion.
6. "It doesn't matter what the dictionary says a word means. What is important is what one means when one uses the word." Explain this statement.
7. Explain the difficulty one would have in using a 1984 dictionary to determine meaning in a book written in 1796.
8. Illustrate the multiple meanings of words with these examples:
   a. Top.
   b. Fall.
   c. Stick.
   d. Run.
   e. Show.
   f. Down.
9. For each of the following words make a list of words which have similar denotative meanings. Explain the connotative meanings of these words as you understand them.
   a. Carry.
   b. Hamburger steak.
   c. Sing.
   d. Cheat.
   e. Look.
10. Discuss how the following statements would have different meanings in different physical environments.
    a. I'll take ten.
    b. Save me.
    c. It's a hit.
    d. He missed a step.
11. Using the context implied in the following sentences, write a definition for a pfitt.

    Mary bought a pfitt last week. She used it briefly Monday before it rained. She likes the way it does the job; but she thought it was too noisy.
12. Explain the map-territory relationship to communication.

6

Some malfunctions of communication

THAT COMMUNICATION is imperfect is clearly evident from our review in the preceding chapters. Specifically, we have seen that some of the difficulty stems from the fact that the reality about which communication is concerned is infinite and complex. Also, we have seen that our minds (filters) are conditioned to receive information in an individual manner based on each mind's accumulations. Further, we have seen that the symbols we use in our efforts to communicate are plagued with imperfections and at best only loosely fit the reality to which they refer. As if these sources of miscommunication were not enough, now we shall see that additional malfunctions are present in our communication effort.

These malfunctions may be described as patterns of miscommunication which are common in human communication effort. Some of these patterns are products of language and result from the language imperfections discussed in the last chapter. Others involve the logical thought patterns which are a part of our cultural heritage—specifically of the system of thinking handed down to us from past generations.

Scholars led by Alfred Korzybski, the founder of the discipline of general semantics, traced these erroneous thought patterns to the teachings of Aristotle.[1] They argue that the Aristotelian system of logic has been the core of our accepted patterns of thought as well as a determinant of the structure of our language. They point out certain aspects of Aristotelian logic which are the sources of our erroneous thought patterns. These arguments are too involved for analysis here, but much of the following material is based on them.

Two-valued thinking

Deeply entrenched in our culture and our language is the pattern of two-valued thinking. It is the pattern in which we recognize two and only two

---

[1] Alfred Korzybski, *Science and Sanity, An Introduction to Non-Aristotelian Systems and General Semantics*, 3d ed., Country Life Publishing Corp., Garden City, N.Y., 1948.

possibilities in a given situation. It is the "either-or" logic—the logic which concludes that something either is or is not. It accepts no middle ground.

The true dichotomy

Now, some situations may be correctly described in two-valued terms. For example, in a lifetime you either will marry or will not marry. You either will make a million dollars or will not make a million dollars. You either will pass this course or will fail this course. Two-valued thinking is quite appropriate in these instances. It fits the realities involved.

Two-way situations are quite common in business. In fact, many business reports concern two-way decisions (to buy or not to buy, to manufacture or not to manufacture, to invest or not to invest, to hire or not to hire, to fire or not to fire). And frequently business writers must report information in either-or terms (profit or loss, sale or no sale, response or no response, machinery running or machinery down, quota met or quota not met). No shortage exists of such examples.

Multivalued situations

Not all situations involve only two values, however. In fact, most involve many values, for most concern an infinite number of gradations between extremes. For example, it is illogical to classify all people as either fat or skinny. True, some are fat, and some are skinny; but most are in between. Also, not all fat people are equally fat, and not all skinny people are equally skinny. If we were to take all the people in the world and group them from the fattest to the skinniest, we would find infinitesimal gradations along the scale. Were we to draw a line dividing the fat from the skinny, we would be separating the groups by an imperceptible weight difference.

It is the same with many other situations. Not all people are either short or tall. The weather is not always either hot or cold. One does not run at only two speeds—fast or slow. Children are not just good or bad. Students are not either intelligent or stupid. Yet in all of these situations we tend to think of just two values. Thus, when we communicate about such situations, we are neither thinking nor reporting accurately. Our words and thought do not match the reality concerned.

Much of the blame for two-valued thinking can be laid on the structure of our language. We have in English an abundance of either-or words and an extreme shortage of words in between. Take the words *sweet* and *sour*. What words do we have for an in-between taste? We could say "slightly sweet," "very sweet," "slightly sour," and the like. But usually we do not. Even if we do, we have only added a few general categories. We could say the same for "stupid or intelligent," "success or failure," "rich or poor," "weak or strong," "happy or sad," "love or hate." The examples are limitless.

The dangers involved

The danger in making two-valued statements, of course, is that they do not fit reality; thus, they can lead to miscommunication. This is not to say, however, that they should be forever eliminated from our vocabularies. Two-valued statements often are convenient devices in communication. They simplify that about which we communicate; hence, they help to make the message understandable. The danger comes in when those involved in the communication think or act as if the two values exhaust the possibilities.

A written evaluation of an employee, for example, may include the words *lazy* or *industrious*. Obviously, there are degrees of laziness and industriousness, and not all people would agree on the dividing line between the two. Thus, any personnel action which fails to take these possibilities into account would be illogical and unfair.

Our thinking patterns on politics and matters of government supply us with an abundance of illustrative material on this point. On candidates for public office or matters of legislation we tend to be either for or against. And we structure our reasoning to support our stand. In structuring our reasoning, there is the tendency to think in terms of right or wrong, good or bad, conservative or liberal, and the like. As a result, we fail to recognize the reality of the situation, which in most cases involves a mixture of good and bad, right and wrong. Thus it is that true Republicans take the stand that all which the Democrats do is wrong and all which their party does is right. A true Democrat takes the opposite position of bias.

Similarly, in viewing the role of unions, representatives of management might conclude that labor unions are bad; and in all their thinking about unions, they are likely to fail to see anything but the bad. True members of labor are likely to view the same situation from a directly opposing viewpoint. Also, on matters of social concern, such as civil rights, drinking, and gambling, dichotomous thinking is apt to be present. In fact, any matter on which viewpoints may be made is a probable topic for two-valued thinking.

Value of specific reference

The only possible solution to the problem of two-valued thinking is a two-step one. First, we must continually be aware of this communication difficulty. We must keep our eyes on the reality with which we are concerned. Second, we must try as well as we can to be specific in our choice of symbols. As the first step involves an awareness of what we have been discussing, it needs no additional comment. The second, however, involves practical techniques which are best presented by illustration.

In choosing symbols that are precise, we are limited by the possibilities of our language, but most of us can do better than we do. Whenever possible, for example, we can use quantitative measures. Instead of saying "She has an excellent academic record," we can say "She has a 3.9 grade-point average." Instead of saying "He is fat," we can say "He carries 345 pounds on a 5-foot, 4-inch frame." Instead of saying "She is a safe driver," we can say "She has driven 500,000 miles without an accident."

In addition, we can use middle-ground words much better than we do. In communicating a qualitative judgment, we can use such gradations as "exceptionally good," "very good," "good," "moderately good," "moderately bad," "bad," "very bad," and "exceptionally bad." In describing taste, we can go far beyond the more general and common symbols such as "good" and "bad" or "sweet" and "sour" with words such as "sugary," "saccharine," "candied," "honeyed," "acid," "tart," "astringent," "vinegary," and "ace-tose." Certainly, many of these words are general, but they do convey some of the gradations of taste.

A somewhat subtle violation of word precision is an expression that falsely implies that you are giving the final word. As mentioned in the discussion of the infinite nature of reality, we cannot say all there is to say about anything. Thus it is illogical to report with implied precision such messages as "the seven characteristics of . . ." or "the four functions of . . . ." Such statements might well end with "etc.," for they are not likely to be complete. To avoid the implied precision in the preceding examples, one could drop the "the." Another solution would be to alter the wording to bring in qualifying words: "There are *at least* four functions of . . . ."

Applications in business writing

The dangers of two-valued thinking are especially a problem in handling certain business writing situations. In writing reports, for example, frequently the assigned goal is to arrive at a yes or a no decision. As we have noted, true dichotomies can and do exist. And they exist in business problems. But often in business, compromise decisions or other alternatives are possible. For example, a problem to determine whether Company X should continue to operate its Middletown plant could be viewed as a yes-no proposition. Other solutions exist—to curtail operations, to renovate, to shift production to other products. For another example, a letter problem concerning answering a request could be viewed as having two response choices—yes or no. But careful review of the facts involved might reveal that a compromise is possible. Or perhaps it can be shown that the no answer really is not the negative answer that first meets the eye—that it has true advantages for the reader. Although such an answer remains a no, it is quite different from a plain and direct refusal.

Fact-inference confusion

Sometimes we are able to communicate about actual experience—things and events we have seen or heard. For example, if we buy a new car for $9,200, we can report factually that "We bought the car for $9,200." Or if we attend a club meeting at which Betty is elected president, we can report factually that "Betty was elected president." When we can do this, it is good, for it tends to produce communication which fits reality.

Unfortunately, we cannot always be factual. Frequently, we need to communicate about something we do not know to be factual. That is, we frequently find it convenient to communicate about things or events we do not know—things we only infer. For example, we may see Bill with a new car. In conversation with Bill, we might say, "How much did you pay for it?" We are, of course, assuming that Bill bought this car. Could it not be that the car belongs to a friend of Bill, or perhaps to his mother? He could have received it as a gift or through an inheritance. He could even have stolen it. In any event, there is at least some likelihood that our inference could be wrong. Thus, our communication would not fit reality and would in effect be a miscommunication.

Necessity of inference

Although inferences sometimes can be wrong, we must make them if we are to engage in human communication. In the first place, we would be severely limited if we could only communicate about that which we have experienced. We could make no interpretations of the events and the reality in the world about us. We could make no predictions. We could make no evaluations. In fact, there would be very little to communicate about. To prove the point, try talking to a friend for five minutes limiting all comments to factual material. If you do it at all, you will find such communication to be dull and difficult.

In the second place, we must make inferences if we are to survive. We cannot know everything with which we must deal in life; yet living requires that we make decisions and take actions based on inferences. If in the days of the Old West two men met on the trail and one went for his gun, the other had no choice but to infer that his life was in danger. If the second man did not draw and attempt to shoot first, the odds were that he would not have lived long. But there was also the slim possibility that all was not as it appeared. Perhaps the first man was only attempting to shoot a rattlesnake coiled and ready to strike the other man.

When we are driving an automobile and sight an approaching car, we infer that the other driver is a normal person who will stay on the prescribed side of the road; but sometimes drivers do not. We infer that cooks and waiters in restaurants are normal, decent human beings who do not put poison in our food; there have been exceptions. If you observe a man entering your home through a window, you infer that he is up to no good; there are other possible explanations. Because there is much we do not know, all of life is filled with risks. If we are to live, we must take them. Thus, we must make inferences.

Effect on communication

As necessary as inferences are to our living, they are a source of human miscommunication. The trouble is not that we make inferences; it is that all too frequently we confuse what is fact and what is inference. More specifically, we tend to make inferences from the facts we perceive, and we tend to treat these inferences as if they were facts. Thus, because we fail to see reality as it is, we cannot communicate accurately.

One of O. Henry's classic short stories illustrates this point well. It is the story of a man who owns one of the world's great jewels. At a dinner party the man shows his famous jewel to his guests, explaining that the jewel is priceless and that it was once a part of a beautifully matched pair. He passes the jewel around the table for all to inspect. The talk then turns to other things. After a time, the host asks for his jewel, but no one has it. Efforts to produce the stone fail; finally, the police are called. A personal search of all guests is called for. Everybody agrees to the search—except one man. As he steadfastly refuses to be searched, suspicion is turned on him. In the minds of all present, he is the guilty one. Why else would he refuse to be searched? As those in the room continue to talk and discuss the case, they label this one man as the guilty party. In time, someone finds the gem in a dish of food. Now the people seek some explanation for their wrong inference. The man explains that, as everyone has been told, his host's gem is one of a matched pair. It just so happens that the suspected man is the owner of the other gem. And he has the matched gem in his pocket.

O. Henry's story, of course, is an unusual one; and the odds of such a coincidence taking place are slim indeed. So let us take a more likely example. Let us assume that we are somehow involved in a sales organization and have observed that three of our top salespeople are bald-headed. From this factual information we may infer that bald-headed people make better salespeople. Now, our communication about bald-headed salespeople or salespeople in general is clouded with this erroneous inference which our filter contains. However, the fact is only that three of our bald salespeople are good. Probably there are many other bald salespeople who are also good, but there are many more who are not as good. In all probability, the reality of this situation does not support the inference we have made.

In the first example, the inference was logical and the odds of its being wrong were long. In the second, the inference was illogical, to say the least. In either event, the result was the same. There was error. The concepts in the mind were not in accord with reality. From this observation one conclusion should be clear: there is risk in inferences. Inferences are not facts of reality. And any communication involving inferences has some probability of not being true.

Calculating the probabilities

Although we must make many inferences in coping with the day-to-day problems of life, we can work to reduce the communication hazards they bring about. Specifically, we can be continually aware of the inferences we make. More specifically, we can attempt to calculate the probability of correctness of each of them.

Thus, when we infer that what appears to be a book on a library shelf contains pages, we should realize that the odds are perhaps a few thousand to one that our inference is correct. But we should be aware that there is always the possibility that it could be a false book—one consisting of a cover and simulated pages with the center cut out to form a secret compartment.

When we infer that because Joan Smith missed work today she is sick, the odds favor our being right. But we should be aware that there is also the possibility that our inference is wrong—that Joan Smith may be playing hooky or attending a funeral; or perhaps she is even dead. When we learn that some thieves are members of a certain organization, we are likely to infer that this organization is made up of immoral people. We should be aware that there is a very good chance that to some degree our inference is incorrect.

Actually, calculating the probability of an inference involves nothing that has not been suggested previously. First, it involves being continually aware of the nature of reality. Second, it involves using our knowledge of reality as a check on our inferences.

Importance in business writing

Fact-inference confusion is a problem in virtually all forms of business writing. Especially is it a concern in report writing. As you will see in following chapters, report writing frequently involves presenting and analyzing data and concluding from the analyses. The emphasis must be on the facts and on the meaning of the facts. In determining meanings, however, report writers sometimes must infer. And they must compute the probabilities of their inferences. They must look with extreme care at the reality represented by the information with which they work. The value of their reports depends on how well they do this task.

For an illustration, take a report on the sales performance of a certain company. The data reviewed show that in recent years company sales have grown steadily. The growth has been fairly uniform in all sales districts except one—District 5. This one district is managed by the oldest member of the sales force—a person who the report writer feels has not kept abreast of change and who generally has become obsolete. So the writer infers that District 5 sales have dropped because of bad leadership. This inference could be true. But other possible explanations exist. Could it not be that District 5 is suffering from an economic decline not affecting the other regions? Or could there not be unusual competitive forces working in this region? The report writer should consider all such possible explanations and assign to each its probability of being true.

Inference-observation confusion is also a factor to be considered in handling the day-to-day letter writing chores in business. In a letter refusing a request, for example, a bluntly worded answer is likely to lead the reader to infer that the writer is hard, unfriendly, unsympathetic, or the like. A sloppily prepared application letter produces inferences of the writer's lack of standards, carelessness, and general inability to do the work. Negative facts given too much emphasis in an employee evaluation letter may lead a reader to make unfair inferences. Similar inference errors are possible in most letter situations.

The blocked mind

A miscommunication pattern which affects us all is that of the blocked mind. As the term implies, a blocked mind is one which is closed to reality. It works on limited information, and it ignores or refuses to accept additional information. Thus, because it uses only a part of the information available, its communication efforts are necessarily only partially correct.

A result of opinions, attitudes, and beliefs

One of the causes of this form of miscommunication was covered in Chapter 4 with our review of opinions, attitudes, and beliefs. There it was pointed out that our minds tend to reject or ignore information which runs contrary to our viewpoints. Our opinions, attitudes, and beliefs tend to become rigid and to resist all information which is contrary to them. As a result, they may severely impair the fidelity of our communication.

A result of allness

A second contributor to the blocked mind is our tendency to judge the whole by a part—to assume that the part is the whole. This tendency is called "allness," and all of us are victims of it from time to time.

More specifically, allness is an attitude implying what one knows or says about something is all there is to know or say about it. In view of our previous discussions of reality, this is a most illogical attitude. As was explained in Chapter 3, reality is too complex, too filled with detail for any human being to know all there is to know about something. It is so detailed that, in communicating about it, we must select (abstract) some of its characteristics. We ignore all the others.

For example, in talking about Wilma Cuppenheimer, we could abstract many things. We could say that she is a devoted mother, a civic worker, a Protestant, a Democrat, a college dropout, a dentist, a gardener, a friend of animals, a music lover, a heavy drinker, a tennis player, a glutton, and a spendthrift. Wilma Cuppenheimer is all of these, and hundreds of others as well. But when we communicate about Wilma, we are likely to refer to only one or two of these characteristics, at least in a single statement.

This practice of selecting one characteristic to communicate about is necessary, for communication would be meaningless if only the broadest and most general references could be made. Such narrow references, however, tend to block our minds to the reality involved. All too often, in selecting limited numbers of characteristics for communicating, we tend to think that our limited reference is the whole.

If, for example, Wilma Cuppenheimer moves into the house next door, the first information reported about her might be that she is a heavy drinker. As we have noted, this is only one of many characteristics one could communicate about the woman. Yet when we communicate about this one characteristic, we tend to consider it as being the whole and to ignore the others. As the news that Wilma is a heavy drinker is communicated through the neighborhood, opinions are likely to be formed. Thus, the whole of Wilma Cuppenheimer is considered by this one part, although the other parts would present a much more favorable impression. But unless the other characteristics are specifically brought out, there is the tendency of the mind to be blocked to their existence.

This attitude may be illustrated further by a woman who comments that a certain detergent is no good. It ruined some of her fine clothes, she may reason. Her reasoning may be entirely valid, but it may be based on incomplete evidence—on only one of the many characteristics involved. The truth may be that although it is not good for finery, the detergent may be excellent for washing greasy work clothes, for killing fleas on dogs, for removing road film from cars, for cleaning rugs, and the like. In view of these many characteristics of the detergent, the woman's comment is not in accord with reality.

Extreme effects of the blocked mind

The problems of the blocked mind that stem from rigid viewpoints or from our tendency toward allness are with us in everyday living. And in a multitude of minor forms they tend to distort the fidelity of our communication. Some extreme forms of the pattern, however, are more likely to lead to serious communication problems.

In its most extreme form, the blocked mind typifies the attitude of the dogmatist and of those among us who "know it all." All of us have had experiences with people who are adamant in their stand on certain issues. They imply that only they have the true facts—that only they are right. These attitudes are appropriately criticized by the old adage "A little learning is a dangerous thing." Until these persons realize how much there is to know about everything and how little they really know, they are not likely to unblock their minds.

Most arguments are to some extent a result of blocked minds—or more precisely, two blocked minds. The point is illustrated by almost any argument you have witnessed. For our purposes here, select any one. Unless you have selected a rare one involving people with super-objectivity, you have selected a contest of blocked minds. In all likelihood, you have selected an argument in which all participants presented their own viewpoints with more vigor than they received the views of their opponent. Probably each did more talking than listening, if they listened at all. In fact, the participants are likely to use their listening time preparing the comments they will make next. At the end of the argument neither of the participants has received much additional information; and if their viewpoints have changed at all, probably they have become more rigid than before.

Unblocking the mind

Unblocking the mind from the effects of our viewpoints and our tendency to allness is no simple undertaking. And explaining how it can be done involves the most general of instructions. Nevertheless, it can be done, at least to some extent; and if we are to improve our communication, we must try.

In unblocking our minds for the effects of our opinions, attitudes, and beliefs, we are striving to do nothing new. Since the beginning days of civilization, intelligent human beings have sought to free their thinking from the grip of their human limitations. They have sought truth. They have striven for rational approaches to their problems. To date, however, even the best of them have failed miserably; and there is likely to be no change in the foreseeable future.

Because we cannot change the fact that we are human beings, about all we can do is to be conscious of the role our opinions, attitudes, and beliefs play in our thinking. We can be conscious of the fact that we acquire many of them through nonrational means. And most important of all, we can strive to be rational, always questioning our viewpoints and checking them with reality.

As is the case with most of the causes of miscommunication, combating the attitude of allness requires that we continually be aware of the nature of reality. More specifically, it requires that we keep in mind the fact that in communicating we must select some of the details of reality while omitting others. This is much the same advice Alfred Korzybski[2] gave in developing his discipline of general semantics when he suggested that all statements end with "etc." This symbol, he argued, keeps communicants aware of the fact that whatever is said about anything, there always is much more that could be said. Perhaps following Korzybski's suggestion would be impractical—at least until many people are aware of this device and of its meaning. But Korzybski's device is sound, and we would be wise to place a silent mental "etc." at the ends of the statements we communicate.

Effects in business communication

As you would expect, the blocked mind can be a problem in any business communication situation. And it can involve any or all of the people involved. In a letter writing situation, for example, the reader's blocked mind may be the major obstacle. If the letter's goal is to sell an idea that may appear to run contrary to the reader's self-interest, the situation calls for careful strategy and writing skill. And the writer's blocked mind on the matter could produce weak or illogical persuasion.

In a report writing situation, a writer's blocked mind can lead to disastrous results. By their nature, reports seek truth. They should emphasize facts whenever possible. They should not be influenced by the set of the mind. Obviously, a wrong decision concluded because of a blocked mind can be costly to a business.

---

[2] *Ibid.,* p. xxxiii.

The static viewpoint

The failure of language and our concept of reality to account for time changes leads us to hold a static view of things. That is, we tend to ignore the fact that all things change, and our language assists us in doing this. Such a static view of the process world in which we live, of course, is not true to fact. Thus, it contributes to miscommunication.

The unstatic nature of things

The fact that all of reality is in a state of perpetual change was explained in Chapter 3. It is a condition of fact about which we all are fully aware. Even so, we are likely to ignore it in our thinking and our communicating.

To illustrate, when we communicate about people we knew in the past, our minds hold references formed in the past. It is these images which become a part of our communication—not the true images of the people as they are now. The truth of this communication error can be vividly described by an ex-convict who has tried to go straight. No matter how hard this person may try, in the minds of many she or he remains the criminal they knew in the past.

Such miscommunication is not limited to references to persons. Two people talking about a place—say Chicago—may apparently agree that "It's one great town." Their filter references, however, may be from different times. One might recall her or his happy days living there 40 years ago; the other's references might be current. Perhaps the first person might not even like the current Chicago. And so it is with all places. The California of today is not the California of 1900, or 1875, or 1849, or of any other time. The England of today is not the England of the 1500s. Yet, in our references to these places the symbols remain the same.

The contributing factor of language

Our language contributes to our tendency to hold static viewpoints of reality, for it fails to give adequate emphasis to the timing of events. Of course, we have tense differences which give some timing to the events about which we communicate; and when there is a special need for time references, we can state specific times and dates. But these are a small part of the whole. Everything we communicate about has a place in time, and usually our language does not provide for it.

For example, when we want to communicate that "Henry Hobson is a scoundrel," there is no natural way of indicating whether we mean Henry Hobson at age 10, 21, 35, or 60. When we read that a certain eminent economist feels "that government subsidies are needed to solve the farm problem," the economist's words do not indicate the time to which they apply. They might be quite inappropriate to the economic situation and the economist's viewpoint a few years earlier or later.

The static viewpoint can occur in any business writing situation in which time is an element. In writing a letter evaluating a former employee, for example, an executive reports on the past. But both writer and reader are likely to assume nonchange. As we know, some change has occurred. In writing a collection letter, one may use techniques that he or she found to be successful in past years. Over time people change, and so do techniques which move them to pay bills. And so it is with various other letter writing situations.

Business people who write reports often use information which changes over time. Especially is this a problem with economic information. Dollar amounts for this year are far from dollar amounts of yesteryear. It could also be true in reporting production information. A production technique that was the best available a few years back is likely to have been made inefficient by technological change. Similarly, information on product comparisons becomes obsolete as soon as one of the products is changed. Report writers deal in facts such as these. If they are not alert to the changes that affect these facts, their reports will contain error.

Failure to discriminate[3]

All too often in our communication we fail to distinguish adequately between the objects and events about which we communicate. We fail to see the differences involved and instead see the similarities. As we have noted, uniqueness is common to all events and objects. Thus, seeing similarities rather than differences is contrary to the nature of things. Such failures to discriminate are common to all of us. The result is some degree of miscommunication.

Probably our language is the major cause of this error in viewing reality. As we noted in Chapter 5, words must do multiple duty if we are to keep their number manageable. Reality is too complex and involved for it to be otherwise. Thus, in forming our language, we have to categorize the events and objects in nature. As a result, we are conditioned to think in terms of similarities.

Miscommunication from stereotypes

In thinking in terms of similarities, we frequently form stereotyped impressions. That is, we view a category of reality as having a common mold. We see a typical or common group of characteristics for the category. Because everything in reality is unique, stereotypes cannot be true to fact.

To illustrate the point, the word *professor* is used to refer to tens of thousands of people. The one major thing professors have in common is that they teach at some institution of higher learning. As with all such

---

[3] Adapted from William V. Haney, *Communication and Interpersonal Relations: Text and Cases,* 4th ed., Richard D. Irwin, Inc., Homewood, Ill., 1979, pp. 386–96.

groups, the differences among professors are infinite. Yet we are conditioned to think in terms of the similarities the word conveys. Most likely, the term *professor* conveys a generally common meaning to the minds of most of us. He is an absentminded, long-haired, bearded gentleman, slight of build and sharp of feature. How well does this description fit your professor in this course—or any of the professors you have had?

Numerous such stereotypes are held by all of us. We are likely to picture a farmer as a tall, slender, rugged man dressed in bib overalls and with tousled hair. But how many farmers actually fit this image? We may see a business executive as a cigar-smoking, bald-headed, pot-bellied, girl-chasing man. How many actually fit this mold? We may see a show girl as a statuesque, unlettered, giddy, partying type. In reality, this type is the exception. Likewise, in our minds there are stereotypes of detectives, poets, wrestlers, students, police officers, gangsters, cowboys, and hundreds of others. Such stereotyped views of the members of any group are a gross distortion of reality, for few of the items in any classification approximate the common mold.

The effect of stereotypes on communication is that they tend to take the place of reality. Stereotyped images are in our mental filters, and they have some effect on our determination of meaning. Thus, when Professor White is mentioned in a communication, our stereotype of "professor" is a part of the meaning we give to the communication. When someone says that "Henry Hatton is a poet," that stereotype plays a role in determining the meaning we give to the statement. And so it is with other stereotypes. Each plays a part in determining meaning, and usually each tends to distort reality.

Judgments by category

An extreme form of discrimination failure is the making of common judgments to cover all things within a category. Rarely are such judgments supported by fact, for rarely are all things in a group sufficiently similar to deserve a common judgment. Most such judgments are based on very limited observation. Almost never are they based on knowledge of all members in the group. Unfortunately, we all make such judgment errors in our day-to-day communication.

The most common judgments by category spring from an incident or two—or at most, very limited observation. A professor may catch a couple of students in the act of cheating. This incident plus news of a few other incidents involving cheating might lead her to react with the judgment that "Students just don't seem to have much regard for honesty." The same professor driving home from work might be passed by a speeding carload of students. Her reaction might be that "Students drive like maniacs." And when she gets home and sees a note from her husband telling her that he is out fishing, she might respond with a judgment "Men have an easy life!"

On all three of these judgments the professor is in error, for she bases her judgments on a very small part of the whole. Certainly, there is good likelihood that at least some, if not all students, are honest. Most are safe, level-headed drivers. And there are many hardworking men who would vigorously refute her last judgment.

Such judgments are so commonplace that we make them and use them without giving them much thought. You have heard such statements as "Women are poor drivers," "Sailors are wild," "Salespeople are deceitful," and "Artists are temperamental." In varying degrees, all of these judgments are wrong, for there are exceptions to every one. In every case a failure to discriminate among the members of the category has resulted in a communication that is inconsistent with reality. Thus, some degree of miscommunication is the result.

Developing an awareness of differences

The solution to the problem resulting from failures to discriminate is to be continuously aware of the differences that exist within all categories. By thoroughly understanding the uniqueness of reality, and by making this understanding a permanent part of our filtering process, we are not likely to make discrimination errors—at least not so many as we do now.

Again, Alfred Korzybski in his work in general semantics suggested a solution for this communication problem. His suggestion is to index our references[4]—to distinguish between the object and events about which we communicate. For example, he would distinguish between the professors communicated about, referring to them as professor$_1$, professor$_2$, professor$_3$, and so on. Parties given by a certain person might be labeled party$_1$, party$_2$, and so forth. Unquestionably, such a system would help to avoid the confusion which develops. But like some of the other suggestions of Korzybski, they are not yet widely accepted. Until they are accepted, their meanings would not be clear to all concerned.

Even so, the suggestion is a good one, and we would be wise to follow it mentally. That is, we can each look for the differences in all things about which we communicate. So the next time you hear someone make a reference to labor leaders, students, bookies, or cabdrivers, keep in mind that everyone in the group is different and that stereotypes will not fit them all. And the next time you hear a general judgment of all members of a category such as "Women are fickle" or "Italian men are romantic," index the statements yourself. Ask yourself "Which women are fickle?" and "Which Italian men are romantic?" By doing so, you will be gaining a more realistic understanding of the reality about which we communicate.

Discrimination failure and business writing

Awareness of the role of discrimination failure is useful to us as business writers in a number of ways. In letter writing situations which require tactful handling, we select words to produce just the right effect. In selecting such words, we should know that stereotypes convey messages beyond their real-

---

[4] Korzybski, *Science and Sanity*, p. 381.

world references. Thus we should use stereotypes with caution. As letter writers we should know also that people make judgments by category—that in trying to influence people we must use words and strategies which account for these judgments. If, for example, we feel that a consumer-reader is likely to think that "business is anticonsumer," we should choose words which overcome this feeling. And when the situation is reversed and we are on the receiving end, we must make certain that we do not think that "consumers are antibusiness."

Report writing is the area of business writing where discrimination failure applies most. As we have noted, report writing involves presenting data, analyzing them, and concluding from the analyses. The process clearly involves discrimination. Our task in report writing is to search for differences, to analyze the differences, and to conclude from the analyses of differences. Failure to seek and find the differences is a most basic error.

Miscommunication summarized

This review of patterns of miscommunication is by no means exhaustive. At best, we have pointed out the major communication violations which can be placed in categories. In forming these categories, we should take some of our own advice. We must note that wide variations occur within each category. Some violations are so mild that they hardly warrant classification as miscommunication. Others are flagrant.

In summarizing the suggestions given for correcting these miscommunication patterns, one basic bit of advice stands out. It is the advice to keep our eyes on reality. If we are to communicate better, we must become better acquainted with the real world, and we must check our communications with this real world. When our communication and the real world are not in harmony, we have miscommunication. Thus, the watchword for ridding ourselves of the miscommunication habit is "Keep in touch with reality."

Questions & Problems

1. Classify each of the following concepts as truly dichotomous or multivariate:
   a. Semester grades.
   b. Swimming across a river.
   c. Succeeding in one's profession.
   d. Honesty.
   e. Happiness.
   f. Living.
   g. Sleeping.
2. What can one do to correct the error of two-valued thinking?
3. How clear is the distinction between fact and inference? Would all of us agree on what is fact and what is inference?
4. What inferences have you made as you studied this chapter? What facts have you observed?
5. Explain how our minds can become blocked.
6. What can we do to avoid blocking the mind?
7. From your experience give an example that illustrates the effects on communication of the static viewpoint.
8. How does language contribute to the static viewpoint?
9. What can we do to overcome the effects of the static viewpoint?
10. Select three stereotypes that are widely held by your associates. Discuss how correct they are and how they developed.

11. For the past 20 years, the Shannon Manufacturing Company has been making a unique garden cart. At a meeting of the board of directors, the chairperson of the board recommended that the company discontinue the product, backing the recommendation with the claim that the product had been a failure from the very beginning. The company's president then came to the defense of the product, claiming that it had been a success. A member of the board entered the discussion with the comment, "One thing is clear. You both cannot be right." Discuss.

12. The president of a manufacturing plant announced that rather than give across-the-board raises the company would give uniform $100-a-month raises to one-half of the workers. Those that would get the raises would be those with the best records of productivity. Discuss the executive's thinking from a communication viewpoint.

13. Give examples of specific wordings which describe each of these multivariate concepts:
    a. Quality of work done on a job.
    b. Profitability of a sales outlet.
    c. Effectiveness of an insecticide.
    d. Odor of gases.
    e. Adhesive strength of a glue.

14. Evaluate this comment: "Some of the workers are doing a good job; but the rest are not earning their pay."

15. Point out and comment on the probability of each of the inferences made in these statements:
    a. Messenger to his boss: "Yes, I delivered the memo to the supervisor personally. I handed it to the only one who was wearing a suit."
    b. A supervisor's memorandum to her workers: "There's been too much talking on the job. Tomorrow we are all going to work."
    c. One customer to another: "This place is a real money maker. Did you ever see so many people buying?"
    d. Waiter to a customer: "I'll give you this choice seat by the orchestra where you can enjoy the music."
    e. Credit manager to assistant: "Turn down Mr. Culberson. He doesn't list one reference from a town he lived in only last year."

16. Discuss the communication malfunction illustrated by each of these statements:
    a. Executive to a salesperson: "Sorry, but we've been buying only Drago office machines for the past 20 years. We tried the others; but none compared with Drago."
    b. One director to another: "The person selected for this administrative job must be an engineer. Sure she or he has to know finance, management, marketing, and all that stuff. But we're an engineering company."
    c. A male interviewer to a female job applicant: "Sorry, Miss Clary. The only jobs we have are on the production line."

17. Discuss this comment: "No, I wouldn't hire Bruce for this job. He's just not the serious type. Back when we were in college together he always was the clown."

18. Evaluate this conclusion: "We have kept records of our company automobiles for over 30 years. Clearly the Curry is the most economical all-around automobile."

19. Describe the stereotype these words convey in your mind:
    a. Politician.
    b. Cabdriver.
    c. Bellhop.
    d. Lifeguard.
    e. Accountant.
    f. Stockholder.

two

Applications to business

General principles of business writing

7

F ROM THE PRECEDING REVIEW it should be evident that a knowledge of communication theory can help you in your business career. Such knowledge gives you a better understanding of the business world of which you will be a part. It will help you to understand the people with whom you will work. And it will help you to understand and to solve the problems you will encounter in business. In addition to these broader benefits, you will also be able to apply communication theory to the more specific, practical tasks of communicating in business. Thus, it is to the practical applications of communication that our analysis now turns.

Any manageable analysis of the application of communication theory to business must be selective, for the area is very broad. For this reason, the material in this chapter and following ones is limited to those phases of applied communication in which you will need the most help. Specifically, we shall cover the area of business writing, especially the writing of correspondence and reports. Following this review of writing we shall cover briefly the more important methods of oral communication in business. Space and time limitations do not permit us to give additional coverage to the important area of interpersonal oral communication. Fortunately, however, this area received some emphasis in the preceding chapters.

The basic principle of adaptation

In applying communication theory to business writing, one basic principle emerges. It is the principle of adaptation—of fitting the symbols to the specific reader or readers. It is the underlying principle upon which many of the rules of good business writing are based, and it serves to temper these rules in their applications.

The filter as the basis for adaptation

As we noted in our study of the communication process (Chapter 2), the meanings we give to the symbols we receive are determined by the filters of our minds. As every filter is made up of all that the mind has retained from all the perceptions that have passed through it, no two are alike. No two can be alike, for no two can possibly have precisely the same knowledge, experience, bias, emotions, and so on. No two have the same knowledge of words, nor do any two give the same meanings to all the words held in common. The differences are so great that they present a major problem in communication.

Because filter makeups differ, especially in the knowledge of words and meanings, you must adapt your communication to fit the individual filter or filters concerned. That is, you must use symbols and concepts which have similar meanings in your filter and in the filters with which you communicate. Not to do so would be much like communicating in a foreign tongue.

The technique of adapting

Adapting your words and concepts to your reader will not come naturally to you. If you are like most of us, you are not likely to adapt without conscious effort. Most of us consider writing something of a chore. We work hard to find words which express our thoughts. We work so hard that we are content to accept whatever word choices come first to mind. Such choices of words, however, are likely to communicate only with those with mental filters similar to our own. The words may completely miss the filters of our readers.

In adapting your writing, you should begin by visualizing your readers. You should get clearly in mind the answers to such questions as who they are, how much they know about your subject, what their educational levels are, and how they think. Then, when an image of your readers is in mind, you should select the symbols which will communicate to them.

In many business situations, adapting to your readers will mean writing to a level lower than your own. Frequently, you will find yourself in situations in which you wish to communicate with people below your educational level, or you will be communicating with readers less knowledgeable than you are on the subject concerned. In both instances you will need to simplify your message. That is, you will need to write in the simple words and concepts your readers understand. If, for example, you must write a memorandum to a group of laborers, you would need to communicate in the everyday words of this group. Or if you must communicate on a technical subject to educated but nontechnical readers, you would need to simplify the concepts in your message. Not to do so would be to miscommunicate, or at least to make communication difficult.

Your task in adapting is relatively simple when you are writing to a single reader or to a homogeneous group of readers. But what if you must write to a number of people with widely varying mental filters? What should you do, for example, if your readers range from college graduates to those with almost no formal education? The answer is obvious. You would have no choice but to aim at the lowest level of the group. If you write at a higher level, you will be likely to miscommunicate with those at the lower levels.

Illustrating this fundamental principle are the financial sections of the annual reports of some of our major corporations. In attempting to communicate the financial information, some companies see their stockholders as being uninformed on matters of finance. Perhaps they see their rank-and-file readers as widows, housewives, and others who have not had business experience. Their communication might read like this:

> Last year your company's total sales were $117,400,000, which was slightly higher than the $109,800,000 total for the year before. After deducting for all expenses, we had $4,593,000 left over for profits, compared with $2,830,000 for 1982. Because of these increased profits, we were able to increase your annual dividend payments per share from the 50 cents paid over the last ten years.

Some companies visualize their stockholders in an entirely different light and see them as being well informed in the language of finance. Perhaps they misjudge their readers, or maybe they fail to consider the readers' knowledge. In any event, these companies present their financial information in a somewhat technical and sophisticated manner, as illustrated by this example:

> The corporation's investments and advances in three unconsolidated subsidiaries (all in the development stage) and in 50 percent owned companies was $42,200,000 on December 31, 1983, and the excess of the investments in certain companies over net asset value at dates of acquisition was $1,760,000. The corporation's equity in the net assets as of December 31, 1983, was $41,800,000 and in the results of operations for the year ended December 31, 1983, and 1982, was $1,350,000 and $887,500. Dividend income was $750,000 and $388,000 for the years 1983 and 1982, respectively.

When you write to someone who is about as well-educated and informed on your subject as you are, your communication task is relatively easy. You need only to write to one like yourself, using language that is easy for you to understand. Likewise, if you are a technical person writing on a technical subject to a technical person who will understand the subject, you should write in the technical language both of you know and use. As technical language is the everyday language of the technician, this is the language which communicates quickly. Also, it is the language the technician expects. As we shall see later, however, such writing can be too technical even for the technical reader.

Care in word choice

Writing in language which is adapted to your reader is not so simple as it may at first appear. To do the job well, you will need to become a student of language as well as a student of people. You can be guided in your efforts, however, by certain rules of word selection.

Selecting words the reader understands

In general, these rules suggest that you simplify your writing. Although adaptation does not always mean simplification, in most business situations it does, and for good reason. In the first place, if you are like the typical business person, you tend to write at too difficult a level. Perhaps subconsciously you seek to impress; or maybe you just have a tendency to become stiff and formal when you write. In any event, the resulting words are not likely to make sharp, clear meanings in the reader's mind.

In the second place, usually the writer knows the subject of the message better than does the reader. Thus, the minds of the two are not equally equipped to communicate on the subject. The writer has no choice but to present the message in the more elementary words and concepts that will make meaning in the reader's mind.

A third reason for simplifying writing is the conclusion drawn from exhaustive studies on readability—that writing which is slightly below the reader's level makes the most comfortable reading. According to the findings of such notables as Robert Gunning and Rudolph Flesch, such writing communicates best (Appendix G). Even if we are able to comprehend the more difficult words, we do so with effort.

Use the familiar words. The first rule of word selection is to use the familiar everyday words. Of course, the definition of familiar words varies by person. What is everyday usage to some people is likely to appear to be high-level talk to others. Thus, the suggestion to use familiar language is in a sense a specific suggestion to apply the principle of adapting the writing to the reader.

Unfortunately, many business writers do not use everyday language enough. Instead, they tend to change character when they begin to put their thoughts on paper. Rather than writing naturally, they become stiff and stilted in their expression. For example, instead of using an everyday word like "try," they use the more unfamiliar word "endeavor." They do not "find out"; they "ascertain." They "terminate" rather than "end," they "demonstrate" rather than "show," and they "utilize" instead of "use."

Now, there is really nothing wrong with the hard words—if they are used intelligently. They are intelligently used when they are clearly understood by the reader, when they are best in conveying the meaning intended, and when they are used with wise moderation. Perhaps the best suggestion in this regard is to use words you would use in face-to-face communication with your reader. Another good suggestion is to use the simplest words which carry the thought without offending the reader's intelligence.

The communication advantages of familiar words over the far more complex ones are obvious from the following contrasting examples:

Unfamiliar Words	*Familiar Words*
The conclusion ascertained from a perusal of the pertinent data is that a lucrative market exists for the product.	The data studied show that the product is in good demand.
The antiquated mechanisms were utilized for the experimentation.	The old machines were used for the test.
Company operations for the preceding accounting period terminated with a substantial deficit.	The company lost much money last year.

Unfamiliar Words	Familiar Words
This machine has a tendency to develop excessive and unpleasant audial symptoms when operating at elevated temperatures.	This machine tends to get noisy when it runs hot.

Prefer the short to the long word. Because short words tend to communicate better than long ones, you should prefer them in your writing. As has been borne out by readability studies, a heavy proportion of long words confuses the reader. Some of the explanation, of course, is that the long words tend to be the more difficult ones. In addition, however, the readability studies indicate that long words give the appearance of being hard; thus, our mental filters receive them as hard words. The studies give evidence that even when the long words are understood, a heavy proportion of them adds to the difficulty of comprehension.

There are, of course, many exceptions to this rule. Some words like *hypnotize, hippopotamus,* and *automobile* are so well known that they communicate easily; and some short words like *verd, vie,* and *gybe* are understood by only a few. On the whole, however, word length and word difficulty are correlated. Thus, you will be wise to use long words with some caution. And you will need to be certain that the long ones you use are well known to your reader.

The following contrasting sentences clearly show the effect of long words on writing clarity. Most of the long words are likely to be understood by most educated readers, but the heavy proportion of long words makes for heavy reading and slow communication. Without question, the simple versions communicate better.

Long Words	Short and Simple Words
The decision was *predicated* on the *assumption* that an *abundance* of *monetary* funds was *forthcoming.*	The decision was *based* on the *belief* that there would be *more money.*
They *acceded* to the *proposition* to *terminate* business.	They *agreed* to *quit* business.
During the *preceding* year the company *operated* at a *financial deficit.*	*Last* year the company *lost money.*
Prior to accelerating productive operation, the supervisor inspected the machinery.	*Before speeding up production,* the supervisor inspected the machinery.
Definitive action was *effected subsequent* to the reporting date.	*Final* action was *taken after* the reporting date.
The unanimity of current forecasts is not *incontrovertible evidence* of an *impending* business *acceleration.*	*Agreements* of the forecasts is not *proof* that business *will get better.*

Use technical words with caution. Whatever your field will be in business, it will have its own jargon. In time, this jargon will become a part of your everyday working vocabulary. So common will this jargon appear in your mental filter that you may assume that others outside the field also know it. And in writing to those outside your field, you may use these words. The result is miscommunication.

Certainly, it is logical to use the language of a field in writing to those in the field. But even in such instances you can overdo it, for an overuse of technical words can be hard reading even for technical people. Frequently, technical words are long and hard-sounding. As we noted in the preceding rule, such words tend to dull the writing and to make the writing hard to understand. Also, the difficulty tends to increase as the proportion of technical words increases. Illustrating this point is the following sentence written by a physician:

> It is a methodology error to attempt to interpret psychologically an organic symptom which is the end result of an intermediary change of organic processes instead of trying to understand those vegetative, nervous impulses in their relation to psychological factors which introduce a change of organic events resulting in an organic disturbance.

No doubt the length of this sentence contributes to its difficulty, but the heavy proportion of technical terms also makes understanding difficult. The conclusion that we may draw here is obvious. When you write to your fellow technicians, you may use technical words, but you should use them moderately.

In writing to those outside the field, you should write in layman language. For example, a physician might well refer to a "cerebral vascular accident" in writing to a fellow physician, but she or he would do well to use the word *stroke* in writing to the public. An accountant writing to a nonaccountant might also need to avoid the jargon of the profession. Even though terms like *accounts receivable*, *liabilities*, and *surplus* are elementary to the accountant, they may be meaningless to some people. So, in writing to such people, the accountant would be wise to use nontechnical descriptions such as "how much is owed the company," "how much the company owes," and "how much was left over." We can draw similar examples from any specialized field.

Bringing the writing to life with words

As we noted in our analysis of the communication process, our sensory receptors and our minds do not give equal attention to all our perceptions. Some they completely ignore. Others they give varying degrees of attention, ranging from almost none to the strong and vigorous. Obviously, it is the strong and vigorous perceptions which communicate best.

Applied to written communication, this observation means that symbols which are strong and vigorous are more likely to gain and hold the interest of your reader. Subject matter, of course, is a major determinant of the interest quality of communication; but even interesting topics can be presented in writing so dull that an interested reader cannot keep her or his mind on the subject. If you wish to avoid this possibility, you will need to bring your writing to life with words.

Bringing your writing to life with words is no simple undertaking. In fact, it involves techniques which practically defy description—techniques which even the most accomplished writers never completely master. In spite of the difficulty of this undertaking, however, you can bring your writing to life by following four simple but important suggestions: (1) You can select the strong and vigorous words, (2) you can use the concrete words, (3) you can prefer the active verbs, and (4) you can avoid overuse of the camouflaged verbs.

Use strong, vigorous words. Like people, words have personality. Some words are strong and vigorous, some are dull and weak, and others fall in between these extremes. In improving your writing skill, you should be aware of these differences whenever you write. You should become a student of words, and you should strive to select words which will produce just the right effect in your reader's mind. You should recognize, for example, that "tycoon" is stronger than "eminently successful business person," that "bear market" is stronger than "generally declining market," and that a "boom" is stronger than a "period of business prosperity." As a rule, you should make the strong words predominate.

In selecting the strong word, you should be aware that the verb is the strongest part of speech, and it is closely followed by the noun. The verb is the action word, and action by its very nature commands interest. Nouns, of course, are the doers of action—the characters in the story, so to speak. As doers of action, they attract the reader's attention.

Contrary to what you may think, adjectives and adverbs should be used sparingly. These words add length to the sentence, thereby distracting the reader's attention from the key nouns and verbs. As Voltaire phrased it, "The adjective is the enemy of the noun." In addition, adjectives and adverbs both involve subjective evaluation; and as previously noted, the objective approach is necessary in many forms of business communication.

Use the concrete word. Interesting business writing is marked by specific words—words which form sharp and clear meaning in your reader's brain. Such words are concrete. Concrete words are the opposite of abstract words, which are words of fuzzy and vague meaning. In general, concrete words stand for things the reader perceives—things the reader can see, feel, hear, taste, or smell. Concrete words hold interest, for they move directly into the reader's experience. Because concrete words are best for holding interest, you should prefer them to abstract words wherever possible.

Among the concrete words are those that stand for things that exist in the real world. Included are nouns like *chair, desk, typewriter, road, automobile,* and *flowers.* Included also are words that stand for creatures and things: *John Jordan, Mary Stanley, Mickey Mouse, Spot,* the *Metropolitan Life Building,* and *Mulberry Street.*

Abstract nouns, on the other hand, cover broad meanings—concepts, ideas, and such. Their meanings are general, as in these examples: *administration, negotiation, wealth, inconsistency, loyalty, compatability, conservation, discrimination, incompetence,* and *communication.* Note how difficult it is to visualize what each of these words stands for.

Concreteness also involves how we put words together. Wordings that are exact or specific are concrete; those that are vague and general are abstract. For example, take the case of a chemist who must describe in a research report the odor of a particular mixture of chemicals. The chemist could use such general words as "It had an offensive, nauseating odor." Now note how much more is communicated with more concrete language: "It had the odor of decaying fish." As the latter example recalls an exact odor from the memory, it is concrete.

Notice the difference in communication effect in these contrasting pairs of wordings:

Abstract	Concrete
A significant loss	A 53 percent loss
Good attendance record	100 percent attendance record
The leading company	First among 3,212 competitors
The majority	Sixty-two percent
In the near future	By Thursday noon
A labor saving machine	Does the work of seven workers
Light in weight	Feather-light
Substantial amount	$3,517,000

Now let us see what difference concreteness can make in the clarity of longer passages of writing. Here is an example of some abstract wording:

It is imperative that the firm practice extreme conservatism in operating expenditures during the coming biennium. The firm's past operating performance has been ineffectual for the reason that a preponderance of administrative assignments have been delegated to personnel who were ill equipped to perform in these capacities. Recently instituted administrative changes stressing experience in operating economies have rectified this condition.

This message written for concreteness might read like this:

We must cut operating expenses at least $2,000,000 during 1984–85. Our $1,350,000 deficit for 1982–83 was caused by the inexperience of our two chief administrators, Mr. Sartan and Mr. Ross. We have replaced them with Ms. Pharr and Mr. Kunz, who have had 13 and 17 years, respectively, of successful experience in operations management.

Prefer active to passive verbs. Of all the parts of speech, the verbs are the strongest, and verbs are at their strongest when they are in the active voice. Thus, for the best in vigorous, lively writing, you should make good use of active-voice verbs. Certainly, this suggestion does not mean that you should eliminate passive voice, for passive voice has a definite place in good writing, especially when you wish to give emphasis to words other than the verb. But it does mean that you should use as much active voice as you logically can.

Active-voice verbs are those which show their subject doing the action. They contrast with the dull, passive forms which act upon their subjects. The following contrasting sentences illustrate the distinction:

Active: The auditor inspected the books.
Passive: The books were inspected by the auditor.

The first example clearly is the stronger. In this sentence the doer of the action acts, and the verb is short and clear. In the second example, the helping word *were* dulls the verb, and the doer of the action is relegated to a role in a prepositional phrase. The following sentences give additional proof of the superiority of active over passive voice:

Passive	Active
The results were reported in our July 9 letter.	We reported the results in our July 9 letter.
This policy has been supported by our union.	Our union supported this policy.
The new process is believed to be superior by the investigators.	The investigators believe the new process is superior.
The policy was enforced by the committee.	The committee enforced the policy.
The office will be inspected by Mr. Hall.	Mr. Hall will inspect the office.
A gain of 30.1 percent was reported for hardware sales.	Hardware sales gained 30.1 percent.
It is desired by this office that this problem be brought before the board.	This office desires that the secretary bring this problem before the board.
A complete reorganization of the administration was effected by the president.	The president completely reorganized the administration.

The suggestion to prefer active voice does not mean that passive voice is incorrect or that you should never use it. Passive voice has a place. It most certainly is correct. The point is that many writers tend to overuse passive voice, especially in report writing. Our writing would be more interesting and it would communicate better if we used more active voice.

Your decision on whether to use active or passive voice is not simply a matter of choice. Sometimes passive voice is preferable. For example, when identification of the doer of action is unimportant to the message, passive voice gives this part of the sentence its proper deemphasis.

Advertising often is criticized for its effect on price. *(passive)*
Petroleum is refined in Texas. *(passive)*

Passive voice also may be preferable when the performer is unknown, as in these examples:

During the past year, the equipment has been sabotaged seven times.
Anonymous complaints have been received.

Yet another situation in which passive voice may be preferred is one in which the writer prefers not to name the performer:

The interviews were conducted on weekdays between noon and 6 P.M.
Two complaints have been made about you.

There are other instances in which for reasons of style passive voice is preferable.

Avoid overuse of camouflaged verbs. An awkward construction that we should avoid is the camouflaged verb. When we camouflage a verb, we take the verb describing the action in a sentence and change it into a noun. Then we have to add action words. For example, suppose you want to write a sentence in which *eliminate* is the action to be expressed. You change *eliminate* into its noun form, *elimination*. Now in order to have a sentence, you must add action words—perhaps *was effected.* Your sentence would then be something like this: "Elimination of the surplus was effected by the staff." The sentence is indirect and passive. You could have avoided the camouflaged construction with a sentence using the verb *eliminate:* "The staff eliminated the surplus."

Here are some additional examples. We could take the good action word *cancel* and make it into a noun, *cancellation.* Then we would have to say something like "to effect a cancellation" in order to communicate the action desired. We could take *consider,* change it to *consideration,* then say "give consideration to." So it would be with these examples:

Action Verb	Noun Form	Wording of Camouflaged Verb
acquire	acquisition	make an acquisition
appear	appearance	make an appearance
apply	application	make an application
appraise	appraisal	make an appraisal
assist	assistance	give assistance to
cancel	cancellation	make a cancellation
discuss	discussion	have a discussion
reconcile	reconciliation	make a reconciliation
investigate	investigation	make an investigation
record	recording	make a recording
liquidate	liquidation	effect a liquidation

Note the differences in overall effect in these contrasting sentences:

Camouflaged Verb	Clear Verb Form
Amortization of the account *was effected* by the staff.	The staff *amortized* the account.
Control of the water *was not possible.*	They *could not control* the water.
The new policy *involved the standardization of* the procedures.	The new policy *standardized* the procedures.
Application of the mixture *was accomplished.*	They *applied* the mixture.
We must *bring about a reconciliation* of our differences.	We must *reconcile* our differences.
The *establishment* of a rehabilitation center *has been accomplished* by the company.	The company *has established* a rehabilitation center.

From these illustrations you can see that the suggestion to avoid camouflaged wording overlaps two preceding suggestions. First, the camouflaged words made from the verbs are abstract nouns. We suggested that you prefer the concrete over the abstract words. Second, camouflaged wordings frequently require passive voice. We suggested that you prefer the active.

You can comply with these related suggestions if you will follow two helpful writing hints. The first is make the subjects of most sentences either persons or things. For example, rather than write "consideration was given to . . ." you should write "we considered. . . ." The second is to write most sentences in normal (subject, verb, object) order and with the real doer of action as the subject. It is when writers attempt other orders that involved, strained, passive structures are most likely to result.

Obviously, writing requires some knowledge of language. In fact, the greater your knowledge, the better you are likely to be able to write. Unfortunately, all too many of us treat language routinely. We use the first words that come to mind without thinking about other ways of saying things. We use words without thinking of the meanings they convey. We use words we are not sure of. The result is fuzzy, indefinite writing.

If you want to be a good writer, you will need to study words carefully. You will need to learn their precise meanings. Especially you will need to know the shades of difference in meanings of similar words. For example, *weary, tired, pooped, fagged out,* and *exhausted* are all words referring to the same thing. Yet there are differences in meaning in many minds. Certainly *weary* would be more acceptable in a rather formal letter than *pooped* or *fagged out.* Similarly, *fired, dismissed, canned, separated,* and *discharged* refer to the same action. They also have different shades of meaning. So it is with each of these groups of words:

die, decease, pass on, croak, kick the bucket, check out, expire, go to one's reward
money, funds, cash, dough, bread, finances
boy, youth, young man, lad, shaver, stripling
fight, brawl, fracas, battle royal, donnybrook
thin, slender, skinny, slight, wispy, lean, willowy, rangy, spindly, lanky, wiry
ill, sick, poorly, weakly, delicate, cachectic, unwell, peaked, indisposed, out of
sorts

Knowledge of language also enables you to use words which come close to giving the meanings you want to communicate. For example, *fewer* and *less* mean the same to some people. But careful users select *fewer* to mean "smaller number of items"; and they choose *less* to mean "value, degree, or quantity." The words *affect* and *effect* often are used as synonyms. But those who know language select *affect* when they mean "to influence" and *effect* when they mean "to bring to pass." Similarly, careful writers use *continual* to mean "repeated but broken succession" and *continuous* to mean "unbroken succession." They write *farther* to express geographic distance; *further* to indicate "more, in addition." They know that *learn* means "to acquire knowledge" and *teach* means "to impart knowledge."

In your effort to be a precise writer, you will want to use the correct idiom. By *idiom* we mean the way we say things in our language. Much of our idiom has little rhyme or reason. But if we want to be understood correctly, we should follow it. For example, what is the logic in the word *up* in this sentence: "Look up her name in the directory"? There really is none. This is just the wording we have developed to cover this meaning. It is good idiomatic usage to say "independent of," not good to say "independent from." What is the justification? Similarly, you "agree to" a proposal, but you "agree with" a person. You are "careful about" an affair, but you are "careful with" your money. So it is with these additional illustrations:

Faulty Idiom	Correct Idiom
authority about	authority on
comply to	comply with
enamored with	enamored of
equally as bad	equally bad
in accordance to	in accordance with
in search for	in search of
listen at	listen to
possessed with ability	possessed of ability
seldom or ever	seldom if ever
superior than	superior to

Emphasis on short sentences

Arranging your words into sentences which form meaning in your reader's mind is a major part of your task as a business writer. As with using words, this task is one of adaptation—of fitting the message to the unique mental filter of a particular reader or readers.

Largely, your task of adapting sentences to your readers is a mental one. On the one hand you visualize your readers; on the other you structure words into sentences which produce the intended meanings in their minds. In structuring your words, you are guided by your own best judgment, for constructing sentences clearly is a product of the thinking mind. The sentence is the form we human beings have devised to express our thought units. Thus, clear and orderly sentences are the products of clear and orderly thinking; vague and disorderly sentences represent vague and disorderly thinking.

The technique of good thinking cannot be reduced to routine steps, procedures, formulas, or the like, for the process is too little understood. But sentences which are the products of good thinking have clearly discernible characteristics. These characteristics suggest the general guidelines for good sentence construction which appear in the following paragraphs.

More than any other characteristic of a sentence, length is most clearly related to sentence difficulty. The longer a sentence is, the harder it is to understand. This relationship is convincingly borne out by the readability studies previously cited. And it is a logical conclusion which we may draw from an analysis of the operation of the mind. We all know that our minds have limitations. We know that they are limited in their abilities to handle complex information. Some minds, of course, can handle more complex information than others, but each one has its maximum limit.

Complexity in communicating with words is largely determined by the number of relationships and the volume of information expressed in the sentence. When an excess of information or relationships is presented in a single package, our minds have to work hard to grasp the message. In written communication, repeated readings may be needed; and in the more extreme cases, even these may not produce results. Thus, like food, information is best consumed in bite sizes.

What is bite size for the mind, however, depends on the mental capacity of the reader. Most of the readability studies conclude that writing aimed at the middle level of adult American readers should have an average sentence length of around 16 to 18 words. For more advanced readers the average can be higher. It must be lower for those of lower reading abilities. Of course, these length figures do not mean that short sentences of 6 or so words are taboo, nor do they mean that one should avoid long sentences of 30 or more words. Occasionally, short sentences may be used to emphasize an important fact, and long sentences may be skillfully constructed to subordinate some less important information. It is the average which should be in keeping with the readability level of the reader.

The following sentence from an employee handbook illustrates well the effect on communication of long sentences:

> When an employee has changed from one job to another job, the new corresponding coverages will be effective as of the date the change occurs, provided, however, if due to a physical disability or infirmity as a result of advanced age, an employee is changed from one job to another job and such change results in the employee's new job rate coming within a lower hourly job-rate bracket in the table, the employee may, at the discretion of the Company, continue the amount of group term life insurance and the amount of accidental death and dismemberment insurance which the employee had prior to such change.

The chances are you did not get a clear message from this sentence on the first reading. The explanation is not in the words used, for probably you know them all. Neither is it in the ideas presented, for they are relatively simple. The obvious explanation is the length of the sentence. So many words and relationships are in this one unit that they confuse the mind. The result is fuzzy communication at best—complete miscommunication at worst.

Writing in simple, short sentences involves two basic techniques. First is the technique of limiting sentence content. Second is the technique of expressing thoughts in fewer words—that is, of economizing in words used. You will find specific suggestions and illustrations of these techniques in the following pages.

Limiting sentence content

Limiting sentence content is largely a matter of mentally selecting the thought units and making separate sentences of most of them. Sometimes, of course, you should combine thoughts into one sentence. But you should do this only when you have good reason to do so. You have good reason, for example, when thoughts are closely related, or when you want to deemphasize content. The advantage of following this practice is evident from the following contrasting examples:

Long and Hard to Understand	*Short and Clear*
This memorandum is being distributed with the first-semester class cards, which are to serve as a final check on the correctness of the registration of students and are to be used later as the midsemester grade cards, which are to be submitted prior to November 16.	This memorandum is being distributed with the first-semester class cards. These cards will serve now as a final check on student registration. Later, they will be used for midsemester grades, which are due before November 16.

Long and Hard to Understand	*Short and Clear*
Some authorities in personnel administration object to expanding normal salary ranges to include a trainee rate because they fear that probationers may be kept at the minimum rate longer than is warranted through oversight or prejudice and because they fear that it would encourage the spread from the minimum to maximum rate range.	Some authorities in personnel administration object to expanding the normal salary range to include a trainee rate for two reasons. First, they fear that probationers may be kept at the minimum rate longer than is warranted, through oversight or prejudice. Second, they fear that it would, in effect, increase the spread from the minimum to the maximum rate range.
Regardless of their seniority or union affiliation, all employees who hope to be promoted are expected to continue their education either by enrolling in the special courses to be offered by the company, which are scheduled to be given after working hours beginning next Wednesday, or by taking approved correspondence courses selected from a list which may be seen in the training office.	Regardless of their seniority or union affiliation, all employees who hope to be promoted are expected to continue their education in either of two ways. 1. They may enroll in special courses to be given by the company. 2. They may take approved correspondence courses selected from the list which may be seen in the training office.

Without question, the long sentences in the examples are difficult to understand and the shorter versions are easy. In each case the difference is primarily in sentence length. Clearly, the shorter sentences fit into the mind better. They give more emphasis to content and to organization of the subject matter.

As with all writing suggestions, however, you can carry short sentences to excess. A succession of short sentences can give the impression of elementary writing as well as draw attention from the content to the choppy effect of the sentences. You should work to avoid these effects by varying the length and ordering of parts of your sentences. But you would be wise to keep the lengths of your sentences within the easy grasp of your readers.

Economizing on words

A second basic technique of shortening sentences is to use words economically. Anything you write can be expressed in many ways, some shorter than others. In general, the shorter wordings save the reader time, are clearer, and make more interesting reading. You should prefer them.

Learning to use words economically is a matter of continuing effort. You should continuously be aware of the need for word economy. You should carefully explore and appraise the many ways of expressing each thought. You should know that the possibility of word economy depends on the subject matter in each case. You should know also that there are certain ways of expression which simply are not economical. These you should avoid. The more common of the uneconomical ways of expression are discussed in the following paragraphs.

Cluttering phrases. Our language is cluttered with numerous phrases which are best replaced by shorter expressions. Although the shorter forms may save only a word or two here and there, the little savings over a long piece of writing can be significant. As the following sentences illustrate, the shorter substitutes are better.

The Long Way	Short and Improved
In the event that payment is not made by January, operations will cease.	If payment is not made by January, operations will cease.
In spite of the fact that they received help, they failed to exceed the quota.	*Even though* they received help, they failed to exceed the quota.
The invoice was *in the amount of* $50,000.	The invoice was *for* $50,000.

Here are other contrasting pairs of expressions:

Cluttering Phrase	Shorter Substitution
Along the lines of	Like
At the present time	Now
For the purpose of	For
For the reason that	Because, since
In accordance with	By
In the meantime	Meanwhile
In the near future	Soon
In the neighborhood of	About
In very few cases	Seldom
In view of the fact that	Since, because
On the basis of	By
On the occasion of	On
With regard to, with reference to	About
With a view to	To

Surplus words. You should eliminate words which add nothing to the sentence meaning. In some instances, however, eliminating the words requires recasting the sentence, as some of the following examples illustrate:

Contains Surplus Words	Surplus Words Eliminated
He ordered desks *which are of the executive type.*	He ordered executive-type desks.
It will be noted that the records for the past years show a steady increase in special appropriations.	The records for past years show a steady increase in special appropriations.
There are four rules *which* should be observed.	Four rules should be observed.
In addition to these defects, numerous other defects mar the operating procedure.	Numerous other defects mar the operating procedure.
His performance was good enough to *enable him* to qualify him for the promotion.	His performance was good enough to qualify him for promotion.
The machines *which were* damaged by the fire were repaired.	The machines damaged by the fire were repaired.
By *the* keeping *of* production records, they found the error.	By keeping production records, they found the error.

Contains Surplus Words	Surplus Words Eliminated
In the period between April and June we detected the problem.	Between April and June we detected the problem.
I am prepared to report *to the effect* that sales increased.	I am prepared to report that sales increased.

Roundabout construction. Of the many ways of saying anything, some are direct and to the point; others cover the same ground in a roundabout way. Without question, the direct ways are usually better, and you should use them. Although there are many forms of roundabout expressions (some of them overlap the preceding causes of excess wording), the following illustrations clearly show the general nature of this violation:

Roundabout	Direct and to the Point
The department budget *can be observed to be decreasing* each new year.	The department budget *decreases* each year.
The union is *involved in the task of reviewing* the seniority provision of the contract.	The union is *reviewing* the seniority provision of the contract.
The president is *of the opinion that* the tax was paid.	The president *believes* the tax was paid.
It is essential that the income be used to retire the debt.	The income *must* be used to retire the debt.
It is the committee's assumption that the evidence has been gathered.	The committee *assumes* that the evidence has been gathered.
The supervisors should *take appropriate action to determine* whether the time cards are being inspected.	The supervisors *should determine* whether the time cards are being inspected.
The price increase will *afford* the company *an opportunity* to retire the debt.	The price increase will *enable* the company to retire the debt.
During the time she was employed by this company, Miss Carr was absent once.	*While* employed by this company, Miss Carr was absent once.
He criticized everyone he *came in contact with*.	He criticized everyone he *met*.

Unnecessary repetition. You should work to avoid unnecessary repetition of words or thoughts. Exception to this rule, however, is justified when you wish to repeat for special effect or for emphasis.

Needless Repetition	Repetition Eliminated
The provision of Section 5 provides for a union shop.	Section 5 provides for a union shop.
The assignment of training the ineffective worker is *an assignment* we must carry out.	Training the ineffective worker is an assignment we must carry out.
Modern, up-to-date equipment will be used.	Modern equipment will be used.
In the office they found supplies *there* which had never been issued.	In the office they found supplies which had never been issued.

Needless Repetition	Repetition Eliminated
He reported for work Friday *morning* at *8 A.M.*	He reported for work Friday at 8 A.M.
In my opinion I think the plan is sound.	I think the plan is sound.
The *important essentials* must not be neglected.	The essentials must not be neglected.
The *consensus of opinion* is that the tax is unfair.	The consensus is that the tax is unfair.
By acting now we can finish *sooner than if we wait until a later date.*	By acting now we can finish sooner.
At the present time we are conducting two clinics.	We are conducting two clinics.
As a matter of interest, I am interested in learning your procedure.	I am interested in learning your procedure.
We should *plan in advance for the future.*	We should plan.

Determining emphasis in sentence design

Writing sentences also involves giving the right emphasis to content. Any written business communication contains a number of items of information, not all equally important. Some are very important, such as a conclusion in a report or the objective in a letter. Some are relatively unimportant. Your task as writer is to determine the importance of each item and then to form your sentences to communicate this importance.

Sentence length affects emphasis. Short, simple sentences carry more emphasis than long, involved ones. The short ones stand out and call attention to their contents. Thus, the reader gets one message without the interference of related or supporting information.

Longer sentences give less emphasis to their contents. When two or more ideas are in one sentence, the ideas share emphasis. How they share it depends on how the sentence is constructed. If the two ideas are presented equally (in independent clauses, for example), they get about equal emphasis. But if they are not presented equally (for example, in an independent and a dependent clause), one gets more emphasis than the other.

To illustrate the varying emphasis you can give information, consider this example. You have two items of information to write. One is that the company lost money last year. The other is that its sales reached a record high volume. You could present the information in at least three ways. First, you could give both facts equal emphasis by placing them in separate short sentences:

The company lost money last year. The loss occurred in spite of record sales.

Second, you could present the two facts in the same sentence with emphasis on the lost money. Note that the information about sales is in a dependent clause.

Although the company enjoyed record sales last year, it lost money.

Third, you could present the ideas in one sentence with emphasis on the sales increase:

The company enjoyed record sales last year, although it lost money.

Which would you use? The answer depends on how much emphasis each item deserves. You would think the matter through and follow your best judgment. But the point is clear: your choice of arrangement makes a difference.

The importance of logical thinking in determining emphasis is illustrated in the following paragraphs. In the first, separate sentences present each item of information. Thus each item gets the emphasis of a short sentence. But because all items are treated the same, none stands out. As the items are not equally important, they do not deserve equal emphasis. Notice, also, how the succession of short sentences produces a choppy effect.

The main building was inspected on October 1. Mr. George Wills inspected the building. Mr. Wills is a vice president of the company. He found that the building has 6,500 square feet of floor space. He also found that it has 2,400 square feet of storage space. The new store must have a minimum of 6,000 square feet of floor space. It must have 2,000 square feet of storage space. Thus, the main building exceeds the space requirements for the new store. Therefore, Mr. Wills concluded that the main building is adequate for the company's needs.

In the next illustration some of the items are subordinated, but not logically. The really important information does not receive the emphasis it deserves. Logically, these two points should stand out: (1) the building is large enough, and (2) storage space exceeds minimum requirements. But these points do not stand out in the following version.

Mr. George Wills, who inspected the main building on October 1, is a vice president of the company. His inspection, which supports the conclusion that the building is large enough for the proposed store, uncovered these facts. The store has 6,500 square feet of floor space and 2,400 square feet of storage space, which is more than the minimum requirement of 6,000 and 2,000 square feet, respectively, of floor and storage space.

The third illustration shows good emphasis of the important points. The short beginning sentence emphasizes the conclusion. The supporting facts that the building exceeds the minimum of floor and storage space requirements receive main-clause emphasis. The less important facts, such as the reference to George Wills, are treated subordinately.

The main building is large enough for the new store. This conclusion, made by Vice President George Wills following his October 1 inspection of the building, is based on these facts: The building's 6,500 square feet of floor space are 500 more than the 6,000 set as the minimum. The 2,400 square feet of storage space are 400 more than the 2,000 minimum requirement.

The preceding illustrations show how sentence construction can determine emphasis. You can make items stand out, you can treat them equally, or you can deemphasize them. The choices are yours. What you do must not be simply a matter of chance, but the result of good, sound thinking.

Good sentences must have unity. For a sentence to have unity, all of its parts must combine to form one clear thought. In other words, everything that is put together as a sentence should have a good reason for being together.

Violations of unity in sentence construction fall into three categories: (1) unrelated ideas, (2) excessive detail, and (3) illogical constructions.

Unrelated ideas. Placing unrelated ideas in a sentence is the most obvious violation of unity. Of course, putting two or more ideas in a sentence is not grammatically wrong. But the ideas must have a reason for being together. They must combine to complete the single goal of the sentence. It is not enough that the ideas just be on the same subject.

There are three basic ways of giving unity to sentences that contain seemingly unrelated ideas. 1. You can put the ideas in separate sentences. 2. You can make one of the ideas subordinate to the other. 3. You can add words that show how the ideas are related. The revisions of this sentence illustrate the first two of these techniques:

Mr. Jordan is our sales manager, and he has a degree in law.

Perhaps the two ideas are related, but the words do not tell how. It might be better to make each into separate sentences:

Mr. Jordan is our sales manager. He has a law degree.

Or the two ideas could be kept in one sentence by subordinating one idea to the other. In this way, the main clause provides the unity of the sentence.

Mr. Jordan, our sales manager, has a law degree.

Adding words to show relationship of the thoughts is illustrated in this example:

Our production increased in January, and our equipment is wearing out.

The sentence has two ideas which do not seem to be related. One way of improving the sentence is to make separate sentences of each idea. A further look reveals, however, that the two ideas are related. The words just do not show how. Thus, the sentence could be corrected by changing the words to show how:

Even though our equipment is wearing out, our production increased in January.

The following contrasting pairs of sentences further illustrate the technique:

Unrelated	*Improved*
Our territory is the southern half of the state, and our sales people cannot cover it thoroughly.	Our territory is the southern half of the state. Our sales people cannot cover it thoroughly.
Operation of the press is simple, but no machine will work well unless it is maintained.	Operation of the press is simple; but, like any machine, it will not work well unless it is maintained.
We concentrate on energy-saving products, and 70 percent of our business is from them.	As a result of our concentration on energy-saving products, 70 percent of our business comes from them.

Excessive detail. Putting too much detail into one sentence tends to hide the central thought. If the detail is important, it is better to put it in a separate sentence.

This suggestion strengthens another given earlier in the chapter. As you will recall, you were advised to use short sentences. Obviously, short sentences do not have much detail. We repeat this good advice primarily for completeness, for long sentences definitely lead to lack of unity, as illustrated in these contrasting sentences:

Excessive Detail	*Improved*
Our New York offices, considered plush in the 1960s, but now badly in need of renovation, as is the case with most offices that have not been maintained, have been abandoned.	Considered plush in the 1960s, our New York offices have not been maintained properly. As they badly need repair, we have abandoned them.
We have attempted to trace the Ply-tec insulation which you ordered from us October 1, and about which you inquired in your October 10th letter, but we have not yet been able to locate it, although we are sending you a rush shipment immediately.	We are sending you a rush shipment of Ply-tec insulation immediately. Following your October 10 inquiry, we attempted to trace your October 1 order. We were unable to locate it.
In 1978, when I, a small-town girl from a middle-class family, began my studies at State University, which is widely recognized for its accounting program, I set my goal for a career with a major accounting firm.	A small-town girl from a middle-income family, I entered State University in 1981. I selected the school because of its widely recognized accounting program. From the beginning my goal was a career with a major accounting firm.

Illogical constructions. Illogical constructions destroy sentence unity. Primarily, illogical constructions result from illogical thinking. Although illogical thinking is too complex for meaningful study here, a few typical examples of this violation should acquaint you with the possibilities involved. Then by using logical thinking you should be able to reduce this problem in your writing.

The first example contains two main thoughts, both in correct clauses. But one clause is in active voice *(we cut);* the other is in passive voice *(quality was reduced).*

First we cut prices, and then quality was reduced.

Unity can be given by making both clauses active, as in this example:

First we cut prices, and then we reduced quality.

Another example is the following sentence. Its mixed constructions do not make a clear and logical thought. (The technical explanation here is that the beginning clause is for a complex sentence and the last part is the predicate of a simple sentence.)

Because our salespeople are inexperienced caused us to miss our quota.

Revised for good logic the sentence might read like this:

The inexperience of our salespeople caused us to miss our quota.

These sentences further illustrate the point:

Illogical Construction	*Improved*
Job rotation is when you train people by moving them from job to job.	Job rotation is a training method involving moving people from job to job.
Knowing that she objected to the price was the reason we permitted her to return the goods.	Because we knew that she objected to the price, we permitted her to return the goods.
I never knew an executive who was interested in helping his workers who had got into problems which caused them to worry.	I never knew an executive who was interested in helping worried workers with their problems.
My education was completed in 1983, and then I began work as a sales representative for Xerox.	I completed my education in 1983, and then I began work as a sales representative for Xerox.

Arranging sentences for clarity

Words alone do not make a message, for their arrangement also plays a role in the meanings given by our minds. All languages have certain rules of arrangement which help to determine meaning. These rules are generally fixed in our minds, and they are a part of our filter operation. Thus, to violate them is to invite miscommunication.

As we all know, scholars of the past have thoroughly cataloged the rules of our language. And all of us have been exposed to these rules in our study of language. Contrary to what many of us may think, however, these rules of language are not merely arbitrary requirements set by detail-minded scholars. Rather, the rules are statements of logical relationships between words. Dangling participles, for example, confuse meaning by modifying the wrong words. Unparallel constructions leave erroneous impressions of the parts. Pronouns without clear antecedents have no definite meaning. The evidence is quite clear: The business writer must know and follow the conventional standards of language.

Unfortunately, too many of us know too little about the conventional rules of English grammar. Why so many people have resisted this subject through years of drill at all levels of education is a mystery to educators.

Obviously, the area is too broad for complete coverage in this book. Some of the points with which most of us have trouble, however, are presented for quick review in the appendix. You should not ignore their importance.

Care in paragraph design

In writing, we do not communicate by words and sentences alone. Paragraphs also play a major role. As we shall see, how a paragraph is designed helps to organize its information as the information goes into our mental filter. In addition, the rest stop provided by paragraphing gives a psychological if not real boost to our receptiveness to messages.

How we should go about designing paragraphs is not easily put into words. Much of paragraph writing depends on the writer's mental ability to organize and to relate facts logically. Thus, it is a mental process about which we know little. There are, however, some general suggestions you would be wise to follow. They are summarized for you in the following paragraphs.

Giving the paragraph unity

A first suggestion in paragraph design is to give the paragraph unity. Unity, of course, means oneness. When applied to paragraph construction, it means that you should build the paragraph around a single topic or idea. That is, you should include only this major topic or idea plus the supporting details which help to develop it. Exceptions to the rule of unity are the transitional paragraphs whose objectives are to relate preceding and suceeding topics.

Just what constitutes unity is not always easy to determine. All of a report, for example, may deal with a single topic and therefore have unity. The same could be said for each major division of the report as well as for the lesser subdivisions. Paragraph unity, however, concerns smaller units than these—usually the lowest level of a detailed outline. That is, in reports written with detailed outlines, each paragraph might well cover one of the lowest outline captions. In any event, one good test of a paragraph is to reduce its content to a single topic statement. If this statement does not cover the paragraph content, unity is not likely to be there.

Keeping the paragraph short

In most forms of business writing, you would be wise to keep your paragraphs short. Short paragraphs help your reader to follow the organizational plan of the paper. Specifically, they emphasize the beginning and ending of each item covered, and they give added emphasis to the facts covered. In addition, short paragraphs are more inviting to the eye. People simply prefer to read material which gives them frequent breaks. This is true as long as the breaks are not too frequent. A series of very short paragraphs would leave an equally offensive choppy effect.

A glance at Figure 7–1 quickly shows the psychological effect of paragraph length. The full page of solid type appears to be more difficult and generally less inviting than the one marked by short paragraphs. Even if both contained exactly the same words, the difference would be present. Perhaps this difference is largely psychological. Psychological or not, it is real.

Just how long a paragraph should be is, of course, dependent upon the topic. Some topics are short; others are long; still others are in between. Even so, a general rule can be given as to paragraph length. Most well-organized and well-paragraphed business papers have paragraphs averaging around eight or nine lines. Some good paragraphs may be quite short—even a single sentence. And some may be well over the eight-to-nine-line average.

One good rule of thumb to follow is to question the unity of all long paragraphs—say those exceeding 12 lines. If inspection shows you that only one topic is present, you should make no change. But if the paragraph covers more than one topic, you should make additional paragraphs.

Putting topic sentences to good use

In organizing your paragraphs, you will need to make effective use of the topic sentence. A topic sentence, of course, is the sentence in a paragraph which expresses the main idea. Around this topic sentence, the details which support or elaborate the main idea build in some logical way. Exactly how a given paragraph should build from the topic sentence depends on the

Figure 7–1
*Contrasting Pages Showing Psychological Effects of
Long and Short Paragraphs*

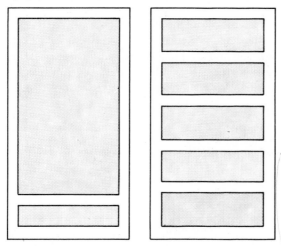

Heavy paragraphs make the
writing appear to be dull
and difficult.

Short paragraphs give well
organized effect—invite the
reader to read.

information to be covered and on the writer's plan in covering it. Obviously, much of paragraph design must come from your mental effort. You would profit, however, by being generally acquainted with the paragraph plans most commonly used.

Topic sentence first. The most widely used paragraph plan begins with the topic sentence. The supporting material then follows in some logical order. As this arrangement gives good emphasis to the major point, it will be the most useful to you as a business writer. In fact, some company manuals suggest that this arrangement be used almost exclusively. As the following paragraph illustrates, this arrangement has merit.

Illustration

A majority of the economists consulted think that business activity will drop during the first quarter of next year. Of the 185 economists interviewed, 13 percent looked for continued increases in business activities; and 28 percent anticipated little or no change from the present high level. The remaining 59 percent looked for a recession. Of this group, nearly all (87 percent) believed the down curve would occur during the first quarter of the year.

Topic sentence at end. Another logical paragraph arrangement places the topic sentence at the end, usually as a conclusion. The supporting details come first and in logical order build toward the topic sentence. Frequently, such paragraphs use a beginning sentence to set up or introduce the subject, as in the following illustration. Such a sentence serves as a form of topic sentence, but the real meat of the paragraph is covered in the final sentence.

Illustration

The significant role of inventories in the economic picture should not be overlooked. At present, inventories represent 3.8 months supply. Their dollar value is the highest in history. If considered in relation to increased sales, however, they are not excessive. In fact, they are well within the range generally believed to be safe. *Thus, inventories are not likely to cause a downward swing in the economy.*

Topic sentences within the paragraph. Some paragraphs are logically arranged with the topic sentence somewhere within. These paragraphs are not often used, and usually for good reason. In general, they fail to give proper emphasis to the key points in the paragraph. Even so, they may sometimes be used with good effect, as in this example:

Illustration

Numerous materials have been used in manufacturing this part. And many have shown quite satisfactory results. *Material 329, however, is superior to them all.* Built with material 329, the part is almost twice as strong as when built with the next best material. Also, it is three ounces lighter. And, most important, it is cheaper than any of the other products.

Making the paragraph move forward

Each paragraph you write should clearly move an additional step toward your objective. Such forward movement is a good quality of paragraph design. Individual sentences have little movement, for they cover only a single thought. An orderly succession of single thoughts, however, does produce movement. In addition, good movement is helped by skillful use of transition, by smoothness in writing style, and by a general proficiency in word choice and sentence design.

Perhaps the quality of movement is easier to see than to describe. In general, it is present when after reading the paragraph, the reader has been moved one sure step toward the objective. Although many arrangements can illustrate good paragraph movement, the following does the job exceptionally well:

> Three reasons justify moving from the Crowton site. First, building rock in the Crowton area is questionable. The failure of recent geological explorations in the area appears to confirm suspicions that the Crowton deposits are nearly exhausted. Second, distances from Crowton to major consumption areas make transportation costs unusually high. Obviously, any savings in transportation costs will add to company profits. Third, obsolescence of much of the equipment at the Crowton plant makes this an ideal time for relocation. New equipment could be scrapped in the Crowton area.

The flow of thought in the preceding paragraph is orderly. Note how the first sentence sets up the paragraph structure and that the parts of the structure follow.

A word of caution

Like most elements of writing, the foregoing principles must be tempered with good judgment. If followed blindly to an extreme degree, they can produce writing which takes on the appearance of being mechanical or which in some way calls attention to writing style rather than to content. For example, slavish application of the rules for short sentences could produce a primer style of writing. So could the rules stressing simple language. Such writing could be offensive to the more sophisticated reader. Your solution is to use the rules as general guides, but clear and logical thinking must guide you in your use of them.

The writing principles presented in this chapter are by no means all we may derive from communication theory. We have reviewed only the most general ones—those which may be applied in most everyday business writing situations. The more specific applications we have reserved for coverage at the points of their best application in business writing situations. They are liberally sprinkled throughout the application chapters which follow.

Questions & Problems

1. Discuss how adaptation is supported by communication theory.
2. Discuss the relationship of short and familiar words to adaptation.

3. Distinguish between active and passive voice. Discuss the advantages of emphasizing active voice.
4. Find a paragraph on some business subject that

is heavy in technical words. Rewrite it for a nontechnical audience.

5. How is the suggestion to use concrete words supported by communication theory?
6. List five commonly used camouflaged verbs and rewrite them. (Do not repeat any of those given in the text.)
7. Discuss the role of sentence length in the readability of writing. Include comments on exceptions to the rule.

8. Explain the role of the topic sentence in paragraph design.
9. What is meant by paragraph unity?
10. Read the description of the Gunning Fog Index in Appendix G.
   (a) Explain how it relates to the writing principles presented in this chapter.
   (b) Apply the Gunning Fog Index to the last two paragraphs of this chapter.

Instructions for questions 11 through 55: Revise the following sentences to make them conform with the principles discussed in the text. They are grouped by the principles they illustrate.

Using understandable words

(Assume that these sentences are written for high school level readers.)

11. We must terminate all deficit financing.
12. The most operative assembly-line configuration is a unidirectional flow.
13. A proportionate tax consumes a determinate apportionment of one's monetary inflow.
14. Business has an inordinate influence on governmental operations.
15. It is imperative that the consumer be unrestrained in determining his preferences.
16. Mr. Casey terminated John's employment as a consequence of his ineffectual performance.
17. Our expectations are that there will be increments in commodity value.
18. This antiquated mechanism is ineffectual for an accelerated assembly-line operation.
19. The preponderance of business executives we consulted envision signs of improvement from the current siege of economic stagnation.
20. If liquidation becomes mandatory, we shall dispose of these assets first.

Selecting concrete words

21. We have found that young men are best for this work.
22. He makes good grades.
23. John lost a fortune in Las Vegas.
24. If we don't receive the goods soon we will cancel.
25. Profits last year were exorbitant.

Limiting use of passive voice

26. Our action is based on the assumption that the competition will be taken by surprise.
27. It is believed by the typical union member that his or her welfare is not considered to be important by management.
28. We are serviced by the Bratton Company.
29. Our safety is the responsibility of management.
30. You were directed by your supervisor to complete this assignment by noon.

Avoiding camouflaged verbs

31. It was my duty to make a determination of the damages.
32. Harold made a recommendation that we fire Mr. Shultz.
33. We will make her give an accounting of her activities.
34. We will ask him to bring about a change in his work routine.
35. This new equipment will result in a saving in maintenance.
36. Will you please make an adjustment for this defect?

Keeping sentences short

37. Records were set by both the New York Stock Exchange industrial index, which closed at 67.19, up 0.16 points, topping its previous high of 67.02 set Wednesday, and Standard & Poor's industrial indicator, which finished at 123.61, up 0.20, smashing its all-time record of 123.41, also set in the prior session.

38. Dealers attributed the rate decline to several factors, including expectations that the U.S. Treasury will choose to pay off rather than refinance some $4 billion of government obligations that fall due next month, an action which would absorb even further the available supplies of short-term government securities, leaving more funds chasing skimpier stocks of the securities.

39. If you report your income on a fiscal-year basis ending in 1983, you may not take credit for any tax withheld on your calendar year 1983 earnings, inasmuch as your taxable year began in 1982, although you may include, as a part of your withholding tax credits against your fiscal 1984 tax liability, the amount of tax withheld during 1983.

40. The Consumer Education Committee is assigned the duties of keeping informed of the qualities of all consumer goods and services, especially of their strengths and shortcomings, of gathering all pertinent information on dealers' sales practices, with emphasis on practices involving honest and reasonable fairness, and of publicizing any of the information collected which may be helpful in educating the consumer.

Using words economically

41. In view of the fact that we financed the experiment, we were entitled to some profit.
42. We will deliver the goods in the near future.
43. Mr. Watts outlined his development plans on the occasion of his acceptance of the presidency.
44. I will talk to him with regard to the new policy.
45. The candidates who had the most money won.
46. There are many obligations which we must meet.
47. We purchased coats which are lined with wolf fur.
48. Mary is of the conviction that service has improved.
49. Sales can be detected to have improved over last year.
50. It is essential that we take the actions that are necessary to correct the problem.
51. The chairperson is engaged in the activity of preparing the program.
52. Martin is engaged in the process of reviving the application.
53. You should study all new innovations in your field.
54. In all probability, we are likely to suffer a loss this quarter.
55. The requirements for the job require a minimum of three years of experience.

8

Correspondence: The basic elements

AS YOU MOVE UP the executive ladder in business, probably you will spend more and more of your time writing. And of all the writing you do, letters are likely to take up most of your time. In fact, if you are to be like the typical business executive, your work routine will include a period for handling the daily mail. Little that you will do the remainder of the day will be more important to your company. Yet, if you follow the practices of today's typical executives, the quality of your letter writing will rank at or near the bottom of your work activities. If you will study them diligently, this and the following three chapters will make you an exception to this statement.

Objectives of the business letter

Our study of business letters appropriately begins with an analysis of letter objectives. By objectives we mean what the writer wants to achieve by writing the letter. As we shall see, the objectives of a letter determine the techniques we should use in writing the letter.

The primary goal

Primary among a letter's objectives is the immediate purpose for communicating. This goal is the one which moves us to write the letter in the first place. Perhaps we write a letter to get certain information; maybe we seek to collect money; or it could be that we are merely communicating routine information to our readers. In each of these instances there is a definite need to communicate, and fulfillment of that need becomes the primary objective of the letter.

This primary objective is the obvious one, and no normal business executive would quarrel about its existence. It is not universally known, however, that it is not the only objective of a letter. There is at least one more objective in the typical business letter situation—one which may be equally important in some cases. This is the public relations objective.

The public relations goal of the letter

In analyzing the public relations objective of the business letter, we need first to look at the overall public relations goal of the firm. It is a fundamental fact in the field of public relations that the success of a business organization is to a large extent determined by what the public thinks of the organization. In a retail operation, for example, the customer's inclination to buy again and again from the store is influenced by what she or he thinks of the store. Purchasers of brand products are guided in their selection among brands by the images their minds hold of the companies involved. Clients of service organizations are influenced to use organizations by the impressions they have accumulated. And so it is with all business organizations. Their customers form mental images of them. Some customers like them; some dislike them; some hold opinions somewhere between these extremes. The important point is that the more the customers like the organization, the more successful the organization is likely to be.

Whether or not a company is liked is determined by the total of the impressions its public has received of it. Throughout its existence each company makes countless impressions on the minds of its customers. Each time customers visit a company's place of business, their mental filters record information about the company—information about such things as the cleanliness and tidiness of the place, the friendliness of the workers, the quality of the goods and services. They register thoughts also from what they read about the organization in the newspapers and by the advertisements the company runs. They form mental notes each time they see the company's delivery trucks come by, each time they meet a company employee socially, and each time they hear comments about the organization. They also form notions about the company from the letters they receive from it.

The total of all these impressions in the minds of the company's public determines the company's public relations. If the overall effect of these public relations is favorable, people will like the organization, and they will want to do business with it. On the other hand, if the total is heavily weighted by negative reactions, people will not be so favorably inclined to do business with the company. The obvious conclusion is that a company's public relations are important. They have a direct bearing on success and profit. Thus, organizations should work to improve their images in the minds of their public. Their effort should be a total one, covering all areas in which they make impressions.

One of the areas of impression in which a company should work for improvement is correspondence. This suggestion is valid even with companies which maintain relatively little communication with their public. As a rule, the letters that are written make strong impressions—strong for a number of reasons. In the first place, letters are highly personalized messages, for they single out a special reader. They have a more formal effect than most face-to-face situations. They receive the added impetus of the printed word, and they have the quality of permanence. Because letters make strong impressions, all organizations should work to get the maximum public relations benefit from them. Thus, we may conclude that every business letter should have the secondary objective of enhancing the company's public relations.

In determining what we should do to give our letters the optimum public relations effect, we need only to explore our own mental filters. Specifically, we need to ask ourselves such questions as how we like to be treated, what effects words produce on us, and what company images we like most. The answers to such questions suggest the techniques we should use to get the best public relations effort from our letters. Some of the more significant of these techniques are presented in the following pages.

Conversational style

Because people like people, for optimum public relations effect you should make your letters sound human. That is, you should write in words which have the effect of good conversation. This is not to say that you should write letters exactly as you would talk to your readers if you were face to face with them. Writing demands more correctness. But the words you use should be from your speaking vocabulary, and the tone of your writing should be that of good conversation. Such writing produces a warmth which all of us like. It recalls to our minds pleasant experiences with friendly people. In addition, as it uses the familiar words of our language. It is the kind of language which communicates best.

Tendency to be formal

Contrary to what you may think, writing in a conversational manner is not easy for all of us. In most of us there is the tendency to stiffen up, to become formal whenever we write. Instead of being the warm, friendly people we are, we become stiff and stilted. We tend to write in an unnatural manner. The results are letters which convey the impression of a cold and formal institution rather than that of a group of friendly folk doing business.

The old "language of business"

Adding to the natural difficulty we have of writing in a conversational manner is an inherited tradition of stiff, unnatural writing. Unfortunately, the pioneer business writers using the English language developed a highly formal, unnatural style. Borrowing heavily from the legal language of the courts and the flowery expressions of the aristocracy, they developed a style of writing which became known as the "language of business." It was a highly stereotyped and cold manner of communicating and had little of the warmth that is so essential for friendly human relations. Typifying this manner of writing were such expressions as these:

In Openings	In Contents	In Closings
Your letter of the 7th inst. received and contents duly noted.	Please be advised	Thanking you in advance
We beg to advise	Said matter	Trusting this will meet with your favor
In compliance with yours of even date	In due course	We beg to remain
Your esteemed favor at hand	Inst., prox., ult.	Anticipating your favorable response
This is to inform you	Kind favor	Assuring you of our cooperation
We have before us	Kind order	Hoping to receive
Responding to yours of even date	Re:	I am, Dear Sir, yours respectfully
Yours of the 10th ultimo to hand	In re	Trusting to be favored by your further orders, we are, Gentlemen, yours faithfully
Your favor received	Said matter	
	Deem it advisable	
	Wherein you state	
	Wherein you state as per your letter	
	In reply wish to state	
	Attached hereto	

This style of writing business letters reached its peak in the last half of the 19th century and was still very much with us in the early years of this century. In fact, the classic letter guide, *Pitman's Mercantile Correspondence*, which was a popular reference during this period, is filled with such expressions. Its introductory instructions go so far as to list this rule as the first one a correspondent should follow: "He must respect the generally recognized commercial modes of expression."[1] Illustrating this manner of word choice, the book presents this typical example:

> Gentlemen,
> We have to thank you for yours of 28th inst., enclosing cheque for $95.12 in payment of our invoice of 17th inst. Formal receipt enclosed herewith. Trusting to be favoured with your further orders,
>
> We are, Gentlemen,
Yours faithfully,[2]

Fortunately, the old language of business no longer receives authoritative support. In fact, it has been under relentless attack by writing authorities for the last half century. That these efforts have been effective is unmistakably clear, for rarely do we see letters like the Pitman example in today's business. As we would expect, however, even a half century of effort is not enough to change completely the habits of business people. There are still writers among us who end their letters with "Thanking you in advance, I remain," "Trusting that you will understand my position," or the like. And there are still outcroppings of bromides such as "enclosed please find," "we wish to thank," "permit me to say," and "take the liberty."

Use of "rubber stamps"

The language-of-business carry-overs plus some more recent additions comprise a group of words and expressions we refer to as "rubber stamps." By rubber stamps, we mean expressions we use somewhat automatically in a

---

[1] *Pitman's Mercantile Correspondence*, Sir Isaac Pitman & Sons, Ltd., London, n.d., p. 2.

[2] *Ibid.*, p. 18.

certain type of situation. They are expressions we use without thought. They do not fit the one case, for we would use the same expressions in any similar situations. They are used as their name implies—as rubber stamps. Because our filters have received them many times, these words produce the feeling that we are being given routine treatment. And routine treatment is far less effective than special attention in bringing about good public relations.

In addition to the language-of-business illustrations previously given, some more modern rubber stamps are commonly used. Perhaps most widely used is the "thank you for your letter" variety of opening sentence. Sincere as its intent may be, its overuse tends to place it in the routine category, and routine treatment has nowhere near the goodwill-building effect that would result from specially selected words to fit the one situation involved. Also in the category is the "if I can be of any further assistance, do not hesitate to call on me" type of close. Like the preceding examples, its sincere intent may suffer from routine use. Other examples of modern-day rubber stamps are the following:

I am happy to be able to answer your letter.
I have received your letter.
This will acknowledge receipt of. . . .
According to our records. . . .
This is to inform you. . . .
In accordance with your instructions. . . .

To eliminate the timeworn expressions as well as the more modern rubber stamps, it is not necessary first to memorize long lists of the taboo words and expressions and then to avoid them. You need only to write in the language of good conversation. The worn-out words and expressions are not a part of your everyday vocabulary. If you use them at all, you have acquired them from reading the letters of others—not from your oral communicating experience. So if you will rely on your conversational vocabulary, you will be safe, and you will be writing in a style which will make a most favorable impression on your reader.

The stilted and conversational styles of writing are perhaps best described by contrasting illustrations. As you read the examples which follow, note the effects they have as they filter through your mind. Try to visualize the people who wrote each, and record your impressions of the companies they represent. You should detect marked differences.

Dull and Stiff	*Friendly and Conversational*
This is to advise that we deem it a great pleasure to approve subject of your request as per letter of the 12th inst.	Yes, you certainly may use the equipment you asked about in your August 12 letter.
Pursuant to this matter, I wish to state that the aforementioned provisions are unmistakably clear.	These contract provisions are quite clear on this point.
This will acknowledge receipt of your May 10 order for 4 dozen Hunt slacks. Please be advised that they will be shipped in accordance with your instructions by Green Arrow Motor Freight on May 16.	Four dozen Hunt slacks should reach your store by the 18th. As you instructed, they were shipped today by Green Arrow Motor Freight.

Dull and Stiff	Friendly and Conversational
Thanking you in advance. . . .	I'll sincerely appreciate. . . .
Herewith enclosed please find. . . .	Enclosed is. . . .
I deem it advisable. . . .	I suggest. . . .
I herewith hand you. . . .	Here is. . . .
Kindly advise at an early date. . . .	Please let me know soon. . . .
The undersigned wishes to advise that the aforementioned contract is at hand.	I have the contract.
Please be advised that you should sign the form before the 1st.	You should sign the form before the 1st.
Hoping this meets with your approval.	I hope you approve.
Submitted herewith is your notification of our compliance with subject standards.	Attached is notification of our compliance with the standards.

You-viewpoint ✳

As we know from an analysis of our own mental filters, we human beings are self-centered creatures. In part, our natural tendency toward self-preservation explains this characteristic, but our self-centered nature goes beyond this. Perhaps the explanation is that basically we are selfish beings. We have structured our thinking (the whole area of our attitudes, opinions, and biases) to conform with our best interests. We want recognition; we want good things to happen to us. We like to talk about ourselves, and we like others to say good things about us. In general, we like ourselves better than we like anyone else.

Because we are self-centered, we tend to see each situation from our own point of view. In letter writing situations this attitude may lead us to a writer-oriented, "we-viewpoint" approach—an approach which places emphasis on us and our interests rather than on our readers and their interests. Such approaches obviously do not bring about the most positive responses in our readers, for they also are self-centered. The resulting effect is not conducive to building goodwill, nor does it help in getting them to do things you want them to do. You can achieve more positive results by writing in the reader's point of view.

What it is

Called the "you-viewpoint" or the "you-attitude," this approach involves seeing situations from your readers' standpoint and choosing words and strategy which will bring about a favorable response in their minds. To some extent it involves using second-person pronouns, for the words *you* and *your* clearly call attention to the readers and their interests. But the you-viewpoint goes much deeper. It is an attitude of mind. As an attitude of mind, the you-viewpoint can take many forms. It involves seeing situations from the readers' point of view rather than from your own. It involves placing your readers in the center of things—talking to them and about them. Sometimes it may involve just being friendly and treating people the way they like to be treated. And at times it may involve skillfully handling people with carefully chosen words in order to get a desired reaction from them. It involves all these things and more.

The you-viewpoint illustrated

Like most techniques of writing, the you-viewpoint may be understood best through illustration. First, take the case of someone writing a letter with the objective of presenting a favorable message. This person could write from an I centered point of view, heralding the message with words such as "I am happy to report. . . ." A you-oriented writer, on the other hand, would write something like "You will be happy to know. . . ." The messages are much the same, but the effects are different.

In a letter reporting to a new customer that a charge account has been approved, the we-viewpoint approach might take this form: "We are pleased to have your new account." The words might be favorably received by some readers, but some may see a self-centered retailer gleefully clapping his hands at the prospect of more business. The you-viewpoint approach would use words like this: "Your new charge account is now open for your convenience."

Perhaps no group is more aware of the technique of you-viewpoint presentation than the advertising copywriters. Although no one from this group would do so, a writer-oriented presentation of the message of a razor manufacturer might go like this: "We make Willett razors in three weights—light, medium, heavy." Instead, the professional copywriter would bring the reader into the center of things and talk about the product in terms of the reader's satisfaction. Probably the correspondent would come up with something like this: "So that you may choose the one razor that is just right for your beard, Willett makes razors for you in three weights—light, medium, and heavy."

Even in fairly negative messages, the you-viewpoint may be effectively used to help the reader see the most positive aspect of the situation. For example, take the case of the executive who must write a letter denying a professor's request for assistance on a research project. The answer, of course, is bad news; but it is even worse when presented in these we-viewpoint words: "We cannot comply with your request to use our office personnel on your project, for it would cost us more than we can afford." A writer skilled in word selection and the advantages of you-adaptation could cover the same ground but with much more positive results. A good strategy might be to view the situation from the reader's point of view, find the one explanation which would be most convincing to this one reader, and then present this explanation in you-viewpoint language. The response might take this form: "As a business professor well acquainted with the need for close economy in all phases of office operation, you will understand why we must limit our personnel to work in our office."

The following contrasting examples provide additional proof of the different effects changes in viewpoint produce. Although they are given without explanation, with a bit of imagination you should be able to supply information on the situations they cover.

We-viewpoint	You-viewpoint
I have seven years' experience as a direct-mail copywriter.	Seven years of practical experience as a direct-mail copywriter will equip me to cultivate your mail solicitations.
We are happy to have your order for Kopper products, which we are sending today by Railway Express.	Your selection of Kopper products should reach you by Saturday, as they were shipped by Railway Express today.
We sell the Forever cutlery set for the low price of $4 each, and suggest a retail price of $6.50.	You can reap a nice $2.50 profit on each Forever set you sell at $6.50, for your cost is only $4.
Our policy prohibits us from permitting outside groups to use our equipment except on a cash rental basis.	As our office is financed by your tax dollar, you will appreciate our policy of cutting operating costs by renting our equipment.
We have been quite tolerant of your past-due account, and must now demand payment.	If you are to continue to enjoy the benefits of credit buying, you have no choice but to clear your account now.
We have received your report of May 1.	Thank you for your report of May 1.
So that we may complete our file records on you, we ask that you submit to us your January report.	So that your file records may be completed, please send us your January report.
We have shipped the two dozen Crown desk sets you ordered.	Your two dozen Crown desk sets should reach you with this letter.
We require that you sign the sales slip before we will charge to your account.	For your protection, we charge to your account only after you have signed the sales slip.

A point of controversy

Use of the you-viewpoint is a matter of some controversy. Its critics point out two major shortcomings. They say that it is insincere; and they say that it is a manipulative technique. In either event, they argue the technique is dishonest. It is better, they say, to just "tell it as it is."

These arguments have some merit. Without question the you-viewpoint can be used to the point of being insincere. It can be and usually is used in obvious flattery. Proponents of the technique argue that insincerity and flattery need not, in fact should not, be the result of you-viewpoint effort. The objective is to treat people courteously—the way they like to be treated. People like to be singled out for attention. They naturally are more interested in themselves than in the writer. Overuse of the technique, they argue, does not justify disuse. Their argument is supported by recent research on the subject. The findings of one major study[3] show that a majority of personality types, especially the friendlier and more sensitive, react favorably to you-viewpoint treatment. A minority, mainly the less sensitive and harsh personalities, are less susceptible.

On the matter of the use of the you-viewpoint to manipulate, we must again concede a point. It is a technique of persuasion. And persuasion may

---

[3] Sam J. Bruno, *The Effects of Personality Traits on the Perception of Written Mass Communication*, doctoral dissertation, Louisiana State University, Baton Rouge, 1971.

have illegitimate goals. Supporters of the you-viewpoint counter this argument by saying that it is the goal and not the technique that should be condemned. Goals can be legitimate, and persuasion techniques used to reach legitimate goals are legitimate.

The answer to the question appears to be somewhere between the extremes. As is the case in most controversies, this question is not a two-valued one. You do not have to use the you-viewpoint exclusively; neither do you have to eliminate it. You can take a middle ground. You can use the you-viewpoint when it is the friendly, sincere thing to do. And you can use it in persuasion when your goals are legitimate. In such cases, using the you-viewpoint is not deceptive. It is "telling it as it is"—or at least, as it should be. We suggest that you take this position. It is with this position in mind that we apply the technique in the following chapters.

Accent on positive language

Whether your letter achieves its goal often will depend to a large extent on the words you use to carry your message. As you know, there are many ways of saying anything, and each way conveys a meaning different from the others. Much of the difference, of course, lies in the meanings of the words.

Effects of words

Words which stir up positive meanings in the reader's mind usually are best for achieving your letter objectives. This is not to say that negative words have no place in business writing. They do. They are strong, and they give emphasis. There are times when you will want to use them. But most of the time your need will be for positive words, for such words are more likely to produce the effects you seek. If you are seeking some action, for example, they are the words most likely to persuade. They tend to put a reader in the right frame of mind; and they place emphasis on the more pleasant aspects of the objectives. In addition, positive words create the goodwill atmosphere we seek in most letters.

On the other hand, negative words produce the opposite effect. The negative meanings they produce in the mind may stir up your reader's resistance to your objective. Also they are likely to be highly destructive of goodwill. Thus, in reaching your letter writing goals, you will need to study carefully the degree of negativeness and positiveness your words convey. You will need to select those words which do the most for you in each case.

In selecting your words, generally you should be wary of those with strongly negative connotations. These are the words which convey meanings of unhappy and unpleasant events; and usually such thoughts detract from your goal. Included in this group are words such as *mistake, problem, error, damage, loss,* and *failure*. Included also are words which deny—words such as *no, do not, refuse,* and *stop.* Additional negative words are all those which by their sounds or connotations have unpleasant effects. Although not all of us hold similar connotations of such words, probably we would agree on these: *itch, guts, scratch, grime, sloppy, sticky, bloody, nauseous.* Or how about *gummy, slimy, bilious,* and *soggy?* Run all of these negative words through your mental filter. Study the meanings they produce. You should have no difficulty seeing how they tend to work against some of the objectives you may have in your letters.

Examples of word choice

To illustrate the positive-to-negative word choices you have in handling letters, take the case of a corporation executive who must write a local civic group denying its request to use the company's meeting facilities. To soften the refusal, however, the executive can let the group use a conference room, which may be somewhat small for its purpose. Of the many ways of wording his response, the executive could come up with this totally negative one:

> We *regret* to inform you that we *cannot* permit you to use our clubhouse for your meeting, as the Ladies Book Club asked for it first. We can, however, let you use our conference room; but it seats *only* 60.

Review of the word connotations clearly brings out the negative words (in italics); first, the positively intended message "We *regret* to inform you" is an unmistakable sign of coming bad news. "Cannot permit" has an unnecessarily harsh meaning. And notice how the one good-news part of the message is handicapped by the limiting word "only."

By searching for a more positive way of covering the same situation, the writer might have written this tactful response:

> As the Ladies Book Club has reserved the clubhouse for Saturday, the best we can do is to offer you our conference room, which seats 60.

Not a single negative word appears in this version. Both approaches achieve the letter's primary objective of denying a request, but the effects on the reader differ sharply. There is no question as to which technique does the better job of building and holding goodwill for the company.

For a second illustration, take the case of a correspondent who must write a letter granting the claim of a woman for some cosmetics damaged in transit. Granting a claim, of course, is the most positive ending such a situation can have. Even though she has had a somewhat unhappy experience, the customer is receiving what she wants. An unskilled writer, however, can so thoroughly recall the unhappy aspects of the problem with negative language that the happy solution is moved to the background. As this negative-filled version illustrates, the effect on the reader is destructive of goodwill:

> We received your claim in which you *contend* that we were responsible for *damage* to three cases of Madame Dupree's lotion. We assure you that we sincerely *regret* the *problems* this has caused you. Even though we feel in all sincerity that your receiving clerks may have been *negligent,* we shall assume the *blame* and replace the *damaged* merchandise.

Obviously, this version grants the claim grudgingly, and only if there were extenuating circumstances would the company profit by such an approach. The words "in which you contend" clearly imply some doubt of the legitimacy of the claim. Even the sincerely intended expression of regret serves only to recall to the reader's mind the ugly picture of the event that has caused all the trouble. And negatives like "blame" and "damage" serve only to strengthen this recollection. Certainly, such an approach is not conducive to goodwill.

In the following version of the message the writer uses only positive aspects of the situation—what can be done to settle the problem. The writer does it without a single negative word. There is no reference to the situation being corrected or to suspicions concerning the legitimacy of the claim. The goodwill effect of this approach is likely to maintain good business relations with the reader.

Three cases of Madame Dupree's lotion are on their way to you by Rocket Freight and should be on your sales floor by Saturday.

For additional illustration, compare the differing results obtained from the following contrasting positive-negative versions of letter messages. Italics mark the negative words.

Negative	Positive
You *failed* to give us the fabric specifications of the chair you ordered.	So that you may have the one chair you want, will you please check your choice of fabric on the enclosed card?
Smoking is *not* permitted anywhere except in the lobby.	Smoking is permitted in the lobby only.
We *cannot* deliver until Friday.	We can deliver the goods on Friday.
Chock-O-Nuts don't have that *gummy, runny* coating that makes some candies *stick* together when it gets hot.	The rich chocolate coating of Chock-O-Nuts stays crispy good throughout the summer months.
You were *wrong* in your conclusion, for paragraph 3 of our agreement clearly states. . . .	You will agree after reading paragraph 3 of our agreement that. . . .
We *regret* that we *overlooked* your coverage on this equipment and apologize for the *trouble* and *concern* it must have caused you.	You were quite right in believing that you have coverage on the equipment. We appreciate your calling the matter to our attention.
We *regret* to inform you that we must *deny* your request for credit.	For the time being we can serve you only on a cash basis.
You should have known that the Peyton fryer *cannot* be submerged in water for it is clearly explained in the instructions.	The instructions explain why the Peyton fryer should be cleaned only with a cloth.
Your May 7 *complaint* about our Pronto minidryer is *not* supported by the evidence.	Review of the situation described in your May 7 letter explains what happened when you used the Pronto minidryer.

Overall tone of courtesy

If you can develop a courteous relationship with your reader, you will have the ideal atmosphere for success in most letter situations. Friendly people working together are likely to solve the problems they may have and to want to do business with each other. In developing a courteous tone in your letter, the techniques previously discussed will help. Certainly, writing in conversational tone, strategically emphasizing the reader's viewpoint, and carefully selecting positive wordings all generate courtesy. They all do much toward putting the reader in a favorable frame of mind. But your efforts should go beyond this.

Singling out your reader

Courteous treatment in a letter involves many things. For one, it involves singling out and writing directly to your reader. Letters that appear routine, that sound like form letters which could be used for any number of similar readers in a similar situation, simply do not affect us positively. They produce cold and impersonal effects as they filter through the mind. They leave us with the negative impression of routine treatment.

In individually tailoring your letter, you can refer to the reader by name within the letter. Our names are dear to us, and a strategic sprinkling of references such as "as you will agree, Ms. Smith," adds to the effectiveness of the letter. A basic technique is to make your letter fit the facts of the one case rather than to use broad statements that cover a variety of similar situations. For example, a writer of a letter granting a professor permission to quote company material in the professor's book could close with this catchall comment: "If we can be of any further assistance, please call on us." Or the writer could make a specific reference to a fact from the one case: "We wish you the best of success on the book." Without question, the latter approach does the better job.

Refraining from preaching

Unless you are careful, sometimes your words will take on a lecturing tone—much like that of the traditional sermon. Except in rare cases in which the reader looks up to the writer, such a preaching tone is offensive. We tend to be somewhat independent creatures. We want to be treated as equals. We do not want to be bossed. Any implication that our relationship with our reader is otherwise would be likely to stir up negative impressions in the reader's mind. With the reader antagonized, the chances for our letter's success are dimmed.

Preaching usually comes about unintentionally, frequently when the writer is attempting to explain or justify something. A writer of a sales letter may insult a reader with these preachy words:

You must take advantage of savings like this if you are to be successful. The pennies you save pile up, and in time you will have dollars.

Perhaps the point made is quite appropriate, but telling something one knows very well as if one does not know it is insulting. If the words "As you know" had prefaced this message, the offense would be lessened. Merely letting the reader know that you know she or he knows reduces the effect of the preachiness.

Likewise, flat obvious statements fall in the preachy category. Statements like "Rapid turnover means greater profits" are very obvious to the experienced retailer and would be likely to produce negative reactions. So would most statements including words such as "you need," "you want," "you must," for they tend to talk down. Another form of the preaching tone takes this obvious question-answer pattern: "Would you like to make a deal that would make you a 38 percent profit? Of course you would!" What intelligent, self-respecting reader would not be offended by such an obvious question?

Doing more than is expected

One sure way for you to gain goodwill is to do a little bit more than you have to for your reader. We are all aware of what the little extra acts can do in other areas of our personal relationships. Too many of us, however, do not use them in our letters. Perhaps in the mistaken belief that we are gaining conciseness, we include only the barest of essentials in our letters. The result is letters which give the effect of brusque, hurried treatments. Such treatments are inconsistent with our efforts to build goodwill and frequently with our primary objectives.

The writer of a letter refusing a request for use of some of the company's equipment, for example, needs only to say no to accomplish the primary objective. This curt answer, of course, would be blunt and totally devoid of courtesy. A goodwill-conscious writer would take the time to explain and justify the answer. She or he might even suggest alternative steps the reader might take. The wholesaler who uses a brief extra sentence to wish a retailer good luck on a coming promotion has productively used the time. So has the insurance agent who includes a few words of congratulations in a letter to a policyholder who has earned some distinction. Likewise, a salesperson uses good judgment by including in an acknowledgment letter some helpful suggestions about using the goods ordered. And the writer for a retail operation could justifiably include in letters to customers a few words about new merchandise received, new services provided, price reductions, and such.

To those who will say that these suggestions are inconsistent with the need for conciseness, we must answer that the information we speak of is needed to build goodwill. Conciseness concerns the number of words needed to say what you must say. Never does it involve leaving out information that is vital to any of your objectives. On the other hand, nothing we have said should be interpreted to mean that anything or any amount of extra information is justified. You must take care that you use no more nor less than you need to reach your goals.

Avoiding anger

Perhaps it is unnecessary to say that you should hold your temper in your letters. There may be times when anger is justified, and letting off steam may benefit us emotionally. But anger helps us to achieve a goal of a letter only when the goal is to make the reader angry. The effect of angry words is obvious. Angry words destroy goodwill. They make the reader angry. And with both writer and reader angry, little likelihood exists that the two can get together on whatever the letter is about.

To illustrate the effect, take the case of an insurance company correspondent who must inform a policyholder that the policyholder has made a mistake in interpreting the policy and is not covered on the case in question. Feeling that any fool should be able to read the policy, the correspondent used these angry words:

> If you had read Section IV of your policy, you would know that you are not covered on accidents which occur on water.

In a sense, we might say that this statement "tells it as it is." The information is true. But as it shows anger, it lacks tact. A more tactful writer would refer to the point of misunderstanding in a positive and impersonal manner:

> As a review of Section IV of your policy indicates, you are covered on accidents which occur on the grounds of your residence only.

Most statements made in anger do not concern information needed in the letter. They are comments which let the writer blow off steam. They may take many forms—sarcasm, insults, or exclamations. You can see from the following examples that it is better to omit them from your letters:

> No doubt you expect us to hold your hand.
> I cannot understand your negligence.
> This is the third time you have permitted your account to be delinquent.
> We will not tolerate this condition.
> Your careless attitude has caused us a loss in sales.
> We have had it!
> We have no intention of permitting this condition to continue.

Showing sincerity ✓

If your letters are to be effective, people must believe you. You must convince your readers that you mean what you say and that your efforts to be courteous and friendly are well intended. That is, your letters must have the quality of sincerity.

The best way of getting sincerity into your letters is to believe in the techniques you use. If you honestly want to be courteous, if you honestly feel that you-viewpoint treatments lead to harmonious relations, and if you honestly feel that tactful treatment spares your reader's sensitive feelings, you are likely to apply these techniques sincerely, and your sincerity will show in your writing.

Overdoing the goodwill technique. In writing sincerely you should keep in mind two major check areas. First, you will need to avoid overdoing any of your goodwill techniques. Perhaps through insincerity in what you are doing, or perhaps as a result of an overzealous effort, you can easily overdo the goodwill techniques. It is easy, for example, to make too many references to your reader by name in your efforts to write to the one reader. And as shown in the following example, the you-viewpoint effort can go beyond the bounds of reason:

> So that you may be able to buy Kantrell equipment at an extremely low price and sell at a tremendous profit, we now offer you the complete line at a 50 percent price reduction.

Likewise, this one, included in a form letter from the company president to a new charge customer, has a touch of unbelievability:

> I was delighted today to see your name listed among Morgan's new charge customers.

Or how about this one, taken from an adjustment letter of a large department store?

> We are extremely pleased to be able to help you and want you to know that your satisfaction means more than anything to us.

Avoiding exaggeration. As a second check area for sincerity, you will need to watch out for exaggerated statements. Most exaggerated statements are easy to see through; thus, they can give a mark of insincerity to your letter. Exaggerations, of course, are overstatements of facts. Although a form of exaggeration is conventional in sales writing, even here there are bounds of propriety. The following examples clearly overstep these bounds:

> Already thousands of new customers are beating paths to the doors of Martin dealers.
> Never has there been, nor will there ever be, a fan as smooth-running and whispering-quiet as the North Wind.
> Everywhere women meet, they are talking about the amazing whiteness Supreme gives their clothes.

Probably most exaggerated comments involve the use of superlatives. All of us use them, and only rarely do they fit the reality about which we communicate. Words like *greatest, most amazing, finest, healthiest,* and *strongest* are seldom appropriate and not often believed. Other strong words may have similar effects—for example, *extraordinary, stupendous, delicious, more than happy, sensational, terrific, revolutionary, colossal,* and *perfection.* Such words cause us to question; rarely do we really believe them.

Techniques of emphasis

The letters you write will contain a number of points of information, and all of them may be vital to the message. They do not all play equally important roles in achieving the letter's objectives. Some points, such as the statement of the letter's primary objective, are more important than others, such as the supporting information. Likewise, for goodwill effect the pleasanter information requires more emphasis than do the more negative aspects of your message.

As we know from our study of the communication process, the alert mind continuously receives information, but some of the information it records with greater emphasis than others. The process is the same when the mind receives the information in a letter. That is, the mind will give different degrees of stress to the points in a letter. Because it is vital to the success of a letter that the reader give each point its due stress, we need to use certain techniques to assist in determining the importance of points. Specifically, we need to use certain emphasis techniques. There are four major ones: position, space, structure, and mechanical devices.

Emphasis by position

The beginnings and ends of a unit of written communication carry more emphasis than do the center parts. This is true whether the unit is the letter, a paragraph of the letter, or a sentence within the paragraph. Perhaps the fresh mental energy of the reader as she or he begins reading each unit explains the beginning emphasis, and the recency of impression of the ending points may explain ending emphasis. Whatever the explanation, exhaustive research on advertising copy has borne out this conclusion.

Viewing the letter as a whole, the beginning sentence and the closing sentence are the major emphasis positions. Thus, you must be especially mindful of what you put in these places. The beginning and ending of the internal paragraphs are secondary emphasis positions. Your design of each paragraph should take this matter into account. To a lesser extent, the first and last words of each sentence carry more emphasis than the middle ones. So even in the design of your sentences, you can help determine the emphasis your reader will give the points in your message. In summary, your organization plan should place the points you want to stand out in these beginning and ending positions. Those points you do not want to emphasize you should bury within these emphasis positions.

Space and emphasis

How much you say about something determines how much emphasis you give it. The more you say about something, the more emphasis you give it; and the less you say about it, the less emphasis you give it. If your letter devotes a full paragraph to one point and a scant sentence to another, the former receives more emphasis. Thus, in giving the desired effect in your letter, you will need to take care to say just enough about each bit of information you have to present.

Sentence structure and emphasis

As we noted in Chapter 7, short simple sentences call attention to their content. Conversely, long involved ones do not. In applying this emphasis technique to your writing, you should consider carefully the possible sentence arrangements for your information. The more important information you should place in short simple sentences so that it will not have to compete with other information for the reader's attention. The less important information you should combine, taking care that the relationships are logical. In your combination sentences the more important material should be cast in independent clauses. The less important information should be relegated to subordinate structures.

Mechanical means of emphasis

Perhaps the most obvious of the emphasis techniques are those using various mechanical devices. By "mechanical devices," we mean any of those things we can do physically to give the printed word emphasis. Most common of these devices are the underscore, quotation marks, italics, and solid capitals. Lines, arrows, and diagrams drawn on the page can also call attention to certain parts. So can the use of color, special type, and drawings. For obvious reasons of propriety, these techniques are rarely used in letters, with the possible exception of sales letters.

Coherence in the letter

Your letters are made up of independent bits of information. But these bits of information do not communicate the whole message through your reader's mental filter. A part of the message is told in the relationships of the facts presented. Thus, if you are to communicate your message successfully, you must do more than communicate information. You must also make these relationships clear. Making these relationships clear is the task of giving coherence to your letter.

The one best thing you can do to give your letter coherence is to arrange the information in an order of logic—an order appropriate for the strategy of the one case. So important is this matter of letter organization that it is the primary topic of discussion in the three following chapters. Thus, we shall postpone discussion of this vital part of coherence. But logical organization usually is not enough. Various aids are needed to bridge across or tie together the information presented in the plan. These aids are known as transitional devices. We shall discuss four of the major ones: tie-in sentences, repetition of key words, use of pronouns, and link words and phrases.

Tie-in sentences

By so structuring your strategy that one idea sets up the next, you can skillfully relate the ideas. That is, you can design sentences to tie in two successive ideas. Notice in the following example how a job applicant tied together the first two sentences of the letter:

> As a result of increasing demand for precision instruments in the Billsburg boom area, won't you soon need another experienced and trained salesperson to call on your technical accounts there?
> With seven successful years of selling Morris instruments and a degree in civil engineering, I believe I have the qualifications to do this job.

Contrast the smooth connecting sentence above with the abrupt shift this second sentence would make:

> I am 32 years of age, married, and am interested in exploring the possibilities of employment with you.

For another case, compare the following contrasting examples of sentences following the first sentence of a letter refusing an adjustment on a trenching machine. As you can see, the strategy of the initial sentence is to set up the introduction of additional information which will clear the company of responsibility:

The Initial Sentence
> Your objective review of the facts concerning the operation of your Atkins model L trencher is evidence that you are one who wants to consider all the facts in a case.

Good Tie-in	*Abrupt Shift*
In this same spirit of friendly objectivity, we are confident that you will want to consider some additional information we have assembled.	We have found some additional information you will want to consider.

Repetition of key words

By repeating key words from one sentence to the next, you can make smooth connections of successive ideas. The following successive sentences illustrate this transitional technique. The sentences come from a letter refusing a request to present a lecture series for an advertising clinic.

> Because your advertising clinic is so well planned, I am confident that it can provide a really *valuable* service to practitioners in the community. To be truly *valuable*, I know you will agree, the program must be given the *time* a thorough preparation requires. As my *time* for the coming weeks is heavily committed, you will need to find someone who is in a better position to do justice to your program.

Use of pronouns

Because they refer to words previously used, pronouns make good transitions between ideas. Thus, you should use them from time to time in forming idea connections. Especially should you use the demonstrative pronouns *(this, that, these, those)* and their adjective forms, for these words can be used clearly to relate ideas. The following examples illustrate this technique:

> Ever since the introduction of our model V 10 years ago, consumers have suggested only one possible improvement—automatic controls. During all this time, *this* improvement has been the objective of Atkins research personnel. Now we proudly report that *these* efforts have been successful.

Transitional words

In your oral communication you make many of your thought connections with transitional words. You should also use these words to bridge the ideas in your letters. By transitional words we mean words that link or tie together the thoughts in the message. Included are words such as *in addition, besides, in spite of, in contrast, however, likewise, thus, therefore, for example,* and *also.* A more complete list appears in Chapter 14 where we review transition in report writing. That these words bridge across ideas is easy to see. Each gives a clue to the nature of the connection between what has been talked about and what comes up next. "In addition," for example, lets the reader know that what is to be discussed next is an enumeration which builds on what has been discussed. "However" clearly indicates a contrast in ideas. "Likewise" shows that what has been said and what is coming next are similar.

A word of caution

Nothing that has been said should imply that you should use these transitional devices automatically or arbitrarily. In fact, much of your subject matter will flow smoothly without them. When you use them, however, they should sound natural. They should blend in with the writing inconspicuously. They are devices all of us use. The trouble is that we do not always use them enough.

Perhaps the best advice concerning how to use transition is to review your writing, looking for abrupt shifts of subject matter. At these points you should consider using some form of transition. You should make the transition blend into your writing so that it does not appear to be stuck in.

International correspondence

As business becomes more international, increasingly we will need to write to readers whose first language is not English. Fortunately for us, the primary language of international business is English. Even so, the problem of communicating with people from other cultures in our language is great. Much of what has been said in the preceding pages, as well as much of what will be said in following chapters, is inappropriate for international communication.

Effects of culture

131

Chapter 8
Correspondence:
The Basic
Elements

One reason for the problem is that cultural differences exist. And even though the message may be communicated in a language both reader and writer understand, some miscommunication may result because of cultural differences. As we know from our knowledge of communication theory, our minds contain information acquired through our experiences, our values, our beliefs, our customs, and such. Through what has been stored in our minds we filter the incoming messages. Thus, even when we generally agree on word meanings, the meanings when filtered through our minds can differ.

This problem is explained by two Japanese authorities in business communication in these words: "For international business, Japanese businessmen write mostly in English. But their mother tongue, customs, and manners concerning communication in general, and cultural background are so different from those of English-speaking people that they cannot get away from their native ways even when they communicate in English, unless they have thoroughly mastered English and other Western habits of saying things."[4] The authors illustrate the point by noting that the Japanese tend to follow a traditional pattern of beginning with what appears to be empty greetings and thanks followed by lengthy reasons before a final and often ambiguous refusal. They use a yes answer to signify agreement, whether the original sentence is negative or positive. For example, take the question "You are not Chinese, are you?" A response of "yes" means "I am not." Also, the Japanese writers point out that their culture does not accept the hard-sell American style of sales writing. For this reason alone, much of what is acceptable in our business communication must be modified when the reader is Japanese.

Similarly, cultural differences cause problems with people from Western cultures. For example, as reported by Hilderbrandt, Germans are deeply bothered by the informality that is so common in our culture.[5] To illustrate, they tend to be offended when addressed by first names, even by close business associates. As the Germans tend to view such situations, "Informal first names are reserved for close intimates, family friends, and relatives."[6]

These differences between us and the Japanese and Germans are but a few of those that could be discussed. Suffice it to say that cultural differences are many. And the Japanese and Germans have been used merely as examples. We could make similar comparisons with every language-culture on earth. In fact, the differences are not only between people with different languages; they exist between people who use the same language. For example, even though England and the United States have a common language, the cultural differences between the two countries cause communication problems. This point is supported by an English writer in this comment about American

---

[4] Saburo Haneda and Hirosuke Shima, "Japanese Communication Behavior as Reflected in Letter Writing," *Journal of Business Communication,* vol. 19, Winter 1982, p. 19.

[5] Herbert W. Hilderbrandt, "Cultural Communication Problems of Foreign Business Personnel in the United States," *Journal of Business Communication,* vol. 13, Fall 1975, p. 16.

[6] *Ibid.,* p. 17.

business communication textbooks: "It is almost impossible to recommend them to students for reasons other than academic interest because the 'cultural gap' is so great that, for example, the language and tone advocated are frequently inappropriate for an English reader."[7]

Two basic suggestions

The obvious question to us as international business communicators is how to overcome such problems. There is no simple answer, although two suggestions appear to have merit. One is to become a student of culture—to learn the cultures of the people with whom we communicate. The task is not simple. And one is not likely to succeed completely in the effort.

The second suggestion also is not a solution; but it is an aid in communicating with international readers. It is a point stressed previously: "Write simply and clearly." Keep in mind the fact that most international business people learned English in school. They are acquainted mainly with primary dictionary meanings. Often they do not understand slang words or the shades of difference in the meanings which we give words. The one best way of communicating with them is to use matter-of-fact, straightforward, basic English.

An approach to letter problems

Your approach to planning each letter should also make good use of your knowledge of communication theory. Your efforts should be largely mental. You should analyze the communication process in the one situation, looking at the one message and its effect on the one reader. On the basis of your analysis, you should build the one letter which will do the best possible job in the one case.

Determination of primary objective

You should begin your mental effort by getting clearly in mind your primary objective—that is, your main reason for writing the letter. It may be that you need information, that you seek to collect money, that you wish to acknowledge an order, or the like. You may even have more than one objective, as when you wish both to give information and to ask for information in the same letter, or when you must both acknowledge an order and clear a vague order in the same message. Then, of course, there is always the secondary public relations objective which all good business letters have.

---

[7] Nicki Stanton, "Business Communication in England," in Herbert W. Hilderbrandt, editor, *International Business Communication,* Division of Research, Graduate School of Business Administration, University of Michigan, Ann Arbor, 1981, p. 16.

Selection of direct or indirect plan

133

Chapter 8
Correspondence:
The Basic
Elements

After determining what your letter must do, your next logical step is to visualize the communication process as your objectives are conveyed to your reader. You must look into your reader's mental filter to see what the reaction to your message is likely to be. If your analysis reveals that your message will be well received, you have no major obstacle to successful communication. You can move directly to your objective without slow explanation or other introductory remarks. This plan of presentation we shall call the "direct" plan, and it will be our choice for most of the letters we write in business.

At the other extreme, if your analysis reveals that your reader is not likely to receive your objective favorably, you have obstacles to overcome before your communication can be successful. That is, in some way you will need to prepare your reader to receive your message. Perhaps you will try to overcome the reader's resistance to your objective through persuasion. Or maybe you will seek to soften the effect of your message with explanation. In any event, you will have to precede talk about your objective with some form of conditioning matter. Such a plan we shall refer to as "indirect."

Choice in the middle ground

Obviously, some letter situations are neither bad news nor good news. They lie somewhere between these extremes. They could even vary in their effects on individual readers, for as we have seen, mental filters and their reactions to reality vary sharply. In this broad middle ground you will have to use your best judgment as to whether the direct or the indirect approach will be best for the individual case.

Your decision should be based primarily on how it appears that the reader's mind will receive the message. If the decision is a close one, however, you will have to base your choice on what you think will be the response in the one case. Frequently, the information in your message will be a routine business matter and will have neither very positive nor very negative effects on your reader. In such cases, you will be wise to use directness, for directness is the timesaving approach. If, however, it appears that a direct presentation of the information is startling to the reader or that the reader's filter would expect some kind of explanation or introductory comment, some manner of indirectness is advisable. More specific analyses of the approach choices are discussed in the chapters which follow.

The plans illustrated

To illustrate these two basic plans, we may use the case of a letter written by an oil company president to a customer, telling that the customer has won $50,000 in a contest sponsored by the company. Certainly, the news is good. There is no question about how it will be received. The writer of the letter should not dally one moment with explanation or other comment. He or she should move directly into the primary message with words like

"The enclosed $50,000 check is your first-prize money for our contest." Any introductory comment such as "We received your contest entry" or "It has been a great pleasure for us to conduct a contest" merely slows down the message and wastes the time of all concerned. Even a positive "It gives me great pleasure to be able to give you good news" is slow and time-wasting.

When the news is bad, as in the case of a correspondent who must refuse a claim for adjustment, a direct approach would be hard on goodwill. Such beginning words as "I must refuse your claim" certainly make a negative impression in the reader's mind. They are exactly opposite to what the reader had hoped to hear. If the writer hopes to convince the reader that the decision is a just one, these harsh words do not put the reader in a frame of mind to listen. In many negative-news letters, only by conditioning the reader's mind with justifying information can the writer move the reader to accept the basic objective.

Contrasting examples in two good-news letters. Perhaps the advantages of these approaches can be seen better by contrasting applications to good-news and bad-news situations. For a good-news situation, we shall use the case of a company which is writing a college professor telling her that the company is granting her request for certain production records for use in a research project. Even though the company asks that its name not be used in any publication, the news is basically good. Now let us see what the slow and indirect approach would do to the message.

Dear Professor White:
We have received your May 2 inquiry in which you ask for our January–March production records for use in your study. As this request has been referred to me for attention, we are pleased to report that we are very much impressed with the work you are doing. We want to help, so we are sending you all of the record sheets you asked for.

We regret to say, however, that we cannot permit you to use our name in your printed results or to identify the statistics as ours in any way. Our industry is a very competitive one, and we work hard to keep our production secret. We must insist that you comply with this restriction.

We are happy to assist you in this instance and regret again that we must ask you to guard our identity.

Sincerely yours,

The letter, of course, illustrates more than indirectness. It makes overuse of negatives which stir up antagonisms in the reader's mind. Its slow approach to the good news, however, is painfully obvious. Almost a full paragraph of introductory trivia precedes the favorable answer. The result is wasted words and wasted time. Compare this slow approach to the timesaving directness of the following version:

Dear Professor White:
Enclosed with our compliments is a copy of the production records you asked for in your May 2 letter. We hope you will find it useful in your project. As you will understand, much of the information concerns company secrets which our competitors should not know. So we must request that our identity be kept anonymous in any published use of the data.

The work you are doing will be valuable to all of us in the industry. We wish you the best of luck in your work and look forward to reading your results.

Sincerely yours,

There should be no question about it. This is the superior plan. In addition to using more positive language, it gets directly to the point. Thus, it wastes no words. Its directness and tact produce a goodwill effect.

Contrasting examples of bad-news letters. A contrasting pair of letters presents equally convincing proof of the value of the indirect approach in handling bad-news problems. The case concerns a department store correspondent who must write a charitable organization denying a request for a contribution. The following is the direct approach an unschooled letter writer might use:

Dear Ms. Smith:

We regret to inform you that we cannot grant your request for a donation to the Association's scholarship fund.

There are so many requests for contributions made of us each year that we have found it necessary to budget a definite amount each year for this purpose. Our budgeted funds for this year are exhausted, so we simply cannot consider additional requests. However, we shall be able to consider your request next year.

We deeply regret our inability to help you and trust that you understand our position.

Sincerely yours,

Part of the bad effect produced by this letter is traceable to the overuse of negative wording. But the direct opening statement of the refusal certainly does not put the reader in the right frame of mind to hear the explanation the writer makes. Her mind receives the bad news, and the resulting negative reaction serves as a barrier to all else that may follow. In fact, she may not even read beyond the first sentence.

The more deliberate indirect approach used in the following version certainly does a better job:

Dear Ms. Smith:

Your efforts to build the scholarship fund for the Association's needy children are most commendable. We wish you good success in your efforts for this worthy cause.

We here at Aaron's are always willing to assist worthy causes whenever we can. This is why each January we budget for the year the maximum amount we feel we are able to contribute to worthy causes. Then we distribute this among the various deserving groups as far as it will go. As our budgeted contributions for this year have been made, the best we can do is to place your organization on our list for consideration next year.

We wish you the best of luck in your efforts to help educate the deserving children of the Association members.

Sincerely yours,

The superiority of this letter is also determined in part by its use of more positive wording. In fact, it makes the refusal without so much as using a single negative word. But its major advantage lies in its indirect approach. Its friendly opening contact sets the explanation which follows. Then Ms. Smith hears the explanation before the refusal—while she is in a mood to listen. Thus, when she receives the refusal, she knows why it must be so. If it is possible to get her to understand the writer's position, this approach is likely to succeed.

The structure of the letter

With the general approach of your letter determined, your next step is to build the specific structure of your letter. This is largely a creative effort. It is an effort in which you construct your letter in your mind. You analyze the facts involved in your one case. You explore the strategy possibilities, keeping in mind your one reader and how his or her mental filter will react to the alternative strategy possibilities. In the end you should develop a specific plan—a strategy which will solve the problem at hand.

The general strategy plans discussed in the following chapters illustrate this mental effort in some detail. As you will see, these discussions are arranged by letter situations which are grouped in three broad categories. First are those situations which can best be handled by directness. Primarily, these are the good-news situations. Second come the indirect letter situations involving bad-news messages. And third are those letter situations requiring more persuasive efforts. Although the second two groups have much in common, they have sufficient differences to justify separate analysis.

Selection of the words

After you have built the plan of your letter in your mind, your final step is to select the words which will produce your message. It is at this stage that you use the writing principles previously described. Especially will you be concerned with those principles which will produce the goodwill tone, for building goodwill is a vital part of the plan you have created. This final step should produce for you the letters which will accomplish the objective which prompted you to begin the letter writing effort.

A concluding and forward look

From the preceding review you should have a general idea of how business letters should be written. But to this point you have reviewed only the general tools with which to work. Now your task is to apply them—to fit them to particular letter situations. As you will see, each letter situation is an individual case to be solved, requiring a particular strategy and application of the basic elements discussed.

Questions & Problems

1. If it were not for the need to maintain goodwill, business letters would be much easier to write. Discuss.

2. What is conversational style, and how do we acquire it?

3. "The you-viewpoint is dishonest. It's not sincere." Discuss.
4. Distinguish between positive and negative words. When would you use each?
5. Discuss the various ways we can achieve courtesy in a letter.
6. Explain how the goodwill techniques discussed in this chapter are supported by communication theory.
7. Is anger ever justified in a business letter? Discuss.
8. Can the goodwill technique be overdone? Explain.
9. Look through letter examples in the following three chapters and find three examples of good transition.
10. Explain and illustrate the primary emphasis techniques available to the business writer.
11. Write three pairs of contrasting sentences illustrating *(a)* positive and negative wording, and three pairs illustrating, *(b)* we- and you-viewpoint. (Avoid using examples similar to those in the text.)

9

Correspondence: Situations requiring directness

FORTUNATELY, you will be able to write most of your business letters in the direct order. This is good because it will save time for both you and your reader. It will save you time because it is a relatively simple letter arrangement. It will save your reader time because it presents the message concisely and quickly. Without question, this order has advantages. You will want to use it whenever your letter objective permits.

As we noted in the preceding chapter, the direct order clearly is advisable for good-news messages. Such messages find no resistance in the reader's mental filter; thus, there is no reason for delay. The plan is also advisable for most neutral messages—that is, messages that basically are neither good nor bad news. Usually such messages concern the routine exchanges of information businesses need. Businesses recognize such needs, and they participate in the exchanges willingly and routinely. Thus, such letters need little or no explanation or persuasion to get action. A simple and direct-to-the-point presentation is sufficient.

In covering the direct order of letter arrangement, we shall review the most common situations which normally require this treatment. Our coverage will not be complete, but it will include most of the types of direct letter problems you will encounter in business. In covering these situations, we shall point out suggested plans for treating them. You should consider these plans as flexible guides to problem solving and not as rigid patterns to follow. As we shall stress again and again, each problem must be thought out and solved on its own unique facts. Even so, a similarity exists within problem types; and you will find that these plans work with most similar problems.

The routine inquiry

Letters which seek information are among the most common written in business. Because the exchange of information is common, the people involved are likely to conclude that such requests are reasonable, and they probably will grant them. Thus, when you are involved in such a situation, your analysis of the effects your objective will have on the reader is likely to lead to the conclusion that a direct plan is in order. Exceptions, of course, should be made when your request is negative, or when it requires explanation or conditioning. As we shall see, you can handle such problems better with an indirect plan.

After you have made the general conclusion that your request can be handled better through a direct approach, your thoughts should shift to developing the specific plan. In your mind you should organize your letter from beginning to end. And as you did in reaching your decision to use the direct approach, you should base your organization of the letter on your analysis of your reader's reactions to your message. Your analysis generally will lead you to proceed as follows.

A question beginning

Because you have decided to use the direct approach, you will begin the routine inquiry with words that get right down to the main objective. Or, more specifically, since your objective is to ask for information, you will start out asking for information. Such directness is commendable, for it moves fast—just as most people in business want their routine to move. Also, it has the provocative form of a question. Because questions stand out from other sentences, they command extra attention in the mind. Thus, they are likely to communicate better than other sentence forms.

The nature of the question you use depends upon the nature of the problem involved, but two basic approaches are available to you. First, you could begin with a question that is a part or all of the letter's objective. If the objective involves just one question, it could be that question. If it involves a number of questions, it could be one of that number—preferably a major one. For example, in a problem in which the objective is to get answers to five questions about a company's product, the opening question could be one of the five: "Does Duro-Press withstand high temperatures and long exposure to sunrays?"

Second, should you feel that such a beginning sentence produces a startling effect, you may use a general question covering the more specific one—for example: "Will you give me, please, the answers to the following questions about your new Duro-Press products?" This general-question approach is not so direct and timesaving as the other, for all the specific questions still must be asked. But because it uses the question form of sentence, it has a mind-arresting effect. Also, it appears to be more logical to some people.

Probably the direct approach appears somewhat illogical to some because our minds have been conditioned to the indirect approach traditional writers use for such cases. The traditional inquiry begins with an explanation of the situation, and it follows the explanation with the questions to be asked. Obviously, the approach is slower than the direct one. Its effect in the mind is likely to be somewhat passive, and passive impressions frequently communicate weakly or not at all.

139

Chapter 9
Correspondence:
Situations
Requiring
Directness

Adequate explanation

Because your reader is likely to need information to assist in answering your questions, you may need to include some explanation. As you attempt to visualize how your question will be received in the mind, you should be aware of just how much or how little knowledge your reader already has and how much he or she needs to have about your situation in order to answer. If you misjudge this knowledge, your reader may not be able to answer, or may have some difficulty answering. An inquiry about a certain product, for example, might go to a person who knows all the answers to your questions. The answers which apply in your case, however, may be determined by the specific use you plan to give the product. Unless you explain this specific use, the person cannot tell you what you want to know.

Where and how you include the necessary explanation information depend on the nature of your letter. Usually, general explanatory material that fits the entire letter is best placed following the direct opening sentence. Here it helps to reduce any startling effect a direct opening question might have. Frequently, it fits logically into this spot, serving as a qualifying or justifying sentence for the entire letter. Sometimes, in letters which ask more than one question, you will need to include explanatory material with some of the questions. If this is the case, the explanation fits best with the questions to which it pertains. Such letters may take on an organization pattern of alternating questions and explanation.

Structured questions

If your inquiry involves just one question, you have achieved your primary objective with the initial sentence. After any necessary explanation, and after a few words of friendly closing comment, your letter is done. If you must ask a number of questions, however, you will need to give some thought to their organization.

Whether you ask one or many questions, you will need to make certain that each question stands out. You can make them stand out in a number of different ways. First, you can make certain that each question is in a sentence to itself. Combining two or more questions in a single sentence de-emphasizes each and invites the reader's mind to overlook some.

Second, you can structure your questions in separate paragraphs whenever this practice is logical. It is logical only when you have enough explanation and other comment about each question to justify a paragraph.

Third, you can number your questions, either in words (first, second, etc.) or with arabic numerals (1, 2, 3, etc.). Either form of number calls special attention to the words which follow. Also, numbers serve as a convenient check and reference guide to answering the inquiry.

Fourth, you can structure your questions in question form. True questions stand out. Sentences that merely hint at a need for information are not likely to get much attention. The "It would be nice if you would tell me . . ." or "I should like to know . . ." forms really are not questions. They do not ask—they merely suggest. Questions that stand out are those written in question form—those using question words such as "Will you please tell me . . . ?" "How much would one be able to save . . . ?" "How many contract problems have you had . . . ?" and the like.

141

Chapter 9
Correspondence:
Situations
Requiring
Directness

Goodwill in the ending

Because it is the natural thing for friendly people to do, you should end routine inquiry letters with some appropriate, friendly comment. This is how you would end a face-to-face communication with the reader, and there is no reason to do otherwise in writing. To just end your letter after asking the questions would be like turning your back on someone after a conversation without saying goodbye. Such an abrupt ending could register negative meanings in your reader's mind and could defeat your goodwill efforts.

Just what you should say in the close to make a goodwill impression is a matter to be determined by the facts of the case. Your letter will receive a more positive reaction in your reader's mind if you use words selected specifically for the one case. The general "A prompt reply will be appreciated" or "Thank you in advance for your answer" varieties do little to create a sense of personal attention in the reader's mind. A much more positive reaction results from something like "If you will get this refrigeration data to me by Friday, I shall be most greateful."

Routine inquiries illustrated

The following three letters illustrate the two general plans for making a routine inquiry. The first letter follows the plan of beginning with one of the specific questions. The second two begin with a general request and explanation which set up the specific questions.

The first letter concerns a routine request for information by a real estate broker. Obviously, the reader will welcome the letter, for it could lead to a profitable sale. Thus, the writer can afford to get right down to the objective, which is to get the answers to specific questions.

The letter begins directly by asking for information. As the reader will welcome the inquiry, no need exists for delaying explanation. Because such a direct opening may have a startling effect, explanatory information which justifies the inquiry follows. Next come the remaining questions, with explanations worked in wherever they help the reader in answering. The letter closes with a courteous request for quick handling. In addition, the close suggests the good news of possible quick action on the property.

Dear Mr. Piper:

Will you please tell me whether the 120-acre tract you advertised in the July 1 *Wall Street Journal* has deep frontage on the river? We are seeking such a site for a new plant, and it appears that your property could meet our needs.

Is the land reasonably level and well drained? A written description of the tract terrain should answer this question. In your description, please include minimum and maximum elevations.

Can the property be reached by an existing all-weather road? If the answer is yes, what is the composition of this road? What is its condition?

If your answers indicate that the site meets our needs, we shall want to inspect the property. As we must move fast on the building project, may I have your answer soon?

Sincerely,

The second illustration is a request for information about hotel accommodations for a meeting. This letter begins with a general question—a sort of topic sentence for the entire letter. Although not so direct as the first letter, this beginning appears more logical in the minds of many people. Thus it may produce better results.

As you will note, following the initial general question and, in fact, worked in with it is some of the explanatory information the reader needs in answering the letter. Next comes the specific question, with additional explanation material where needed. An individually tailored and friendly compliment marks the letter's close.

Dear Ms. Briggs:

Will you please help the National Management Forum to decide whether it can meet at the Lakefront? The Forum has selected your city for its 1986 meeting, which will be held August 16, 17, and 18. In addition to the Lakefront, we of the convention committee are considering the De Lane and the White House. In making our decision, we shall need the information requested in the following questions.

Can you accommodate a group such as ours on these dates? Probably about 600 delegates will attend, and they will need about 400 rooms.

What are your convention rates? We need assurance of having available a minimum of 450 rooms, and we would be willing to guarantee 400. Would you be willing to reserve for us the rooms we shall require?

What are your charges for conference rooms? We shall need eight for each of the three days, and each should have a minimum capacity of 60. On the 18th, for the one-half-hour business meeting, we shall need a large assembly room with a capacity of 500. Can you meet these requirements?

Also, will you please send me your menu selections and prices for group dinners? On the 17th we plan our presidential dinner. About 500 can be expected for this event.

As convention plans must be announced in the next issue of our bulletin, may we have your response right away? We look forward to the possibility of being with you in 1986.

Sincerely,

The third example of a routine inquiry is a letter from a company training director to the director of a university management-training program. The training director has received sales literature on the program, but some specific questions remain unanswered.

As did the preceding example, this letter begins with a broad question which sets up the specific questions to be asked. Next comes a brief reference to the sales literature which the writer already has. This information tells the reader what the writer knows about the program and should be helpful to him or her in responding. For emphasis and ease in answering, the questions are numbered. Note how explanatory information is worked into the questions where needed. The close is friendly, and its favorable forward look is good news for the reader.

143

Chapter 9
Correspondence:
Situations
Requiring
Directness

Dear Ms. Hrozek:

Will you please send me the additional information we need in determining whether to send some of our executives to your Western Management Institute? We have your illustrated brochure and the schedule you mailed August 17. Specifically, we need the answers to these questions:

1. Do you give quantity discounts? We could send about six executives each session.
2. Is the program geared for people with diverse backgrounds? We have engineers, accountants, scientists, and business administrators. Most have college degrees. Some do not.
3. Can college credit be given for the course? Some of our executives are working on degrees and want credit.
4. Please give me names and addresses of training directors of companies that have sent executives to the program.

We shall appreciate your answering promptly. And we look forward to the possibility of sending our executives to you in the years ahead.

Sincerely,

Inquiries about people

Letters asking for information about job applicants fall in the routine inquiry group, but they involve a special problem. Because they are about people, these letters involve certain elements of privileged communication not present in other letters. For obvious reasons of courtesy, we human beings just do not exchange personal information about ourselves indiscriminately. We have moral as well as legal rights which must be protected. Inquiries about us must protect these rights.

Privileged communication

Probably the best guide for you to follow in inquiring and reporting about people is to pursue truth and to act in good faith. In pursuing truth, you distinguish carefully between fact and opinion. For the most part, you should seek and give facts. Opinion, when you must use it, should be clearly labeled as opinion and should be supported by fact. In acting in good faith, you should seek and give only that information which is needed for business purposes. You should give and receive such information only when the person concerned has authorized it. And you should hold all such information in confidence. Because these points are so vital to fair treatment in inquiries about people, you will want to cover them in your letters.

Question content

Letters inquiring about job applicants vary even more in their content. What you will need to know in any given case depends on the job to be done. For sales jobs, for example, you would need to know about personality—how the applicants meet and get along with people, how they talk, how aggressive they are, and the like. Such information might be only incidental in considering people for work as accountants. Thus, the coverage of your content for such letters should fit the one case at hand.

Aside from the need to cover the privileged aspects of communication and the basic content differences, letters about people are much like those previously described and illustrated. As the following examples show, they begin directly, they bring in explanation whenever necessary, and they close in friendly fashion.

Examples of personnel inquiries

The writer of the following letter did an excellent job of analyzing the work her applicant was seeking to do. Then she asked the specific questions which would help her to determine whether this one applicant could do the job. The letter begins directly, with a topic sentence form of question which serves to justify the inquiry as well as to give some needed introductory information. Next, it presents additional introductory information which serves also to cover the privileged aspects of the case. Then in following paragraphs the mixed pattern of question and exposition covers and explains the information needed. The questions are all stated in clear question form. Thus, they stand out and are easy to answer. The courteous and individually tailored close brings in another of the privileged aspects of communication.

Dear Ms. Borders:

Will you help me to evaluate Mr. Rowe W. Hart for the position of office manager? In authorizing this inquiry, Mr. Hart indicated that he worked for you from 197x to 198x. Your candid answers to the following questions will help me to determine whether Mr. Hart is the right person for this job.

Does Mr. Hart have the leadership ability, including human-relations skills, to run an office of eleven?

Can Mr. Hart manage a rapidly expanding office system? Ours is a growing company. The person who manages our office will need not only to know good office procedures but also how to adapt them to changing conditions.

Does Mr. Hart have the stamina and drive to cope with a high-volume, pressure-filled operation?

Is Mr. Hart morally reliable? Our office manager is responsible for much of our company equipment as well as some company funds. We could not consider one who is to the slightest degree a questionable risk.

We shall, of course, hold your answers in strict confidence. And we shall appreciate whatever help you are able to give Mr. Hart and us.

Sincerely,

The next example concerns a freight-line executive who is looking for a manager for one of the company's branches. The top applicant is a shipping clerk for a furniture company. With the applicant's permission, the freight-line executive has written to the applicant's employer.

The letter begins with an interest-gaining question which tells the reader what is wanted. Because such a question about a current employee could be startling, an explanation of the situation follows. Included is the vital note that the inquiry is authorized. The second paragraph clearly explains

145

Chapter 9
Correspondence:
Situations
Requiring
Directness

the kind of person needed. A single question which seeks to learn whether the applicant is this kind of person follows logically. The third paragraph covers the basic information which is needed on most prospective workers. The goodwill close expresses appreciation and assures confidential treatment.

Dear Mr. Dodgson:

Will you do George Barton and me the favor of an evaluative report on him? He is an assistant shipping clerk with you who wants to manage a branch office for us. He has authorized this inquiry.

Does he know packing and hauling techniques thoroughly?

Does he have the administrative skills to run an office of one secretary and a work force of six?

Has he demonstrated the personal qualities required to meet customers and generally build goodwill with the community?

Is there a reason to question his honesty and integrity. Our managers are solely responsible for their branch's assets—equipment as well as all receipts.

As a final question, do you know anything that might make him unfit for this work?

I shall be grateful for your answers. Of course, whatever you report will be held in close confidence.

Sincerely,

The following illustration about a prospective bookkeeping supervisor gets off to a fast start. It opens with a general request. Then it justifies the request with appropriate explanation. Next it sets up the specific questions with an introductory statement. The questions follow with explanations where needed. Note how the questions fit the one job and the one company's needs. The close is both friendly and specially adapted to the one case.

Dear Ms. Gomez:

Will you please give me the benefit of your experience with Ms. Cleo Carpenter, who reports that she worked for you from 1974 to 1983? Ms. Carpenter has authorized this inquiry in applying for a supervisory position in our bookkeeping department. I need the answers to these specific questions:

1. Does Ms. Carpenter have administrative ability? In this supervisory position she would direct the work of four people.
2. Is she honest and reliable? This information is important, for the job involves handling money.
3. Does she know bookkeeping? Although the work she would supervise is routine, she should have a basic knowledge of accounting.
4. How does she get along with people? Our close-knit organization has no place for people with personality problems.

I shall be grateful for these answers and for any other information you feel I should have. I assure you that this information will be held in strict confidence.

Sincerely,

Favorable responses

When you answer an inquiry and can comply with your reader's wishes, you are telling what your reader wants to know. The news is good, and you need not delay it. In such cases you would be wise to choose the direct pattern.

Situation identification

In analyzing reader response to a favorable reply, you should note first that the situation needs to be identified. You are answering a letter from the reader. It may be that she or he has written many letters recently, as is the case with many business executives. The reader's mind may be so crammed with details that the specific inquiry you are answering may not immediately be clear. So for reasons of quick, clear communication, you should identify the letter you are answering somewhere early in your letter.

One good way of identifying the letter is through use of a subject line—a mechanical device usually appearing near the salutation of the letter (see Appendix B). You may place it in any of a number of specific places—on a line between the salutation and the first sentence of the letter, to the right and on the same line as the salutation, between the salutation and the inside address, or in the upper right corner of the letter layout. Usually, the subject line contains some identifying term such as "Subject," "About," or "Reference," followed by appropriate descriptive words. The words take no one correct form, but as a minimum should include the nature of the letter and a by-date reference to the inquiry being answered. Applied to some typical response situations, something like these examples might be used:

> *Subject:* Reply to your January 13 inquiry about the Little Mole trencher
> About your April 27 inquiry concerning Ms. Lois Ray

You may also place the necessary identification material in the body of the letter. Because your reader should know this information early if it is to help in the communication of the basic message, it should come in the first sentence or two. Preferably, you should cover it incidentally, for it does not deserve the importance of a separate sentence. Thus, you should place it as an incidental comment somewhere in the opening. Words like "As requested in your July 7 inquiry" typify this technique.

Good-news beginnings

Because nothing you have to say will make a better impression on your reader, you should begin with the favorable response. If your letter is an answer to a single question asked, your opening words should give this one answer. For example, a letter granting the reader's request to use certain equipment might begin like this: "Yes, you may use our duplicating equipment on the weekend of the 13th."

Your response to an inquiry involving a number of questions can use either of two approaches. One is to begin with an answer to one of the questions asked—preferably the most important one. Certainly, the approach should create a favorable effect in your reader's mind. It tells something the reader wants to know. These specific answers to major questions illustrate this type of opening statement:

147

Chapter 9
Correspondence:
Situations
Requiring
Directness

> We have been using the Atlas lifts in our Wellsburg warehouse since early January with good results.
> The Craft-O-Matic can be adapted to handle the small jobs you mentioned in your April 16 inquiry.

Your second possibility is to begin with a general statement heralding a favorable answer. This approach is not so direct as the first, for it really does not answer the question asked. It does, however, tell that the reader will get what she or he wants. And it has the effect of direct treatment without the risk of startling the reader. These examples illustrate the technique:

> You certainly may have the answers to the questions you ask in your May 3 letter.
> As you requested in your December 1 inquiry, here are the answers to your questions about Tiger-Craft products.

Either of these beginnings is a great improvement over the indirect approach used by altogether too many business people. The almost conventional "Your April 1 letter has been received" or "Thank you for your April 3 inquiry" beginnings certainly do not tell what the reader wants to hear. They delay the main message of the letter. And as in the case of the first example, sometimes they are obvious.

Construction of answers

If your problem concerns just one question, you have little to do after handling it in the opening. You answer it as completely as the situation requires, and you bring in whatever explanation or other information you need to achieve your objective. Then you are ready to close the letter.

If, on the other hand, your problem concerns two or more questions to be answered, you proceed to answer them. Thus, the body of your letter becomes a series of answers—answers to the specific questions asked. As in all clear writing, you should work to place your answers in some logical order, perhaps in the order your reader used in the letter to you. You may even wish to number your answers, especially if your reader numbered the questions. Or you may elect to arrange your answers by paragraphs, so that each will stand out clearly in your reader's mind.

Handling negatives

When your response concerns some bad news along with the good news, you will need to handle the bad news with care. Bad news stands out. Unless you are careful, it is likely to receive more emphasis than it deserves. So, in order to give the bad news its appropriate emphasis, usually you will need to subordinate it. Conversely, you will need to emphasize the good-news part.

In giving proper emphasis to your information, you will of course make full use of the techniques of emphasis. Especially will you use position. That is, you will place good news in positions of high emphasis—at the beginnings and endings of the paragraphs as well as of the letter. The bad news you will place in secondary positions. In addition, you will want to consider the effects of space emphasis by covering the negative news quickly. Also, you will take care in selecting your words and arranging your sentences. That is, you will use wisely the pleasant, happy words that create good feeling. In general, your goal should be to present all of your information so that your reader gets the effect you intend.

Consideration of "extras"

For the optimum in goodwill effect you should consider including with your answers some of the extra comments, suggestions, and so forth, which serve to build goodwill. These are the things you say and do which are not really required of you. Included would be an additional comment or question which shows an interest in the reader's problem, some extra information which may prove to be valuable, or a suggestion for use of the information supplied. In fact, it could be anything which does more than skim the surface with hurried, routine answers. Such "extras" frequently make the difference between success and failure in the goodwill effort.

Illustrations of how such "extras" can enhance the goodwill effects of a letter are as broad as the imagination. A business executive answering a college professor's request for information on company operations could supplement the specific information requested with suggestions of other sources of information on the subject. An executive answering questions on his or her experiences with a computer could bring in helpful data not covered in the inquiry. Or a technical writer could take time to supplement some highly technical answers with helpful explanations. Obviously, such extras as these are of genuine service to the reader. Their goodwill effects are equally obvious.

Cordiality in the close

As in most routine business letter situations, you should end the letter with friendly, cordial words which make clear your willing attitude. As much as possible, your words should be adapted to the one case. For example, a writer ending a letter answering questions about the company's experience with duplicating equipment might close with these words:

> If I can help you further in deciding whether to purchase the Multi-Cater, please write me again.

Or an executive writing to a graduate student giving answers to certain questions for a thesis project could use this paragraph:

> If I can give you any more of the information you need for your study of executive behavior, please write me. I wish you the best of luck on the project.

Favorable replies illustrated

149

Chapter 9
Correspondence:
Situations
Requiring
Directness

The following three letter examples show the value of directness in routine responses. The first is a response to a professor's request for production records to be used in some research the professor is doing. The company is giving the professor all that was requested, although it must place a minor restriction on use of the data.

The letter achieves its goal right away by giving its main message in the first sentence. It follows this direct opening with a diplomatic handling of the negative restriction. Notice that this part is handled without the use of a single negative word. The final paragraph is goodwill talk especially adapted to the one case.

Dear Professor Garland:

Enclosed with our compliments is a copy of the production records you asked for in your May 2 letter. We hope you will find it useful in your project. As you will understand, much of the information concerns company secrets which our competitors should not know. So we request that we not be mentioned in any published use of the data.

The work you are doing will be valuable to all of us in the industry. We wish you the best of luck in your work and look forward to reading your results.

Sincerely,

The second letter uses a subject line to identify the inquiry being answered. Thus it frees the text from the need to cover this detail. The letter begins directly, with the most favorable answer. Then it presents the other answers, giving each the emphasis and positive language it deserves. It subordinates the one negative answer by position, volume of treatment, and structure. More pleasant information follows the negative answer. The close is goodwill talk, with some subtle selling strategy thrown in. "We know that you'll enjoy the long-lasting beauty of this mildew-proof paint" points positively to purchase and successful use of the product.

Dear Ms. Motley:

Subject: Your April 3 inquiry about Chem-Treat

Yes, Chem-Treat paint will prevent mildew or we will give you back your money. We know it works, for we have tested it under all common conditions. In every case, it proved to be successful.

If you will carefully follow the directions on each can, Chem-Treat paint is guaranteed safe. As the directions state, you should use Chem-Treat only in a well ventilated room—never in a closed, unvented area.

One gallon of Chem-Treat usually is enough for one-coat coverage of 500 square feet of previously painted surface. For the best results on new surfaces, you will want to apply two coats. For such surfaces you should figure about 200 square feet per gallon for a good heavy coating that will give you five years or more of beautiful protection.

We sincerely appreciate your interest in Chem-Treat, Ms. Motley. We know that you'll enjoy the long-lasting beauty of this mildew-proof paint.

Sincerely,

The third letter is an answer to an inquiry about an executive's experiences with a word processing center. The response letter follows the systematic plan of the inquiry by numbering the answers just as they were numbered in the inquiry. Such a plan calls for an opening which introduces the list and which tells that the reader is receiving what he or she requested. Although this opening is not truly direct (it does not start answering), it is favorable. Also, it sets up an orderly and efficient presentation of the information. The letter appropriately ends with goodwill words. Notice the little extra in the close—the invitation to visit.

> Dear Mr. Casey:
>
> Following is the information about our word processing center which you requested in your August 3 letter. For your convenience, I have numbered my responses to correspond with the sequence you used.
>
> 1. Our executives have mixed feelings about the effectiveness of the center. At the beginning, majority opinion was negative, but it appears now that most of the antagonism has subsided.
> 2. The center definitely has saved us money. After normal attrition has eliminated unnecessary workers, we estimate that the monthly saving will be about $5,400.
> 3. The changeover did create a morale problem among the secretaries, even after we had assured them that we would reduce employment only by attrition.
> 4. We created our center from our own secretarial staff. We lost no one during the changeover period.
> 5. We are quite willing to share our center operating procedures with you. I am enclosing a copy of our procedures directive, which describes center operations in detail.
>
> If after reviewing this information you have other questions, please write me again. And if you feel that an inspection of our operation would help, you are welcome to visit us. I wish you the best of luck in implementing your center.
>
> Sincerely,

Routine acknowledgments

Another good-news letter is the routine acknowledgment. An acknowledgment letter is one sent to those who place an order to let them know the status of that order. An acknowledgment is routine when the order can be handled without problem—that is, when the goods can be delivered. Many routine acknowledgments are routine to the point of being form letters. In fact, some companies use printed, standard notes, sometimes with checkoff or write-in blanks to be filled in with information on the specific order. Some individually written letters are used, however, especially with new accounts and with large orders.

When properly written, individually written acknowledgment letters can do much more than acknowledge orders, although this task remains their primary goal. These letters can serve as good-will building devices. By taking on a warm, personal, human tone, they can reach out and give readers a hearty handshake. They can make readers feel good about doing business with a company that cares about them, and they can make readers continue to want to do business with the company.

Acknowledgment in the beginning

As with other good-news letters, you should begin a routine acknowledgment directly—getting to the point of your objective right away. Because this letter has a more than usual goodwill need, you will want to work especially hard to make the most positive impression with your opening words. You could, for example, report the news directly with words such as these:

> Your July 7 order for assorted Mandy Candies will be shipped Monday by Green Arrow Motor Freight.

This example does not produce the positive effect, however, of words which play up the receiving rather than the sending of the goods:

> Your assorted Mandy Candies which you ordered July 7 should be on your sales floor by Wednesday. They will leave our warehouse Monday by Green Arrow Motor Freight.

Goodwill talk and resale

The typical acknowledgment letter concentrates on the goodwill function and sometimes even does some selling and reselling. It may tell of new products or new services, and it may tell about the goods being ordered. Your goodwill talk could be built from any of these topics which appear to be appropriate in the individual case.

Somewhere in the letter, as a matter of courtesy, you will need to express your appreciation for the order. After all, you are making a sale, and some form of thank-you is appropriate. If you are acknowledging a first order, your new customer deserves a warm welcome.

A friendly, forward look

Your ending of an acknowledgment letter appropriately is a friendly, forward look. What you use here as subject matter depends on what you used in your goodwill and selling efforts earlier in the letter. If you elected to stress resale of the merchandise ordered, your close might well comment about enjoyable and profitable use of the product. If one of your objectives in the letter happens to be sales promotion, you could urge your reader to give an additional order; or if you choose a goodwill, customer-welcome theme, you could look ahead to additional opportunities to serve. In any event, you would do well to make your close tie in with the material which preceded it. And you would do well to make it fit the one case.

Routine acknowledgments illustrated

The following two letters illustrate individually written acknowledgment letters. The first is almost in the form-letter category. It adapts to the specific situation by bringing in the facts of this one order. But obviously, its goals are limited to covering acknowledgment details and saying thank you for the order.

> Dear Ms. Hammond:
>
> You should have your Art-Grain paneling early next week, for it was shipped from our Kalamazoo warehouse this morning. Northern States Transport is the carrier. As you requested, you will be billed for the $368.50 cost on the 1st with the usual 2/10, n/30 terms.

151

Chapter 9
Correspondence:
Situations
Requiring
Directness

We sincerely appreciate your continued business. We look forward to serving you again with quality Art-Grain products.

Sincerely,

In addition to acknowledging the order and expressing gratefulness, the writer of the second letter extends a warm welcome to a new customer, and it includes some resale talk about the product. The writer's apparent objective is to build a friendly relationship with this new customer and to give the information which may help in selling the products concerned. Letters such as this take time. Thus, they are not justified in all acknowledgment situations. Selectively used, however, they can be powerful tools in building profitable accounts.

Dear Mr. Gilmer:

Subject: Shipment of goods on your order No. 3172B

Your selection of Wonder Lures should reach you by Wednesday, for they were sent by Southern Freight this morning. As you instructed, we are sending them c.o.d. Total payment will amount to $42.44, which includes our state sales tax.

As this is your first order from us, I welcome you to the Sports Distributors, Inc., circle of fine dealers. Our representative, Mr. Carl Forman, has told us of the growth your new company has had in the area. We shall be happy to do whatever we can to help you further your success.

Probably we can help you most by continuing to supply you with the best in sports equipment. We work hard to make each Wonder Lure to perfection, and I think we have succeeded. Under Uncle Billy Wonder's careful supervision, each lure is handcrafted, as have been all Wonder Lures for the past 53 years. As you may know, Uncle Billy limits our line to only six lures—every one tested by him personally and guaranteed to be the best. It has to be a mighty good lure to replace one of the six. There is no question about it—Wonder Lures will complement the good reputation you are building.

We genuinely appreciate your order, Mr. Gilmer. And we look forward to a mutually rewarding relationship in the years ahead.

Sincerely,

Personnel evaluation reports

Replies to inquiries about job applicants usually are received favorably. You can expect a favorable reaction regardless of how positive or negative the information in the letter may be. The reader is getting what was asked for. Since the reader's reaction will be positive, you should begin these reports in the direct order.

Directness in the opening

As you would do with the favorable-reply letter, you begin an evaluation report by telling the reader something she or he wants to hear. Preferably, you should answer one of the more significant questions asked you. It should be one which deserves this position of emphasis—one which serves as introductory material for the remainder of the report. For example, a report might begin with a statement of how long the person has worked for you. Such a statement serves to qualify all else which follows. Or for another example, if you are writing a report which contains nine favorable points and one unfavorable one, you would be overemphasizing the negative one by beginning with it. You would do better to select one of the nine—one which is consistent with the overall evaluation of your subject.

Should a direct move to one of the answers appear to produce a startling effect, you may use the less direct approach, which begins by telling the reader that you are complying with the request. Such a beginning might use these words:

> As you requested in your May 8 letter, following is my evaluation of Mr. Garton L. Ford.

Like similar beginnings cited in preceding direct letters, this one tends to explain while retaining the effects of directness.

Employee evaluation reports are written in response to inquiries; so they have some need for early identification to tie in quickly with the correspondence being answered. You may wish to use the subject line for this purpose. Or you may wish to acknowledge the preceding letter incidentally, as is done in the illustration sentence above. Also, since they concern confidential information, these reports require the same privileged communication treatment given to the inquiry letters they answer. Thus, somewhere in the letter you will need to consider labeling the information as confidential; and you will want to make it clear by word or implication that the report has been authorized, that it was requested, and that the information is to be used for business purposes only.

Systematic presentation of facts

Most of the remainder of your report should concern the information the reader wants. If your reader's inquiry includes specific questions, your response should include the answers to these questions. On the other hand, if the inquiry is a general one, you must decide what the reader needs. Your content decision should be guided by your analysis of the work for which the applicant is being considered. You should select for presentation those points which are important in doing the work.

You should present your information in as orderly and systematic a manner as you can devise. If you are only answering a reader's questions, you would do well to organize your information around the questions. If the inquiry is a general one, leaving the content up to you, you will need to find some logical order of organization. Especially should you seek to organize so that you eliminate overlap and repetition. In general, you should work to keep related information together, and you should find a sequence which will permit the information to flow naturally and smoothly.

The problem of fair reporting

As a fair-minded writer, you will want to be careful that your employee evaluation reports convey a correct picture. To present a job applicant in too positive a light would be unfair to your reader, and to present the applicant too negatively would be unfair to the applicant. Your task will be to find

153

Chapter 9
Correspondence:
Situations
Requiring
Directness

just the right picture and to try hard to convey this picture with your words.

Conveying a true picture, as we have noted in our study of words, is no simple undertaking. Words have imprecise and inconsistent meanings in our minds. But words do not present the only difficulties in our efforts to make a truthful report. Perhaps even more important is the material you select for presentation and the emphasis you give this information.

In selecting the information for presentation, you should make a careful distinction between fact and opinion. For the most part, your report should contain fact. But sometimes opinions are sought. If you present an opinion, you should clearly label it as opinion; and you should support it with fact.

Even if every item in your report is verifiable fact, the report could be unfair. The reason is that negative points tend to stand out. They overshadow the positive ones. For example, you could write all day about the merits of a certain person; but if you ended with the comment that this person was arrested for theft, this one negative point would be likely to stand out above everything else. Perhaps in some minds it would erase all else.

The fact that negatives stand out means that in your personnel evaluation letters you will need to be very careful in handling negative points. You will want to give them only the emphasis they deserve—just enough to convey the true picture in your one case. Frequently, this need for fair treatment requires that you subordinate the negative points of your report. Not to do so would be to give these points more emphasis than they deserve.

To illustrate, take a report on a person who, in spite of a personality problem, has a good record. If you place this one negative point in a position of emphasis or if you write too much about it, you make it stand out. So if you are to give this information the emphasis it deserves, you must subordinate it.

Nothing that has been said should be interpreted to mean that you should hide the shortcomings of the subject of your report or that you should communicate any form of wrong information. Quite the contrary is intended. If your subject is a scoundrel, your words should show that he or she is a scoundrel. If your subject is a model human being, your words should reflect this status. Purely and simply, your task is to communicate a true picture, whatever that picture may be. You can communicate a true picture only by giving every fact you report the emphasis it deserves.

Natural friendliness in the close

As you should do in all friendly business letters, you should close employee evaluation reports with some appropriate goodwill comment. A sentence or two usually will do the job. As in other similar situations, you should strive to make it fit the one case. Above all, you should avoid the "rubber stamps" that so often find their way into this type of letter.

Case examples

Illustrating good technique in a personnel evaluation report is the following letter. The writer of this letter has a well-qualified person to write about—

a new holder of a doctoral degree who is looking for work as a university instructor. Although the man is well qualified, he has a number of minor weaknesses which in all honesty must be covered. He is a good but not brilliant scholar; he has a slight speech problem; and he sometimes irritates others with his extreme preoccupation with his work. The writer covers all three of these negative points in subordinate fashion, giving each the emphasis he feels it deserves. The result is a fair appraisal of a generally good applicant.

Especially commendable in the letter is the writer's logical organization of the subject matter. Notice how the direct opening gives a summary evaluation of the applicant. And notice how this evaluation sets up the three areas of discussion which form the organization plan of the letter. The plan is a most orderly one.

Dear Dean Koogan:

Dr. Harlan A. McQueen, about whom you inquired in your January 31 letter, is a competent scholar, a diligent worker, and a capable teacher in the classroom.

His scholarship is evidenced by his 3.7 grade-point record (4.0 basis) with us as well as his good undergraduate record at Southern Illinois University. In the two classes he had with me, he did good work, making A's in each. Although I did not find him to be a brilliant student of management, he did demonstrate a marked degree of scholarly inquisitiveness. With this inquisitiveness I fully expect him to make some normal contribution to his field of research. At times I have felt that he tends to get lost in the minutiae of detail and to overlook the obvious.

Perhaps Dr. McQueen's outstanding quality is his extreme dedication to work. Of all the graduate students I have known, I have observed none who works more diligently than he. What he lacks in native intelligence, he overcomes with tireless dedication. So dedicated and interested in his work is he that he sometimes forgets that all those around him do not share his enthusiasm for his topic of interest.

During the three years I have known him, he served as a graduate assistant under my direction. He does a commendable job in the classroom in spite of a slight hesitancy in speech. He prepares his classwork diligently, and he extracts good work from his students. He is sincerely interested in his students, and he spends much time counseling them.

In summary, Dean Koogan, I recommend Dr. McQueen to you as a teacher of industrial management. If I can help you further in your evaluation of him, please write me again.

Sincerely,

Also showing good technique is the following evaluation of a person who the writer feels is very well qualified. The letter contains no negative information. The letter's strength is in its systematic handling of the information. The opening is not so direct as the preceding two examples, for it follows the technique of announcing a favorable response rather than beginning the report. But the words have the effect of directness. The answers are numbered in the sequence used in the letter being answered.

Dear Mr. Crump:

Subject: Report on Ms. Patricia Heine, requested by you May 10

Following are my answers to your questions about Ms. Heine. For your convenience, I have arranged them in the numbered sequence used in your letter.

1. Ms. Heine worked for us from January 1982 to June 1983.
2. For the first six months Ms. Heine worked as an administrative trainee. Her

155

Chapter 9
Correspondence:
Situations
Requiring
Directness

assignments rotated through the major departments of the company. Following the training period, she was placed in charge of customer services, where she remained until she left the company. On this assignment she demonstrated good administrative ability and a practical knowledge of dealing with people.

3. In all her assignments I found Ms. Heine to be a very capable worker. She worked hard, and she demonstrated good administrative potential. In fact, I had selected her to groom for a position of administrative responsibility.

4. I found Ms. Heine to be a most personable young woman. She got along with all her associates. I believe she is a person of integrity and good morals.

5. Ms. Heine left us for a higher paying job—a job she felt offered her faster advancement. We wanted her to stay with us.

I have a high regard for Ms. Heine. I recommend her to you for any work for which her experience has prepared her.

I am pleased to give you this confidential report on Ms. Heine.

Sincerely,

The third letter begins directly, reporting a significant point in the first sentence. Use of the subject line frees the text of the need to identify the inquiry, resulting in a faster moving letter beginning. The text presents the information in good and logical order, with like things being placed together. Also, the words present the information fairly. The major negative point is presented almost positively, which is the way it should be viewed in regard to the job concerned. The letter ends with an appropriate goodwill comment.

Dear Ms. Brooking:

Subject: Your May 10 inquiry about George Adams

Mr. Adams has been our assistant shipping clerk since March, 1982, and has steadily improved in usefulness to our company. We want to keep him with us as long as he wants to stay. But with things as they are, it will apparently be some time before we can offer him a promotion that would match the branch managership for which you are considering him.

Of course I am glad to give you in confidence a report on his service with us. As first assistant, he has substituted at the head clerk's desk and is thus familiar with problems of rate scales and routing. His main assignment, however, is to supervise the car and truck loadings. By making a careful study of this work he has reduced our shipping damages noticeably within the last year. This job also places him in direct charge of the labor force, which varies from six to ten men. He has proved to be a good boss.

We have always found Mr. Adams to be honest, straightforward, and dependable. He is a man of strong convictions. He has his own ideas and backs them up. He is resourceful and works well without direction.

I recommend Mr. Adams to you highly. If you need additional information about him, please write me again.

Sincerely,

Claim letters

When things go wrong between a business and its customers, usually someone begins an effort to right the wrong. Typically, the offended person begins by calling the trouble to the attention of those responsible. In other words, he or she makes a claim. The offended one can make a claim in person, by telephone, or by letter. Of course, our concern here is how to do it by letter.

Directness in spite of negativeness

157

Chapter 9
Correspondence:
Situations
Requiring
Directness

As you analyze a claim situation, you will see clearly that it is a situation steeped in negativeness. Goods have been damaged or lost, a product has failed to perform, service has proved to be ineffective, or the like. It is truly an unhappy situation for the writer. Usually, when the news you have to present is bad, you will elect to use an indirect approach. In this case, however, you will use a direct one—and for good reason.

In the first place, most business executives want to please their customers. When they do not please, they want to know about it. They want to make the adjustment necessary to make the customer happy. There is no need to persuade the business executive to do the right thing. Neither is there need to break the news gently.

In the second place, directness lends strength to your claim. To begin directly with the trouble emphasizes it and shows your confidence in reporting it. In fact, some readers would interpret indirectness as weakness. Since your chances of getting a favorable adjustment depend in large part on the strength of your claim, you will want to use the arrangement which will contribute to strength.

Need for identifying facts

Because the claim letter is about a particular transaction, item of merchandise, service call, or the like, you will need to bring in the necessary identification material early in the letter. What you bring in depends on what is needed in each case—invoice number, order date or number, serial number of product, or such. You should include enough to permit your reader to determine quickly just what your claim is about.

As was discussed earlier, such identification can be handled incidentally or by subject line. Should you elect to use the subject line, you may be hesitant to identify the situation, since it is negative. Your directness logically can start right here, however, through the use of words which lend strength to your claim. The following examples illustrate this manner of identification:

> *Subject:* Breakage of Tira cologne shipped on invoice No. 317A dated July 5, 1984.
> *Subject:* Failure of model N pump, serial No. 31510, purchased May 15, 1983.
> *Subject:* Damage of fire extinguishers on arrival, your invoice No. 3421.

Forthright statement of what is wrong

In writing the claim that will communicate with the courteous firmness and strength that you want, you should tell the trouble right away. Preferably you should do it in the first main clause, for any other arrangement would weaken your case. Your initial statement should move as far as is possible into the facts of the situation. If there are details of identification not covered in the subject line, you might need to work these into your letter, perhaps somewhere near the beginning. But this you should do incidentally.

In some instances, you may wish to do more than just name the problem.

You may wish to explain also any special effects the problem may have caused. A broken machine, for example, may have stopped an entire assembly line. Or damaged merchandise ordered for resale may have cost the buyer a loss in sales, or perhaps even a loss of customers. By interpreting the breakage, loss, or the like in terms of effect, you strengthen your claim. And sometimes you may need a stronger approach to enable you to get the relief you seek. The following two first sentences of claim letters illustrate this technique:

> The total content of 8 of the 11 cartons of Sea Mist cologne was broken on arrival and could not be used for our advertised promotion.
> The model H freezer (serial No. 71312) we purchased from you last September has suddenly quit working, destroying $312 of frozen food in the process.

Explanation of facts

After indicating what is wrong, your next logical step is to present the supporting facts. This you should do in a straightforward manner, being as factual and objective about it as you can. You will need to take care to tell your reader just what went wrong, what evidence you have, the extent of the damage—in fact, everything you know which could affect the decision.

In presenting the facts of the case, you should choose your words carefully. Words which tend to accuse the reader or which imply distrust will work against your claim. So will words of anger. Although anger may work effectively in some cases, it is not likely to work in cases which require persuasion. Angry and accusing words tend to put the reader on the defensive and to arouse resistance. With resistance aroused, your chances of receiving a good settlement are hurt.

Choice in handling the error

The facts you present should prove your claim. So after you have presented the facts, you logically move to the handling of your claim. How you handle your claim is a matter for you to decide. Quite often the facts of the case point clearly to one of the possibilities as being superior.

One possibility is to state specifically what you want the reader to do to correct the wrong. Perhaps you want your money returned, or new merchandise, or free repairs. Clearly stating what you want strengthens your case, for giving you something short of what you want gives the adjuster an added hurdle to clear.

When you know that your reader has a favorable adjustment reputation, you may wish to let the reader decide what is to be done. Many companies try hard to make equitable adjustments. In fact, they often do more than is necessary and more than you would dare ask them to do.

Doubt-removing friendliness in the close

Your final friendly words should remove all doubt about your cordial attitude. For added strength, when strength is needed to support a claim, you could express grateful appreciation for what you seek. This suggestion does not support use of the timeworn "Thanking you in advance" wording. Instead, something like "I shall be grateful if you can get the new merchandise to me in time for my Friday sale" would be better.

159

Chapter 9
Correspondence:
Situations
Requiring
Directness

Claim letters illustrated

Illustrating the direct approach to establishing a claim, the following letter begins with a clear statement of what went wrong and the effects of the error. Then, in a tone that shows firmness without sign of anger or accusation of wrongdoing, it relates precisely what went wrong. It asks for a specific remedy, and it covers disposition of the damaged merchandise. Its ending uses some subtle persuasion by implying confidence in the reader, yet it leaves no doubt as to the continued friendship of the writer.

Dear Ms. Golby:

Subject: Damage to Fireboy extinguishers, your invoice No. 715C

The corroded condition of all the Fireboy extinguishers received today makes them unfit for use.

At the time of delivery the condition of your shipment was called to the attention of the Red Arrow Freight Company driver by our shipping and receiving supervisor. Upon inspection, we found all boxes thoroughly soaked with fluid. Further investigation revealed that at least six of the extinguishers had leaked acid from the cap screws. As a result, the chrome finish of all units has been badly damaged.

As we are under orders from the fire marshal to have this equipment in our plant by Monday, please get the 24 replacement units to us by that date. Also, will you please instruct me what I should do with the defective units?

I am aware, of course, that errors like this will happen in spite of all precautions. And I am confident that you will take care of this problem with your usual courtesy.

Sincerely,

The second illustration follows the same general plan, but it differs in one application. Its opening does not clearly name the trouble. Instead, it merely reports that the product is defective. Obviously, it is not so direct as the preceding opening. It has some added strength, however, in the moral trap of the words indicating that the reader "will want to know" about the trouble.

Dear Mr. Samuels:

Subject: Malfunction of Stay-Cool model M, serial No. 37471

You will want to know, I feel sure, that the Stay-Cool window air conditioner I ordered from you on May 7 is not performing well.

Apparently, the difficulty is in the thermostat, for the unit will not maintain a consistent temperature. Although the compressor does cut on and off automatically from time to time, the room temperature fluctuates widely between changes.

In addition, the unit arrived with a defective temperature control knob. It was severely cracked, and after short use it broke completely. I had not intended to do anything about so small a matter, but I feel certain that you will want to take care of this matter, also.

As you have no repair representative convenient to me, I should be happy to install these two parts myself. So will you please send them to me? Should you wish, I shall gladly send you the defective ones.

As the weather is becoming unbearable, I shall appreciate your promptness in mailing the parts to me.

Sincerely,

The third case example takes a strong, direct approach. In the beginning it states the trouble—clearly and in terms of effect. It then presents the alternate remedies that the writer considers appropriate. The close is courteous. Its assumption that the trouble will be corrected continues the polite firmness that is present in preceding parts of the letter.

Dear Mr. Ferguson:

Subject: Color fading of your Kota-Tuff carpeting, your invoice 3147 dated January 3, 1984.

The Kota-Tuff carpeting you installed for us last January has faded badly and is an eyesore in our hotel pool area. The original forest green color now is spotted with rings of varying shades of white and green. The spotting is especially heavy in areas adjacent to the pool. Probably water has caused the damage. But your written warranty says that the color will "withstand the effects of sun and water."

As the product clearly has not lived up to the warranty, we ask that you replace the Kota-Tuff with a more suitable carpeting. If you are unable to find a satisfactory carpeting, we request a refund of the full purchase price, including installation.

I shall appreciate your usual promptness in correcting this problem.

Sincerely,

Adjustment grant

When you can grant a claim, the situation is a happy one for your reader. So, when you transmit the decision by letter, there is no reason to justify or explain. Instead, you should present your message in the direct order that is appropriate for other presentations of good news.

Need to overcome negative impressions

Even though your basic objective is a good-news one, the adjustment-grant situation is not all positive. If you will look through your reader's mental filter, you will understand why. As the reader sees it, something bad has happened—goods have been damaged, equipment has failed to work, sales have been lost, and the like. The reader has suffered some unpleasant experiences, and the ugly pictures of them remain in the mind. The reader's ill feelings are likely to be focused in two directions—on your company and on your product or service.

Granting the claim is likely to take care of any ill feelings your reader may have toward you or your company. Certainly, by doing what the reader wants you to do you have helped to improve relations. But just correcting the error is not likely to regain the confidence lost in your product or service. At this state, the reader could conclude that you are good but your products or service is bad.

Direct presentation of decision

161

Chapter 9
Correspondence:
Situations
Requiring
Directness

Because the basic news is good, you should begin adjustment-grant letters with a direct statement of your answer. Since your letter is a response to one the reader wrote, however, you will need to identify the preceding correspondence. This you can do by incidental reference within the first sentence, or by use of a subject line.

The news you have to present is certain to create a favorable response, and you should take full advantage of it. For the best effect, you should select words that add to the positiveness of your answer. You may, for example, present your decision in terms of customer satisfaction, as in this beginning sentence:

> The enclosed check for $82.50 is our way of proving to you that we at Strickland's value your satisfaction highly.

Avoidance of negatives

In the opening as well as throughout the letter, you will want to avoid using words which tend to recall unnecessarily in your reader's mental filter the bad situation you are correcting. Your goal is to change your reader's mental picture of your company and your product from negative to positive, and you do not help your case by recalling memories of what went wrong. Your emphasis should be on what you are doing to correct the wrong— not on the wrong itself.

Illustrating the point are the truly negative words which describe the situation—words like *mistake, trouble, damage, broken,* and *loss.* Also negative are the apologies which begin some letters of this type. Even though well intended, the somewhat conventional "We sincerely regret the inconvenience caused you" type of comment does not produce optimum results. Equally negative are such general references as "problem," "difficulty," and "misunderstanding." Even though you may need to talk about the problem somewhere in the letter, you should try to do so using a minimum of negative words.

Regaining lost confidence

A good-news beginning should put the reader in a happy frame of mind. You are doing what the reader asked. You are correcting the wrong. Now the situation is ideal for you to work on your secondary goal of regaining lost confidence.

Except in those cases in which the cause of the difficulty is routine or incidental, you will need to regain lost confidence. Just what you must do and how you must do it depend on the facts of the case. You will need to survey the situation to see what the facts are. If something can be done to correct a bad procedure or a product defect, you should do it. Then you should present this information to your reader as convincingly and positively as you can. If what went wrong was a rare, unavoidable event, you should explain this situation. Sometimes you will need to explain how a product should be used or cared for. Sometimes you will need to resell the product.

Happiness in the close

Regardless of how positively you handle the preceding parts of the letter, the problem is still filled with negative elements. So, for the best in goodwill effect, you will need to end the letter on a happy note. Your final words should do as much as you can to move your reader's mind away from the unpleasant situation which caused the adjustment problem.

Your choice of subject matter for the close again depends on what is appropriate for the one case. It could be a forward look to happy future relations, a comment about a product improvement, talk about announcements of a coming promotion, and the like. You should include not a word which recalls to your reader's mind the negative situation. Even an apology would be negative, for it would bring back to mind that for which the apology is being made.

Three case illustrations

The logic of this direct approach to granting adjustments is applied in the following illustrations. The first concerns acceptance of a legitimate claim for fire extinguishers damaged in transit. After making proper identification of the transaction involved and of preceding correspondence, it states the good news in words which add to the happiness of the message. With a reader-viewpoint explanation, it leads into a review of what happened. Without as much as a single negative word, it makes clear the cause of the problem and what has been done to prevent its recurrence. After handling the essential matter of disposing of the damaged merchandise, it closes with positive talk which is far removed from the problem of the claim.

Dear Ms. Watson:
Subject: Your December 3 report on invoice 1348

Two dozen new and thoroughly tested Fireboy extinguishers should reach your sales floor in time for your Saturday promotion. They were shipped early today by Red Line Motor Freight.

As your satisfaction with our service is important to us, we have thoroughly checked all the Fireboys in stock. In the past, we have assumed that all of them were checked for tight seals at the factory. We learned, thanks to you, that now we must systematically check each one. Already we have set up a system of checks as part of our normal handling procedure.

When you receive the new Fireboys, will you please return the original group by motor freight? Of course, we shall bear all transportation charges.

As you may know, the new Fireboys have practically revolutionized the extinguisher field. Their compact size and efficiency have made them the top seller in the field in a matter of only three months. We hope that they will play their part in the success of your coming sale.

Sincerely,

The second illustration follows much the same plan. It differs primarily in the nature of its explanation. It can make no face-saving explanation of what happened or what it will do to prevent recurrence of the happening. It can only make a plea of the human error with which all businesses are plagued from time to time. It makes the plea most positively and convincingly.

163

Chapter 9
Correspondence:
Situations
Requiring
Directness

Dear Ms. Brown:

Subject: Your October 3 inquiry concerning order No. A4170

Your Mecca sterling cutlery properly monogrammed with an Old English B should reach you in a day or two. It is our evidence to you that Mecca's century-old record for satisfaction is as genuine as the sterling itself.

Because we value your satisfaction so much, we have carefully looked into the handling of your order. As you probably guessed, we found it was just one of those rare situations which even the most careful human beings occasionally get into. Two people read and checked the order, and two people overlooked the "Old English monogram" specification. You will agree, I feel sure, that even in the best run businesses such things happen. Even so, we are redoubling our efforts to continue to give the fast, dependable service Mecca customers have come to expect over the years.

We know that your Mecca sterling will enhance many a dinner party through the years ahead. And we wish you the best in enjoyment from your set.

Sincerely,

Further illustrating good technique in granting adjustments is the following letter. This one concerns a claim for a damaged suit, one that reached the customer with faded spots on the coat front. The angry customer returned the coat with a demand for money back.

The letter begins with the only news the reader really wants to hear—that he is getting his money back. Then, with the reader's confidence gained, the letter moves to the explanation. Here the suit is relieved of blame. The letter ends with an appeal for giving the blameless suit a chance to prove itself. A fair-minded reader would be likely to conclude that the product has earned this chance.

Dear Mr. McShane:

The attached check for $321.40 is Consort's way of assuring you that your satisfaction is very important to us.

Because we sincerely want to please, we thoroughly examined the suit you returned to us. Our investigation showed that the likely cause of the fading was accidental contact with some form of chemical. We couldn't determine precisely what the chemical was or just how contact was made. But we suspect a liquid spill sometime after packaging, either in our warehouse or during shipment. Such unexpected happenings will occur in spite of our best precautions. Anyway, we were relieved to know that Consort's reputation for quality fabrics and craftsmanship remains good.

We sincerely hope that we have convinced you of Consort's desire to serve you. And we look forward to serving you with Consort suits in the years ahead.

Sincerely,

Order letters

Letters which order goods are not written as often nowadays as they once were. Most orders today either are placed orally with salespeople or are made on standard order forms. Nevertheless, some orders must be made by letter.

Clear and forthright authorization

Order letters carry good news to the reader, for they mean business and profits. So you should use the direct approach which is appropriate for the good-news letter. Your first main words should authorize shipment—in clear, specific language. Your words should say, in effect, "Please send me. . . ." Any wording which merely hints or suggests ("I am in need of . . ." or "I should like . . .") falls short of the ideal.

Specific coverage of the sale

The remainder of your letter is an exercise in clear and orderly coverage of the details your reader needs to know. Your letter is likely to contain many facts, and unless these facts are arranged in good order, they are likely to overwhelm or confuse your reader's mind. As we have noted, the mind can receive only a limited number of facts in one message. So you must work to keep the facts in the best possible order for quick understanding.

No one best arrangement exists for the descriptive information needed in an order. You would, however, be wise to begin with the numbers and units you need. Then, in the following sequence, you may list these descriptive parts:

Catalog number
Basic name (including trade names and brands when helpful)
Points of description (color, size, weight, etc.)
Unit price
Total price

In finished form, a description might read like this:

3 dozen No. 712AC, Woolsey claw hammer,
    drop-forged head, hickory
    handle, 13 inches overall length,
    16 ounces, at $48.24 per dozen $144.72

For quick and easy communication, you will need to arrange this information in orderly and neat fashion. There is no one best form, although the illustration letter below gives one good arrangement. Most acceptable arrangements keep the quantities and units in a clear column to the left. The remaining description is set off to the right with carry-over lines dropping under the preceding beginnings of the description (see example letter). Price extensions appear to the right of the listing and are also set off in a clear column.

In addition to describing the items ordered, you will need to include other vital information. You will need to give whatever shipping instructions are necessary and any information regarding payment (charge, cash, c.o.d.). Some of this information you may work into the beginning of the letter, following the beginning authorization statement. The remainder you may include with your closing remarks. The essential point is that you include all the reader needs to know to fill your order.

A cordial close

You should end the order letter with a short and friendly comment relating to the order. As was mentioned earlier, it could even include some of the shipping instructions not covered previously. It should not demand, command, or talk down. But it would be appropriate to request early action, as in this example:

> As we have promised to make our first delivery on the 17th, will you please get the supplies to us by the 13th at the latest? We shall sincerely appreciate it.

An order illustrated

The specimen order letter which follows shows good form in arranging the detailed facts in an order. It authorizes the shipment right away, as it should; it covers the necessary shipping details clearly and quickly; and it ends with appropriate cordiality. It meets the requirements of a good order letter in every respect.

Dear Ms. Green:

Please send me the office supplies listed below by prepaid parcel post at the address above. I am ordering from your September 7 price list.

10 reams	No. 321A, Scroll bond paper, white, 25%-rag, 8½ by 11 inches, 20-pound, @ 3.25	$ 32.50
4 boxes	No. 106B, carbon paper, 8½ by 11 inches, medium weight, @ $4.40	17.60
5 dozen	No. 1171A, typewriter ribbons, Royal, black record, medium-inked, @ $10.50	52.50
5 each	No. 215H, typewriter stands, Luddell model K, 26 inches high, 161 by 24-inch top, black enamel, @ $9.60	48.00
		$150.60

Please charge the amount to me on the usual 2/10, n/60 terms. As our supplies of these items are nearly depleted, I shall appreciate any rush service you can give this order.

Sincerely,

165

Chapter 9
Correspondence:
Situations
Requiring
Directness

Letter problems–1

Routine inquiries

1. While reading *The Wall Street Journal* you see an advertisement that gains your interest. It is from The Nut House, a business in Atlanta, Georgia, which sells packaged assortments of nuts primarily as business gifts. You are interested because each year your D&Z Industrial Sales, Inc., expresses its appreciation at Christmas time with gifts to about 550 of its good customers. In the past you have given pen sets, candy, cheese packs, desk calendars, and other such conventional products—but never nuts.

The advertisement contains much of the information you need. The nuts are attractively packaged in three sizes, selling for $14, $8, and $6. Probably you would want about 120 of the largest size for your major customers. The $8 size would be sufficient for the others.

Before you commit to the purchase, you need to know more. First, you'll want the descriptive brochure mentioned in the advertisement. Then for a purchase of this size you feel there should be a discount. Is there one? The advertisement makes no mention of it. You'll need to know also whether The Nut House people would send the packages individually to your customers or whether they send the entire order to you. And, if they will ship them individually, is there an extra charge? Of course, you could supply the mailing list of your customers. They are all within 300 miles of your headquarters city (you select it).

If you feel you need additional information, you may supply it. But make it consistent with the facts given in this problem.

2. In the Real Estate Corner of today's *The Wall Street Journal* you read an advertisement describing an Arkansas lodge. Located on 540 acres in the heart of the Ozarks, the lodge accommodates 32 people for sleeping. Its dining area seats 60, and its kitchen is adequate for this number. A 55-acre lake "teeming with fish" is a part of the property. The asking price is $1,250,000.

Your employer, Atlas Manufacturing Company, is looking for such a place for use as a training center. As the Company's director of training, you have the job of leading the search for this facility. Of course, before making a recommendation you will want to visit the place—and probably a few other places. But before you spend time and money on a visit, you will gather additional information. This you can do by letter.

The advertisement does not mention how far from civilization the lodge is. Atlas wants a secluded place, but it should be near an airstrip. Company executives will fly in and out of training sessions. Perhaps a landing strip could be built on the property, but that matter would be determined by the nature of the terrain. The ad doesn't say what the room arrangements are like. Are there 32 individual rooms, 16 double rooms, or dormitory-type rooms? This matter is important, for you would not want your executives staying in crowded quarters. Also, since you will use the lodge for training, a meeting room will be a must. Typically, you run classes of from 16 to 25. And what about the availability of recreational facilities (other than those mentioned in the advertisement)? Are golf courses and tennis courts available? Is there anything else you can think of?

If you feel you need additional background facts, you may supply them. But keep them consistent with the intent of the problem. The address given in the advertisement is P.O. Box 71, Fayetteville.

3. Place yourself in the role of training director, Gadsden Department Stores, Inc. In this month's issue of *Training Journal* you read an interesting article titled "Administrative Training by Mail." The article described a management training program offered by Waterford University through its Division of Extension. For years Waterford and other universities have conducted on-campus programs designed to teach administration to promising executives. For obvious reasons, such programs are costly; and they take the executive-student from his or her work for long periods. Now Waterford has an alternative program.

The Waterford Program covers all the topics of its on-campus programs; but all the teaching is done through a series of 15 lessons mailed to the students. The students study assigned reading materials, write answers to questions, and submit their written answers to Waterford faculty. The faculty members grade the work and return it with abundant comments. A final examination ends the course.

You like the plan, especially the fact that it costs $1,050, which is well under the $3,850 per person charged for Waterford's three-week residence course (you've been considering this option). Before you can decide on the matter, however, you need more information. So you will write a letter to the Waterford people.

Of course, you will ask for any printed matter they may have on their new program—brochures, posters, or such. Also, you would like to know about the possibilities of course credit for those completing the work (a few of your promising executives are working on degree programs). Another matter is the level of the instruction. Your executive students are all bright, you think; but they vary broadly in educational background, ranging from high school to college graduates. Then there is the matter of cost. If the program is bought, about 30 people would be enrolled at once—all paid for by the Company. Are discounts given for such quantities? And what about progress reports? If the Company pays, can they be informed of the grades given to the students? Or is this privileged information available only to the student?

You will ask for all the information in your letter—and possibly more (if you think of additional needs). Address the letter to the person mentioned in the article—Dr. Herta Goode, director of the Division of Extension at Waterford.

4. Assume the role of a member of a three-person interview team for Stanford-Brinks, Inc., an international pharmaceutical manufacturer and distributor. Your team's job is to visit a select group of colleges in your area for the purpose of hiring qualified graduates for the firm's training program. One of the schools on the list is your alma mater (the school you are now attending). Because you and the other members of the team have had no experience interviewing on campuses, you will write the college placement officer for the information you need.

In your letter you will tell what types of people you seek. Actually, you need help from most major business areas: accounting, marketing, management, information systems, and finance. So, you will want the placement officer to arrange interviews in each of these areas for you. If the officer requires you to set up your own interviews, of course you will do so. You would like to know whether it would be possible to get a list of interviewees, with résumés, prior to the interviews. And you would like, also, to talk with some of the school's faculty members—especially those who know the students you will be interviewing. If it can be arranged, you would like to take the professors to lunch on the dates of the interviews.

About the dates for the interviews, you have some flexibility. You would prefer the third Thursday–Friday of next month. As second choice, you would take the Monday–Wednesday of that week. If neither of these dates is available, you would have to do some major rescheduling; but it could be done.

With the foregoing thoughts in mind, draft the inquiry letter that will get you the information you need and will set up the interviews. Direct it to the placement officer of your school.

5. Take over as vice president for administration for Hudnall Industries. On the airplane today, while returning from a business trip, you read an interesting advertisement in *Barron's*. It concerned a new service called Executive Digest—a service which prepares monthly summaries of "all that is important in business literature." As explained in the advertisement, this service saves executives valuable time. It enables them to be current on readings in the field in a minimum of time.

You feel that such a service would be good for the 38 members of your management team. It certainly would keep them informed on the latest management topics, and it would save work time. But you will need some questions answered before buying the service for them. So you will write the Executive Digest people a letter.

Your letter will seek to determine what business fields are covered. And what about types of publications—trade, scholarly, technical? The advertisement mentioned a cost of $72 per year, but you were wondering whether you would get a quantity discount if you bought a subscription for each of the 38 executives. If Executive Digest would send you a sample copy, virtually all of your remaining questions would be answered.

Perhaps you will think of additional questions as you write the letter.

6. In the role of the training director of Apex Electronics, you must write a letter seeking information from Professor Elizabeth Harwell at Northern State University. From an associate, you heard that Professor Harwell is an excellent lecturer—that she performs masterfully in putting over her subject of "The Art of Handling People."

Her topic is one your 43 top executives need to hear; so you are considering inviting Dr. Harwell to present the lecture to them at your annual executive retreat next August. Before you decide on Harwell for certain, however, you need to know more.

First, of course, is the matter of Dr. Harwell's fee. You expect to pay for a quality presentation, but you have some budget limitations. Then, for scheduling purposes, you need to know the length of her presentation. Perhaps she has some flexibility concerning time. If so, you'd like to know, so you can select the arrangement that best fits your schedule.

At the moment, you could schedule Dr. Harwell on any of the three days of the retreat, for you have not committed to any of the other speakers. But you'll need to know her preferences soon. Also, there is the matter of class size. Forty-three executives in one class may be too much for best results—and you do want best results. The professor may prefer to make two presentations. Perhaps she could send you a brochure or such describing her presentation.

7. Move into the position of manager of the Atwell Hotel and write a letter seeking information about Stone Weave carpeting. You read about this unique carpeting in an advertisement in this week's *Inn Keepers' Journal;* and you like what you read.

The advertisement described Stone Weave carpeting as "plush to the touch, yet so tough it will outwear ordinary carpeting two to one." You could use a product like this, especially in the hallways and in the lobby. Because your carpeting in these areas needs replacing badly, you are in the market for about 4,200 square feet.

Before you buy anything, you need more information. So you will write the Stone Weave people for this. You'd like to have descriptive brochures or other literature it might have on the product. You need to know where you can see—and perhaps buy—the product. You want to know what if any guarantees the Stone Weave Company makes to back up its claim of durability. And there is the question of color fading. The lobby area gets quite a bit of sunlight, which has caused fading problems in the past. Also, you'll want to know about price.

You may think of additional questions to ask as you write the letter.

8. As business manager for Rollo Rollins, a leading lecturer on the business-executive circuit, you must write a letter to the sponsors of a Rollins lecture scheduled in Bay City. Your objective is to get the information Rollins needs in planning his presentation.

Rollins uses from 30 to 40 handouts in his presentation, "The Nuts and Bolts of Administration." Thus, it is important that he know about how many people will be in his audience. He travels by commercial air; so it is not easy to carry extra copies.

You'll need to know also the general makeup of the audience—things like executive levels and types of companies. Rollins adapts his presentations to the group whenever possible. Perhaps a list of registrants showing company and position would take care of this matter.

Also, you must know the size of the meeting room and the seating configuration possibilities. Rollins adapts his visual aids to the physical facilities available (overhead projector for small room, feltboard for large room).

You need the information right away because the lecture is scheduled for 7 P.M. a week from Friday. Write the letter to Ms. Ann Cassity, who is coordinator of educational programs for the Bay City Executives Association, sponsors of the event.

9. You are the sales manager for Pen-Southern Chemical Company. Your task of the moment is that of planning the annual sales meeting of all Pen-Southern salespeople.

Although the meeting is primarily for business purposes, you select meeting sites which offer recreational attractions. For this year's meeting, you are considering Coral Cove, a small resort city on the Florida Gulf coast. Reports given you by some of your staff strongly support Coral Cove, especially because of the fishing and swimming available. But you need to know more before you can decide; so you will write a letter to the Coral Cove Chamber of Commerce asking for the information you need.

Any place you select must have hotel accommodations that will take care of the Company's 104 salespeople (two to a room); and you'll need meeting rooms for the group. Since Coral Cove appears on the map to be somewhat isolated, you'll need to know how difficult it would be for people traveling by commercial air to get there. You know about the swimming and fishing that is available, but what about other recreational facilities—golf, tennis, and such? Perhaps Coral Cove could send you descriptive literature on the place to help you decide and to help you sell your decision to your associates.

10. Assume the role of vice president of sales for Moran Business Machines, Inc., manufacturers of computers and other business machines. In your efforts to promote your products, you frequently display them at conventions and other meetings of business groups. One such group was called to your attention today by one of your salespeople. It is the National

Association of Business Managers, which will hold its annual meeting in three months at the Metropolitan Hotel in Kansas City. You know little about this organization,—its size, makeup, anticipated attendance, and such. In fact, you don't even know whether it invites companies to exhibit at its meetings. To get the answers to this and the other questions suggested above, you will write a letter to Conway Deutsch, the Association's executive director.

In addition to asking for the information described above, you'll need to ask some specific ones about exhibiting at this year's meeting. One is the cost of display space (you'll need a minimum of 200 square feet). Another is the matter of protection of your valuable equipment after meeting hours. You would not want it unguarded. Yet another is the beginning and ending times and dates for the displays. You may think of other questions before you finish writing the letter.

11.   At the last meeting of your local Sales Executives Association you heard about a new organization, Continental Travelers Club. One of your associates commented that her company had bought membership in CTC for all its traveling people and that they were well satisfied. CTC provides its members with significant discounts on most travel expenses (air travel, automobile rental, hotel–motel accommodations, and meals). Your associate didn't know all the details, but she gave you CTC's address from her membership card. As sales manager for Global Electronics, Inc., you are interested. So now you will write CTC for the information you need.

First, you'll want any descriptive literature it may have on its organization. Perhaps its literature will cover your other questions, but you'll make certain by asking CTC. Specifically, your questions will cover membership costs; quantity discounts (you would buy 35 memberships); the hotels, restaurants, and automobile rental companies offering discounts. Probably you will add a question or two before you finish writing the letter.

12.   This morning as you read the *The Wall Street Journal,* a classified advertisement under "Business Opportunities" caught your eye:

Sell or Lease: Three convenience stores in thriving New Mexico city. Owner has other interests. Good profit record. For details write P.O. Box 17, Albuquerque, New Mexico 87103.

You have been looking for just such a business ever since you inherited $50,000 a few months back. You know that $50,000 won't buy these stores, but perhaps it will make an acceptable down payment. You think you'd like living in New Mexico. So you decide to write for more information.

You'll ask about the selling price, as well as the leasing terms. You might want to lease rather than buy. Also, what can you expect to make per month; and what is the gross volume of the three stores? And is there competition in the areas of these stores?

As you plan your letter, you decide that these questions will do for a start, but you'll need to ask more. Think clearly so you can get all the information you need with this one letter.

Favorable replies

13. Assume the position of sales manager for The Nut House and answer the letter received from D&Z Industrial Sales (see Problem 1 for background information). You are indeed pleased at the prospect of selling 550 gift packs to this company; so you'll do your best to answer the letter positively.

Of course you'll send D&Z your descriptive brochure. Although it covers prices in detail, including discounts, you will answer the question about the discounts in your letter for extra emphasis. You'll say that you do give discounts for quantity orders—10 percent for orders exceeding $1,000 and an additional 5 percent (total of 15 percent) for orders over $5,000.

You will also tell the sales manager that your prices do not include shipping costs. Thus, these costs would be added to the total. You can ship the entire order to D&Z in bulk and let it send the gifts individually to its customers. Or, if it prefers, D&Z can furnish you a mailing list and you will mail the gifts individually. This service costs an extra 75¢ per box, including postage and handling. Also included, and at no extra charge, is a card bearing the donor's name and a holiday message. The cards from which one may choose are illustrated in the brochure.

You may want to make an additional comment or two enhancing the reader's interest in your product. After all, the fact that a sale is involved makes this more than a routine response letter. Address the letter to Herta M. Silverman, the D&Z president.

14. You are owner of Ozark Realty and today you received an inquiry from the director of training of the Atlas Manufacturing Company (see Problem 2 for background information). The inquiry concerns High Mountain Lodge, one of your choice listings in the mountain area outside Fayetteville. You feel that you have a good prospect here, and you are encouraged by the fact that you can answer the questions favorably.

The property is only 12 miles from the Fayetteville city limits. It is the sort of wooded, secluded place the writer appears to want. In fact, the nearest neighbors are well over a mile away. There is no airstrip on the property (too hilly); but a municipal airport is only nine miles away.

Concerning room arrangements, the information in the advertisement was based on double occupancy. But the rooms are spacious—roughly in the 14-by-16-foot range. All have twin beds and private baths. Although it was not designed to be a meeting room, the sun parlor off the lobby could be converted into one. It is roughly 25 by 30 feet. There are no tennis courts on the grounds; neither is there a golf course. But a check at Holly Hill Country Club, which is just two miles down the road, reveals that it would welcome short-term guests for a minor membership fee. Holly Hills has four tennis courts and a truly exciting golf course. Then, of course, there is the lake on the grounds where "the best fishing in Arkansas may be found."

Now you will draft the letter that will answer the questions of Fredrick

W. Sutton, the Atlas executive who wrote you. Of course, you will be truthful. But you will maintain the friendly, helpful attitude that will lead to a sale.

15. Play the role of Dr. Herta Goode of Waterford University's Division of Extension and answer the letter written by the Gadsden Department Stores' training director (see Problem 3 for background information). You are truly excited about the possibilities of enrolling 30 executives in your program. So you'll try especially hard to handle this one tactfully.

You will send your eight-page brochure on your program to the training director. It describes your program in detail and includes some persuasive description as well. On the matter of course credit, you must report negatively. This course is quite broad in coverage and includes virtually all business subjects. Such a course just does not fit into the typical business curriculum.

The instruction is aimed at the college-level audience. Even so, your experience indicates that bright, noncollege-trained executives are able to handle it.

And yes, you can give a discount. You can reduce the price $100 per person if ten or more students are enrolled by one company in a calendar year. But you cannot give the company periodic progress reports (on advice of the university attorney). However, you can report when one successfully completes the instruction; but these reports do not indicate grades. Perhaps the Gadsden training director could get the grade reports from the students.

Write the letter that will answer the training director's questions and will enhance the chances that Gadsden will buy your program. The training director's name is Charlotte E. Moore.

16. As the placement officer for your school, write the letter responding to the inquiry made by the Stanford-Brinks interviewer (see Problem 4 for background information). You are pleased to know that this major pharmaceutical company will recruit on your campus. You have been inviting the firm to visit you for the past few years. Now that it has decided to do so, you'll do what you can to make its representative's visit successful.

Already you have announced the Stanford-Brinks opening through the campus newspaper and your placement bulletin board. So far the response has been encouraging. You can promise interested applicants for all positions. You would be pleased to schedule the interviews for Stanford-Brinks; and you will send the rep the schedule of interviews with résumés of the interviewees at least a week in advance of the interview date.

About the interview dates, you can give Stanford-Brinks its first choice—the third Thursday–Friday of next month. Typically, you schedule the interviews for 30 minutes each, beginning at 9:00 A.M. and ending at 4:30 P.M. You can promise a full schedule of interested students.

You will be quite willing to arrange a luncheon meeting with two or three professors who are likely to know the students being interviewed. And, unless you are instructed otherwise, you will allow a lunch break of an hour and a half in the interview schedule.

Address the letter to Alice Blinn, personnel specialist, who is in charge of the interview team.

17.   As president of Executive Digest, your new business venture, you have begun to get responses from your advertisement. One of them is from Carlos Avalos (see Problem 5 for background information) of Hudnall Industries. The prospects of selling 38 subscriptions of your service to Hudnall is indeed good news. You'll work especially hard to cultivate this potential customer. You will answer the man's questions with the following information.

Your service primarily covers all the quality management publications—primarily those in the scholarly and technical areas. Specifically, this includes 31 publications, headed by the *Academy of Management Journal, Academy of Management Review, Administrative Science Quarterly, Harvard Business Review, Personnel Psychology, Journal of Business, Industrial and Labor Relations Review,* and *Personnel Administration.* Also included are the more popular trade publications, such as *Journal of Management, Supervisory Management, Personnel Administrator,* and *Advanced Management Journal.*

You will enclose your brochure, which describes coverage in more detail, especially concerning the survey coverage of certain trade publications. Although some of these publications may be rather sophisticated, your service summarizes the articles in terms that are meaningful to practicing executives. Your goal is to make Executive Digest a very practical service.

Although you had not thought of it before receiving Avolos's letter, you certainly can give discounts for quantity orders. After thinking the matter over, you conclude that you can give a 10 percent discount on orders exceeding 5, 15 percent on orders exceeding 10, and 20 percent on orders exceeding 20.

You will be pleased to send the sample copy requested—just as soon as the first issue is ready. It is at the printers and you have a promise that copies will be ready early next week.

18.   Assume the position of Dr. Elizabeth Harwell, and answer the letter from the Apex Electronics training director (see Problem 6 for background information).

Over the past few years you have had good success with your lecture, "The Art of Handling People." Currently you give your standard 90-minute presentation plus 30 minutes of questions and answers for $1,200 plus expenses. You do not give a shorter presentation, for you feel it would require cutting essential material. However, you can expand the subject for one to three hours of experiential exercises. You charge $200 an hour for these. These exercises, you feel, are quite effective in teaching the techniques covered in the lecture.

You have no class size limit for your standard presentation. But as your experiential exercises involve participation, you have set a maximum class size of 20. In this case, you would be willing to handle the 43 executives in two classes.

After looking at your schedule, you find that you are free only on August 7, the first day of the retreat. So that will have to be the date.

You do not have a brochure describing your presentation; so you cannot send one. But you do have an outline, and a copy of an article from *The Administrator* describing your presentation. These you will send.

Write the letter that will give the Apex training director the information needed. His name is Robert E. Marek.

19. Take over as sales manager for the Stone Weave Company and answer the inquiry from Chester Pirollo, manager of the Atwell Hotel, Boulder, Colorado (see Problem 7 for background information).

You can answer Pirollo's letter positively, you think, for Stone Weave carpeting is indeed superior. You will send a copy of your illustrated, descriptive brochure, which answers most of the questions asked. But you will also answer all of Pirollo's questions in your letter as a matter of courtesy and emphasis.

Because Stone Weave is a new product, distributors for it are not yet available in all cities. None is in Boulder; but Davidson Furniture, Inc., of nearby Denver now handles the product. You can't quote Davidson's price, of course, but you can assure Pirollo that Stone Weave is priced competitively.

You can also assure Pirollo that Stone Weave's guarantee is the most concrete in the industry. Although specific time guarantees are not possible, because wear depends on extent and nature of use, the company guarantees that Stone Weave lasts longer than any other carpeting on the market. Stone Weave will give money back if a customer can prove otherwise. The company has tested Stone Weave scientifically against all competition; and the results are clear and convincing. These results are available to all who wish to see them.

Since Stone Weave is made for indoor and outdoor use, its colors are fast. Sunlight will not affect them.

If other questions were asked, you will also answer them—positively, of course.

20. Play the role of Ann Cassity, coordinator of educational programs for the Bay City Executives Association and answer the inquiry from the business manager of Rollo Rollins (see Problem 8 for background information).

The publicity buildup you have been giving to the Rollins lecture has generated good interest in Bay City. You feel that the 120 seats in the Mini-Ballroom of the Bay City Hotel will be filled. About audience makeup, a good cross-section of Bay City executives will be present—bankers, merchants, manufacturers, professional people, and such. You are sending Rollins a list of the 65 who have registered to date, including names, companies, and positions. Of course, registration will continue until room capacity is reached. But this preliminary list should tell Rollins something about audience makeup.

The meeting room (Mini-Ballroom) is rectangular—about 80 by 40 feet. You can arrange whatever seating configuration Rollo wants, but you had planned to place a moveable stage platform about midway along the long wall opposite the main entrance to the room. You have arranged to have an overhead projector available.

Address the letter to Wilburt Perrin, manager of Rollo Rollins.

21. As manager of Coral Cove Chamber of Commerce you have the assignment of answering inquiries about the recreational attractions of the

city. One such inquiry arrived in today's mail. It is from Alice Guidry, who is sales manager for Pen-Southern Chemical Company (see Problem 9 for background information). Your immediate task is to answer it.

You will send Ms. Guidry the glossy, full-color, four-page brochure which you have prepared to describe the attractions of the area. It emphasizes the swimming and fishing to be enjoyed; but Ms. Guidry asked for more information.

There's only one hotel in Coral Cove that could accommodate 104 people. It is the 140-room Light House Hotel. If it can't provide all 52 rooms to one group, the Starfly Motel is only a half block away. And only two blocks away is the Traveler's Inn, another hotel. Between the three, Pen-Southern's needs could be met. The Light House Hotel has four meeting rooms, which have been adequate for similar groups in the past.

Getting to Coral Cove using commercial air involves flying to Tampa and then going by shuttle bus to Coral City. The buses are sponsored by Coral City hotels and meet all flights carrying preregistered hotel guests.

There is no shortage of golf and tennis facilities in the area. Hotel guests have temporary memberships in the adjacent Coral Cove Country Club. Its 18-hole golf course is one of the best in the state. Its eight tennis courts are of championship calibre.

You may want to tell more about the attractions of your beautiful city. Write the letter that will give Ms. Guidry all she needs for her decision.

22. For this assignment you are Conway Deutsch, executive director of the National Association of Business Managers. Your immediate task is to answer the inquiry from Sheila Madden, who is the sales manager for Moran Business Machines (see Problem 10 for background information).

Your organization does indeed welcome exhibitors to its meetings. In fact, at last year's meeting 57 exhibitors were present. Among those represented were manufactures of office furniture, business services, computers, and duplicators. You expect a larger number this year.

The Association's membership is an ideal group for promoting such products. It comprises the cream of the nation's office managers. Association membership totals 7,512. About 1,500 can be expected to attend the annual meeting.

Display space rents for $300 a stall (about 100 square feet). Probably the Moran people will need two stalls. Security (24 hours a day) is provided by uniformed police, paid by the Association. In addition, the display area is securely locked after convention hours. As the convention runs from Wednesday through Friday, most displays are set up Tuesday afternoon. They are dismantled Friday afternoon, after the luncheon that concludes the convention.

If there is other information you think Ms. Madden needs, give it to her.

23. Today at your desk at the Continental Traveler's Club you received an inquiry from Basil H. Buckingham, sales manager for Global Electronics, Inc. (see Problem 11 for background information).

You do have a descriptive brochure that you can send to Buckingham. It gives much of the information the man requests; but for added emphasis, you'll answer all his questions in your letter.

You will tell how the Continental Traveler's Club was founded by traveling people to give them the benefits of organization—discounts on travel, hotels, automobile rentals, and such. The cooperating companies are listed in the brochure; but you can note that included are three major motel chains, two of the major automobile rental companies, and three airlines. (You may use your imagination in naming the companies and in describing these benefits.)

Continental Traveler's Club plans to greatly increase the number of cooperating companies in the years ahead. Memberships sell for $50 per year. Because the membership costs are based on costs of operations, no discounts are given. But the Club is a nonprofit operation; and if ever operating costs per member can be reduced, membership costs also will be reduced.

Answer any other questions you feel Buckingham should have asked.

24. Today's mail brings good news—a letter inquiring about the three convenience stores you advertised for sale in *The Wall Street Journal*. The letter is from Veronica Sabatini of Toledo, Ohio (see Problem 12 for background information).

Although you had expected more, her suggestion of a $50,000 down payment is acceptable to you. You would be willing to carry the remaining amount at the current bank rate. Your asking price for the three is $325,000. You would lease the stores for $1,000 per month each (total of $36,000 per year). You would be willing to give a one-year renewable lease. The specific details would have to be worked out through your attorney.

You'll want to be careful in telling about sales and profits, for you don't want to misinform Ms. Sabatini. You would be quite willing to show her your accounting records. The store grossed $1,641,500 in sales last year; and you paid taxes on income of $52,500. (You may create any additional financial information you feel is necessary.)

Ms. Sabatini's question about competition is somewhat difficult to answer. Not one of the three stores is within a half mile of another convenience store; but all are near competing stores (grocery stores, drug stores, and such).

There is much more information that Ms. Sabatini would need to know before buying. You feel she will want to come to Albuquerque to inspect the stores and the records first. Your letter will tell her enough to help her decide whether the trip would be worthwhile.

Inquiries, prospective employees

25. You, the new owner of Round-the-Clock Stores are looking for a qualified person to serve as manager. Round-the-Clock is a chain of five convenience stores, all located in your community. When you bought the

operation last month, you had expected the old manager to continue, but soon you learned that he had other plans.

Your search for a replacement produced a number of good applicants. Kevin D. Stumpf appears to be the best qualified of the lot. But you'll need to check his references before taking action. He lists a Ms. Cindy Rashka as his last supervisor. Ms. Rashka is the manager of Toby's Corner, a convenience store in Central City. Stumpf reported that he worked as assistant manager at Toby's for over two years, and that he left because of personal problems (a divorce) that led to a decision to move back to his home town (your city).

The person you need as your manager will have to know all aspects of convenience-store operations—buying, selling, record-keeping, personnel, maintenance, inventory control. He or she will have to be willing to work hard and to put in long hours. And he or she must be honest beyond question, for money handling is involved. And so is handling people, for Round-the-Clock has 11 employees—all under the control of the manager.

You think Stumpf can handle the job. Before you hire him you'll write Ms. Rashka to see if she has information that will support your belief. You will ask her the questions which will get all the appropriate information she can give you.

26.   In your office as manager of Empire Department Stores you have just completed interviewing Sherry Cohen for the position of head of your sporting goods department. She is the best of the applicants you have seen— well qualified by experience, personable, enthusiastic. And she appears to have a genuine interest in sporting goods and sports (especially golf, tennis, fishing, and skiing).

Before you hire anyone for the job, you will check his or her references carefully, so now you must write Belford A. Washington of Canyon City. Mr. Washington formerly owned and operated a small sporting goods store (The Sports Shop), and he was Ms. Cohen's boss for four and a half years. As Ms. Cohen explained it, she was Washington's assistant and was involved in most store operations—buying, selling, record-keeping. During the last year she practically ran the store, because Washington was in poor health through this period. She left only when Washington closed the store and retired.

The person who takes over as head of your sporting goods department must know sporting goods inside and out. He or she must know how to buy and to sell. He or she must have an appreciation for precise record-keeping, for maintaining inventories, and generally for maximizing profits. Because the department has two other employees, the head also must be able to manage people; and he or she must be self motivated, for Empire's departments operate almost as independent units. The head is free to buy and sell and to hire and fire, with a minimum of interference from top management.

Now you will write Mr. Washington at his Canyon City home. You will ask all the right questions—those that will help you decide whether Sherry Cohen is right for this one job.

27.   Play the role of president of the Singing Woods Country Club and write a letter inquiring about the qualifications of Doyle D. Brasher, an applicant for the position of Club manager. For the past few days, you and your board have been interviewing applicants for the position; and Basher appears to be the best of the lot. Before you take action, however, you will check the man's record on the job he has held for the past seven years—that of manager of the Sunset Racquet Club.

In his interview, Brasher explained that, although he is satisfied with his job at Sunset, he would prefer a larger operation such as yours. His salary at Sunset is well below what you can offer; so you see his explanation as a logical one.

Managing a club such as Singing Woods is no small undertaking. The Club manager directly supervises 27 employees, ranging from unskilled kitchen help to administrative specialist. He or she must also be knowledgeable in all areas of restaurant operations, for running the Club dining facility is a major function of the manager. Especially important is the manager's ability to get along with the Club's membership, for each considers the manager to be working for her or him. Then, of course, there is the overriding need for the manager to have good general administrative knowledge and ability. Running a club with a $5 million budget is indeed a challenging assignment.

With the managers job requirements in mind, you must now write the letter that will get for you and the board the information needed from the people at Sunset. Address the letter to Ms. Molly O. Cooter, Club president. Brasher has informed her of his interest in your job.

28.   Debbie Ramsey appeared to be a highly qualified person when you interviewed her for a sales job with the Silver Shield Insurance Company. The job involves calling on company executives and selling Silver Shield's group medical insurance program. The field is highly competitive; but although sales are made infrequently, they result in big commissions.

Silver Shield salespeople must be of high quality, for primarily they call on high-level business executives. They also must be aggressive and personable. And, of course, they must have good oral communication skills. Silver Shields people are paid solely on a commission basis, so you seek only people who are highly motivated. All in all, the person you seek must be a super salesperson.

You think Debbie Ramsey may meet these requirements. You hope to confirm your appraisal with evaluations by people who know her abilities. One of these people is Geoffrey Gotfried, who supervised her work for six years on the sales force of Doodley-Cross, Inc., seller of office furniture and supplies. At Doodley-Cross she called on business accounts. She quit Doodley-Cross, she explained, because she wanted a more challenging and rewarding assignment.

Now you must write Gotfried and ask all the appropriate questions about this promising applicant.

29.   As the principal of J. F. Baily Academy you think you have found the ideal person for the history teaching vacancy. She is Ms. Helen Vorman,

a true professional with 17 years experience with the Oak Hills Independent School District. She has moved to your community to be near her ailing mother.

Baily Academy is a private boarding school with classes ranging from junior-high through high school. Emphasis is on scholarship and character-building. Strict discipline is expected from all faculty. Only teachers of the highest character and impeccable morals are considered. Because its primary benefactor, J. F. Baily, was a deeply religious man, the school places high emphasis on Christian values and expects its faculty to do likewise.

You think Ms. Vorman meets all your requirements. But you'll want to get the appraisal of her last superior. So you will write a letter to Ms. Tina Martinez, principle of the Oak Hills High School. You will ask all the questions needed to get the information you should have to make your decision.

30. Assume the role of manager of Royal Towers, a large modern office building in Big City. You are in the process of hiring a new maintenance superintendent, and you think you have found the right person. He is Timothy Hornsby, until recently assistant maintenance manager at Central State University. Hornsby reports that he left Central to go into business for himself. Now that his business has failed, he is seeking employment.

The work for which you are considering Hornsby requires good administrative ability as well as some general technical knowledge. It involves supervising three technicians plus a janitorial staff of 15. And past experience has shown that managing such a group requires strong leadership qualities. Although outside technicians (such as electricians and plumbers) are called in for major problems, the maintenance staff handles all the minor emergencies. Thus the maintenance superintendent should know something about the electrical equipment, plumbing, heating, and such. From what Hornsby told you, you feel that his work at Central equipped him for the job. In addition, the job requires a high dedication to duty. When emergencies occur, the maintenance superintendent must be thoroughly dependable.

You will now write Mr. Daniel Q. Adamic, the superintendent of maintenance at Central State University to find out whether Hornsby is right for the job. You will ask all the specific questions required to get the information you must have.

31. Assume the role of administrator for the Elway Foundation. Founded by the late Elsie Elway, the Foundation consists of approximately $70 million in various assets. Among them is the Woodlands—the 140-year-old ancestral home of the Elway family. This palatial 54-room structure and its well-kept gardens and surrounding 1,200 acres of wilderness is maintained by the Foundation and is open to the public during daytime hours. For the past 30 years, maintenance of the gardens and surrounding grounds has been performed by able George Coppersmith, who unfortunately announced his retirement. So now you are looking for a replacement.

Among the applicants is Mary Ellen Gann, who reports 20 years of experience as a gardener with the Delta City Parks Department. She appears to be the best qualified of the applicants, but you will verify your impressions through an inquiry to her former supervisor. On her application she identifies this person as Nelson E. Overmiller, who is the director. Ms. Gann explained that she resigned from the Delta City job because her husband's failing health forced the family to move to your city so her husband could be admitted to the local Veterans Administration Hospital.

The person selected as caretaker of the Woodlands must have expert gardening skills, of course. But also, because the caretaker works without direct supervision, he or she must be self-motivated—and one who takes pride in maintaining a showplace. The estate has an elaborate security system; but the caretaker is privy to its operations and has access to all of the house and grounds. Thus he or she must be a highly respectable person and honest beyond question.

Now you must write the letter that will get what Mr. Overmiller knows about Ms. Gann's qualifications for the job. Make certain that you ask all the appropriate questions.

32.   Write a letter that will get the information you need in deciding whether Dirk Steiner should be a sales clerk for The Man's Store. You are the manager of this exclusive clothing store in your city.

The sales clerks in The Man's Store must be from the right cultural background. They must fit in with the store's customers, most of whom are business executives and professional in the upper-middle and high-income groups. They must know quality merchandise and have a current knowledge of men's fashions. They must be personable and intelligent; and, of course, they must know how to sell—but not with high pressure. At The Man's Store the customer's satisfaction comes first.

In Steiner's application he noted that he last worked for Herb's Clothiers in Prairie Town. Following the death of his mother, he moved back to his home (your city) to take care of the family home and other properties he inherited. He listed Mr. Herbert E. Durflinger as his superior at Herb's Clothiers. So you will write Herb for all the information you need on this good prospect.

Personnel reports

33.   Place yourself in the role of Cindy Rashka, manager of Toby's Corner and answer the inquiry about Kevin Stumpf from the Round-the-Clock owner. (See Problem 25 for background information.)

You know Kevin Stumpf well, and you can recommend him highly. In fact, you'd like to have him back as an employee. During the two years he worked for you, he proved to be a hard and willing worker. He displayed good initiative and learned the convenience-store business fast. He often worked extra hours when need dictated, and he never complained. You have no reason to question his honesty.

About his potential as a manager, you can only speculate. You feel he has sufficient knowledge of the operations of a convenience store to do this part of the manager's work. But you don't know how well he could handle people. He had no supervisory duties with you. Judging from your observations, however, you feel he has the qualifications. He gets along well with his associates. Perhaps his one shortcoming is his somewhat quiet personality. He gives the appearance of being shy and distant. You discussed this matter with him and feel that he has improved.

With the information presented above forming the basis of your message, you will write a report that will be fair to all concerned. Address it to Calvin Fontenot, the Round-the-Clock owner.

34. It is satisfying to you, Belford A. Washington, to write a report on Sherry Cohen in response to an inquiry from the manager of the Empire Department Stores (see Problem 26 for background information).

Sherry was an excellent employee throughout her four and a half years with you. You can report that she knows sports and sporting goods well, and she has a genuine interest in keeping her knowledge current. No doubt her active interest in a wide variety of sports contributes to her knowledge.

During the latter part of her time with you, you practically turned over store operations to her. Overall, she performed well. She made a few buying mistakes, which resulted in excessive inventory losses. But she accepted your criticisms of her mistakes, and you feel she learned from them. You regret that she had to lose her job when you closed the business.

On whether she can manage subordinants, you can only judge from what you know about her, for she had no supervisory assignments with you. She gets along well with people, and she appears to have good leadership characteristics. She is aggressive and personable. And she has an appreciation for fairness and duty. Thus, you feel that she could handle subordinates well.

Using the information above, as well as other information you may think of which is consistent with it, write the report that will present a fair appraisal of Sherry Cohen. Address it to Cynthia Roundtree, the Empire manager.

35. Assume the role of Molly O. Cooter, president of Sunset Racquet Club, and answer the inquiry about Doyle B. Brasher, the club's manager. (For background information, see Problem 27.)

You have known that Brasher has been looking into the position at Singing Woods, for he has kept you posted. You like Brasher, and you like the job he has done for Sunset. But you want to do what is right for all concerned, and you can't blame the man for wanting to move up to a better position.

When Brasher came to Sunset seven years ago, the Club was losing money, primarily through its restaurant operation. Within a year Brasher turned the operation around, and the Club's finances have been in the black ever since. In turning operations around, Brasher made a number of personnel changes—hiring and firing until he had the staff he wanted. He streamlined the menus, initiated tighter controls on food inventories, reduced serving hours, and shopped frugally for better prices. In the process, he kept the

quality of the food high. The volume of sales increased. In general, the
Club has become a well-organized, efficient, and productive operation under
Brasher's management.

In all fairness, however, you must concede that not all Club members
like Brasher. Probably because he is a strong administrator, he has angered
some members. Some feel he was ruthless in firing the old employees; and
some did not like his policy of restricting hours for food service. You like
the man personally; but there are those who feel that he is too quiet—
that he does not have an outgoing personality. You agree that he does not
have a sparkling personality. He is not loud and gregarious. But you think
that he is a pleasant enough fellow. You'll want to cover his personality in
your report, but you'll choose your words carefully. Brasher doesn't deserve
to be eliminated on this point.

The foregoing comments will form the basis of your response to the
questions asked. You may add more information as long as it is consistent
with the information given. Address the letter to Emanuel A. Timms.

36. You, Geoffrey G. Gotfried, have received an inquiry about Debbie
Ramsey. For six years Debbie worked under your direction selling office
furnishings and supplies for Doodley-Cross, Inc. (See Problem 28 for background information.) Now she is seeking employment on the sales force of
the Silver Shield Insurance Company.

You'll write a good report on Debbie, for she is a good salesperson as
well as a good human being. She is highly intelligent and can meet and
talk with people at the highest professional levels. She has the charm, wit,
and communication skills that are needed for an ideal sales personality. You
are especially impressed with her self-motivation. She worked hard and she
was successful. In fact, at the time she left, she was leading the force. You
feel she has great potential in sales.

Perhaps because she is highly motivated, you sometimes felt that Debbie
was too aggressive in her sales approach. She knew how to apply pressure
in selling, and sometimes she may have gone too far. In fact, some of your
old-time customers complained to you about her. But apparently most of
her customers did not object to her tactics, for her sales continued to increase
throughout her six years with you. You'll want to be careful in handling
this point, for it should not eliminate Debbie from the job. In fact, it could
be that aggressive selling is just what Silver Shield wants.

Write the letter, making sure that you answer all questions and that
you are truthful and fair to all. Address it to Henrietta Buffington, who is
the sales manager at Silver Shield Insurance.

37. Now you are Tina Martinez, principal of Oak Hills High School.
You have the assignment of answering an inquiry about one of your former
subordinants, Helen Vorman (see Problem 29 for background information).

You can give a good report on Ms. Vorman, for she performed her
job well. She is a highly competent teacher of history. She likes teaching
and she likes children. Her standards were consistently high, and she got
good results from her students. She got good results without being a strong

disciplinarian in the classroom. Rather, she had a way of gaining the students' respect and stimulating them without cracking the whip. By some standards she may be regarded as soft. But her classes were orderly, and the students learned history.

As far as you know, her morals are high; and you feel that over the years she contributed to the character-building of her students. Certainly she set a role-model for them. She especially enjoyed working with the problem children and often spent after-duty hours counseling and helping them. You don't know much about her religious convictions. Because yours is a public school, you have had no occasion to inquire into this aspect of her life. But you know that she lives by Christian principles. She is truly a good person. The fact that she resigned her position to take care of her terminally ill mother is evidence of her goodness.

Address your letter to Cecil B. Laughton, the principal of J. F. Baily Academy. If you feel that additional facts are needed, you may supply them; but keep them consistent with the other information.

38. Answer the inquiry from the Royal Towers manager about your former assistant, Timothy Hornsby. (See Problem 30 for background information.) You are Daniel Q. Adamic, superintendent of maintenance at Central State University.

Although Hornsby left Central about two years ago to set up his own appliance repair business, you remember him well. You are surprised that his business failed, for the man has a good knowledge of mechanical things. You feel that he has the technical knowledge that the Royal Towers job requires.

For the 11 years Hornsby was at Central, he worked hard. He was highly dependable. As well as you can remember, he never missed a day of work; and he willingly worked overtime when he was needed.

While he was with you, Hornsby was assigned the duty of supervising some of the maintenance workers. He performed reasonably well, you feel; but he had a few minor problems. Apparently he expected and demanded work from his subordinates; and when he didn't get it, he reacted with anger. Some felt that he was crude and autocratic in his actions. But he got results. Overall, you feel that he did a reasonably good job of supervising.

With the facts presented above in mind, write the response that will give the Royal Towers manager (her name is Shannon Deere) what she needs. You may bring in additional details if needed, but keep them consistent with the information given.

39. In the role of Nelson E. Overmiller, director of the Delta City Parks Department, write an objective personnel report on Mary Ellen Gann. (See Problem 31 for background information.)

Ms. Gann is indeed a competent gardener. She knows gardening and she is a willing and able worker. Her performance record indicates that she works well without supervision. You could count on her to carry out an assignment as long as her husband's health permitted. She did miss work occasionally when he became seriously ill. Perhaps, now that he is under full-time care in the Veterans Administration Hospital, this situation won't recur. You regard Ms. Gann as one who takes genuine pride in her work. You regretted losing her when she resigned to be near her husband, whose failing health forced him to be hospitalized.

As far as you know, Ms. Gann is honest. You have no reason to believe otherwise. All the evidence you have indicates that she has good character. And although it may not be important for the caretaker's job at the Woodlands, she is a very friendly and pleasant person.

Your report will be based on the information presented above. If necessary, you may add information as long as it is consistent with the other facts. Address the report to Bettie Flores, administrator of the Elway Foundation.

40.   Assume the role of Herburt E. Durflinger and write an evaluation of Dirk Steiner. (See Problem 32 for background information.) Steiner worked for you for four years. He quit about a month ago because he felt it necessary to move following his mother's death. As you understand his situation, Steiner has properties to take care of in your city.

You can recommend Steiner for the position at The Man's Store. While he worked for you, he developed a thorough and current knowledge of men's fashions. He was a dependable worker who rarely missed work; and he got along well with his associates. In addition, he proved to be a personable, cultured, and mature young man with a good gift of conversation. You feel he'll fit in well with the high-level customers of The Man's Store.

The one possible negative bit of information you can think of is Steiner's sales technique. Although he is a good salesperson, at times he can become a bit aggressive—more so than you felt was appropriate for your store. You discussed the matter with him a few times and feel that he responded well to your suggestions. You feel that this is a matter that can be corrected— if it hasn't already been corrected.

Address your letter to Horris T. Ruiz, manager of The Man's Store. If other information is needed, you may supply it; but keep it consistent with the other facts.

Claims

41.   You have just learned that there was a mix-up on the gifts your Midway Industrial Sales Company gave to its customers for Christmas last month. You, Midway's director of marketing, had ordered the five-pound assorted cheese packages from the Land O' Lakes Cheese Company. Your sales people report they are getting thank-yous for the three-pound packages. After checking your records carefully, you find that you ordered and paid for the five-pound packages—$14.95 each, including mailing. The Land O' Lakes brochure shows the three-pound packages selling for $9.95.

Obviously, something went wrong. Somebody at Land O' Lakes apparently made an error, probably inadvertently. Something has to be done. Besides the difference in money, you are concerned about what your good customers think of you. Midway always has given quality gifts at Christmas, as do its competitors. So you will write a letter to the Land O' Lakes people. You will explain what went wrong and what you want them to do about it. Even though it is well after Christmas, you think the firm should send every one of your 1,462 customers a two-pound cheese package with an explanatory letter that clears Midway of all blame for the error. As you see it, Land O' Lakes should bear any losses and inconveniences involved. Address the letter to the Land O' Lakes sales manager (you don't know the name).

42. You are Veronica Chubbock, owner of Veronica's Gift Shop. Today you received from Manhattan Imports, Inc., the shipment for which you have been waiting for the past few days. You were hoping it would arrive in time for your advertised sale, which begins a week from Friday.

When you opened the carton you found inside almost total destruction. The two dozen sets of gilded Venetian glass wine decanters with six matching goblets were mainly pieces of glass. In fact, only 3 of the 24 decanters escaped damage and 21 of the 72 goblets. You don't know the value of the individual pieces, for you bought complete sets. The price per set was $192.

Inspection of the packaging quickly revealed the problem. Whereas in past shipments the glass was securely packed in shredded paper, these packages had very little. The decanters and goblets were carelessly stacked together and had extra space that left room for jostling. Also, the boxes were not marked "fragile." So probably they received no special handling by the freight company. Apparently, someone in the shipping department slipped up.

You are confident that Manhattan will make good the loss, but that isn't your total concern. Your advertised sale begins next week, and these decanters and goblets are one of your features. So you will write a claim letter that will tell what happened and ask for a rush replacement in time for the sale.

43. You have been very busy over the past week getting your City Furniture ready for its annual spring sale. This sale has become a tradition in the area, attracting hundreds of the local citizens. They come because they like the genuine discounts that are offered and because they can count on City Furniture for service and quality.

Your plans were running smoothly until today's delivery of patio furniture from Outside Living, Inc. Your local advertising had featured six-foot carrousel patio umbrellas at $79.50. And you had ordered six dozen—enough, you thought, to satisfy the demand. You received six dozen umbrellas, all right, but they are not fit for sale. All of them bear fire or smoke damage. Some have badly scorched fabric; and all have a strong odor of smoke. Not one is fit for sale. You can't explain what happened, and neither can the shippers. Apparently the problem originated with Outdoor Living.

Now you must write the Outdoor Living people for correction of the problem. You'd like rapid replacement of the umbrellas—in time for your sale, which begins in nine days. If they can't make it, you'll just cancel the order. You don't expect to pay freight charges again, and you'll need to know what to do with the damaged umbrellas.

44. Assume you are visiting your crusty great-aunt Myrtle, owner of Myrtle's Clothiers in Big Beaver Junction. Last month she sent a rush order to Bronco, Inc., for three dozen Bronco Jr. jeans in assorted sizes—"like your Mr. Moody sold me last June," she specified in her order.

A short time later the order arrived, and immediately she displayed the jeans. She sold some. But, in short time, some of the purchasers returned their jeans in badly faded condition. Obviously, the colors are not fast. Aunt Myrtle became very upset, went to her desk in the back of the store, and wrote this letter to the Bronco sales manager:

> Dear Mr. Brady:
> What are you people trying to put over on me? Here I've been buying from you for 35 years and you push some cheap jeans on me. That last shipment of 3 dozen of Bronco Jr. jeans faded something terrible. I got customers bringing them back as fast as I sell them. I am taking what's left off the shelf. I want my money back on all of them. Tell me what to do with the 30 I got left.
> Sincerely,

Aunt Myrtle showed you the letter with some pride. "But I'm not educated like you," she said. "Why don't you rewrite it for me—like they teach you to do in college." So now you will rewrite the letter. Use your good logical imagination to help you with any additional details which you might need.

45. Play the role of Professor Cynthia Crabtree. Last month you took a group of 16 industrial management students on a 15-day tour of Japanese industry. You worked up the tour through Asian Tours, Inc., of Tokyo. You bargained for a package costing $2,800 per person, including all travel, housing, and food.

The trip turned out to be excellent in most respects. There was one drawback. Luncheons (except for one sponsored by the university you visited) were not covered. The agreement with Asian clearly specified that they would be covered. You conclude that the out-of-pocket cost for luncheons for each of the participants was about $8 per day—a total of $112 per person for the trip.

You will insist that Asian return this part of the total cost. It can do this individually (to each of the 16 students plus you), or it can send the total to you and you will give the students their shares. Write the letter that will get this action.

46. Things have not gone well for you today in your work as manager of the Bon Voyage Motel. It has been one problem after another. Now, early this morning, your maintenance worker comes in with another broken patio chair from the swimming pool area.

Reports of broken chairs are nothing sensational in your business; but four chairs in one week are! Especially is it unusual since the Ironware Furniture Manufacturing Company described these chairs as ones that "can take all you can give them." On the basis of this claim, you bought two dozen; and now after only one week four have become unusable. All seem to have the same problem: the metal tubing forming the legs has been bent or broken.

So you decide to write the Ironware people about their product. You want immediate replacement of the four damaged chairs, and you will expect replacement of others that break within the year covered by the warranty. If this arrangement is not satisfactory, you want to return all the chairs ·and get your money back. If you need additional details, you may supply them.

47. Assume the role of manager of The Clothes Horse, a leading men's store in your city. Your order from the Sabre Shirt Company arrived this morning. When you unpacked the carton you were terribly disappointed at what you saw.

The five dozen Sabre shirts in assorted sizes are all badly soiled. It appears that some type of liquid spilled on them, causing scattered large blotches of stain. Apparently, the damage occurred before the shirts were packed, for the cartons show no evidence of the liquid. And clearly the freight company is not at fault.

You certainly can't sell these shirts, and you won't pay for them. But you do need shirts to sell—and in a hurry. Your stock is very low. So you will write the Sabre people telling them what happened and asking for a quick correction of the problem. You'll also need to cover the disposition of the unwanted shirts.

48. Ten months ago you ordered from the Stone Weave Carpet Company 70 square yards of its Stone Weave, Jr., carpeting for your office suite. You thought you had made a wise choice, especially since you got the 20 percent sale discount (total cost of $1,470). In addition, you thought you could believe all the advertising claims you had heard the Stone Weave people make—about how their product would wear almost forever and never fade.

In recent weeks, however, you have noticed a change in color near the entrance area. This area is bathed in sunlight every sunny afternoon; but you expected Stone Weave to withstand the sun's rays. It is now apparent that this product doesn't stand up to their claim, and you want something done about it.

So you decide to write the company and ask for your money back. You'll forget installation charges as payment for the ten months of use you got from the carpeting. Of course, there is the chance that you got a bad batch. So you would consider replacement of the carpeting—with a written guarantee against fading.

Adjustment grants

49. You, the sales manager for Land O' Lakes Cheese Company, are embarrassed. After receiving the claim letter from Midway Industrial Sales (see Problem 41 for background information), you checked the records. Its claim is correct. You sent its 1,462 customers three-pound packages instead of the five-pound packages it ordered. Apparently the person in charge of assembling the shipment misread the hand-written order. Your inspection

of the order shows that the five does resemble a three; but the listed price should have cleared the confusion. You discussed the matter with the shipping crew and instituted a procedure to double check all orders in the future. You are confident that such errors will not recur.

Your attention now turns to correcting the damage done to your relations with Midway. You would like to keep this lucrative account, but to do so you'll have to change its thinking about your company's service. So you will do your very best to regain the goodwill lost.

You feel that you have no choice but to agree to Midway's request to send two-pound packages to each of its 1,462 customers. By doing this, Land O' Lakes will suffer a small loss; but you feel that it will profit in the long run. Also, you'll send an explanatory letter with each gift package. In fact, you'll write the explanatory letter now and send a copy along with the claim-granting letter. Then, to regain any lost confidence in your service, you'll explain how your double-checking system should eliminate such errors in the future.

Address this goodwill-restoring adjustment letter to Rebecca Wunderlich, who is director of marketing for Midway.

50.   You are genuinely concerned about Veronica Chubbock's problem with the Venetian glass decanters and goblets you shipped her. And it's a costly error for Manhattan Imports as well (see Problem 42 for background information). You will do what you can to correct the situation in time for her coming promotion.

Investigation of your shipping operation reveals one possible explanation. The goods were shipped last Thursday when two of your experienced packers were on sick leave. Apparently the overworked shipping crew sealed the cartons before the protective packaging material was placed around the glass. And in their haste to get out the day's shipment, the crew failed to stamp the packages "fragile." There is really no excuse for such negligence, you know. But this was the first time two regular shipping clerks have ever been absent at any one time. If ever it happens again, you personally will see to it that proper procedures are used.

You will assemble immediately the replacements for all the broken merchandise. And you will send them out this afternoon by Blue Darter Motor Freight. The Blue Darter people have assured you that their driver will deliver the goods no later than Wednesday—in time for the sale, which begins Friday.

51.   Play the role of manager of customer relations for Outdoor Living, Inc. You have received a claim for adjustment from City Furniture Company. (See Problem 43 for background information.)

Your review of the facts of the case show that the claim is legitimate. In fact, it is embarrassing to Outdoor Living. Somehow, through error, fire-damaged umbrellas were sent. Six weeks ago there was a fire in the warehouse. The damage was significant. Supposedly, the damaged goods were moved to a secondary warehouse where they would be inspected and either destroyed or sold for salvage. Apparently, the umbrellas City Furniture received came from this damaged lot.

You are unable to explain the mistake further. The shipping personnel simply made a mistake. But, as one might expect, there has been a lot of confusion in the warehouse since the fire. Such a problem is not likely to recur.

You will ship the replacement umbrellas this very day—and in time to reach City Furniture for its annual sale. You have the guarantee of the Rocket Transfer Company that the goods will arrive Tuesday—three days before the sale begins. You will monitor the shipment personally to assure that it arrives on time. Also, you will do what you can in the letter to assure the City Furniture Company owner that this is a very unusual problem—that City can continue to expect the dependable service you have given it in the past.

Address the letter to Cyrus A. Vinitis, owner of City Furniture Company.

52. That last shipment of jeans you sent Myrtle's Clothiers was indeed as defective as she claimed in her letter to you. (See Problem 44 for background information.) The trouble stems from a purchase of defective material. You have confronted your supplier with the problem, and this company has given you a satisfactory adjustment. But that doesn't solve the problem with your customers who have been affected.

You will replace all three dozen of the jeans sent Myrtle's Clothiers with jeans of Bronco's traditional high quality. You want the defective jeans back, for you don't want them sold under your brand name. You will pay shipping expenses. You hope that you can make Myrtle understand that what happened was most unusual. It has not happened before. It won't happen again, your production people assured you, for they now test each bolt of fabric before using it.

In an additional effort to correct the damage done to your relations with Myrtle, you will send her a coupon good for a 10 percent discount on her next purchase. Perhaps it will help to compensate her for the inconvenience caused.

Now you must answer Myrtle Wilson's letter, granting her the adjustment and doing what you can to repair damaged relations.

53. As Tetsuro Hayanari, manager of Asian Tours, Inc., you must answer the claim letter made by Professor Cynthia Smythe. (See Problem 45 for background information.) Professor Smythe does indeed have a valid claim, and you will correct the problem. But you want to go further than just correcting the error, for you want to protect the good reputation your company has built over the years. What happened just isn't representative of your operation.

Apparently the new tour guide assigned to Professor Smythe's group confused this group with one scheduled for Ronald R. Smith and a group of American industrialists. The Smith group did not have luncheons included in their tour. When the tour guide called at the home office to determine whether lunches were included, the clerk answering the call pulled the Smith records rather than the Smythe records. So no lunches were included.

Now you will write Professor Smythe. You will send her a check for the $112 owed her personally. And you will send that amount to each of her tour members—with an appropriate explanation absolving the professor of any blame. You'll explain what happened as convincingly as you can in an effort to regain any lost confidence in your company.

54. In the role of Millicent Isaacs, manager of customer relations for Ironware Furniture Manufacturing Company, you must respond to the claim letter from Ivan K. Boros, manager of the Bon Voyage Motel. (See Problem 46 for background information.)

You are disappointed, of course, to learn that a customer has had a bad experience with your chairs. You will send replacements immediately, and you will promise replacements for any others that break within the 12-month warranty.

Because your chairs have been thoroughly tested to withstand more abuse than any competing chair on the market, you are curious to find the cause of the problem. So you discuss the matter with Ironware's production superintendent. From him you learn that a few weeks ago a lighter metal tubing was used in some chairs by mistake. Before the problem was detected, some chairs were completed and shipped out. No doubt the Bon Voyage Motel got some of these. This problem won't occur again, the production superintendent assures you, for recently instituted quality-control checks would quickly detect such product shortcomings.

Because you want to keep this good customer thinking favorable about your good product, you also want to explain what happened. Thus, a part of your letter will be devoted to an effort to regain lost confidence.

55. Play the part of the customer relations manager of Sabre Shirt Company. The claim letter from Owen A. Babbington, owner of The Clothes Horse, has reached your desk. You are thoroughly embarrassed. (See Problem 47 for background information.)

Immediately you figured out what happened. Someone in shipping sent The Clothes Horse those damaged shirts that had been returned by the freight company. These were scheduled to be given to charity. But apparently someone in shipping put them in the wrong cartons. After a quick check at the warehouse, your speculation is supported by fact.

Of course, someone should have checked the shirts before they were shipped; and because of this incident, a change in checking procedure has been made. The contents of every package will be checked against each order prior to sending any package. Thus, you can promise that such an error won't happen again.

You will send The Clothes Horse the five dozen Sabre Shirts as ordered. And you'll get them on the way today by Red Arrow Freight. The goods will arrive day after tomorrow, the trucker assured you. As for the soiled shirts, Babbington can send them back to you at your expense. Or, if he prefers, he can give them to a local charity.

56. Today you received a letter from Charmane George making a claim about unsatisfactory service from your Stone Weave carpeting. (See

Problem 48 for background information.) You are surprised, for Stone Weave is truly a remarkable product. Laboratory tests have shown conclusively that it is far better than its competition. It is particularly resistant to color fading, which is the basis for Ms. George's claim.

Because you have a one-year satisfaction-or-money-back guarantee, you'll honor this claim. So you elect to send her 70 square yards of Stone Weave to replace the faded carpeting. You will let her dispose of the old carpeting as she sees fit. But because you want to get to the cause of the problem, you will ask her to send you a sample of the faded area so you can run it through the laboratory. You feel that she must have got a bad run of carpeting, for mistakes can happen. You know your normal output just doesn't fade.

In addition to giving her new carpeting, you will attempt to regain any lost confidence in your product. This you will do through explanation and assurance that the new carpeting will hold its color. You'll back this claim with a money-back guarantee in writing.

Orders

57. As Maria Juarez, owner of Maria's Gift Shop, you are interested in several items described in an advertisement of The Bidell House, manufacturer of a line of reading accessories. The advertisement appears in this month's issue of your trade journal, *Novelty*. The advertisement urges that you buy the items from your suppliers; but "if they don't carry our products, order directly from us." Your suppliers don't carry Bidell products; so you will order from the manufacturer. The descriptions of the items you want read as follows:

> Pin-up expansion lamp, gold trimmed. Color choices: red, gold, black, olive, ivory (the gold has brown trim). $29.95 each (You want 2 each of the gold, red, and olive.)
>
> Magazine racks, choice of pecan or oak, 14 inches high by 15 inches wide, $32.95 each. (You want 3 of the oak.)
>
> Reader's end tables, with angled front piece, choice of pine or oak, 22 inches high by 19 inches wide, $64.50 each. (You want 3 of the oak.)

The advertisement states that shipping costs are extra and that you should allow $2 per item for shipping and handling cost for the lamp and magazine racks and $3 for each of the tables.

58. Assume that you are a buyer for Bigg City Department Store. You are looking over some of the sales literature you picked up at the National Toy Show in New York last week. You decide to order the following items from Fun and Games, Inc.:

> No. 717A. Jungle. A game for ages 9–90. Involved chance and wits as each player races to escape from the perils and density of the jungle. Games for 4, $8.45. Games for 8, $12.37. (You want four dozen of the small sets, two dozen of the large sets.)

No. 725C. Knock-out. Electronically controlled boxing figures respond to players' finger tip commands. Accumulation of blows landed leads to knock out victory. A game of skill for ages 8 and up. $32.40 each. (You want 25.)

No. 913D. Bugsy. Assortment of fuzzy parts (eyes, legs, bodies, wings, antenas, etc.) that can be put together to form a wide variety of funny bug-like creatures. For ages 4–10. Small kit $4.45, medium kit $6.25, large kit $7.75. (You want 60, 40, and 20, respectively, of the three sizes.)

The Fun and Games people advertised that they will ship COD; so you'll take them up on it.

59.   Among your various duties as training director at Haywood Chemical Company is that of getting current books for the company library. Periodically, you send out memos to the company executives for suggestions for new books. You now have accumulated enough to order. Four of the books wanted are published by Business Books, Inc., which is headquartered in San Francisco. So you will write this company an order for these four books. The descriptions as you received them from the executives read like this:

Why Japanese Management Won't Work in America, written by Katherine B. Boyd. It's listed as $24.95 on the jacket—a hardcover. There is a paperback, but don't know the price.

Peter A. Hollingsworth and Florence Devlin, *Profiles of Success,* sells for $7.95 in paperback and $19.95 in hardcover.

Lorain F. Schwartz's *Personal Characteristics and Management Style;* sells for $25.50 in hardcover.

Success Stories of American Business Executives, 3d ed., $21.95 in hardcover, $12.95 in paperback.

Because you have purchased from Business Books in the past, it will bill you for the total cost of the books plus shipping costs. You will order only one copy each of the first two books listed; but, because the last two are currently very popular, you will order three of each of them. Also, library policy is to order hardcover books rather than the paperbacks whenever there is a choice.

60.   From an advertisement in a newspaper, trade publication, or the like (your instructor will select the ad), write an order for a minimum of three items. Make sure that you have given all information needed to complete the sale, such as size, color, weight, and so on. Take care to cover the cost portion, including shipping cost and manner of payment. In addition, you will want to give proper shipping instructions.

Write the order in letter form and ask for rush shipment.

10 Correspondence: Indirect letters

AS EXPLAINED in Chapter 8, when the main message of a letter is bad news, usually you should write in the indirect order. Especially is this true when you must say no to a request or when the message tells of other disappointing news. The reason for this approach is that negative messages are received better when explanation precedes them. Explanation prepares the reader for the bad news. Also, it cushions the shock. Not to cushion the shock makes the letter unnecessarily harsh, and harshness destroys goodwill.

Of course, sometimes you may want to use directness in bad-news situations. If, for example, you feel that the negative answer will be accepted routinely, you may choose to use directness. Likewise, you may choose directness when you know your reader well and feel that he or she will appreciate frankness. Also, you may choose directness any time you are not concerned about goodwill. But such instances are not the rule. Usually, you will be wise to use indirectness in refusals.

In the following pages are analyses of the more common situations usually requiring indirect order. As in preceding chapters, the letter situations reviewed do not cover all possibilities; but they are the major ones. If you learn how to handle them, you should be able to apply your knowledge to the others.

Refused request

Refusal of a request definitely is a bad-news message. Your reader has asked you for something, and you must say no. How bad the news is, of course, varies from case to case. Even so, one has to strain the imagination to find a refusal that is good news. So, because the news is bad, usually you should write the request refusal in the indirect order.

Your reason for refusing indirectly has been mentioned, but its importance justifies repeating it. In the refusal letter you have two goals. The main one is to say no. The other is the goodwill goal. You could achieve the first goal simply by saying no—plainly and directly. Maintaining goodwill, however, requires more. It requires that you explain your decision, that you justify it. It requires that you convince your reader that the no answer is fair and reasonable. If you were to begin with the no answer, you would put the reader in an unhappy frame of mind. Then the unhappy reader would not be in the best mood to read your explanation. Your best strategy is to explain or justify first. Then from your explanation or justification you can move logically to your answer.

Strategy development

Developing the strategy which will maintain goodwill and justify your decision is largely a mental process. You will need to search through the facts of the one case for the best possible explanation to use. You will need to place yourself in your reader's position and attempt to view the situation as perceived through the reader's mental filter. Then you will have to work out something to say that will lead the reader to accept your decision as a fair and logical one.

It may be that your decision must be made because of a policy of your company. In such a case, you will be wise to think through the justification of your policy. If the policy is a fair one, as all policies should be, you should see reasons why it benefits your reader as well as your company. For example, a policy of refusing to accept returns on goods bought on sale obviously benefits the house; but it also benefits the customer. Only by cutting the costs of returns can the house give the customer the low sale price. A policy of selling only through retail outlets can be justified on the basis of providing better service to the customer. Such reasoning makes a convincing explanation.

In some instances, you may need to refuse simply because the facts of the case justify a refusal. When this is the case, your task of building goodwill is more difficult, for you can use little reader-viewpoint reasoning. You can only review the facts of the case which justify your decision, taking care not to accuse or insult. Probably your best strategy would be to appeal to the reader's sense of fair play.

Each letter situation, of course, will have its own set of facts for you to evaluate. In the end, you should develop a reasoning which should work on your one reader in the one case.

Opening contact and setup of the plan

With your strategy in mind, you should next turn to the task of putting it into letter form. Usually, you cannot just blurt out your explanation or justification, for such directness would be just as awkward as beginning with the refusal. Instead, your best course is to begin with some comment which meets the reader on neutral ground. It should imply neither a yes nor a no answer. It should be on the subject enough to clearly inform that you are writing about the reader's request. In this regard, you may also include an incidental reference to the reader's letter somewhere in the opening. Most important of all, the opening should set up the presentation of your strategy which will justify your decision.

How to meet these requirements is explained best through illustration. So let us look at some. First, take the case of refusing an association's request for a donation to its scholarship fund. This opening would meet the requirements well:

> Your organization is doing a commendable job of educating its needy children. It deserves the help of those who are in a position to give it.

The beginning on-subject comment clearly marks the letter as a response to the inquiry. It implies neither a yes nor a no answer. With the statement "It deserves the help of those who are in a position to give it," the opening sets up the explanation. The explanation will point out that the company is not in a position to help.

Or take another example—this one the beginning of a letter refusing a professor's request for personnel information. The request must be denied because too much work would be involved in assembling the information. The company simply cannot spare the workers for the task. The best it can do is to permit the professor or his staff to go through company records and get the information. The following words set up the strategy:

> Your interesting study of executive characteristics described in your July 3 letter should be a helpful contribution to management literature. Certainly it is a project deserving as much help as businesses are able to give it.

Note how these words begin on subject so that the reader recognizes them as a response to the inquiry. Note, also, that the words are neutral. They give no indication of the answer. Finally, note how the strategy of the letter is set up with the words saying that the project is one "deserving as much help as businesses are able to give it." The plan of the following explanation is to show that in this case the company is not able to help to the extent of the request.

Presentation of the reasoning

As we have implied, the reasoning which justifies your decision should flow logically from your opening. Your opening sets it up; so now you present whatever facts and reasoning you have selected to justify your decision. You present it as convincingly as you can.

In presenting your strategy convincingly, you will need to make good use of the rules of emphasis. You may need to highlight the happier aspects of your problem and to subordinate the gloomier ones. You will need to watch your words carefully, working to avoid the negatives which may offend a sensitive reader. Also, you will need to make good use of the you-viewpoint in your presentation. Since your effort will be designed to change your reader's thinking (more specifically, to convince him or her of your way of thinking), you will need to consider carefully the effects of every word and thought which go into this part of your letter.

Positive handling of the refusal

Your handling of the refusal logically follows your reasoning. If you have built the groundwork of explanation and fact convincingly, the refusal comes as a logical conclusion. And it comes as no surprise. If you have done your job well, it may even be supported by your reader. Even so, because it is the most negative part of your message, you will need to avoid overemphasizing it. You will want to say it quickly, clearly, and positively. And you will want to keep it away from positions of emphasis.

In stating your refusal quickly, you should use a minimum of words. To labor the point for three or four sentences, when a single clause would do the job, emphasizes the refusal. You should use not one word more than is necessary.

In stating the refusal clearly, you will need to make certain that there is no doubt about your decision. Sometimes, in the effort to be positive, we become evasive and unclear. For example, the writer who uses the words "it would be better if . . ." to carry the refusal would not communicate the decision to all people. Equally vague would be refusals made with words like "these facts clearly support the policy of. . . ."

In making your refusal positive, you need to study carefully the effects of your words. Harsh negatives, such as "I refuse," "will not," and "cannot," clearly stand out. So do the timeworn apologies like "I deeply regret to inform you . . ." and "I am sorry to say. . . ." Usually, you can make your stand clear by a positive statement of policy. For example, do not write that your "policy does not cover damage to buildings not connected to the house." Instead, say that your "policy covers damage to the house only." Or instead of using words like "We must refuse," a wholesaler could deny a discount with something like "We can grant discounts only when. . . ."

If you can make a compromise of any kind, you may use it to cover your refusal. That is, by saying what you can do, you can clearly imply what you cannot do. For example, if you write "The best we can do is . . . " you make it clear that you cannot do what the reader has requested. Yet you do it in the most positive way the situation will permit.

Off-subject goodwill close

Even though you handle the refusal skillfully, it is the most negative part of your message. The news is disappointing, and it is likely to put your reader in an unhappy state of mind. If you are to achieve your goodwill objective, you must move the reader from this unhappy state. So, in the close of your letter, you should shift to thoughts that are more pleasant— to off-subject material about happier things.

What you may include as subject matter for a particular letter depends, again, on the facts of the situation. It should be positive talk appropriate to the one case. If you have made a counterproposal, for example, you could discuss some aspect of it. If the reader's request concerns a project, you could make some suggestion concerning it, or perhaps express a wish for its success. In fact, you may use anything which makes appropriate subject matter for the situation, as long as it serves your goal of goodwill building.

Ruled out are the timeworn but negative final apologies or requests for understanding. To end with "Again, may I say that I regret that we must refuse . . ." or "I sincerely hope that you understand why we make the decision" clearly parades the negative views through the reader's mind.

Cases in refusal strategy

Good tact and strategy in a refusal are illustrated by the case of an office manager who refuses the request of a trade-book author. The author has asked the office manager for some of the best letters in the company's files. She wants to use them as examples in a correspondence guidebook she is writing. The request is an unreasonable one, for it would require going through many file drawers—perhaps all 40,000 of the company's letters on file. So the office manager must refuse.

In building the strategy for her refusal, the office manager concludes that the author will certainly want quality letters in the book, for the book will be no better than the letters. But not just any clerk can recognize quality letters. The work will require someone with ability. And because of the volume of work needed, it will require time. So the office manager selects a compromise. She will invite the author to use the files personally.

Her letter follows the general plan suggested in preceding pages. It begins away from the request—on neutral ground as far as the answer is concerned. But it is on the subject of the inquiry, and it sets up the explanation which follows. The explanation proceeds quickly, using a positive you-view-point approach. It presents the refusal without using a single negative word. It tells what the company can do and clearly implies what it cannot do. The close moves away from the refusal to more positive talk about the book.

Dear Ms. Howard:

Your *Correspondence Guidebook* should be a worthy contribution to business literature as well as a really practical aid to the business executive.

The practical value of the book, as I see it, depends largely on the quality of its illustrations. Your book demands illustrations that meet all the criteria of good correspondence. But getting the quality of illustration you need will require careful checking by someone who knows good writing, and going through the 40,000 letters in our files will take considerable time. For these reasons, I am sure you will understand why the best we can do is to make our files open to you or your staff. We would, of course, be happy to provide working space for you, and we assure you our very best cooperation. If you wish to use our files in this way, please let us know.

Please let us know, also, if we can help you further. We look forward to seeing the book. It is likely to get good use in the office here at Merrit & Company.

Sincerely,

The next illustration letter is a company's refusal of a request for a donation. The letter's opening words are on subject and clearly tell that this letter responds to the request. But the words are neutral. Note how the opening sets up the explanation which follows. The clear and logical explanation ties in with the opening. Using no negative words, the explanation leads smoothly to the refusal. The refusal is handled without negative words; yet it is clear. To say "the best we can do is . . ." also tells what cannot be done. The friendly close fits the one case.

Dear Ms. Cangelosi:

Your efforts to build the scholarship fund for the Association's needy children are most commendable. We wish you good success in your efforts for this worthy cause.

We here at Cottle's are always willing to assist worthy causes whenever we can. That is why every January we budget for the year the maximum amount we feel we are able to contribute to worthy causes. Then we distribute this amount among the various deserving groups as far as it will go. As our budgeted contributions for this year already have been made, the best we can do is to place your organization on our list for consideration next year.

We wish you the best of luck in your efforts to help educate the deserving children of the Association members.

Sincerely,

The following refusal illustrates good strategy in turning down a request to speak before a convention group. The letter begins on subject with a flattering comment about the meaning of the invitation. Then it sets up the explanation with a comment about the quality of the audience. Such a quality audience, the following explanation points out, deserves and expects a good presentation. But preparing good presentations takes time, which the writer does not have. The refusal is clear, even though it is implied by a suggestion for an alternate speaker. The wording is positive. The friendly close fits the one case.

Dear Mr. Gooch:

Your January 13 invitation to address the National Association of Administrators is a most distinct honor to me personally. I am well aware of the high quality of NAA's membership.

Presenting a major paper to this quality group deserves a thorough and competent effort. Obviously, such an effort requires time. Because my time is fully committed to a writing project for the months ahead, I must suggest that you get someone who has the time to do the job right. May I recommend Ms. Paula Perkins of my staff? Paula is an outstanding speaker and an expert on the subject of women's progress in management.

If I can help you further in your efforts to get speakers, please write me again. I wish you good luck with the program.

Sincerely,

Adjustment refusals

Claims which you must refuse make another bad-news situation. Fortunately, most claims are legitimate, and most companies try hard to do what they can to correct any damage or mistakes they may have caused. But sometimes claims are not well founded. They may be based on wrong information. They may even approach fraudulence. On such occasions the company is likely to say no.

Saying no clearly and diplomatically in such cases requires your utmost effort in strategy and writing skill. You may be dealing with someone who is worked up emotionally about the situation giving rise to the claim—someone whose mental filter contains incomplete knowledge and biased judgments on the case. This person may honestly feel wronged, and that the only right action is for you to come through with an adjustment. Of course, some will know that their claims are weak, perhaps even fraudulent. Even these people have biased opinions on the matter. All are likely to resist any effort to justify a claim refusal.

Determination of basic strategy

Your strategy in refusing a claim involves finding some way of overcoming your reader's negative mental reaction to your message. Your refusal, of course, is based on legitimate reasons. The facts support you, but your reader is not aware of them. To win your case, you must present these facts; and you must make the reader believe them. In your presentation, you must appeal to the reader's basic human honesty. Because you are dealing with a matter on which there is initial disagreement, you will need to select your words with great care, giving thought to the connotations they are likely to form in your reader's mind. Unquestionably, the problem requires the indirect approach and the utmost in strategy.

You should begin planning your strategy in adjustment refusal situations by reviewing all the facts involved. Your review should bring out the facts of the case as completely and clearly as you can identify them. Of course, they should support a refusal; otherwise, your action is not justified. Then, with the facts in mind, you should search for possibilities of presenting them so that they will be accepted. This effort is a mental one. You should place yourself in the reader's position, limit yourself to the reader's knowledge of the situation, and search for means of presenting your case to him or her. You should look for reader-viewpoint reasoning wherever it logically can be supported. Then, with your strategy in mind, you should fit it into the general plan presented in following paragraphs.

Opening setup of the reasoning

Your objective in the opening is to set up the review of facts which will justify your decision. Because you are answering a letter the reader has written to you, you will need to make this matter clear. Probably the best way of doing this is through an incidental reference to the reader's letter early in your letter. A subject line would also do the job; but because the letter has a bad-news message, it would have to be neutral about the decision. Nothing like "Refusal of your July 19 claim" would be appropriate.

In setting up a review of the facts involved, you will need to exercise your logical imagination. You will need to find some point on which you can begin communicating. It should be a point which in no way implies a yes or a no answer. It should be pertinent to the situation, for something far afield would create a startling effect. And perhaps most important of all, it should lead to the review of facts which will follow.

The subject matter for your opening contact could be almost anything which fits the situation. It could be some point on which you and the reader can agree—perhaps some point in the claim letter. For example, in a claim letter about an air-conditioning unit which was not cooling a house satisfactorily, the adjustment correspondent used this opening sentence:

> You are correct in believing that a two-ton Deep Kold window unit should take care of the ordinary five-room house.

The sentence makes contact on a point of common agreement. At the same time, it sets up the reasoning which will justify the refusal: that the house in question has many features which make it far from the ordinary five-room house. A statement showing concern for the reader's well-being might be effective in some cases. An interior decorator might begin a refusal with these contact words:

> Assisting young couples to enjoy beautifully decorated homes at budget prices is one of our most satisfying goals. We do all that we reasonably can to reach it.

From this goodwill contact, the writer could shift smoothly to reasoning which shows that the company does all one can reasonably expect of it, and that making the adjustment is beyond that reasonable limit.

In some cases a statement showing mutual respect for honest intentions could form the basis for opening contact:

> Your straightforward report of the 13th shows that you are one who wants to get all the facts and to base a fair decision on them. That is why I am confident that you will want to consider the following information.

Clearly, the statement sets up a review of the new information which follows. The new information, of course, will justify the refusal.

Presentation of reasoning

The reasoning which supports your decision should follow your opening as a logical outgrowth of it. Your objective in this part of your message is to convince. To convince, you should first have sound logical reasoning. Far-fetched facts and unsupported claims just will not do the job. Your information should be believable.

In addition to using information that convinces, you should use your best skill in writing to make your facts sound convincing. Especially should you use positive language, for negatives have an irritating effect on the mind and thereby work against conviction. For similar reasons, you should avoid any inclination to question the reader's sincerity or honesty or to talk down or insult. Statements such as "If you had read the contract, you would have known . . ." or "Surely you knew that . . ." do little to convince. Instead, they do much to antagonize.

Positive coverage of refusal

Your reasoning, of course, should build up your case. It should take your reader logically and systematically to the refusal. Then you should refuse. If you have done your job well, your refusal should appear to be the logical outcome of what you have given beforehand. It should have no startling effect. In fact, if you have done your job well enough, your decision should be the only one that the facts of the case support.

As with all similar refusal problems, you should word your refusal clearly and positively. To be clear, your refusal should leave no doubt in anyone's mind. There should be no need to question. To be positive, you again will need to study the effect of your words. You may find it possible to refuse without using a single negative word. Perhaps you can imply what you can do. Also, you will need to keep your refusal words away from emphasis positions.

Although it is hard to judge refusal sentences without the explanations which precede them, the following three generally do a good job:

> For these reasons you will understand why we can pay only when our employees pack the goods.
>
> Although the contract clearly ended our responsibility on the 1st, we will do whatever we can to help repair the equipment.
>
> In view of these facts, the best we can do is to repair the equipment at cost.

Off-subject closing talk

Because your refusal is negative, you should follow it with some appropriate comment which is away from the subject of the refusal. No negative apologies are in order. Neither are any words which recall the problem giving rise to the claim. Probably a good general topic would be some more agreeable aspect of customer relations—new products, services, uses of products, industry news, or the like. Any friendly comment which appears logical in the one case will suffice.

Adjustment refusals illustrated

In the following example of a refused adjustment, a small manufacturer of furniture has made a claim to the Do-Craft Company, manufacturer of heavy fabrics. The claim contends that a certain Do-Craft fabric bought numerous times over the past year has badly faded and discolored. The furniture manufacturer includes with the claim three faded samples of the fabric, and they prove the point. Already the manufacturer had a number of complaints from buyers, and the claims total $545. The furniture manufacturer wants cash payment on these claims.

Inspection by the fabric manufacturer reveals that the fabrics were exposed to strong sunlight for long periods. The fabrics in question are strictly for inside use, and all of Do-Craft's advertising and catalog descriptions clearly emphasize the point. Do-Craft is not responsible and does not intend to pay the claim. Because the furniture manufacturer is a good customer, however, Do-Craft hopes to make her see the justice of the decision and to remain friends.

The Do-Craft letter begins in a friendly tone and on a point of agreement. In addition, the beginning sets up the review of facts. Without accusations, anger, or negative words of any kind, it relates the facts of the case—facts which clearly free the Do-Craft people from any blame. The refusal is clear, although more by implication than by direct wording. It is skillfully handled, without resort to negative words or undue emphasis. The close shifts to helpful suggestions which apply to the one case. Friendliness permeates the entire letter.

Dear Ms. Sanderson:

Subject: Your May 3 letter about Do-Craft fabric

Certainly you have a right to expect the best possible service from Do-Craft fabrics. Every Do-Craft product is the result of years of experimentation. And we manufacture each yard under the most careful controls we know how to impose. We are determined that our products will do for you what we say they will do.

Because we do want our fabrics to please, we carefully ran the samples of Do-Craft fabric 103 you sent us through our laboratory. Exhaustive tests show that each has been subjected to long periods in extreme sunlight. As we have known this limiting feature of Do-Craft from the beginning, we have clearly noted it in all our advertising, in the catalog from which you ordered, and with a stamped reminder on the back of every yard of the fabric. Under the circumstances, all we can do concerning your request is to suggest that you change to one of our outdoor fabrics. As you can see from our catalog, all in the 200 series are recommended for outdoor use.

Probably you will be interested also in the new Duck Back cotton fabrics listed in our 500 series. These plastic-coated cotton fabrics are most economical, and they resist sun and rain remarkably well. If we can help you further in your selection, please call on us.

Sincerely,

The next illustration letter is a refusal by a mail-order nursery of an unjustified claim for plants that died. The plants died ten months after the sale—too long a period for the nursery to be responsible. Whether a plant survives depends much on the treatment it gets from the purchaser. Proper planting and watering are vital. Even so, the nursery replaces all plants that die within the first 90 days. But it does this more as a goodwill gesture than because it is responsible. In the case at hand, the facts show no reasonable basis for granting the claim.

The letter begins on a point from the claim letter. Then it sets up the explanation. The explanation is an honest review of the nursery's policy, including a justification of it. Next comes the refusal—clearly and positively worded. Notice the appeal to the reader's sense of fair play. The close is goodwill.

Dear Mr. Huddleston:

You were right in assuming in your August 30 letter that we would want to know about the plants you bought from us. We are always interested in doing whatever we can to make our sales satisfactory.

That is why we inspect every outgoing shipment. Of course, after the plants leave us, we no longer can give them our personal attention. As you know, the first weeks after planting are critical for plant survival. Proper planting is essential. And so is regular watering, especially during the hot summer months. Even though this vital care is out of our hands, we guarantee survival for the first 90 days, which is more than enough time to make certain that all plants delivered were healthy. In view of this explanation, we feel sure you will understand why we must stand by our guarantee policy in this case. It is a fair policy—for you and for us.

Thank you for this opportunity to explain. We shall continue to work hard to provide you with the healthy plants and good service you have a right to expect.

Sincerely,

Refusal of an apparently dishonest claim is shown in the following letter. The case concerns an out-of-town customer who has bought an expensive dress from an exclusive shop. Three weeks after the purchase, the customer mailed back the dress, asking for a refund. She explained that after getting the dress home, she decided that she really did not like it. She explained, also, that it was not a good fit. Inspection of the dress shows that the woman has not told all. The dress has been worn—no question about it. It is dirty. Perspiration stains under the arms are evident. It cannot be accepted for refund.

The letter shows good restraint in refusing. It contains no accusation, no anger. It begins on subject, with a neutral point taken from the claim letter. Notice how the opening sets up the explanation. The explanation is a straightforward review of the fairness of the store's policy. Then comes the application of the facts of the reader's case. The refusal follows logically in clear and positive words. The letter ends with emphasis on what the store is able to do. It is as friendly a close as the facts permit.

Dear Ms. Krumpleman:

We at Wayland's understand your concern about the exclusive DiVella dress you returned February 15. As always, we are willing to do as much as we reasonably can to make things right.

What we can do in each instance is determined by the facts of the case. With returned clothing, we generally give refunds. Of course, to meet our obligations to our customers for quality merchandise, all returned clothing must be unquestionably new. As you know, our customers expect only the best from us; and we insist that they get it. Thus, because the underarm stains on your dress would prevent its resale, we must consider the sale final. We are returning the dress to you. With it you will find a special alteration ticket, which assures you of getting the best possible fit free of charge.

So, whenever it is convenient, please come by and let us alter this beautiful DiVella creation to your requirements. We look forward to serving you.

Sincerely,

Vague and back orders

Not all orders can be acknowledged as positively as we illustrated in Chapter 9. Sometimes the persons ordering do not specify all of the information needed to complete the transactions; so you have to write them letters to clear up their vague orders. Then, sometimes you are out of the goods wanted, and you have to write those who order, telling them when they will receive the goods. Both situations are in the bad-news category. Those placing the order are not getting what they want right away. They must wait.

Consideration in handling

In some areas of business, back orders and vague orders are somewhat routine. They are accepted as normal, and no one gets excited about them. In such situations, the news is reported routinely, perhaps on printed forms or as notations on a copy of the order form. When the customer clearly will be disappointed in the news, however, a more tactful means of presentation is needed. In such cases, you will want to write a letter; and you will be wise to write it in the indirect order used for most bad-news messages.

In planning your strategy for this form of acknowledgment letter, you should first review the facts of the case. If the order is vague, the fault is the reader's. In such cases, you are free of blame; but the situation is still negative. The reader is not getting what she or he wants now. Also, any tactless reference to the error could bring about resentment. If some of your reader's goods must be placed on back order, the fault may be yours; at least, it is not the reader's. In either event, you will need to give careful thought to the handling of the negative points.

Variations in opening possibilities

Your opening for the letter will depend on how much your letter must do. If a number of items were ordered, you could have to acknowledge any combination of goods that you are shipping, goods that you must place on back order, and goods that were vaguely described. When you are sending some of the goods (the usual case), you may begin with this good-news part of your message, as illustrated in this beginning sentence:

> Your durable Rockwood roofing, which you ordered October 1, should be in Oxford well before your Wednesday deadline, as the shipment left our Cleveland warehouse this morning.

When you have only vague orders or back orders to handle, your opening should make a positive, friendly contact and serve as a buffer for the following bad news. Probably the most appropriate possibility is to begin with a grateful acknowledgement of the order. Or if the order is the first one, a new-customer welcome would be appropriate. Whatever you say, however, should be sincerely and individually written for the one case. The rubber stamp "Thank you for your order" long ago lost its personalized effect. So has the "We are happy to have your order" variety. A more effective approach is one like this:

> Your January 31 order of Williams janitorial supplies is receiving our best attention, and we are sincerely grateful to you for it.

Other opening possibilities include a wide range of friendly, pertinent conversation topics that might go on between reader and writer. It could be some comment on the significance of the order:

> Your large April 9 order appears to indicate continued good business in the Burtville area.

It could also be some friendly remark reflecting business relationships:

> It's always good to receive an order from our friends at Morrison's Supply.

Tact in handling the delayed shipment

After the friendly opening comment, you will need to move into the bad-news part. Your work here is largely an exercise in positive writing and writing in the you-viewpoint. In handling the vague order, for example, you should ask for the information you need without pointing an accusing finger at the reader for leaving out necessary information. Certainly, the reader made a mistake; but nothing is gained by saying "You failed to specify the color of umbrella you want." You gain much more in goodwill by something like this:

> So that you may have just the right color of umbrella to complement your wardrobe, will you please check your choice of the colors listed on the enclosed card?

The sentence not only handles the matter diplomatically; it makes the action easy to take. The reader has only to check and mail a card. In cases in which additional information would be helpful to the decision, you would be wise to supply it. In the illustration above, for example, a color chart or fabric samples could be sent.

Your handling of any back-order information should place primary emphasis on the most positive part of this bad news. That is, rather than say that you "can't ship the goods until the 9th," you can get the goods moving to the reader with words like "We shall be able to rush the Old New Orleans pralines to you by the 9th." Of course, since the back order is your fault, it may deserve some explanation. If there is a logical one, present it—especially if the explanation shows good demand for the product or in some other way enhances the demand for it. Words like "As our supply of this very popular product should be replenished by rush shipment due Friday" do the job well. Should your back order be for a long period of time, you may choose to give your reader a way out if she or he wishes. Something like "Unless we hear from you by the 10th" following the back-order handling should take care of this matter.

A pleasant ending picture

Like all good acknowledgment letters, you should end this one on some positive topic. If you are handling a vague order, you might choose to end with a request for the information you seek. If skillfully handled, this question can make a positive ending. In other situations you will need to find some specifically adapted goodwill talk. It could be talk about enjoyable use of the product. If you have not already done it earlier in the letter, it could be an expression of your gratefulness for the order. It could even be some resale talk about the products ordered—something which will enhance your reader's interest in the product. In some cases, such resale talk may be sprinkled appropriately throughout the letter, especially if there is some likelihood that the reader will not wish to wait for the goods.

Illustrated handling of delayed order

Good technique in handling order delays is illustrated in the following letter. The case concerns an order for a number of items of individual equipment. Some can be sent right away. One item must be placed on back order. Another requires additional information before it can be sent.

Generally, the letter follows the plan just described. Since some goods are being sent, it uses this information to form the good-news opening contact. It handles the vague order without mentioning the reader's negligence. Instead, it presents the choice from the reader's point of view, and it gives the reader information which should help to make a choice. The back-order news is presented in its most positive light, with emphasis on receipt of the goods rather than on the delay, and with reselling words which tend to make the product more desirable. The close is a sincere expression of gratefulness, with a forward look to continued friendly relationships.

Dear Mr. Fletcher:

By noon tomorrow, your three new Baskin motors and one Dawson 110 compressor should reach your Meadowbrook shop ready to use on the production line. As you requested, we marked them for your West Side loading dock and sent them by Warren Motor Express.

So that we can be certain of sending you the one handcart for your special uses, will you please review the enclosed description of the two models available? As you will see, the model M is our heavy-duty design, but its extra weight is not justified for all jobs. When you have made your choice, please mark it on the accompanying card and mail the card to us. We'll send your choice to you as soon as we know it.

Your three dozen 317 T-clamps should reach you by the 13th. As you may know, these very popular clamps have been in short supply for some time now, but we have been promised a limited order by the 11th. We are marking three dozen for rush shipment to you.

It is always a pleasure to do business with your fine organization. We look forward to serving you again with quality industrial equipment.

Sincerely,

Credit refusals

Letters which refuse an application for credit carry an unusually negative message. Their major objective of denying credit to someone who wants it obviously is negative, for it goes against the reader's wishes. The situation is made more negative, however, by the very nature of the subject. Credit is tied to things a person holds dear—morals, acceptance in society, character, and integrity. Unless skillfully handled, a refusal of credit is likely to be interpreted as a reflection on the person personally. A situation as negative as this clearly requires that you use the indirect order of organization in handling it.

Perhaps some people will argue that there is no need to be concerned about the sensitive feelings of your reader. You are declining the reader's business, they may say, so why spend time trying to be nice? Why not just give a quick, curt no and let it go at that? If you will carefully study the situation, the answer should be clear to you.

In the first place, being nice to people is personally gratifying to us all—at least, it should be. All the rewards in business are not measured in cold dollars and cents. There are emotional satisfactions to be gained, and kind treatment—by us and to us—produces one of them.

In the second place, being nice to people is profitable in the long run, and perhaps even in the short run. All prospective credit customers who are turned down have needs, and they are going to satisfy them somewhere. The chances are that they will have to buy for cash. If you turn them down, others are likely to turn them down also. So someone is going to get their cash business; and if you handle them positively, it might be you. In addition, the fact that you must turn them down now does not mean that they never will be good credit customers. Many good credit accounts today were bad risks sometime in the past. By not offending credit applicants now, you may keep them as friends of your company until they become good credit risks.

Strategy and the reason for refusal

In studying your case to find the best strategy for breaking the bad news, you should first consider the reason for your refusal. If your applicant is a bad moral risk, you have a most negative situation. You cannot tell the applicant bluntly that you are refusing because her or his character is not up to par. The mental filters of even the lowest characters would be likely to react negatively to such moral accusations. Instead, your plan will need to be more roundabout. Probably you will be wise only to imply the reason, and you will not want to promise any future credit extension. As your only interest in the applicant would be as a cash customer, you might want to work for whatever cash business she or he might be able to give.

If you are refusing because your applicant has a weak capital position, your task is an easier one. Short capital is not a reflection on one personally. In fact, one's ability to pay hardly is related to one's personal qualities.

Thus, you can broach the subject more directly. And you can talk more optimistically about future credit possibilities should the applicant's financial situation change.

The buffer beginning

As in the preceding refusal patterns, the beginning of a credit refusal should meet these requirements: (1) it should set up the strategy; (2) it should be neutral; (3) it should be on subject.

Your specific choice of subject is again a matter for you to think out. Almost anything will do which sounds sincere if it also meets the three requirements listed above. For example, if an order was included with the request for credit, you could say something about the order. Perhaps it could be a compliment, a statement about the significance of the order, some words about the goods ordered, or the like. The following opening illustrates such possibilities:

> Your January 22 order for Rock-Ware roofing shows good planning for the rush months ahead. As you will agree, it is good planning which marks the path of business success.

This opening ties in with the inquiry being answered. It is neutral, and it sets up the refusal strategy with the reference to planning. The following discussion will show that the best planned businesses hold down their debts— something the reader also needs to do.

If no order accompanies the request for credit, any appropriate comment that fits the situation can make a good opening. An expression of appreciation for the request for credit is one such possibility. But it has been used so often that probably it has lost some effectiveness. Even so, it is almost always appropriate. If you use it, try to vary the wording from the timeworn "Thank you for your application" variety. Something like this would be better:

> We are sincerely grateful for your credit application, Ms. Spangler, and will do all that we reasonably can to help you in getting your business started.

As they should be, these words are on subject and neutral. In addition, they set up the explanation that giving credit is beyond what the company reasonably can do.

Justification of the refusal

Your explanation logically follows the opening which sets it up. How you explain depends on why you are refusing. If you are refusing on moral grounds, you need to say little. As bad moral risks know their records, you need only to imply that you also know. You do not need to say anything like "Your credit record is bad." A tactful sentence like this will do the job:

> Our review of your credit record requires that we serve you only on a cash basis at this time.

Refusing an applicant with good credit morals but weak finances justifies a more open approach. You can discuss the reasons for refusing with as much frankness as your relationship with the applicant permits. In your explanation, you can justify your credit policy, and you can say that the reader does not qualify. Of course, your words here should be carefully chosen. They should not talk down, nor should they imply moral wrongdoing. They might well show concern for the reader's credit problem. They might even suggest ways how the reader can get out of the current financial problem. Whatever your explanation, it should be sound, believable, and convincing. It should lead logically to the refusal that follows.

Tact in the refusal

Your wording in the refusal also depends on the strategy you have selected. If your refusal is for moral reasons, after a brief incidental reference or two to the reasons for the refusal, you can refuse, probably through implication rather than direct words. Words like these do the job clearly yet positively:

> As our credit check gives us insufficient evidence to grant you credit at this time, we invite you to join the tens of thousands who save on Deal's discount prices.

Applicants being turned down because of weak finances likewise should be refused positively. In such cases, however, you can look hopefully to the future. For a study in contrasting effects, read carefully the following sentences. The first one is blunt and tactless:

> For these reasons, we must refuse all applicants whose current assets-to-liabilities ratio falls below 2 to 1.

This one does the job well:

> Thus, for the best interests of both of us, we must postpone credit buying until your current assets-to-liabilities ratio reaches 2 to 1.

A closing forward look

Because the refusal is bad news, you should follow it with some more pleasant talk. It could be on a variety of topics, as long as they fit the one case and accomplish the goodwill objective. Perhaps the best choice is something that will suggest cash buying. In fact, you might invite the applicant to buy for cash with you, perhaps supporting your invitation with talk about low prices, merchandise, service, and the like. How much you say and how far you go toward driving for a cash sale should depend on your judgment of the reader. This goodwill talk might well mark the end of your letter, with your last words taking a forward look to whatever future relations appear to be appropriate. Two such closes are these:

> As one of Myers' cash customers, you will continue to receive the same courtesy, quality merchandise, and low prices we give to all our customers. We look forward to serving you soon.

For your buying convenience, we are sending you our new spring catalog. We look forward to serving you through your orders.

Cases in review

Illustrating variation in credit refusal are the three following letters. The first is a routine refusal used by a department store. Because the store must handle its credit applications on a mass basis, it does not choose to write individual letters in each case. Thus, the letter is general, and it is short. Yet it covers all that needs to be covered. It explains the reasons for the refusal in positive language, and it ends with a pleasant forward look.

Dear Mr. Sands:

We sincerely appreciate your interest in an account with White-Horton & Company. Whenever we can, we are always willing to serve you.

In determining what we can do for you regarding your December 9 request for credit, we made the routine checks you authorized. The information we have received permits us to serve you only as a cash customer. But as you know, cash buying here at White-Horton's discount prices can make a very real saving for your budget.

We hope to see you in the store again very soon, and we look forward to the opportunity of serving you.

Sincerely,

The second letter refuses credit to a mercantile customer who is short of finances. Under the "sound business practice" theme, the letter explains the refusal in a you-viewpoint manner that is meaningful to this one reader, the owner of a laboratory supply business. The letter covers the refusal without harsh, negative words, but through telling what can be done rather than what cannot be done. It does more than is usually expected in such a case: It suggests an alternative. In addition, it works for cash buying in the off-subject close.

Dear Ms. Haines:

Your June 3 order for Bell precision instruments suggests that Technicians Supplies is continuing to make progress. We sincerely hope that this is the case and that the good growth of the past will continue.

To assure yourself of that continued growth, we feel certain you will want to follow the soundest business procedures wherever possible. As you may know, most financial experts say that maintaining a reasonable indebtedness is a must for sound growth. About a 2-to-1 ratio of current assets to liabilities is a good minimum, they say. In the belief that the minimum is best for all concerned, we extend credit only when this ratio is met. In your case, perhaps we shall be able to review the application soon. At the rate your organization is growing, your current assets-to-liabilities ratio should reach this sound status soon.

Some companies we know have achieved sound status in record time by taking advantage of every possible saving. One in particular is the very significant 5 percent discount we and most firms like us give for timely cash payments. Your saving on your current order, for example, would amount to $87.30. This percentage added to your cash holdings would help a lot to improve the ratio. Even if you would need to borrow locally, the cash saving on the volume of your purchases would be significant.

We hope that you will soon find it possible to reap these savings with us. We hope also that Bell Instruments will be your partner in progress through the years ahead.

Sincerely,

The third credit refusal illustration is also a form letter. It is a letter sent by a mail-order company to credit applicants who have overused their credit. The letter uses the explanation that these people would be better off if they cut back their credit buying.

Generally, the letter follows the plan of the others. Its on-subject, neutral opening sets up the explanation with its stress on service. The following explanation frankly discusses the need to hold down debt. Notice the you-viewpoint emphasis here. The close is a friendly, courteous appeal for cash business.

Dear Ms. Goetz:

Your order and request for credit are sincerely appreciated. We are always grateful for the opportunity of serving you in the best way we can.

Serving you well means many things to us. Among them, it means looking out for the best interests of you and of all the other customers we serve. This task of looking out for our customers' best interests prompts us to carefully limit credit to only those people who are in a position to benefit from it. As you know, credit can be a dangerous thing. Sometimes all of us are better off with less of it. In your case, we sincerely feel that this time by buying for cash you will be acting in your own best interest.

Knowing that you are eager to get the goods you ordered, I am having them assembled and made ready for shipment at a moment's notice. So won't you please send the cash amount of the purchase in the enclosed, addressed envelope? We'll rush your merchandise to you the moment it reaches us.

Sincerely,

Letter problems–2

Refused requests

1. Assume the role of the executive assistant to the president of Colonial Insurance Company and say no to a request from Calvin Coonrad, sponsor of the Woodville Youth Club. Mr. Coonrad has requested that Colonial permit the 31 members of his Club to use the Company's Sea Pines Lodge for a weekend at no cost.

For the past eight months, the Company has freely permitted such organizations to use this recreational facility. From the beginning the policy appeared to be a mistake. Almost without exception each group left the place in a mess. On some occasions even windows, doors, and furniture were broken. The situation became so bad that last week your boss, the president, decided to limit use of the facility to Company groups only.

Your job now is to convey your boss's decision to Mr. Coonrad. And since Coonrad and all his Youth Club members are a part of the public with which Colonial wants to maintain a positive image, you will handle the situation positively. Perhaps you can suggest an alternate site for the outing.

2. You, the owner of the City Office Supply Company, have just received a persuasive letter from Ms. Hilda Hubnic, president of Alert, a powerful local political action organization. She wants you to buy advertising space in Alert's annual election publication, *Voice of Reason*. As she worded it, "A $150 contribution would display your company's name prominently in a 2-column 4-inch space and would mark you as one who stands up for good government."

Your political sympathies lie with Alert. You know that many of your customers also sympathize with the organization. But you also know that many of your customers do not sympathize with it. As you see it, you cannot afford to take a stand publicly. It would be bad for business.

Thus, you decide to refuse the request—politely and with convincing explanation. The organization may get your support at the polls, but not in print.

3.   You were flattered when you received a letter from Shelly Tomes, chairperson of Career Day activities at Central State University. In her letter she asked you to make a 30-minute presentation on "How to Prepare for a Career in Business Leadership." You were especially pleased because you know you were selected for your record of achievement in your business and in your community. You were pleased also when you read: "We can promise you 600 attentive listeners who will be guided by your words."

Normally, you would accept the assignment; but on the second Wednesday of next month, the date they want you, you have scheduled a business trip. Because changing trip plans would also change the plans of a number of other people, you will just have to say no to Ms. Tomes.

Perhaps you will suggest one of your very capable business associates as a substitute. Whatever you do, you will convey the message positively; and you will show appreciation for being chosen.

4.   Take the place of Professor Carmen De Loren and answer the persuasive request from Wilmer A. Vandiver of the Crescent City Executives Club. For the past three years you have said yes to the request for your lecture on "Determining Your Management Style" for the Club's Executive Seminar Series. This time you must say no.

Just as in the past, Vandiver explains how the Executive Club holds a weekly series of six two-hour seminars for business leaders in the area. The business leaders pay for the seminars, and the money collected (after expenses) goes to support the Club's summer camp for underprivileged children. Lecturers are requested to contribute their time, although expenses are covered.

You strongly support the program and its goals; but you just cannot participate a fourth year. The trip to Crescent City and back would take a full day from your very tight schedule over the next two months. You have a heavy schedule of consulting engagements over the coming weeks. Then there is a manuscript that you must complete by the semester's end. And on top of this is a teaching load made heavy by a new preparation. You simply cannot help the Executive Club this year.

You like the Crescent City people, so you will try extra hard to say no positively. Since you are well acquainted with business professors, you may be able to help them find someone else.

5.   As owner of the Planter's Farm Implement Company you have just received a very persuasive request from Mary O. Pockrus, president of the Tri-County Fair Association. Ms. Pockrus seeks your Company's active participation in the opening-day parade. Specifically, she wants you to enter a float for your Company.

After thinking over the matter carefully, you conclude that you cannot afford it. The entry fee of $250 is one reason. Another is the cost of preparing a float that would be of the quality you would want. You know that most firms spend hundreds of dollars—some a few thousand. Your young, struggling business just won't stand it.

Anyway, it's not as if you weren't involved in fair activities. You have volunteered to work with the Association's livestock judging committee, although you haven't been asked to do anything yet. Also, you will participate in the farm implement displays and have paid the $200 participation fee. You feel you have done enough.

Now you will write Ms. Pockrus giving her your answer and justifying it. You don't want to offend any of the public-spirited people who are giving their time freely. So you will be tactful.

6. It will be hard to say no to Patricia Neuman, but you must. She was one of the 17 who applied for the position as manager of your Old New Orleans Restaurant. Your refusal is especially difficult because Patricia's father is an old college friend of yours.

You considered Patricia very carefully. The evidence, however, did not justify hiring her. She has worked in restaurant operations only three years and has served as an assistant manager (never a manager) for only the past eight months. Your restaurant is a major operation ($2,300,000 gross annually), and you must have someone with a proven record of managerial experience to run it. It would be some time before Patricia could qualify for such an assignment. In fact, the person you hired has managed restaurants for nine years and has been in the business for 15.

Because of the friendship involved, you will try to handle this letter with extra-special skill. You know that you can't make Patricia like your decision. But you want her (and her father) to understand it and to not hold it against you.

7. Today you received a rather unusual request from Abe Lutz, who is president of the Valley City Boy's Club. Mr. Lutz explained in his persuasive letter that the Boy's Club is looking for a place to construct a recreational area—primarily a softball field. The Club has its eye on a lot on the outskirts of town—a lot which its investigation shows you own.

So, since the lot is vacant, the Club would like you to permit it to construct a recreational facility, for free of course. It cannot afford to buy a lot.

The Club's budget would permit it to take care of all the work and expenses involved in clearing the lot, building temporary bleachers, installing lights, building a scoreboard, and such. It would promise to take care of the property. And the Club assures you that all the construction would be temporary and could be moved with six-month's notice. "The kids of Valley City would be forever grateful to you," the letter concludes.

Normally, you would be quite willing to say yes to such a request. But this time you must say no. This is no ordinary vacant lot. It is the proposed site of your future retirement home. Valley City is your old home town, and you have planned to return to it since college days. After buying the lot last year, you have begun getting it ready. Across the back (probably hidden by weeds) are a dozen small fruit trees that you planted. And you also planted the small oaks scattered around the street side of the lot. A softball field would require destroying all of this. You don't want just a barren place for your future home.

You will refuse the request, but you'll try hard to be diplomatic.

8.   There is no way that you will permit the Tidwell Lumber Company to use the private road across your Wilderness Trails property. The 130-acre piece of property is the site of your recreational home, and you like its rugged, wilderness qualities. Anyway, the old road Tidwell wants to use is hardly a road. It hasn't been used for ten years. It is now only a trail, and you're letting it return to a wilderness state. You like the place as it is—without a road and without noisy trucks.

In the letter to you, the Tidwell representative explained how use of the road would save its logging trucks three miles each trip. Tidwell would be quite willing to pay for the privilege of taking this shortcut across your property. You see Tidwell's point, and you hope it can see yours.

You will say no to Tidwell, but you'll do so in a friendly, neighborly way. After all, it is your neighbor. It owns a few thousand acres of forest adjacent to Wilderness Trails. Address the letter to Thomas A. Toomey, who is superintendent of the local operations.

9.   The request you received from Ms. Tizzy T. Tibbits, who is chairperson of the Board of Directors of National Youth Clubs, Inc., flatters you. It is no small honor to be asked to serve as a member of the Board.

As Ms. Tibbits points out in her letter, your past record of service to the organization marks you as a dedicated worker and a friend. You have earned the appointment, and the organization is pleased to honor you with this recognition.

Although Ms. Tibbits is most persuasive, you cannot accept. At any other time, you would be pleased to take the assignment; but now your work schedule will not permit it. Over the next year or two you will have to travel extensively. Your company is expanding operations, and you will have to do much of the work in planning and implementing the expansion. You just would not have the time to make the six to eight meetings that Board membership would require.

Write the letter which will so present the refusal that Ms. Tibbits and the Board will understand.

10.   Assume the position of owner-manager of the Heidleberg Motel and answer the request of Ms. Janice Guajardo, special representative of the Travelers Association. About a month ago, Ms. Guajardo visited you in your office. She explained that her association of traveling people had a network of cooperating motels, hotels, automobile rental companies, restaurants, and such that gave discounts to members. As a result, they got the members' business. She used her best persuasion in an effort to get you to join. Not being one to make hasty decisions, you asked for time to think over the matter.

Today, you received a letter from Ms. Guajardo. In it she reviewed the points she made earlier, and again she asked you to join. Now is the time that you give her an answer.

The answer must be no. It is likely that a 20 percent discount would indeed influence some travelers to stay at your motel. As you see it, however, you really do not need the extra demand for your units. For some time now, you have had no vacancies on most peak days. You doubt that additional customers at a lower price would add to the profit picture.

Write Ms. Guajardo giving her the answer. You like this personable, sincere woman; so you will work to handle the matter skillfully.

11. For the past few weeks, all your spare time has been spent working on arrangements for the annual convention of the National Association of Merchandizers. You are the arrangements chairperson.

In today's mail comes a letter from Wingate A. Bueller, III, president of Bueller-Moore and Company. The man asked for a special favor. Bueller-Moore will have 22 people at the meeting, and all of them will attend the Friday night banquet. The Company wants them seated together—"at a long table as near the speaker's platform as possible." The Company feels the request is appropriate because Mr. Bueller is scheduled to become a member of the Association's Board of Directors at the banquet.

You will have to deny the request. It just is not practical to reserve seats at the banquet. If you did it for one Board member, you would have to do it for all. And there are 16 members of the Board. Anyway, the Board considered such a possibility at last year's meeting and concluded that making reservations would be a problem. About 800 people milling around a banquet room looking for their seats simply would be impractical. Also, forcing the members to sit with people they do not know improves the fellowship the Association seeks.

With the information above in mind, you will now write the letter refusing Bueller's request. Remember that soon he will be a member of the Board and will be working with you.

12. A few months ago, Ms. Joanne Zanbrano agreed to join your Adventures to the Orient tour. You accepted her $500 deposit and saved for her one of the 24 spaces on this 20-day guided tour. She signed the terms-and-conditions statement, which required 30 days' notice before departure for cancellation without sacrificing the deposit. Today, just eight days before departure, you receive a note from her saying that she cannot go. She presents a distressing story of family problems, including the severe (probably terminal) illness of her mother. The letter ends with an impassioned plea for money back.

You must be firm and say no. It is too late to fill the spot. You could have filled it earlier, had there been a vacancy; so now you will not make as much as you might have made. You would make even less if you gave back the $500. In fact, if you did not have the deposit for just such cases, you'd have to charge more for the total package to make a profit. Anyway, you advised Ms. Zanbrano, as you did all others, to take out trip insurance. She did not take your advice.

Now you will write the letter. You feel sorry for the woman; but right and reason are on your side. Try to make her understand.

13. Play the role of the public relations director of the National Oil and Refining Company and answer a letter written by the president of the State University Free Enterprise Association. This association of business students is seeking financial support for its exhibit in the forthcoming Free Enterprise Fair, a national competition for free enterprise clubs. The State University Club plans to spend about $1,500 on its exhibit. As the Club reasons in its letter, "Since National is the leading business in this area, we are confident you will want to help us in our effort to promote free enterprise."

You support the goals of the Free Enterprise Club, and you are personally pleased to see college students involved in such projects. Even so, National cannot comply in this case. It gets many more such requests than it can support, and some good ones have to be turned down. It is not as if the Company does not do its share for education. Currently, National is sponsoring an executive-in-residence professor on the State University faculty. It is supporting six State University students through its scholarship program. Its Executive Lecture Series is providing, on request, free classroom lectures on energy matters. And there are other examples you can think of.

Address the letter to Ms. Carolyn Capola, president of the Association.

14. It will be hard to say no to the persuasive request of Mr. Miles Madden's Westlake Junior-High School basketball team; but you must. Your Westlake Department Store may be the biggest store in town, but it has to draw the line somewhere.

Yesterday you received a letter signed by all 12 of the squad members and Madden. In the letter they asked you for a contribution to help pay for warm-ups and uniforms for the team. As they explained, "The school's budget provides little for basketball. And if you will help us with say about $200, you'll gain the goodwill of every kid and parent at Westlake."

You don't like the pressure, and you don't like the request. It is not that you and your store aren't community-minded. You give more than your share to community charities. It's just that you have to draw the line somewhere; and you don't see basketball on the plus side of the line.

In presenting your refusal to Mr. Madden and his team, you'll be very careful with your words. You don't want to offend. You'll try to so present your reasoning that they will accept and understand your decision.

Adjustment refusals

15. Six months ago, your High Mountain Kennels (High Mountain, Colorado) sold two AKC registered Doberman pinscher puppies to Ms. Kathy Donlic of Atlanta. The price was $500 each. You shipped them by air and assumed that all was well.

Today's mail brings a letter from Ms. Donlic. "The dogs were sick from the start," she writes. "One died yesterday, and the other is also sick and will have to be destroyed. I must ask that you refund the purchase price. I should ask you to pay the $120 in vet bills, but will forget about that."

You cannot accept the blame. You sent the woman two healthy pups. They had been given all the required shots and were carefully inspected prior to shipment by your veterinarian, T. A. Talifero. You have his signed statement supporting the dogs' health. You do not feel responsible for what happened. After all, a lot can happen in six months.

Now you must write the woman refusing her request. You will try to so word your reply that she will understand and respect your position.

16. Assume the role of manager of customer relations, Dependable Power Mower Company. Yesterday you received a brief note from Fred Chote of Chote's Hardware Company in Prairie City. Fred wrote that he overordered when he asked for nine of your seven-horsepower riding mowers. "I am sending two of them back by Eastern Flyer. When you get them, send me my $1,680 back."

Today the Eastern Flyer truck delivered the two riding mowers. To your surprise, both had been used—and more than just to demonstrate. Each has telltale nicks and scratches that can come only from hours of use in the field. Apparently, an attempt was made to clean up the mowers, but the evidence cannot be hidden.

You simply could not resell these machines. They are not new. If by chance they were returned as defective, you would be pleased to correct the problem; but you cannot accept them as returned, unused merchandise.

Even though you suspect that Chote may be trying to put something over on you, you value his business. You would like to protect your rights and keep him as a customer. Write the letter.

17. Play the role of manager of customer relations of Svetlic Uniform Company and answer the claim letter of Mildred Pfluger of Carson's Drilling Company. Last month Carson's ordered eight dozen coverall uniforms in assorted sizes with the Company name embroidered across the shoulders. As Pfluger explains in her letter, "The uniforms have just arrived—with the company name misspelled. The name should be Carson—not Carton."

Your first reaction is that of embarrassment. Your company never makes errors like that. So you check further. After much talk and investigation, Mike Wells, the superintendent of production, discovers the cause of the error. On the original order, in the spot for the name information, appears the misspelled name—Carton. Apparently the Carson employee who typed the order made the mistake. Your workers followed precisely the instructions on the order.

Because the error is not your fault, you do not feel you should comply with Ms. Pfluger's request to correct all uniforms at no charge. It is a time-consuming process to take out the wrong letter and to embroider the correct one. But you will do the work at cost—which Mike Wells estimates to be

$2 per uniform. If Carson will get the uniforms to you right away, you'll have them on the way back the next day. Write your letter positively.

18.   Last week your Old New Orleans Restaurant served a banquet for Travelers Incorporated, an association of traveling salespeople. The organization made reservations for 120; only 91 meals were consumed. Now the organization wants some money back—28 meals at $18.50 each. You do not feel it is entitled to its claim.

As the group's president, Suzanne Havaland, explained in her letter, the stormy weather that came up on the day of the banquet was responsible for the poor attendance. She informed you "well in advance" that attendance would suffer. "Because of my warning," she reasons, "you should have allowed for decreased attendance."

You do not see it Suzanne's way. About an hour before serving time, she left word with your secretary that the storm might affect attendance. But it was too late, for you had already begun to prepare the 120 meals. Even if there had been time, she said nothing about how many meals to cancel. As you see it, you carried out your end of the agreement. Now she and her group must carry out theirs. You cannot be expected to pay for happenings which you did not cause.

You would like to maintain the goodwill of these people; so handle the refusal delicately.

19.   Last year Paul E. Tabor bought from your Tampa Bay Pool Supply Company sufficient Kool-Coat material to cover the 1,200 square feet of deck surrounding his pool. He had seen this heat-resistant material on his brother's pool in Tampa Bay, liked it, and decided to get it for his pool. He told you that he planned to put it down himself, because he had carefully watched the workers do his brother's pool. What Tabor did not tell you, however, was that he was visiting in Tampa Bay and that he would take the material back to his home (and pool) in Chicago.

Today, almost eight months after the sale, you receive a letter from Tabor. He wants his money back (all $960 of it). "The material didn't stick!" he writes. "Following the cold winter weather it came loose from the concrete base in big chunks."

You know what happened. The expanding and contracting caused by freezing moisture broke up the material. Kool-Coat won't take extremely cold weather. Every Kool-Coat advertisement makes this point clear—as does a statement prominently placed on every can. You cannot understand how Tabor missed the warnings, but apparently he did.

But you cannot be responsible for Tabor's shortcomings. You are not obligated, and neither is the manufacturer. So you must refuse. Even so, you feel for the man. You will tell him about Duro-Coating, an epoxy-based coating that costs more but will withstand freezing weather. You would be glad to get the material for him at your cost plus shipping expenses (about $581, you estimate).

20.   Assume that you are the director of Campus Europe, a foreign study program operating out of Stonewall University. In today's mail comes

a letter from Sylvester T. Abernathy, who was enrolled last semester in the six-week Greek History course conducted by Professor Gregorio Vozikus.

Abernathy claims in his letter that he is entitled to a refund for most of his tuition payment and for most of his room and board. According to Abernathy, the course was worthless; so he dropped out at the end of the second week. He did not use his room, nor did he eat meals after that date. He did rejoin the group for the trip home, however. As Abernathy sees it, he is entitled to two thirds of the $600 tuition cost and the four-week room and board at $120 per week.

After reading Abernathy's letter, you check with Professor Vozikus and learn some additional facts. Abernathy did drop out, as he claims; but it was after the first test, on which he made a score of 32. The class average was 84. The man displayed little interest in the class. In fact, he was absent at least three days during the first two weeks; and rarely, if ever, did he do his homework. According to the other students, Abernathy spent most evenings "on the town." About his claim that the class was worthless, Vozikus pointed to the students' evaluations. Not one of the 26 other students rated it lower than eight on a ten-point scale.

As you see it, the man has no right to a refund. Stonewall University kept its end of the bargain. The course was run on a break-even basis. If refunds were permitted, losses would result. About meals and rooms, they were included in Stonewall's contract with the hotel. Stonewall had to pay for them even if they were not used.

Write the letter that will give this illogical young man your answer. And as much as you'd like to tell him off, resist the temptation and maintain the dignity that is appropriate for Stonewall University.

21. Assume that last week you bought a new automobile. Rather than trade in your old one, you sold it to Marilyn McMillan, a close friend throughout your college days. Marilyn had just completed her studies and bought the auto to take her to her new job some 1,200 miles away. She paid you $4,200 cash for the car, which was precisely what you could have gotten as a trade-in on the new car. You thought you were doing Marilyn a favor.

Today's mail brings a letter from Marilyn. In it she writes that the car started giving her trouble about two hours out of town. It broke down completely after 500 miles, and she had to be towed in. "The transmission is shot," she explains. "It cost $325 to fix, and I had to pay a $50 fee for towing. The mechanic said it had been going bad for some time. Since it was already bad when you sold it to me, I really think you should pay for the repairs and the towing."

You are keenly disappointed. You thought you were doing Marilyn a favor. As you see the matter, you are in no way responsible. You made no guarantees. And it is common knowledge that a used car can develop problems at any moment. You are not going to give her the money. But you'll try to explain in such a way that she will understand and respect your decision.

22. "What Patrick A. Traweek is trying to do to me borders on fraud," you think as you read his claim letter. Three months ago the man bought

by mail order a pair of your King Tex western boots. They were top quality boots made of specially selected ostrich skin and artistically decorated by Jose Ramirez, your master bootmaker. Traweek paid $465 for the pair.

Along with his letter he has sent the boots back to you. "I am returning the boots," his letter says, "because they are faulty. As you can see, the stitching is coming loose on both boots and the ostrich leather appears to be breaking down. I want either my money back or a new pair."

Your inspection of the boots shows that what happened is no fault of yours. Very obviously some substance (lye you suspect) was spilled on the boots. It dissolved and defaced the leather wherever it hit, and apparently it weakened the stitching. What happened is so clear to you that you find it hard to believe that Traweek expects you to believe his claim. But he confidently ends his letter with the optimistic words: "As I have been buying your boots for over 20 years, I know you are one who will want to do what is right in this matter."

You do want to do what is right, and you will. You will refuse. But you will hold your temper and try to handle the matter diplomatically.

23. Cheryl Materiste, owner of Cheryl's Fashions, is not happy with the four dozen Water Shed coats she bought from your clothing manufacturing company last week. In her letter she writes that these coats were not at all like those she saw at your market showing of last year—"the kind I thought I was buying." She wants her money back—all $1,764 of it. You cannot give it to her.

The reason you can't give her her money back is that she bought from your "close-out special." Because you are no longer making coats, you advertised your remaining merchandise for sale at cost. If she would reread the mailing piece from which she ordered, she would know this—as well as your stated condition that all sales are final. You just could not sell this product, or any other, at such a low price if you had to allow for return.

You don't really know how the woman was confused about the Water Shed brand. It is precisely what you displayed at market last year. It is the only coat you have ever displayed. In fact, it is the only coat you've ever manufactured. Now you are getting out of coat manufacturing to concentrate on sportswear, which has been your primary product over the years.

You cannot give the woman her money back. But she got a good product at a very good price.

Credit refusals

24. Play the role of credit manager for the New England Furniture Manufacturing Company and handle the credit application of the Schlimer Furniture Company. Your sales representative in the area submitted the application from this new, struggling store, noting that a good sale (over $10,000) would result if credit is approved.

Your review of the financial information submitted and of the report of credit references shows a dangerously weak financial picture. Apparently, Wilfred Schlimer started the business on the proverbial shoestring. His liabilities are much too high, and his cash flow is low. It would be very risky for you to join Schlimer's group of creditors.

From the information you have assembled, you judge that Schlimer is a very honorable person. He has a long record of honest business dealings, and he is a highly respected citizen in his community. The simple fact is that his business is in financial trouble.

You must turn down the request, of course. But you'll want to do what you can to keep this company as a possible outlet for your furniture. After all, financial conditions can and do change over time.

25. Last week Gina Calouette applied for credit from Manor's Fashions, your exclusive dress shop. You remember talking to this young professional woman. She's bright, gregarious, intelligent—all that you would expect of a young lawyer. You expected her to have no difficulty getting credit.

Now your credit checks are in, and the results are not at all what you expected. It appears that Ms. Calouette has been living well beyond her means. She has bought heavily and paid sparingly. Four of the stores where she has credit have reported her as delinquent, and one of the four has referred the account to its legal department. Clearly, she has overextended her credit, which probably explains why she is seeking credit from you.

Because of the current status of her credit, you cannot open an account for her. This wouldn't be good for you, and it wouldn't help her. So you will write her a tactful letter telling her your decision. You'd like to have her cash business, of course. And probably, in time, she could become a good credit customer.

26. Jessica McTavish is starting a sporting goods store, and she wants the Walton Company to help finance her. In her application for credit she noted that she was opening the Athlete's Locker in her city's new shopping mall. After working 11 years in the sporting goods field, she feels she is ready to start her own business. From the information she supplied you, it is evident that she has everything going for her except money.

The financial information she sent you with her credit application does not justify credit. She has very little cash, and apparently plans to finance her business mainly through her suppliers. The Walton Company simply does not do business this way. She should get local financing first. After all, her home-town bankers are in a position to understand her situation and take care of her needs better than a far-away supplier.

Your information doesn't tell you much about Ms. McTavish. Your salesperson in the area knows her only casually. He reports that she appears to be quite competent and that she has a good reputation in the community. He feels that her new store is in a good location, but there is no shortage of sporting goods stores in the city.

Now you must write a letter refusing credit. In time you hope to be able to grant it. Meanwhile, you'd like to get the Athlete's Locker's cash business.

27. Assume that you have just been promoted to credit manager of Stafford's Department Stores, Inc. One of the first things you will do is to revise the credit letters used by your predecessor. First you will work on the credit refusal letters.

One in particular offends you. It has been used for low- to middle-income credit applicants whose records for payment are not good. It reads like this:

> Dear——
> Stafford's regrets to inform you that your application for credit cannot be honored. The credit check we ran on you does not show the satisfactory record of payment which is required of all Stafford's credit holders. Even though we cannot give you credit at this time, we invite you to shop Stafford's.
> Sincerely,

You will write a unique and original letter, and it will not borrow plans and wordings in the textbook or from any other such source.

28. Assume that you are ten years out of college and beginning your own business—a hardware store. You have selected an ideal location in a small shopping center serving a middle-income neighborhood. You've had eight years' experience in the hardware business, and you have an excellent reputation in the community. There is no nearby competition. The situation appears to be good, you think, even though you are beginning without as much capital as you'd like—and certainly not as much as is considered sufficient by the financial experts.

Last week you mailed an application for credit to the Top Grade Company, manufacturers of a line of products you hope to carry. You explain how you would need about $14,000 of merchandise and would like 90 days to pay for them. Apparently your effort failed, for today you received this response:

> Dear——
> Thank you for your credit application. However, I regret to report that our policy does not permit us to grant credit in cases like this. Your capital position is too weak to justify credit at this time.
> If I can be of additional service to you, please do not hesitate to ask.
> Sincerely,

You are keenly disappointed in the letter. "It is not written the way I would write it," you think. But how would you have written it? Write that letter.

29. Your investigation of Stephanie Underwood's credit background produced unexpected results. Last week, when she visited your Slim and Trim Health Studio, you figured you had another good customer. She appeared to be an upright and dependable person; and when she asked for credit for use of your facilities, you thought granting it would be routine. But not so.

Following good business practices, you asked her to fill out an application form. Then you checked her record. What you learned is not good. She had been reported as delinquent on her payments by three local businesses. One of the three is Xerciz, Inc.—your only local competitor. Her bad payment record dates back a number of years—to the time she lived in Lincoln. With a record such as hers, you wonder how she has been able to get credit locally. Anyway, she won't get more from you.

Now you will write Ms. Underwood your answer. Because she is an exercise advocate, possibly she'll exercise somewhere—perhaps on a cash basis. Keep this in mind as you write the letter.

30.   Assume the position of credit manager for Beemans, an exclusive department store with an international reputation. Most of your customers are from society's upper crust, although you have some who mistakenly think they are in this group. In the past, you have granted credit liberally, on the assumption that people who buy expensive merchandise can and will pay. In recent months, however, your credit rolls have attracted more and more people who don't qualify. Because your deliquent accounts have increased, now you must handle your credit applications carefully. And you must refuse more often.

In tightening credit, you see the need to develop a model credit-refusal letter. It will have to be written most diplomatically, for Beemans wants no negative messages appearing under its letterhead. Also, it must not appear to be a form letter, for Beemans takes pride in the individual attention it gives. Use your best imagination to develop the letter that will fit this one company and its would-be credit customers.

Vague and back-order acknowledgments

31.   Your China Imports has been highly successful in recent months. So successful has it been that shipments from Shanghai haven't kept up with sales. So you have had to handle a number of back orders.

One back order is from Gifts Galore. Because Gifts Galore is a new customer, you feel it deserves special attention, which you'll give. From your catalog, Gifts Galore ordered two dozen of the Magnificent Tiger jade sculptures at $144.50 each; three dozen assorted 12-inch cloisone vases at $48 each; and four dozen assorted hand-painted snuff bottles at $41 each.

You can send only the snuff bottles now. The remaining items are on order and should be in within three weeks. Handle the matter skillfully, for you want to make a good impression on this new customer.

32.   As manager of mail-order sales for the ABC Sales Company, you have the task of handling the "rush" order of Mr. Elijah P. Gronzy. The man's handwriting is almost illegible. As you read his order, he wants one #714 kangaroo leather jacket, size M, $132. But he specifies no color. You have it in brown, black, or tan. He wants one #517A Kingco bedroom slippers, brown, at $24.50; but you can't be certain about the size. Is that a 7M? or could it be a 9M?

So you must write the man to get the correct information before sending him anything. The delay is his fault, as you see it; but there is little need to emphasize this point. Your letter will display the friendly, customer-service attitude for which ABC is noted.

33. You are the sales manager of The Book Factory, a company that sells books by mail. Your full-page ad in last week's *Populace*, a magazine section appearing in many leading newspapers, is producing good results. But, as usually is the case, some of the orders present problems.

One is from a Ms. Petunia Pettibon, who orders four books. You have and can send her immediately Cal Crump's *Night Flower* ($12.95) and *Portrait of a Scoundrel* ($14.95). But Mildred A. Bedicek's *The Broom Sweeps Clean* ($15.95) is completely sold out. This current best seller is hard to keep in stock, but you expect to have more within two weeks. Rodney Kilroy's *Living Art Legends* is available in cloth binding ($44.50) or gold-embossed leather ($55.95). Ms. Pettibon didn't say which.

Now you must write Ms. Pettibon handling all parts of her order in the goodwill manner that The Book Factory stresses.

34. Play the role of sales manager of the Forever Green Greenhouse Company. In today's mail you received an order in letter form from Ms. Johana DuBoise of Route 1, Farmersville, Missouri. Ms. DuBoise writes that she is ordering your 10-by-12 model 10K greenhouse kit, and that she wants it right away "before cold fall weather." She explains that she is ordering from your brochure—"the one you mailed to those who responded to your ad in the July issue of *Home and Family Magazine.*" She enclosed her check for $1,480.

You would be happy to send the greenhouse kit right away; but you can't. Apparently Ms. DuBoise has confused the information in the brochure. The 10-by-12 model K sells for $1,680. It is the model L (also 10-by-12) that sells for $1,480. The difference is that the model L must be assembled adjacent to a building—preferably on the south side. Its north wall is the wall of the adjacent building. The model K is a free-standing structure.

You can't send Ms. DuBoise anything until you find out what she wants. Write the letter that will get the information you need.

35. Take over as shipping manager for the Beverly Brass Works. For years your sales representative of the southern region has been trying to sell to Mammoth Department Stores, and finally she has succeeded. You now have Mammoth's first order. Unfortunately, there are problems.

Mammoth wants 38 of your solid brass Heirloom regular-size beds at $315 each; 24 king-size beds, solid brass, Heirloom, at $385 each; 48 solid brass floor lamps at $125 each; and 48 serving trays, 30-inch circular, at $68 each. It's a very nice order, totaling $33,624.

It's so nice, in fact, that you cannot handle it right away. You can send the serving trays and the floor lamps, for they are in stock. But it will be two weeks before you can manufacture the regular-size brass beds, and four weeks before you can get the king-size beds made. Demand for these two beds has been so good that you just haven't been able to produce them fast enough.

Now you must write the Mammoth purchasing manager and tell him the status of this order. You will try to convince him to wait for your product, but you know he could go to another manufacturer. You may use your imagination logically to create any background facts you may need.

36. Assume the role of manager of mail-order sales for Dennis-Wampole, Inc., a large department store in Bigg City. In each Sunday edition of *Bigg City News*, Dennis-Wampole runs an advertisement of specials for the week; and in each advertisement appears the caption "mail-order sales accepted." As a result, the store has built a regular and sizable direct-mail business.

One of your regular customers is Ms. Connie Mae Bowes of Valley View. Her dainty handwritten orders have become well known to your mail-order personnel. Today's mail brings another one.

This order is for three items, and two of them present a problem. You can send the solid brass wall swinger lamp with textured white shades ($32.95). The set of six plates with hand-painted roses on Seto porcelain ($29.95 a set) comes in pink on white or yellow on white. She didn't specify which. The solid marble rolling pins, hardwood handles, at $27.95 are sold out. You hope to have your stock replenished within two weeks.

Now you must write this good customer telling her the status of her order. Since this is the first time you've had a chance to communicate with her, you'll also express your appreciation for her business.

37. Place yourself in the position of owner-president of the True-Fit Uniform Company. Your sales representative in the southern district has just filled in an order from one of the big accounts in his area, Pueblo Oil Company. The order is a big one by your standards. It is for 300 sets of shirts and trousers in assorted sizes. At $32.50 the set, the order comes to $9,750.

The order specifies that the first 100 must be delivered in two weeks and the remaining 200 a week later. You cannot do it, for the kelly green fabric the Pueblo people want isn't in stock. A quick check with your supplier tells you that you can get more in 14 days. Then you'll need another five days to make the uniforms and two more days for delivery. Thus, you could deliver a week late.

Write the Pueblo Oil Company purchasing manager (Ms. Marvel Dominik) explaining the situation. Try to get her to wait. (You may use your imagination logically to supply additional information about your products.)

Nonexistent

11 Correspondence: Persuasive requests and collections

SOME OF YOUR business letter goals will require that you overcome the resistance of your readers. Perhaps your readers will resist because your goals are opposed to their best interests or wishes. Or perhaps the readers have little concern for your goals. Whatever the explanation, if you are to succeed, you must overcome resistance. Usually you must use persuasion to overcome resistance.

Persuading your readers to accept your goals involves changing the content of their mental filters. As things stand at the outset, their mental filters contain knowledge, impressions, and viewpoints which run contrary to your goals. Your task is to communicate information which will change this mental set. To do this job well will require your best in human evaluation, logical reasoning, and persuasive writing.

The specific organization plan you should use in persuasion problems will vary depending on the facts of the case. In general, however, you should follow the indirect order. The indirect order is justified because, in persuasive situations, you anticipate that your reader's first reaction to your objective will be to oppose it. The message your letter brings is unfavorable; and as we know, unfavorable messages are best handled indirectly. In fact, we may view persuasion letters as just a special type of unfavorable letter. We discuss them in a separate chapter because they have some unique problems.

Our plan for study of this form of letter is again to take up some of its representative types. In this chapter we analyze routine persuasive request letters. This is the basic type of persuasion letter, and our approach to it sets the pattern for the other persuasion letters. The first of these other types is the collection letter, which also is discussed in this chapter. In the following chapter we cover two additional persuasion letter types: sales and job applications. If you will study the analyses presented in each of these situations, you should have little difficulty adapting to any other situation requiring persuasion.

Persuasive requests

Requests which are likely to encounter resistance require a slow, deliberate approach. As we noted in Chapter 9, the fast-moving direct order is preferable in most inquiries; but to begin with a request the reader is likely to oppose would be to invite failure. Very obviously, you must change this negative mental attitude if you are to achieve your objective. Thus, in such cases you should sacrifice the speed and simplicity of directness. You should elect the slower approach of persuasion.

Determination of persuasion

Your planning of the persuasive request letter is a matter for your logical imagination. You will need to place yourself in your reader's position, and you will need to think through her or his mind as well as your own. Specifically, you will need to determine any objections the reader might have. Then you will have to build arguments or explanations which will overcome them.

In some cases your thinking will be comparable to that used by the orderly and logical debater. You will think through the problem noting the points of opposition; and you will develop the counterpoints and arguments to these points. In other cases, you may need to sell your reader on your objective through the use of basic appeals. For example, you may be able to build an argument showing how your reader stands to gain directly from your objective in time, money, and such. Or perhaps you can show how the reader stands to gain in goodwill or prestige. Sometimes you may be able to persuade by appealing to the aesthetic side—to love of beauty, excitement, serenity, and the like. When such appeals as these will not do the job, you may be able to use the altruistic appeal—the pleasant feeling one gets from doing a good turn. In any event, your task is to build the most convincing strategy you can devise for your specific situation.

Attention in the opening contact

Armed with the strategy which will convince your reader to grant your request, you are ready to fit it into a plan for presentation. As we have noted, the best plan for such letters is an indirect one. Thus, your opening will not give away your goal. Instead, it will serve as a form of buffer for your main objective.

As in other indirect letters, your opening has the basic objective of setting up the strategy of your presentation. In persuasion situations, however, it has a second objective. Because you usually are writing to someone who has not invited your correspondence, and who may not even care to see it, your opening must also gain interest. A flat, dull statement would do little to begin the change which must be made in your reader's mind. You can get better results from some interest-arresting question or statement which will start the reader's mental activity. Because of its natural interest value, a question form of beginning is especially good, if, of course, it is appropriate to your strategy. The following beginning sentences illustrate some of the possible variations.

From a covering letter of a questionnaire seeking medical doctors' opinions:

> What, in your opinion as a medical doctor, is the future of the private practice of medicine?

From a letter requesting contributions for handicapped children:

> While you and I dined heartily last night, 31 orphans at San Pablo Mission had only dried beans to eat.

From a letter seeking cooperation of business leaders in promoting a fair:

> What would it mean to your profits if 300,000 free-spending visitors were to come to our town during a single week?

Presentation of the persuasion

Following your interest-arresting opening, you should proceed with your objective of persuading your reader. Your task here involves a logical and orderly presentation of the reasoning you have selected.

As in all convincing arguments, you should do more than merely list points. You should help to put over your points with words and structures which add to their persuasiveness. Since you are trying to penetrate a resisting mind, you will need to make good use of you-viewpoint adaptation in your discussion. You will need to pay careful attention to the connotations of your words and the clarity of your expression. And because your reader may tend to become impatient if you delay your objective for long, you will need to make your words travel fast.

Goodwill and action in the close

After you have done the selling job, you logically move to the action you seek. You have prepared the reader for what you want. If you have done a good job, the reader is ready to accept your proposal.

As with all negative parts, your request requires care in word choice. You will want to avoid all words which tend to detract from it. You will want to avoid words which bring to mind ugly pictures and things which might work against you. Words which bring to mind reasons for refusing are especially harmful, as in this example:

> I am aware that business people in your position have little free time to give, but will you please consider accepting an assignment to the board of directors of the Children's Fund?

The following positive tie-in with a major point in the persuasion strategy does a much better job of asking:

> Because your organizing skills are so desperately needed, will you please serve on the board of directors of the Children's Fund?

Whether your request should end your letter will depend on the needs of the case. In some cases you will need to follow your request with additional words of explanation and conviction. Especially is this procedure effective when your persuasion effort must be long and you simply cannot keep your objective from your reader through the presentation of all your reasoning. On the other hand, you might well end less-involved presentations with the request. Even in this latter case, however, you may want to follow the request with a reminder of the appeal used. As illustrated at the end of the following letter, this procedure associates the request with the advantage the reader will enjoy by agreeing to the request.

Approach variations illustrated

That persuasive requests make good use of the imagination is illustrated by the following examples. All generally follow the plan just described, yet each adapts to the specific situation and readers involved. The first is a request sent to prospective contributors by the solicitation committee of a city's Junior Achievement program. The letter's opening has good interest appeal, and it sets up the overall plan. Perhaps its special need for explanation slows the movement to the persuasion effort somewhat. But the explanation helps in the persuasion effort. Its strength comes from a strong you-viewpoint slant, and it leads directly to the action close.

Dear Mr. Williams:

Right now—right here in our city—620 teenage youngsters are running 37 corporations. With their only adult help being advice from some of your business associates who work with them, the kids run the whole show. Last September they applied for a charter and elected officers. They selected products for manufacture—antifreeze, candles, and chairs, to name a few. They issued stock— and they sold it, too. With the proceeds from stock sales, they set up a production operation. Now they are producing and marketing their products. This May they will liquidate their companies and account to their stockholders for their profits or losses.

You, as a public-spirited citizen, will quickly see the merits of the Junior Achievement program. You know the value of such realistic experience to the kids—how it teaches them the operations of business and how it sells them on the merits of our American system of free enterprise. You can see, also, that it's an exciting and wholesome program—the kind we need more of to combat delinquency. After you have considered these points and others you will find in the enclosed brochure, I know you will see that Junior Achievement is a good thing.

Like all good things, Junior Achievement needs all of us behind it. During the three years the program has been in our city, it has had enthusiastic support from local business leaders. But with the over 900 students on the waiting list this year, our plans for next year call for expansion. That's why I ask that you help make the program available to more youngsters with a $50 contribution (it's deductible). Please make your check payable to Junior Achievement, and send it right away. You will be doing a good thing for the kids in our town.

Sincerely,

The next letter uses the interest-gaining narrative approach to gain the attention of prospective contributors for Father Flanagan's Boys Town. Its appeal is subtle, coming mainly through the sympathy aroused from the story told. It is powerful persuasion. It illustrates how far the imagination may range in finding an effective approach.

My Dear Friend:

A knock at the door—a swirl of snow over the threshold and standing in the warm glow of the hall light was little Joe. His thin jacket was drawn tightly around his small body. "I'm here, Father. I'm here for an education," he blurted out.

Like other homeless boys, Joe dropped out of school at an early age. He had made his lonely way over hundreds of miles to Boys Town, determined to better himself by continuing his education. Now he stood there, cold, hungry, and forlorn, his big eyes pleading. A hot meal and a warm clean bed for the night—again I had found a room for one more boy. Joe proved to be an adept student and now, a leading citizen in his community, he follows his profession like other Boys Town graduates as shown on the back of this letter.

During the past 47 years about 11,000 homeless boys have come to Boys Town. They were sad at heart, sensitive, and with many hidden heartaches because some tragedy had robbed them of their home and parents. Here they begin life all over again, in clean, healthy surroundings. Through understanding and individual counseling we give them a feeling of contentment and a sense of dignity. They receive an excellent education in our well equipped and fully accredited schools.

As Christmas approaches our hearts go out to these unfortunate boys and for the other homeless ones who will be coming to Boys Town. Will you help me provide for them? Here are your Boys Town Christmas seals. Please keep them and use them and send me in the enclosed envelope $1, $2, $5, or more as your heart dictates.

In appreciation of your kind generosity our boys will elect you an Honorary Citizen of Boys Town and I will send your certificate with my acknowledgment. May your Christmas be especially happy since you have extended a helping hand to our unfortunate and helpless boys. Thank you and God bless you!

Sincerely,

The next letter is from the editor of a trade magazine to a business executive. The editor is seeking information for an article on desirable application procedures for new college graduates.

The letter begins with an interest-gaining question which sets up the explanation. The following explanation is straightforward, yet it appeals subtly to the good feeling one gets from helping others (the young job seekers). After the appeal has had its effect, the request comes. It is clear and direct. The final words strongly recall the basic appeal of helping young people.

Dear Ms. Romano:

What clues have you found in application letters which help you to estimate a person's character and desirability to your firm?

Young people entering the field of business are eager for any clue that will put them on the other side of the fence. They want to know what goes on in your mind when you are judging the people behind the letters. In our column, "Letters That Talk," we want to send a message especially to those people. In order to make the article as practical as possible, we are drawing out information from people in the field who really know.

A mutual friend of ours told me of your recent problem of finding the most desirable person back of 260 application letters. What specific points did you look for in these letters? What were those clues that distinguished some people from the others? When the going got hard, what fine points enabled you to make your final choice? The young people of today are eager for you to answer these questions.

You can help solve the young person's problem if you will jot down your personal comments on these letters and allow me to study them in confidence as the basis for an article. Will you do this for us—and them? It is just possible, you know, that through your help in this article to the young business people you may contribute to the success of a future leader in your own company. At least, you will be of service to the mass of young people who are trying to get "that" job which is so important to them right now.

Sincerely,

Collection letters

When your customers do not pay their bills on time, you must try to collect. If you follow conventional business practice, you are likely to use letters in your efforts. You could use other ways—for example, telephone or personal visits. But letters are the most common.

A series of efforts

In studying collection letters, first you should understand how businesses usually collect past-due bills. Typically, their collection efforts consist of a series of steps. Each step is a contact (usually by mail) with the delinquent customer. The first step is the bill that is sent on the due date. If this bill is not paid, a second bill may be sent—maybe a third. Sometimes for added strength a few reminder words, such as "Please," "May we remind you?" "Probably you have forgotten," are added to a past-due bill. These reminders may be in various forms—printed enclosures, stickers, stamped words.

If the reminders fail to bring in the money, the efforts get stronger. Typically, a letter is sent urging payment. If this one fails, another one is sent—and another—and another. The letters get progressively stronger. As we shall see, how many letters are written depends on company policy. When the buildup of letters fails to bring in the money, a final letter ends the mail effort. Additional action through credit bureaus or the courts could follow.

In a sense, the buildup of collection efforts resembles a stairway (see Figure 11–1). Each step represents a collection effort. The first steps are called *early-stage* collection efforts. Mainly these are the reminders. The assumption at this stage is that the debtors *will* pay. The company needs only to remind them.

Following the early (will-pay) stage comes the middle stage of collection. Here the company's attitude becomes that of having to convince the readers that they *should* pay. This truly is a persuasion stage. The company's goal is to sell the debtors on the idea of paying. This stage makes up the bulk of most collection series.

After all persuasive efforts to collect have failed, the letters must stop. So a final stage must end the collection-letter series. In this stage the company's attitude becomes that of having to convince the debtors that they *must*

Figure 11–1
Diagram of the Collection Procedure

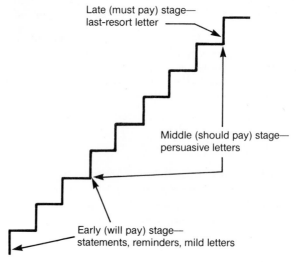

Late (must pay) stage—
last-resort letter

Middle (should pay) stage—
persuasive letters

Early (will pay) stage—
statements, reminders, mild letters

Note: Number of steps depends on policy of the firm

pay. Called last-resort, this stage consists of just one letter. Because this letter is so different from the others, it justifies being a stage by itself.

Determining the collection series

How many steps you may choose to use in a collection effort or how much time should elapse between steps should be based primarily on the class of credit risk with whom you are dealing and on the conventions of your business. For example, if you are collecting for an exclusive dress shop catering to good credit risks, you would probably move slowly in your efforts. You would send a number of reminders before resorting to persuasive effort. Then you would move slowly through a series of persuasive letters, reaching last-resort action only after giving the reader every opportunity to respond. Your collection efforts might extend over a long period—perhaps even a year or more.

On the other hand, if you are collecting from a bad credit risk, you would move faster through your collection efforts; and you would not take many steps. In extreme cases, you might jump quickly from routine statements to strong persuasion. Then, should the persuasion not work, you might move just as quickly to last-resort action. Such a series could reach its end in a matter of a few weeks.

Convention requires that your collection efforts with mercantile accounts move at a faster rate than those for the individual consumer. You will find that businesses expect and receive payments on a timely basis from other businesses; and when payments lag, collection efforts move fast. Because business dealings are more impersonal, your collection efforts with business accounts can be more matter-of-fact and more calm and rational in their approach.

Individual consumer accounts vary greatly in the treatment you should give them. Probably you would be wise to classify them on some basis. Some classification by type of risk would fit most collection operations. Also, some classification by type of account may be helpful. Open accounts represent the most selective type of credit risk; thus, they are handled slowly and tactfully. Budget accounts, cycle accounts, and other credit plans used for more questionable risks require a more aggressive collection effort. Installment accounts traditionally permit little laxness in payment, and move to strong action quickly.

Early-stage efforts

As long as it appears that your customers have good intentions of paying but have forgotten or have just put it off, you should use tact in dealing with them. At first, you will be wise to follow the lead of most companies by sending a duplicate of the original bill. For added strength, you might elect to add a few reminder words to the bill, perhaps as a sticker, a rubber-stamp message, or a printed insert. Such reminders can take many forms. Typically, they carry such messages as "Please," "May we remind you," "Probably you have forgotten," and "Just a friendly reminder."

If your reminders fail to bring in the money, you will need to begin your collection letter efforts. Except in cases in which your series must move quickly, your first letter should be in the reminder stage. Actually, such letters are not truly persuasive. At least, they do not follow the conventional persuasion pattern covered in this chapter. But because they are a part of the overall persuasive buildup of the series, we shall discuss them here.

If you follow the lead of most companies, your first collection letter will use a direct pattern of organization. At the beginning you will courteously come to the point and remind your reader of the past-due account. Because your assumption at this stage is that the reader *will pay,* your goal is to remind more pointedly than you have done in the past. But because the account is not long past due, you have no cause to use strong appeals for payment. Your message may contain some appropriate goodwill talk—as much as is necessary to convince your reader of your friendly intent. Obviously, such messages need not be long. Usually, two or three short paragraphs are adequate.

Although such letters follow no definite pattern, the following three are typical. The first is a form letter which reminds directly of the past-due bill, but it does so with courtesy and tact. It gives the reader a face-saving explanation (that he or she forgot). It includes the subtle suggestion that paying is something the reader will want to do. Appropriate goodwill talk ends the letter.

Dear Mr. Beloit:

This is just a friendly reminder that your account with us is now two months past due (see enclosed statement). No doubt you just overlooked it. If you're like me, you'll appreciate my calling it to your attention.

Loren's genuinely appreciates your business. We look forward to serving you in the years ahead.

Sincerely,

The second letter is quite direct in its beginning, getting right down to the basic question. But its tactful words clear it of any overly negative effect. Its goodwill content and closing invitation to trade clearly mark it as a friendly reminder.

Dear Ms. Adams:

Won't you take a brief moment to write a check for the $148.50 now four months past due on your account? We know how easy it is to let such matters slip by, and we are confident that you will appreciate this friendly reminder.

If you choose to bring your check into the store personally, you'll enjoy seeing the new fall suits which are beginning to arrive. Perhaps you will want to take advantage of the preseason discounts Loren's charge customers can get on purchases made before the 15th.

We look forward to seeing you in the store again soon.

Sincerely,

The third letter, which is from a major publisher to a subscriber, reminds the reader while helping her or him to save face by offering a possible explanation. Its positive words clearly mark it as a friendly reminder.

Dear Subscriber:

Like many other subscribers, you probably have the systematic habit of settling your accounts at a regular time every month.

For this reason, we almost wish the enclosed bill were larger—then you wouldn't have overlooked it. The amount is so small, you must have lost sight of it the last time you cleaned up your monthly bills.

If so, won't you send us your check today?

This will clear your books . . . ours, too . . . and will be much appreciated. Many thanks!

Cordially,

A milder type of reminder letter is one which appears to have some other purpose for being sent than to collect money. Usually, such letters are basically goodwill letters. They may tell of new merchandise, promotions, services, and such. But in telling of these goodwill topics, they slip in the reminder of the past-due account. Such letters truly follow a sandwich pattern, with the payment reminder placed between two sections of noncollection material.

Obviously, this type of letter is best used when the accounts can be handled on an individual, personal basis. Because not many companies feel that they can afford to give their accounts such treatment, this approach is not widely used. Nevertheless, it has merit, and it is worthy of your consideration whenever the situation will permit.

The following illustration shows how this form of letter begins away from the subject of collection and on a topic which justifies the letter's being sent. After some discussion of this topic, it slips into a reminder of the past-due account, and then it moves back to the other friendly talk.

Dear Ms. Vinton:

As one of Brock's discriminating charge customers, you will be well pleased when you see the new fashions we have selected for the fall. They're coming in fast now and will be ready for our annual preseason preferred-customer sale next week. As you would expect, our buyers have made their usual careful selections from the creations of both Arno and d'Antoni, as well as the leading American fashion houses.

You may inspect these exciting fashions on the 15th or 16th from 7–9:30 p.m. As a preferred customer, you will be entitled to the usual 10 percent preseason discount; and of course, you may add it to your account. While you are doing it, perhaps you will wish to pay the $178.40 now four months past due, which no doubt you have just overlooked. We know you will enjoy this annual event and that you will find something made especially for you.

We look forward to having you with us.

Sincerely,

The middle (persuasion) stage

If your reminders do not collect the money, you will need to write stronger letters to convince the debtors that they *should* pay. Your procedure here is first to select a basic appeal. Then you present this appeal convincingly. That is, you persuade.

Analysis of the strategy. As in other cases requiring persuasion, the delinquent customers' wishes run contrary to yours. You want them to pay. They have shown by ignoring your reminders that at best they are not eager to pay. Thus, they are not likely to receive favorably your persuasive letter to collect. More than likely, they do not want to hear from you at all. As you know, in such situations you must gain reader attention at the beginning. If you do not, the odds of getting across your message are slim.

In persuading debtors to pay, you should use strategy. As in other persuasion cases, you should begin by looking at the situation as the reader sees it. Then you should select appeals which will work with your particular reader. You may, for example, feel that a fair-play appeal will work in a particular case. Or perhaps you would select an appeal to pride, to the value of a good credit record, or to the protection of social standing. The point is, you should select the appeal you feel will work best in the one case.

After selecting your appeal, you should develop it by thinking out the reasoning that will convince the debtor to pay. If, for example, you selected the fair-play appeal, you might show that the debtor got something for the promise to pay. Now it is only fair that the debtor keep his or her end of the bargain. You would go through similar strategies with the other appeals.

How strong you make your appeal depends on how far along in the collection effort you are. Usually, your first persuasion letter is mild and has much goodwill content. The following letters get stronger and stronger, and the goodwill content becomes less and less.

Attention in the opening. This letter is not invited—probably not even wanted. Thus, your first words have a special need to gain attention. As your readers have received your reminders, they know that they owe you. More than likely, most of them intend to pay—in time—when it is convenient. They may quickly label your letter as just another dun and put it aside. So, if this letter is to have a chance of succeeding, it must gain attention right away.

In gaining attention, you will need to use your imagination to find some interesting opening words. Whatever words you select, they should also help to set up your basic appeal. The possibilities are unlimited and are explained best by example.

One successful letter begins with this question:

When they ask about you, what shall we tell them?

Written late in the collection series, the letter uses the appeal of the danger of losing a good credit reputation. The opening truly is a persuasive question. It makes one want to read further to learn just what is to be told. Clearly, it sets up discussion of the appeal.

Another successful beginning asks a question about the product for which the debtor owes:

How are you and your Arctic air-conditioning system making it through these hot summer months?

This opening has the subtle advantage of working on the reader's conscience through a friendly human question. The appeal it sets up is that of fair play—of persuading the reader to carry out his or her end of a bargain for goods now being enjoyed.

Another interest-gaining question is this one:

How would you write to a good friend on an embarrassing subject?

The question is personal. It is interesting. It sets up the persuasion of the letter. This persuasion, of course, builds around the human situation of friends communicating on a subject that hurts friendships. The appeal it sets up is that of the reader's moral obligation to a friend.

Persuasive presentation of the appeal. Following the opening contact, you should present the appeal you have selected. Your beginning sentence has set it up. So presenting the appeal is the logical thing to do. Because the opening has set up the appeal, the shift in thought at this point should be smooth.

Presenting the appeal requires adapting to the reader's point of view. You study the appeal for its you-viewpoint possibilities. Then you present it in these terms. The technique is much like that of selling. You have searched through your imagination for reasoning that will move your reader to take the action you want taken. You try to show the advantages to be received from taking it. And you present it all in the carefully selected language that will convince.

In writing this part, you should be careful that your words carry just the right degree of force for the one case. Early in the collection series, the facts of the case may call for mild persuasion. The farther along the collection series you progress, however, the more forceful you can afford to be. In addition, you will need to take care that you do not insult, talk down to, lecture, or show anger. As we have noted in other related situations, an angry reader tends to resist; and resistance leads to failure. Instead, your tone should be wholesome and friendly. You will need to keep in mind that throughout this stage of collection you hope to collect, to maintain cordial relations, and perhaps even to continue business with the debtor. If you did not feel this way, you would move to the last-resort letter.

The closing drive for payment. After you have made your persuasive appeal, the logical follow-up is to ask for the payment. In doing this, you should bring in a reference to the reader's past-due account (how much, how long past due, perhaps even what for). In form letters, however, often this information goes outside the letter—at the bottom of the page or as a separate statement. Next, you should ask for payment. You should ask directly, in words that form a clear question, not merely hint at payment. "Won't you please write a check for $77.88 today and mail it to us right away?" meets this requirement. "We shall appreciate your writing and sending your check for $77.88" does not.

In collection letters as in sales letters, a closing reminder of a benefit to be gained by taking the action strengthens the appeal. For example, a letter which stresses an appeal to the advantages of a prompt-pay record for a business could effectively end with these words:

> Won't you please write out and mail a check for the $275.30 right now while you're thinking about it? It's your best insurance of keeping your invaluable prompt-pay record.

Or a letter appealing to the moral principle of paying might have this ending:

> Won't you write us a check for the amount owed and prove that you're the kind of person we think you are?

Illustrations of approach variations. Because collection letters are so much a product of the creative mind, the variations possible are best shown by illustration. As you would expect, the examples selected do not cover all the variations which might be used. They represent only a small selection from a whole that is limited only by the imagination.

The first example comes early in the collection series of a distributor to a retail customer. It builds around an appeal to the reader's pride. By beginning with an excerpt from the debtor's credit report, it ranks high in interest value.

Dear Mr. Black:

He is of Scotch-Irish descent, a native of Springfield, Illinois. Twenty-seven years of experience in retail hardware operations. Hard working, reliable, and competent manager. Pays promptly, usually discounts. . . .

This is a part of the report we received on you when you applied for credit with us. It's an excellent report, and you have every right to be proud of it. It shows that you are a man of your word—that when you promise to pay, you come through with the payment. And you have proved it over a period of 27 years.

In view of your good record, we are concerned that your account has slipped into the delinquent group. Certainly, a man of your reputation will want to take care of this matter right away. So won't you please write and mail a check for the $488.50 now 60 days past due on invoice 704A? Your good record tells us that you will.

Sincerely,

Using an appeal to the advantages to be derived from prompt payment, the following letter proved to be very effective with a retail account. Part of its effectiveness may be explained by its interest-gaining question opening as well as the straightforward, logical approach it takes.

Dear Ms. Carr:

Have you wondered how we are able to sell quality hand tools at 10 percent under our competitors? As you know, the low price permits you to take an additional markup and still beat competition.

A part of the explanation lies in our selective credit policy. We grant credit only to the most reliable firms—those that have earned their good credit reputation. As they pay us promptly, we can keep down collection costs. And we can pass these savings on to you.

As you were reported to us as an excellent credit risk, we know that you will want to join our other prompt-pay customers. So will you please send us a check today for the $845.53 now 30 days past due on your order for assorted hand tools? You will be helping all of us to profit.

Sincerely,

The next letter builds around an appeal to pride supported by the advantages of a prompt-pay record. Although much of the persuasion is presented without actual you-references, its you-viewpoint adaptation is clearly implied.

Dear Mr. Stevenson:

You don't belong in that group!

Every day Massey's deals with hundreds of charge customers. More than 99 percent of them come through with their obligations to pay. We mark them as "prompt pay," and the doors to credit buying are opened to them all over town. Less than 1 percent don't pay right away. Of course, sometimes they have good reasons, and most of them tell us about it. And we work something out. But a few allow their good credit records to tarnish.

Somehow, you have permitted your account to place your name in this last group. We don't think it belongs there. Won't you please remove it by writing us a check for the $137.75 now over four months past due? It would place you in the group in which you belong.

Sincerely,

Written near the end of the collection series, the next letter uses an appeal to the value of a good credit reputation. Its short and direct question opening quickly gains attention. It talks directly to the reader, interpreting the effects of her credit record on her personally.

Dear Ms. Matson:

How much is it worth to you? It's your credit record I am referring to, and it's a most important question to you now that it hangs in the balance.

The good reports we got on you when you opened your account told us that you have handled your promises to pay promptly for a long time. We know that you must want to maintain this good rating, for it means so much to you. Aside from the obvious advantages of credit buying, it is important to you personally. The community and your friends judge you by how you fulfill your promises. It is vital to your own peace of mind to know that you have fulfilled your promises to pay.

Because your credit record means so much to you, it is hard to understand how you have permitted your account of $371.43 to run six months past due. Won't you please save your good credit record by sending us payment today?

Sincerely,

A next-to-last letter to a retail customer is the following illustration. Obviously, it is stronger than the preceding one, for it talks more of the effects of nonpayment than of the advantages of paying. It presents a rather doleful picture of the consequences of not paying.

> Dear Ms. Carmichel:
>
> What shall we report about you?
>
> As you may know, all members of the Capital Credit Bureau must report their long-past-due accounts for distribution to the members. At the moment your own account is in the balance, and we are wondering whether we shall be forced to report it. We are concerned because what we must say will mean so much to you personally.
>
> A slow-pay record would just about ruin the good credit reputation you have built up over the years. You wouldn't find it easy to buy on credit from Capital Bureau members (and this includes just about every credit-granting business in town). Probably your credit privileges would be cut off completely. It would take you long years to regain the good reputation you now enjoy.
>
> So won't you please avoid all this by mailing a check for the $474.80 now nine months past due? It would stop the report and would save your credit record.
>
> Sincerely,

Last-resort letters

Hard as you may try, not all of your collection letters will bring in the money. Some of your debtors will ignore your most persuasive efforts. Because you cannot continue your collection efforts indefinitely, you will need to take some last-resort action with these debtors. And you will use your final letter in the collection series to inform them of this action.

A number of last-resort actions are available to you at this stage. One of the most common ones is to report the account to some credit interchange group, such as the credit bureau in the community to which most retailers belong. Another is to sell the account to a collection agency, with full authority to take legal steps if necessary. Yet another is to take the delinquent to court. You will need to decide on the action appropriate to your case. In making your decision, you should consider the customs in the field, the nature of the account, and the image of your organization.

Justification of directness. In selecting the letter plan for the last-resort letter, you should consider what must be done to collect the money. Up to this point, you have tried the milder persuasive methods. They have not worked. Something stronger is needed.

As we learned earlier, there is strength in directness. We have not used it through the middle stage of the series because directness in such cases can destroy goodwill. Until now, we have been concerned about keeping goodwill. We have wanted to save the account. But now we have reached the point where we are more interested in collecting the money. So we can justify using the strongest plan—the plan of directness.

Direct presentation of last-resort action. For the strongest effect, as well as for interest-gaining purposes, you should begin the last-resort letter with a clear statement of your action. That is, you should tell the reader right away just what you are going to do. Although your reader probably knows very well why you are taking the action, it is likely to help your case if you can bring in some justification of your decision. It could be that the reader has delayed later than she or he thinks. Something like this would do the job well:

> Your failure to pay the $378.40 now seven months past due on your account leaves us no choice but to report you to the Omaha Credit Bureau.

Interpretation of the action. Following your direct opening should come your persuasion. Again, in selecting it, you need to place yourself in your reader's position. You need to think through your last-resort action to see just how it will affect the reader. It may mean that she or he will lose credit-buying privileges. Or it may mean court costs, loss of prestige, personal embarrassment, and the like. Whatever the effects, you should reason them out, and you should think about how you can best present them to make your reader understand them. Then you should describe these effects in clear, convincing language.

In describing the doleful effects of the last-resort action, you will need to watch the tone of your words. Certainly, you are no longer handling the reader with the tact you used in earlier efforts. But you still wish to avoid inviting his or her anger, for even at this stage anger invites resistance. So, instead of a tone of exasperation, your words should show a genuine concern for the predicament the reader is in. You wish it had not turned out this way, but the reader's actions leave you no other course.

The action close. After you have described the effects of the last-resort action, you should give your reader a last chance to pay. Thus, in your close you should set a deadline for payment, or perhaps for other arrangements; and you should urge the reader to meet this deadline. As in other persuasive efforts your final words should recall what the reader will gain (or avoid) by taking the action. The following close meets these requirements well:

> We won't report you to Capital Credit Bureau until the 15th; so won't you please help yourself by sending us your check by that date? It's the one way you can save your credit reputation.

Last-resort illustrated. The effectiveness of the direct approach to collection is well illustrated by the following letter. Its opening strength is high in interest value, and its interpretation of the effects of the action is vividly described in terms of the reader's viewpoint. In spite of its sternness, it reflects a spirit of helpfulness and concern for the reader's welfare.

> Dear Mr. Perry:
>
> Your failure to answer all of our seven requests for payment of the $317.10 now 12 months past due leaves us no choice but to take you to court for collection. We sincerely want to avoid this action, for it would be unpleasant for both of us. Especially would it be unpleasant for you.
>
> For you, it would mean that you would be forced to pay. You would pay not just the $317.10 you owe, but court costs also. In addition, you would pay attorneys' fees.
>
> Also, legal action would be embarrassing to you. As you know, it's the kind of information people talk about. Your friends would pick it up. So would other

business people. Results might well be an end to your credit buying. And your credit reputation would be injured permanently.

You can avoid the effects of court action only by paying before the 17th— the day we shall turn your account over to our attorney. Won't you please help yourself by mailing your check by that date? It's the only way you can avoid the cost and embarrassment of going to court.

Sincerely,

As illustrated in the next example, last-resort letters to industrial accounts can be much like those to consumers. This one begins directly. In addition to naming the action, it justifies taking it by reviewing past collection efforts. Explanation of the effects of the action is concrete, convincing, and without anger. Strong you-viewpoint is evident throughout. The close urges the debtor to pay, thereby avoiding the bad things described.

Dear Mr. Waldon:

Since our five previous requests for payment of your four-months past-due bill for $3,587.31 have received no response, we are forced to turn your account over to the Merchants' Credit and Collections Agency, unless payment is in our office by July 19.

As a business executive, you are well aware of just what this action can mean to you. The collection agency would be empowered to take this case to court. And court action would be both costly and embarrassing to you. You would be forced to pay not only the full $3,587.31, but court costs as well. Your friends around Millville would be quick to learn of a collection suit against you, for such news travels fast. Your other creditors also would pick up the news. Thus your future credit buying would be severely restricted—maybe even cut off completely. And with limited credit, chances are your business operations—and your profits—would be cut down.

We sincerely urge you to avoid this agency's forced collection, Mr. Waldon. We'll hold them off until July 19. You can hold them off permanently by mailing us your check for $3,587.31 so that it will reach us by that date. Won't you pay this honest debt right away and avoid the unpleasantness of court action?

Sincerely,

Letter problems—3

Persuasive requests

1.   At last week's public meeting, the leading citizens of the rural community of Green Meadows organized the Green Meadows Volunteer Fire Fighters. The goal of this new organization, of course, is to provide fire protection for the community.

Money contributions by those present provided enough to make a down payment on "Old Red," a somewhat old but efficient fire engine. And one citizen donated a vacant building (formerly a general store) which can be remodeled to be a suitable garage and fire department headquarters. Much more is needed from the community.

As the elected president of the Green Meadows Fire Fighters Association, you now have the task of getting additional help from the community. You will solicit this help by way of a persuasive letter addressed individually to the heads of household of the 756 families in the community.

In your letter you will appeal to the reader's sense of civic responsibility. You will ask for financial help (which will be needed on an annual basis). And you will ask for volunteer labor. From those young and vigorous and with the time required for training and practice, you will seek time as volunteer fire fighters. From others, you will seek help on the telephone relay network needed to assemble fire fighters. And you will seek help for working on the various auxiliary projects (fairs, raffles, and such) which will be used to raise money for the organization. There is enough work for everyone who is willing.

Write the letter that will convince your neighbors to work with you on this worthwhile project. You may use your logical imagination to furnish any additional information you feel you need, but don't change the nature of the assignment.

2.   Play the role of organization chairperson for the Tri-Cities Automobile Show. This newly formed organization was founded to give the automo-

bile dealers in the area an opportunity to display the new models in a festive atmosphere.

The plan is to rent the Pennebrook Convention Center in Bigg City, assign display areas to each brand of automobile, and promote the event heavily. Live entertainment, activities, free soft drinks, and contests will serve as added attractions throughout the one-day affair. But the biggest attraction of all will be the display of next year's models; and, periodically, all entertainment will cease so the people can inspect the automobiles without conflicting attractions. At the moment the idea is shared by 5 of the 28 auto dealers in the Tri-Cities area. You'd like to get the other 23 to cooperate, so you will attempt to persuade them to join you. You will do it by letter.

The plan you and your four associates worked out calls for a total budget of $42,000 for the show. If all 28 dealers participate, the cost will be $1,500 each. Of course, it could be higher if some do not participate. Any money left over would be returned to the dealers.

Since a number of the dealers sell the same brands, it would be necessary to so coordinate efforts that a complete display of models, without duplication, would be set up. A plan for coordinating displays will be worked out at the organizational meeting scheduled for next Thursday at 7:30 P.M. in room 113 at the Pennebrook Convention Center.

Filling in with any additional specific information you feel you need, write the form letter which will persuade the dealers to join in the activity. Use whatever appeals you feel will be most effective with this group. After you've convinced the dealers, ask that they attend the organizational meeting. Address the first letter to Maybell Popek, president of City Motor Company.

3. You are the advisor for the Senior Class Council of your area's high school. This year the Council is promoting a "Counsel a Kid" program.

The project is simple. It involves the counseling of graduating seniors by executives and professionals in the area of each senior's career interest. More specifically, it involves getting for a would-be physician a counseling session with a practicing physician, a would-be lawyer with a practicing lawyer, a would-be scientist with a practicing scientist, and so on. Through such contacts, each student should learn about the career he or she is considering and, thus, should be better prepared to make a career decision.

The Council has asked you to get the executives and professionals for it, and you have consented. Your effort will consist of writing a letter to a list of such people in the area. You will use whatever persuasive appeal you feel would be most effective in this case. You may make up any additional facts you feel are needed.

Address the letter to Amos Anderly, a lawyer and the first name on your list.

4. As administrative assistant to the president of Universal Refining Company, you have just been assigned a special problem. It seems that residents in the area of the Company's suburban headquarters do not like the way Company employees have used their streets for parking automobiles.

As their petition (signed by 29 residents) states, "even our driveways are regularly used."

Universal's management regrets that its employees are parking in the area streets, but it can't command its employees not to park there. Such parking is legal. It is not that the company doesn't provide adequate parking space. There is plenty, although it is to the back of the building and is not as convenient as the streets in front.

On the instructions of your president, you will write a form letter to all employees. The goal of the letter will be to persuade the employees to use the lots provided by the Company. Probably you will use an appeal to pride, although you will think through the problem before deciding.

5. The smoking problem has raised its head at the Sentry Insurance Company headquarters. For some time now nonsmokers have been complaining to management that they are bothered by the smoking of their neighbors in the work areas.

Management has considered various ways of solving the problem. It considered isolating the smokers, but this would destroy the functional work arrangement that has proved to be efficient. And it isn't quite ready to institute a rigid no-smoking-on-the-job rule. For the moment, it has decided to use persuasion. Its plan is to persuade the smokers to smoke only during designated break periods, and in a designated smoking area (the snack rooms on the second and fourth floors).

You, the Company's director of employee relations, have the job of persuading the workers to accept the plan. You will use a persuasive letter addressed to each employee to carry the message. Before you write it, you will think through the situation thoroughly. The appeal (or appeals) you will use will be those most likely to convince an irritated group of workers to give in to the demands of their fellow workers.

6. Ten months ago the Fenimore Manufacturing Company started a fitness program for its employees. It built an exercise room and a 1⅛-mile track at its Employee Recreation Center. With these new additions and the 120-by-50-foot swimming pool and four tennis courts which the Center already had, participants in the program had excellent facilities.

In addition to providing excellent facilities, the Company hired Anita Olsen, a qualified exercise specialist, to run the program and to develop individually tailored exercise programs for each participant. And it arranged for all participants to have a free preliminary physical examination at the North Side Clinic. But in spite of these efforts, participation in the program has been weak.

As head of employee relations, your job is to get the program moving. After considering various alternatives, you decide to write a letter that will be individually typed and mailed to each worker. It will present your best persuasive explanation of the values of the exercise program to the workers and their families. You may add additional information if you need it. Try to get the readers to respond by coming to your office to sign the participation forms.

7. At its last meeting, the board of directors of Mammoth Petroleum Company agreed to sponsor an educational program for employees.

The program that resulted consisted of a variety of course offerings. For those whose basic knowledge of mathematics, English, and science is weak, there were basic courses offered after work hours in the Company training center. Qualified public school teachers in the area were brought in to teach these courses. For those desiring college course work, the Company offered to underwrite all tuition costs at nearby Waterfield University. And for those wanting to study interesting and exciting topics, the Company offered short courses at its training center. Currently, the Company is offering courses in ceramics, music appreciation, and public speaking. It plans to offer courses in investments, automotive repair, interior decorating, and landscaping in the near future.

Clearly, the plan was to offer something for everyone. In spite of the Company's best efforts, however, very few of the employees have taken advantage of the courses. In fact, the whole program has been a miserable failure.

Before writing off the program as a lost cause, the Company will make one last effort to increase participation. To this point, bulletin-board announcements and a feature story in the Company house organ have been the primary means of promoting the courses. Now a persuasive letter sent to each worker will be used. And you, the assistant to the training director, have been assigned the task of writing the letter.

In the letter you will present your most persuasive arguments of why the workers should take advantage of the educational opportunities being offered. You will enclose a brochure describing the courses scheduled for the coming months and giving the details of the program.

If you need additional facts, you may supply them as long as they are consistent with the information given. Address the letter to the first name on the employee list: Morene E. Abbott. Type the letter for the signature of Durwood C. Cornwell, director of training.

8. Assume the role of administrative assistant to J. Jerome Bergeron, president of Night and Day Stores, Inc., a chain of 14 convenience stores in your city. Mr. Bergeron has just returned from a meeting sponsored by the local Chamber of Commerce designed to kick off a "Clean Up Our City" campaign.

At the meeting, Mr. Bergeron pledged the support of the Night and Day organization toward the campaign. Now he must get this support. The logical way of getting it is to work through the store managers. But because the managers are really independent operators working under a lease arrangement, Mr. Bergeron can't just order them to clean up their stores. Instead, he will have to persuade them. He will attempt to persuade them by means of a letter, and he has asked you to write the letter for him.

In planning the letter, you first must think through the situation to determine why one should want to participate in such a campaign. It is important also to determine just what is involved in a clean-up campaign.

Keeping the premises free of litter is one part of it. Another is improving the appearance of the stores—painting, repairing, and generally giving the place a fresh, neat appearance.

After you have thought through the matter, write the letter. Although you will write just one letter, it will be individually typed for each manager. Address the first one to Rose McCarnak, manager of the 12th Street store.

9. As president of the Bay City Historical Society, you are faced today with a very perplexing situation. An out-of-town realtor has bought the historic Thompson House and is planning to tear it down and build an apartment building on the site. You shudder at the thought of destroying this landmark.

You recall the background of the house—how it was built by pioneer settler Bill Thompson in the early 1800s. It was the scene of the Thompson massacre in 1848, when renegades killed the Thompson family after a three-day seige. During the Civil War it served briefly as a command post for Colonel Wilfred Watson and his staff of the 104th Confederate cavalry. It was a stagecoach stop in the post-Civil War period. Bought by Truman Carpenter in 1882, the house served as a residence for various members of the Carpenter family until it was bought last year by Penny Pennbrooke, the realtor who plans to destroy it.

You must attempt to persuade Ms. Pennbrooke not to tear down the structure. Thus, you will write her a letter in which you will present the Society's (and your) case. Of course, you cannot expect her to lose the money she has invested. So in the name of the Society you'll offer to buy the property at her cost. You'll send along with the letter a petition signed by 2,600 Bay City residents supporting your cause.

10. Project yourself into the future about ten years and assume that you are the College of Business Administration representative on the board of directors of your Alumni Association—a position you hold in addition to your full-time job as vice president of public relations for Micro Instruments, Inc. Today you received a packet of information from O. L. Davis, chairman of the board of the Alumni Association. The packet includes plans for a new Alumni House to be built on the campus. This imposing new structure will serve as a focal point for all Alumni activities; and each college is to have its own room in the building for meetings, social gatherings, and other activities.

Each college is asked to solicit donations from its own graduates to provide the interior furnishings for the college's room. Naturally, your college's room should be one of the nicest in the new building, and it's your job to collect the $12,000 necessary to make the room a real showplace. Since all the graduates have done well in the real world of business, you know everyone can make a donation; but you also know that, since they are traditionally money-oriented, you will have to be very persuasive in the form letter you design to be sent out.

Your letter will have the letterhead of the Alumni Association and will be sent to individual addresses.

Although a major appeal will be directed to the pride of graduates in their alma mater, you can include any appeals that might be appropriate. You might include the fact that they'll want their room to be first class in every respect, the potential uses for the room, how they might benefit from the room when they're on campus, the potential for forming a private club to utilize the room year round, the public relations advantages of such a room, and so on.

Be creative and original, but keep your persuasive request realistic. Contributions to such causes are tax deductible and can be in any amount, but you might encourage $10 as a minimum. Stocks and bonds would also be welcome, and special arrangements can be made for them.

11. As student chairman of the homecoming activities of Hallsford College, it is your duty to line up some big-name talent for this year's traditional stage show. Various faculty members and students have requested that you try to get Ric Dorson, an alumnus of Hallsford, to agree to appear on the program and to sing some of his hit recordings. Dorson, a current rage in the world of popular music, and generally in the "with-it" set, was graduated from Hallsford in 1961. Since that time, his popularity in the singing world has skyrocketed.

But a problem presents itself. Dorson may not have too many fond memories of his college days. It took him six years to get through the degree requirements. And he was constantly in trouble with the administration.

Yet, because of pressure to try to get Dorson to be a part of this year's festivities, you're going to use your best persuasive writing personality. Try your hand at getting Dorson to fly to Simpson, Virginia, the home of Hallsford College, at his expense (you have no funds available for paying him). Write to him at his Hollywood address: International Studios, 1819 Pacific Boulevard.

12. As manager of the western division (Phoenix) of Great National Automobile Insurance Company, you have a ticklish situation concerning your agents facing you this morning. More and more policyowners are writing your office and asking questions about their policies. Most of the questions could best be answered by the agents who sell the insurance. It seems, however, that many agents tell their clients to write to the western division if they have questions.

The work load in answering these letters is becoming staggering. So you've decided to try to put an end to the problem. Write a form letter which will go to all the agents in your territory. Persuade them to have their customers contact them—not your office—when these policyowners have questions or complaints. After all, that's part of each agent's job. In effect, he's shirking his responsibility when he asks policyowners not to deal principally with him concerning their insurance needs.

You've found through the years that agents can get their feelings hurt rather easily. So you vow to write a letter that will get your mission accomplished but will not create ill will between the division office and the agents.

Collections

(These problems are arranged by series. The stage in the series is identified at the beginning of each problem.)

Regal Office Furniture Company Series

13. *(Early stage.)*   The local office of Sentry Realtors (Mary Mahoney, manager) owes your Regal Office Furniture Company $1,689 for an assortment of desks and chairs. You sent this firm the original invoice 75 days ago, with terms of 2/10, 10/30. Thirty days later (on the due date) you sent the first formal notice, and thirty days later you sent the second formal notice.

Today you're ready to try your first letter. You suspect Ms. Mahoney needs to be reminded, but you will try to make it a gentle one. This account has been a good one over the years.

14. *(Middle stage.)*   It is now 21 days after your first letter to Mary Mahoney and her Sentry Realtors. You have not received payment. So it is time to try again to collect the $1,689—now over two months past due.

You will write the company a somewhat stronger letter this time. For a basic appeal you'll stress the value of a prompt-pay record. Because the customer is a valued one with a long history of profitable relations with you, you'll be careful not to insult or offend. But you will be strong enough to convince the woman that she should pay.

15. *(Middle stage.)*   Your last letter to Sentry Realtors didn't work. Now, another 15 days later, you will write again.

This time you will try a stronger appeal. You will stress the fair-play theme—that is, you will emphasize how you did something for Sentry when it was in need. Now, it's only fair that Sentry takes care of its end of the bargain. Use your best persuasion to drive home the point; but remember, you are not yet ready for threatening talk.

16. *(Middle stage.)*   Mary Mahoney and her Sentry Realtors still haven't paid. Fifteen days after you wrote Sentry stressing the fair-play appeal, you wrote again. Now, another 15 days later, you'll have to write yet another letter.

In this letter you will use negative appeal for the first time. You will talk about the danger of losing a good credit reputation. Even so, the letter won't be threatening; nor will it show anger. If this one does not bring in the money, the next letter will be the last one.

17. *(Last resort.)*   After five futile attempts you will try one more letter to collect from Sentry Realtors. If it does not pay you, you will turn over the case to your attorney for collection. Your letter will show Ms. Mahoney how essential it is that she come through with payment. Not to do so would cost her heavily in court fees as well as damage to reputation. You will give Ms. Mahoney and Sentry 15 days from today before you will take final action.

The Esquire Limited Series

18. *(Early stage.)* Esquire Limited, your exclusive gentleman's clothing store, has served the high-income buyers of your community for seven months. So far, business has been good. Especially have credit sales been good. But recently you have been faced with a problem that was certain to occur sooner or later—the problem of collection. To your disappointment, you find that some of your elegant gentlemen are slow to pay.

Now, you are in the process of working out a collection procedure for these customers. You have decided on the following plan. First, you will send your monthly statement. You will send a second statement the next month. The following month (when the bill is two months past due) you will send a statement with a printed reminder. If this reminder does not bring in the money, you will send a first-reminder form letter the next month. The reminder letter will follow a "knowing you have been very busy, we thought you'd appreciate a reminder" theme. Its reasoning will be that you know the reader must have forgotten and will appreciate a reminder.

19. *(Middle stage.)* If the first letter doesn't do the job, 30 days later Esquire Limited will send a second form letter. This one will get down to collection talk, but it will take a positive approach. Its appeal will be to the social rewards of keeping an impeccable credit record.

Write this letter. Make some provisions for mentioning the amount owed and time past due.

20. *(Middle stage.)* Your collection plan for Esquire Limited is to write a third letter 30 days later and a fourth after another 30 days. By this time, the account is six months past due. A stronger appeal is in order.

In this fourth letter you will stress fair play. As in the other letters, make some provision for mentioning the amount owed and the time past due. Write this fourth letter.

21. *(Last resort.)* Fifteen days after the fourth letter in the Esquire Limited series comes another persuasive letter. This one talks rather directly about the advantages of maintaining a good credit record, and asks for the money with some force. If it doesn't work in 15 days, a last-resort letter is sent.

Because Esquire doesn't want the negative publicity associated with forced collection, it sells its long-overdue accounts to the City Collection Agency with full authorization to take legal action. Thus, the last letter Esquire writes warns of this impending action. It talks with friendly directness of what this action will mean to the reader. And it urges the reader to pay within 15 days and avoid these consequences. Write this last letter.

U-Pay-Less Series

22. *(Middle stage.)* U-Pay-Less is a department store that caters primarily to low-income families. It grants credit on a selective basis. But because of the income level of its customers, it maintains a vigorous collection procedure.

If payment is not made within 15 days of the initial statement, the store sends a second statement with a printed reminder. If this does not do the job in 15 days, it sends a persuasive form letter. By most standards, this letter would be classified as middle stage. It talks rather directly about the value of maintaining a good credit reputation. Write this letter.

23. *(Middle stage.)*   If U-Pay-Less's first letter doesn't collect in 15 days, it moves to a second persuasive form letter. This one talks rather directly and negatively about the consequences of losing a good credit reputation. And it makes clear that this is likely to happen to the reader if he or she doesn't pay up. Write this letter.

24. *(Last resort.)*   U-Pay-Less doesn't believe in waiting long. If it doesn't collect in another 15 days, it is ready for last-resort action. So it writes a third form letter. This one points out clearly that, unless payment is made within 15 days, it is turning the account over to its attorney with full authorization to go to court. And it talks convincingly and with concern about the consequences of this action. Write this letter.

Valley Fruit and Vegetable Supplies, Inc., Series

25. *(Early stage.)*   As collection manager for Valley Fruit and Vegetable Supplies, Inc., handle the account of Chapman's Grocery. This small-town grocery store made a $527.80 initial purchase from you 60 days ago on terms of 2/10, n/30. On the due date, you sent the statement; and, 15 days later, sent another statement with a printed reminder. Now, an additional 15 days later, you still have not received its money. So you will write a first letter.

This first letter will be a friendly reminder, for you're not yet ready to do anything to hamper relations with this new customer. Your letter will stress the theme that probably the store has overlooked this matter. Much of the letter will concern goodwill material. Address the letter to Marty A. Chapman, owner.

26. *(Middle stage.)*   The friendly reminder to Marty A. Chapman didn't work. Now, 20 days later, you have to write again.

This time your letter will have to be persuasive. You'll appeal to the man's pride, showing how a good credit record is a part of one's character.

27. *(Middle stage.)*   Try again to collect from Marty A. Chapman and his Chapman's Grocery. It's another 20 days later. In this letter you'll talk about the value of a good credit rating to one's success in business. You'll try to present the case so convincingly that he'll want to pay. But take care not to threaten. You'll do that next time—if he doesn't pay.

28. *(Last resort.)*   Unfortunately, Marty Chapman didn't respond to your persuasive request. So you'll have to take drastic action. This $527.80 account now is 90 days past due. If payment is not received within 15 days of the date of your letter, you will turn the matter over to your lawyers. They will then force collection through the courts.

Write a letter to Chapman telling him of this action, describing its consequences, and giving him a chance to pay up and avoid the consequences.

M & N Market Research, Inc., Series

29. *(Early stage.)* Your M & N Market Research, Inc., has had some difficulty collecting from Garner-Gomez Home Development, Inc. Some five months ago, president Cindy Gomez came to your firm with a market research problem concerning the development of Shady Shores, a 300-unit retirement village. You worked with Ms. Gomez personally for three eight-hour days. And you conducted a market study that consumed 84 hours of employee time. Then you submitted the finished report to Garner-Gomez. You were satisfied that your study gave the firm the information it needed for its project.

After submitting the report, you billed Garner-Gomez $8,470 for services rendered. Thirty days later it had not paid; so you sent a duplicate bill. Now, an additional 30 days later, Garner-Gomez still hasn't paid.

You feel it's time to send a gentle reminder. Because you had very friendly relations with Cindy Gomez, you will take the approach that payment has been overlooked and that a friendly reminder will be appreciated. Write the letter.

30. *(Middle stage.)* You are disappointed that your reminder to Cindy Gomez didn't bring in the money. Now, 60 days later, you will write a second letter. This one will stress the fair-play appeal (We've given you something you needed; now how about doing something for us?). Write the letter.

31. *(Middle stage.)* Thirty days after sending the second letter to Garner-Gomez, you had to write another letter. It didn't work. Now, 15 days later, you are ready to try your hand at letter writing again. If this letter doesn't work, the next letter will threaten last-resort action.

This fourth letter will stress the advantages of keeping a good credit record. And it will give convincing argument to support the appeal. Write the letter.

32. *(Last resort.)* You don't like to do it, but you feel that you must take last-resort action to collect the $8,470 Garner-Gomez owes you. If the firm doesn't pay within 15 days, you will take the matter to court. The letter will explain vividly the effects of this action. It will make Garner-Gomez see that it has no choice but to pay. Write the letter.

12

Correspondence: Sales and applications

BECAUSE THEY ARE very similar, sales and application letters are combined in this chapter. The similarities of the two letter situations should be apparent. For all practical purposes, both have the same general objective: to sell. The sales letter sells a product or service. The application letter sells one's ability to work.

Sales letters

Probably you will never write a sales letter—a real one, that is. With small exceptions, sales letters are written by professional writers who specialize in selling by the written word. They get to be professionals, first, by having a talent for writing and, second, by long, hard practice. Why then, you might ask, should you know how to write sales letters?

Value of sales writing

The answer should be obvious. Even though you are not likely to have to write sales letters in business, you benefit from the experience of writing them now as a student. You benefit even though your efforts may appear amateurish. Especially do you benefit from experience in using the techniques of selling which all sales letters employ. This experience will help you in writing other letters; for, in a sense, every letter you write is a sales letter. In every letter case you are selling something—an idea, a line of reasoning, your company, yourself. And to do this selling in each of these letter situations, you use the general techniques of selling.

Even in your daily life you will find good use for the selling technique. From time to time, all of us are called on to sell something. If we are engaged in selling goods and services, our sales efforts will, of course, be frequent. In other areas of business, our selling effort may consist only of selling such intangibles as an idea, our own competency, and the goodwill of the firm. In all such cases, you can make good use of the selling techniques. Thus, sales writing and the techniques used in it actually are more valuable to you than you might at first think. After you have studied the section, you should see why.

Need for preliminary knowledge

Before you can begin writing, you must know something about your product or service and your readers. You simply cannot sell most goods and services unless you know something about them. To sell, you have to tell your prospects what they need to know. You must tell how the product is made, how it works, what it will do, what it will not do, and the like. Thus, as an initial step in sales writing, you should study your product or service.

Next, you will need to know something about the people who will read your message. Especially will you need to know their needs for your product or service. In the progressive business organization, a marketing research department or agency will gather this information. If you do not have such a source of information, you will need to gather the information yourself. The nature of the product or service should give you some of the guidance you need. For example, industrial equipment would be likely to be bought by people with technical backgrounds. Expensive French perfumes and cosmetics would be most attractive to people in high-income brackets. And burial insurance would appeal to older members of the lower economic strata.

Determination of appeal

With your product or service and prospect in mind, you are ready to write the letter. Although this is the area about which even the experts know little, it does involve selecting the appeals you will use. By appeals, we mean the strategies you use to present a product or service favorably to the readers. You could, for example, introduce a product in terms of its beauty. You could present its taste qualities. You could stress the fun the product will give, or how it will make one more attractive to members of the opposite sex. Or you could attempt to sell your readers through appeals to profits, savings, durability, and the like.

For convenience of study, we may divide appeals into two broad groups. In one group are the emotional approaches to persuasion—those which affect how we feel. Included here are all the appeals to our senses—tasting, smelling, feeling, hearing, and seeing. They include, also, all strategies designed to arouse us through love, anger, pride, fear and enjoyment. Rational appeals are the appeals to reason—to the thinking mind. Included in this group are persuasion efforts based on saving or making money; doing a job better, or more efficiently; and getting better use of a product.

In any given case, the possible appeals available to you are many. You need to consider all that fit your product or service. Which ones you select should be based on an analysis of product or service and prospect. Some products or services, for example, are well suited to emotional selling. Products and services, such as perfume, travel, style merchandise, candy, and exotic food, lend themselves to emotional reasons for buying. On the other hand, products like automobile tires, tools, or industrial equipment are best sold through rational appeals. Automobile tires, for example, are not bought because they are beautiful. People buy them for very rational reasons—because they are durable, because they grip the road, because they are safe.

How the product will be used by the buyer may be a major determinant of the best sales strategy to use. Cosmetics sold to ultimate users might well be sold through emotional appeals. The same product sold to retailers (who are interested only in reselling the product) would require rational appeals. Such readers would have an interest in the emotional qualities of the product only to the extent that these qualities would influence customers to buy. The main concerns of retailers about the product involve such questions as the following: will it sell? what is the likely turnover? how much money will it make?

An approach to the subject

After selecting the appeal, you should write the letter. At this point, your imagination comes into the picture. Writing sales letters is as creative as writing short stories, plays, and novels. In addition to imagination, it probably involves applied psychology and the skillful use of words. There are as many different ways of handling sales letters as there are ideas in the brain. The only sure way of judging each is by the sales the letter brings in.

Because sales letters can vary so much, it is hard to describe their order. Even so, most follow a conventional pattern. In addition, most use conventional techniques. This pattern and these techniques are the subjects of discussion in the following paragraphs. As you study them, however, keep in mind that in actual practice only your imagination will limit the possibilities open to you.

Some mechanical differences

Planning the sales letter also involves determining the physical structure of the letter. As you may know from your personal experiences, sales letters often differ in many ways from other business letters. Usually they are mass-produced; and they appear to be mass-produced. Some direct-mail sellers try to overcome the impersonal appearance problem by personalizing the letter. Using sophisticated electronic typewriting and printing equipment, they address each letter individually. They even refer to the reader by name inside the body of the letter. Although such efforts to personalize sales letters apparently are effective, most direct-mail sellers continue to use impersonal mass mailings with such salutations as "Dear Student," "Dear Homeowner," and "Dear Investor." Some use the technique of eliminating the salutation and the inside address and placing the beginning words of the letter in the form of these parts. As shown below, this arrangement gives the letter what appears at first glance to be a normal layout. The letters can be mass-produced without the cost of individually typed inside addresses.

IT'S GREAT FOR PENICILLIN
BUT YOU CAN DO WITHOUT IT
ON YOUR ROOF. . . .

We're referring to roof fungus, which, like penicillin, is a moldlike growth. However, the similarity ends there. Unlike penicillin, roof fungus serves. . . .

Sales letters may use a variety of mechanical techniques to gain attention. Pictures, lines, diagrams, and cartoons are common; so is the use of varying colors of ink. Devices, such as coins, stamps, sandpaper, rubber bands, pencils, and paper clips, may be affixed to the letter to gain interest and help put over the appeal. One letter, for example, was mailed on scorched pages to emphasize the theme of "some hot news about fire insurance." A letter with a small pencil glued to the page used the theme that "the point of the pencil is to make it easy to order" a certain magazine. As you can see, the imagination possibilities in sales writing are boundless.

The attention opening

Although how you begin the sales letter can vary to the extent of your imagination, your words must meet one fundamental requirement. They must gain attention. Not to do so would insure the failure of your letter. The reason for the attention need of the opening should be apparent from your own experience. Sales letters are sent without invitation. They are not likely to be received favorably, and, in fact, may even be unwanted. So, unless the opening words do something to overcome the barriers and gain the reader's attention, the letter travels to the wastebasket unread.

Your plan for gaining attention is a part of your creative effort. But whatever you do, it should assist in presenting the sales message. That is, it must help to set up your strategy. It should not be just attention for attention's sake. Attention is really easy to get if nothing else is needed. For example, a small explosion set off when the reader opens the envelope would gain attention. So would an apparatus which would give an electric shock, or a miniature stink bomb. But these devices would not be likely to assist in the selling. Unless the attention is favorably directed, anger is likely to build up, and the letter is doomed.

One of the most effective attention-gaining openings is a statement or question which introduces a need the product will satisfy. For example, a rational-appeal letter to a retailer would clearly tap the reader's strong needs with these words:

Here is a proven best seller—and with a 12 percent greater markup!

Another rational-appeal beginning is this first sentence of a letter seeking to place metered typewriters in hotel lobbies:

Can you use an employee who not only works free of charge but who also pays you for the privilege of serving your clientele 24 hours a day?

Yet another rational-appeal beginning is this opening device from a letter selling a trade publication to business executives:

How to move more products,
Win more customers,
And make more money
. . . for less than $1 a week

For an illustration of a need-fulfilling beginning of an emotional-appeal approach, study these words, which begin a letter selling a fishing vacation at a lake resort:

Your line hums as it whirs through the air. Your lure splashes and dances across the smooth surface of the clear water as you reel in. From the depths you see the silver streak of a striking bass. You feel a sharp tug. And the battle is on!

As you can see, the preceding paragraph begins to cast an emotional spell around the reader, which is what emotional selling should do. It puts a rod in the hand, and it takes the reader through the thrills of the sport. To an addicted fisherman, the need is clearly established. Now the reader will be willing to listen to see how the need can be fulfilled.

As was mentioned previously, gimmicks sometimes are used to gain interest; but a gimmick is effective only if it supports the theme of the letter. One company made effective use of a penny affixed to the page top, with these words:

Most pennies won't buy much today, but this penny can save you untold worry and money—and bring you new *peace of mind.*

A paper manufacturer used a letter with small samples of sandpaper, corrugated aluminum, and smooth glossy paper fastened to the top of the page with these first words:

You've seen the ads—
you've heard the talk—
now feel for yourself what we mean by *level-smooth.*

Another opening approach is the story technique. Most people like to read stories; and if you can start one interestingly, your reader should want to hear the rest of it. Following is the interest-catching beginning of a four-page masterpiece used by *Time* magazine:

The girl in my office doorway was blonde . . . real blonde.
Her dress was as short as a cop's temper and tighter than a landlord's pocketbook. Her coat had orphaned a lot of little minks . . . and the ice on her wrists was the non-melting kind.

Thus far the attention-gaining techniques illustrated have been short. But longer ones are used—and used effectively. In fact, a technique currently popular in direct-mail selling is to place a digest of the total sales message at the beginning—usually before the salutation. The strategy is to communicate quickly the full impact of the sales message before the reader loses interest. If any of the points presented attract interest, the reader is likely to continue reading.

Illustrating this technique is the following beginning of a letter selling subscriptions to *Change*. These lines appeared before the salutation, and after the salutation came four pages of text:

> A quick way to determine whether you should read this letter:
>
> If you are involved in or influenced by higher education—and you simply don't have the time to read copiously in order to "keep up"—this letter is important. Because it offers you a money-saving shortcut (plus a free gift and a money-back guarantee).
>
> As a subscriber to CHANGE, the leading magazine of higher learning, you'll have facts and feelings at your fingertips—to help you form opinions. On today's topics: tenure, professors' unions, open admissions, the outlook for new PhDs . . . On just about any subject that concerns academe and you.
>
> CHANGE has the largest readership of any journal among academic people.
>
> To find out why 100,000 people now read CHANGE every month, take three minutes to read the following letter: . . . .

Presentation of the sales material

After your attention-gaining opening has set up your sales strategy, you develop this strategy. What you do in this part of the letter is the product of the thinking and planning you did at the beginning. In general, however, you should show a need and present your product or service as fulfilling this need.

The plan of your sales talk will vary with your imagination. But it is likely to follow certain general patterns determined by your choice of appeals. If you select an emotional appeal, for example, your opening probably has established an emotional atmosphere which you will continue to develop. Thus, you will sell your product in terms of its effects on your reader's senses. You will describe your product's appearance, texture, aroma, and taste so vividly that your reader will mentally see it, feel it—and want it. In general, you will seek to create an emotional need for your product.

If your appeal is rational, your sales description is likely to be based on factual material. In such a case, you should describe your product in terms of what it can do for your reader, rather than how it appeals to the senses. You should write matter-of-factly about such qualities as durability, savings, profits, and ease of operation. Differences in these two sharply contrasting appeals are shown in the illustrations near the chapter end.

The writing which carries your sales message can be quite different from your normal business writing. Usually, sales writing is highly conversational, fast moving, and aggressive. It even uses techniques that are incorrect or not appropriate in other forms of business writing—incomplete sentences, one-sentence paragraphs, folksy language, and such. It uses mechanical emphasis devices (underscore, capitalization, exclamation marks, color) to a high degree. Often its paragraphing appears choppy. Apparently, the direct-mail professionals feel that whatever will help to sell is appropriate.

Stress on the you-viewpoint

In no area of business communication is you-viewpoint writing more important than in sales writing. As we noted in our discussion of the makeup of
our mental filters, we human beings are selfish creatures. We are persuaded
best through our own self-interest. Thus, in sales writing, you would do
well to present the sales points in terms of reader interest. More specifically,
you should make good use of the pronoun *you* and the implied *you* throughout the letter.

The techniques of you-viewpoint writing are best described through
illustration. For example, in a sales letter to a retailer, one may wish to
stress what the manufacturer will do through advertising to help the retailer
sell the product. One could do this in matter-of-fact fashion: "Star mixers
will be advertised in *Time* for the next four issues." Or one could present
the information in terms of what it means to the reader: "Your customers
will read about the new Star mixers in all January issues of *Time.*" For
another example, one could quote price in impersonal language like "a 4-
ounce bottle costs $2.25 and you can sell it for $3.50." But one would
serve the reader's interests better with something like this: "You can sell
the 4-ounce size for $3.50 and make almost a 55 percent profit on your
$2.25 cost." The following examples further show the value of the technique:

Matter-of-fact Statements	*You-viewpoint Statements*
We make Aristocrat hosiery in three colors.	You may choose from three lovely shades. . . .
The Regal has a touch as light as a feather.	You'll like its feather-light touch.
Lime-Fizz tastes fresh and exciting.	You'll like the fresh, exciting taste of Lime-Fizz.
Baker's Dozen is packaged in a rectangular box which has a bright bull's eye design.	Baker's Dozen's new rectangular package fits compactly on your shelf, and its bright bull's eye design is sure to catch the eyes of your customers.

Completeness of the sale

Of course, the information you present and how you present it is a matter
for your best judgment. But you must make sure that you present enough
information to complete the sale. You should leave none of your reader's
questions unanswered. Nor should you fail to overcome any likely objections.
You must work to include all such basic information in your letter. And
you should present this information in a clear and convincing way.

In your effort to include all necessary information, you may choose to
use any of a variety of supplementary sales material—booklets, leaflets, brochures, and the like. When you use such supplements, you should take
care to coordinate all the parts of your mailing. In other words, all the
information mailed should fit together. The parts should form a unified
sales message.

As a general rule, you should use the letter to carry your basic sales
message. This means that in your letter you should not shift a major part

of your sales effort to an enclosure. Instead, you should use the enclosures mainly to supplement the sales letter—to supply the descriptive, pictorial, and other information that is too detailed for inclusion in the letter. To have all the parts of your mailing fit together into a unified sales effort, you might well direct the reader's attention to each of them. You can do this best through incidental references in the text of the letter.

Clearness and motion in the action

After you have sold your reader on your product or service, the next logical step is to drive for the sale. After all, this is what you have been working for all along; and it is a very natural conclusion to the sales effort you have made.

How you should word your drive for the sale depends on your strategy. If your selling effort is strong, your action may also be strong, even approaching a command. If you use a milder selling effort, you could make it a direct question. In any event, the drive for action should be crystal-clear—in no way resembling a hint. For best effect, it should take the reader through the motions of whatever will be necessary to complete the transaction, as is shown in these examples:

Just check your preferences on the enclosed stamped and addressed order form. Then drop it in the mail today!
Won't you please permit us to deliver your Tabor recorder on approval? The number is 348–8821. Dial it now, while it's on your mind.
Mail the enclosed card today—and see how right the *Atlantic* is for you!

Urgency in the action

Because action is sometimes delayed and forgotten, you would do well to include in your request some urge for immediate action. "Do it now," "While it's on your mind," or "Act today" illustrate some of the possible versions of this technique. Especially can you use this technique effectively when you tie it in with a practical reason for taking the action, such as "to take advantage of this three-day offer," "so that you can be ready for the Christmas rush," or "so that you will be the first in your community."

Recall of the appeal

Yet another effective technique for the close of a sales letter is to insert a few words which bring the basic appeal back to the reader's mind. The strategy here should be clear. By associating the action with the benefits your reader will gain by taking the action, you add strength to your sales effort. Illustrating this technique is a letter selling Ever-Flame cigarette lighters to retailers. After building its sales effort around a high-turnover, high-profit theme, the letter makes a drive for action and follows it with these words:

. . . and start taking your profits from the fast-selling Ever-Flame lighter.

Or, for another example, a letter selling a fishing resort vacation could follow its action words with these words recalling the joys described earlier in the letter:

> It's your reservation for a week of battle with the fightingest bass in the Southland.

Addition of a postscript

Because sales letters often are written in an informal, breezy style, a postscript (P.S.) is acceptable. It can be used effectively in a number of ways—to urge the reader to act, to emphasize the major appeal, to invite attention to other enclosures, and to suggest that the reader pass along the sales message to others. Examples of postscripts effectively used by professionals are the following:

> P.S. Don't forget! If ever you feel that *Action* is not for you, we'll give you every cent of your money back. We are that confident that *Action* will become one of your favorite magazines.
>
> P.S. Hurry! Save while this special money-saving offer lasts.
>
> P.S. Our little magazine makes a distinctive and appreciated gift. Know someone who's having a birthday soon?

A study of examples

Evidence of the creative nature of sales letter writing is shown best by example. A thorough review of possibilities, however, would be voluminous and could not possibly fit into the space requirements of this book. Our course, therefore, is to select a limited number of diverse types of letters to illustrate some of the variations possible.

First is a letter selling the services of a restaurant consultant. Because of the very nature of the service, a strongly rational appeal is justified. Notice especially how the description of the service is presented in you-viewpoint language.

> Dear Ms. Collins:
> "Killshaw is adding $15,000 a year to my restaurant's profits!"
> With these words, Bill Summers, owner of Boston's famed Pirate's Cove, joined the hundreds of restaurant owners who will point to proof in dollars in assuring you that I have a plan that can add to your profits.
> My time-proven plan to help you add to your profits is a product of 28 years of intensive research, study, and consulting work with restaurants all over the nation. I found that where food costs exceed 40 percent, staggering amounts slip through restaurant managers' fingers. Then I tracked down the causes of these losses. I can find these trouble spots in your business—and I'll prove this to you in extra income dollars!
> To make these extra profits, all you do is send to me, for a 30-day period, your guest checks, bills, and a few other things I'll tell you about later. After these items have undergone my proved method of analysis, I will write you an eye-opening report that will tell you how much money your restaurant should make and how to make it.
> From the report, you will learn in detail just what items are causing your

higher food costs. And you will learn how to correct them. Even your menu will receive thorough treatment. You will know what "best sellers" are paying their way—what "poor movers" are eating into your profits. All in all, you'll get practical suggestions that will show you how to cut costs, build volume, and pocket a net 10 to 20 percent of sales.

For a more detailed explanation of this service, you'll want to read the enclosed information sheet. Then won't you let me prove to you, as I have to so many others, that I can add money to your income this year? This added profit can be yours for the modest investment of $500 ($200 now and the other $300 when our profit plan report is submitted). Just fill out the enclosed form and place it along with your check in the addressed and stamped envelope that is provided for your convenience.

That extra $15,000 or more will make you glad you did!

Sincerely,

Written on clear plastic in red, black, and blue type, the following letter seeks to sell *Popular Science* subscribers on renewing their subscriptions. Although the words may appear to place undue emphasis on the writer, the slant deftly brings out the reader's point of view. The personal tone of the writing adds to its effectiveness.

Dear Friend:

Here's an honest-to-goodness attempt to make everything between us as CLEAR as CRYSTAL—

Frankly, I'm thoroughly confused because out of the thousands of readers whose subscription expired with yours several months ago, you're one of the very small handful who have not renewed yet. Whatever it is that's holding up your renewal, I wish you'd let me know about it because you're a good customer and we miss you.

I'm sure you haven't lost your hearty interest in the latest news on cars and car repairs, inventions, home workshop projects and ideas, aviation, mechanics, and the hundreds of other exciting things POPULAR SCIENCE brings to your doorstep every month. I'm sure you'll find the lively new features and money-saving home repair articles lined up for coming issues of POPULAR SCIENCE even *more* inviting than ever!

Chances are you've been intending to renew all along, but just keep putting it off. To make certain you don't delay another minute, I'm going ALL OUT with a special bargain offer that can't be *repeated!*

I'm going to SLASH the regular rate of $8.40 a year DOWN TO ONLY $6—SAVING YOU A FULL 28%! That means you'll get 12 crisp, new issues of POPULAR SCIENCE for only 50¢ a copy. You save even more by renewing for 2 or 3 years!

So get on the band wagon. Join the vast majority who have already renewed their subscriptions. All you have to do is fill in and return the enclosed postage-free order card TODAY. If it isn't convenient to send your remittance now, don't worry about it because your credit is TOPS with me.

This is CLEARLY a bargain you shouldn't miss!

Sincerely,

Letters to dealers typically are all rational appeal, as is the next example. Because dealers are always interested in profit makers, this one starts out with a direct statement of a claim. The remainder of the letter is devoted to proving the claim. It does it with good you-viewpoint description which interprets the product features in terms of customer satisfaction, sales, turnover, profits, and the like.

Dear Ms. Sullivan:

Here's a new, fast-selling profit maker that's a "must" for the progressive automobile accessory store. It's Drive-Rest—a long-needed support for the driver's right arm that will sell to your comfort-seeking truck- and car-owner customers.

Your customers will like the fast, easy adjustment that moves Drive-Rest up or down, right or left, and into the desired position (a Drive-Rest solution to a problem that has long kept major automobile manufacturers from placing permanent drivers' right arm rests in their cars). Best of all, they'll be sold on the relaxed, "easy-chair" ride the Drive-Rest will give them.

Your salespeople will have smooth sailing in selling customers on Drive-Rest's overall construction. Its sturdy support bar of special alloy aluminum is insulated for fullest protection to clothing and upholstery. The rest itself is cushioned with foam rubber and upholstered with a durable material in several colors.

Drive-Rest will be a "natural" to sell to the throngs of vacationers who will soon be shopping for items that will add comfort and pleasure to summer driving. There will be additional sales to the front- and backseat riders, too. We'll furnish the mats that will bring them in for the sale.

Profitable sales will continue beyond the vacation period. Weekend drivers, salespeople, truck drivers—in fact, all who want driving comfort on those long straightaway drives—will keep your profits coming in the year round. And profits are good, too. You get the Drive-Rest for 50 percent and 10 percent off the suggested selling price of $12.95 (no excise tax added) on terms of 2/10, n/30, f.o.b. Houston, Texas. All armrests are packed in individual boxes. Shipping weight is 36 per 100 pounds, and they take third-class freight rate. Look over the enclosed catalog sheet—then mail your order for Drive-Rest.

The profits will make you glad you did.

Sincerely,

Some products, such as travel, jewelry, and perfume, lend themselves to purely emotional appeals. Because the reader must be approached in terms of his or her own enjoyment of the product, as many senses as possible are brought into play in the writing. Such a situation is shown in the next example, which seeks to stimulate reservations for an airline's special weekend package tours. Throughout the letter, as many descriptive words as possible are used to paint vivid mental pictures of desirable aspects of the tours. The rather negative aspect of cost is subordinated in the middle of a paragraph, surrounded by pleasantly positive material. Finally, the action-drive close pushes the reader to act *now* for his or her own enjoyment, and the final words bring back to mind the appeals developed in the sales pitch.

Dear Mr. Pettit:

You slide back in the deep plush chair, champagne tickles your nose, the hills of Georgia float swiftly away 30,000 feet below—and cares of the week are left far behind in the steady whine of the jets.

Three more glasses, a mouth-watering selection of hors d'oeuvres, and suddenly you're deplaning and swept up in the never-ending excitement of America's fun capital—New Orleans. As the uniformed doorman of the world famous Royal Orleans welcomes you to the understated elegance of the hotel's crystal chandeliered and marbled lobby, you understand why this "city that time forgot" is the perfect place for a completely carefree adventure—and that's what you're on—a fabulous Delta Jet-Set Weekend. Every detail is considered to give you the ultimate in enjoyment. You'll savor New Orleans as it's meant to be experienced—gracious living, unsurpassed cuisine, jazz-tempo excitement.

After settling in your magnificent Royal Orleans "home," you're off to dinner at Antoine's—spicy, bubbling Oysters Bienville, an exotic salad, trout almondine, selected fromages, all mellowed with a wine from one of the world's most famous cellars, and topped off with spectacular cherries flambé. A memorable meal sets you up for the night spot tour of many splendored delights—the spots where jazz was born, the undulating strippers, Pete Fountain's chic club, and the rollicking sing-a-long of Pat O'Brien's where a tall, frosty Hurricane signals the close of a perfect evening. Then, just before returning to the hotel, time for a steaming cup of dark, rich French Market café au lait and some extra special doughnuts.

Saturday morning dawns bright and crisp—perfect for casual browsing through the "treasure" shops of the Quarter—the world of artists, antiques, and astonishing sights awaits you. From noon, you are escorted through some of the famous areas of the city—the Garden District (where the elegance of the past lives on), the lake area, and the most famous historical sights of the Quarter. Late afternoon finds you approaching famed Elmwood Plantation for an exclusive cocktail party and dinner—you'll practically hear the moan of ol' river steamers on the mighty Mississippi before you.

Night ends back in the Quarter—with the particular pleasure of your choice. But don't sleep too late Sunday! Unforgettable "breakfast at Brennan's" begins at 8:30 and two hours later you'll know why it is the most famous breakfast in the world! Wrap up your relaxed visit shopping in the afternoon, then the mighty Delta jet whisks you back to Atlanta by 7:00. This perfect weekend can be yours for the very special price of only $175, which includes transportation, lodging, and noted meals. Such a special vacation will be more fun with friends, so get them in on this bargain—you owe yourself the pleasures of a Jet-Set Weekend in America's fun capital.

This Jet-Set Weekend to dream about becomes a reality starting right now— a quick call to the Delta Hostess at Peachtree 4-0663 confirms your reservation to escape to the fun, the food, and the fantasy of New Orleans, land of excitement. The city is swinging—waiting for you!

Sincerely,

The following letter is out of the ordinary, for it uses a sample of the product being sold as an attention-gaining device. The opening words tie into the sample. Next, description of the product brings out the benefits that the product can give the reader. It presents these benefits with the reader in the center of things. The words are light and fast, and they present the product and its qualities clearly and concretely. After conviction is achieved, the drive for action comes. It is not a drive for an immediate sale but a request to let the company's salesperson call. Such endings are common in industrial sales. The final words urge the reader to act now.

Dear Mr. Buchstein:

Before you read the rest of this letter, won't you pick up that sample strip of Burlon and give it the works? It's *two* strips—see? Stuck together like two cockleburs. But pick up the tabs at the bottom and pull them apart. Press them back together. Test for the *side* pull, to see how firmly they hold together. Now the tabs again—how easily they slip apart.

Now you know—it's a pushbutton zipper—a closer with no gadgets.

Already you see what to do with it—what it can mean for your line of children's jackets . . . raincoats . . . shirts . . . any garment that has to be fastened somewhere.

Picture your sales copy to mothers of children who have trouble starting the fastener, to the man in a hurry to button up the raincoat, "Fingertouch fastening—no buttons, no slides, no metal, no plastic teeth. Press the edges together—they are fastened to hold. Pull up gently from the bottom—they come apart so quickly and quietly."

Your engineering curiosity will be shooting questions at us like "How does it work, anyway? How *good* is it?"

Well, it works like a cocklebur—like ten thousand of them, in fact. That gray top strip is packed with microscopic nylon hairs with infinitesimal fish-hook tips—so small that you can rub them on soft skin without feeling the points. The blue strip's surface is merely soft nylon yarn. Press the two together and your nylon-cockleburs, or Burlon, grasp the yarn firmly. That's all there is to it. They pull apart so easily from the bottom up.

How *good*? Well, you'll find you can wash or dry-clean Burlon. It won't corrode. It won't jam. It holds its grip indefinitely. And try it now to see how light and flexible it feels and works. In strips ranging from a half inch to 2 inches wide, it is adaptable to any garment-closure problem you might have.

In order to work this startling new fastener into your fall-production specifications, wouldn't you like to have one of our representatives come and show you the whole range of demonstrations and tests and help figure your needs for different garments and fabrics? Just use the handy air-mail-paid card to describe your needs and tell us that you'd like to see the Burlon representative.

Mail it this morning to get in an early itinerary.

Sincerely,

Probably you have observed that most sales letters are longer than the preceding illustrations. In practice, letters of two, three, and four pages are common. Direct-mail people appear to reason that interested readers will read long messages—that they will read at least long enough to satisfy their interest. And sometimes much information is necessary to satisfy their interest.

The illustration below typifies this form of letter. It ran three full pages; and it was accompanied by a descriptive brochure, order card, return envelope, and a supplementary letter (see page 268). The mailing produced excellent results.

Note that the letter begins with a gift offer—one especially interesting to those who like fishing. From the beginning the letter talks fishing, whetting the interest of those who enjoy the sport. Then it moves the magazine into the picture, describing its contents in detail. The description is long, filled with convincing facts and figures. The letter ends with a drive for action. For those who may not fit the mold of the intended reader, a postscript suggests an alternate use of the free gift.

Yours free!
Texas Saltwater Big 3
That's right, fellow outdoorsman:

With your tryout subscription to THE TEXAS FISHERMAN I will send you this big 112-page book that tells you how to take home more redfish, trout, and flounder—the "saltwater big 3" in Texas—FREE!

If you're headed for the Gulf anytime soon, you'll want to tuck this guidebook in your tacklebox—and refer to it often.

A. C. Becker, Jr., wrote it. He hails from Galveston and knows saltwater fishing. He ought to. He's traveled and fished the entire Gulf Coast—plus Mexico—plus the Bahamas! And he's authored more than 500 feature-length articles. This is his ninth book!

So my advice is to pay attention to A. C.'s advice. You'll get more out of your next Gulf trip and you'll bring home bigger catches than ever before.

THIS IS MY GIFT TO YOU AS A NEW SUBSCRIBER

267

Chapter 12
Correspondence:
Sales and
Applications

Along with your FREE "Big 3" guidebook, you'll start receiving the newsmonthly Texas fishermen and boaters swear by. It's THE TEXAS FISHERMAN—you've seen it at your local newsstand and in coin racks around town. Fact is you've probably bought a copy now and then and intended to subscribe, but just haven't gotten around to it.

It's a whopper of a monthly—gives you all the latest know-how and know-where when it comes to Texas fishing and boating.

And it's a big handsome monthly, too. Full of super-size photography of big catches, big boats, big smiles—plus to-the-point articles on every subject that interests you.

Saltwater fishing your thing? We take you out on the Gulf through words and pictures. Prefer freshwater? We help you have the time of your life out on your favorite lake or stream. You'll want to try some new ones we'll tell you about.

Or, if you'd just as soon make some waves and forget the fish, concentrate on the helpful boating articles (how to pick the right one for you; what to pay; how to keep yours in A-1 shape; and much, much more).

Every issue, every page, every column is chock-full of "how to" advice you can't find anywhere else. What's more, you can rely on what our writers say. They are tops in their fields—in Texas. And when I say TOPS I mean guys like:

A. C. Becker, Jr., Dale Branam, John Clift, Joe Doggett, Al Eason, Max Eggleston, Earl Golding, Morris Gresham, Billy Halfin, Bob Hood, Anton Husak, Dan Klepper, Bob Lanier, A. W. McLaughlin, C. C. Risenhoover, Stan Slaten, John Thompson, Russell Tinsley, L. A. Wilke. . . .

. . . AND IF THOSE AREN'T ENOUGH, there's our regular boating column by none other than DAVE ELLISON! And what Texas outdoorsman hasn't heard of Dave! (See more about this on page 4 of this letter.)

THE TEXAS FISHERMAN WILL BE YOUR "GOODTIME GUIDE"

Let's face it. You've got quite an investment. When you consider your boat and gear and equipment of all kinds, it adds up pretty fast.

This means one thing: You are serious about having fun.

And this is why we make sure you get your money's worth with each monthly issue. You want experienced advice from experts who know Texas lakes, rivers, ponds, and puddles like the back of their hand—and you get it. You want evidence of where the big ones are biting—and you get it. You want all the latest news about boats and boating—and you get it.

How? With articles like these:

** Dave Ellison tells you about the almost indestructible boat now on the market—a boat so tough you can't dent it with a sledge hammer!
** The way you play the fish can make a difference in the number you catch.
** How and when to fish for snapper.
** Avoiding or treating snakebite.
** How to fish the birds for speckled trout.
** How you winterize your boat will affect next season's performance.
** How to catch bass with crappie jigs.
** Wadefishing the surf . . . and the list goes on and on.

NO MATTER HOW LONG . . .

. . . you've been fishing or boating in Texas—10 years, 20, 30, you-name-it—I guarantee you'll pick up more new tips and "tryout ideas" than you have in a month of Sundays. That's what our subscribers tell me. And we've got a lot of them!

34,237—at last count!

If you'd like to join your fellow Texas outdoorsmen and make it 34,238—and receive your FREE guidebook besides—here's what you do:

Mail back the enclosed FREE BOOK CERTIFICATE today.

Hurry! I have only a limited supply on hand, and when they're gone, that's it.

AND YOU ENJOY A SAVINGS, TOO.

At newsstands and in coin racks, you pay 50¢ an issue. Over 24 months (2 years), you'd be out $12. But RIGHT NOW, during our limited-time Money-Saving Get-Acquainted Offer, you get 24 rip-roarin' action-packed issues—two whole years' worth—for only $9.50. You SAVE $2.50 right off the bat.

Or—save even more! Send for 36 issues (3-year subscription) for only $12. You save a whopping $6.00 off the newsstand price!

Anyway you look at it, here's a real bargain.

You get your FREE book, your money-saving subscription and this ironclad guarantee: If you ever believe we're letting you down, just write. I'll see that you immediately get your money back on all unmailed issues. Just that simple. No questions asked.

There's an old saying that goes, "Thunder is impressive, but lightning does the work." If you think my letter is all thunder and no lightning, now you can find out for yourself. I'm betting that THE TEXAS FISHERMAN becomes the best-read monthly around your house.

Return your FREE BOOK CERTIFICATE today. Thanks.

Sincerely, Marvin Spivey, Editor

P.S.   If you're a boater who doesn't fish, pass along your FREE book to a fishing buddy. Watch his eyes light up. And you still save money on your subscription!

Use of a second letter in the mailing

A currently popular way of adding strength to the sales effort is to use a second letter (or note, or memorandum) as a part of the mailing. Usually, this second letter is headed with a boldly displayed message saying something like "don't read this unless you've decided not to buy." Apparently, the technique is effective. At least, direct-mail professionals think it is, for they use it widely. An example of such a message follows.

Accompanying the preceding letter (THE TEXAS FISHERMAN), this memorandum reviews the main sales message of the letter. As you can see, it is really another sales letter. It even ends with a drive for action and has a postscript which intensifies the action. As noted earlier, this mailing was highly successful. Perhaps this second message contributed to this success:

DON'T READ THIS UNLESS YOU HAVE DECIDED NOT TO CLAIM YOUR FREE TEXAS SALTWATER BIG 3 BOOK.

Frankly, I'm puzzled.

I just don't understand why every fisherman and boat owner in Texas doesn't run—not walk—to the nearest mailbox and return the enclosed FREE BOOK CERTIFICATE.

Here's a guidebook that will bring you better times and better catches each and every time you head for that big beautiful Gulf.

PLUS, you get a money-saving bargain on a subscription to THE TEXAS FISHERMAN—the newsmonthly that Texas outdoorsmen swear by.

Month after month you'll be in on all the latest tips about where the big ones are biting. Each issue sports super-big photographs of fishermen grinning their heads off, holding up the catch for the day.

And Dave Ellison is there each month telling you the latest there is about boating. Plus many other boating articles every month.

Over 34,000 Texas boaters and fishermen are subscribing now. And the yearly renewal rate is just fantastic!

But those 34,000 aren't important this morning. The important person to me today is YOU. I want YOU as a new subscriber— because I know you'll find more helpful advice here than in any other publication in the state today.

Do yourself a favor. Send off your FREE BOOK CERTIFICATE now, today, while you're thinking about it. Have more fun and catch more fish!

Sincerely for better fishing and boating.

Bob Gray, Publisher
P.S. Please hurry! We have only a limited supply of this FREE BOOK. Get yours now!

Applications for employment

Of all the business communications you will ever write, probably the data sheet and application letter will be the most important to you. Their importance should be obvious. Data sheets and application letters are the written forms you are likely to use in finding a job. And finding a job most certainly will be among the important activities in your life.

Of course, you can get a job without applying for it in writing. You can get a job through a recruiter who visits your campus. Or you can get one through an employment agency or a company's employment office. But when you cannot find a job through these routes, you are likely to apply for jobs by using data sheets and letters.

Other reasons may lead you to write data sheets and application letters. Perhaps you will want to work for a company that does not send representatives to your campus or that does not have an employment office nearby. Maybe you will want to change jobs at various stages in your career. Such situations frequently require applications in writing.

Actually, preparing the data sheet and application letter is much like preparing a sales mailing. Both situations involve selling. In one case, you are selling a product or service; in the other, you are selling your ability to do work. The data sheet is much like the supporting material that accompanies the sales letter. The application letter is much like the sales letter. These similarities should become obvious to you as you read the following paragraphs.

Preliminary planning

As you would do in preparing a sales mailing, you begin work on a written application for a job by studying what you are selling. What you are selling, of course, is you.

Studying yourself involves taking personal inventory. You should begin by listing all the information about you that you feel an employer would want to know. In addition to studying yourself, you should study the work. Studying the work means learning as much as you can about the company—its plans, its policies, its operations. It also means learning the requirements of the work the company wants done. Sometimes you can get this information through personal investigation. More often, you will have to develop it through your own logical thinking.

With this preliminary information assembled, you are ready to plan the application. First, you will need to decide just what your application will consist of. Will it be just a letter, or will it be a letter and a data sheet (also called vitae and résumé)? The data sheet is a summary of background facts in list form. Probably you will select the combination letter and data sheet, for this arrangement is likely to do the better job. But some people prefer to use the letter alone. Such one-piece mailings usually contain much detail, for they must do the whole sales job.

The data sheet

After you have decided what your mailing will be, you turn to constructing the parts. Perhaps you will choose to begin with the data sheet, for it is a logical next step from the personal inventory discussed above. In fact, the data sheet is a formal arrangement of this personal inventory.

You will want to include in the data sheet all the background information you feel the reader should know about you. This means including all that is reviewed in an accompanying letter plus supporting and incidental details. Designed for quick reading, the data sheet lists facts. Rarely does it use sentences—just facts, tabulated and arranged for the best possible appearance.

Data sheets may be arranged in many ways. In general, two basic types are common. One, the *general* type, is designed to cover a variety of jobs. It is the type one would send to a dozen different companies when applying for a dozen different jobs. The *personalized* data sheet is the second type. It is written for one company and one job. Most of its contents are similar to those of a general data sheet, but the information is specially selected for the one case, and the wording is made to fit the one case. Because it fits the one case, the personalized type probably is the more effective.

Selection of the background facts. Your first step in writing the data sheet is to review the information you have assembled about yourself. Then you select the information you feel will help your reader evaluate you. You should include all that is included in an accompanying letter, for this is the most important information. In addition, you should include the significant supporting details. These details are not covered in the accompanying letter, for they would clutter it. Yet you want to report them for completeness.

Arrangement by groups. After you have selected the background facts you want to include, you should arrange them into logical groups. Many arrangements are possible. The most conventional is the four-part grouping: experience, education, personal qualities, and references. As shown in some of the following examples, these four areas may be further subdivided. Education, for example, may include an overall summary (schools, dates, degrees), courses and areas of concentration, and honors and awards. Personal qualities may be arranged as two areas: vital statistics (age, marital status, sex) and professional and social activities (organization memberships, hobbies, community service).

In some instances, other organization plans may be effective. One such possibility is an organization by job requirements (for example: personality, industriousness, intelligence). Another possibility is to arrange the information on a time basis—perhaps by years, from most recent to earliest. You may be able to work out other plans through your imagination. Any plan which favorably presents the information and which communicates the information clearly is all right.

Wording of the headings. Your next step is to write captions (headings) for each of the groups of information as well as for the data sheet itself. By far the most commonly used form is the topic caption, which merely identifies the subject covered in a word or two. For example, *"Education," "Experience," "Personal Details,"* and *"References"* are topic captions for the subject divisions of a data sheet. A typical topic caption covering the entire data sheet is "Résumé of Wilma T. Triggs" or "Personal Data Sheet of John D. Potts."

Some authorities favor another form of caption—the talking (or popular) caption. Talking captions use additional words in the effort to draw favorable attention to the items covered. Their form is explained best by illustration. For the main caption of a data sheet, you might adapt to the one company and the one job with words such as these:

PREPARATION OF DIANE S. HANDY
TO SELL ILCO PRODUCTS
WHY WILMA WINN IS QUALIFIED AS A FASHION BUYER
WILLIAM O. HOBSON'S QUALIFICATIONS
FOR GENERAL ACCOUNTING WORK
WITH HUGGINS, INC.

Similarly, you could use talking captions for the information areas of the data sheet. Instead of writing a topic caption such as "Education," you could write "Specialized Training in Accounting." Rather than "References," you could use "Administrators Who Know Her Work." These are but a few of the possibilities available to you. Your imagination should produce good ones for your background facts.

Presentation of the data. The information you present under each of the captions will depend on your good judgment. You should list all that you think are important. You will want to make certain that you include enough information to permit the reader to judge you. As a minimum, your coverage of working experience should identify jobs completely. You should include dates, places, firms, and duties; and you should say whether the work was full- or part-time employment. Also, you will want to present this information in words that do the most for you. For example, in describing a job, you could write "1980/83: office manager for Carson's, Inc." But it would be more helpful to you to give this fuller description: "1980/83: office manager for Carson's, Inc., supervising a staff of 14."

Because your education is likely to be your strongest selling point for your first job after college, probably you will cover it in some detail. As you gain experience, education gets less and less emphasis in your applications. As a minimum, your coverage of education should cover institutions, dates, degrees, and areas of study. For some jobs, you may want to list specific courses. Especially are you likely to do this when you have little other information to present or when your course work has uniquely prepared you for a job.

What personal information to list is a matter for your best judgment. Probably race, religion, and sex should be omitted in all cases; and age and marital status are questionable. The reason is that current laws prohibit hiring based on this information. But not everybody agrees on this matter. Some authorities feel that at least some of these items should be included. They argue that the law only prohibits employers from considering such information in hiring—that it does not prohibit applicants from presenting the information. The illustrations shown in this chapter support both viewpoints.

Personal information that generally is appropriate includes all those items which tell about the applicant's personal qualities. Information on one's organization memberships, civic involvement, and social interests is evidence of experience and interest in working with people. Hobbies and athletic participation tell of one's balance of interests. Such information can be quite useful to some employers, especially when personal qualities are important to the work involved.

Authorities disagree on whether to list references on the data sheet. Some feel that references should not be bothered until negotiations are further along. Others feel that references should be listed for those employers who want to check them early in the screening process. Perhaps the best advice is to list them unless a good reason exists not to do so—such as when the applicant is employed and wants to keep the job search secret. If you choose not to list references, you should explain their absence. You can do this in the accompanying letter. Also, you can do it on the data sheet by listing the caption "References" and following it with an explanation, such as "will be furnished on request."

How many and what kinds of references to include will depend on your background. If you have an employment record, you should list one for every major job you have held—at least for the recent years. You should include all that are related to the work you seek. If you base your application heavily on your education or your personal qualities, or both, you should list people who can vouch for these areas—professors, clergy, community leaders, and such. Your goal is to list those people who can verify the points which form the basis for your appeal for the job. As a minimum, you should list three references. Six is a good maximum.

Your list of references should include accurate mailing addresses, with appropriate job titles. Complete addresses are important because the reader is likely to write the references. Job titles (office manager, president, supervisor) are helpful because they show what the references are able to tell about you.

Other vital information. Although not a category of background facts, a statement of the applicant's career objectives (work goals) is appropriate on the data sheet. Many employers like to see it. Such a statement is especially valuable in data sheets not submitted with a letter—for example, ones submitted to a company representative interviewing on campus. A statement of career goals forms a good beginning for a data sheet.

Perhaps it is so obvious that it need not be mentioned, but your address is another vital part of the data sheet. In some cases, two addresses are necessary: permanent and temporary. If you are a student, for example, your current address is likely to be temporary and may not be valid by the time an employer responds to your application. Usually, the address appears at the top of the page, directly below the main heading of the page. Another popular placement is at the end.

Some points on wording. Because the data sheet is a listing of information, you should write without personal pronouns (no I's, we's, you's). Also, you should write all equal-level captions in the same grammatical form. Likewise, you should write the parts under each caption in the same grammatical form. For example, if one caption in the data sheet is a noun phrase, all other captions should be noun phrases. The following four captions illustrate the point. All but the third one (an adjective form) are noun phrases. The error can be corrected by making the third one into a noun phrase, as in the examples to the right:

Not Parallel	*Parallel*
Specialized study	Specialized study
Experience in promotion work	Experience in promotion work
Personal and physical	Personal and physical qualities
Qualified references	Qualified references

Illustrating grammatical inconsistency in the parts of a group are the following items:

> Born in 1964
> Single
> Have good health
> Active in sports
> Ambitious

Inspection of these entries shows that they do not fit the same understood words. The understood words for the first one are "she was" (*She was* born in 1964). For the second they are "she is" (*She is* single). "I," "I am" (or "she is"), and "she is" are the understood words for the remaining entries.

Figure 12–1
Thoroughness and Good Arrangement in a Data Sheet

CYRUS C. SYLVESTER'S QUALIFICATIONS

FOR LABOR RELATIONS WORK

Address   Telephone
3117 North Hawthorne Boulevard   AC 914, 967-3117 (home)
Olympia, NY 12507   AC 914, 938-4449 (work)

Employment goal: To obtain entry-level work in labor relations which
will lead to development as a labor relations specialist

Experience as a Part of Labor

1980-84 Equipment repair worker, Davidson Electric Company
         Olympia, NY (part time)
1978-80 Driver, Wayland Trucking Company, New York, NY (was a member
         of Local 714, International Brotherhood of Teamsters,
         Chauffeurs, Warehousemen, and Helpers of America)
1976-78 Shipping and receiving clerk, Kiawa Garment Company,
         New York, NY (part time)

Training for Labor Relations Work

1980-84 Olympia University; Bachelor of Business Administration
         degree with major in labor relations; overall grade point
         average of 3.7 (4.0 basis), 3.9 average in major field;
         24 semester hours of labor and management courses, electives
         in business report writing advanced statistics, labor law,
         industrial psychology, industrial sociology
1974-78 C. H. Aldridge High School, New York, NY, pursued college
         preparatory program

Personal Qualities

Physical: 5 ft. 11 in., 165 lbs.   Memberships: Delta Sigma Pi
 brown hair and eyes   (professional); Sigma Iota
Nativity: born March 7, 1958   Epsilon (honorary), served
Interests: tennis, fishing, reading,   as treasurer and president;
 jogging   First Methodist Church,
Family status: married, one daughter   Olympia, serving on board of
 (age 1)   stewards; League of Olympia,
                                          served as registration leader

People Who Know His Abilities

Ms. June Rojas, Service Manager   Professor Helen K. Robbins
Davidson Electric Company   Department of Management
7114 East 71st Street   Olympia University
Olympia, NY 12509   Olympia, NY 12507

Mr. Todd E. Frankle, Manager   Professor Carl A. Cueno
Wayland Trucking Company   Department of Economics
47712 Beecher Road   Olympia University
New York, NY 10029   Olympia, NY 12507

Any changes which would make all five items fit the same understood words
would correct the error.

Attractive physical makeup. The attractiveness of your data sheet will
say as much about you as the words. Perhaps it is unfair, but the appearance

of the typed information the reader sees forms part of his or her judgment. A sloppy, poorly designed presentation may even ruin your chances of getting the job. Thus, you have no choice but to give your data sheet (as well as the letter) a physical arrangement that will be pleasing to the eye.

Designing the data sheet for best eye appeal is no routine matter. Because there is no one best arrangement, your best procedure is to approach the task as a printer would. Your objective is to work out an arrangement of type and space that looks good to the eye. Even so, you would do well to use the following general plan for arranging the data sheet.

Your overall margins on top, left, and right sides of the page look better if they are at least an inch. A minimum margin of about 1½ inches is good for the bottom. Your listing of the items looks best by rows (columns) if the items are short and can be set up with two uncrowded rows, one on the left and one on the right side of the page. Longer items of information are more appropriately set up in lines extending across the page. In any event, you will do well to avoid long and narrow columns of data with large sections of wasted space showing on either side. Likewise, any arrangement which gives a heavy, crowded effect offends the eye. Extra spacing between subdivisions and indented patterns for subparts and carry-over lines are especially effective in pleasing the eye.

Some examples of data sheets. The four examples of data sheets shown in this section generally follow the content and form instructions given. The first (Figure 12–1) is attractively arranged. The information is not crowded; nor is it strung out. The balance is good, and so is the content. Additional words give a measure of the quality of Mr. Sylvester's work experience and education. They emphasize points that make the man suited for the work he seeks. Note, also, the additional personal information about memberships. It tells something specific about the man—how he works successfully with people. Complete mailing addresses permit the reader to contact the references easily. Job titles tell how each is qualified to evaluate the subject.

A unique narrative review of qualifications adds to the effectiveness of the next example (Figure 12–2). In reviewing his experience, the writer tells what he did on each job. Note how he brings out qualifications that fit him for the job he seeks. The narrative review is especially good for covering the writer's educational experience. Because the writer's studies include part-time and extension work, the extra comments help to present an accurate summary. Perhaps the review of personal details is somewhat scant, but it brings out the most important information. An identifying caption preceding each reference tells what area of background the person can evaluate. This data sheet is well balanced and generally appealing to the eye.

A general-purpose form of data sheet popular with personnel people is the next example (Figure 12–3). Its arrangement is orderly, although somewhat mechanical. It contains no frills—no special wording to add to the effects of the information. In other words, the facts stand alone. Notice how placement of captions in the margins helps display the information—

Figure 12–2
A Personalized Narrative Data Sheet

DON R. ANDERSON'S PREPARATION FOR WORK AS A LEGAL SECRETARY

WITH BORROW, OTIS, BORROW, AND DELAHAYE

Permanent address: 1366 Hyacinth Street
Baton Rouge, LA 70803
Telephone: AC 512, 433-6605

Job objective: To work as a legal assistant and secretary while
completing law school preparation for a career in
the practice of law.

Versatile Experience

1973-74   Worked part time while in high school as office clerk for
Nowotny Construction Company, Houston, TX. Work involved
typing, filing, and preparing reports.

1974-76   Manuscript typist and editor for Kenyon Publishing Company,
Houston, TX. Responsible for editing, typing, and proof-
reading manuscripts.

1976-82   Active duty with United States Navy, two years of which
were in rating of yeoman, first class. Navy work was
primarily clerical and administrative in nature, involving
shorthand (100 w.p.m.) and typing (70 w.p.m.). One of
rating requirements was understanding of court-martial
procedure. As senior petty officer, assumed responsibility
for offices assigned to, both ashore and afloat.

Specialized Education

1970-74   Attended Reagan High School, Houston, Texas, graduating
in upper twenty-five percent of class.

1974   Developed skills in typewriting, shorthand, and office
procedures through six months intensified study at
Barker Business College, Houston, TX.

1980-82   While on active duty with Navy, commenced part-time prelaw
study at Iowa State University, Ames, Iowa.

1982-84   Completed prelaw curriculum in General Business at
Louisiana State University with a scholastic standing of
3.53 out of a possible 4.00. Courses studied included
Business Statistics, Business Management, Elementary French,
General and Labor Economics, Business Law, Business
Communication, and other courses designed for a broad business
background for the legal profession.

Personal Characteristics

Facts and figures: Age, 27; weight, 175 pounds; height, 72 inches;
no known defects other than slight visual
impairment which is corrected by glasses.

Memberships: Delta Sigma Pi (professional business), Beta Gamma
Sigma (honorary business), University Presbyterian
Church, Baton Rouge Forensic Society.

Marital status: Married, one daughter three years old.

Interests: Golf, fishing, reading, bridge.

Figure 12–2 *(continued)*

277

Chapter 12
Correspondence:
Sales and
Applications

Resume of Don R. Anderson - page 2

References (by permission)

From last job:
  Rear Admiral Eli T. Swabb
  171 North Riverside Drive
  Ames, IA 50010

From early employment:
  Ms. Gala S. Strelski
  Kenyon Publishing Company
  3131 West Parker Road
  Houston, TX 77007

From childhood background:
  Rev. Bill E. Gallagher
  1171 Pennington Road
  Houston, TX 77019

From college training:
  Professor Mary A. Gann
  Department of Finance
  Louisiana State University
  Baton Rouge, LA 70803

how the captions help the eye through the material. Note, also, there are no references. The reason is that the writer still is employed and does not want her employer to know that she is job seeking.

Another widely used arrangement is displayed in the data sheet in Figure 12–4. Although it lists the form of work the writer seeks, it aims at no

Figure 12–3
A Popular Form of General-purpose Data Sheet

```
                              Resume
                        DONNA MARIE CRENSHAW


    Employment         To obtain entry-level work which offers
      Objective        development opportunity for a career in office
                       administration

    Education

      1983-present     Metropolitan Community College, New York, NY;
                       major in office administration; coursework in
                       office practices, shorthand, typewriting,
                       business communication, basic management,
                       computer programming; grade-point average of 3.3
                       (4.0 basis); Associate of Arts degree

      1977-81          Elmer Hughes High School, Northport, NY

    Experience

      1983-present     Payroll clerk, Guynes Manufacturing Company, New
                       York, NY; handles time keeping and payroll for 235
                       workers; performs general office administration
                       assignments; supervises two clerks

      1980-83          Salesperson, Billows Department Store, New York,
                       NY; sold cosmetics and costume jewelry (part time)

      1979-80          Office assistant, Pennington Insurance Agency,
                       New York, NY; performed general office
                       administration assignments (part time)

    Professional       Typewriting speed, 75 wpm
      Skills           Shorthand speed, 140 wpm

    Activities         Active member of Metro Big Sister Association,
                       works with orphaned children

                       Member of Metropolitan Curtain Club, participates
                       as actor and stagehand

                       Member of Metropolitan Business Club, serves as
                       secretary-treasurer

    Interests          Golf, swimming, tennis, reading

    References         Will be furnished on request

    Telephone          AC 212, 381-7797 (home); AC 212, 381-1114 (office)

    Address            74173 West 118th Street
                       New York, NY  11057
```

Figure 12–4

A General-purpose Data Sheet

279

Chapter 12
Correspondence:
Sales and
Applications

```
                    PERSONAL DATA SHEET OF
                      LOUISE E. MASSEY

        Candidate for Bachelor of Business Administration Degree
                    The University of Texas
                         June 1984

    OCCUPATIONAL PREFERENCES
       Type of Work:  Retail Advertising, Manufacturer's Advertising
       Department, Manufacturer's Salesperson
       Location:  No preference
       Travel:  Willing to travel


    PERSONAL DATA
       Date of birth:  June 13, 1963
       Hobbies and Sports:  ceramics, reading, tennis, swimming


    SCHOOLS ATTENDED
       1980-1984,  The University of Texas, Austin, Texas
       1977-1980,  Waco High School, Waco, Texas


    ACADEMIC PREPARATION
       Major:  Advertising.  24 semester hours
          Fundamentals of advertising, retail advertising (writing and
          production), selling, advanced advertising, marketing research,
          sales management, principles of retailing, psychology in
          advertising
       Other Business Administration Courses Included:
          Accounting - 9 hours, business law - 6 hours, business writing -
          5 hours, management - 3 hours, finance - 6 hours, statistics -
          7 hours, basic marketing - 3 hours
       Outside the College of Business Administration:
          Economics - 6 hours, mathematics - 8 hours, engineering drawing
          - 3 hours, psychology - 6 hours, chemistry - 8 hours
       Grade-Point Averages:  Major - 3.3 out of 4.  In all courses - 3.2
          out of 4


    COLLEGE HONORS AND ACTIVITIES
       The University of Texas:  Member, Alpha Delta Sigma; Co-Chairman
       of Round-Up Committee; President, Royal Co-Operative House; Delta
       Sigma Pi - Senior Vice-President, Historian, Outstanding Member
       Award; Inter-Coop Council; Senior Class Secretary; CBA; College of
       Business Council; American Marketing Association


    BUSINESS EXPERIENCE
       June-August 1983, Assistant Co-ordinator for Summer Entertainment,
       Student Activities Office, The University of Texas, Austin, Texas
       June-September 1982, Cashier, Raleigh Hotel, Waco, Texas
       June-September 1981, Cashier, Mammoth Hotel, Yellowstone National
       Park, Wyoming
```

Figure 12–4 *(continued)*

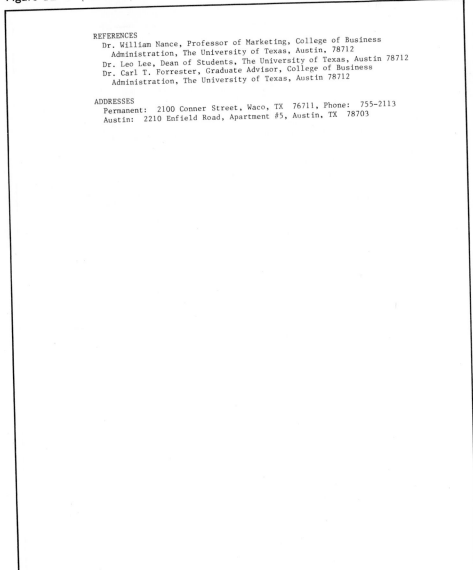

REFERENCES
Dr. William Nance, Professor of Marketing, College of Business
Administration, The University of Texas, Austin, 78712
Dr. Leo Lee, Dean of Students, The University of Texas, Austin 78712
Dr. Carl T. Forrester, Graduate Advisor, College of Business
Administration, The University of Texas, Austin 78712

ADDRESSES
Permanent: 2100 Conner Street, Waco, TX 76711, Phone: 755-2113
Austin: 2210 Enfield Road, Apartment #5, Austin, TX 78703

specific company or job. It is typical of the type that is printed and used for an extensive job-seeking effort. Because the writer's strongest qualification is her education, this area gets most attention (three information areas). This heavy coverage of education overcomes an otherwise scant record. In general, the coverage is thorough; the arrangement is attractive.

Letters of application

281

Chapter 12
Correspondence:
Sales and
Applications

As in sales writing, the opening of the application letter has two requirements: it must gain interest; it must set up the review of information that follows.

The need to gain interest is especially important in prospecting letters (those not invited). These letters are likely to reach the desk of a busy executive who has many other things to do than reading application letters. Unless the letter grasps favorable interest right away, the executive probably will not read the letter at all. Even invited letters must command attention, because they will compete with other invited letters. The letters that stand out favorably from the beginning have a competitive advantage.

Because this letter is a creative effort, you should use your imagination in writing the opening. But the nature of the work you seek should guide your imagination. Take, for example, work which requires an outgoing personality and vivid imagination, such as sales or public relations. In such cases, you would do well to show these qualities in your opening words. At the opposite extreme is work of a conservative nature, such as accounting or banking. Openings in these cases normally should be more restrained.

In choosing the best opening for your one case, you should consider whether the letter is invited or prospecting. If it has been invited, a good choice is to refer to the work to be done. Your words should begin qualifying you for the work. They also should refer incidentally to the invitation, as in this example:

> Will an honor graduate in accounting with experience in petroleum accounting qualify for the work you listed in today's *Post?*

In addition to fitting the work sought, your opening words should set up the following review of qualifications. The preceding example meets this requirement well. It structures the review of qualifications around two areas— education and experience.

Of course, you can gain attention many ways in the opening. One possibility is to use a topic which shows understanding of the reader's operation, or of the work to be done. Employers are likely to be impressed by applicants who make the effort to learn something about the company, as in this example:

> Now that Taggart, Inc., has expanded operations to Central America, can you use a broadly trained business administration graduate who knows the language and culture of the region?

Another possibility is a statement or question which gives attention to a need of the reader. The need is one which the writer seeks to fill. The following opening illustrates this approach:

> When was the last time you interviewed a young college graduate who wanted to sell and who had successful sales experience?

If you seek more conservative work, you would be wise to use less imaginative openings. For example, a letter answering an advertisement for a beginning accountant might open with this sentence:

> Because of my specialized training in accounting at State University and my practical experience in petroleum accounting, I feel I have the qualifications you described in your advertisement in the *Journal.*

Sometimes, one learns of a job possibility through an employee of the company. Mentioning the employee's name can serve to gain interest, as in this opening sentence:

On the suggestion of Ms. Martha S. Hawkes of your staff, I submit the following summary of my qualifications for work as your loan supervisor.

Many other possibilities exist. In the final analysis, you will have to use what you feel will be best for the one case. But you would be wise not to use the dull and overworked beginnings that were popular a generation or two ago. Included in this group are "This is to apply for . . ." and "Please consider this my application for. . . ."

Selection of content. Following the opening, you should present the information which qualifies you to do the work. You should begin this task by reviewing the requirements for the job. Then you should select the facts about you which qualify you for the job.

If your letter is invited, you may learn about the job requirements from the source of the invitation. If you are answering an advertisement, you should study it for requirements the employer seeks. If you are writing following an interview, you should review the interview for information about job requirements. Or if you are prospecting, your research and your logical analysis should guide you.

In any event, you are likely to present facts from three background areas: education, experience, and personal details. You may also include a fourth—references. But it is not exactly an area of background information. If you include references, probably they will go in the data sheet.

How much you include from each area and how much you emphasize each should depend on the job and on your background. Most jobs you will seek as a new college graduate will have strong educational requirements. Thus, you should stress your education. When you apply for work after you have accumulated experience, probably you will need to stress experience. As the years go by, experience becomes more and more important—education, less and less. Your personal characteristics are of some importance for some jobs, especially when the job involves working with people (as in sales or public relations).

If a data sheet accompanies the letter, you may rely too much on it. You should remember that the letter is the persuasive part of the mailing. It does the selling. The data sheet summarizes the significant details. Thus, your letter should contain all the major points around which you build your case. The data sheet should include these points, plus the supporting details. As the two are parts of a team effort, somewhere in the letter you should refer the reader to the data sheet.

An order for conviction. You will want to present the facts about yourself in the order that does the most for you. In general, the plan you select is likely to follow one of three general orders. The most common one is an order based on some logical grouping of the information, such as education, personal details, and experience. A second possibility is a time order. For example, you could present the information to show a year-by-year preparation for the work. Third is an arrangement based on job requirements. For example, an advertised job might list character, personality, intelligence, and industriousness as requirements.

Merely presenting facts does not assure conviction. You will need also to present the facts in words which make the most of what you have to say. You could say, for example, that you "held a position" as a sales manager; but it is much more concrete and convincing to say that you "supervised a sales force of 14." Likewise, you do more for yourself by writing that you "earned a degree in business administration" than by saying that you "spent four years in college." And it is more effective to say that you "learned cost accounting" than to say that you "took a course in cost accounting."

You can help your case, also, by presenting your information in reader-viewpoint language whenever it is practical. More specifically, you should work to interpret the facts in terms of what they mean to your reader and to the work to be done. For example, you could present a cold recital of facts like this:

> I am 21 years old and have an interest in mechanical operations and processes. Last summer I worked in the production department of a container plant.

Or you could interpret the facts, fitting them to the one job:

> The interest I have held in things mechanical over most of my 21 years would help me to fit into one of your technical manufacturing operations. And I submit last summer's experience in the production department of Moyse Container Company as evidence that I can and will work hard.

Since you will be writing about yourself, you may find it difficult to avoid overusing I-references. But you should try. An overuse of I's sounds egotistical, and it focuses too much of the attention on the often-repeated word. Some I's, however, should be used. The letter is a personal one. To strip it of all I-references would be to rob it of some of its personal warmth. Thus, you should be concerned with the degree of I-references. You want not too many, not too few.

Action drive in the close. The presentation of your qualifications should lead logically to the action which comprises the close of the letter. You should use whatever action is appropriate in your case. It could be a request for an interview, if distance permits. It could be an invitation for further correspondence, perhaps to answer the reader's questions. Or it could be an invitation to write references. Rarely would you want to ask for the job, at least not in a first letter. You are concerned mainly with opening the door to further negotiations.

Your action words should be clear and direct. Preferably you should put them in question form. As in the sales letter, you may make the action request more effective by following it with words which recall a benefit the reader will get by taking the action. The following close illustrates this technique:

> If I have described a promising personnel trainee, Mr. Sellers, may I have an interview? A collect wire or a letter will bring me in at your convenience to talk about how I can help in your personnel work.

Review of examples. The following application letters generally illustrate the techniques we have described. The first letter begins with an interesting question that sets the stage for the following presentation. The review of experience is interpreted in terms of how it would help in performing the job sought. The review of education is similarly covered. Notice how the interpretations show that the writer knows what the job requires. Notice, also, how reader-viewpoint is stressed throughout. Even so, a moderate use of I's gives the letter a personal quality. The closing request for action is a question. It is clear, direct, and courteous. The final words recall a main appeal of the letter.

Dear Mr. Stark:

Is there a place in your labor-relations department for a person who is specially trained in the field and who knows working people and can talk with them on their level? I feel that my background, experience, and education have given me these unique qualifications; and I submit the following brief review of background facts in support.

All my life I have lived and worked with laboring people. I was born and reared by working parents in a poor section of New York City. While in high school, I worked mornings and evenings in New York's garment district, primarily as a shipping and receiving clerk. For two years, between high school and college, I worked full time as a truck driver for Wayland Trucking; and I was a member of the Teamsters. Throughout my four years of college I worked half time as an equipment repairperson for Davidson Electric. From these experiences, I feel that I know and understand labor. I speak labor's language, and laboring people understand and trust me.

My college studies at Olympia University were specially planned to prepare me for a career in labor relations. Pursuing a major in industrial relations, I studied courses in labor relations, labor law, personnel administration, organizational behavior, administrative management, business policy, and collective bargaining. In addition, I studied a wide assortment of supporting subjects: economics, business writing, industrial psychology, human relations, and operations management. My studies, I feel, have given me the foundation of knowledge from which to learn the practical side of labor-relations work. I hope to begin the practical side of my development in June after I receive the Bachelor of Business Administration degree, with honors (3.7 grade-point average on the basis of 4).

If this brief description and the additional information on the accompanying résumé meet your requirements, may I hear from you soon? I could visit you any time at your convenience to talk about how I could help in your labor relations work.

Sincerely,

The next illustration is a form prospecting letter written by a young college graduate seeking her first job. She mailed the letter to a number of companies, and ultimately she received three job offers. Thus, the letter must be regarded as successful.

Perhaps the letter's success is explained by its directness, its good selection of highlight information, and its organization. The opening directly names the writer's goal; and it establishes the three bases of appeal for the job. The following review presents the highlights of the writer's credentials in good order. Where helpful, interpretations are used to enhance the values of the facts. Although there is not much obvious you-viewpoint adaptation, good adaptation is present. The information selected shows the writer's understanding of the qualifications needed in an administrative trainee. The close courteously requests an appropriate action and leaves the suggestion of a person wanting to work for the company.

Dear Mr. Shannon:

Will you please review my qualifications for work in your administrative trainee program? I base my case on my training, work attitude, and personal skills.

My training for administration consists primarily of four years of business administration study at State University. The Bachelor of Business Administration degree I will receive in June has given me a broad foundation of business knowledge. As a general business major, I studied all the functional fields (management, marketing, finance, accounting) as well as the other core business subjects (communication, statistics, law, economics, production, and personnel). I feel that I have the knowledge base that will enable me to be productive now. And I feel that I can build upon this base through practical experience.

As I am seeking my first full-time job, I must use other than work experience to prove my work attitude. I submit my grade-point record at State as evidence that I took my studies seriously and that I worked hard. My 3.3 overall average (4.0 basis) placed me in the top ten percent of my graduating class. I also worked diligently in student associations. As you will see in the following paragraph, my efforts were recognized by the special assignments and leadership roles given me. I assure you that I would bring these work habits with me to General Electric.

Throughout my college years I devoted time to the development of my personal skills. As an active member of the student chapter of the Society for the Advancement of Management, I served as treasurer and program chairperson. I participated in intramural sports (golf and volleyball). And I was an active worker in the Young Republicans, serving as publicity chairperson for three years. All this experience, I feel, has helped me to have the balance you seek in your administrative trainees.

If these highlights and the details on the enclosed résumé describe a potential career administrator, may I please have an interview? I could be in your office at your convenience to talk about working for General Electric.

Sincerely,

Using the name of a company executive to gain interest in the opening, the following letter applies for work as a correspondence supervisor. Overall, the letter is conservative in style and tone. Its primary strength is in its presentation of background facts with interpretations which show that the writer knows the field. Little obvious you-viewpoint is present in the review of background facts, yet you-viewpoint is there. It is implied through words which show the writer's understanding of the work and the qualifications needed to do it. The final paragraph brings the preceding review of qualifications to a head. Here, in summary fashion, the writer fits the qualifications to the job. The close appropriately moves for action with a clear question.

Dear Ms. O'Daniel:

On the suggestion of Mr. Victor O. Krause of your staff, I submit the following summary of my qualifications for work as your correspondence supervisor.

Presently I am in my fifth year as correspondent for Atlas Insurance. Primarily my work consists of writing letters to Atlas policyholders. This work has made me a student of business writing. It has sharpened my writing skills. And more important, it has taught me how to gain and keep friends for my company through writing.

Additional experience working with business people has given me an insight into the correspondence needs of business. This experience includes planning and presenting a correspondence-improvement course for local civil service workers, a course in business writing for area business executives, and a course in bank correspondence for employees of Columbia National Bank.

My college training was carefully planned to prepare me for work in business writing. Advertising and public relations were my areas of concentration for my B.S. degree from Northern State University. As you will see in the enclosed résumé, I studied all available writing courses. In addition to the business writing and advertising copywriting courses in my degree plan, I studied elective writing courses in journalism and English.

In summary, Ms. O'Daniel, I feel that my studies and my experience have equipped me for work as your correspondence supervisor. I know business writing. I know how it should be practiced to benefit your company. If after reviewing my credentials you feel that I might meet your needs, may I have an interview? I could be at your office at any time convenient to you.

Sincerely,

The following prospecting letter is bland when compared with preceding examples. Its style is somewhat artless. Even so, its straightforward, matter-of-fact quality is favored by some personnel people. The letter begins directly, and this directness should serve as an effective attention device. The information presented is well organized around the major areas of information covered, and highlights are appropriately emphasized. The direct question in the close should be effective.

Dear Mr. Butler:

Can Darden, Inc., use a hard-working young woman who wants a career in office administration? I am that woman, and I feel my education, training, and personal qualities justify my application for office administration work.

My five years of work experience (see attached data sheet) have taught me to do all phases of office work. For the past two years I have been in charge of payrolls at Gynes Manufacturing Company. As the administrator of payrolls, I have had to handle all types of office operations, including records management and general correspondence. Although I am happy on this job, it does not offer the career opportunity I seek with Darden.

Complementing my work experience are my studies at Metropolitan Community College. In addition to studying the prescribed courses in my major field of business administration, I selected electives to help me in my career objective. And I believe I have succeeded. In spite of full-time employment through most of my time in college, I was awarded the Associate of Arts degree last May with a 3.3 grade-point average. But most important of all, I learned from my studies how office work should be done.

In addition, I believe I have the personal qualities that would fit me harmoniously into your organization. I like people, and through experience I have learned how to work with them.

If my qualifications appear to meet your needs, Mr. Butler, may I talk to you about working for Darden? I could arrange a visit to your office at any time convenient to you.

Sincerely,

Three qualifications listed in the advertisement being answered determine the plan for the next letter. Repetition of the three points of the reader's words is sure to gain interest in the opening. In addition, the words serve to set up the structure of the remainder of the letter. The review of qualifications includes good interpretations. Each of the parts ends with you-viewpoint words which relate qualifications to the job. As it should, the letter ends with a request for action. The final thought is of the benefit the reader will receive by taking the action.

> Dear Ms. Alderson:
>
> Sound background in advertising . . . well-trained . . . work well with others. . . .
>
> These key words in your July 7 advertisement in the *Times* describe the person you want, and I believe I am that person.
>
> For the past four years I have gained experience in every phase of retail advertising working for the *Lancer*, our college newspaper. I sold advertising, planned layouts, and wrote copy. During the last two summers I got more firsthand experience working in the advertising department of Wunder & Son. I wrote a lot of copy for Wunder, some of which I am enclosing for your inspection; but I also did just about everything else there is to do in advertising work. I enjoyed it, and I learned from it. I am confident that this experience would help me to fit in and contribute to the work in your office.
>
> In my concentrated curriculum at the University I studied marketing, with a specialization in advertising. As you will see from the attached data sheet, I studied every course offered in advertising and related fields, and I believe that my honor grades give some evidence that I worked hard and with sincerity. I am confident that upon my graduation in June I can bring to your organization the firm foundation of knowledge and imagination your work demands.
>
> Understanding the importance of being able to get along well with people, I actively participated in Sigma Chi (social fraternity), the First Methodist Church, and Pi Tau Pi (honorary business fraternity). From the experience gained in these associations, I am confident that I can fit in harmoniously with your close-knit advertising department.
>
> If I have convinced you of my sincerity and capability, may I meet with you and talk with you? I could visit your office at any time convenient to you to talk about doing your advertising work.
>
> Sincerely,

Other letters about employment

The job-application procedure may require other correspondence than the traditional application letter and data sheet. For example, there may be a need to say thank-you for an interview, to accept a job offer, to inquire about the status of an application, or to refuse an offer. Such correspondence is not persuasive. Primarily, it falls into the letter situations described in Chapters 9 and 10. Even so, because these letters may be very important to you, a brief review of them follows.

Thank-you letters. After an interview you would be wise to write a thank-you letter. It is the courteous thing to do, even if you are not interested in the job. If you are interested, the letter can help your case. It singles you out from the competition, and it shows your interest in the job.

Typically, such letters are short. They begin with an expression of gratefulness. They say something about the interview, the job, or such. They take care of any additional business (such as submitting information requested). They end on a goodwill note—perhaps a hopeful look to the next step in the negotiations. Such a letter is the following:

Dear Ms. Chubbuck:

I genuinely appreciate the time you gave me yesterday. You were most helpful. And you did a first-rate job of selling me on Graystone-Brune, Inc.

As you requested, I have enclosed samples of the advertising campaign I developed as a class project. If you need anything more, please write me.

I look forward to the possibility of discussing employment with you before long.

Sincerely,

Constructing a follow-up to an application. When a prospective employer is late in responding to an application, you may need to write. Sometimes employers are just slow, but sometimes they may lose the application. Whatever the explanation, a letter may help to produce action.

Such a letter is a form of routine inquiry. Perhaps it can use, as an excuse for writing, the need to make a job decision. Or perhaps it can use some other good explanation. Such a letter is the following:

Dear Mr. Lemon:

As the time is approaching when I must make a job decision, may I please ask the status of my employment application with you?

You may recall that you interviewed me in your office November 7. You wrote me November 12 indicating that I was among those you had selected for further consideration.

Barrow, Inc., remains one of the organizations I would like to consider in making my career decision. I'll very much appreciate an early response.

Sincerely,

Planning the job acceptance. Job acceptances in writing are merely favorable response letters. Usually they include an extra amount of goodwill. Because the letter should begin directly, a yes answer in the beginning is appropriate. The remainder of the letter should be comments about the work, the company, the interview—whatever you would say if you were face to face with the reader. The letter need not be long. This one does the job well:

Dear Ms. Polansky:

I accept your offer of employment. After my first interview with you, I was convinced that Allison-Caldwell was the organization for me. It is good to know that you feel I am right for Allison-Caldwell.

Following your instructions, I shall be in Atlanta on May 28, ready to begin a career with you.

Sincerely,

Writing a letter refusing a job. Letters refusing a job offer follow the normal refusal pattern. One good technique is to begin with a friendly comment—perhaps something about past relations with the company. Next, explain and present the refusal in words that are clear yet positive. Then end with more friendly talk. This example illustrates the plan:

Dear Mr. Segura:

Meeting you and the other fine people at Northern was a genuine pleasure. All that I saw and heard impressed me most favorably. I was especially impressed to receive the generous job offer which followed.

In considering the offer I naturally gave some weight to these favorable impressions. Even though I have accepted a job with another firm, these favorable impressions remain strong in my mind.

Thank you for the time and courteous treatment shown me.

Sincerely,

Letter problems—4

Sales

1.   Combining the knowledge gained from his business studies and his extraordinary ability in the kitchen, Roger Wascom has done quite well for himself over the past six years. His Grandma's Bakery has established an enviable reputation in the area, especially for his Grandma's Old Fashioned Fruitcakes. But Roger isn't content to rest on the profits of local sales. Following the lead of a bakery he observed while on vacation last year, he has decided to cash in on the mail-order market. As he sees it, his fruitcakes are a natural for the Christmas season.

With a mail-order sales campaign in mind, Roger approached your small advertising agency. After discussing the pros and cons of direct-mail selling, Roger decided to give you the job of handling the campaign. And so you could write the sales copy with first-hand knowledge, he gave you a two-pound fruitcake.

After tasting the cake, you can understand Roger's enthusiasm—and that of his local customers. There is no shortage in quality fruits—candied pineapple, cherries, figs, dates, and raisins. Then there are the nuts—black and English walnuts, pecans, almonds—all in ample quantity. Over the top is a heavy assortment of pineapple slices, cherries, and almonds. Although you can't see it, Roger told you that he uses honey in his recipe as well as in his secret assortment of spices. Positively, this is the best fruitcake you have ever tasted.

The fruitcakes are packaged in a round tin attractively decorated in a Christmas design. They're available in two sizes—two pounds and three pounds. They sell for $14.95 and $20.95, respectively—postpaid anywhere in the nation. Purchases exceeding $100 receive a 10 percent discount.

As specified by Roger, this first mailing will go to business executives and will present the cakes as ideal business gifts. Included in the mailing will be an attractive brochure picturing and describing the fruitcakes in detail; order forms and postage-paid envelopes; and, of course, the accompanying sales letter. Your task now is to write the letter.

You haven't yet decided what appeals to use, but probably you will stress the quality of the product—the favorable impression this truly delicious cake will make for the one who gives it. Your letter will carry the basic sales message, and it will refer to the brochure for details.

Address the letter to Ms. Beatrice Kanuth, one of the executives on the mailing lists.

2. Roger Wascom (see preceding problem for background) is excited again. After successfully marketing his Grandma's Old Fashioned Fruitcake to executives as business gifts, he has his eyes on selling his products through quality gift shops in the region next Christmas season. Roger plans to promote his product further in the three months prior to Christmas with weekly two-column, four-inch advertisements in the two regional newspapers. In addition, he has prepared a good supply of eye-catching, point-of-purchase, easel-type cards that call attention to the fruitcakes as they are displayed in the stores. (You may imagine their appearance.) Roger will send these displays with all orders.

This mailing will also consist of a brochure, order forms, and sales letter (the part you must write now). Because it will go to people interested in fruitcakes only if the fruitcakes will sell at a profit, your appeal will be rational. You'll play up the quality and taste, of course, but in terms of satisfying customers and enhancing profits. You will offer the two-pound cakes for $9.80 and the three-pound cakes for $13.95 plus shipping costs. The suggested retail prices of the cakes are $14.95 and $20.95. Shipments will be made by motor freight and with 2/10, net 30 terms.

You may add any other information you feel is needed, as long as it is logical. Address the letter to Ms. Candy Yoder, owner of the Treasure House. And write it for Roger's signature.

3. You are the founder of *Regional Sports,* a new monthly magazine for your region (southwest, midwest, northeast, etc.—your choice). The plan of the publication is simple. It will cover all competitive sports in the region—football, basketball, hockey, track, tennis, golf. On occasion, it will even cover lesser ones. It will preview the coming seasons for the major sports, giving detailed reviews and predictions for each team. It will report on activities during the season, and it will carry feature stories on leading personalities.

Last week you came out with the first issue. You are pleased with it, generally—that is, with everything except sales. You badly need more readers. So you have decided to promote the magazine through a mail campaign to area sports enthusiasts.

Since you have some talent as a writer, you will prepare the mailing. It will consist of a persuasive letter, an order form, and a copy of the first issue of the magazine. Your letter will describe the reading pleasures the magazine will bring to genuine sports enthusiasts. And it will point to features in the sample copy to support the description. (You may use your imagination to develop the content of this issue.) After making your appeal, you will lead the reader through the motions of filling out and mailing the order blank. Subscription price is $12 a year, which is half the retail price of $2 an issue. Subscribers can pay now, or they can pay later by way of a major credit card merely by writing the card number and expiration date on the order form.

The first letter will go to Thomas Ahern, the first name on the list of area sports enthusiasts you purchased from the Dooley Mailing Service Company.

4. Write a letter selling a packaged golf vacation to Whispering Hills Lodge. Located in a resort area near you (your instructor may select the place), Whispering Hills features one of the nation's most beautiful and challenging 18-hole golf courses. Designed by Jack Nicklaus, it is the scene of a major event on the professional tour.

The lodge facilities are equally as good. The lodge contains 144 luxurious rooms. In addition, there are 22 individual cottages, a club house with restaurant and lounge, a swimming pool, and two Har-tru surfaced tennis courts. The resident golf pro is Carol Topping, a former world-class professional player. She has a qualified staff of assistants.

Package rates per person are $90 per day (double occupancy) and $105 per day (single occupancy). Included in the price are breakfast and dinner, unlimited use of the golf course, and one hour of instruction. Additional instruction is available at the rate of $40 an hour.

Using your imagination logically to supply additional information about the place, write the letter. It will be mailed to a list of affluent golfers. Include an illustrated brochure and a postage-paid reservations-request card.

5. The Schwartz Portrait Studio, long established in Kansas City, makes a specialty of children's pictures. It is now prepared to offer parents a contract whereby the studio agrees to take eight 8-by-10-inch portraits of a child over a period of five years for $150. The pictures will be taken in the studio when the child is three months, six month, one year, one year and a half, two years, three years, four years, and five years old. Each time the parents will have at least four good proofs from which to make their selection. The studio will keep a file and notify parents of the date when each picture should be taken.

Write the letter. Assume that you will have an illustrative panel of eight pictures of a child across the top of the sheet on which the letter is typed. Parents are to telephone or fill out a return card to make an appointment for the first sitting.

6. Assume you are the special shopping consultant for a local department store. You are excited over the new perfume to which your cosmetic department has acquired the exclusive rights for this area—select a scent of your choice. This new product should be just the item for any gift occasion. Since the holiday season coming up is loaded with sales possibilities, you want to write a letter which will be sent out to your list of 1,000 best male customers. If you can convince these 1,000 men to purchase the perfume

for the women in their lives, then the product line should be well launched, as you're sure repeat sales will occur when the women discover this exotic scent.

Your letter will have to be tasteful, but can be loaded with emotion. Your main effort will be to convince the receivers that this perfume is just what the woman (or women—don't forget sisters, daughters, even mothers-in-law as possible recipients of such a gift) in his life wants. You won't enclose a mailer, but you can assume that the stationery will be scented. Each letter will be individually typed. You can use people's names; but basically it's a form letter, so don't include personal references to their specific situations, families, and so on.

Some sales pointers are as follows: exclusive new perfume, choice of four ways to give, a wide price range, the high-fashion and snob-appeal aura of a French perfume, the possible reaction of the female receiver of such a gift, the fact that the reader can charge it and have it mailed with a gift card just by phoning the store, and so on.

This is a chance for you to really use your imagination, so go to it! But be sure to include the basic essentials necessary to complete the sale.

7. Assume that you are a direct-mail writer with the assignment of selling the perfume in Problem 6 to retailers. You must prepare a sales letter, which will be addressed to buyers in the more exclusive places where perfumes are sold.

As in the preceding problem, you will gather the facts about the product. You will need also to determine prices, sales terms, and such. And you may assume that the perfume will be advertised in appropriate quality publications; you may supply these details. When you have assembled all this information, you will be ready to write.

Writing this letter will be somewhat different from writing the preceding one. In this case, you must use a more rational approach. Although the aesthetic qualities of the product are important, they are better interpreted in terms of sales, turnover, satisfied customers, and profits.

A brochure giving prices and shipping details as well as a description of the product will accompany the letter. So will a postage-paid order form. Address the letter to any of the buyers on your list.

8. Willie Williams and Terry Hopkins, two former stars with the Bay City Pirates professional basketball team, have opened a camp for boys in the San Juan Mountains of southwestern Colorado. The camp is located in a beautiful valley filled with white-bark aspen and tall green firs. Peaks exceeding 14,000 feet mark the landscape. Without question, it is a delightful place for a boy to spend a summer. There are fish to be caught, horses to ride, trails to be hiked. Then there is the special basketball clinic and body-building program Willie and Terry conduct personally. The food is the very best, tasty and nutritious. In fact, the camp has a full-time dietitian (Willie's wife) on the staff. And for the boys' safety, there is a full-time registered nurse (Terry's wife) available 24 hours a day.

All Willie and Terry need to do now is to tell people about their camp, and that's where you come in. As business manager for the camp, you will write a sales letter that will get parents to send their 12- to 16-year-old boys to Camp Wilderness (that's what they named it). There will be three four-week sessions, beginning the first Sunday in June. The price is $900 per session. Transportation to and from the camp is extra, although Willie and Terry will pick up the boys at the airport or bus depot at Durango at no extra charge. Because each session will be limited to 30 boys, the reader will need to act fast.

9. Gear up for selling a Christmas vacation ski holiday to students at your school. The $375[1] package trip originates from your campus on December 27 and returns from Aspen, Colorado, via Denver on January 3. Price includes all transportation, two meals per day (breakfast and lunch), lodging at Aspen House Inn at Snowmass-at-Aspen (new luxury inn with heated pool, ski instructors, sauna, and ski lounges), ski lift tickets for two days, instruction for two days, a one-day ski-daddle rental. Reservations are made through the University Tour Committee (Union Building Lobby), or call 342-6754.

Air transportation is via chartered 707 leaving from __ (airport near you).

Snowmass-at-Aspen is America's newest, most complete total ski resort. It has lighted slopes for night skiing. The Colorado snow is some of the finest powder in the world. Aspen itself abounds with fine bars, shops, and food. The night life rivals anything found in the United States.

Use your creative imagination to make this an outstanding letter that will sell this package to your fellow students.

10. Come to the rescue of Joe E. Horowitz, promotion manager for Dacy's Department Store, Ottawa, Ontario. Each year shortly before Easter he writes a letter to all of Dacy's better charge customers selling them on doing their Easter shopping at Dacy's. Frankly, his letters haven't been very successful. And you can see why, now that you've read some of them. They're unimaginative, dull, and flat, in your opinion.

Now that you're the new management trainee in the department, Joe gives you the assignment. You are determined to do a good job. Anyway, it would be hard to do worse. You put your very best imagination to work. What can you say to a wide assortment of customers that will sell them on doing their Easter shopping at Dacy's? It's a challenging assignment.

Address the letter to any one of your charge customers. You don't plan to use any of those "dear customer" salutations Horowitz used.

11. Select from a current magazine an advertisement on a product that could be sold profitably to business executives. Preferably select an advertisement that presents a thorough description of the product. Then write a sales letter for this product. Be careful that your writing does not borrow the wording in the advertisement. In other words, make your letter original

---

[1] You may need to change this if distance varies much from 1,000 miles.

in its wording from start to finish. Include a descriptive brochure and an order card with your letter. Address it to the first business executive on your list. (For class purposes clip the advertisement to your letter).

Applications

12. Assume that you are completing your degree requirements this semester and are looking for a job. Find an advertisement for a job for which you would be qualified. Then write a letter of application for the job. (For class purposes, clip the advertisement to your letter. Assume that a data sheet accompanies the letter.)

13. Write the data sheet to accompany the letter in Problem 12, above.

14. Move yourself ten years into the future. Your career development has been fairly successful, though not sensational. To this point you have been employed by one major firm (you name it) and have gained excellent experience. But the road to advancement with this firm appears to have only limited possibilities. So you have decided to look elsewhere for a suitable position.

Your search for a new position turns up one good possibility. The job is with a major competitor of your present employer; and the position would represent a logical move up from your present status.

Making only logical assumptions about your development and experience over the ten-year period, write the letter. Assume that a data sheet accompanies the letter.

15. Write the data sheet that accompanies Problem 14, above.

16. Assume that you are in your last term of school and that graduation is just around the corner. Your greatest interest is in finding work which you like and in which you could support yourself now and a family later as you win promotions.

No job of your choice is revealed in the want ads of newspapers and trade magazines. No placement bureau has provided anything to your liking. So you decide to do as any good salesman does: survey the product (yourself), then the market (companies which in the scope of their operations could use a person who can do what you are prepared to do), then advertise (send the company a data sheet with a covering application letter). Such a procedure sometimes creates a job where none existed before; sometimes it establishes a basis for negotiations for the "big job" two, three, or five years after graduation. And, very frequently, it puts you on the list for the good job which is not filled through advertising or from the company staff. Assume that a data sheet accompanies the letter.

17. Write the data sheet to accompany Problem 16, above.

18. Move the calendar to your graduation date so you're now ready to sell your working ability in the job market for as much as you can get

and still hold your own. Besides your wide canvass of likely firms with the aid of prospecting letters and your diligent follow-ups of family "contacts," you've decided that you won't overlook anything especially good in the ad columns of newspapers and magazines. A look through the library copies of the latest issues available of big town publications turns up the following prospects worth looking over that you think you could handle. (You may change publication and place names to fit your section of the country.)

A. *Banking trainee.* Major big-city bank seeks recent finance graduate for training program. Opportunities for careers in all areas of bank operations. Applicants should show evidence of sincerity, maturity, and dedication to work. Excellent pay and benefits. Write Personnel Director, P.O. Box 4557 *(your city)*.

B. *Personnel trainee.* Recent business graduate wanted to train in personnel department of major manufacturing company. Knowledge of personnel department activities and general administration necessary. Good communication skills. Must be easy to work with, dependable, and personable. Send credentials to P.O. Box 1421, City.

C. *Marketing graduate.* Developing telecommunications company has career opening for one interested in becoming marketing systems development analyst. Work will involve coordinating strategic and tactical pricing, analyzing competition capabilities, and implementing marketing systems. Will work directly under and will be trained by founder-owner until ready for position. Marketing degree and commitment to work required. Box DY-3, *The News.*

D. *Sales representative.* Fortune 500 company in computer sales and systems has openings for sales representatives. Company will train. Work involves heavy customer contact, consulting on and servicing computer products. Degree in engineering, marketing, computer science, or information systems desired. Should be outgoing and personable. Must have good communication skills. Outstanding compensation plan. Write Box A-19, *The News.*

E. *MIS graduate.* Expanding energy company seeks MIS graduate for work in data-processing functions, including systems design, programming, data center operations, telecommunications, mini computers, and word processing. Excellent pay and opportunity for those who can produce. Write Box E-7, *Business Journal.*

F. *EDP specialist.* Very profitable savings and loan company needs a college-trained person to work in data processing. Knowledge of CICS, teleprocessing monitor on IBM 4341, DOS-VSE. Top pay and benefits. Write Box 2-127, *Daily News.*

G. *Office administrator trainee.* College graduate with general business knowledge to train for position as manager of corporate office of major real estate development company. Should have basic knowledge of personnel management, data processing, accounting, systems and procedures. Good communication skills necessary. Must be personable, mature, and hard-working. Write Personnel Manager, P.O. Box 5511, *(your city)*.

H. *Market research.* Growing marketing research company needs recent graduate in marketing. Should have good foundation in research methodology, quantitative analysis, and computers. Good writing skills. Excellent compensation. Send application to Box C-717, *Daily News.*

I. *Executive secretary.* College-trained secretary for work as secretary to high-level administrator of major insurance company. Must be personable, willing to work, and highly skilled. Knowledge of modern office systems and word-processing equipment necessary. Write Box B-91, *The Daily Telegram.*

J. *Assistant to hospital administrator.* Large health care facility seeks assistant to administrator. Excellent training opportunity for recent business graduate. Basic knowledge of administration, accounting, personnel, and finance required. Must have good communication skills and a willingness to work and learn. Send application to Box H-77, *Health Care Journal.*

K. *Securities representative.* Business graduates wanted to train as securities representatives and for Series Securities License. Work involves setting up accounts by phone, accepting orders, transmitting orders to clearing brokers, answering customer inquiries, and maintaining accounts and month-end reports. Good oral communication skills required. Challenging and responsible work. Must be a self-starter. Excellent pay and benefits. Write Box D-11, *Business Journal.*

L. *Administrative assistant.* VP of Fortune 500 manufacturing company needs bright college graduate to relieve her of detail work. Management, production, or general business majors preferred. Good communication skills and initiative necessary. Only the serious, hard-working, ambitious need apply. Send application to Personnel Director, P.O. Box 2399, *(your city)*.

M. *Merchandising trainee.* National department store chain seeks marketing graduates for trainee program. Must be willing to relocate throughout career. Advancement dependent on ability and achievement only. Must be self-motivated, personable, and dependable. Write Personnel Manager, P.O. Box 779, *(your city)*.

N. *Hotel management trainee.* Young college graduate for career in hotel administration. Training covers all phases of hotel operations. Applicants must be personable, hard-working, mature, and intelligent. Write Placement Officer, DeVoe Hotels, Inc., 3175 Burgess Avenue, City.

O. *Office manager.* Local insurance agency needs bright young college graduate. Will train for position. Must know office administration and have good letter-writing ability. Excellent salary and fringe benefits. Box 3007, City.

P. *Management trainee.* Business administration or engineering gradu-
ate preferred. Must be intelligent, hard-working, and personable.
Apply by letter only to Personnel Department, Moran Chemical
Company, Box 1001.

Q. *Banking trainee.* Large bank has openings for college graduates with
good foundation in finance. Training programs designed to give
thorough foundation in all areas of bank operation. Applicants must
be mature, intelligent, and personable. Good salary and fringe benefits. Excellent opportunity for advancement. P.O. Box 171, City.

R. *Banking opportunity.* Small-town bank seeks recent college graduate
to train for No. 2 position. Finance major preferred. Should have
good managerial skills and a basic knowledge of bank operations.
Must be personable, hard-working, and intelligent. Good pay and
benefits. Write Box X-12, *Daily Telegram.*

S. *Tax-Shelter Salesperson.* Business graduate to train for sales work
with highly successful tax-shelter organization. Must be a self-starter,
personable, intelligent, and able to talk with successful people. Shel-
ters are in equipment leasing. Good pay while training. Unlimited
earnings potential. Write Box A-13, *Daily Telegram.*

Assume that you *do* want a job, and concentrate on the ad describing
the work you would like most or could do best—then write a letter which
will get that job. Your letter will first have to survive the siftings which
winnow out the dozens (sometimes hundreds) of applicants who lack the
expected qualifications. Toward the end you'll be getting into strong competition, in which small details may make the little extra margin of superiority
that will get you an interview and a chance to campaign further.

Study your ad for what it says—and even more for what it implies
between the lines. Weigh your own preparation even more thoroughly than
you weigh the chosen ad. You may imagine far enough ahead to assume
completion of all the courses which are blocked out for your degree. You
may build up your case a bit on what you actually have. Sort out the things
that line up for the *one* job, organize them strategically, and then present
them. Assume that you've attached a complete data sheet (possibly with
picture).

19. Write the data sheet to accompany Problem 18, above.

Reports: The problem and its organization

13

HOW MUCH you will communicate through reports in business will depend on the nature of your organization. But the odds are that you will use reports and that you will use them a lot. Reports are vital to the communication needs of all large organizations; and the larger the organization, the greater the need for reports is likely to be. Also, the more technical and complex the work within the organization is, the more likely it is that reports will be needed. As today's movement is toward progressively larger and more technical business operations, your likelihood of communicating extensively through reports is good.

An orientation to reports

The special needs of reports

Communicating through reports involves applying many of the principles of clear writing used in letters, especially those discussed in Chapter 7. Certainly, there is much in common in all forms of writing. Reports, however, have some special needs which make it desirable that you study them separately. The most important of these needs are those related to the special communication problems caused by the extent of information some reports must present. Although many reports are no longer than a long business letter, many others contain great masses of information. Presenting vast quantities of data for the best possible communication results involves many problems worthy of study.

From a review of the communication process, we can see easily the difficulty of communicating voluminous material. The sensory receptors are selective, and the mental filters are deficient in giving meaning to what the receptors pick up. As a result, much of any involved message will be missed. Thus, you, as a report writer, must do whatever you can to help in the communication of the mass of information which makes up your report.

As you will learn from the following pages, you can help to communicate voluminous material in a number of ways. You can present the information in an order carefully worked out to give maximum clarity to the information. You can work hard to show the relationships of various parts of the report, making them fit logically together in the reader's mind. You can make good use of visual helps when words alone would not do the best job. You can summarize from time to time; and you can mark the reader's path through the information with forward-guiding references and concluding remarks. These, and other things you can do to overcome the major communication barrier of a report, make up the bulk of the discussion which appears in the following pages.

Reports defined

Most of us know, or think we know, what business reports are, for they are commonplace in 20th-century life. But probably we would be hard pressed to find words to define them. In fact, definitions in current use range from one extreme to the other. Some are so broad as to include almost any presentation of information. Others limit reports to only the most formal types. For our purposes, this middle-ground definition is adequate: A business report is an orderly and objective communication of factual information which serves some business purpose.

Careful inspection of this definition reveals the identifying characteristics of the business report. As an *orderly* communication, a report is given some care in preparation. And care in preparation distinguishes a report from the casual, routine exchanges of information which continually occur in business. The *objective* quality of a report is its unbiased approach to the facts presented. The report seeks truth, regardless of its consequences. The word *communication* is broad by definition, covering all ways of transmitting meaning (speaking, writing, drawing, gesturing, and so on). The basic ingredient of the report is factual information—events, records, and the various forms of data that are communicated in the conduct of business. Not all reports are business reports. Research scientists, medical doctors, ministers, students, and many others write reports. To be classified as a "business report," a report must *serve some business purpose*.

Even though this definition of a business report is specific enough to be meaningful, it is broad enough to take into account the variations to be found in reports. For example, some reports do nothing more than present facts. Others go a step further by including interpretations. Still others proceed to conclusions and recommendations. There are reports that are formally dressed both in writing style and in physical appearance. And there are reports that evidence a high degree of informality. The definition given permits all of these variations.

Determining the report purpose

Your work on a report logically begins with a need. Someone or some group (usually your superiors) needs information for a business purpose. Perhaps the need is for information only. Perhaps it is for information and analysis. Or perhaps it is for information, analysis, and recommendation. Whatever the case, persons with a need will authorize you to do the work. Usually, they will authorize the work orally. But they could do it in a letter or a memorandum.

After you have been assigned the task of writing a report, your first step should be to get the problem clearly in mind. As elementary and basic as this step may appear to be, all too often it is haphazardly done. All too often it is the cause of the failure of a report to reach its goal.

The preliminary investigation

Getting a problem in mind is largely a matter of gathering all the information needed to understand it, and then applying your best logic to the problem. Gathering the right information involves many things, depending on your problem. It may mean gathering material from company files, talking over the problem with experts, searching through printed sources, and discussing the problem with those authorizing it. In general, you should conduct the preliminary investigation until you have the information necessary for understanding the problem.

Needs for a clear statement of problem

After you understand your problem, your next logical step is to state it clearly. Preferably, you should state it in writing. Stating the problem in writing is good for many reasons. A written statement is preserved permanently; thus, you may refer to it time and again without danger of changes occurring in it. In addition, other people can review, approve, and evaluate a written statement; and their assistance sometimes may be valuable. Most important of all, putting the problem in writing forces you to get the problem clearly in mind. In this way, this practice serves as a valuable form of self-discipline.

The problem statement normally takes one of three forms: infinitive phrase, question, or declarative statement. Illustration of each should make the meaning clear. To illustrate each, we shall use the case of determining why sales at a certain store have declined.

1. *Infinitive phrase:* "To determine the cause of decreasing sales at Store X."
2. *Question:* "What are the causes of decreasing sales at Store X?"
3. *Declarative statement:* "Store X sales are decreasing and management wants to know why."

Determination of factors

From the problem statement you should next turn to the mental task of determining the problem's needs. Within the framework of your logical imagination, you should look for the factors of the problem. That is, you should look for the subject areas that must be investigated to satisfy the overall objectives. Specifically, these factors may be of three types. First, they may be merely subtopics of the broader topics about which the report is concerned. Second, they may be hypotheses that must be tested. Third, in problems that involve comparisons, they may be the bases on which the comparisons are made. Obviously, the process of determining factors is a mental one, involving the intricate workings of the mind. Thus, we can describe it only in a most general way. You begin the process by applying your best logic to the problem. The same mental process that helped you to comprehend your problem now should assist you in determining how to solve it.

Use of subtopics in information reports

If the problem concerns primarily a need for information, your mental effort should produce the main areas about which information is needed. Illustrating this type of situation is the problem of presenting for Company X a report that reviews the Company's activities during the past quarter. Clearly, this is an informational report; that is, it requires no analysis, no conclusion, no recommendation. It requires only that information be presented. The mental process in this case is concerned simply with determining which subdivisions of the overall subject should be covered. After thoroughly evaluating the possibilities, you might come up with the following factor analysis.

> *Problem statement:* To review operations of Company X from January 1 through March 31.
> Factors:
> 1. Production.
> 2. Sales and promotion.
> 3. Financial status.
> 4. Plant and equipment.
> 5. Product development.
> 6. Personnel.

Hypotheses for problems of solution

Some problems by their nature seek a solution. Typically, such problems seek an explanation of a phenomenon or the correction of a condition. In analyzing such problems, the researcher must seek possible explanations or solutions. Such explanations or solutions are termed *hypotheses.* Once they are determined, hypotheses are tested and their applicability to the problem is either proved or disproved.

To illustrate this type of situation, assume that you have the problem of determining why sales at a certain retail store have declined. In preparing this problem for investigation, you logically would think of the possible explanations (hypotheses) of the decline in sales. You would be likely to think of more explanations than would be workable, so your task would be one of studying, weighing, and selecting. After such a study session, you would come up with explanations such as these:

Problem statement: Why have sales declined at the Milltown store?

Hypotheses:

1. Activities of the competition have caused the decline.
2. Changes in the economy of the area have caused the decline.
3. Merchandising deficiencies have caused the decline.

Logically, in the investigation that follows you would test each of these hypotheses. Perhaps you would find that one, two, or all apply. Or perhaps you would find that none is logical. Then you would have to advance additional hypotheses for further evaluation.

Bases of comparison in evaluation studies

When the problem concerns evaluating something, either singly or in comparison with others, the researcher seeks to determine the bases for the evaluation. That is, you would determine what characteristics you will evaluate. In some cases, the procedure may concern more than naming the characteristics. It also may include the criteria to be used in evaluating each characteristic.

The problem of a company that seeks to determine which of three cities would be best for opening a new factory illustrates this technique. Such a problem obviously involves a comparison study of the cities, and the bases for the comparison are the factors that determine success for the type of factory involved. After careful mental search for these factors, you would be likely to come up with a plan such as the following:

Problem statement: To determine whether Y Company's new factory should be built in City A, City B, or City C.

Factors:

1. Availability of labor.
2. Abundance of raw material.
3. Tax structure.
4. Transportation facilities.
5. Nearness to markets.
6. Power supply.
7. Community attitude.

Need for subbreakdown

Each of the factors selected for investigation may have factors of its own. In the last illustration, for example, the comparison of transportation in the three cities may well be covered by such subdivisions as water, rail, truck, and air. Labor may be compared by categories such as skilled and unskilled. These breakdowns may go still further. Skilled labor may be broken down by specific skills: machinists, plumbers, pipe fitters, welders, and such. The subdivisions could go on and on, and they should be made so far as it is helpful to the investigator.

The value of this step of finding the factors of the problem is obvious: it serves as a guide to the investigation that follows. In addition, it gives the problem order, and the value of order is apparent.

Gathering the information needed

With the problem clearly in mind, your next step is to gather the information you need. How you get the information is determined by the nature of your problem. For most business problems, your research is likely to involve gathering information from company sources. Perhaps you will need to get information by talking to other employees. Or perhaps you will get what you need from records or reports. In rare instances, you may need to conduct some form of primary research, such as a survey or experiment. Maybe you will need to look through printed sources: books, periodicals, and such.

Whatever method is required, it is likely to be one for which your work has prepared you. For this reason, and because research methods is a complex subject, we shall move past this major step in report preparation. Thus, we shall assume that the research has been done—that you now have collected all the information your problem requires.

Selecting the information

With your research completed, you next find yourself with a mass of information on your subject. But not all the information you have gathered may be what you need. In fact, you probably have more information than you need. As you know from your study of reality, information about anything is infinite. So much information exists about everything that it is easy to get more than you need for your problem.

Your next step, then, is to select the information you need from what you have gathered. Thus, you must go through what you have gathered applying each item of information to the needs of the problem. If the information helps answer a need, you keep it. If it does not, you discard it. The whole process is a mental one—a process of judgment. We can tell you little about how to do it. We can say only that in the end you should be able to justify retaining every item of information you choose to keep.

Organizing the report information

After you have determined what information you will use in the report, you are ready to give this information the order in which it will appear in your report. That is, you are ready to organize the report.

Preliminary steps in determining order

In all likelihood, your research findings will be in some form of disorder. They may be in the form of stacks of note cards, reams of questionnaires, sheets of recordings, and such. In this condition they are almost useless. You must do something to them before they can be made meaningful in your report.

What you do to give your findings their first semblance of order depends on the nature of the information you have assembled. If you have conducted library research, for example, you will need to assort your findings by some means of grouping or classifying. If you have conducted a survey or an experiment, it may mean entering findings on a computer and organizing them for analysis. It may mean constructing tables, computing statistical measurements, or the like. Or, if your research is from your memory, this step of putting the information in orderly form would mean only logically arranging the thoughts in your mind.

With your information organized for better understanding, you may now begin to apply it to your problem. This, of course, is a mental task, and we can give no formula for doing it. Generally, it involves fitting your findings to your problem—that is, analyzing them and applying them to your objectives in the one case. Your task is one of good, hard thinking—of using good logic and good knowledge in giving meaning to your research. The end result will be that from this thinking the report story will begin to emerge. You will decide what you are going to say and how you will say it.

Need for a written outline

After you have given your findings meaning and know generally what your report will say, you are ready to begin arranging your material in the order it will take in your report. Your work here will involve constructing an outline. As you know, an outline is simply a plan for the writing task which follows. It is to you, the writer, what the blueprint is to the construction engineer or what the pattern is to the dressmaker. In addition to guiding your efforts, the outline compels you to think before you write. And when you think, your writing is likely to be clearer.

Although your plan may be written or mental, you will be wise to use a written plan for all but the shortest problems. In longer reports, where tables of contents are needed, the outline forms the basis of this table. Also, in most long reports, and even in some short ones, the outline topics may serve as guides to the reader when placed within the report text as captions (or heads) to the paragraphs of writing they cover.

Patterns of report organization

After you have made your information ready for outlining, and before you begin the task, you should decide on the writing sequence, or pattern, you will use in your report. The possible sequences are many, but they fall into these definite patterns: logical, direct, and chronological. Although the emphasis at this stage of report preparation is on the selection of a sequence for the whole of the report, these patterns may be followed in any writing unit, be it sentence, paragraph, major section, or the whole.

In the *logical* arrangement, you present the findings in inductive order—moving from the known to the unknown. You preface the report findings with whatever introductory material is necessary to orient the reader to your problem. Then you present the facts, possibly with their analyses. And from these facts and analyses, you derive concluding or summary statements. In some problems you may include a recommendation section. Thus, in report form this arrangement is typified by an introductory section, the report body (usually made up of a number of sections), and a summary, conclusion, or recommendation section.

Illustrating this plan is the following report of a short and rather simple problem concerning a personnel action on a subordinate. For reasons of space economy, only the key parts of the report are presented.

> Numerous incidents during the past two months appear to justify an investigation of the work record of Clifford A. Knudson, draftsman, tool design department. . . .
> The investigation of his work record for the past two months reveals these points:
> 1. He has been late to work seven times.
> 2. He has been absent without acceptable excuse for seven days.
> 3. On two occasions he reported to work in a drunken and disorderly condition.
> 4. Etc.
> The foregoing evidence leads to one conclusion: Clifford A. Knudson should be fired.

Contrasting with the logical sequence is the *direct* arrangement. In this sequence, you present the subject matter in deductive fashion. First, you present conclusions, summaries, or recommendations; and you follow them with the facts and analyses from which they are drawn. A typical report following such an order would begin with a presentation of summary, conclusion, and recommendation material. The report findings and the analyses from which the beginning section is derived comprise the following sections. Written in direct order, the same report recommending that Knudson be fired would look like this:

> Clifford A. Knudson, draftsman, tool design department, should be fired. This conclusion is reached after a thorough investigation brought about by numerous incidents during the past two months. . . .
> The recommended action is supported by this information from his work record for the past two months:
> 1. He has been late to work seven times.
> 2. He has been absent without acceptable excuse for seven days.
> 3. On two occasions he reported to work in a drunken and disorderly condition.
> 4. Etc.

In the *chronological* arrangement, you present the findings in the order in which they happened. Obviously, such an arrangement is limited to problems of an historical nature or to problems which in some other way have a relation to time. The time pattern followed may be from past to present, from present to past, from present to future, or from future to present. A report following an order of time might begin directly with the chronological review of facts (see examples below), with an introductory section, or with a conclusion, summary, or recommendation. In other words, the chronological order may be combined with either of the two preceding orders. In such cases, it is the arrangement of the findings (the report body) to which the chronological sequence applies. Again, the report on Knudson illustrates this arrangement.

> Clifford A. Knudson was hired in 1981 as a junior draftsman in the tool design department. For the first 18 months his work was exemplary, and he was given two pay increases and a promotion to senior draftsman. In January of 1983, he missed four days of work, reporting illness, which was later found to be untrue. Again, in February. . . .
>
> All of these facts lead to the obvious conclusion: Clifford A. Knudson should be fired.

System of outline symbols

In constructing your outline, you will use some system of symbols to designate the levels of importance of your parts. Thus, a word about systems of symbols is necessary at this point. The most common system of outline symbols is the conventional form with which you are familiar:

I. First degree of division
    A. Second degree of division
        1. Third degree of division
            a. Fourth degree of division
                (1) Fifth degree of division
                    (a) Sixth degree of division

A second system of symbols is the numerical (sometimes called *decimal*) form. This system uses whole numbers to designate the major sections of a paper. Whole numbers followed by decimals and additional digits indicate subsections of the major sections. That is, an additional digit to the right of the decimal designates each successive step in the subdivision. Illustration best explains this procedure:

1. First degree of division
    1.1 Second degree of division
        1.11 Third degree of division
            1.111 Fourth degree of division
2. First degree of division
    2.1 Second degree of division
        2.11 Third degree of division (first item)
        2.12 Third degree of division (second item)
            2.121 Fourth degree of division (first item)
            2.122 Fourth degree of division (second item)

You should take care with numbers over ten. For example, 1.19 shows that this is item 9 of the third degree of division—not the 19th item of the second degree. The latter division would be written 1.(19).

The nature and extent of outlining

In general, you should build the outline around the objective of the investigation and the findings. With the objective and findings in mind, you build the structure of the report in imagination. In this process you hold large areas of facts and ideas in your mind, shifting them about until the most workable arrangement becomes clear. A workable arrangement is that order which will enable you to present the findings in their clearest and most meaningful form.

The extent of the task of outlining will differ from problem to problem. In fact, in many instances much of the work may be done long before you consciously begin the task of constructing an outline. The early steps of defining the problem and determining its subproblems may lay the groundwork for final organization. If you use a questionnaire or other form in gathering information, possibly its structure has given the problem some order. The preliminary analysis of the problem, the task of classifying and tabulating the findings, and possibly the preliminary interpretations of the findings may have given you the general idea of the report's story. Thus, when you begin to construct the outline, the work before you may be in varying degrees of progress. Obviously, the task of outlining will never be the same for any two problems. Even so, the following general and systematic procedure for outlining may prove helpful.

Organization by division

This procedure is based on the concept that outlining is a process of dividing. The subject of division is the whole of the information you have gathered. Thus, you begin the task of organizing by surveying the whole for some appropriate and logical means of dividing the information.

After you have divided the whole of the information into comparable parts, you may further divide each of the parts. Then you may further divide each of these subparts, and you may continue dividing as far as it is practical to do so (see Figure 13–1). Hence, in the end, you may have an outline of two, three, or more levels (or stages) of division. You designate these levels of division in the finished outline by some system of letters or numbers, such as by one of the two systems we have discussed.

Division by conventional relationship

In dividing the information into subparts, you have the objective of finding a means of division that will produce equal and comparable parts. Time, place, quantity, and factor are the general bases for these divisions.

Whenever the information you have to present has some chronological aspect, organization by *time* is possible. In such an organization, the divisions are time periods. Usually, the periods follow a time sequence. Although a past-to-present or present-to-past sequence is the rule, variations are possible. The time periods you select need not be equal in length, but they should be comparable in importance. Determining comparability is, of course, a subjective process and is best based on the facts of the one situation.

A report on the progress of a research committee serves to illustrate this possibility. The time period covered by such a report might be broken into the following subperiods:

The period of orientation, May–July.

Planning the project, August.

Implementing the research plan, September–November.

The happenings within each period might next be arranged in the order of their occurrence. Close inspection might reveal additional division possibilities.

If the information you have collected has some relation to geographic location, you may use a *place* division. Ideally, the division would be that similar characteristics concerning the problem exist within each geographic area. Unfortunately, place divisions are hampered by the fact that political

Figure 13–1

Procedure for Constructing an Outline by Process of Division

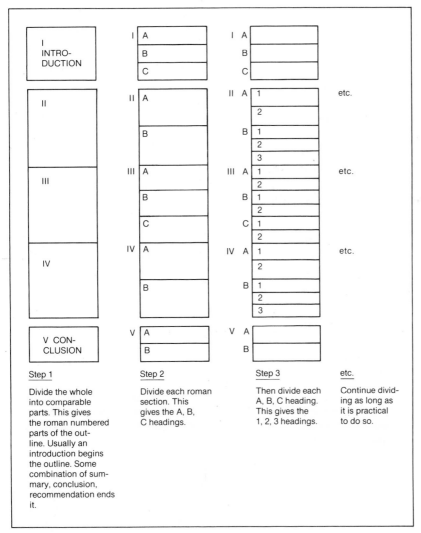

boundary lines and geographic differences in characteristics do not always coincide.

A report on the sales program of a national manufacturer illustrates a division by place. The information in this problem might be broken down by these major geographic areas:

New England
Atlantic Seaboard
South
Southwest
Midwest
Rocky Mountain
Pacific Coast

Another illustration of organization by place is a report on the productivity of a company with a number of manufacturing plants. A major division of the report might be devoted to each of the company's plants. The information for each of the plants might be further broken down by place, this time by sections, departments, divisions, or the like.

Quantity divisions are possible whenever your information has quantitative values. To illustrate, an analysis of the buying habits of a segment of the labor force could very well be divided by income groups. Such a division might produce the following sections:

Under $5,000
$5,000 to under $10,000
$10,000 to under $15,000
$15,000 to under $20,000
$20,000 to under $25,000
$25,000 and over

Another example of division on a quantitative basis is a report of a survey of men's preference for shoes. Because of variations in preferences by ages, an organization by age groups might be used. Perhaps a division, such as the following, would be appropriate:

Youths, under 18
Young adult, 18–30
Adult, 31–50
Senior adult, 51–70
Elderly adult, over 70

Factor breakdowns are not as easily seen as the preceding three possibilities. Frequently, problems have little or no aspects of time, place, or quantity. Instead, they require that certain information areas be investigated to meet the objectives. Such information areas may consist of a number of questions which must be answered in solving a problem. Or they may consist of subjects which must be investigated and applied to the problem.

An example of a division by factors is a report which seeks to determine the best of three cities for the location of a new manufacturing plant. In arriving at this decision, one would need to compare the three cities on the basis of the factors which affect the plant location. Thus, the following organization of this problem would be a logical possibility:

Worker availability .
Transportation facilities
Public support and cooperation
Availability of raw materials
Taxation
Sources of power

Another illustration of organization by factors is a report advising a manufacturer whether to begin production of a new product. This problem has few time, place, or quantity considerations. The decision on the basic question will be reached by careful consideration of the factors involved. Among the more likely factors are these:

Production feasibility
Financial considerations
Strength of competition
Consumer demand
Marketing considerations

Combination and multiple division possibilities

Not all division possibilities are clearly time, place, quantity, or factor. In some instances, combinations of these bases of division are possible. In the case of a report on the progress of a sales organization, for example, the information collected could be arranged by a combination of quantity and place:

Areas of high sales activity
Areas of moderate sales activity
Areas of low sales activity

Although not so logical, the following combination of time and quantity is also a possibility:

Periods of low sales
Periods of moderate sales
Periods of high sales

The previously drawn illustration about determining the best of three towns for locating a new manufacturing plant shows that a problem may sometimes be divided by more than one characteristic. In this example, the information also could be organized by towns. That is, each town could be discussed as a separate division of the report. This plan, however, is definitely inferior, for it separates physically the information which must be compared. Even so, it serves to illustrate a problem with multiple organization possibilities. The presence of two characteristics is common. The possibility of finding three or even four characteristics by which the information may be grouped is not remote. When multiple division possibilities exist, those not used as a basis for the major division might serve to form the second and third levels of division. In other words, the outline to this problem might look like this:

II. Town A
    A. Worker availability
    B. Transportation facilities
    C. Public support and cooperation
    D. Availability of raw materials
    E. Taxation
    F. Sources of power
III. Town B
    A. Worker availability
    B. Transportation facilities
    C. Public support and cooperation
    D. Availability of raw materials
    E. Taxation
    F. Sources of power
IV. Town C
    A. Worker availability
    B. Etc.

Or it might look like this:

II. Worker availability
    A. Town A
    B. Town B
    C. Town C
III. Transportation facilities
    A. Town A
    B. Town B
    C. Town C
IV. Public support and cooperation
    A. Town A
    B. Town B
    C. Town C

The plan of organization selected should be the one which best presents the information gathered. Unfortunately, the superiority of one plan over the others will not always be as clear as in the illustration above. Only a careful analysis of the information and possibly trial and error will lead to the plan most desirable for any one problem.

Introductory and concluding sections

To this point, the organization procedure discussed has concerned arrangement of the information gathered and analyzed. It is this portion of the report which comprises what is commonly referred to as the report "body." To this report body may be appended two additional major sections.

At the beginning of a major report may be an introduction to the presentation (the reason why the examples above begin with II, rather than I), although some forms of today's reports eliminate this conventional section. Appended to each major report may be a final major section in which the objective is brought to a head. Such a section may be little more than a summary in a report, when the objective is simply to present information. In other instances it may be the section in which the major findings or analyses are drawn together to form a final conclusion. Or possibly it might lead to a recommended line of action based on the foregoing analysis of information.

Wording the outline for report use

Because the outline in its finished form is your table of contents, and may also serve as caption guides to the paragraphs throughout the written text, you should take care in constructing its final wording. In this regard, you should consider a number of conventional principles of construction. Adherence to these principles will produce a logical and meaningful outline for your report.

Topic or talking caption? In selecting the wording for the outline captions, you have a choice of two general forms—the topic or the talking caption. *Topic captions* are short constructions, frequently one or two words in length, which do nothing more than identify the topic of discussion. The following segment of a topic-caption outline is typical of its type:

II. Present armor unit
    A. Description and output
    B. Cost
    C. Deficiencies
III. Replacement effects
    A. Space
    B. Boiler setting
    C. Additional accessories
    D. Fuel

Like the topic caption, the *talking caption* (or "popular" caption, as it is sometimes called) also identifies the subject matter covered. But it goes a step further: It also indicates what is said about the subject. In other words, the talking caption summarizes, or tells the story of, the material it covers, as in the following illustration:

II. Operation analyses of armor unit
    A. Recent lag in overall output
    B. Increase in cost of operation
    C. Inability to deliver necessary steam
III. Consideration of replacement effects
    A. Greater space requirements
    B. Need for higher boiler setting
    C. Efficiency possibilities of accessories
    D. Practicability of firing two fuels

Following is a report outline made up of captions that talk:

I. Orientation to the problem
    A. Authorization by board action
    B. Problem of locating a woolen mill
    C. Use of miscellaneous government data
    D. Logical plan of solution

II. Community attitudes toward the woolen industry
    A. Favorable reaction of all cities to new mill
    B. Mixed attitudes of all toward labor policy
III. Labor supply and prevailing wage rates
    A. Lead of San Marcos in unskilled labor
    B. Concentration of skilled workers in San Marcos
    C. Generally confused pattern of wage rates
IV. Nearness to the raw wool supply
    A. Location of Ballinger, Coleman, and San Marcos in the wool area
    B. Relatively low production near Big Spring and Littlefield
V. Availability of utilities
    A. Inadequate water supply for all but San Marcos
    B. Unlimited supply of natural gas for all towns
    C. Electric rate advantage of San Marcos and Coleman
    D. General adequacy of all for waste disposal
VI. Adequacy of existing transportation systems
    A. Surface transportation advantages of San Marcos and Ballinger
    B. General equality of airway connections
VII. A final weighting of the factors
    A. Selection of San Marcos as first choice
    B. Recommendation of Ballinger as second choice
    C. Lack of advantages in Big Spring, Coleman, and Littlefield

The report outline below is made up of topic captions:

I. Introduction
    A. Authorization
    B. Purpose
    C. Sources
    D. Preview
II. Community attitudes
    A. Plant location
    B. Labor policy
III. Factors of labor
    A. Unskilled workers
    B. Skilled workers
    C. Wage rates
IV. Raw wool supply
    A. Adequate areas
    B. Inadequate areas
V. Utilities
    A. Water
    B. Natural gas
    C. Electricity
    D. Waste disposal
VI. Transportation
    A. Surface
    B. Air
VII. Conclusions
    A. First choice
    B. Alternate choice
    C. Other possibilities

Parallelism of construction. Because of the many choices available, you are likely to construct an outline which has a mixture of grammatical forms. Some report writers believe that such a mixture of forms is acceptable, and that each caption should be judged primarily by how well it describes the material it covers. The more precise and scholarly writers disagree, saying that mixing caption types is a violation of a fundamental concept of balance.

This concept of balance they express in a simple rule—the rule of parallel construction: All coordinate captions should be of the same grammatical construction. That is, if the caption for one of the major report parts (say part II) is a noun phrase, all equal-level captions (parts III, IV, V, etc.) would also have to be noun phrases. And if the first subdivision under a major section (say part A of II) is constructed as a sentence, the captions coordinate with it (B, C, D, etc.) would have to be sentences.

The following segment of an outline illustrates *violations* of the principle of parallel construction:

A. Machine output is lagging (sentence)
B. Increase in cost of operation (noun phrase)
C. Unable to deliver necessary steam (decapitated sentence)

You may achieve parallelism in any one of three ways—by making the captions all sentences, all noun phrases, or all decapitated sentences. If you desire all noun phrases, you could construct such captions as these:

A. Lag in machine output
B. Increase in cost of operations
C. Inability to deliver necessary steam

Or, as all sentences, you could make them like this:

A. Machine output is lagging
B. Cost of operations increases
C. Boiler cannot deliver necessary steam

Variety in expression. In the report outline, as in all forms of writing, you should use a variety of expressions. You should not overwork words and expressions, for too-frequent repetition tends to be monotonous, and monotonous writing is not pleasing to the discriminating reader. The following outline excerpt illustrates this point well:

A. Chemical production in Texas
B. Chemical production in California
C. Chemical production in Louisiana

As a rule, if you make the captions talk well, there is little chance of such monotonous repetition occurring, for it is unlikely that your successive sections would be presenting similar or identical information. That is, captions which are really descriptive of the material they cover are not likely to use the same words. As an illustration of this point, the outline topics in the foregoing example can be improved simply through making the captions talk:

A. Texas leads in chemical production
B. California holds runner-up position
C. Rapidly gaining Louisiana ranks third

Questions & Problems

1. For each of the following problem situations, write a clear statement of the problem and list the factors involved. When necessary, you may use your imagination logically to supply any additional information needed.
   a. A manufacturer of breakfast cereals wants to determine the characteristics of its consumers.
   b. The manufacturer of a toothpaste wants to learn what the buying public thinks of its product in relation to competing products.
   c. Southwestern Oil Company wants to give its stockholders a summary of its operations for the past calendar year.
   d. A building contractor engaged to build a new factory for Company X submits a monthly report summarizing its progress for the period.
   e. The Able Wholesale Company must prepare a report on its credit relations with the Crystal City Hardware Company.
   f. The supervisor of Department X must prepare a report evaluating the performance of his secretary.
   g. Baker, Inc. wants a study made to determine why turnover of its employees is high.
   h. An executive must rank three subordinates on the basis of their suitability for promotion to a particular job.
   i. The supervisor of production must compare three competing machines for a particular production job.
   j. An investment consultant must advise a client on whether to invest in the development of a lake resort.
   k. A consultant seeks to learn how a restaurant can improve its profits.

2. Explain the concept of outlining as a division process.

3. Select a hypothetical problem with a time division possibility. What other division possibilities does it have? Compare the two possibilities as the main bases for organizing the report.

4. Assume that you are writing the results of a survey conducted to determine what styles of shoes are worn throughout the country for various occasions by women of all ages. What division possibilities are present here? Which would you recommend?

5. For the problem described above, use your imagination to construct topic captions for the outline.

6. Select one of the divisions formed in Question 4 and construct the subcaptions. Use talking caption form.

7. Point out any violations of grammatical parallelism in these captions:
   a. Region I sales lagging
   b. Moderate increase seen for Region II
   c. Region III sales remain strong

8. Point out any error in grammatical parallelism in these captions:
   a. High cost of operation
   b. Slight improvement in production efficiency
   c. Maintenance cost is low

9. Which of the following captions is logically inconsistent with the others?
   a. Agricultural production continues to increase
   b. Slight increase is made by manufacturing
   c. Salaries remain high
   d. Service industries show no change

10. Select an editorial, feature article, book chapter, or the like that has no captions. Write talking captions for it.

Reports: Determination of makeup

AFTER YOUR OUTLINE is in finished form, you next turn to the task of planning the makeup of your report. This task is complicated by the fact that reports are far from standardized in regard to their physical arrangement. The variations existing among reports are countless. In fact, report types in use are so numerous as to almost defy meaningful classification. Even so, if you are to determine the makeup of a specific report, you should know the possibilities of choice available. Thus, you should be acquainted with some workable approach to the makeup of all reports.

Overall view of content

Such an approach is presented in the following paragraphs. It should be pointed out, though, that the concept of this approach is quite general. It does not account for all possible reports nor the countless minor variations in report makeup. But it does serve to help you grasp the relationship of all reports.

To understand this relationship, you might view the whole of reports as resembling a stairway, as illustrated in Figure 14–1. At the top of this stairway is the formal, full-dress report. This is the form used when the problem is long and the problem situation is formal. This report contains a number of prefatory parts (parts that appear before the report text). The typical prefatory parts included are the title fly, title page, letter of transmittal and authorization, table of contents, and synopsis.

As the need for formality decreases and the problem becomes smaller, the makeup of the report also changes. Although these changes are far from standardized, they follow a general order. First, the somewhat useless title fly drops out. This page contains nothing other than the title, and the title information appears on the next page. Obviously, the title fly is used strictly for reasons of formality. Next in the progression, the synopsis (summary) and the transmittal letter are combined. When this stage is reached, the report problem usually is short enough to permit its summary in a relatively short space. A third step down, the table of contents drops out. The table of contents is a guide to the report text, and such a guide serves little value in a short report. Certainly, a guide to a 100-page report is necessary, but a guide to a 1-page report is illogical. Somewhere between these extremes a dividing point exists. You should follow the general guide of including a table of contents whenever it appears to be of some value to the reader.

Another step down, as formality and length requirements continue to decrease, the combined letter of transmittal and synopsis drops out. Thus, the report now has only a title page and report text. The title page remains to the last because it serves as a very useful cover page. In addition, it contains the most important of the identifying information. Below this short-report form is a report which reinstates the letter of transmittal and summary and presents the entire report in the form of a letter—thus, the letter report. And finally, for short problems of even more informality, the memorandum (informal letter) form may be used. Illustrated at the end of the chapter

Figure 14–1
Progression of Change in Report Makeup as Formality Requirements and Length of the Problem Decrease

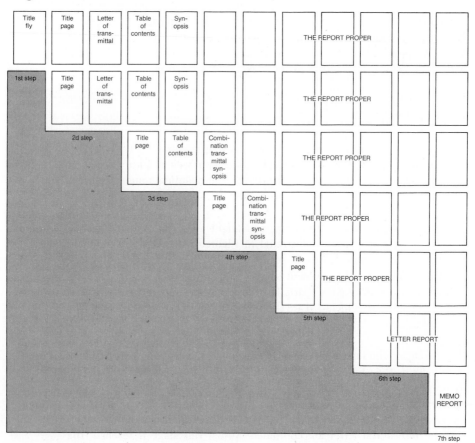

are these steps in the progression: Step 1, Figure 14–3; Step 5, Figure 14–4; Step 6, Figure 14–6; Step 7, Figures 14–5 and 14–7.

As previously mentioned, at best this analysis of report change is general, and perhaps it oversimplifies changes in report structure. Few of the reports actually written coincide exactly with its steps. Most of them, however, fit generally within the framework of the diagram. Knowledge of this relationship of length and formality should help you as you plan your reports.

Greater importance of the short types

Of all the reports described in the foregoing review, by far the most important are those at the bottom of the stairway (see Figure 14–1). Specifically, these are the short, letter, and memorandum reports. These are the reports that organizations use most of all to communicate the internal operational information they need to function. And in all likelihood, they are the types of reports you will write most often in the years ahead.

Although the shorter reports are the most numerous and important, the plan in the following pages is to first review the long, formal report. This is the one depicted at the top of the stairway. We take this approach because much of the subject matter of this review applies equally well to the shorter, less formal plans. In a sense, the shorter, informal report forms are adaptions of the longer, formal forms. Much of what we must know about overall organization, introduction, contents, concluding-summary sections, and about writing in general is most thoroughly covered through a review of the long, formal report. When you have acquired this information, you should be able to adapt it easily to the lesser report forms.

Organization and content of longer reports

Although not as numerous as the shorter forms, the longer, more formal reports tend to be highly important. They usually concern major investigations, which explains their length. And usually they are written for high-level administration—which explains their formality.

In constructing the long, more formal reports, you should view your task much as an architect views a design problem. You have a number of components with which to work. Your task is to select and arrange components to meet the requirements of the given situation.

The components in your case are the report's prefatory parts. As we noted in our review of the structure of reports (Figure 14–1), the longest, most formal report contains all of these parts. As length and formality requirements decrease, some of the parts drop out. Thus, it is your decision as the architect of the report to determine which of these parts are needed to meet the length and formality requirements of your situation.

To make this decision and, in fact, to carry it out, you need first to know the parts. Thus, in the following paragraphs we shall review them.

In addition, we shall review the remaining structure of the longest, most formal report. For convenience, the following review arranges the parts by groups. First are the prefatory parts—those which are most related to the formality and length of the report. Then comes the report proper, which, of course, is the meat of the report: It is the report story. The final group consists of appended parts. These parts contain supplementary materials—information that is not essential to the report but which may be helpful to some readers. In summary, the review follows this pattern:

Prefatory parts:

Title fly
Title page
Letter of authorization
Letter of transmittal, preface, or foreword
Table of contents and table of illustrations
Synopsis

The report proper:

Introduction
The report findings (usually presented in two or more major divisions)
Conclusions, recommendations, or summaries

Appended parts:

Bibliography
Appendix
Index

The prefatory parts

Title fly. First among the possible prefatory report pages is the title fly (see page 335). It contains only the report title. A simple page to construct, the title fly is included solely for reasons of formality. Because the title appears again on the following page, the title fly really is somewhat useless. But most books have one. And so do most formal reports.

Even though constructing the title fly is simple, composing the title is not. In fact, on a per-word basis, the title typically requires more time than any part of the report. This is as it should be, for titles should be carefully worded. Their goal is to tell at a glance what is covered in the report—and what is not. A good title fits the report like a glove. It covers all of the report information snugly, no more, no less.

For completeness of coverage, you should build your title around the five *W*s: *who, what, where, when, why.* Sometimes, *how* may be added to this list. In some problems, however, not all of the *W*s are essential to complete identification; nevertheless, they serve as a good checklist for completeness. For example, a title of a report analyzing the Lane Company's 198x advertising campaigns might be constructed as follows:

Who:	Lane Company
What:	Analysis of advertising campaigns
Where:	Not essential
When:	198x
Why:	Implied

Thus, the title emerges: "Analysis of the Lane Company's 198x Advertising Campaigns."

Obviously, you cannot write a completely descriptive title in a few words—certainly not in a word or two. Extremely short titles are as a rule vague. They cover everything; they touch nothing. Yet it is your objective to achieve conciseness in addition to completeness; so you must also seek the most economical word pattern consistent with completeness. Occasionally, in your effort to be concise and complete, you may want to use subtitles.

Title page. Like the title fly, the title page presents the report title. But, in addition, it displays other information essential to the identification of the report. In constructing your title page, you should include the complete identification of yourself and the authorizer or recipient of the report. You may include also the date of writing, particularly if the time identification is not made clear in the title. The page is mechanically constructed and is precisely illustrated in Appendix A and in the report illustration on page 336.

Letter of authorization. A report may be authorized orally or in writing. If yours is authorized in writing, you should insert a copy of this document (usually a letter or memorandum) after the title page. If your report is authorized orally, you may review the authorization information in the letter of transmittal or the introductory section, or both, of the report.

The primary objective of the letter of authorization is that of authorizing the investigator to begin the investigation. In addition, the letter contains a brief statement of the problem, with some indication of the limiting factors, together with the scope of the investigation and the limitations (if there are any). Perhaps the use of the report might also be mentioned, as well as when the report is needed and how much the cost of preparation is to be. The letter may follow any of a number of acceptable organization patterns. The outline below describes one acceptable arrangement and content:

1. Direct, clear authorization of the investigation.
2. Explanation of the objective in clear, unmistakable words.
3. Description of areas of the problem requiring investigation. This description may be an explanation of the subdivisions of the problem.
4. Limitations (such as time and cost) and special instructions.

Letter of transmittal, foreword, preface. Most formal reports contain some form of personal communication from writer to reader (see page 337). In most business cases, the letter of transmittal makes this contact. In some formal cases, particularly where the report is written for a group of readers, a foreword or preface performs this function.

The letter of transmittal, as its name implies, is a letter which transmits the report to the reader. Since this major message is essentially positive, you should write the letter in direct style. That is, in the beginning you should transmit the report directly, without explanation or other delaying information. Thus, your opening words should say, in effect, "Here is the report." Tied to or following this statement of transmittal usually comes a brief identification of the subject matter of the study and possibly an incidental summary reference to the authorization information (who assigned the report, when, etc.).

If you choose to combine the letter with the synopsis, as may be done in some forms of reports, the opening transmittal and identification may be followed by a quick review of the report highlights, much in the manner described in the following discussion of the synopsis. But whether the letter of transmittal does or does not contain a synopsis of the report text, you should generally use the letter to make helpful and informative comments about the report. You may, for example, suggest how the report information may be used. You may suggest follow-up studies, point out special limitations, or mention side issues of the problem. In fact, you may include anything which helps your reader to understand or appreciate the report.

Except in very formal instances, the letter allows you to more or less chat with your readers. Such letters may well reflect the warmth and vigor of your personality. Generally, you should use enough personal pronouns *(you, I, we)* to make a friendly impression. A warm note of appreciation for the assignment or a willingness and desire to further pursue the project may mark your close.

Minor distinctions sometimes are drawn between forewords and prefaces, but for all practical purposes they are the same. Both are preliminary messages from writer to reader. Although usually they do not formally transmit the report, forewords and prefaces do many of the other things done by letters of transmittal. Like the letters of transmittal, they seek to help the reader appreciate and understand the report. They may, for example, include helpful comments about the report—its use, interpretation, follow-up, and the like. In addition, prefaces and forewords frequently contain expressions of indebtedness to those helpful in the research. Like the letters of transmittal, they usually are written in the first person, but seldom are they as informal as some letters. Arrangement of the contents of prefaces and forewords follows no established pattern.

Table of contents and list of illustrations. If your report is long enough for a guide to its contents to be helpful, you should give it a table of contents. This table is the report outline in its finished form with page numbers. If the report has a number of tables, charts, illustrations, and the like, a separate table of contents may be set up for them. The mechanics of construction of both of these contents units are fully described in Appendix A.

Synopsis. The synopsis (also called the epitome and précis) is the report in miniature. It concisely summarizes all the essential ingredients of the report. It includes all of the major facts as well as major analyses and conclusions derived from these facts. Primarily, it is designed for the busy executive who may not have time to read the whole report; but it may also serve as a preview or review for those who very carefully read the report text.

In constructing the synopsis, you simply reduce the parts of the report in order and in proportion. Because your objective is to cut the report to a fraction of its length (usually less than one eighth), much of your success will be determined by your skill in directness and word economy. With space at a premium, loose writing is obviously costly. But in your efforts to be concise, you are likely to find your writing style dull. Thus, you must work hard to give this part a touch of color and style.

Although most synopses simply present the report in normal order (normally from introduction to conclusion), there is some usage nowadays of a more direct opening (see Figure 14–2). Such a plan shifts the major findings, conclusions, or recommendations (as the case may be) to the major position of emphasis at the beginning. From this direct beginning, the summary moves to the introductory parts and thence through the report in normal order.

The report proper

Your presentation of the report contents may follow any of a number of general arrangements. Most companies prefer the more conventional arrangements (direct, logical, chronological) discussed earlier. Some companies prefer to prescribe a definite arrangement for all reports, particularly for the technical ones. Descriptions of two such reports, the technical research paper and the staff study, appear at the chapter end. Most of the variations, however, are only rearrangements of the same general information. Thus, you should be able to adapt to other arrangements the following review of the makeup of the body of a conventional logical-order report.

Introduction. The purpose of the introduction of the report is to orient the reader to the problem at hand. In this undertaking you may include scores of possible topics, for you may include anything which will help your

Figure 14–2
Diagram of the Synopsis in Normal Order and in Direct Order

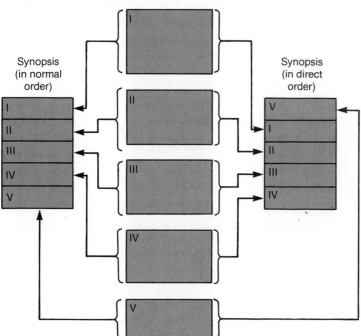

reader to understand and appreciate the problem. Although the possible contents are varied, you should consider the following general topics.

1. Origin of the report. The first part of your introduction might well include a review of the facts of authorization. Some writers, however, leave this part out entirely. If you decide to use this section, you will present such facts as when, how, and by whom the report was authorized, who wrote the report, and when the report was submitted. This section is particularly useful in reports which have no letter of transmittal.

2. Purpose. A vital part of almost every report you will write is a description of the purpose of your investigation. Called by other names (objective, problem, object, aim, goal, mission, assignment, proposal, project, and so on), the purpose of the report is the value to be attained by solving the problem. It may be a long- or short-term value, or a combination of both.

You may state the purpose of your report in an infinitive phrase (". . . to propose standards of corporate annual reports"), or in the form of a well-phrased question ("What retail advertising practices do Centerville consumers disapprove of?") Usually, you will need no more than a single sentence for this major purpose.

You also may need to state collateral, or secondary, purposes in this section. If a major problem is solved, collateral values are achieved. By stating these values, you help to convince the reader of the worthwhileness of your report. In other words, you should use a positive approach by telling what the solved problem can do for your reader.

3. Scope. If the scope of the problem is not clearly covered in any of the introductory sections, you may need to include it in a separate section. By "scope," we mean the boundaries of the problem. In this section, in good, clear language you should describe the exact coverage of the problem. Thus, you tell your reader exactly what is and what is not a part of the problem.

4. Limitations. With some problems, you will find limitations which are of sufficient importance to warrant presenting them as a separate section of the introduction. By limitations, we mean anything that in some way has worked to impede the investigation or in some way has a deterring effect on the report. The illustrative list of limitations to a report investigation problem might include an inadequate supply of money for conducting the investigation, insufficient time for doing the work, unavoidable conditions which hampered objective investigation, or limitations existing within the problem under investigation.

5. Historical background. Sometimes a knowledge of the history of the problem is essential to understanding the report. Therefore, you may need to include in your introduction a section on the history of the problem. Your general aim in this part should be to acquaint your reader with some of the issues involved, some of the principles raised, and some of the values which might be received if more research were done. Also, in this section, you may orient the readers and help to give them a better understanding of the report situation. This better understanding will help the readers and you to solve some of the problems which may arise in the future.

6. Sources and methods of collecting data. It is usually advisable to tell the readers how you have collected the report information, whether through library research, through interviewing, and the like. If you used library research, for example, you may mention the major publications consulted. Or, as another example, if you used interviewing to get your information, your description would cover such areas of the survey as sample determination, construction of the questionnaire, procedures followed in interviewing, facilities for checking returns, and so forth. Whatever the technique used, you should describe it in sufficient detail to allow the reader to evaluate the quality of your research.

7. Definitions. If in the report you use words likely to be unfamiliar to the reader, you should define these words. One practice is to define each such word at the time of its first use in the report text. A more common practice, however, is to set aside a special section in the introduction for definitions.

8. Report preview. In long reports, you should use a final section of the introduction to preview the report layout. In this section, you should tell the reader how the report will be presented—what topics will be taken up first, second, third, and so forth. And of even greater importance, you should give the reasons why you follow this plan. Thus, you give your readers a clear picture of the road ahead, so they may logically relate the topics of the report as they come to them.

As previously noted, the sections discussed are listed only for the purpose of suggesting possible introduction content. In few reports will you need all of the topics mentioned. And in some instances you will be able to combine some of the topics; in other instances you may further split them into additional sections. In summary, you should tailor your introduction to fit the one report.

The report body. The part of the report which presents the information collected and relates it to the problem is the report body. Normally, it comprises the bulk of the content of a report. In fact, in a sense this part is the report. With the exception of the conclusion or recommendation section which follows, the other parts of the report are merely trappings. It is the report body to which most of the comments in this chapter and the following ones pertain.

The ending of the report. You may end your report in any of a number of ways: with a summary, a conclusion, a recommendation, or a combination of the three.

1. Summary. For some reports, particularly those which do little more than present facts, the end may consist of a summary of the major findings. Frequently, these reports follow the practice of having minor summaries at the end of each major division of the report. When you follow this practice, your final summary should simply recap these summaries. This form of summary, however, should not be confused with the synopsis. Like the summary, the synopsis presents a review of major findings; but unlike the summary, it contains the gist of the major supporting facts.

2. Conclusions. You draw your conclusions by inference (induction or deduction) from the facts and discussion in the body. Conclusions follow facts, even though in some reports they are placed at the beginning (the psychological arrangement).

Your conclusion should flow logically from the facts; but since this is a human process of interpretation, faulty conclusions may result. Consequently, conclusions are subject to opinions, be it rightly so or not.

For easy reference, you may tabulate your conclusions. But the arrangement of them is open to question. Sometimes, you will feel that the most important ones should be placed first; sometimes, you will want to list them according to the arrangements discussed in the findings. Also, you may combine them with recommendations. In some cases, where the conclusion is obvious, you may omit it and present only a recommendation.

3. Recommendations. The recommendations are the writer's section. Here you state your opinion based on the conclusions. Of course, you may not state your recommendations if you are not asked to; but if you are asked, you state them completely, including who should do what, when, where, why, and sometimes how.

You may include alternative courses of action. But you should state your preferences. Since you are familiar with the findings, you should not leave your readers on the horns of a dilemma. You should state the desired action and then leave the readers to choose their own course. Since you are likely to be in a subordinate position, you should give your advice for your superiors to accept.

Appended parts. Sometimes it is desirable that you append special sections to the report. The presence of these parts is normally determined by the specific needs of the problem concerned.

1. Appendix. The appendix, as its name implies, is a section tacked on. You use it for supplementary information which supports the body of the report but which has no logical place within the body of the report. Possible contents might include questionnaires, working papers, summary tables, additional references, other reports, and so on.

As a rule, you should not include in the appendix the charts, graphs, sketches, and tables which directly support the report. Instead, you should place them in the body of the report where they support the findings. Reports are best designed for the convenience of the reader. Obviously, it is not convenient for readers to thumb through many pages to find appendix illustrations to the facts they read in the report body.

2. Bibliography. When your investigation heavily uses library research, you should include a bibliography (a list of the publications consulted). The construction of this formal list is described in Appendix C.

3. Index. An index is an alphabetical guide to the subject matter of a piece of writing. It is used primarily with long manuscripts in which it would be difficult to find a specific topic were a subject guide not available. But few, if any, of the reports you will write will be of a length sufficient to justify an index.

Major differences in short and long reports

The foregoing discussion of report parts obviously concerns the longer and more formal types. Certainly these types are significant in business, and we cannot know report writing without knowing how to construct them. Even so, we should keep in mind that most reports written in industry are shorter and more informal. As you can see by inspecting the examples at the chapter end, these shorter forms of reports appear to be quite different.

Even though much of what we learned concerning the long, formal report applies equally well to the other forms, certain differences exist. By concentrating on these differences, we can adapt quickly our knowledge of report writing to the wide variety of short, informal reports. Four areas of such differences stand out as most significant: (1) less need for introductory material, (2) predominance of direct (psychological) order, (3) more personal writing style, and (4) less need for a coherence plan.

Less need for introductory material

One major content difference in the shorter report forms is their minor need for introductory material. Most reports at this level concern day-to-day problems. Thus, these reports have a short life. They are not likely to be kept on file for posterity to read. They are intended for only a few readers, and these few know the problem and its background. The reader's interests are in the findings of the report and any action they will lead to.

This is not to say that all shorter forms have no need for introductory material. In fact, some have very specific needs. In general, however, the introductory need in the shorter and more informal reports is less than that for the more formal and longer types. But no rule can be applied across the board. Each case should be analyzed individually. In each case, you must cover whatever introductory material is needed to prepare your readers to receive the report. In some shorter reports, an incidental reference to the problem, authorization of the investigation, or such will do the job. In some extreme cases, you may need a detailed introduction comparable to that of the more formal report. There are reports, also, that need no introduction whatever. In such cases, the nature of the report serves as sufficient introductory information. A personnel action, for example, by its very nature explains its purpose. So do weekly sales reports, inventory reports, and some progress reports.

Predominance of direct order

Because they usually are more goal-oriented, the shorter more informal reports are likely to use the direct order of presentation. That is, typically such reports are written to handle a problem—to make a specific conclusion or recommendation of action. This conclusion or recommendation is of such relative significance that it overshadows the analysis and information that support it. Thus, it deserves a lead-off position.

As noted earlier, the longer forms of reports also may use a direct order. In fact, many of them do. The point is, however, that most do not. Most follow the traditional logical (introduction, body, conclusion) order. As one moves down the structural ladder toward the more informal and shorter reports, however, the need for direct order increases. At the bottom of the ladder, direct order is more the rule than the exception.

Your decision on whether to use the direct order is best based on a consideration of your readers' likely use of the report. If the readers need the report conclusion or recommendation as a basis for an action they must take, directness will speed their efforts. A direct presentation will permit them to receive quickly the most important information. If they have confidence in your work, they may not choose to read beyond this point; and they can quickly take the action the report supports. Should they desire to question any part of the report, however, it is there for their inspection. The obvious result would be to save the valuable time of busy executives.

On the other hand, if there is reason to believe that your readers will want to arrive at the conclusion or recommendation only after a logical review of the analysis, you should organize your report in the indirect (logical) order. Especially would this arrangement be preferred when your readers do not have reason to place their full confidence in your work. If you are a novice working in a new assignment, for example, you would be wise to lead your readers to your recommendations or conclusions by using the logical order.

More personal writing style

Although the writing in all reports has much in common, the writing in the shorter reports tends to be more personal. That is, the shorter reports are likely to use the personal pronouns *I, we, you,* and such rather than a third-person approach.

The explanation of this tendency toward personal writing in short reports should be obvious. In the first place, short-report situations usually involve personal relationships. Short reports tend to be from and to people who know each other—people who normally address each other informally when they meet and talk. In addition, the shorter reports by their nature are apt to involve a personal investigation. The finished work represents the personal observations, evaluations, and analyses of their writers. These writers are expected to report them as their own. A third explanation is that the shorter problems tend to be the day-to-day routine ones. They are by their very nature informal. It is logical to report them informally, and personal writing tends to produce this informal effect.

As will be explained in Chapter 15, your decision on whether to write a report in personal or impersonal style should be based on the circumstances of the situation. You should consider the expectations of those who will receive the report. If they expect formality, you should write impersonally. If they expect informality, you should write personally. Second, if you do not know the readers' preferences, you should consider the formality of the situation. Convention favors impersonal writing for the most formal situations.

From this analysis, it should be apparent that either style can be appropriate for reports ranging from the shortest to the longest type. The point is, however, that short-report situations are most likely to justify personal writing.

Less need for coherence plan

As is pointed out in Chapter 15, the longer reports need some form of coherence plan to make the parts stick together. That is, because of the complexities brought about by length, the writer must make an effort to relate the parts. Otherwise, the paper would read like a series of disjointed minor reports. What the writer does is to use summaries and introductory forward-looking sentences and paragraphs at key places. In this way, the reader is able to see how each part of the report fits into the whole scheme of things.

The shorter the report becomes, the less is its need for such a coherence plan. In fact, in the extremely short forms (such as memorandum and letter reports), little in the way of wording is needed to relate the parts. In such cases, the information is so brief and simple that a logical and orderly presentation clearly shows the plan of presentation.

Although coherence plans are less frequently used in the short forms of reports, the question of whether to include them should not be arbitrarily determined by length alone. Instead, the matter of need should guide you in your choice. Whenever your presentation contains organization complexities that can be made clear by summarizing, introducing, and relating parts, these coherence elements should be included. Thus, need rather than length is the major determinant. But it is clearly evident that need for coherence plans decreases as the report length decreases.

Short forms of reports

As was noted earlier, the short forms of reports are by far the most numerous and important in business. In fact, the three types represented by the bottom three steps of the stairway (Figure 14–1) make up the bulk of the reports written in business. Thus, a review of each of these types is in order.

The short report

One of the more popular of the less imposing reports is the conventional short report. Representing the fifth step in the diagram of report progression, this report consists of only a title page and the report text. Its popularity may be explained by the middle-ground impression of formality it gives. Inclusion of the one most essential of the prefatory parts gives the report at least a minimum appearance of formality. And it does this without the tedious work of preparing the other prefatory pages. It is ideally suited for the short but somewhat formal problem.

Like most of the less imposing forms of reports, the short report may be organized in either the direct or indirect order, although direct order is by far the more common plan. As illustrated by the report at the chapter end (Figure 14–4), this plan begins with a quick summary of the report, including and emphasizing conclusions and recommendations. Such a beginning serves much the same function as the synopsis of a long, formal report.

Following the summary come whatever introductory remarks are needed. As noted previously, sometimes this part is not needed at all. Usually, however, there follows a single paragraph covering the facts of authorization and a brief statement of the problem and its scope. After the introductory words come the findings of the investigation. Just as in the longer report forms, the findings are presented, analyzed, and applied to the problem. From all this comes a final conclusion and, if needed, a recommendation. These last two elements—conclusions and recommendations—may come at the end, even though they also may appear in the beginning summary. Sometimes, not to include a summary or a conclusion would end the report abruptly. It would stop the flow of reasoning before reaching its logical goal.

The mechanics of constructing the short report are much the same as those for the more formal, longer types. As illustrated at the chapter end, this report uses the same form of title page and the same layout requirement. Like the longer reports, it uses captions. But because of the report's brevity, the captions rarely go beyond the two-division level. In fact, one level of division is most common. Like any other report, its use of graphic aids, appendix, and bibliography is dependent on its need for them.

Letter reports

As the wording implies, a letter report is a report written in letter form. Primarily, it is used to present information to someone outside the company, especially when the report information is to be sent by mail. For example, a company's written evaluation of one of its credit customers may well be presented in letter form and mailed to the one who requests it. An outside consultant may write a report of analyses and recommendations in letter form. Or an organization officer may elect to report certain information to the membership in letter form.

Normally, letter reports present the shorter problems—typically, those that can be presented in three or four pages or less. But no hard and fast rule exists on this point. Long letter reports (ten pages and more) have been used successfully many times.

As a general rule, letter reports are written personally (using *I, you, we* references). Exceptions exist, of course, as when one is preparing such a report for an august group, such as a committee of the United States Senate or a company's board of directors. Other than this point, the writing style recommended for letter reports is much the same as that for any other report. Certainly, clear and meaningful expression is a requirement for all reports (see Figure 14–6).

Letter reports may be arranged either in the direct or indirect order. If the report is to be mailed, there is some justification for using an indirect approach. Because such reports arrive unannounced, an initial reminder of what they are, how they originated, and such is in order. A letter report written to the membership of an organization, for example, may appropriately begin with these words:

As authorized by your board of directors last January 6, this report reviews member company expenditures for direct-mail selling.

If one elects to begin a letter report in the direct order, a subject line would be appropriate. The subject line consists of some identifying words, which appear at the top of the letter, usually immediately after or before the salutation. Although subject lines are formed in many ways, one acceptable version begins with the word "Subject" and follows it with descriptive words that identify the problem. As the following example illustrates, this identifying device helps to overcome any effect of confusion or bewilderment the direct beginning may otherwise have on the reader.

Subject: Report on direct-mail expenditures of association members, authorized by board of directors, January, 1984.
Association members are spending 8 percent more on direct-mail advertising this year than they did the year before. Current plans call for a 10 percent increase for next year.

Regardless of which beginning is used, the organization plan for letter reports corresponds to those of the longer, more formal types. Thus, the indirect order letter report follows its introductory buildup with a logical presentation and analysis of the information gathered. From this presentation, it works logically to a conclusion or recommendation, or both, in the end. The direct order letter report follows the initial summary-conclusion-recommendation section with whatever introductory words are appropriate. For example, the direct beginning illustrated above could be followed with these introductory words:

These are the primary findings of a study authorized by your board of directors last January. As they concern information vital to all of us in the association, they are presented here for your confidential use.

Following such an introductory comment, the report would present the supporting facts and their analyses. The writer would systematically build up the case that supported the opening comment. With either order, when the report is sent as a letter it may close with whatever friendly goodwill comment is appropriate for the one occasion.

Memorandum reports

Memorandum reports are merely informal letter reports. They are used primarily for routine reporting within an organization, although some organizations use them for external communication. Because they are internal communications, often they are informally written. In fact, they frequently are hurried, handwritten messages from one department or worker to another department or worker. The more formal memorandum reports, however, are well-written and carefully typed compositions (see Figure 14–5).

As far as the writing of the memorandum is concerned, all the instructions for writing letter reports apply. But memorandum reports tend to be more informal. And because they usually concern day-to-day problems, they have very little need for introductory information. In fact, they frequently may begin reporting without any introductory comment.

The memorandum report is presented on somewhat standardized interoffice memorandum stationery. The words *To, From,* and *Subject* appear at the page top, usually following the company identification. Sometimes, the word *Date* also is included as a part of the heading. Like letters, the memorandum may carry a signature. In many offices, however, no typed signature is included, and the writer merely places initials after the typed name in the heading.

Special report forms

As noted previously, this review describes only generally the forms of the reports used in business. Countless variations exist. Of these variations, a few deserve special emphasis.

The staff report

One of the most widely used reports in business is the staff report. Patterned after a form traditional to the technical fields, the staff report is well adapted to business problem solving. Its arrangement follows the logical thought processes used in solving the conventional business problems. Although the makeup of this report varies by company, the following arrangement recommended by a major metals manufacturer is typical:

Identifying information: As the company's staff reports are written on intercompany communication stationery, the conventional identification information *(To, From, Subject, Date)* appears at the beginning.

Summary: For the busy executive who wants the facts fast, a summary begins the report. Some executives will read no further. Others will want to trace the report content in detail.

The problem (or objective): As in all good problem-solving procedures, the report text logically begins with a clear description of the problem—what it is, what it is not, what its limitations are, and the like.

Facts: Next comes the information gathered in the attempt to solve the problem.

Discussion: Analysis of the facts and applications of the facts and analyses to the problem follow. (Frequently, the statement of facts and the discussion of them can be combined.)

Conclusions: From the preceding discussion of facts come the final meanings as they apply to the problem.

Recommendation: If the problem's objective allows for it, a course of action may be recommended on the basis of the conclusions.

The audit report

The short-form and long-form audit reports are well known to accountants. The short-form report is perhaps the most standardized of all reports—if, indeed, it can be classified as a report. Actually, it is a stereotyped statement verifying an accountant's inspection of a firm's financial records. Its wording seldom varies. Illustrations of this standard form can be found in almost any corporate annual report.

Composition of the long-form audit report is as varied as the short form is rigid. In fact, a national accounting association, which made an exhaustive study on the subject, found practices to be so varied that it concluded that no typical form exists. Although the audit report illustrated at the chapter end (Figure 14–7) covers a somewhat simple and limited audit, it shows one acceptable form.

The technical report

Although it generally follows the plan of the conventional formal report, the technical research report has some identifying characteristics. Exact makeup of the research report differs from company to company, but the following description is typical of this form.

The beginning pages of the research report are much like those of the traditional formal report. First come the title pages; although frequently a routing or distribution form for intercompany use may be worked into them, or perhaps added to them. A letter of transmittal is likely to come next, followed by a table of contents and illustrations. From this point on, however, the technical report is likely to differ from the traditional one. These differences are mainly in the treatment of the information usually presented in the synopsis and the introduction of the conventional formal report.

Instead of the conventional synopsis, the technical report may present the summary information in various parts, such as "findings," "conclusions," and "recommendations." Parts of the conventional introductory material also may be presented in prefatory sections. The "objective" is the most likely part in this area, although "method" is also a widely used section.

The text of the technical report usually begins with introductory information. The remaining information may be organized much like any conventional report, or it may follow a predetermined and somewhat mechanical arrangement. One such arrangement is "facts," "discussion," "conclusions," and "recommendations."

Questions & Problems

1. Discuss the effects of formality and problem length on the model of report makeup described in the chapter (Figure 14–1).
2. A good report title should be complete and concise. Are not these requirements contradictory? Explain.
3. Discuss the relative importance of the title fly and the title page in a report.
4. Distinguish among letter of transmittal, foreword, and preface.
5. Describe the role and content of a letter of transmittal.
6. Why is personal style typically used in the letter of transmittal?
7. What is the basis for determining whether a report should have a table of contents?
8. Discuss the construction of the synopsis.
9. Why do you think the synopsis includes the facts and figures in addition to the analyses and conclusions drawn from them?
10. Some reports need little or no introduction; others need very long ones. Why is this so?
11. Give examples of report problems that would require introductory coverage of methods of collecting data, historical background, and limitations.
12. Give examples of report problems that require an ending summary. An ending conclusion. An ending recommendation.
13. Why is direct order usually used in the shorter types of reports? When is indirect order desirable for such reports?
14. Give examples of short forms of reports that are appropriately written in personal style. Do the same for impersonal style.
15. Is it correct to say that the shorter forms of reports have little need for coherence? Discuss.
16. What determines the need for coherence aids in the short forms of reports?
17. Describe the organization of the conventional short report.
18. What types of problems are written up as letter reports? As memorandum reports? Explain the differences.
19. What is meant by saying that the order of the staff study report is a problem-solving order?
20. Discuss the differences between technical reports and the other business reports.

Figure 14–3
*Illustration of a Long, Formal Report**

335

Chapter 14
Reports:
Determination of
Makeup

RECOMMENDATIONS FOR 19-- REPLACEMENTS

IN ALLIED DISTRIBUTORS, INC., SALES FLEET

BASED ON A COMPARISON OF FOUR SUBCOMPACT AUTOMOBILES

* The illustration which appears in the following pages typifies the long, formal report. Because of the need to disguise the names of the branded products involved, perhaps the report has lost some of its realism. Nevertheless, it represents an orderly, thorough, and objective solution to a somewhat complex problem.

Figure 14–3 *(continued)*

RECOMMENDATIONS FOR 19-- REPLACEMENTS

IN ALLIED DISTRIBUTORS, INC., SALES FLEET

BASED ON A COMPARISON OF FOUR SUBCOMPACT AUTOMOBILES

Prepared for

Mr. Norman W. Bigbee, Vice President
Allied Distributors, Inc.
3131 Speedall Street, Akron, Ohio   44302

Prepared by

George W. Franklin, Associate Director
Midwestern Research, Inc.
1732 Midday Avenue, Chicago, Illinois   60607

April 13, 19--

Figure 14–3 *(continued)*

337

Chapter 14
Reports:
Determination of
Makeup

April 13, 19--

Mr. Norman W. Bigbee
Vice President in Charge of Sales
Allied Distributors, Inc.
3131 Speedall Street
Akron, Ohio   44302

Dear Mr. Bigbee:

Here is the report on the four makes of subcompact automobiles you asked me to compare last January 3.

To aid you in deciding which of the four makes you should buy as replacements for your fleet, I gathered what I believe to be the most complete information available. Much of the operating information comes from your own records. The remaining data are the findings of both consumer research engineers and professional automotive analysts. Only my analyses of these data are subjective.

I sincerely hope, Mr. Bigbee, that my analyses will aid you in making the correct decision. I truly appreciate this assignment. And should you need any assistance in interpreting my analyses, please call on me.

Sincerely,

George W. Franklin

George W. Franklin
Associate Director

Figure 14–3 *(continued)*

TABLE OF CONTENTS

Figure 14–3 *(continued)*

339

Chapter 14
Reports:
Determination of
Makeup

Figure 14–3 *(continued)*

Epitome

The recommendation of this study is that Gamma is the best buy for Allied
Distributors, Inc., authorized by Mr. Norman W. Bigbee, Vice President,
on January 3, 19--, this report is submitted on April 13, 19--. This study
gives Allied Distributors an insight into the problem of replacing the approximately 50 two-year-old subcompact cars in its present sales fleet. The
basis for this recommendation is an analysis of cost, safety, and construction
factors of four models of subcompact cars (Alpha, Beta, Gamma, and Delta).

The four cars do not show a great deal of difference in ownership cost
(initial cost less trade-in allowance after two years). On a per-car basis,
Beta costs least for a two-year period -- $3,216. Compared with costs for
the other cars. Beta is $370 under Gamma, $588 under Alpha, and $634
under Delta. For the entire sales fleet, these differences become more
significant. A purchase of 50 Betas would save $18,500 over Gamma,
$29,400 over Alpha, and $31,700 over Delta. Operation costs favor
Gamma. Cost per mile for this car is $0.13970, as compared with
$0.14558 for Alpha, $0.14785 for Delta, and $0.15184 for Beta. The
totals of all costs for the 50-car fleet over the two-year period shows
Gamma to be least costly at $385,094. In second place is Alpha, with
a cost of $400,208. Third is Delta with $406,560, and fourth is Beta
with a cost of $417,532.

On the qualities that pertain to driving safety, Gamma is again superior
to the other cars. It has the best brakes and is tied with Alpha for the
best weight distribution. It is second in acceleration and is again tied
with Alpha for the number of standard safety devices. Alpha is second
over-all in this category, having the second best brakes of the group.
Beta is last because of its poor acceleration and poor brakes.

Construction features and handling abilities place Gamma all by itself.
It scores higher than any other cars in every category. Alpha and
Delta are tied for second place. Again Beta is last, having poor
steering and handling qualities.

vi

Figure 14–3 *(continued)*

341

Chapter 14
Reports:
Determination of
Makeup

RECOMMENDATIONS FOR 19-- REPLACEMENTS

IN ALLIED DISTRIBUTORS, INC., SALES FLEET

BASED ON A COMPARISON OF FOUR SUBCOMPACT AUTOMOBILES

1. ORIENTATION TO THE PROBLEM

A. The Authorization Facts

This comparison of the qualities of four brands of subcompact automobiles
is submitted April 13, 19--, to Mr. Norman W. Bigbee, Vice President,
Allied Distributors, Inc. At a meeting in his office January 3, 19--, Mr.
Bigbee orally authorized Midwestern Research, Inc., to conduct this
investigation. Mr. George W. Franklin, Research Director for Midwestern
Research served as director of the project.

B. Problem of Selecting Fleet Replacements

The objective of this study is to determine which model of subcompact
automobiles Allied Distributors, Inc., should select for replacement in
its sales fleet. The firm's policy is to replace all two-year-old models.
It replaces approximately 50 automobiles each year.

The replacements involve a major capital outlay, and the sales fleet expense
constitutes a major sales cost. Thus, the proper selection of a new model
presents an important problem. The model selection must be economical,
dependable, and safe. Allied is considering four subcompact automobiles
as replacement possibilities. As instructed by Mr. Bigbee, for reasons
of information security, the cars are identified in this report only as
Alpha, Beta, Gamma, and Delta.

1

Figure 14–3 *(continued)*

2

C. Reports and Records as Sources of Data

The selection of the replacement brand is based on a comparative analysis of
the merits of the four makes. Data for the comparisons were obtained from
both company records and statistical reports. Operating records of ten
representative cars of each make provide information on operating costs.
These reports are summaries compiled by salesperson-drivers and represent
actual performance of company cars under daily selling conditions. Additional material enumerating safety features, overall driving quality, and
dependability comes from the reports of the Consumers Union of the United
States, Inc., Automotive Industries, and Bond Publishing Company's
periodical, Road and Track. Mr. Bigbee furnished the trade-in allowance
granted on the old models. From this material extensive comparisons of
the four makes are presented.

D. A Preview to the Presentation

In the following pages of the report, the four cars are compared on the basis
of three factors: operating costs, safety features, and total performance.
Operating costs receive primary attention. In this part the individual cost
items for each car are analyzed. This analysis leads to the determination
of the most economical of the four cars.

Safety features make up the second factor of comparison. In this part the
analysis centers on the presence or absence of safety features in each
car and the quality of the features that are present. From this analysis
comes a safety ranking of the cars. The third factor for comparison is
total performance and durability. As in preceding parts, here the analysis
produces a ranking of the cars.

II. THE MAJOR FACTOR OF COST

As cost is an obvious and generally accepted requirement of any major
purchase, it is a logical first point of concern in selecting a car to
buy. Here the first concern is the original cost--that is, the fleet

Figure 14–3 *(continued)*

343

Chapter 14
Reports:
Determination of
Makeup

3

discount price. Of second interest in a logical thinking process are the
cash difference after trade-in allowance for the old cars. These figures
clearly indicate the cash outlay for the new fleet.

A. <u>Initial Costs Favor Beta</u>

From Table I it is evident that Beta has the lowest window sticker price
before and after trade-in allowances. It has a $634 margin which must
be considered in the light of what features are standard on Beta in comparison with those standard on the other cars. That is, the Beta may
have fewer standard features included in its original cost and, therefore,
not be worth as much as the Alpha, Gamma, or Delta.

TABLE I
ORIGINAL COST OF FOUR BRANDS
OF SUBCOMPACT CARS IN 19--

Make	Window Sticker Prices	Trade-in Value for Two-Year-Old Makes*	Cash Costs After Trade-in Allowance
Alpha	$7,318	$3,514	$3,804
Beta	$6,716	$3,500	$3,216
Gamma	$7,140	$3,552	$3,588
Delta	$7,700	$3,850	$3,850

*Trade-in value for Alpha and Beta are estimates
Sources: Primary and <u>Road and Track</u>, 19--

It is clear that where features are listed as standard they do not add to
original cost, but where listed as options they do. As will be shown in a
later table, the Delta has many more standard features than do the other
makes. In addition to a study of standard features, a close look at trade-
in values and operating costs will also be necessary to properly evaluate
original cost.

Figure 14–3 *(continued)*

4

Further discussion of standard features of the cars appears in following discussions of safety and per-mile operating costs.

B. Trade-in Values Show Uniformity

Original costs alone do not tell the complete purchase-cost story. The values of the cars at the ends of their useful lives (trade-in values) are a vital part of cost. In this case, the trade-in value is $3,850 for Delta, and the lowest is $3,500 for Beta (see Table 1). Only $350 separates the field.

Although fairly uniform, these figures appear to be more significant when converted to total amounts involved in the fleet purchases. A fleet of 50 Betas would cost $160,800. The same fleet of Gammas, Alphas, and Deltas would cost $179,376, $190,222, and $190,500, respectively. Thus, Allied's total cost of purchasing Betas would be $18,550 lower than Gammas, $29,216 lower than Alphas, and $31,676 lower than Deltas.

C. Operating Costs Are Lowest for Gamma

Gamma has the lowest maintenance cost of the four, 1.970 cents per mile. But Delta is close behind with 2.0650 cents. Both of these are well below the Beta and Alpha figures of 2.7336 and 2.7616, respectively. As shown in Table II, these costs are based on estimates of repairs, resulting loss of working time, tire replacements, and miscellaneous items.

It should be stressed here how greatly repair expense influences the estimates. Actually, two expenses are involved, for to the cost of repairs the expense of time lost by salespeople must be added. Obviously, a salesperson without a car is unproductive. Each hour lost by car repairs adds to the cost of the car's operation.

The time lost per repair is the same for each car--five hours. Thus, the important consideration is the number of repairs and the costs of these repairs. On this basis, the Gamma has the lowest total cost burden at $1,086 (see Table II). Delta ranks second with $1,038. Beta is third with $1,506, and Alpha is last with $1,520.

Figure 14–3 *(continued)*

5

TABLE II
COMPARISON OF REPAIRS AND RELATED
LOST WORKING TIME FOR FOUR MAKES
OF CARS FOR TWO YEARS

Make	Number of Repairs	Repair Expense	Working Hours Lost*	Total Burden
Alpha	8	$820	40	$1,520
Beta	8	806	40	1,506
Gamma	6	560	30	1,086
Delta	6	612	30	1,138

*Based on hourly wage of $17.50
Source: Allied Distributors, Inc., Operating Records

Alpha has the best record for oil and gas economy with a per–mile cost of 6.228 cents (see Table III). Second is Gamma with a cost of 6.654 cents. In third and fourth positions are Beta, 6.910 cents , and Delta, 7.336 cents. Figured on the basis of the 55,000 miles Allied cars average over two years, Alpha's margin appears more significant. Its total margin over Delta is $610.22 per car-- or $30,512 for the fleet of 50 cars. Compared with Gamma,

TABLE III
COST–PER–MILE ESTIMATE OF OPERATION

Depreciation	$.05566	$.05540	$.05344	$.05384
Gas	.05800	.06482	.05800	.06482
Oil	.00428	.00428	.00854	.00854
Tires	.00452	.00326	.00168	.00122
Repairs	.01450	.01446	.01054	.01278
Miscellaneous	.00862	.00962	.00750	.00666
Total	$.14558	$.15184	$.13970	$.14786

Source: Allied Distributors, Inc., Operating Records

Figure 14-3 *(continued)*

6

Alpha's margin is $1,034 per car and $11,742 for the fleet total. Alpha's per-car margin over Beta is $356.12, and its fleet margin is $17,806.

D. Cost Composite Favors Gamma

Gamma is the most economical of all cars when all cost figures are considered (see Table III). Its total cost per mile is 13.970 cents, as compared with 14.558 cents for Alpha, 14.786 cents for Delta, and 15.184 cents for Beta. These figures take on more meaning when converted to total fleet cost over the two-year period the cars will be owned. As shown in Chart 1, a fleet of 50 Gammas would cost Allied a total of

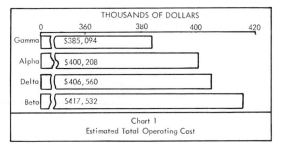

Chart 1
Estimated Total Operating Cost

$385,094. This figure is under all the other car totals. It is $15,114 below Alpha's $400,208, $21,466 below Delta's $406,560, and $32,436 under Gamma's $417,532.

III.   EVALUATION OF SAFETY FEATURES

Even though cost receives major emphasis in this analysis, safety of the cars also is important. How much importance safety should receive, however, is a matter for Allied management to decide. Allied salespeople spend a large part of their working time driving. And

Figure 14–3 *(continued)*

347

Chapter 14
Reports:
Determination of
Makeup

7

unquestionably driving is a hazardous assignment. Certainly Allied
management wishes to minimize these hazards. Thus, it may be willing
to sacrifice some cost in order to get safer vehicles.

A. Delta Is Best Equipped with Safety Devices

Only Delta has as standard equipment all five of the extra safety devices
considered desirable by The Consumers Safety Council. The Delta is
fully equipped with front disc brakes, vacuum brake assist, adjustable
seatbacks, flow-through ventilation, and anti-glare mirrors, as shown
in Table IV. The Delta's braking system differs from that of the Alpha

TABLE IV LIST OF STANDARD SAFETY FEATURES				
FEATURE	Alpha	Beta	Gamma	Delta
Front Disc Brakes	Yes	No	Yes	Yes
Vacuum Brake Assist	No	No	No	Yes
Adjustable Seatback	No	No	No	Yes
Flow-through Ventilation	Yes	No	Yes	Yes
Anti-glare Mirror	No	No	No	Yes
Source: Road and Track				

and Gamma in that it provides vacuum assistance. The Beta does not
equip its cars with either disc brakes or vacuum assistance.

Alpha and Gamma are tied in the field of safety features with two out
of the possible five shown in Table IV. The Beta, although offering
three of these features as options, does not provide any of the possible
five.

Now that the Federal Government has legislated the basic safety
requirements, such as seat belts, padded dashboards, collapsible
steering column, and shatter-proof windshields, the extra safety
features of the Delta are even more welcome.

Figure 14-3 *(continued)*

8

B. Acceleration Adds Extra Safety to Delta

A life-saving factor that differs greatly among the four makes is acceleration.
It is important as a safety "on-the-spot" need--something to have when in a
pinch. Especially is it important in low-powered subcompact automobiles.
When needed, acceleration should be available in the safest car. It should
never be depended on by a driver to the extent of his taking chances because he knows that it is available. But acceleration must be included in
any brand comparison.

While Gamma's acceleration time from 0 to 30 miles per hour is the fastest
in the group, the Delta leads in both 0 to 60 mph times and in the 1/4
mile acceleration runs. As shown in Chart 2, Gamma reached 30 mph
.3 seconds sooner than Bets, and .5 and 1.5 seconds sooner than Delta

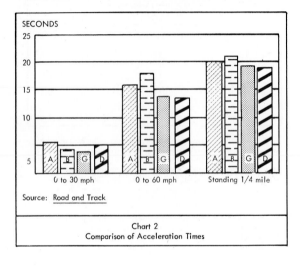

Source: Road and Track

Chart 2
Comparison of Acceleration Times

Figure 14–3 *(continued)*

349

Chapter 14
Reports:
Determination of
Makeup

9

and Alpha, respectively, Delta reached 60 mph .4 seconds sooner than
Gamma, which is not a very significant length of time. The Delta,
however, achieved this same speed a full 3 seconds faster than Alpha,
and 4.5 seconds sooner than Beta.

C.   Weight Distribution Is Best in Alpha and Gamma

Weight distribution affects not only the acceleration of an automobile,
but also the effectiveness of its brakes and its handling abilities. The
correct proportion of weight on the rear wheels balances the car. In
doing so it controls body movements in cornering and braking. The
problem is generally caused by the placement of the engine in the
front of the automobile. The arrangement of the other essential heavy
items at the best places on the chassis results in the best distribution.

As shown in Table V, Alpha and Gamma are tied in this category.

TABLE V
COMPARATIVE WEIGHT DISTRIBUTIONS,
BRAKING DISTANCES, AND CORNERING ABILITIES

	Alpha	Beta	Gamma	Delta
Distribution, rear, %	47	45	47	43
Braking, 80-0 mph, ft.	330	331	321	390
Brake fade, % increase				
in pedal effort	30	33	14	43
Control, panic stop	good	fair	excel	fair
Lateral acceleration,				
in g units	0.680	0.685	0.611	0.614
speed achieved, mph	32.0	32.1	30.2	30.3

Source: Road and Track

Their 47 percent is near the 50 percent automotive experts consider best.
In contrast, Delta carries a relatively low proportion (43 percent) of
its weight on the rear wheels. This low proportion of weight is not
good from the the the standpoint of traction on slippery roads that seem to be
common throughout the Allied sales territory. The Beta is between the
two extremes with 45 percent of its weight on its rear wheels.

Figure 14-3 *(continued)*

10

D. Gamma Has Best Braking Quality

At speeds of 80 miles per hour, Gamma stops in the shortest distance (321 feet); but Alpha (330 feet) and Beta (331 feet) are not far behind. Delta is well back (390 feet). In tests simulating panic-stop situations, Gamma's brakes also prove superior to the others, rank "excellent" by test standards. On the same test scale, Alpha's brakes rank "good" and Beta's and Delta's brakes rank "fair." Gamma's brakes also are more resistant to fade than are the other three. In stops from 80 miles per hour, all makes exhibit good braking control except Beta. Its stops are far less consistent than the others.

An overall review of safety features shows Gamma to have a very slight advantage over the other cars. Its brakes, weight distribution, and stopping distance lead to this conclusion. Alpha is second, scoring high in all categories except acceleration and standard safety features. Delta is third with the best acceleration but poor braking action. Beta is last, having only scored highly in cornering ability.

IV. RIDING COMFORT AND OVERALL CONSTRUCTION

Few things affect the day's work of a traveling salesperson more than the ride in the car. Thus, the factors of handling ease and general riding quality should be considered in selecting a car. Somewhat related to these factors are the overall qualities of construction of the cars in question.

A. Gamma Ranks First in Handling

The Gamma, with near perfect steering, is overall best handling car of the group. As shown in Table VI, Gamma exceeds all of the other makes when values are assigned to each category. Alpha, which is second in this area, is quick and predictable in handling. During emergency situation tests, however, it jarred and rocked severely around bumpy corners. Delta, while exhibiting normal handling characteristics during routine driving, performed miserably when subjected to emergency handling tests. Beta suffered from being knocked off course by almost any small bump. When smoother roads were encountered, Beta's handling was judged somewhat below average.

Figure 14–3 *(continued)*

351

Chapter 14
Reports:
Determination of
Makeup

11

	Front Seating	Rear Seating	Ride Light Load	Ride Full Load	Hand-ling	Steering Effort
TABLE VI COMPARATIVE COMFORT AND RIDE						
Excellent						
Good					Gamma	
Fair-to-good	Gamma Alpha Delta	Gamma	Alpha		Delta Alpha	
Fair	Beta		Gamma		Beta	
Fair-to-poor		Delta	Delta	Gamma Delta		
Poor		Alpha Beta	Beta	Beta Alpha		
Low						
Low-to-moderate						Beta Alpha Gamma
Moderate						Delta

Source: Consumers Union of United States, Inc.

B. Gamma Gives Best Ride

While it is true that Alpha's ride has been judged superior to Gamma's when loaded lightly, Gamma comes out first overall because of the quickly deteri-orating ride Alpha exhibits when its load is increased. Gamma's superior ride and directional stability are the best in the group primarily because of its fully independent suspension. A rarity in any front engined car, much less a car in this price field, Gamma's front bucket seats are judged fair-to-good in comfort--relatively high rating in economy car circles. As shown in Table VI, Gamma's rear seating comfort is the best in the group.

C. Gamma Is Judged Most Durable

The Gamma is assembled with better-than-average care. In fact, Consumer Research engineers have found only 16 minor defects in the car. In addi-tion, the Gamma has a better-than-average record for frequency of repairs.

Figure 14–3 *(concluded)*

12

Delta, second in this category, has only 20 problems. Some of these problems are judged serious, however. For instance, in the tests run the starter refused to disengage after a few hundred miles had accumulated on the car. The car's ignition timing, idle mixture, and idle speed were incorrectly set. An optically distorted windshield and inside mirror were discovered. In spite of all these defects, the Delta ranks above Alpha and Beta on durability.

Clearly, Gamma leads in all categories of riding comfort and overall construction. It handles best. It gives the best ride. And it has some definite construction advantages over the other three.

V. RECOMMENDATION OF GAMMA

Normally, this simulation cannot be merely a count of rankings on the evaluations made, for the qualities carry different weights. Cost, for example, is the major factor in most such decisions. In this instance, however, weighting is not necessary for one automobile is the clear leader on all three of the bases used for evaluation. Thus, it would lead in any arrangement of weights.

From the data presented, Gamma is the best buy when all costs are considered. The total difference on a purchase of 50 automobiles is a significant $15,114 over the second-place brand. Gamma has a slight edge when safety features are considered. And it is the superior car in handling ease, ride quality, and construction. These facts point clearly to the recommendation that Allied buy Gammas this year.

Figure 14–4
*Illustration of a Short Report**

353

Chapter 14
Reports:
Determination of
Makeup

RECOMMENDATIONS FOR DEPRECIATING DELIVERY TRUCKS

BASED ON AN ANALYSIS OF THREE PLANS

PROPOSED FOR THE BAGGET LAUNDRY COMPANY

Submitted to

Mr. Ralph P. Bagget, President
Bagget Laundry Company
312 Dauphine Street
New Orleans, Louisiana 70102

Prepared by

Charles W. Brewington, C.P.A.
Brewington and Karnes, Certified Public Accountants
743 Beaux Avenue, New Orleans, Louisiana 70118

April 16, 19--

* In the following pages appears a short report written in the direct order (recommendation and summary first). As its introduction reviews the background facts of the problem, most of which are known to the immediate reader, the report apparently is designed for future reference. For reasons of convention in the accounting field, the writing style of the report is somewhat reserved and formal.

Figure 14–4 *(continued)*

RECOMMENDATION FOR DEPRECIATING DELIVERY TRUCKS

BASED ON AN ANALYSIS OF THREE PLANS

PROPOSED FOR THE BAGGET LAUNDRY COMPANY

I. Recommendations and Summary of Analysis

The Reducing Charge method appears to be the best method to depreciate Bagget Laundry
Company delivery trucks. The relative equality of cost allocation for depreciation and
maintenance over the useful life of the trucks is the prime advantage under this method.
Computation of depreciation charges is relatively simple by the Reducing Charge plan
but not quite so simple as computation under the second best method considered.

The second best method considered is the Straight-Line depreciation plan. It is the simplest to compute of the plans considered, and it results in yearly charges equal to those
under the Reducing Charge method. The unequal cost allocation resulting from increasing
maintenance costs in successive years, however, is a disadvantage that far outweighs the
method's ease of computation.

Third among the plans considered is the Service Hours method. This plan is not satisfactory for depreciating delivery trucks primarily because it combines a number of undesirable features. Prime among these is the complexity and cost of computing yearly charges
under the plan. Also significant is the likelihood of poor cost allocation under this plan.
An additional drawback is the possibility of variations in the estimates of the service life
of company trucks.

II. Background of the Problem

Authorization of the Study. This report on depreciation methods for delivery trucks of
the Bagget Laundry Company is submitted on April 16, 19-- to Mr. Ralph P. Bagget,
President of the Company. Mr. Bagget orally authorized Brewington and Karnes, Certified
Public Accountants, to conduct the study on March 15, 19--.

Statement of the Problem. Having decided to establish branch agencies, the Bagget Laundry
Company has purchased delivery trucks to transport laundry back and forth from the central
cleaning plant in downtown New Orleans. The Company's problem is to select from three
alternatives the most advantageous method to depreciate the trucks. The three methods
concerned are Reducing Charge, Straight-Line, and Service-Hours. The trucks have an
original cost of $7,500, a five-year life, and trade-in value of $1,500.

Method of Solving the Problem. In seeking an optimum solution to the Company's problem,
we studied Company records and reviewed authoritative literature on the subject. We
also applied our best judgment and our experience in analyzing the alternative methods.
We based all conclusions on the generally accepted business principles in the field.
Clearly, studies such as this involve subjective judgment, and this one is no exception.

1

Figure 14–4 *(continued)*

355

Chapter 14
Reports:
Determination of
Makeup

2

Steps in Analyzing the Problem. In the following analysis, our evaluations of the three depreciation methods appear in the order in which we rank the methods. Since each method involves different factors, direct comparisons by factors is meaningless. Thus our plan is that we evaluate each method in the light of our best judgment.

III. Marked Advantages of the Reducing Charge Method

Sometimes called Sum-of-the-Digits, the Reducing Charge method consists of applying a series of decreasing fractions over the life of the property. To determine the fraction, first compute the sum of years of use for the property. This number becomes the denominator. Then determine the position number (first, second, etc.) of the year. This number is the numerator. Then apply the resulting fractions to the depreciable values for the life of the property. In the case of the trucks, the depreciable value is $6,000 ($7,500 - $1,500).

As shown in Table I, this method results in large depreciation costs for the early years and decreasing costs in later years. But since maintenance and repair costs for trucks are higher in the later years, this method provides a relatively stable charge over the life of the property. In actual practice, however, the sums will not be as stable as illustrated for maintenance and repair costs will vary from those used in the computation.

	Table I		
	DEPRECIATION AND MAINTENANCE COSTS FOR DELIVERY TRUCKS OF BAGGET LAUNDRY FOR 19X0-19X4 USING REDUCING CHARGE DEPRECIATION		
End of Year	Depreciation	Maintenance	Sum
1	5/15 ($6,000) = $2,000	$ 100	$ 2,100
2	4/15 ($6,000) = 1,600	500	2,100
3	3/15 ($6,000) = 1,200	900	2,100
4	2/15 ($6,000) = 800	1,300	2,100
5	1/15 ($6,000) = 400	1,700	2,100
	$6,000	$4,500	$10,500

In summary, the Reducing Charge method uses the most desirable combination of factors to depreciate trucks. It equalizes periodic charges, and it is easy to compute. It is our first choice for Bagget Laundry Company.

Figure 14–4 *(continued)*

3

IV. Runner-up Position of Straight-Line Method

The Straight-Line depreciation method is easiest of all to compute. It involves merely taking the depreciable value of the trucks ($6,000) and dividing it by the life of the trucks (5 years). The depreciation in this case is $1,200 for each year.

As shown in Table II, however, the increase in maintenance costs in later years results in much greater periodic charges in later years. The method is not usually recommended in cases such as this.

Table II

DEPRECIATION AND MAINTENANCE COSTS FOR
DELIVERY TRUCKS OF BAGGET LAUNDRY FOR 19X0–19X4
USING STRAIGHT-LINE DEPRECIATION

End of Year	Depreciation	Maintenance	Sum
1	1/5 ($6,000) = $1,200	$ 100	$1,300
2	1/5 ($6,000) = 1,200	500	1,700
3	1/5 ($6,000) = 1,200	800	2,100
4	1/5 ($6,000) = 1,200	1,300	2,500
5	1/5 ($6,000) = 1,200	1,700	2,900
	Totals $6,000	$4,500	$10,500

In addition, the Straight-Line method generally is best when the properties involved are accumulated over a period of years. When this is done, the total of depreciation and maintenance costs will be about even. But Bagget Company has not purchased its trucks over a period of years. Nor is it likely to do so in the years ahead. Thus, Straight-Line depreciation will not result in equal periodic charges for maintenance and depreciation over the long run.

Figure 14–4 *(concluded)*

357

Chapter 14
Reports:
Determination of
Makeup

4

V. Poor Rank of Service-Hours Depreciation

The Service-Hours method of depreciation combines the major disadvantages of the other ways discussed. It is based on the principle that a truck is bought for the direct hours of service that it will give. The estimated number of hours that a delivery truck can be used efficiently according to automotive engineers is one-hundred thousand miles. The depreciable cost ($3,000) for each truck is allocated pro rata according to the number of service hours used.

The difficulty and expense of maintaining additional records of service hours is a major disadvantage of this method. The depreciation cost for the delivery trucks under this method will fluctuate widely between first and last years. It is reasonable to assume that as the trucks get older more time will be spent on maintenance. Consequently, the larger depreciation costs will occur in the initial years. As can be seen by Table III, the periodic charges for depreciation and maintenance hover between the two periodically discussed methods.

The periodic charge for depreciation and maintenance increases in the later years of ownership. Another difficulty encountered is the possibility of a variance between estimated service hours and the actual service hours. The wide fluctuations possible make it impractical to use this method for depreciating the delivery trucks.

The difficulty of maintaining adequate records and increasing costs in the later years are the major disadvantages of this method. Since it combines the major disadvantages of both the Reducing Charge and Straight-Line methods, it is not satisfactory for depreciating the delivery trucks.

Table III

DEPRECIATION AND MAINTENANCE COSTS FOR
DELIVERY TRUCKS OF BAGGET LAUNDRY FOR 19X0-19X4
USING SERVICE-HOURS DEPRECIATION

End of Year	Estimated Service-Miles	Depreciation	Maintenance	Sum
1	30,000	$1,800	$ 100	$1,900
2	25,000	1,500	500	2,000
3	20,000	1,200	900	2,100
4	15,000	900	1,300	2,200
5	10,000	600	1,700	2,300
	100,000	$6,000	$4,500	$10,500

Figure 14–5
Illustration of a Memorandum Report

THE MURCHISON CO. INC.

MEMORANDUM

July 21, 19--

TO: William T. Chrysler
Director of Sales

FROM: James C. Colvin, Manager
Millville Sales District

SUBJECT: Quarterly Report for Millville Sales District

SUMMARY HIGHLIGHTS

After three months of operation I have secured office facilities, hired and developed three salesmen, and cultivated about half the customers available in the Millville Sales District. Although the district is not yet showing a profit, at the current rate of development it will do so this month. Prospects for the district are unusually bright.

OFFICE OPERATION

In April I opened the Millville Sales District as authorized by action of the Board of Directors last February 7th. Initially I set up office in the Three Coins Inn, a motel on the outskirts of town, and remained there three weeks while looking for permanent quarters. These I found in the Wingate Building, a downtown office structure. The office suite selected rents for $340 per month. It has four executive offices, each opening into a single secretarial office, which is large enough for two secretaries. Although this arrangement is adequate for the staff now anticipated, additional space is available in the building if needed.

PERSONNEL

In the first week of operations, I hired an office secretary, Ms. Catherine Kruch. Ms. Kruch has good experience and has excellent credentials. She has proved to be very effective. In early April I hired two salespersons--Mr. Charles E. Clark and Ms. Alice E. Knapper. Both were experienced in sales, although neither had worked in apparel sales. Three weeks later I hired Mr. Otto Strelski, a proven salesman who I managed to attract from the Hammond Company. I still am searching for someone for the fourth subdistrict. Currently I am investigating two good prospects and hope to hire one of them within the next week.

PERFORMANCE

After brief training sessions, which I conducted personally, the sales people were assigned the territories previously marked. And they were instructed to call on the accounts listed on the sheets supplied by Mr. Henderson's office. During the first month

Figure 14–5 *(concluded)*

359

Chapter 14
Reports:
Determination of
Makeup

Memorandum   -2-   July 21, 19--

Knapper's sales totaled $17,431 and Clark's reached $13,490, for a total of $30,921.
With three sales people working the next month, total sales reached $121,605. Of the
total, Knapper accounted for $37,345, Clark $31,690, and Strelski $52,570. Although
these monthly totals are below the $145,000 break-even point for the three subdistricts,
current progress indicates that we will exceed this volume this month. As we have
made contact with only about one half of the prospects in the area, the potential for
the district appears to be unusually good.

Figure 14–6
Illustration of a Letter Report

INTERNATIONAL COMMUNICATIONS ASSOCIATION

3141 Girard Street • Washington, D.C.

January 28, 19--

Board of Directors
International Communications Association

Dear Members:

Subject: Recommendation of Convention Hotel for the 1985 Meeting

RECOMMENDATION OF THE LAMONT

The Lamont Hotel is my recommendation for the International Communications Association
meeting next January. My decision is based on the following summary of the evidence
I collected. First, the Lamont has a definite downtown location advantage, and this
is important to convention goers and their spouses. Second, accommodations, including
meeting rooms are adequate in both places, although the Blackwell's rooms are more
modern. Third, Lamont room costs are approximately 15% lower than those at the
Blackwell. The Lamont, however, would charge $400 for a room for the assembly meeting.
Although both hotels are adequate, because of location and cost advantages the
Lamont appears to be the better choice from the members' viewpoint.

ORIGIN AND PLAN OF THE INVESTIGATION

In investigating these two hotels, as was my charge from you at our January 7th meeting,
I collected information on what I believed to be the three major factors of consideration
in the problem. First is location. Second is adequacy of accommodations. And third is
cost. The following findings and evaluations form the basis of my recommendation.

THE LAMONT'S FAVORABLE DOWNTOWN LOCATION

The older of the two hotels, the Lamont is located in the heart of the downtown business
district. Thus it is convenient to the area's two major department stores as well as the
other downtown shops. The Blackwell, on the other hand, is approximately nine blocks
from the major shopping area. Located in the periphery of the business and residential
area, it provides little location advantage for those wanting to shop. It does, however,
have shops within its walls which provide virtually all of the guest's normal needs.
Because many members will bring spouses, however, the downtown location does give
the Lamont an advantage.

Figure 14–6 *(concluded)*

361

Chapter 14
Reports:
Determination of
Makeup

Board of Directors   -2-   January 28, 19--

ADEQUATE ACCOMMODATIONS AT BOTH HOTELS

Both hotels can guarantee the 600 rooms we will require. As the Blackwell is new
(since 1982), however, its rooms are more modern and therefore more appealing.
The 69-year-old Lamont, however, is well preserved and comfortable. Its rooms
are all in good repair, and the equipment is modern.

The Blackwell has 11 small meeting rooms and the Lamont has 13. All are adequate
for our purposes. Both hotels can provide the 10 we need. For our general assembly
meeting, the Lamont would make available its Capri Ballroom, which can easily
seat our membership. It would also serve as the site of our inaugural dinner. The
assembly facilities at the Blackwell appear to be somewhat crowded, although the
management assures me that it can hold 600. Pillars in the room, however, would
make some seats undesirable. In spite of the limitations mentioned, both hotels
appear to have adequate facilities for our meeting.

LOWER COSTS AT THE LAMONT

Both the Lamont and the Blackwell would provide nine rooms for meetings on a
complimentary basis. Both would provide complimentary suites for our president and
our secretary. The Lamont, however, would charge $400 for use of the room for the
assembly meeting. The Blackwell would provide this room without charge.

Convention rates at the Lamont are $55-$65 for singles, $65-$75 for double-bedded
rooms, and $68-$80 for twin-bedded rooms. Comparable rates at the Blackwell are
$65-$75, $75-$85, and $80-$95. Thus the savings at the Lamont would be approximately 15% per member.

Cost of the dinner selected would be $16.00 per person, including gratuities, at the
Lamont. The Blackwell would meet this price if we would guarantee 600 plates.
Otherwise, they would charge $18. Considering all of these figures, the total cost
picture at the Lamont is the more favorable one.

Respectfully,

Willard K. Mitchell
Willard K. Mitchell
Executive Secretary

Figure 14–7
Illustration of a Long-Form Audit Report

To: William A. Karnes   Date: May 3, 19--

From: Auditing Department

Subject: Annual Audit, Spring Street Branch

Introduction

Following is the report on the annual audit of the Spring Street branch. Reflecting conditions existing at the close of business May 1, 19--, this review covers all accounts
other than Loans and Discounts. Specifically, these accounts were proofed:

Accounts Receivable	Savings
Cash Collateral	Suspense
Cash in Office	Series "E" Bonds
Collections	Tax Withheld
Christmas Club	Travelers Checks
Deferred Charges	

Condition of Accounts

All listing totals agreed with General Ledger and/or Branch Controls except for these:

Cash in Office . . . .$1.17 short
Tax Withheld . . . . .21 short
Travelers Checks . . . . .97 short

Exceptions Noted

During the course of the examination the following exceptions were found:

Analysis. The branch had 163 unprofitable accounts at the time of the audit. Losses on
these accounts, as revealed by inspection of the Depositors Analysis Cards, ranged from
$7.31 to $176.36 for the year. The average loss per account was $17.21.

Proper deductions of service charges were not made in 73 instances in which the accounts
dropped below the minimum.

Bookkeeping. From a review of the regular checking accounts names were recorded of
customers who habitually write checks without sufficient covering funds. A list of 39 of
the worst offenders was submitted to Mr. Clement Ferguson.

Figure 14–7 *(continued)*

363

Chapter 14
Reports:
Determination of
Makeup

A check of deposit tickets to the third and fourth regular checking ledgers revealed six accounts on which transit delays recorded on the deposit tickets were not correctly transferred to the ledger sheets.

During the preceding month on 17 different accounts the bookkeepers paid items against uncollected funds without getting proper approval.

Statements. Five statements were held by the branch in excess of three months:

Account	Statement Dates
Curtis A. Hogan	Sept. through April
Carlton I. Breeding	Dec. through April
Alice Crezan	Nov. through April
Jarvis H. Hudson	Jan. through April
W. T. Petersen	Dec. through April

Paying and Receiving. During the week of April 21–27, tellers failed to itemize currency denominations on large (over $100) cash deposits 23 times. Deposits were figured in error 32 times.

Savings. Contrary to instructions given after the last audit, the control clerk has not maintained a record of errors made in savings passboooks.

The savings tellers have easy access to the inactive ledger cards and may record transactions on the cards while alone. When this condition was noted in the last report, the recommendation was made to set up a system of dual controls. This recommendation has not been followed.

Safe Deposit Rentals. Rentals on 165 safe deposit boxes were in arrears. Although it was pointed out in the last report, this condition has grown worse during the past year. Numbers of boxes by years in arrears are as follows:

2 to 3 years	87
3 to 4 years	32
4 to 5 years	29
over 5 years	17
Total	165

Stop payments. Signed stop payment orders were not received on three checks on which payment was stopped:

Account	Amount	Date of Stop Payment
Whelon Electric Company	$317.45	Feb. 7, 19--
George A. Bullock	37.50	April 1, 19--
Amos H. Kritzel	737.60	Dec. 3, 19--

Figure 14–7 *(concluded)*

Over and Short Account. A $23.72 difference between Tellers and Rack Department was recorded for April 22. On May 1 this difference remained uncorrected.

William P. Bunting

William P. Bunting
Head, Auditing Department

Copies to:

W. F. Robertson
Cecil Ruston
W. W. Merrett

Reports: Techniques of writing

15

WHEN YOU HAVE collected and organized your information and have determined the arrangement your report will have, you next turn to the task of writing. This task, of course, is the primary one in your effort to communicate the report contents, although the others certainly have their effects. As you know, communication is not easy. In a report it is unusually difficult because of the complex mass of information that must be communicated in most cases. Unless you make a very special effort to communicate the mass of information in your report, you are likely to fall short of your communication objective.

Much of what you can do in communicating the information in your report we discussed in our analysis of clear writing (Chapter 8). All of these principles of clear writing apply to report writing, and you would do well to keep them in mind as you write your report. In addition, however, there are some general characteristics of good report writing that you should know. These are adaptation, objectivity, time viewpoint, transition, and interest. We shall discuss them in the pages which follow.

Need for adaptation

From our analysis of the communication process, we know that the communication abilities of people differ. Thus, you and your reader will not have precisely the same communicating ability. In fact, you are likely to differ sharply. The fact that you and your reader differ in communication ability is perhaps the major barrier to successful report communication—or to any other form of communication, for that matter. Obviously, if you use words which are not in the mental filter of your reader, communication does not occur. For written communication to be successful, the words used must mean the same to both you and your reader.

From this analysis, one fundamental requirement for report writing is clear. This is the need for adapting the writing to the specific reader or readers. Unfortunately, you are not likely to adapt your writing to the reader without conscious effort. If you are like most of us, you find writing to be such a chore that you are content to accept whatever wording comes first to mind. Such wording may communicate with someone like you, but not so well with your readers.

To adapt your writing, you should begin by visualizing your readers. You should determine such things as who your readers are, how much they know about the subject, what their educational level is, and how they think. Then, keeping this image of your readers in mind, you tailor your writing to these specific people.

Your task is relatively simple when you write to a single reader or to a homogeneous group of readers. But what if you write to a group with varying characteristics? What if, say, your audience comprises people ranging from college graduates to grade school graduates? The answer should be obvious. In such cases you have no choice but to aim at the lowest level of the group. To aim higher would be to exclude the lower levels from your message.

In cases in which you are better educated or better informed on the subject area than your readers, adaptation means simplification. A company executive writing to rank-and-file employees, for example, would need to write in the simple words the readers understand. Likewise, a technical person writing to nontechnical readers would need to simplify the writing. But when this technical person writes to fellow technicians, she or he would do well to use the technical vernacular which is easily understood and expected by such people. As the following examples show, few technical writers were better aware of this fundamental rule than the late Albert Einstein. In writing on a technical subject to a nontechnical audience, he skillfully wrote down to their level:

> What takes place can be illustrated with the help of our rich man. The atom M is a rich miser who, during his life, gives away no money (energy). But in his will he bequeaths his fortune to his sons M' and M", on condition that they give to the community a small amount, less than one thousandth of the whole estate (energy or mass). The sons together have somewhat less than the father had (the mass sum M' and M" is somewhat smaller than the mass M of the radioactive atom). But the part given to the community, though relatively small, is still so enormously large (considered as kinetic energy) that it brings with it a great threat of evil. Averting that threat has become the most urgent problem of our time.[1]

But when writing to fellow scientists, Einstein wrote in words which they understood and expected.

> The general theory of relativity owes its existence in the first place to the empirical fact of the numerical equality of the inertial and gravitational mass of bodies, for which fundamental fact classical mechanics provided no interpretation. Such an interpretation is arrived at by an extension of the principle of relativity to co-ordinate systems accelerated relatively to one another. The introduction of co-ordinate systems accelerated relatively to inertial systems involves the appearance

---

[1] Albert Einstein, *Out of My Later Years*, Philosophical Library, Inc., New York, 1950, p. 53.

of gravitational fields relative to the latter. As a result of this, the general theory of relativity, which is based on the equality of inertia and weight, provides a theory of the gravitational field.[2]

Requirement of objectivity

The communication objective in a report is difficult enough without your own opinions, biases, and attitudes becoming a part of it. Your readers' mental filters will have your readers' biases, and their biases will become a part of their interpretations of meaning. Over this you have little control. But you do have control over your own writing effort. Thus, you should do whatever you can to present truth as well as it is humanly possible to do so. More specifically, you should strive to maintain an attitude of objectivity in your writing.

Maintaining an attitude of objectivity concerns both your attitude and your writing style. You can have an objective attitude by divorcing your own prejudices and emotions from your work and by fairly reviewing and interpreting the information you have uncovered. Thus, you should approach your problem with an open mind and look at all sides of each question. Your role is much like that of a judge presiding over a court of law. You are not moved by personal feelings. You seek truth, and you leave no stone unturned in quest of it. You make your decision only after carefully weighing all of the evidence uncovered.

Objectivity as a basis for believability

A report built on the quality of objectivity has another ingredient that is essential to good report writing: believability. Perhaps biased writing can be in language that is artfully deceptive and may at first glance be believable. But such writing is risky. If at any spot in the report the reader detects bias, she or he will be suspicious of the whole work. Painstaking objectivity, therefore, is the only sure way to believable report writing.

Objectivity and the question of impersonal versus personal writing

Recognizing the need for objectivity in their work, the early report writers strove to develop a writing style which would convey this attitude. They reasoned that the source of the subjective quality in a report is the human being. And they reasoned that objectivity is best attained by emphasizing the factual material of a report, rather than the personalities involved. So they worked to remove the human being from their writing. Impersonal writing style was the result. By impersonal writing is meant writing in the third person—without *I*s, *we*s, or *you*s.

---

[2] Albert Einstein, *Essays in Science*, Philosophical Library, Inc., New York, 1934, p. 50.

In recent years, some report writing authorities have questioned impersonal writing. They point out that personal writing is more forceful and direct than is impersonal writing. They contend that writing which brings both reader and writer into the picture is more like conversation and therefore more interesting. And they answer to the point of objectivity with a reply that objectivity is an attitude of mind and not a matter of person. A report, they say, can be just as objective when written in personal style as when written in impersonal style. Frequently, these critics counter with the argument that impersonal writing leads to an overuse of passive voice and a generally dull writing style. This last argument, however, lacks substance. Impersonal writing can and should be interesting. Any dullness it may have is wholly the fault of the writer. As proof, one has only to look at the lively style used by writers for newspapers, newsmagazines, and journals. Most of this writing is impersonal—and usually it is not dull.

As in most cases of controversy, there is some merit to the arguments on both sides. There are situations in which personal writing is better. There are situations in which impersonal writing is better. And there are situations in which either style is appropriate. You must decide at the outset of your work which style is most appropriate for your one situation.

Your decision should be based on the circumstances of each report situation. First, you should consider the expectations or desires of those for whom you are preparing the report. More than likely, you will find a preference for the impersonal style, for business people have been slow to break tradition. Next, you should consider the formality of the report situation. If the situation is informal, as when the report is really a personal communication between business associates, you should use personal writing. But if the situation is formal, as is the case with most major reports, you should use the conventional impersonal style.

Perhaps the distinction between impersonal and personal writing is best made by illustration.

Personal	*Impersonal*
Having studied the various advantages and disadvantages of using trading stamps, I conclude that your company should not adopt this practice. If you use the stamps, you would have to pay out money for them. Also, you would have to hire additional employees to take care of the increase in sales volume.	A study of the advantages and disadvantages of using trading stamps supports the conclusion that the Mills Company should not adopt this practice. The stamps themselves would cost extra money. Also, use of stamps would require additional personnel to take care of the increase in sales volume.

Logic of present-time viewpoint

A major problem in keeping order in a report is that of fitting all of the details into their proper places in time. Not to do so would be to confuse the reader and to bring up unnecessary barriers in the communication effort. Thus, it is important that in your report you maintain a proper time viewpoint.

You have two choices of time viewpoint, past and present. Although some authorities favor one or the other, either viewpoint can produce a good report. The important thing is to be consistent. You should select one time viewpoint and stay with it. In other words, you should view all similar information in the report from the same position in time.

If you adopt a past-time viewpoint, you treat all findings as well as the research and the writing of the report as past. Thus, you would report the results (in italics) of a recent survey in past tense: "22 percent of the managers *favored* a change." You would write a reference to another part of the report this way: "In Part III, this conclusion *was reached.*" Your use of past-time viewpoint would have no effect on references to future happenings. It would be proper to write in a following sentence "If the current trend continues, by 1995 30 percent *will favor* a change." Prevailing concepts and proven conclusions are exceptions. You would present them in present tense. For examples, take these two sentences: "Solar energy *is* a major potential source of energy" and "The findings *show* conclusively that managers *are* not adequately trained."

Writing in the present-time viewpoint presents as current all information which may logically be assumed to be current at the time of writing. All else is in its proper place in the past or future. Thus, you would write the results of a recent survey in these words: "22 percent of the managers *favor* a change." You would refer to another part of the text like this: "In Part III, this conclusion *is* reached." In referring to an old survey you would write "In 1980 only 12 percent *held* this opinion." And in making a future reference you would write, "If this trend continues, by 1990 30 percent *will hold* this opinion."

Structural aids to report coherence

Smooth flow of thought and clear relationships between the facts presented are essential to successful communication of the report information. Unless you make clear the relationships of the details, unless you make the readers see the logic of your presentation, your readers are not likely to receive the full communication effect of the report message. The writing technique which gives your report this desired effect is coherence.

Perhaps the one best contributor to coherence is good organization—a topic discussed in detail in Chapter 13. By relating facts in a logical, natural sequence, you can give some degree of coherence to the writing. But logical arrangement of facts alone is not always enough. Particularly is this true in the long and involved report in which the relationships of the parts are complex and are not so easily grasped by the readers. In such a report, you need to make a special effort to so structure the report that the relationships are clear. Specifically, you can structure the report story by using concluding and summary paragraphs to mark the report's progress. You can use introductory and preview paragraphs to show major relationships. And you can use transitional sentences and words to show relationships between the lesser parts.

The use of introductory, concluding, and summarizing sections

The extent of use of introductory, concluding, and summarizing sections depends on the report. Perhaps the best rule for you to follow is to use them whenever they are needed to relate the parts of the report or to move the report message along. In general, these sections are more likely to be needed in the longer and more involved reports. In such reports, you are likely to follow a traditional plan of connecting structure.

This plan, as described in Figure 15–1, uses these special sections to tie together all the parts of the report. Because it serves to keep the readers aware of where they have been, where they are, and where they are going, the plan helps them to find their way through complex problems. Also, placement of forward-looking and backward-glancing sections permits casual readers to dip into the report at any place and quickly get their bearings.

As noted in Figure 15–1, you may use three types of sections (usually a paragraph or more) to structure the report. One is the introductory preview.

Figure 15–1
Diagram of the Structural Coherence Plan of a Long, Formal Report

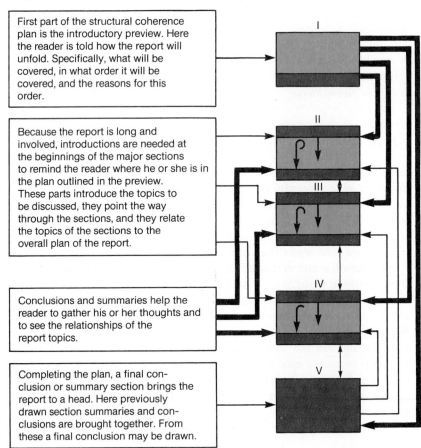

First part of the structural coherence plan is the introductory preview. Here the reader is told how the report will unfold. Specifically, what will be covered, in what order it will be covered, and the reasons for this order.

Because the report is long and involved, introductions are needed at the beginnings of the major sections to remind the reader where he or she is in the plan outlined in the preview. These parts introduce the topics to be discussed, they point the way through the sections, and they relate the topics of the sections to the overall plan of the report.

Conclusions and summaries help the reader to gather his or her thoughts and to see the relationships of the report topics.

Completing the plan, a final conclusion or summary section brings the report to a head. Here previously drawn section summaries and conclusions are brought together. From these a final conclusion may be drawn.

Another is the section introduction. And still another is the conclusion or summary section, either for the major report parts or for the whole report.

For a long report, you may use a section of the report introduction (see Chapter 14) to tell the reader of the report's organization plan. Generally, this preview covers three things: topics to be discussed, their order of presentation, and the logic for this order. Having been informed of the basic plan, the readers are then able to understand quickly how each new subject they encounter in the following pages fits into the whole. Thus, a connection between the major parts is made. The following paragraphs do a good job of previewing a report comparing four brands of automobiles for use by a sales organization:

> A comparison of data on cost, safety, and dependability serves as the bases for the decision as to which light car Allied should buy. The following analysis breaks down each of these factors into component parts and applies each part to the three brands considered.
>
> Because it is the most tangible factor, cost appears first. This section compares initial and trade-in values. Then it takes up the matter of operating costs as determined by gasoline mileage, oil usage, and repair expense. In a second major section, similar comparisons determine care safety. Here driver visibility, special safety features, braking, steering quality, acceleration rate, and traction serve as major considerations. A third section measures car dependability on the basis of repair records and salespeople's time lost because of automobile failure. A final section reaches the decision as to the best brand to buy through a procedure of assigning weights to the foregoing comparisons.

In addition to the introductory preview, you may help show relationships between the major report topics by introductory and summary sections placed at convenient spots throughout the report. You may use sections occasionally to remind the readers of where they are in the progress of the report. Also, you may use these sections to elaborate on the relationships between the report parts and, in general, to give detailed connecting and introductory information. The following paragraph, for example, serves as an introduction to the final section of a report of an industrial survey. Note how the paragraph ties in with the preceding section, which covered industrial activity in three major geographic areas, and justifies covering secondary areas.

> Although the great bulk of industry is concentrated in three areas (Grand City, Milltown, and Port Starr), a thorough industrial survey needs to consider the secondary, but nevertheless important, areas of the state. In the rank of their current industrial potential, these areas are the Southeast, with Hartsburg as its center; the Central West, dominated by Parrington; and the North Central, where Pineview is the center of activities.

The following summary-conclusion paragraph gives an appropriate ending to a major section. The paragraph brings to a head the findings presented in the section and points the way to the subject of the next section.

> These findings and those pointed out in preceding paragraphs, all lead to one obvious conclusion. The small-business executives are concerned primarily with subject matter which will aid them directly in their work. That is, they favor a curriculum slanted in favor of the practical subjects. They do, however, insist on some coverage of the liberal areas. Also, they are convinced of the

value of studying business administration. On all of these points they are clearly out of tune with the bulk of big-business leaders who have voiced their positions in this matter. Even the most dedicated business administration professors would find it difficult to support such an extremely practical concept. Nevertheless, these are the small-business executives' opinions on the subject; and as they are the consumers of the business education product, their opinions should at least be considered. Likewise, their specific recommendations on courses (subject of the following chapter) deserve careful review.

Proper use of such paragraphs as these forms a network of connection throughout the work. The longer the report, the more effective they are likely to be.

Communication value of transition

Transition, which literally means "a bridging across," may be formed in many ways. In general, transitions are made by words, or sentences, placed in the writing to show the relationships of the information presented. They may appear at the beginning of discussion on a new topic and may relate this topic to what has been discussed. They may appear at the end as a forward look. Or they may appear internally as words or phrases which in various ways tend to facilitate the flow of subject matter.

Whether you should use a transition word or sentence in a particular place depends on the need for relating the parts concerned. Because the relationship of its parts may be seen merely from a logical sequence of presentation, a short report, on the one hand, might require only a few transitional parts here and there. A long and involved report, on the other hand, might require much more transitional help.

A word of caution. Before more specific comments on transition are given, one fundamental point must be made clear. You should not make transitions mechanically. You should use them only when there is need for them, or when leaving them out would produce abruptness in the flow of report findings. You should not make them appear to be stuck in; instead, you should make them blend naturally with the surrounding writing. For example, you should avoid transitional forms of this mechanical type: "The last section has discussed topic X. In the next section topic Y will be analyzed."

Transitional sentences. Throughout the report, you can improve the connecting network by the judicious use of sentences. You can use them especially to form the connecting link between secondary sections of the report, as illustrated in the following example of transition between sections B and C of a report. The first few lines of this illustration draw a conclusion for section B. Then, with smooth tie-in, the next words introduce section C and relate this topic to the report plan.

[Section B, concluded]
   . . . Thus the data show only negligible difference in the cost for oil consumption [subject of section B] for the three brands of cars. [Section C] Even though costs of gasoline [subject of section A] and oil [subject of section B] are the more consistent factors of operations expense, the picture is not complete until the cost of repair and maintenance [subject of section C] is considered.

Additional examples of sentences designed to connect succeeding parts are the following. By making a forward-looking reference, these sentences set up the following subject matter. Thus, the resulting shifts of subject matter are both smooth and logical.

These data show clearly that Edmond's machines are the most economical. Unquestionably, their operation by low-cost gas and their record for low-cost maintenance give them a decided edge over competing brands. *Before a definite conclusion as to their merit is reached, however, one more vital comparison should be made.*

(The final sentence clearly introduces the following discussion of an additional comparison.)

. . . *At first glance the data appear to be convincing, but a closer observation reveals a number of discrepancies.*

(This final sentence logically sets up a discussion of the discrepancies.)

Placement of topic sentences at key points of emphasis is another way of using a sentence to improve the connecting network of the report. Usually, the topic sentence is best placed at the paragraph beginning. Note, in the following example, how the topic sentences help the flow of thought by emphasizing the key information.

Brand C accelerates faster than the other two brands, both on level road and on a 9 percent grade. According to a test conducted by Consumption Research, brand C attains a speed of 60 miles per hour in 13.2 seconds. To reach this same speed, brand A requires 13.6 seconds, and brand B requires 14.4 seconds. On a 9 percent grade, brand C reaches the 60-mile-per-hour speed in 29.4 seconds and brand A in 43.3 seconds. Brand B is unable to reach this speed.

Because it carries more weight on its rear wheels than the others, brand C has the best traction of the three. Traction, which means a minimum of sliding on wet or icy roads, is most important to safe driving, particularly during the cold, wet winter months. As traction is directly related to the weight carried by the rear wheels, a comparison of these weights should give some measure of the safety of the three cars. According to data released by the Automobile Bureau of Standards, brand C carries 47 percent of its weight on its rear wheels. Brands B and A carry 44 and 42 percent, respectively.

Transitional words. Although the major transition problems concern connection between sections of the report, there is need also for transition between lesser parts. If the writing is to flow smoothly, you will need to relate clause to clause, sentence to sentence and paragraph to paragraph. Transitional words and phrases generally serve to make these connections.

The transitional words you may use are too numerous to relate, but the following review is a clear picture of what these words are and how you can use them. With a little imagination to supply the context, you can easily see how such words relate succeeding ideas. For better understanding, the words are grouped by the relationships they show between subjects previously discussed and those to be discussed.

Relationship	*Word Examples*
Listing or enumeration of subjects	In addition
	First, second, etc.
	Besides
	Moreover
Contrast	On the contrary
	In spite of
	On the other hand
	In contrast
	However
Likeness	In a like manner
	Likewise
	Similarly
Cause-result	Thus
	Because of
	Therefore
	Consequently
	For this reason
Explanation or elaboration	For example
	To illustrate
	For instance
	Also
	Too

The role of interest in report communication

Like all forms of good writing, report writing should be interesting. Actually, the quality of interest is as important as the facts of the report; for without interest, communication is not likely to occur. If their interest is not held— if their minds are allowed to stray—the readers cannot help missing parts of the message. And it does not matter how much the readers want to read the report message; nor is their interest in the subject enough to assure communication. The writing must maintain this interest. The truth of this reasoning is evident to you if you have ever tried to read dull writing in studying for an examination. How desperately you wanted to learn the subject, but how often your mind strayed!

Perhaps writing interestingly is an art. If so, it is an art in which you can gain some proficiency—if you work at it. If you are to develop this proficiency, you need to work watchfully to make your words build concrete pictures; and you need to avoid the "rubber-stamp" jargon or technical talk so often used in business. You must cultivate a feeling for the rhythmic flow of words and sentences. You must remember that, back of every fact and figure, there is some form of life—people doing things, machines operating, a commodity being marketed. The secret of quality writing is to bring, as far as possible, the real life to the surface—by concrete diction and vigorous active-voice verbs. But, at the same time, you should work to achieve interest without using more words than are necessary.

Here a word of caution may be injected. Attempts to make writing style interesting can be overdone. Such is the case whenever the reader's attention is focused on how something is said, rather than on what is said. Good style, to be effective, simply presents information in a clear, concise, and interesting manner. Possibly the purpose and definition of style can best be summarized by this objective of the report writer: Writing style is at its best when the readers are prompted to say "Here are some interesting facts," rather than "Here is some beautiful writing."

Questions & Problems

1. Are adaptation and simplification the same? Explain.
2. Find a paragraph written for a high level of readership. Rewrite it for a lower level. Point out the differences.
3. Certainly not all reports written in business are written objectively. In fact, many have deliberate bias. In the light of this information, why should we stress objectivity in a college course in report writing?
4. Explain how the question of personal and impersonal writing is related to objectivity.
5. Explain the differences between present- and past-time viewpoints.
6. Is it incorrect to have present, past, and future tense in the same report? In the same paragraph? In the same sentence?
7. Using your imagination to supply the information needed, write an introductory paragraph for a section of a long, formal report.
8. For the same report, write a typical summary paragraph bringing to a close one of the major sections.
9. For the same report, show your knowledge of transition by writing three pairs of connecting sentences. In each pair, one sentence will end a paragraph and the other will begin the next paragraph.

16 Reports: Visual communication aspects

PERHAPS CONFUCIUS was not precisely correct when he said "a picture is worth a thousand words." But we can quarrel only with the number in the statement. As we know from our study of communication theory, words are imprecise conveyors of meaning. We know that this is so, for we must make a limited number of words cover an infinite number of variations in reality. At best, they fit reality loosely. Thus, there is little wonder that we frequently have difficulty communicating through words.

Because your reports often must communicate complex and voluminous information, you are likely to have difficulty making words do the job. In a statistical analysis, for example, you are likely to get your reader lost in a maze of data as you tell the report's story in words. Or, in a technical report, you are likely to have difficulty attempting to use words to describe a process or a procedure. Frequently, in such cases, you will need to use pictures of one kind or other to help communicate your information.

Pictures, or "graphic aids," as we call them in report writing, are an essential part of many reports. Rarely do they take the place of words, for words are essential for communicating the information in most reports. Their role is more a supplementary one—one of assisting the words to communicate the report content. In addition to this communication role, graphic aids also serve to present minor supporting details not covered in words. They help to give emphasis to the key points of coverage. Also, they serve to improve the physical appearance of the report, thereby making the report more inviting and readable.

Foresight in planning

If you are to use graphic aids effectively, you must plan them with foresight and care. Such planning is a part of the task of organizing the report.

As you approach the task of planning your graphic aids, you should keep in mind your fundamental purpose of communicating. Thus, you should never arbitrarily select some random number of illustrations to include. Nor should you judge the completeness of graphic presentation in a report by the number of illustrations used. Instead, you should plan each graphic aid for a specific communication reason. Each one should help to present your report information. Each one should be included because it is needed.

Relationship of need to the plan

Just what graphic aids you will need to communicate a report's story, however, is not easy to determine. Much depends on your overall plan. If you plan to cover the subject in detail, the role of the graphic aids is to emphasize and to supplement. Specifically, the graphic aids point up the major facts discussed and present the detailed data not covered in the writing. On the other hand, if you plan to present the facts in summary form, you may use the graphic aids to work more closely with your text.

The first of these arrangements (complete text supplemented by graphic aids) is conventional and is best for all studies in which completeness is a main requirement. The second plan (summary text closely helped by graphic aids) is gaining in importance. It is used especially in popular types of reports, such as those addressed to the general public. As illustrated in Figure 16–1, this plan produces fast-moving, light reading—the kind the public likes. In addition to the public, many top executives prefer this plan. With the increasing demands on their time, these executives prefer that the reports they read give them the facts quickly and easily. Short, summary reports, helped by an abundance of clear graphic aids, do this job best. Frequently, because of the need for a complete report for future reference and the need for presentation of summary information to the top executives, both kinds of reports are written for the same problem.

Preferred placement within the report

For the maximum communication effect, you should place the graphic aids, which help tell the report story, within the report and near the text they will illustrate. In such positions, they are likely to be seen at the time they need to be seen.

Exactly where you should place each illustration is determined by its size. If the graphic aid is small, taking up only a portion of the page, you should so place it that it is surrounded by the writing covering it. If the graphic aid requires a full page for display, you should place it immediately following the page on which it is discussed. When the discussion covers several pages, however, the full-page illustration is best placed on the page following the first reference to its content.

There is some acceptance of the report arrangement in which all of the illustrations are placed in the appendix. Aside from the time saved by the typist, little can be said for this practice. Certainly, it does not work for the convenience of our readers, who must flip through pages each time they wish to see the graphic presentation of a part of the text.

The graphic aids which you wish to include, but which do not tell a

Figure 16–1

*Page from a Popular Report Illustrating Use of a Summary Text Closely
Helped by Graphic Aids*

Long Industry Lead Times

In considering measures to ease the energy supply situation (section VI), the importance of long lead times cannot be overemphasized. In some activities a sufficient concentration of brains and money can solve problems through "crash" action. In the oil industry, however, as the diagram below shows, planners must think in terms of several years, not months. An understanding of the time factor in oil operations is fundamental.

CHART 15

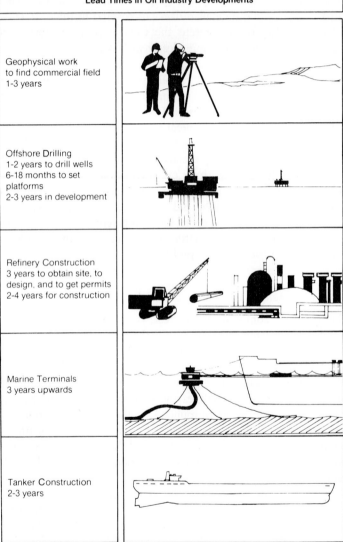

Lead Times in Oil Industry Developments	
Geophysical work to find commercial field 1-3 years	
Offshore Drilling 1-2 years to drill wells 6-18 months to set platforms 2-3 years in development	
Refinery Construction 3 years to obtain site, to design, and to get permits 2-4 years for construction	
Marine Terminals 3 years upwards	
Tanker Construction 2-3 years	

specific part of the report's story, you should place in the appendix. Included in this group are all graphic aids which belong within the report for completeness, yet have no specific spot of coverage within the study. As a rule, this group is comprised of long and complex tables which may cover large areas of information. These tables may even cover the data displayed in a number of charts and other more graphic devices which generally are constructed to illustrate very specific spots within the report.

Whether you place the illustrations within or at the end of the text, you should key them to the text portions they cover by means of references. That is, you might well call the reader's attention to illustrations which cover the topic under discussion. Such references you can make best as incidental remarks in sentences containing significant comments about the data shown in the illustration. You may use numerous incidental wordings, such as these:

. . . , as shown in Chart 4. . . .
. . . , indicated in Chart 4. . . .
. . . , as a glance at Chart 4 reveals. . . .
. . . (see Chart 4). . . .

General mechanics of construction

In planning the illustrations, and later in the actual work of constructing them, you will be confronted with numerous questions of mechanics. Many of these questions you must solve through intelligent appraisal of the conditions concerned in each instance. But the mechanics fall into general groups, the most conventional of which are summarized in the following paragraphs.

Size determination. One of the first decisions involved in constructing a graphic aid is that of determining how large the graphic aid should be. The answer to this question should not be arbitrary, nor should it be based solely on your convenience. Instead, you should seek to give the illustration the size that its contents justify. If, for example, an illustration is relatively simple, comprising only two or three quantities, a quarter page might be adequate. Certainly, a full page would not be needed to illustrate the data. But if a graphic aid is made up of a dozen or so quantities, more space would be justified—possibly even a full page.

With extremely complex and involved data, it may be necessary to make the graphic aid larger than the report page. Such long presentations must be carefully inserted and folded within the report so they open easily. The fold selected will, of course, vary with the size of the page, so there is no best fold that can be recommended. You would do well to survey whatever possibilities are available to you.

Layout arrangement. The layout of any graphic aid is influenced by the amount of information being illustrated. But whenever it is practical, it is best to keep the layout of the illustration within the normal page layout.

Rules and borders. You should arrange rules and borders of any form of graphic presentation to help display and to make clear the data presented. Thus, you should determine their use chiefly through careful planning. As a general practice, however, you should set off graphic aids of less than a page from the text by a lined border which completely encloses the illustration and its caption. You may use this arrangement for full-page illustrations as well, although with such pages the border does not serve so practical a purpose. You should not extend the borders beyond the normal page margins. An exception to this rule is, of course, the unusual instance in which the volume of data to be illustrated simply will not fit into an area of less than the normal page layout.

Color and cross-hatching. Color and cross-hatching appropriately used help the reader to see the comparisons and distinctions. In addition, they give the report a boost in physical attractiveness. Color is especially valuable for this purpose, and you should use it whenever practical.

Numbering. Except for minor tabular displays which are actually a part of the text, you should number all illustrations in the report. Many schemes of numbering are available to you, depending on the makeup of the graphic aids.

If you have many graphic aids which fall into two or more categories, you may number each category consecutively. For example, if your report is illustrated by six tables, five charts, and six maps, you may number these graphic aids Table 1, Table 2, . . . Table 6; Chart 1, Chart 2, . . . Chart 5; and Map 1, Map 2, . . . Map 6.

But if the illustrations used are a wide mixture of types, you may number them in two groups: tables and figures. To illustrate, consider a report containing three tables, two maps, three charts, one diagram, and one photograph. You could group these graphic aids and number them Table I, Table II, and Table III, and Figure 1, Figure 2, . . . Figure 7. By convention, tables are never grouped with other forms of presentation. *Figures* represent a sort of miscellaneous grouping, which may include all illustration types other than tables. It would not be wrong to group and number as figures all graphic aids, other than tables, even if the group contained sufficient subgroups (charts, maps, and so on) to warrant separate numbering of each of these subgroups.

As the preceding examples illustrate, tables are conventionally numbered with capital roman numerals (I, II, III, etc.). All other forms of illustration use the arabic numerals (1, 2, 3, etc.). But some people prefer using arabic numerals for all forms. Obviously, the most important rule to follow in regard to numbering is that of consistency.

Construction of title captions. Every graphic aid should have a title caption which describes its contents. Like the captions used in other parts of the report, the title to the graphic aid has the objective of concisely covering the contents. As a check of content coverage, you might well use the journalist's five Ws—*who, what, where, when, why.* Sometimes you might include *how* (the classification principle). But as conciseness of expression is also desired, it is not always necessary to include all of the Ws in the caption constructed. A title of a chart comparing annual sales volume of Texas and Louisiana stores of the Brill Company for the 197X–198X period might be constructed as follows:

Who:	Brill Company
What:	Annual sales
Where:	Texas and Louisiana
When:	197X–198X
Why:	For comparison

The caption might read, "Comparative annual sales of Texas and Louisiana branches of the Brill Company, 197X–198X."

Placement of titles. Titles of tables conventionally appear above the tabular display. Titles to all other graphic presentations usually are below the illustration. Convention exists also for placing table titles in a higher type (usually solid capitals without the underscore in typewritten reports) than titles of all other illustrations. But nowadays these conventional forms are not universally followed. The tendency is growing to use lowercase type for all illustration titles, and to place titles of both tables and charts at the top. These more recent practices are simple and logical; yet for formal reports you should follow the conventional arrangement.

Footnotes and acknowledgments. Occasionally, parts of a graphic aid require special explanation or elaboration. When these conditions come up, just as when similar explanations are made within the text of the report, you should use footnotes. Such footnotes are nothing more than concise explanations placed below the illustration and keyed to the part explained by means of a superscript (raised number) or asterisk, as shown in Figure 16–2. Footnotes for tables are best placed immediately below the graphic presentation. Footnotes for other graphic forms follow the illustration when the title is placed at the bottom of the graphic.

Usually, a source acknowledgment is the bottom entry made on the page. By source acknowledgment is meant a reference to the body or authority which deserves the credit for gathering the data used in the illustration. The entry consists simply of the word *source* followed by a colon and the source name. A source note for data based on information gathered by the United States Department of Agriculture might read like this:

Source: United States Department of Agriculture.

If the data were collected by you or your staff, two procedures may be followed. You may give the source as "primary," in which case the source note would read:

Source: Primary.

Or you may omit the source note.

Construction of tables

A table is any systematic arrangement of quantitative information in rows and columns. Although tables are not truly graphic in the literal meaning of the word, they are instrumental in communicating information. Therefore, you may appropriately consider them a part of the graphic-aids planning of your report. The purpose of a table is to present a broad area of information

Figure 16–2
Good Arrangement of the Parts of a Typical Table

Stub head	Spanner head			
	Column head	Column head	Column head	Column head
TABLE NO. TITLE OF TABLE				

Stub	X X X	X X X	X X X	X X X
Stub	X X X	X X X	X X X	X X X
Stub	X X X	X X X	X X X	X X X
Stub	X X X	X X X	X X X	X X X
"	"	"	"	"
"	"	"	"	"
"	"	"	"	"
"	"	"	"	"
"	"	"	"	"
"	"	"	"	"
TOTAL	X X X	X X X	X X X	X X X

Footnotes

Source:

in convenient and orderly fashion. By such an arrangement, the information is simplified, and comparisons and analyses are made easy.

Two basic types of tables are available to you—the general-purpose table and the special-purpose table. *General-purpose tables* are arrangements of a broad area of data collected. They are repositories of detailed statistical data and have no special analytical purpose. As a rule, general-purpose tables belong in the report appendix.

Special-purpose tables, as their name implies, are prepared for a special purpose—to help to illustrate a particular phase of the text. Usually, they consist of data carefully drawn from the general-purpose tables. Only those data are selected which are pertinent to the analysis, and sometimes these data are rearranged or regrouped to better illustrate their special purpose. Such tables belong within the text near the spot they illustrate.

Aside from the title, footnotes, and source designation previously discussed, the table consists of stubs, captions, and columns and rows of data, as shown in Figure 16–2. Stubs are the titles to the rows of data, and captions are the titles to the columns. The captions, however, may be divided into subcaptions—or column heads, as they are sometimes called.

Because the text tables should be specially planned, their construction is largely influenced by their illustration purpose. Nevertheless, a few general construction rules may be listed.

1. If rows tend to be long, the stubs may be repeated at the right.

2. The dash (—) or the abbreviation "n.a.," but not the zero, is used to indicate data "not available."

3. Footnote references to numbers in the table should be keyed with asterisks, daggers, double daggers, and such. Numbers followed by footnote reference numbers may cause confusion.

4. Totals and subtotals should appear whenever they help the purpose of the table. The totals may be for each column and sometimes for each row. Usually, row totals are made at the right; but, when the totals need emphasis, they may be placed at the left. Likewise, column totals generally appear at the bottom; but they may appear at the top of the column when writers want to emphasize them. A ruled line (usually a double one) separates the totals from their data.

5. Units in which the data are recorded must be clear. Unit descriptions (bushels, acres, pounds, and such) appropriately appear above the columns, as part of the captions or subcaptions. If the data are in dollars, however, the dollar mark ($) placed before the first entry in each column is sufficient.

Tabulated information need not always be presented in formal tables. In fact, short arrangements of data may be presented more effectively as parts of the text. Such arrangements generally are made in either of two ways: as leader work or as text tabulations.

Leader work is the presentation of tabular material in the text without titles or rules. (Leaders are the repeated dots.) Typically a colon precedes the tabulation, as in this illustration:

August sales for representatives of the Western Region were as follows:

Charles B. Brown	$13,517
Thomas Capp	19,703
Bill E. Knauth	18,198

Text tabulations are simple tables, usually with headings and some rules. But they are not numbered, and they have no titles. They are made to read with the text, as in this example:

August sales for the representatives in the Western Region increased sharply from the preceding month, as these figures show:

Representative	July Sales	August Sales	Increase
Charles B. Brown	$12,819	$13,517	$ 698
Thomas Capp	17,225	19,703	2,478
Bill E. Knauth	16,838	18,198	1,360

The simple bar chart

Simple bar charts are graphic means of comparing simple magnitudes by the lengths of equal-width bars. You should use such charts to show quantity changes over time, quantity changes over geographic distance, or quantitative distances.

The principal parts of the bar chart are the bars and the grid. The bars may be arranged horizontally or vertically, and each has in its beginning a title identifying the quantity being illustrated. The grid upon which the bars are placed is simply a field carefully ruled by line marks arithmetically scaled to the magnitudes illustrated. Usually, a finely marked grid is made as a preliminary step in constructing a bar chart, and the bars are then placed on the grid. But the final drawing of the chart is best made to show only sufficient grid lines to help the reader's eye measure the magnitudes of the bars. These scaled grid lines are carefully labeled with numerals, and the unit in which the values are measured is indicated by a scale caption appearing below the values in a vertical bar chart and above the values in a horizontal bar arrangement.

Although there are numerous acceptable variations in bar-chart construction, a basic pattern should be helpful to you. Such a pattern, as illustrated in Figure 16–3, is generally adequate.

Figure 16–3
Illustration of Good Arrangement of the Parts of a Simple Bar Chart

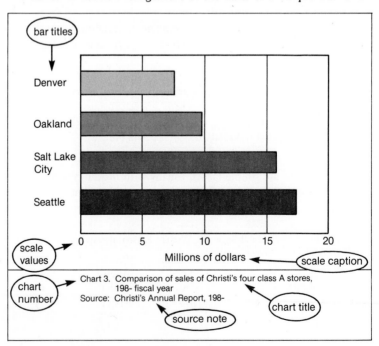

Variations of the bar chart

385

Chapter 16
Reports: Visual
Communication
Aspects

In addition to the simple bar chart just described, you may use a number of other types of bar charts in presenting a report. The more commonly used of these variants are the multiple bar chart, the bilateral bar chart, and the subdivided or component-part bar chart.

Multiple bar charts. Comparisons of two or three variables within a single bar chart are made possible by the use of multiple bars distinguished by cross-hatching, shading, or color. That is, the bars representing each of the variables being compared are distinguished by these mechanical means, as illustrated in Figure 16–4. The key to the variables is given in a legend, which may be placed within the illustration or below it, depending on where space is available. Generally, it is confusing and, therefore, inadvisable to make multiple comparisons of this type for more than three variables.

Figure 16–4
Multiple Bar Chart

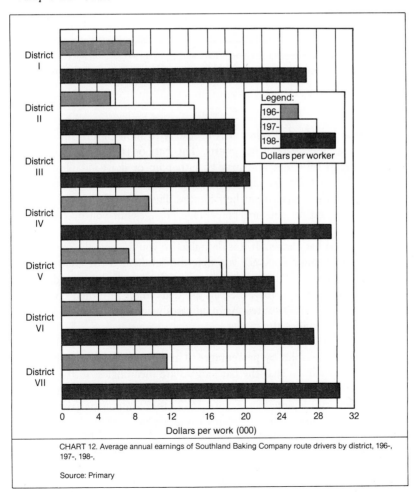

CHART 12. Average annual earnings of Southland Baking Company route drivers by district, 196-, 197-, 198-,

Source: Primary

Figure 16–5
Bilateral Bar Chart

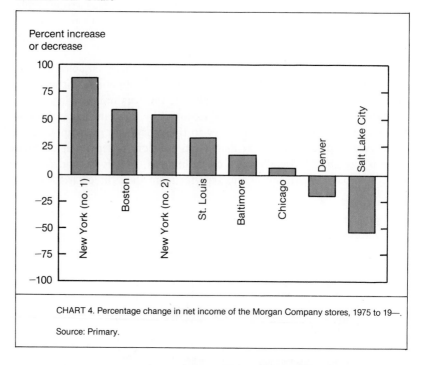

CHART 4. Percentage change in net income of the Morgan Company stores, 1975 to 19—.

Source: Primary.

Bilateral bar charts. When it is necessary to show plus or minus deviations, you may use bilateral bar charts. The bars of these charts begin at a central point of reference and may go either up or down, as illustrated in Figure 16–5. Bar titles may appear either within, above, or below the bars, depending on which placement best fits the illustration. Bilateral bar charts are especially good for showing percentage change, but you may use them for any series in which minus quantities are present.

Subdivided bar charts. If it is desirable for you to show the composition of magnitudes being compared, you may use subdivided bar charts. In this form of chart, cross-hatchings, shadings, or colors are first assigned to each of the parts to be shown; then the bars are marked off into their component parts, as Figure 16–6 illustrates. As in all cases where cross-hatching or color is used, a legend guides the reader.

A form of the subdivided bar chart frequently is used to compare the composition of variables by percentages. This chart differs from the typical bar chart principally in that the bar lengths are meaningless in the comparisons. All the bars are of equal length, and only the component parts of the bars vary. As depicted in Figure 16–7, the component parts may be labeled; but they may also be explained in a legend.

Pie-chart construction

Also of primary importance in comparing the percentage composition of variables is the pie chart (Figure 16–8). As the name implies, the pie chart

Figure 16–6
Illustration of a Subdivided Bar Chart

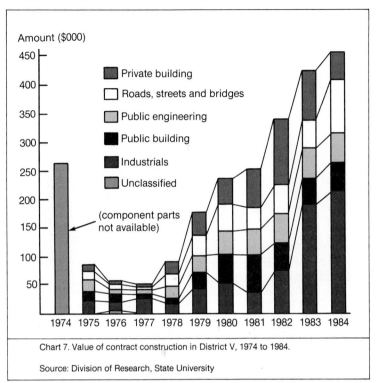

Chart 7. Value of contract construction in District V, 1974 to 1984.

Source: Division of Research, State University

shows the whole of the information being studied as a pie, and the parts of this whole as slices of this pie. The slices may be individually labeled, or cross-hatching or coloring with an explanatory legend may be used. Because it is difficult to judge the value of each slice with the naked eye, it is advisable to include the units of value within each slice. A good rule to follow is to begin slicing the pie at the 12 o'clock position and to move around clockwise. It is usually best to show the slices in descending order of magnitude.

You should never use pie diagrams to show comparisons of two or more wholes by varying the areas of wholes. Such comparisons are almost meaningless. The human eye is totally inadequate to judge the relative areas of most geometric shapes.

Arrangement of the line chart

Line charts are best used to show the movements or changes of a continuous series of data over time. They are especially useful for showing changes in prices, weekly sales totals, and periodic employment data. You may plot line charts on an arithmetic, semilogarithmic, or logarithmic grid; but since the arithmetic plot is most common to business reports, it is described here.

In constructing a line chart, you should plot the item to be illustrated as a continuous line on a grid. On the grid, you should plot time on the

Figure 16–7
Illustration of a Subdivided Bar Chart

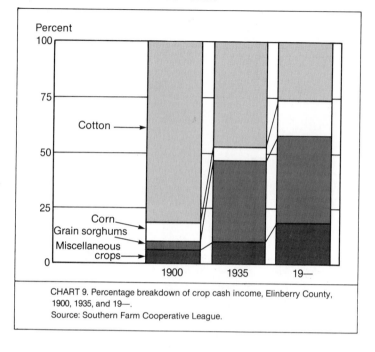

CHART 9. Percentage breakdown of crop cash income, Elinberry County, 1900, 1935, and 19—.
Source: Southern Farm Cooperative League.

Figure 16–8
Illustration of a Pie Chart

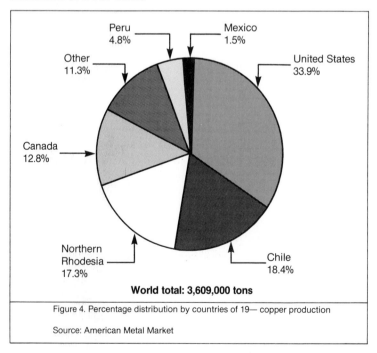

Figure 4. Percentage distribution by countries of 19— copper production

Source: American Metal Market

Figure 16–9
A Line Chart with One Series

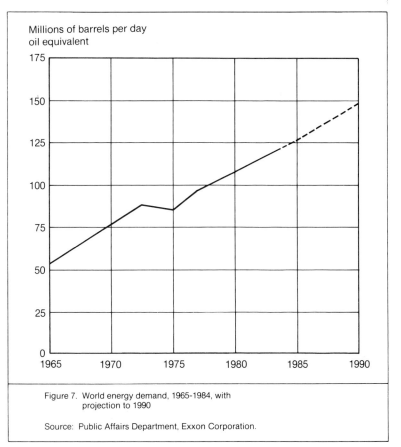

Millions of barrels per day
oil equivalent

Figure 7. World energy demand, 1965-1984, with
projection to 1990

Source: Public Affairs Department, Exxon Corporation.

horizontal axis (*X*-axis). You should plot the values of the series on the vertical axis (*Y*-axis). You should mark clearly the scale values and time periods on the axis lines, as shown in Figure 16–9.

You may also compare two or more series on the same grid on a line chart (Figure 16–10). In such a comparison, you should clearly distinguish the lines by color or form (dots, dashes, dots and dashes, and the like). You should clearly label them by a legend somewhere in the chart. But the number of series that you may compare on one chart is limited. As a practical rule, four or five series should be a maximum.

It is possible, also, to show component parts of a series by use of a line chart—sometimes called a belt chart. Such an illustration, however, is limited to one series to a chart. You should construct this type of chart, as shown in Figure 16–11, with a top line representing the total of the series. Then, starting from the base, you should cumulate the component parts,

Figure 16–10
Line Chart Comparing more than One Series

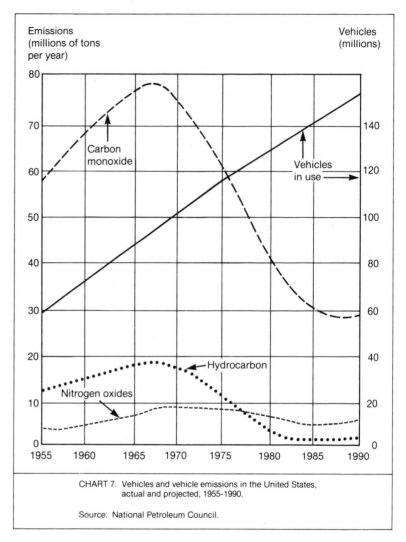

CHART 7. Vehicles and vehicle emissions in the United States,
actual and projected, 1955-1990.

Source: National Petroleum Council.

beginning with the largest and ending with the smallest. You may use cross-hatching or coloring to distinguish the parts.

Even though the line graph is one of the simplest charts to construct, you should be aware of three common pitfalls. First of these is the common violation of the rule of the zero origin. The *Y*-scale (vertical axis) should begin at zero, even though the points to be plotted are relatively high in value. If most of the points to be plotted are relatively high in value, the comparison may be facilitated by breaking the scale somewhere between zero and the level of the lowest plotted value. Of the numerous means of showing scale breaks, these two techniques are recommended:

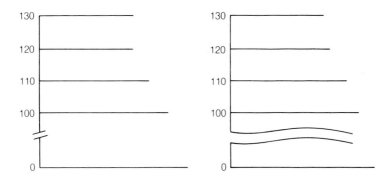

Second, equal magnitudes on both *X*- and *Y*-scales should be represented on the grid by equal distances. Any deviation from this rule would distort the illustration, thereby deceiving the reader.

A third common violation of good line-chart construction concerns the determination of proportions on the grid. It is easy to see that by expanding one scale and contracting the other, impressions of extreme deviation can be made. For example, data plotted on a line chart with time intervals one sixteenth of an inch apart certainly appear to show more violent fluctuations than the same data plotted on a chart with time intervals plotted a half inch apart. Only the application of common sense can prevent this violation. The grid distances selected simply must be such as will tend to make the presentation of the data realistic.

Figure 16–11
Illustration of a Component-Part Line Chart

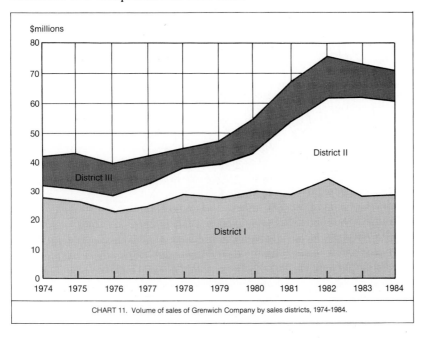

CHART 11. Volume of sales of Grenwich Company by sales districts, 1974-1984.

Design of the statistical map

Maps may also be used to help communicate quantitative information. They are primarily useful when quantitative information is to be compared by geographic areas. On such maps, the geographic areas are clearly outlined; and the differences between areas are shown by some graphic technique. Of the numerous techniques that may be used, four are most common.

1. Possibly the most popular technique is that showing quantitative differences of areas by color, shading, or cross-hatching (Figure 16–12). Such maps, of course, must have a legend to explain the quantitative meanings of the various colors, cross-hatchings, and so forth.

2. Some form of chart may be placed within each geographic area to depict the quantities representative of that area, as illustrated in Figure 16–13. Bar charts and pie charts are commonly used in such illustrations.

3. Placing the quantities in numerical form within each geographic area, as shown in Figure 16–14, is another widely used technique.

4. Dots, each representing a definite quantity (Figure 16–15), may be placed within the geographic areas in proportion to the quantities to be illustrated for each area.

Figure 16–12
Illustration of a Statistical Map Showing Quantitative Differences of Areas by Cross-hatching

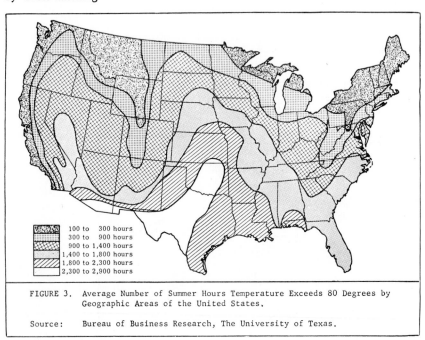

	100 to 300 hours
	300 to 900 hours
	900 to 1,400 hours
	1,400 to 1,800 hours
	1,800 to 2,300 hours
	2,300 to 2,900 hours

FIGURE 3.   Average Number of Summer Hours Temperature Exceeds 80 Degrees by Geographic Areas of the United States.

Source: Bureau of Business Research, The University of Texas.

Figure 16–13
Statistical Map Showing Comparisons by Charts within Geographic Areas

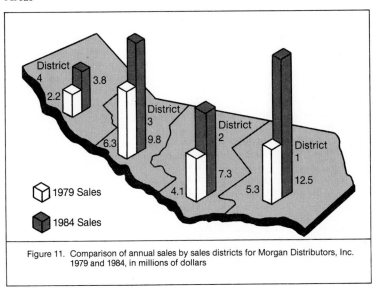

Figure 11. Comparison of annual sales by sales districts for Morgan Distributors, Inc. 1979 and 1984, in millions of dollars

Figure 16–14
Statistical Map Showing Quantitative Differences by Means of Numbers Placed within Geographic Areas

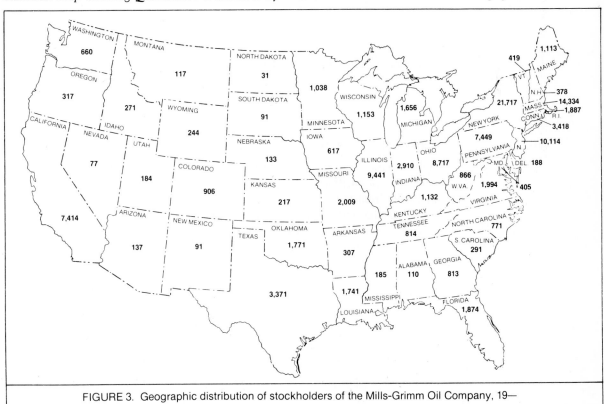

FIGURE 3. Geographic distribution of stockholders of the Mills-Grimm Oil Company, 19—

Figure 16–15
Illustrations of a Statistical Map Using Dots to Show Quantitative Differences by Geographic Areas

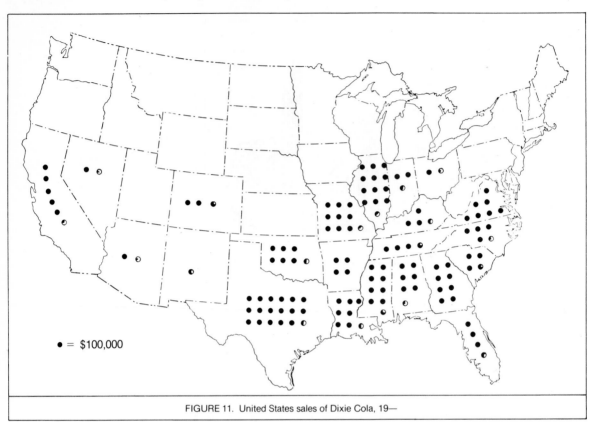

● = $100,000

FIGURE 11. United States sales of Dixie Cola, 19—

Construction of the pictogram

A pictogram is a bar chart which uses pictures, rather than bars, to get across the information. For example, a company seeking to show graphically its profits from sales could use a simple bar chart for the purpose. Or the firm could use instead of bars a line of coins equal in length to the bars. Coins might be selected because they depict the information to be illustrated. This resulting graphic form, as illustrated in Figure 16–16, is the pictogram.

In general, when constructing a pictogram, you should follow the procedure you used in constructing bar charts. In addition, you should follow two special rules. First, you must make all of the picture units of equal size. That is, you must make the comparisons wholly on the basis of the number of illustrations used and never by varying the areas of the individual pictures. The reason for this rule is obvious. The human eye is grossly inadequate in comparing areas of geometric designs. Second, you should select

Figure 16–16
Illustration of the Pictogram

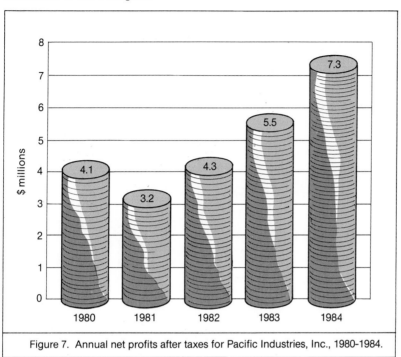

Figure 7. Annual net profits after taxes for Pacific Industries, Inc., 1980-1984.

pictures or symbols which appropriately depict the quantity to be illustrated. A comparison of the navies of the world, for example, might use miniature ship drawings. Cotton production might be shown by bales of cotton. Obviously, the drawings used must be immediately interpreted by the reader.

Miscellaneous graphic aids

The graphic aids discussed thus far are those most commonly used. Others are sometimes helpful. Photographs and drawings may serve a useful communication purpose. Diagrams (see Figure 16–17), may help to make simple a complicated explanation or description, particularly when technological procedures are being communicated. For all practical purposes, any form of graphic design is acceptable as long as it helps to communicate the true story. The possibilities are almost unlimited.

Figure 16–17
Example of the Use of a Diagram

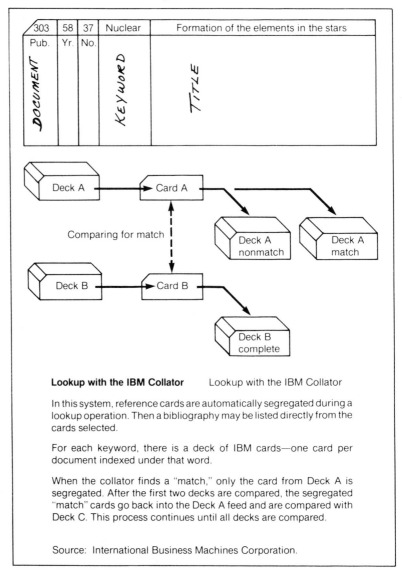

303	58	37	Nuclear	Formation of the elements in the stars
Pub.	Yr.	No.		

DOCUMENT KEYWORD TITLE

Deck A → Card A

Comparing for match

Deck A nonmatch   Deck A match

Deck B → Card B

Deck B complete

Lookup with the IBM Collator   Lookup with the IBM Collator

In this system, reference cards are automatically segregated during a lookup operation. Then a bibliography may be listed directly from the cards selected.

For each keyword, there is a deck of IBM cards—one card per document indexed under that word.

When the collator finds a "match," only the card from Deck A is segregated. After the first two decks are compared, the segregated "match" cards go back into the Deck A feed and are compared with Deck C. This process continues until all decks are compared.

Source: International Business Machines Corporation.

Questions & Problems

1. For the past 20 years, Professor Kupenheimer has required that his students include five graphic aids in the long, formal report he requires them to prepare. Evaluate this requirement.

2. Because it is easier to do, a report writer prepared all of her graphic aids on separate pages. Each one took the full page. Some of these graphic aids were extremely complex; some were very simple. Comment on this policy.

3. "I have placed every chart near the place I write about it. The reader can see it without any *additional* help from me. It just doesn't make sense to direct attention to them with words." Evaluate this comment.

4. A report has five maps, four tables, one chart, one diagram, and one photograph. How would you number these graphic aids?

5. How would you number this composition of graphic aids in a report: seven tables, six charts, nine maps?

6. Construct a complete, concise title for a bar chart which shows annual attendance at home football games at your school from 1965 to the present.

7. The table prepared in Question 6 requires an explanation for the years 1975 to the present. In these years one extra home game was played. Explain how you would do this.

8. For each of the areas of information described below, which form of graphic aid would you use? Explain your decision.
   a. Record of annual sales for the Kenyon Company for the past 20 years.
   b. Comparison of Kenyon Company sales, by product, for this year and last year.
   c. Monthly production in units for the automobile industry.
   d. Breakdown of how the average middle-income family in your state disposes of its income dollar.
   e. Comparison of how middle-income families spend their income dollar with similar expenditures of low-income families.
   f. A comparison of sales for the past two years for each of the B&B Company's 14 sales districts. The districts cover all 50 states and Puerto Rico.
   g. National production of automobiles from 1930 to the present, broken down by manufacturer.

9. Discuss the logic of showing scale breaks in a chart.

10. Discuss the dangers of using illogical proportions in constructing a grid for a chart.

11. Discuss the techniques that may be used to show quantitative differences by area on a statistical map.

12. Select some data that are ideally suited for presentation in a pictogram. Explain why a pictogram is good for this case.

13. Discuss the dangers of using a pictogram.

14. For each of the following sets of facts (a) determine the graphic aid (or aids) that would be best, (b) defend your choice, and (c) construct the graphic aid.

(1) **Average (mean) amount of life insurance owned by Fidelity Life Insurance Company policyholders. Classification is by annual income.**

Income	Average Life Insurance
Under $10,000	$ 5,245
$10,000–14,999	14,460
15,000–19,999	26,680
20,000–24,999	39,875
25,000–29,999	51,440
30,000 and over	76,390

(2) **Profits and losses for D and H Food Stores, by store, 1980–1984, in dollars.**

Year	Store Able City	Baker	Charleston	Total
1980	13,421	3,241	9,766	26,428
1981	12,911	−1,173	11,847	23,585
1982	13,843	−2,241	11,606	23,208
1983	12,673	2,865	13,551	29,089
1984	13,008	7,145	15,482	35,635

(3) **Share of real estate tax payments by ward for Bigg City, 1979 and 1984, in thousands of dollars.**

	1979	1984
Ward 1	17.1	21.3
Ward 2	10.2	31.8
Ward 3	19.5	21.1
Ward 4	7.8	18.2
City total	54.6	92.4

(4) Percentage change in sales by salesperson,
1983–1984, District IV, Abbott, Inc.

Salesperson	Percentage Change	Salesperson	Percentage Change
Joan Abraham	+ 7.3	Wilson Platt	+ 7.4
Wilson Calmes	+ 2.1	Carry Ruiz	+11.5
Todd Musso	− 7.5	David Schlimmer	− 4.8
Mary Nevers	+41.6	Helen Dirks	− 3.6

(5) Net income from operations of seven
largest U.S. banks, with percentage
of profit derived from foreign
operations, 1983–1984.

Bank	1983 Operations Net (Millions)	Foreign (Percent)	1984 Operations Net (Millions)	Foreign (Percent)
Bank America	$178.4	25%	$166.5	20%
1st Nat'l City	168.2	42	145.1	38
Chase Manhattan	147.7	20	139.3	15
J. P. Morgan	109.1	30	102.0	25
Mfgrs. Hanover	77.9	28	85.2	24
Chemical	72.5	15	77.4	10

Report problems

Short problems

1. **Advising on whether to buy new or used automobiles.** Since taking over as sales manager for Hamm Distributors, Inc., Loomis H. Hogan has introduced a number of revolutionary ideas for helping this regional sales organization get out of financial difficulties. The current idea is to buy used automobiles, rather than new ones, for its sales representatives. Hogan argues that the salespeople have small territories and average only 10,000 miles per year. He acknowledges that the old cars are likely to be less dependable and less prestigious. But he feels that the main problem now is one of finances and that the used automobiles would save money.

Because he seeks support for his ideas, Mr. Hogan turned to you, a research associate with Morrison Research, Inc. Thus, it is your task to gather information on the subject and to submit the information to your client along with your analyses and recommendation.

Gathering the information was easy, for you had only to find the file copy of research your office did for Econo-Kar Auto Rental, Inc. (The Econo-Kar people have authorized you to use these data.) As summarized in Table 1, these data show clearly the costs of automobiles and their operation. The information is not as current as you'd like. But you feel the conclusions they support are valid. In addition to these data, you will include in your analysis the other considerations involved in the problem—dependability of old automobiles, prestige, image, and such.

Your task now is to present your information with appropriate analyses, conclusions, and recommendations. Of course, you will present the information in appropriate report form—probably as a conventional short report (title page plus text).

2. **Reporting on energy conservation to the Board of Regents.** Seven years ago the Board of Regents of State University authorized the Office

Table 1
Per-Mile Ownership and Operating Costs

Age of Automobile at Purchase	Purchase Price	Car Kept 3 Years	Percent Saving	Car kept until Junked	Percent Saving
New	$7,296	42.1	—	26.8	—
1 year	5,968	37.9	10%	26.0	6%
2 years	3,881	29.5	30	22.5	21
3 years	2,061	21.9	48	20.4	32
4 years	1,547	20.9	51	20.1	37
5 years	1,250	20.3	52	19.8	43
6 years	923	19.8	53	19.8	49
7 years	693	19.7	53	—	53

Note: All figures are based on prices and costs of an intermediate-sized car driven 10,000 miles a year. The percentage saved until junked at ten years reflects driving the used car the same number of years as the new car is driven; that is, the saving for a year-old car driven nine years and then junked is the saving over the cost of driving a new car for nine years.

of Physical Plant to begin a massive energy-saving program. Physical Plant responded by taking a number of energy-saving actions. It raised thermostats in summer months and lowered them in winter. It installed a computer-controlled power management system. It conducted extensive energy conservation campaigns. And it did other things. All available information indicates the efforts were reasonably successful.

Now the Board of Regents wants a report on these energy-saving efforts. And as chief engineer, Office of the Physical Plant, you have the job of doing the reporting.

You begin by collecting the data for energy consumption over the seven-year period. Since the university has added some buildings during the period, you are careful to distinguish between energy used for the buildings existing seven years ago and for buildings added since. You will report on costs, also; but here you will be careful not to confuse. Energy costs have almost tripled over the seven-year period. Your data are summarized in Table 2.

Make your report to the Board and point out what has happened. Probably the Board also will want some words on the future. Here you cannot be optimistic. State Utility Company projects costs to increase to $0.09

Table 2.
State University Energy Consumption for Past Seven Years

	Therms* of Energy Consumption		Energy Costs ($000,000)
	Old Buildings	New Buildings	
Last year	9.1	2.5	$5.8
2 years ago	8.8	2.1	4.2
3 years ago	8.7	2.2	3.3
4 years ago	9.6	0.3	2.3
5 years ago	9.5	0.2	2.0
6 years ago	9.7	—	1.8
7 years ago	11.2	—	1.6

* Therm = 100,000 Btu's.

per kwh. (today's cost is $0.03). Although you and your office have done most of the easy things to conserve, you could do some of the more difficult. You will gladly report on these suggestions to the Board—if it wants such a report.

Now you are ready to begin writing the report. You will present consumption data so they form a picture of the success of the conservation plan. And you will report cost data, taking care to emphasize the effects of price changes over the years. Present your information in the form of a short report (title page plus text). You probably will use some graphic aids to emphasize the data. Address the report to the Board of Regents, Wilma L. Sullivan, Chairperson.

3. Presenting and analyzing differences in grades of dorm and nondorm students. As director, Office of Campus Housing, State University, your current task is to report on grade point averages of dorm and nondorm students. You have the data neatly assembled (Table 3). Now you must organize the data for analysis and presentation in a report to Dr. Theodore Hobbs, dean for Academic Affairs.

Table 3
Grade Point Averages (4.0 Basis)

	Freshmen	Sophomores	Juniors	Seniors
Men				
Dormitory	2.15	2.40	2.51	2.78
Nondormitory	1.90	2.14	2.39	2.66
Women				
Dormitory	2.34	2.54	2.68	3.06
Nondormitory	2.17	2.36	2.60	2.91

As you review the data, you quickly see that dorm students perform better than nondorm students. You will present this information fully, of course; and you will also explain why. Here you will move into the area of subjective interpretation. That is, you will use your best judgment to explain the grade differences. You will take care to label your judgments for what they are.

Write the report on State University's memorandum stationery.

4. Recommending a scholarship recipient. Assume the role of executive secretary, the DeLong Foundation. It is your job to recommend to the Foundation's Board of Directors a recipient for the DeLong Scholarship at your school. This scholarship is one of the better ones. It pays well, and it covers the remaining years of the recipient's undergraduate education.

Following the initial announcement of the scholarship award four weeks ago, 31 applications came in. You carefully evaluated all of them, and you interviewed the top 11. Now you have narrowed the selection to two people: Hazel McNutt and Mark Klammer. You will present these two students to the Board, along with a comparative review of their background facts and your recommendation. In summary form, the facts you have assembled on your note pad are as follows:

> *Hazel McNutt.* Age 19. Second semester sophomore. Grade point average, 3.6. Memberships: University Methodist Church (president Wesley Foundation Association), Young Republicans (secretary-treasurer), Marketing Club (membership chairperson). Dean's List all semesters. Major in Marketing. Father deceased and mother works as secretary. Two younger sisters at home. Mother unable to help with finances. Hazel works 20 hours a week busing tables at local cafeteria. An attractive woman—an extrovert. Very pleasing personality. Friendly smile. Polite. Respectful. Check of professors reveals only favorable comments— good student, hard worker. Character references all report favorably—a young woman of good character and high morals.

> *Mark Klammer.* First semester junior. Grade point average, 3.8. Memberships: Accounting Club, University Choral Club, Southside Baptist Church. Major in Accounting. Age 20. Works 30 hours per week as night clerk in downtown hotel. From large family (five younger brothers and sisters). Father employed as mechanic; mother works as salesclerk in department store. Parents able to give only limited financial help (20 percent). A small, slightly built young man. Friendly but somewhat reserved. Appears to be timid. Evaluations by professors are exceptionally high—a diligent, intelligent, outstanding scholar. Character references attest to his high morals and ideals—a truly fine young man.

Using your very best objectivity, now you will evaluate the two people. You will present your evaluations in an objective memorandum report addressed to Kenneth Kendall, chairperson of the Board.

5. Justifying the purchase of a typewriter with magic correcting tape. You are the manager of the executive typing pool at Cherokee Manufacturing Company. Under your supervision are 15 typists who handle the typewriting needs of all except the Company's highest executives. (These have their own secretaries.) Mainly your employees type letters, memoranda, and reports.

At the moment it is time to order five new typewriters (you replace the machines routinely at three-year intervals). You have decided to purchase Continental Business Machines' new Standard III model with magic correcting tape feature. The Company has used the Continental Standard III for years, but not with the correcting tape feature. In fact, the Company's purchasing agent has negative opinions on such "expensive frills" (his words).

It is true, the correcting tape adds $92 to the basic cost of $680 (plus tax) for the Standard III. You think the extra feature is worth the difference by enabling the typist to make corrections without erasing (merely by setting the machine in a split second and typing over the error). And the corrections cannot be detected with the naked eye.

Knowing that you will have to sell Mr. Cecil W. Tweedy (the purchasing agent) on the idea, you will write him a report justifying the purchase and, of course, seeking his approval.

In order to build a convincing case, you conducted a brief observation study of your typists at work. After a total of three hours of uninterrupted watching, you found that the average typist makes about nine errors per hour. Total lost time for erasures and retyping is about three minutes per hour (20 seconds per error). The magic correcting tape would make each correction easily in five seconds. You believe the time saved will soon pay for the added cost, considering the fact that the typists now average $5.20 per hour in salary.

So your task now is to look over the facts you have assembled, organize them logically, and present them in a report which will convince Mr. Tweedy that this purchase is justified.

6. Recommending dress and grooming regulations. Move into the role of director of employee relations for City National Bank and write a memorandum on dress and grooming regulations for all employees (male or female, or both, as your instructor directs). At last week's executive committee meeting the discussion centered on the inappropriate attire and grooming of too many of the employees. The general feeling was that the Bank's image is suffering.

The meeting concluded with President Lorraine Wukash directing you to prepare appropriate dress and grooming regulations. "Be careful not to make us appear to be prudes," she warned you. "But give us something that will protect the image of City Bank. Send your recommendations to me first. I'll send them to the employees over my signature."

Now you must use your best judgment in preparing these regulations. Be careful to cover all important matters. And make the regulations so clear that all will understand. Write them in a memorandum report addressed to President Wukash.

7. Writing the results of an evaluation study of a department head. You are personnel director of Conway Industries, Inc., and your office has just completed a performance evaluation of all department heads. These evaluations were made using a nine-statement questionnaire, which was distributed to all subordinates of each department head. The subordinates were instructed to mark on a scale of 0–100 the position his or her department head would place relative to the statement.

Now you have tabulated all the data and have the results for each department head. For purposes of comparison, you also have the averages of all department heads at Conway. Your next step is to present this information to each department head, pointing out his or her strengths and weaknesses. You will present this review in a memorandum report. The first department head to be reported is Eilene Abernathy. (Table 4)

8. Selecting the best outlet for Cerdan's Cravats. Assume the role of special assistant to Mr. Julian P. Pitts, sales manager for Cerdan's Cravats, Inc. Your present assignment is to investigate two retail outlets in Metroville, and to recommend to Mr. Pitts the one you think should be awarded the Cerdan dealership for the city. Each of the two stores has indicated an interest in handling Cerdan's quality products, but the Cerdan dealership policy forbids more than one outlet in a city the size of Metroville (60,000 population).

For the past two days you have been in Metroville, where you very

Table 4
Subordinates' Evaluations of Eilene Abernathy

Statement	Rating for Eilene Abernathy*	Average Ratings for All Department Heads*
1. The quality of human relationships, such as being fair, objective, honest	59	71
2. Quality of leadership	52	54
3. Quality of communication in both oral and written forms and the willingness to be communicative	55	58
4. Quality of support of employee development	66	71
5. The way in which the budget is planned and administered in regard to both equity and efficiency	41	55
6. The way in which the administrative unit is represented to higher administration	92	87
7. The efficiency of operation of the administrative offices	67	80
8. The extent to which this administrator keeps abreast of matters within the department	58	78
9. Your personal estimate of the confidence which your colleagues have in this administrator	56	54

* Scale of 0 to 100.

carefully inspected the two stores involved. As you conducted your investigation, you kept foremost in mind that Cerdan's enviable sales record and its reputation as a tie for style-conscious men are attributed to careful selection of outlets. Cerdan's customers are men of some means, usually coming from the upper middle- and high-income groups. So, traditionally, Cerdan has selected outlets catering to these groups.

Exclusiveness of customers, however, is not your only consideration. Certainly, you are seeking an outlet that can move Cerdan's Cravats in volume; and you want an outlet that gives the kind of service for which Cerdan dealers are noted. You will also want to consider a number of other factors—things like store location, growth potential, and physical plant. Now you are ready to begin your analysis of the facts. The facts, in the garbled form in which you noted them, look like this:

Metroville Man's Shop

A small, exclusive shop. Sells only quality lines of men's and boys' clothing. Stocks two other brands of ties—Pennington (middle to high quality), and the popular High Fashion (middle quality). Is willing to drop the Pennington brand if given Cerdan dealership. Store is owned by its founder, Cornelius W. Hodge, who appears to be in mid-60s. Mr. Hodge is very personable and gregarious—

likes to wait on customers personally. Stresses service and quality. Two other salespeople, both in their 20s. Selling atmosphere is leisurely—no pressure. Customers appear to be mostly mature, conservative, and successful business executives and professionals. Only high-quality merchandise sold. Annual sales approximately $550,000. Advertises weekly (usually in Sunday edition of local daily)—average a quarter page per week. No TV or radio. Ads are dignified and stress quality and style. Sales floor is small (40 x 75 feet) and old, but clean and well-maintained. Store located at heart of downtown. Downtown merchants have suffered from development of suburban shopping centers; but this store has prospered, probably because of presence of business executives and professionals in area. Store opened 37 years ago. Building has attractive, modern front. The fixtures are old but well kept. Mahogany-paneled walls give dignified but dreary appearance. Stock is neatly arranged, but store has crowded appearance.

Clifton's Haberdashery

A new men's store located in the West End Shopping Center, the new shopping mall. Floor space about 45 x 130 feet. Modern design—bright and attractive interior. Neat arrangement of merchandise. Spacious. Store owned by Hansel Sylvester—young (mid-30s) and aggressive. Sales force consists of three full-time and one part-time salespeople. Sales tactics involve some pressure; but service also stressed. Merchandise ranges from top quality to low-middle. Four brands of ties now carried:Dapper Dan (low-middle), Paree (middle), King's Crown (middle), and Bayman (middle-high). Not willing to drop any of these brands if Cerdan dealership awarded. Store sales about $1 million annually. It caters heavily to young business executives and college students. Emphasizes young (mod) styles, but also carries some conservative clothing. Advertises heavily—total of 1¼ pages per week—usually ¼ page on Thursdays and full page on Sundays. Some radio spot ads. Ads are smart, smooth, appealing. Stress style and price.

You will write up the analysis and your recommendation in the company memorandum form Mr. Pitts will expect. Because Pitts is a man who likes his answers fast, you plan to present your recommendation right off. And because he is the thorough man that he is, you plan to follow your recommendation with a logical analysis of the facts which will support your decision.

9. Justifying the purchase of a riding mower. As manager of the operation and maintenance department at the Macon Tire & Rubber Company, you recently purchased a riding lawn mower for the department. Because Company policy requires that all expenditures over $250 be justified in writing, you must write a justification report to Mr. Benjamin Cox, director of purchasing. Mr. Cox will then keep the report on file for the auditors or for whomever may wish to see it.

Here are the facts around which you will build your case. Previously, you had been using two self-propelled, walking-type mowers, 24-inch cut. They cost $345 new, have a three-year life and a trade-in value of $50. The mowers were used about 120 hours each year. The two operators received $4.10 per hour for this work. Average annual repair cost for each mower is $68.

The riding mower, which has a life of about six years, was purchased for $1,140. Because it has a 60-inch cut, it can more than do the work of the two other mowers. With it, one operator can take care of all the Company's lawn in about 100 hours each year. But one of the smaller mowers will be kept for close work. With such limited use, this one old mower should last another three years. Upkeep costs for this mower are apt to be $120 per year. The difference in operating costs between the mowers is negligible. Write up the report in Macon's standard memorandum form.

10. **Recommending a sales manager for Mason-Platt Pharmaceuticals, Inc.** As sales manager for the Western region of Mason-Platt Pharmaceuticals, Inc., you must recommend one of your better salespeople for the vacant position of district manager for the Valley City area. After carefully screening the records of your seven eligibles, you determine the top three. Now you have to evaluate them, rank them for the job, and pass on your recommendation to Naomi Guerra, the marketing vice president for Mason-Platt. You know the three top candidates fairly well. All three are personable, ambitious people. Judging from impressions you have of them, there is not much to choose between them. So you will make your recommendation on the basis of the factual information you have assembled from their personal records (see summary below). You will write up your analysis and recommendations in the standard memorandum form used for all Mason-Platt intercompany reports. And you will use the conclusion-first approach which you know Ms. Guerra prefers.

	George MacFarren	Mary Toops	Joe W. Rush
Age	33	28	35
Sales experience	3½ years, Glad Publishing Co.; 4 years, Mason-Platt	6 years, Mason-Platt	4 years, Central Insurance; 5 years, Lund Pharmaceutical; 4 years, Mason-Platt
Education	High School diploma; City Community College, Associate of Arts in general business	B.B.A. degree, Northern State University, major in marketing	B.S. degree, Steward University, major in psychology
Record with Mason-Platt (percent of sales quota)	1st yr., no quota 2d yr., 117 3d yr., 106 4th yr., 121	1st yr., no quota 2d yr., 105 3d yr., 98 4th yr., 121 5th yr., 107 6th yr., 137	1st yr., no quota 2d yr., 137 3d yr., 141 4th yr., 140
Score on Management Potential Test (60 = passing, 70 = above average, 80+ = outstanding)	81	88	77

11. **Writing a personnel action report on an erring subordinate.** You don't like to do such things, but you must report one of your subordinates for general inefficiency and neglect of duty. In fact, you conclude that you must recommend discharge of the fellow.

As supervisor of Department 7 (the office supply department of the Boulder Insurance Company), you have been putting up with the antics of Wingate P. Throckmorton III for nearly all of the seven months he has been with your company. The two quarterly evaluation reports on Throckmorton showed that his work was below standard from the start. He received "inferior" ratings both times. These were not your judgments, but those of Throckmorton's immediate superior, Martha Kay Bennett. Perhaps Throckmorton has the ability (he made a fair score on the company's aptitude test), but he just has not produced. He has made numerous costly errors in his assignment of writing purchase orders (you may use your imagination to bring in these details); and he resents, to the point of belligerence, any criticism of his errors.

During the past three months he has been absent from work 13 days. Only one of these absences was excusable. Twice he reported to work intoxicated and had to be sent home. On one of these occasions (it happened just yesterday) he had to be forcibly ejected. This last act was the final straw. Although he reported to work today all apologetic and promising to do better, you have no more hope for him. He made similar promises the last time you had him in your office for frank discussions of his problems.

Now you will write a personnel action report recommending that Throckmorton be discharged. You will use the Company's memorandum form and will address your report to Eleanor A. Gandy, director of personnel. Standard practice in the Company is to write such reports with the conclusion first and then to justify the conclusion with facts and analyses.

12. Investigating a personnel problem in Department 77. Today's assignment in your role as special assistant to Mildred Kammer, director of employment relations, Southwestern Aircraft, Inc., takes you to Department 77. Your objective is to investigate charges brought to you by Tim Cory, the union steward representing the workers of this department. According to Cory, union members in Department 77 have been discriminated against in the awarding of overtime work. Nonunion workers have been getting the lion's share of overtime.

Upon arriving at the department, you discuss the matter with Stanley Krause. Krause's version of the story goes like this. Of the eight workers in the department, five are members of the union and three are not. The three nonunion workers have had more overtime than the others; but they deserve it. Krause claims that he gave overtime on the basis of seniority and productivity—nothing else. This policy, he points out, is permitted in the contract with the union. If the nonunion employees got more of the overtime, it is because they have seniority and are better workers.

After talking to Krause you go to the files containing the department's records. Here you find data that should prove or disprove Krause's claim, and in fact, should point to the solution to the whole problem. After an hour or more of poring over these records covering the past six months, your summary notes look like this:

Employee and Union Status*	Hours of Overtime Work	Years Employed	Productivity (Average Daily Units Performed)	Percent Rejection (not Meeting Inspection)
George Graves (U)...........	0	14	30	0.08
W. Wilson Davis (U)	0	1	21	0.09
Kermit Crowley (U)..........	10	3	32	0.07
Walter H. Quals (U)	60	8	26	0.01
Hugo Detresanti (U)	60	7	30	0.03
Ralph A. Andrews (NU)	40	35	26	0.02
Will O. Rundell (NU)........	70	17	35	0.03
Thomas A. Baines (NU)	90	12	43	0.03

* U—union, NU—nonunion.

Now your task is to analyze these data and to present your findings to Ms. Kammer in the form of the standard memorandum report used by the company. In addition to analyzing the data, you will recommend a course of action on the problem.

13. Which commercial is better for EZ-Clean? The research department of the Alman-Beaty Advertising Agency has completed an experiment with two 60-second TV commercials for EZ-Clean, a liquid window cleaner. Not being able to decide between two approaches for promoting the product, the agency decided to try out each commercial in a different test city. Petro-ville and River City were selected for the test. After the commercials were run, a representative sample of viewers was interviewed by telephone in an attempt to determine the effectiveness of the advertisements.

One of the commercials (Commercial A) is a humorous cartoon strip depicting the use of the product by popular comic-strip characters. It depicts one character, an animated mouse, gleefully cleaning a large plate of glass with an "old-fashioned" glass cleaner. Then the mouse runs into the next room, gets the attention of his perpetual adversary, a cat, and gets the cat to chase him. His plan to get the cat to run into the plate glass fails when the cat sees dirt on the glass. The cat lectures to the mouse on the virtues of EZ-Clean and then walks away. While walking out of the room, however, the cat runs into a glass door, knocking himself out. The commercial ends with the mouse standing by the door, holding a can of EZ-Clean, and winking at the TV viewers.

The second commercial (Commercial B) is a conventional family scene. It shows a husband and wife sitting in their parlor and looking out of the "largest picture window in town." Their view is limited, however, for the window is dirty. They try everything—ammonia, soapy water, other products; but nothing does the job until they try EZ-Clean. The final scene shows the couple watching a parade as it passes by their clean window.

The results of the test are now in (see Tables 5 and 6) and it is your job to study them and to report on your analyses and conclusions to the Agency. Your conclusions will be based on which ad will be likely to sell

Table 5

Commercial A, Recall of Viewers 24 Hours Later; Test Sample of 1,000 Female Viewers, Petroville

	Percent
Remembered commercial 24 hours after viewing	88.3
Product story recall	72.3
Video (recall of specific incidents)	
Mouse cleaning window with "old-fashioned" cleaner	68.5
Cat detecting glass	70.0
Cat lecturing to mouse about EZ-Clean	64.3
Mouse gleefully viewing scene	60.2
Cat running into glass door	71.3
Mouse holding can of EZ-Clean	36.4
Audio (recall of specific appeals)	
Simple/easy to use	8.3
Not messy	2.3
Gets glass clean, cleaner	11.7
Cleans well/best cleaner	3.2
Glass stays clean, clear longer	6.3
Leaves no film/leaves glass clean, clear	16.1
Glass seems to disappear	2.3

Table 6

Commercial B, Recall of Viewers 24 Hours Later; Test Sample of 1,000 Female Viewers, River City

	Percent
Remembered commercial 24 hours after viewing	68.4
Product story recall	56.4
Video (recall of specific incidents)	
Demonstration: Saw window being cleaned/couple man and woman clean window	45.1
Window cleaned with EZ-Clean	21.1
Window cleaned with old-fashioned cleaners, ammonia, soap and water, vinegar	18.8
Saw couple in living room/couldn't see out of dirty windows	21.8
Saw outdoor scene, parade passing by after cleaning window	12.0
Different sizes of EZ-Clean	5.3
Spray can	3.8
Audio (recall of specific appeals)	
Simple/easy to use	36.8
Not messy	7.5
Gets glass clean, cleaner	28.6
Cleans well/best cleaner	11.3
Glass stays clean, clear longer	10.5
Leaves no film/leaves glass clean, clear	9.8
Glass seems to disappear	5.3

more EZ-Clean. And, of course, you will present your work in good report form.

14. **Determining the advertising effectiveness of a cooking school.** Until recently the manufacturers of Mrs. Walker's Shortening have depended almost totally on newspaper and magazine advertising to sell their product.

Six months ago, however, the Company's management decided to try a new form of advertising—a televised cooking school.

Before going into this form of advertising on a big scale, the Company management decided to experiment with the plan. Thus, they designed a before-after with control group experiment, using Millville (65,000 population) as the test city and Harrisburg (61,000 population) as the control city. In each city they selected 20 comparable stores for the study.

Sales of Mrs. Walker's Shortening were recorded for all stores for one week. Then the cooking school was conducted over the Millville television station. Directed by a nationally prominent cooking authority, the school was held during a daytime hour that is popular for consumers' viewing. Although the school was primarily educational, Mrs. Walker's Shortening was subtly suggested in the instructions and strongly recommended in the commercials which were included in the 30-minute program. Weekly results of sales were kept for all of the stores in the experiment during and immediately after the program. Then, to determine long-run effects, additional records were collected 12 weeks and 24 weeks later. This information (Table 7) holds the key to the question of whether television cooking schools are effective means of advertising Mrs. Walker's Shortening.

As director of research for Mrs. Walker's Products, Inc., you have the task of analyzing the results of the experiment and of reporting your conclusions to management. Write your report in memorandum form, using the company's standard memorandum stationery. Address your report to President George E. Walker.

15. Recommending a secretary to Ms. Sicili. As an interviewer in the personnel department of the Mashack-Karner Manufacturing Company, write a memorandum report to Ms. Beatrice Sicili, supervisor, production planning department.

Some days ago Ms. Sicili requested that you find her an experienced secretary as a replacement for one who is resigning. Today, after carefully screening application blanks, test scores, and your own interview notes of the nine applicants for the job, you select what appear to be the top three people. Now, following standard Company policy, you must summarize your

Table 7
Records of Sales for Test and Control City Stores before, during, and after the Experiment

	Pounds Sold in Test City Stores	Pounds Sold in Control City Stores
January 3–9, before school	2,371	2,031
January 10–16, week of school	2,893	2,076
January 17–23, week after school	2,964	2,047
January 24–30, 2d week after school	2,981	2,088
April 4–10, 12th week after school	2,521	2,107
June 27–July 3, 24th week after school	2,503	2,142

analysis on a standard memorandum (To, From, Subject form). This report will rank the three people and will concisely evaluate their suitability for the job in question. Ms. Sicili, however, will make the final decision. As is customary in your Company, the report will be written in the direct order and in personal style.

The following are the facts which will form the basis of your evaluation. If you think it is necessary, you may supplement this information with reasonable imagination so long as you do not alter the general picture presented.

Mary Beth Jenkins: Age 41; husband disabled; children 16, 11, and 9; five years as secretary with Butler Realty, lost job when company closed business, excellent references from superiors; neat and fairly attractive; high school and business college graduate; test scores: typing—84 words per minute; shorthand speed—121 words per minute; secretarial aptitude—95 (excellent); good health.

Joe W. Whatley: Age 24; single; high school diploma; Associate of Arts degree from community college, secretarial studies; typing speed—71 words per minute; shorthand speed—108 words per minute; secretarial aptitude test—85 (good); three years secretarial experience with Bentley Electric—excellent references. Neat and personable.

Marie Shaver: Age 21; married, no children; high school, three years' college (major in secretarial studies); no working experience; typing speed—94 words per minute; shorthand speed—133 words per minute; secretarial aptitude test—94 (excellent); very attractive and personable.

16. The coffee break problem at Bruin, Inc. As office manager of Bruin, Inc., you are disturbed over the fact that your 85 office workers are taking long rest periods at 10:00 A.M. and 2:30 P.M. You feel that since Bruin is paying its office workers an average of $280 a week, the company is losing money.

A bit of discreet checking revealed to you that 41 of the 50 workers you observed left the office for their rest period. You observed also that these 41 workers average breaks of 27 minutes. Those taking their breaks within the office area all were back within the 15 minutes allotted. The cause of the long breaks is clear to you. Those going outside the office must wait for a very crowded elevator on their way to the downstairs coffee shop.

An office manager friend of yours recently circumvented a similar problem by installing a vending machine in his office. He told you that the machine he installed has the following characteristics:

1. It costs $1,260, installed, and includes a unit for dispensing instant mixes and a unit for dispensing very hot and very cold water. Mixes dispensed include instant coffee (with a packet of sugar and a packet of instant cream), instant cocoa, and instant chicken or beef bouillon.
2. The two-unit arrangement occupies 20 square feet of floor space.
3. The machines support themselves insofar as cost is concerned, and they provide a small profit which can be distributed to such funds as the Employee Annual Picnic Fund.

The machines are sold by the Bollon Company, which will supply the necessary coffee, cocoa, and bouillon mixes. The Bollon Company will service the machines as necessary.

On the basis of your personal observation and what your friend told you, you are now prepared to write a memorandum report of your findings to the vice president, administration. You want to write your report in good form, and you will want to cover such essentials as estimated money and work-hours saved as possible justification for installing a vending machine.

17. Should Fidelity use a janitorial service? As assistant to the president of Fidelity Insurance Company, you have been asked to look into the possibility of using a janitorial service instead of the two full-time janitors employed by the Company. In recent years the firm has had much difficulty keeping janitors. In fact, five people have filled the two $175-a-week positions within the past two years, the longest lasting ten months. The two janitors currently employed have been with the Company for only three and five weeks, respectively.

As you gather the facts, you learn that, in addition to the two salaries, the Company must pay about $27 a week for janitorial supplies. Then, of course, there are the workers' fringe benefits, which amount to an extra 20 percent. And once each year for major housecleaning extra help costing about $1,600 has to be hired. The Perkins Janitorial Service has offered to do all of the Company's work for $475 per week. Your job is to analyze all of the facts involved and to arrive at a decision. You will give the cost factors heavy weight, but you must remember that there are other less tangible reasons which should be considered. Write up your analysis and recommendation in a standard memorandum report addressed to President Joseph E. Ward.

18. Who should be Raeder Manufacturing Company's new office manager? As director of personnel for the home office of the Raeder Manufacturing Company, you must recommend someone to serve as office manager. Following Company procedure you narrow your selection to the three leading contenders. Next you must evaluate them, determine which one should have the job, and submit your decision with your reasons to Mr. Preston P. Puffer, vice-president in charge of administration.

You know the top three candidates very well. They are all section heads, and they are all competent. Thus the decision will be a close one. Because you will want to keep personalities out of your analysis, you will make your recommendations largely on the basis of factual information you have assembled from the personnel records (see summary below). You will write up your analysis and recommendations in the standard memorandum form used for all Raeder intercompany reports, and you will use the conclusion-first approach, which you know Mr. Puffer prefers.

Malvina Krenek
Age: 49.
Education: high school graduate, one-year business college course (certificate).
Experience: 8 years as bookkeeper with Parr Plumbing Company; 3 years of personnel records work with Kable Manufacturing Company; 20 years with

Raeder in various general office assignments, last 7 as head of personnel records section.

Company ratings*: satisfactory, seven years; very satisfactory, nine years; excellent, four years.

Comments from rating sheets: a hard worker, loyal, somewhat limited in ability to grasp problems quickly, works well under pressure, overemphasizes details.

Test scores†: administrative potential, 70; office procedure, 89.

Stanley Vitek

Age: 30.

Education: B.B.A. from State University, major in personnel management, B+ average.

Experience: two years as pilot in U.S. Air Force; two years of general personnel work with McKee Aircraft, Inc.; five years at Raeder in various general office assignments, last two as head of customer correspondence section.

Company ratings*: very satisfactory, two years; excellent, three years.

Comments from rating sheets: a very bright young man, aggressive, thorough and tireless in his work, will not be content with mediocre assignment, good leadership qualities.

Test scores†: administrative potential, 92; office procedure, 84.

William A. Heine

Age: 39.

Education: high school diploma (completed 12 years ago after 3 years of night school); has been attending evening college for past 7 years, 42 semester hours passed, C+ average, major in general business.

Experience: 9 years in U.S. Army as clerk typist and administrative clerk; 12 years with Raeder in various general office assignments, last 7 as head of sales records.

Company ratings*: very satisfactory, 10 years; excellent, 2 years.

Comments from rating sheets: a very hard worker, a perfectionist, does not delegate work as much as he should, ambitious, works his subordinates hard.

Test scores†: administrative potential, 77; office procedure, 80.

* Company ratings are made annually on each employee by his or her supervisor. Classifications used are as follows: excellent, very satisfactory, satisfactory, barely satisfactory, unsatisfactory.

† Scale for company tests is as follows:
   below 60, below average
   60–69, average
   70–79, above average
   80–89, well above average
   90–100, exceptional

Problems of medium length

19. Recommending on whether to meet on your campus. As education director, International Future Business Leaders, your current assignment is to investigate the site for next year's meeting. Every summer this association of university business students meets on a college campus. The meetings are held on campuses between semesters. Typically, from 80–100 members attend the one-week program. They meet in classroom buildings, union facilities, and such. Usually, they stay in vacant dormitories and eat in campus facilities, although sometimes they have used off-campus lodging and eating facilities.

For next year the organization directors are considering meeting on your campus. They have asked you to gather the pertinent facts for them. Of primary importance are such vital matters as the availability and costs of meeting rooms, dormitory rooms, and meals. The group needs one large meeting room (capacity of 100) and four small rooms (25 capacity). Fifty dormitory rooms will be adequate (two to a room). Men and women will be about equally represented. Meals usually are bought individually, but a weekly rate would be considered.

In addition to these basic needs, organization members are interested in information on after-hours activities. Therefore, you will report on the recreational, sightseeing, and cultural attractions of the area. Of course, you will emphasize the attractions that are likely to interest college people.

After you have gathered the information, you will organize it and present it in appropriate report form. Because the directors must make a decision, you will help them by making your recommendation. Try hard to be objective.

20. **Determining consumer attitudes toward fraudulent practices.** As a research specialist in the Public Relations Office of Central Department Stores, your job is to investigate problems which affect this major department store chain's relations with its customers. Your specific problem of the moment is that of fraudulent behavior of customers (shoplifting, altering price tags, returning worn clothing, and such).

Central management is well aware of the fact that some of its customers deal fraudulently with company stores. Ideas of how to deal with this problem have been numerous, but all involve possible negative results. In fact, it could be that some solutions would produce results worse than the fraud. Before Central management takes any action, it feels that it should know more about the attitudes of consumers toward fraud and how it should be combated. So management has asked you to gather and analyze this information.

You begin the task by surveying 200 Central customers (you may fill in the details of your research procedure). To each of the 200 you presented 15 fraud situations. Then you asked the interviewees for their personal viewpoints on each situation. You asked also for an indication of how their friends would react in each situation—a subtle way of learning the recipients' true feelings on a matter involving morality. The information in Tables 8–10 summarize your findings.

Even though the work was extensive, the information obtained was not. You will present your findings in a short report. Address it to Ms. Madelaine Childs, Director of Public Relations. In general, your report will present and interpret the data you collected. Your goal is to guide management in forming policies regarding fraudulent practices.

21. **Evaluating effects of coupon deals on dairy products sales.** Assume that you are a trainee in the marketing department of Green Valley Dairies,

Table 8
Personal Attitudes of Consumers toward Fraudulent Practices (Percent)

Fraudulent Practice	Attitude			
	Very Wrong	Not Serious	Under-standable	Not Wrong
Shoplifting	97.0	0.3	2.7	0.0
Returning worn clothing	93.7	2.3	3.3	0.7
Changing or switching price tag	96.7	1.3	2.0	0.0
Writing bad checks	82.3	15.3	2.4	0.0
Eating food in store (without paying)	77.7	18.3	4.0	0.0
Ignoring change error at checkout	76.0	16.7	7.3	0.0
Dishonest use of coupons	64.3	27.7	2.7	5.3
Making invalid warranty claim	53.0	35.3	10.0	1.7
Ignoring undercharge	49.3	37.7	8.7	4.3
Ignoring billing error	52.3	35.3	8.7	3.7

Table 9
Percent of Customers Whose Friends Would Engage in Fraudulent Practices when Opportunity Occurs

Fraudulent Practice	Most of Time	Occasionally	Rarely	Never
Shoplifting	10.3	2.3	22.0	65.4
Returning worn clothing	21.0	2.0	4.3	72.7
Changing or switching price tag	12.7	3.7	22.3	67.3
Writing bad checks	5.3	12.0	26.7	56.0
Eating food in store (without paying)	25.7	5.0	37.0	32.3
Ignoring change error at checkout	33.0	17.3	30.7	19.0
Dishonest use of coupons	8.0	21.0	35.3	35.7
Making invalid warranty claim	24.7	36.3	22.3	16.7
Ignoring undercharge	39.3	37.0	15.7	8.0
Ignoring billing error	21.0	20.7	31.3	27.0

Inc. For years this national dairy operation has used with cooperating grocers a coupon plan to promote its products. Specifically, this plan is to include coupons in newspaper advertisements of cooperating grocers. The coupons entitle purchasers to discounts on nine categories of Green Valley products. Green Valley covers the discount costs so the grocers do not lose; but it hopes that the campaign will increase sales, thereby overcoming these costs.

Green Valley management feel the plan has been successful, but it has no hard facts. So it asks your department to come up with some. Your boss, Susan Kron, devised the following research plan (you may add details to this general description).

First, a panel of 500 households was selected. Each was requested to

Table 10

Customers' Viewpoints of Appropriate Actions for Certain Fraudulent Practices

	Action Considered Most Appropriate (Percent of Customers)			
Fraudulent practice	Do Nothing	Take Preventive Action	Give Warning	Take Drastic Action
Shoplifting	1.3	.3	58.7	39.7*
Returning worn clothing . . .	3.0	7.7	11.0	78.3†
Changing or switching price tag	.7	3.7	70.3	25.3*
Writing bad checks	1.0	7.3	59.3	32.3*
Eating food in store (without paying)	4.7	32.3	63.7	.3
Ignoring change error at checkout	1.7	37.0	60.3	1.0*
Dishonest use of coupons . .	2.7‡	7.0	27.0	63.3†
Making invalid warranty claim	3.0‡	14.3	28.7	54.0*
Ignoring undercharge	5.7	76.3	18.0	.0
Ignoring billing error	5.0	31.3	63.7	.0

* Notify authorities.
† Refuse.
‡ Accept coupon or claim.

keep a diary of dairy product purchases. Dairy records were submitted to Green Valley covering three periods: (1) the two-week period ending one month before the discount period, (2) the two-week period in which the discount was offered, and (3) the two-week period beginning one month after the discount period. This plan, Ms. Kron reasoned, should give some of the effects of the offer—short run and long run.

Discount offers were made for each of the nine categories of dairy products over a period of two years (one category at a time). You have the results all neatly arrayed in tables (see Tables 11 and 12). Now your task is to interpret these findings for management. Especially you want to emphasize the long-run effects of the discount coupons by type of dairy product. And if there are any, you'll want to point out any differences in the effects of discount deals on demographic groups.

Of course, you will present your findings, analyses, and conclusions in appropriate report form—one befitting the top executives who will read it.

22. Evaluating a flexible work-hour plan. Six months ago, Hill Manufacturing Company began experimenting with a flexible work-hour plan. Specifically, the Company selected 298 workers from a representative cross section of functions and placed them on flexible work schedules. That is, the workers could come and go as they wished. They are required only to work their usual number of hours per week.

The general feeling at Hill is that the plan is working quite well. At least, this is the information that feeds back to management. But management

Table 11

Average Quantities of Dairy Products Purchased by Households for Two-Week Periods before, during, and after Coupon Promotion

Product Group	Before	During	After
Fluid milk (half gallons)	5.9	7.6	5.9
Cottage cheese (pounds)	1.3	3.7	1.7
Yogurt (half pints)	1.7	5.8	2.2
Ice cream (gallons)	.7	1.5	.9
Ice milk (gallons)	.4	1.2	.6
Process cheese (pounds)	.7	2.9	.7
Natural cheese (pounds)	.7	2.7	1.1
Butter (pounds)	1.2	2.8	1.2
Cream products (pints)	1.2	1.9	1.2

Table 12

Total Effects of Coupon Discount Promotion on Sales of Fluid Milk, by Demographic Characteristic (Percentage Change from before Period)

Demographic Characteristic	During	After
Education		
Grade school	+58	+27
High school	+28	+8
College	+20	−1
Occupation		
Labor and crafts	+41	+5
Professional and clerical	+14	−7
Farmer	+41	−9
Retired and unemployed	+69	+17
Race		
White	+27	−3
Nonwhite	+68	+14
Employment status		
Wife employed	+54	+7
Wife unemployed	+6	0
City size		
Less than 2,500	+28	−1
2,500–49,999	+26	−2
50,000–499,999	+28	+9
500,000–999,999	+47	+17
1,000,000 and over	+33	+13
Income of household		
$25,000 and over	+43	+4
$15,000–$24,999	+17	+2
$10,000–$14,999	+21	+1
$5,000–$9,999	+8	+3
Under $5,000	+49	0

wants some more concrete information on the matter. As one of two management trainees in Hill's employee relations department, you were given a part of the assignment. The other trainee, Marilyn Matson, was given a second part. Marilyn's task is to look at the concrete evidence—at information concerning such items as turnover, productivity, and absenteeism. Your assignment is to look at the attitudinal side—at what the workers think about the plan.

Your first step was to interview the 298 workers involved to get each's reaction. Then you interviewed 100 managers (all closely involved with the 298 workers) to get their reactions. Of course, you got from each group the information you felt it could give, although there was some duplication. Your findings are summarized in Tables 13 and 14.

Now you are ready to present your findings. You will analyze the data as well as reach a general conclusion concerning the effectiveness of the plan as revealed by your findings. Even though the report will be rather short, it will be important to Hill Manufacturing. So you will prepare it in short report form (title page plus text). And you will prepare some graphics to emphasize the highlights. Submit the report to Hudson A. Hill, President.

23. Reporting on international franchise operations. In your job as a research associate for Caldwell Research, Inc., you have been assigned

Table 13

Employees' Viewpoints Concerning Certain Measures of Flexible Working-Hours Plan (Percent)

Measure	Viewpoints		
	Increased	Unaffected	Decreased
Driving time	17	24	59
Pressures related to getting to work	6	20	74
Needs to leave work before quitting time	5	33	62
Leisure time	66	23	11
Morale	86	8	6
Attitudes toward company	67	24	9
Productivity	67	22	11
Need for supervision	27	27	46
Cooperation and coordination between departments	42	37	21
Cooperation and coordination between shifts	53	39	8
Abuses	37	33	30

Table 14

Managers' Viewpoints Concerning Certain Measures of Flexible Working-Hours Plan (Percent)

Measure	Viewpoints		
	Increased	Unaffected	Decreased
Employees' driving time	3	21	76
Sick-leave use	0	54	46
Productivity	45	50	5
Absenteeism	21	72	7
Supervisor-subordinate relations	11	70	19
Employee leisure time	81	18	1
Employee morale	57	40	3

the task of getting information for the Continental Franchise Association. Officers of this organization of Canadian and U.S. franchise owners want information on the expansion of Association members into foreign markets and the factors and problems involved in such expansion.

You gather the data for this study by sending questionnaires to the 221 member firms. Sixty-three responded (representing 46,280 franchise units).

The questionnaire was designed to get six areas of information. First you sought to classify the firms by type of franchise (automotive, fast-food, soft drink, and such). Second, you asked for information on the firms' expansion plans—that is, how many and what ownership forms of new units do they plan to open in the next three years. Third, you asked for reasons why some of the firms had no plans for international expansion. Fourth, from those firms with expansion plans, you sought to determine why they elected to get into foreign markets. Fifth, you tried to determine the major

Table 15

Classification by Respondents' Firms by Type of Franchise System

	Respondents	
Type of Franchise System	Number	Percent
Automotive services	2	3.2
Business services	8	12.7
Car rentals	1	1.6
Recreation services	3	4.8
Fast foods	22	34.9
Retailing (food)	3	4.8
Hotels/motels	6	9.5
Soft drinks	—	—
Other	18	28.5
Total respondents	63	100.0

Table 16

Number of Units Planned in Next Three Years (by Location and Ownership Form)

	Ownership Form					Total	
Location	Franchisee-Owned (No.)	Master or Area (No.)	Company-Owned (No.)	Joint Venture Franchisee/ Majority (No.)	Joint Venture Franchisee/ Minority (No.)	Number	Percent
In United States and Canada	12,576	129	713	24	32	13,474	83.17
In foreign countries	1,932	616	110	24	45	2,727	16.83
Total number	14,508	745	823	48	77	16,201	
Total percent	89.55	4.60	5.08	0.30	0.47		100.0

problems encountered by firms engaged in foreign franchise operations, current and planned. And sixth, you sought to learn where were the foreign franchise operations, current and planned.

The information you have gathered is exhaustive. All of it will go in a long, analytical report, which you will write later. However, because the board wants a preview of findings right away, you will present only the highlights in a summary report. And you will get the report to the board in time for their quarterly meeting next Monday.

For this report you have assembled the key information in Tables 15 through 20. Now you must analyze this information and organize it for presentation. Address the report to the Board of Directors, Wilma Neeley, Chairperson. Give the report the formal preparatory pages its length and formality justify.

24. Reporting on the status of women in Granite's sales force. Seven years ago the executives of Granite, Inc., a large marketer of industrial goods, decided to bring women into its sales force "as quickly and expeditiously as possible." Now they want a progress report. In general, management

Table 17
Reasons for No Franchises at Present in Foreign Countries

	Respondents	
Reason	**Number**	**Percent**
1. Government or legal restrictions......................	14	32.6
2. Insufficient foreign demand for products (goods and/or services)	8	18.6
3. Lack of market information	16	37.2
4. Trademark and/or copyright obstacles	2	4.7
5. Products not adapted to foreign consumers............	3	7.0
6. Excessive geographic distance	20	46.5
7. Other	13	30.2
Total respondents	43*	—

* Multiple answers given by some.

Table 18
Reasons for Involvement in Franchise Activities in Foreign Countries

	Respondents	
Major Problem	**Number**	**Percent**
1. Increase sales and profits	21	77.8
2. Returns on investment usually greater than that from domestic operations	2	7.4
3. Saturated U.S. market for firm's products	1	3.7
4. Market expansion..................................	22	81.5
5. Acquisition	1	3.7
6. Desire to be known as an international firm	14	51.9
7. Other	3	11.1
Total respondents	27*	—

* Multiple answers given by some.

Table 19
*Major Problems Encountered in Establishing Franchises in Foreign
Countries (for Firms Currently Engaged in Foreign Franchise Activities)*

	Respondents	
Reason	**Number**	**Percent**
1. Host government regulations	17	68.0
2. Patent, trademark, and/or copyright protection	7	28.0
3. Inadequate local financing	4	16.0
4. Control of franchisees	8	32.0
5. Recruitment of franchisees	5	20.0
6. Adaption of products to local markets	2	8.0
7. Adaption of franchise package to local markets	4	16.0
8. High import duties and taxes	9	36.0
9. Location problems	3	12.0
10. Training of foreign franchisee personnel	6	24.0
11. Logistics problems	7	28.0
12. Language and cultural barriers	9	36.0
13. Monetary uncertainties and royalty retribution to franchisor	11	44.0
14. Other	3	12.0
Total respondents	25*	—

* Multiple answers given by some.

Table 20
Location of Franchise Units, Current and Planned

	Current	**Planned***
United States and Canada	44,894	14,461
England	481	668
Japan	663	578
West Germany	177	141
France	88	57
Italy	39	31
Remainder of continental Europe	61	88
Other	417	177
Total	46,820	16,201

* Next three years.

wants an overall picture of the status of women in the Granite sales force. More specifically, management wants the answers to such questions as how many women have been hired, what are their characteristics, and how successful they have been.

As administrative assistant to Marvin Stutts, vice president of sales, you have been assigned the chore of doing the reporting. You begin by going through personnel records for each of Granite's 13 sales regions. First, you gather comparative information on the number of men and women salespeople now and for the same time seven years ago (Table 21). Then, from the same source, you get comparative information on absenteeism and turnover (Table 22), sales experience (Table 23), and personal details (Table

Table 21

Number of Men and Women Employed in Sales, by Region, Current Year, and Seven Years ago

Sales region	Current Year		Seven Years Ago	
	Men	Women	Men	Women
A	14	3	11	0
B	19	1	16	0
C	77	12	70	2
D	43	5	39	2
E	92	24	87	1
F	37	10	33	2
G	23	3	19	0
H	51	7	48	1
I	28	3	27	0
J	49	6	43	2
K	35	3	33	1
L	59	17	50	1
M	67	5	61	0
Total	594	99	537	12

Table 22

Absenteeism and Turnover, by Sex (Preceding Year)

	Men	Women
Absenteeism (days):		
None	27%	14%
1–5	62	48
6–10	6	29
11–15	4	7
16+	1	2
	100%	100%
Turnover:		
Employees	11.5%	5.4%

Table 23

Years of Industrial Sales Experience (Percent of Total Male and Female)

Years of experience	Men	Women
0–5	13	37
6–10	26	26
11–15	24	17
16–20	19	19
21–25	11	1
Over 25	7	0

24). Next, you go to the sales records file for data on sales performance (Table 25).

In your judgment, information on customer impressions also is essential; so you conduct brief telephone interviews with 302 Granite customers. It appears that your findings (Table 26) give a clear measure of customer viewpoints toward women in selling. You conduct similar interviews among company sales executives.

Now, with all this information tabulated neatly before you, you are ready to begin work on the report. Because the report will be read by top management, you will give it the appropriate formal trappings (as specified by your instructor). Address it to Mr. Stutts.

25. Determining the meaning given to nonverbal behavior by interview participants. At last year's meeting of the Personnel Officers Association, controversy developed over how nonverbal behavior of job applicants

Table 24
Profile of Salespeople (Percent)

	Men	Women
Age:		
Under 25	11	27
26–35	34	54
36–50	40	19
Over 50	15	0
Marital status:		
Married	81	16
Divorced, widowed, separated	9	25
Single	10	59
Education (year completed, 12 = high school):		
12	8	0
13	13	0
14	19	16
15	12	12
16	48	69
Over 16	0	3

Table 25
Sales Performance of Men and Women Meeting or Exceeding Annual Quota (Percent)

Percent of Annual Quota Met	Men	Women
130 and over	9	2
120–129	7	9
110–119	18	23
100–110	47	51
90–99	9	11
80–89	8	4
70–79	1	0
Under 70	1	0

Table 26

Opinions of Sales Executives and Customers about Overall Performance
of Men and Women Salespeople (Percent)*

	Sales Executives	Customers† Served Only by Men	Customers† Served by One or More Women‡
Believe men perform better	23	3	9
Little or no difference	74	75	80
Believe women perform better	7	2	11
Believe men employees cause more problems	10		
Little or no difference	68		
Believe women employees cause more problems	22		

* 13 regional managers and 37 district managers, all men, all supervising one or more women.
† 99 percent men.
‡ Not necessarily women salespeople from Granite.

should be interpreted. Opinions varied widely on the topic. In fact, the controversy continued on into the meeting of the Board of Directors, which concluded the conference. Thus it was that the Board members voted to provide the necessary funds and authorized you, its executive director, to conduct a study on the subject.

Soon after the meeting you began the work. First, you designed a questionnaire covering ten statements concerning key attitudes toward nonverbal behavior. The design organized answers by degrees of respondent's agreement with the statements. Next, you mailed two copies of the questionnaire to each of 500 members randomly selected from the Association's mailing list of personnel officers (not the association's membership roster, although some on the list are members).[1]

Those receiving the questionnaires were instructed to complete and return one of the two copies and to give the other to a person whom they had interviewed and hired recently. This person also was instructed to complete and return the questionnaire. After receiving 400 usable responses (200 from interviewers and 200 from interviewees), you tabulated the findings. Although you are not convinced that it is meaningful, you organized the responses by sex. Finally, you arranged your findings in an orderly table (Table 27).

Now you are ready to begin the task of analyzing and organizing the findings for presentation in a report. The report will be rather formal; so you will give it appropriate prefatory sections. You probably will make good use of visual aids, because the information is quantitative. In time, probably the content of the report will be printed in monograph form and distributed

---

[1] Actually the data are from Jack D. Eure and Joan Baron, "Nonverbal Cues and the Perceptions of Intelligence in the Employment Interview," *Proceedings of the 1980 Southwest American Business Communication Association Meeting*, San Antonio, Texas.

Table 27
Attitudes toward Nonverbal Behavior in the Employment Interview (Percent)

Attitude Statement		Strongly Disagree		Disagree		No Opinion		Agree		Strongly Agree	
		E	S	E	S	E	S	E	S	E	S
1. A good indicator of intelligence is the length of time a person can hold eye contact during the interview.	M	29	18	50	48	21	14	0	20	0	0
	F	13	18	55	46	13	9	19	27	0	0
2. Applicants who lean forward during the interview are more assertive.	M	0	4	43	40	21	16	36	38	0	2
	F	0	0	75	14	6	5	19	73	0	9
3. Facial twitches are signs of insecurity.	M	7	4	50	30	29	40	14	20	0	6
	F	6	14	62	55	13	18	13	9	6	5
4. Repeated eyebrow movement indicates a short attention span.	M	14	10	58	64	14	14	14	12	0	0
	F	0	14	63	68	31	18	6	0	0	0
5. Frequent hand gestures indicate a high level of energy.	M	7	6	50	28	0	14	43	46	0	6
	F	0	0	38	14	6	14	43	77	13	0
6. Constant fidgeting by the applicant indicates a lack of self-confidence.	M	7	0	21	26	14	4	50	58	7	12
	F	0	0	37	27	6	5	44	55	13	14
7. Interviewees exhibiting fewer eye shifts are more likely to have greater credibility.	M	14	6	29	28	14	18	43	34	0	14
	F	0	9	37	23	13	23	37	46	13	0
8. Frequent smiling during the interview indicates a friendly personality.	M	7	0	22	10	7	14	50	62	14	14
	F	0	0	38	18	0	0	56	50	6	32
9. Applicants who nod their head during the interview are more attentive.	M	7	4	36	34	14	10	36	50	7	2
	F	0	0	31	14	25	18	44	59	0	9
10. A good indicator of character is the applicant's appearance.	M	0	2	28	12	0	6	36	50	36	30
	F	0	0	25	5	0	5	50	55	25	36

Note: M—male; F—female; E—employee; S—student.

to the membership. For the moment, however, you are submitting information to the board. So address the report to the Board of Directors, Ms. Elizabeth Kipper, Chairperson.

26. Interpreting survey results for Giant's advertising department. As assistant to the director, advertising department, Giant Soap and Glycerine, Inc., of Omaha, you are faced with the task of presenting and interpreting some survey statistics. The statistics were given to you by William A. Kennard, director, who had received them from the research department. Kennard's instructions to you were both brief and precise.

"Here are some figures Research handed me," he said. "They're a part of Research's most recent survey—the part they say we should be interested in. Look them over, digest them, and then tell me what they mean to us in advertising. Have it ready for me before our departmental meeting Friday. Better write it up for the record."

The data (Tables 28–31) are quite significant, for they tell what the consumers think of Giant. Giant, of course, is the company's leading product and ranks among the nation's leading detergents. The statistics tell a lot, too, about the image the buyers have of each of Giant's major competitors. It is your job now to present this information to Mr. Kennard in good orderly fashion pointing out those things which are significant from an advertising point of view.

Table 28

Percentages of Households Using Leading Brands of Detergents, by Use (Based on National Sample of 1,000)

Brand Name	For Dishes	For Fine Fabrics	For Laundry
White	220	312	92
Snow	131	94	—
Giant	112	56	251
Surf	83	40	73
Eze	76	—	64
Del	51	261	—
Kleen	—	—	132
Sun	—	—	121

Table 29

Major Reasons Given for Liking Six Leading Brands for Washing Dishes (Samples of 100 for Each Brand)

Reason for Liking	White	Snow	Giant	Surf	Eze	Del
Amount of suds	16	8	14	9	19	13
Superior cleaning	13	16	11	36	9	19
Mild on hands	21	2	19	9	0	34
Pleasant odor	0	1	15	0	6	0
Economical	3	0	21	0	0	0

Table 30
Major Reasons Given for Liking Five Leading Brands for Washing Fine Fabrics, Hand Wash (Samples of 100 for Each Brand)

Reason for Liking	White	Snow	Giant	Surf	Del
Right amount of suds	14	11	15	10	14
Superior cleaning	13	12	24	41	12
Mild on hands	62	29	19	11	52
Mild on clothes	51	24	23	14	50
Pleasant odor	3	1	15	0	0
Economical	4	0	22	0	0

Table 31
Major Reasons Given for Liking Six Leading Brands for Regular Laundry, Automatic Washer (Samples of 100 for Each Brand)

Reason for Liking	White	Giant	Surf	Eze	Kleen	Sun
Amount of suds	33	34	32	15	17	44
Superior cleaning	36	38	39	55	61	67
Mild on clothes	55	52	40	7	3	2
Economical	0	37	0	0	19	0

In analyzing the data, you will want to keep in mind the general advertising Giant has had in recent years. For years the company has promoted Giant as a mild yet extremely effective all-around cleaner—good for dishes as well as for fine and regular fabrics. Giant advertising campaigns have stressed two primary appeals. They have stressed the mildness which makes Giant safe for delicate hands and for the most delicate fabrics. And they have stressed Giant's strong cleaning power—strong enough, they say, to make the dirtiest work clothes come clean without scrubbing. Perhaps the data will show the effectiveness of these claims; or maybe they will point out other appeals which have not yet been used. At least the data will show what consumers like in a soap or detergent.

You plan to write the report in your Company's short-report form—title page and text proper, with captions. Because Mr. Kennard likes his facts fast, you consider presenting the conclusions first—or perhaps you will have a brief summary at the report's beginning. Because this is a subsidiary report to the main one Research will present on the survey, there is no need for you to present a description of the research methodology used.

27. Will contests bring profits to Food King? John H. Gromman, newly appointed advertising and promotion manager for Food King, Inc., has an idea for increasing sales and thereby increasing profits, for the chain of 142 stores. He thinks that contests at each store, with an abundance of prizes, would more than pay off. Such contests, he concludes, have been tried by other stores—and they appeared to work.

Janice Clemmons, however, does not think very much of the plan; and Janice Clemmons happens to be Food King's president. So to prove or disprove the value of contests, Ms. Clemmons suggests that the company conduct an experiment. You, as director of research, get the assignment.

The first step is to devise a contest for the experiment. With Gromman's assistance, you settle on a contest involving a simple drawing for prizes. With each purchase of $10 or more, the customers receive entry blanks, which they endorse and deposit in a large box. Drawings are made weekly to determine the winners of such prizes as washing machines, radios, electric mixers, and toasters.

For your experiment you select two comparable and homogeneous groups of five stores—one group as the experimental group and the other as a control group. In one group of stores (Group A) contests are held; none are held in the other stores (Group B). After one month of contests, with weekly drawings and prizes galore, the contests are stopped. Because you believe the contests may have some long-run effect on sales, you decide to analyze operations for the following months. You later find three months to be adequate. Now you assemble the data in preparation for your analysis.

Although you considered using a variety of data (traffic flow, size and numbers of purchases, cost of the contests) you conclude that net profits tell the whole story in summary fashion. The profit figures you assembled are in Table 32.

Write up your analysis of these data, and then conclude from your analysis. Write up your work in a form that is appropriate for this situation.

28. What will business be like during the months ahead? As assistant to the president, De Berry Stores, Inc., you have drawn the assignment of writing a consensus forecast to be presented at the meeting of the Board next Wednesday. President Nadine De Berry of this chain of 24 major department stores in the East and Midwest gave you the assignment personally. The Company does not employ an economist. De Berry does not believe in such "frills." "Why should we pay for them," she says, "when we can get free forecasts of all the top economists merely by reading through current periodicals."

Ms. De Berry's instructions, as usual, were quite vague; so much of

Table 32
Net Profits ($000)

	Store	Month before Contests	Month of Contests	Month after	Second Month after	Third Month after
A	1	32	29	39	34	32
	2	31	27	38	33	30
	3	30	27	33	31	31
	4	33	25	37	34	33
	5	30	28	38	31	29
B	6	29	30	31	30	32
	7	30	32	31	30	30
	8	31	31	30	30	32
	9	33	34	33	32	32
	10	30	31	31	30	30

what you will do is left to your good judgment. All she said was that she wants you to survey the predictions of the nation's leading economic forecasters for the months ahead and to present your findings in a clear and meaningful report to the Board. She wants the forecasts consolidated as much as it is practical—that is, she does not want merely a succession of individual forecasts. Your coverage will, of course, be largely of a general nature, covering all of the country's economy. But you will give special emphasis to whatever information you can find pertaining especially to department stores and to the eastern and midwestern regions.

In good short-report form your report will begin with a title page. Because the Board will want the facts quickly, you will include a fast-moving synopsis. Whether you will need additional prefatory parts will depend on how voluminous your presentation turns out to be.

29. Should Sage change its formula? Your employer, E. O. Struman, Inc., has for two generations manufactured a leading line of men's toiletries. During the past few years, the company has watched its share of the market diminish. Much of the sales loss, Struman management believes, is a result of the Company's failure to change formulas of its products. With only minor exceptions, Struman products today are the same as they were the day they were introduced. And some were introduced over 40 years ago.

About a year ago, following a reorganization of its management, Struman began a program of product improvement. Its laboratories, heretofore concerned with new product development and production testing, began serious efforts to change the existing products. And to test consumer reaction to their developments, they brought in a research analyst. You are that analyst.

Your first assignment in this capacity is to test a change in formula for Sage, the firm's leading cologne for men. The new formula for this product includes a chemical which produces a cooling, tingling sensation on the skin—something the old formula did not have. According to news in the trade, this sensation is well liked and has been responsible for increased sales of some of Struman's competitors. You have no authentic proof of this effect; so you will need to conduct your own research on the subject.

To test the new product, you designed a primary research project. You constructed a controlled sample of 500 men carefully selected to represent the male users of cologne. You used ages and education as your primary controls. Then your carefully selected and trained investigators approached the men selected; and they determined how each man rated the new product with the old. Each participant was asked to use each product alternately for a two-week period. After this period an interviewer approached each participant and, through questioning, determined his reactions to the two products.

Now the results are in and are neatly tabulated and arranged in Tables 33–36. It is time to analyze them and to report your findings to the firm's management. Your major problem, of course, is to advise management on the critical question of whether to change to the new formula. But your analysis of the reasons why men like and dislike the two products should

Table 33

Comparison of Preferences for New and Old Formulas for Sage

	Number Preferring New Sage	Number Preferring Old Sage	Number with No Preference
Overall preference	273	210	17
Odor preference	168	313	19
Preference for effect on skin	317	166	17

Table 34

Answers to Question: "What, if anything, do you like about each product?"

	New Sage	Old Sage
Odor:		
Mild	34	0
Strong	0	87
Pleasant	109	207
Other comments about odor	23	13
Skin effect, stimulating:		
Invigorating	134	0
Refreshing	83	23
Other	37	3
Skin effect, comforting:		
Soothing effects	7	96
Doesn't burn, mild	0	82
Cooling effect	93	0
Other	17	23

Table 35

Answers to Question: "What, if anything, don't you like about each product?"

	New Sage	Old Sage
Odor:		
Weak	62	3
Strong	17	69
Dislike (in general)	194	48
Other comments about odor	17	23
Harsh effect on skin:		
Stings	66	0
Burns	51	0
Other comments	13	3
Not enough effect on skin:		
Little or no feeling	0	119
Other comments	5	17

Note: Because each respondent could give any number of answers (0, 1, 2, 3, etc.), the totals do not equal 500.

Table 36

Answers to Questions: "What brand of cologne are you now using?" and "How do the two colognes you have sampled compare with your present brand?"

Brand	Number Using	Comparison of Sage (New) with Present Brand			Comparison of Sage (Old) with Present Brand		
		Prefer Sage (New)	Prefer Present Brand	Like about Same	Prefer Sage (Old)	Prefer Present Brand	Like about Same
Sage (old)	118	7	86	25	—	—	—
Royal Purple*	104	21	32	51	2	100	2
Gentry*	86	16	24	46	0	83	3
Sir*	51	9	19	23	2	46	3
Mystic Knight	44	3	40	1	7	21	16
Seven Seas	24	2	18	4	3	13	8
Others	43	4	35	4	8	21	14
Others*	30	7	9	14	0	28	2
Total	500	69	263	168	22	312	48

* Contains chemicals that produce skin tingling effects.

be helpful in promoting the products; so you will want to emphasize these points en route to your conclusion. You will present your report in a form suitable for top management. Because most of the readers will have little interest in the specific details of your methodology, your introduction will contain only a brief description of method. Address the report to Y. A. Ferguson, President.

30. Advising the Board on the question of using deal campaigns to help sell food products. At last week's meeting of the Board of Directors, Warner Foods, Inc., the major topic of concern was Warner's sagging sales of margarine, shortening, and oils. During the past six months, the firm's two major competitors made substantial gains at Warner's expense. So far as Warner can determine, the gains were made through aggressive selling and promotion—factors that the Warner's sales staff feels it can adjust to. But such adjustments take time. What the Warner directors want now is something that will pick up the lost ground in a hurry.

One possible approach, as some of the directors view the situation, is to begin a series of deal campaigns with each product. "Deals" are any form of coupon, gift, or gimmick arrangement designed to stimulate sales. For example, coupons giving a discount on the purchase price of a product may be mass mailed to consumers; or gift certificates may be packed within a product's container. The possible variations are many. They all have one thing in common, however. They are costly, frequently to the point of causing temporary losses. They are effective only if they can cultivate repeat customers.

Although Warner has never used deal campaigns, its competitors have used them extensively. And so have many other manufacturers of foods and other household products. Over the years, however, Warner management has viewed deal campaigns with a high degree of skepticism, especially since

Warner products are high in quality and price and appeal to the higher income and social groups.

Because the directors are skeptical about deal campaigns, they are reluctant to begin them without knowing more about them. So, in an effort to become better informed, they have called on the research department for help. You, the senior research specialist, have been given the assignment.

As Board Chairman Peter Darwin explained it to you, your assignment is to gather the best available information on effectiveness of deals. The Board will expect your recommendation, too; but you may wish to qualify it, since you are not going into the financial aspects of the problem in detail. Also, any consideration of the financial aspects would depend on the nature of the specific campaign selected.

The Board meets again in about two weeks; so there isn't time for primary research. Secondary research will have to be used. After a few hours of fruitless work, you give up on your company library; but you find exactly what you want at a nearby university library. It is a report conducted just last year by Professor Mary Cook at Midlands University. In her somewhat brief but information-packed tables (Tables 37–39), you see the basis of your analysis.

After you have studied the data and made your analysis, prepare the report for the Board. Give the report whatever formality the Board is likely to expect; and, since the information is largely quantitative, you will support your presentation with appropriate graphic aids.

31. **Solving a problem on your campus. (Requires additional research.)** On all college campuses some common problems exist. At least, they exist in the minds of many of the faculty, students, and staff. From

Table 37

Margarine, Shortening, and Oils (Percent of Families Reporting Specified Number of Deals and Percent of Total Deals Accounted for in Each Category, during July 198X, Saint Louis, Missouri)

Number of Deals per Family	Margarine		Shortening		Oils	
	Dealing Families	Portion of Total Deals	Dealing Families	Portion of Total Deals	Dealing Families	Portion of Total Deals
1	29.6	6.6	34.5	11.3	60.2	35.7
2	23.5	10.4	19.5	12.8	24.5	29.1
3	10.7	7.1	17.2	17.0	7.7	13.6
4	8.6	7.7	6.9	9.0	3.4	8.0
5	4.5	5.0	6.9	11.3	3.4	10.1
6	4.1	5.5	6.1	12.1	—	—
7	4.1	6.4	1.1	2.6	0.8	3.5
8	1.7	2.9	2.7	7.1	—	—
9	1.7	3.3	2.7	7.9	—	—
10	1.2	2.8	0.4	1.2	—	—
11	0.4	1.0	0.4	1.4	—	—
12 or more	9.9	41.3	1.6	6.3	—	—
Total	100.0	100.0	100.0	100.0	100.0	100.0

the list of problem areas which follows, select one which you regard as a problem at your institution.

For the problem that you select, you will first gather all of the significant information which concerns it. When you are thoroughly acquainted with the facts of your problem, you will gather whatever authoritative information you can concerning how it might be solved. Perhaps your research will involve looking through bibliographical sources to find out what has been done on

Table 38

Sales Increases Attributed to Deal Campaigns and Effect of Campaigns on Profits (Average [mean] of Six Companies, One Campaign Each)

	Percent Higher Than before Campaign
Sales during campaigns	16.3
Sales after campaigns (months):	
1....................................	9.1
3....................................	5.9
6....................................	3.6
12....................................	1.8

Note: Net profit before and after campaign, 5.1 percent of gross sales; net profit during campaign, 2.1 percent of gross sales.

Table 39
Dealing and Nondealing Households by Characteristics (Percent)

Household characteristics	Buying Households		Purchases by Dealing Households		Purchases by All Households	
	Dealing Households	Nondealing Households	Deal (Pounds)	Nondeal (Pounds)	Deal (Pounds)	Nondeal (Pounds)
Race and nationality:						
Native white	54	46	10.0	90.0	6.4	93.6
Foreign-born white....................	51	49	10.1	89.9	6.0	94.0
Nonwhite	22	78	5.7	94.3	1.6	98.4
Income:						
Low (under $12,000)	39	61	10.0	90.0	4.8	95.2
Medium ($12,000–$25,000)	55	45	9.4	90.6	6.0	94.0
High (over $25,000)...................	53	47	9.9	90.1	6.1	93.9
Size of household:						
Small (1 or 2 persons)	39	61	14.1	85.9	7.0	93.0
Medium (3 or 4 persons)...............	53	47	8.9	91.1	5.4	94.6
Large (5 or more persons)	55	45	8.5	91.5	5.1	94.9
Education:						
8 years or less	43	57	11.0	89.0	5.3	94.7
9–12 years..........................	47	53	7.9	92.1	4.4	95.6
13 years or more	59	41	11.6	88.4	8.5	91.5
Age of housewife:						
Under 45 years......................	54	46	9.2	90.8	5.8	94.2
45–64 years.........................	44	56	11.0	89.0	5.9	94.1
65 years or older....................	38	62	10.8	89.2	4.4	95.6

other campuses. It may involve getting information or opinions from the various people on campus who are involved in the problem. When you have all this information, you will carefully analyze your problem in the light of all available knowledge. Then you will arrive at a recommended solution.

So the situation will appear to be realistic, you may assume whatever role or position at your college that is appropriate. Present your work in appropriate report form.

Your problem area possibilities are as follows (some are broad and will need to be made specific):

> Traffic regulation and control.
> Fire prevention.
> Safety on campus.
> Crime prevention on campus.
> Scholastic honesty.
> Attendance policies.
> Orientation of new students.
> Registration procedures.
> Student government.
> Grades (appeal procedures, grade inflation).
> Faculty-student relations.
> Dress and grooming.
> Library operations.

Long problems

32. Searching for unique characteristics of retail executives. Is there commonality in the backgrounds and characteristics of executives in retail and nonretail companies? This is the question you must answer for the National Retail Merchants Association.

As director of research for the association, you have just completed an extensive survey.[2] Your goal was to gather information which will guide the association's members in selecting personnel for future executive assignments. It would be helpful if the members know whether retail executives are special types or much like other executives. Your survey was designed to do just that; and you think you have been successful.

With your findings neatly summarized before you, your next step is to analyze them for their meaning to your problem. Then you will organize your findings and analyses into the pattern that will produce the most logical and efficient presentation. Certainly, you will want to do more than just present a long succession of questions and answers (which is the form your

---

[2] Actually the survey results presented were gathered by Korn-Frey International, and the UCLA Graduate School of Management. The actual survey comprised responses from 1,708 executives from a cross section of American businesses.

findings are in now). Perhaps you can find some means of arranging the survey questions on the basis of broad types of information involved.

Your analyses will produce an answer to the basic question of whether retail executives are unique. And if they are, it will end with a summary of the major differences—information that retailers can use in selecting people for management training.

The finished report will be rather formal, for it will be duplicated en masse and sent to the membership. It will contain the traditional prefatory parts. But rather than a letter of transmittal, it will have a preface.

Following is a summary of the findings:

Q. How many years have you been employed by your current company?

Average	Nonretail	Retail
19	14.5	23

Q. How many different companies have you worked for during your business career?

Number of Companies	Nonretail	Retail
1	26%	23%
2	19	15
3	23	24
4	27	30
5 or more	5	8

Q. If you have worked for more than one company, which factors were most influential in your decision to change positions?

	Nonretail	Retail
Better compensation package	32%	42%
More desirable location	7	3
Increased responsibility	44	48
Increased status	6	5
Increased creativity	9	9
Increased challenge	42	48
More rapid advancement	19	17

Q. In which function area did you begin your career?

	Nonretail	Retail
Finance/accounting	28%	26%
Marketing/sales	19	35
Personnel	4	4
Professional/technical	31	16
Production/manufacturing	9	8
International	1	0
General management	4	5
No response	4	6

Q. What is your current functional area?

	Nonretail	Retail
Finance/accounting	22%	19%
Marketing/sales	8	10
Personnel	7	10
Professional/technical	12	15
Production/manufacturing	2	0
International	2	2
General management	44	41
No response	3	3

Q. Which functional area do you believe is currently the "fastest route to the top"? Which one will be in ten years?

	Current		Ten Years	
	Nonretail	Retail	Nonretail	Retail
Finance/accounting	33%	32%	30%	35%
Marketing/sales	31	47	20	30
Personnel	0	0	1	2
Professional/technical	7	1	10	7
Production/manufacturing	4	0	4	0
International	2	1	4	2
General management	18	18	23	22
No response	5	1	8	2

Q. Has your workweek increased, decreased, or remained the same over the past ten years?

	Nonretail	Retail
Increased	40%	34%
Decreased	15	15
Remained the same	45	52

Q. Has your business travel time increased, decreased, or remained the same over the past ten years?

	Nonretail	Retail
Increased	47%	52%
Decreased	27	25
Remained the same	26	23

Q. Have you ever been transferred overseas during your business career?

	Nonretail	Retail
Yes	11%	5%
No	89	95

Q. Do you consider overseas business experience valuable in terms of professional growth?

	Nonretail	Retail
Yes	64%	45%
No	34	52
No response	2	3

Q. Have you ever taken a leave of absence from the business community to participate in nonmilitary government service?

	Nonretail	Retail
Yes	2%	3%
No	97	97
No response	1	0

Q. Do you believe that government service enhances one's chances for corporate success?

	Nonretail	Retail
Yes	24%	20%
No	74	79
No response	2	1

Q. Has your interest in participating in government service increased, decreased, or remained the same over the past ten years?

	Nonretail	Retail
Increased	21%	25%
Decreased	28	23
Remained the same	49	51
No response	2	1

Q. Is your present position the highest to which you aspire?

	Nonretail	Retail
Yes	67%	61%
No	33	39

Q. If you were financially independent, would you continue in your present position?

	Nonretail	Retail
Yes	68%	75%
No	31	23
No response	1	2

Q. When do you wish to retire?

	Nonretail	Retail
Before age 65	48%	49%
At age 65	31	24
At age 70	4	3
Work as long as possible	17	23
No response	0	1

Q. If you were starting over, would you pursue the same career, a similar career, or a different career?

	Nonretail	Retail
Same	60%	60%
Similar	28	28
Different	12	12

Q. In retrospect, was your formal education worthwhile as it applies to your career?

	Nonretail	Retail
Not worthwhile	1%	1%
Somewhat worthwhile	24	29
Very worthwhile	75	70

Q. In general, do you believe the chances for advancement are greater for the executive who remains with one company for his or her entire career?

	Nonretail	Retail
Yes	27%	30%
No	71	68
No response	2	2

Q. In general, do you believe the "it's who you know, not what you know" theory of career advancement is still valid?

	Nonretail	Retail
Yes	16%	18%
No	83	82
No response	1	0

Q. In general, which traits do you believe enhance an executive's chances for success?

	Nonretail	Retail
Creativity	45%	46%
Desire for responsibility	58	56
Concern for people	49	56
Concern for results	74	75
Ambition	38	45
Integrity	66	56
Loyalty	23	28
Aggressiveness	36	39
Appearance	15	18
Social adaptability	16	17
Exceptional intelligence	20	20

Q. Which level of education have you attained?

	Nonretail	Retail
No college degree	8%	13%
College degree	85	81
Graduate degree	43	33

Q. If you have a college degree, is it a B.A. or a B.S.?

	Nonretail	Retail
B.A.	66%	74%
B.S.	34	26

Q. From what type of undergraduate institution did you receive your degree?

	Nonretail	Retail
Small private	29%	24%
Large private	24	27
Small public	9	9
Large public	31	40

Q. From what type of graduate institution did you receive your degree?

	Nonretail	Retail
Small private	13%	14%
Large private	52	49
Small public	4	3
Large public	31	35

Q. Were you employed during your undergraduate education?

	Nonretail	Retail
Yes	68%	68%
No	27	23
No response	5	9

Q. In what region did you spend the major portion of your childhood?

	Nonretail	Retail
Northeast	33%	25%
Southeast	9	9
Midwest	38	39
Southwest	7	10
West	9	16
Other	4	3

Q. In what locality did you spend the major portion of your childhood?

	Nonretail	Retail
Urban	42%	39%
Suburban	34	31
Rural	20	25
No response	5	5

Q. With which of your parents did you live during your childhood?

	Nonretail	Retail
Father only	1%	0%
Mother only	8	10
Both	89	88
Neither	1	2
No response	1	0

Q. How would you classify your parents' occupations during your childhood?

	Nonretail	Retail
Professional/technical	22%	18%
Managerial	23	25
Clerical	4	3
Sole proprietor	17	13
Blue collar	21	23
Did not work outside home	0	0
Other	7	7
No response	6	11

Q. Were you an only child, first child, middle child, or last child?

	Nonretail	Retail
Only child	14%	11%
First child	34	37
Middle child	22	18
Last child	29	33
No response	1	1

Q. Was your precollege education primarily public, parochial, or other private?

	Nonretail	Retail
Public	79%	82%
Parochial	12	11
Other private	8	7
No response	7	0

Q. Please indicate your age.

	Nonretail	Retail
Over 60	19%	25%
59–50	48	40
49–40	29	28
Below 40	4	6
No response	0	1

Q. Sex.
The nonretail is 99 percent male. Retail is 98 percent male.

Q. Marital status.
Both the nonretail and the retail groups are 95 percent married.

Q. Number of children.
Both the nonretail and the retail groups have an average of three children, but 8 percent of the nonretail group have one or less children, while 17 percent of the retail respondents have one or less children.

Q. Have you been married more than once?

	Nonretail	Retail
Yes	11%	12%
No	89	88

Q. If currently married, is your spouse employed?

	Nonretail	Retail
Full-time	5%	7%
Part-time	9	16
Not employed	82	73
No response	4	4

Q. Within the past five years, do you find yourself devoting more time to leisure activities?

	Nonretail	Retail
Yes	32%	28%
No	68	72

Q. Do you feel that you are able to spend an adequate amount of time with your family?

	Nonretail	Retail
Yes	67%	66%
No	32	34
No response	1	0

Q. How important is religion in your daily life?

	Nonretail	Retail
No importance	14%	16%
Limited importance	28	18
Moderate importance	34	46
Significant importance	24	20

Q. Religion.

	Nonretail	Retail
Protestant	68%	70%
Catholic	22	14
Jewish	6	13
Other	3	3
No response	1	0

Q. On social issues, how do you consider yourself politically?

	Nonretail	Retail
Conservative	74%	61%
Moderate	25	39
Liberal	1	0

Q. What is your political affiliation?

	Nonretail	Retail
Democrat	13%	15%
Republican	68	61
Independent	18	24
No response	1	0

Q. Do you vote regularly?

	Nonretail	Retail
Yes	95%	93%
No	4	7
No response	1	0

Q. How often do you drink?

	Nonretail	Retail
Never	5%	3%
Seldom	16	28
Moderately	63	53
Often	15	13
Very often	2	3

Q. How often do you smoke?

	Nonretail	Retail
Never	58%	61%
Seldom	9	10
Moderately	13	8
Often	13	17
Very often	6	4
No response	1	0

Q. How often do you use tranquilizers?

	Nonretail	Retail
Never	87%	85%
Seldom	10	9
Moderately	2	5
Often	0	0
Very often	0	0
No response	1	1

Q. Compensation—base salary plus bonus.

	Nonretail	Retail
Under $100,000	53%	47%
$100,000–150,000	27	27
$150,000–200,000	11	21
$200,000–250,000	7	11
$Over $250,000	5	11

Note: Rounding sometimes produces totals not precisely 100 percent.

33. Determining preretirement and retirement practices. Assume the role of research director for the National Association of Administrators. Your current assignment is to conduct a study of preretirement, retirement, and postretirement practices of the nation's organizations. More specifically, your objective is to get answers to such questions as what are organizations doing to prepare employees for retirement, what do they do for employees at retirement, and what relations do they have with retirees after retirement.

The information you gather will go to the membership in a report to the organization's members. Primarily, the report will be informational, but it will contain some analyses; and it will reach whatever conclusions the analyses support.

In your search for the information, you conducted a mail survey of 474 organizations representing the Association's membership. You received 267 usable responses, 47 percent being manufacturing, 31 percent being nonmanufacturing, and 22 percent being nonbusiness organizations (hospitals, universities, government agencies, and such). In your attempt to distinguish among organizations by size, you classified employers of 1,000 or more as large and employers of fewer than 1,000 as small. Based on this classification plan, approximately 40 percent of your respondents were large and 60 percent were small.

You have tabulated your results (Tables 40–45)[3] and are ready to construct the report that will present them. Because the report will be written for the total membership, you will give it the appropriate formal parts. You will need to decide whether to use a preface, rather than a letter of transmittal. Because the information to be presented is quantitative, you will use graphic aids wherever they help to communicate.

34. **Evaluating the performance of a college dean.** Place yourself in the position of assistant dean in the College of Business Administration, Wayward University. Your boss, Dean Alonzo K. Cuevas, is very much concerned with his faculty's perception of his performance. A man who only recently entered the academic field after a highly successful career in business, Dean Cuevas wants badly to know his strengths. He wants even more to know his shortcomings so he can correct them. So, to get this information, he asks you to conduct a survey of the full-time faculty that will reveal the information he seeks.

After long and diligent effort and much consulting with various experts on the faculty, you produced a survey instrument consisting of 30 statements. The statements cover key areas of performance. Responses to each statement are based on the extent to which the faculty members agree. The questionnaire provides for five levels of agreement.

After two weeks of persuasively requesting the faculty to respond, you were able to obtain 68 usable responses (out of a possible 87). Your next step was to tabulate the answers.

Now that the tabulating is done (see Table 46), you are ready to prepare your findings for final presentation. You want something better than just a long list of questions and answers; so you will first arrange the questions by broad areas of similarity. Then you will present the data with meaningful analyses. Remember that the main concern of Dean Cuevas is what he must do to improve his performance. Thus, your report should lead to some specific recommendations.

---

[3] These tables are used with permission from the Bureau of National Affairs and come from a survey of American Society for Personnel Administration members.

Table 40
Preretirement Counseling and Education Programs

| | Percent of Companies | | | | | |
| | By Industry | | | By Size | | All Companies |
	Manufacturing	Nonmanufacturing	Nonbusiness	Large	Small	
Employer has a preretirement counseling program	39	39	25	57	22	36
Employees participate in program:*						
Six months before retirement	6	3	13	5	8	6
One year before retirement	4	13	13	5	14	8
Two years before retirement	0	0	7	0	3	1
Three years before retirement	0	6	7	2	6	3
Four years before retirement	2	0	0	2	0	1
Five years before retirement	8	0	13	3	11	6
At age 55	27	41	40	35	31	33
At age 60	20	22	0	17	19	18
Anytime, at employee's request	33	31	13	25	42	31
Participants include:*						
All employees nearing retirement	82	97	87	85	92	88
Spouse or other family members	62	63	66	72	50	64
Program was developed:*						
Entirely in-house	61	63	67	60	67	63
Using a packaged program	22	25	7	23	17	21
With help of outside consultant	18	9	27	17	17	17
Tuition aid is available for employees near retirement to develop new interests/activities	28	26	20	26	25	25

* Percentages are of companies that have counseling programs. Percentages add to more than 100 because of multiple responses.

Table 41
Topics Covered in Preretirement Counseling Programs

| | Percent of Companies with Programs | | | | | |
| | By Industry | | | By Size | | All Companies |
	Manufacturing	Nonmanufacturing	Nonbusiness	Large	Small	
Social Security benefits	90	94	93	92	92	92
Company pension benefits	94	88	93	93	89	92
Other company benefits/services for retirees	84	81	60	83	81	82
Financial planning	61	59	60	62	58	60
Wills and inheritance provisions	51	59	60	65	39	55
Earning money after retirement	53	50	53	55	47	52
Recreation and hobbies	45	63	53	63	33	52
Health problems of older persons	49	63	33	60	36	51
Organizations for retirees	45	53	60	50	50	50
Mental/emotional aspects of retirement	45	53	47	58	31	48
Where to live after retirement	45	47	27	57	19	43
Volunteer activities	35	53	40	50	28	42
Safety precautions for older persons	22	28	20	33	8	24

Table 42
Flexible Retirement Arrangements

| | Percent of Companies | | | | | |
| | By Industry | | By Size | | All |
	Manufacturing	Nonmanufacturing	Nonbusiness	Large	Small	Companies
Employees may "taper off" working hours prior						
to retirement	10	15	27	14	16	15
All employees eligible	3	5	19	5	9	7
Certain employees eligible	6	10	8	9	7	8
Employees may continue						
working on consultant basis after retirement	55	52	46	55	50	52
Employees may be recalled for temporary work						
after retirement	63	56	66	65	60	62

Table 43

Company Retirement Ceremonies

	Percent of Companies						
	By Industry			By Size			
	Manufacturing	Nonmanufacturing	Nonbusiness	Large	Small	All Companies	
Company sponsors retirement ceremonies	75	89	81	82	80	81	
Types of ceremonies:*							
Informal office parties	48	47	56	49	50	50	
Luncheon	41	37	31	33	40	38	
Dinner	36	37	21	28	36	33	
Reception	14	22	31	25	17	20	
Company gives retirement awards or gifts	54	67	53	54	60	58	

* Percentages are of companies that sponsor retirement ceremonies. Percentages add to more than 100 because of multiple responses

Table 44
Relations with Retired Employees

	Percent of Companies					
	By Industry			By Size		All Companies
	Manufacturing	Nonmanufacturing	Nonbusiness	Large	Small	
Services provided to retired employees:						
Invitations to company functions	68	67	46	66	61	63
Regular employee publications mailed to home	59	63	37	73	44	55
Life insurance coverage	59	56	39	67	45	53
Coverage at reduced amount*	84	87	78	80	88	84
Payment of health insurance to supplement Medicare	39	43	32	48	32	39
Payment of optional Medicare	17	16	5	20	11	14
Company pays all*	45	54	33	52	41	47
Company pays part*	36	23	—	14	47	29
Discounts on company products or services	26	39	12	29	25	27
Membership in company recreation or social club	16	12	5	17	9	12
Special publications for retired persons	10	12	5	14	7	10
Matching gifts to educational institutions	10	2	—	10	2	6
Free use of company medical dept.	4	1	2	4	2	3
Free physical exams	0.7	1	2	2	0.6	1
Company has a retired employees club	14	9	5	20	4	10
Other	11	20	5	16	9	12

* Percent of companies providing benefit.

Table 45
Changes in Retirement Programs

	Percent of Companies					
	By Industry			By Size		All Companies
	Manufacturing	Nonmanufacturing	Nonbusiness	Large	Small	
Impact of change in the mandatory retirement age:						
None	39	31	34	29	40	35
Very little	50	58	45	57	48	51
Some	8	10	14	9	11	10
Great	0	1	2	2	0	1
Increase in number of employees electing not to retire since age 70 amendment	17	26	22	29	16	21
Changes in programs for preretired and retired employees in past two years	29	29	22	33	24	28
Anticipate making changes in near future	30	35	32	37	29	32

Table 46
Number of Faculty Members Rating Dean's Performance at Different Levels under Each of 30 Propositions

	Agree			Disagree		Unable to Evaluate
	Com-pletely	Mostly	Partly	Mostly	Com-pletely	
I. Philosophy and knowledge base:						
1. Possesses knowledge and skills in general administration needed to head the College of Business Administration	19	24	7	5	11	2
2. Has adequate understanding of each functional field and its potential contributions	6	16	19	16	12	3
3. Has clear sense of purpose of College and conveys this to departments	15	17	17	8	9	2
4. Demonstrates balanced concern for teaching, research, public service, and university service	12	19	10	12	14	1
5. Demonstrates strong concern for faculty needs in order to function effectively and to develop professionally	15	17	8	16	12	0
6. Demonstrates awareness and sensitivity to differences in faculty talents and to areas in which each may best contribute	6	14	16	11	16	5
7. Demonstrates strong concern for student needs.......................	7	14	12	7	5	23
II. Planning:						
8. Provides adequate policy statements for collegewide guidance in important decisions that are common to all departments	10	19	16	11	8	5
9. Sees that goals are set, plans are made, and results are evaluated for the College as a whole	12	17	17	10	7	4
10. Sees that goals are set, plans are made, and results are evaluated for each major study area (for programs, curricula, faculty needs, space needs, budgets, etc.)	11	10	20	13	8	6
11. Maintains continuing program for planning improvements and innovations, both long range and short range	13	17	14	7	5	12
12. Involves people effectively in planning, actively soliticing ideas from all faculty members, or from all who may have useful inputs regarding particular issues	8	14	8	11	23	4
III. Organizing work and providing resources:						
13. Sees that faculty resources are used effectively, considering different types and levels of instruction, research and service, and considering strengths and limitations of individual faculty members...........................	7	13	14	14	14	6

450

Table 46 *(continued)*

| | Agree | | | Disagree | | Unable to Evaluate |
	Com-pletely	Mostly	Partly	Mostly	Com-pletely	
14. Provides adequate policy governing control of class size for type of class, multiple section coordination, load adjustment where justified, instructor assistance where justified, and other support where both needed and feasible	5	11	17	8	12	14
15. Supports research to extent needed and possible and gives general encouragement to development of individual creative effort	11	16	17	13	9	2
16. Supports a faculty recruiting program that is based upon carefully planned needs and that generates adequate numbers, quality, university representation of applicants, and diversity of background to prevent either inbreeding or limited perspective; and that screens and attracts as many as possible of the best qualified from throughout the nation	14	21	7	12	6	7
IV. Leadership, communication, and evaluation:						
17. Is action-oriented, a real doer, a person who gets things done	24	20	11	4	6	2
18. Delegates effectively to assistant administrators most of the responsibilities for ongoing operations, yet stays in touch and monitors results	16	19	13	5	5	9
19. Encourages (either directly or through chairmen) each faculty member to realize and utilize individual potential—takes personal interest and is easily approachable	10	13	7	16	18	2
20. Administers reward system fairly and objectively and in terms of preannounced standards; encouraging chairmen and others involved to recognize and reward diverse contributions, not allowing biases to dominate, not playing favorites; also explains his recommendations to chairmen and faculty	9	11	11	11	16	8
21. Keeps faculty members informed on university, college, departmental, and individual developments likely to be of interest and value to them	15	21	14	10	6	1
22. Invites faculty suggestions and other inputs regarding plans, operating problems, and possible improvements, is genuinely receptive, and considers suggestions seriously and objectively	10	12	12	12	19	1

451

Table 46 *(concluded)*

	Agree			Disagree		Unable to Evaluate
	Completely	Mostly	Partly	Mostly	Completely	
23. Welcomes differences of opinion and deals with these with an open mind	7	13	10	19	15	3
24. Uses democratic procedures wherever possible and appropriate (gets people involved in making decisions that affect them)	7	10	8	18	21	3
25. Holds well-planned meetings for distributing information, holding constructive group discussions of College problems and needs, and reaching group decisions where appropriate	12	16	20	10	7	2
26. Is sensitive to student needs and suggestions, including feedback regarding current operations and unfilled needs	7	8	10	8	4	31
V. External representation:						
27. Represents College effectively at university levels	20	26	3	6	5	8
28. Represents College effectively in relations with business groups	25	23	4	3	3	9
29. Represents College effectively in relations with professional groups	18	24	2	6	4	13

	Considerably above Average	Somewhat above Average	Average	Somewhat below Average	Considerably below Average	Unable to Evaluate
30. Compared to other deans in your knowledge and experience, how would you evaluate the overall performance of Dean Cuevas	19	14	8	7	14	2

As you are hopeful that a good job on this report will get you the advancement you seek, you will give it your best effort. You will dress it up with appropriate prefatory parts. And you will use visual aids wherever they help to communicate.

35. Determining what makes a Mufti service center successful. The management of the Mufti Muffler Company wants to know why some of its automotive service centers are doing much better than others. Your job is to find out.

You, as research supervisor for Dobbs Research Associates, have been working on the problem for the past four weeks. As orally authorized by Mufti's vice president for sales, Rene C. Cullen, you and your crew have visited 200 manager-owned Mufti operations in the 27-state area served by the Company. The stations visited were selected by Mufti executives to be about equal insofar as physical facilities and location are concerned. All are predominantly community stations—that is, they are off main highways. All are about equal in traffic flow past the station; and all have nearly equal competitive situations. But they differ in one major respect—sales volume. One half (100) of the stations have had unusually good sales volumes; the other half (100) have had low volumes.

To find the reasons for high or low volumes, you worked out a detailed plan for collecting data. First you had your investigators visit each station posing as customers. They then observed and recorded such things as the attendants' courtesy, services rendered, and conditions of the stations. Some of these observations were factual. Others were subjective. But the subjective evaluations were based on definite guide points on which each observer was very carefully instructed. Later, the investigators returned to the stations and observed and interviewed the managers. From the managers they received some pertinent factual information on the personnel employed at each station.

Now the research is done, and you have the summary tabulations before you. Your next step is to put these data into some meaningful order. Then you will analyze them in the light of your problem. From these analyses you hope to be able to draw some conclusions as to why some stations are successful and others are not. Of course, you will present all of this work in a report befitting the formality of your professional relationship with Mufti. (Your instructor may specify these requirements.)

Your summary tables are presented below. Should you require other information, you may use your good, logical imagination. For example, in describing your research procedure in the introduction section, you will need to fill in with steps that are consistent with good research methodology.

	S	U
Courtesy of attendants:		
Unusually courteous	18	3
Above average	44	23
Average	32	42
Below average	4	20
Discourteous	2	12
Customer services:		
Muffler	100	100
Wash and lube	7	23
Brakes	74	37
Carburetor	54	32
Ignition, tune-up	61	33
Wheels and shocks	81	34
Heavy repairs	2	21
Condition of stations:		
Overall appearance:		
Clean and neat	82	10
Fair, but could be improved	18	62
Dirty	0	28
Rest rooms:		
Clean and neat	92	22
Fair	8	47
Dirty	0	31

	S	U
Age of building:		
Less than 5 years	31	33
5–10 years	41	38
Over 10 years	38	29
Overall appearance of stock:		
Neatly arranged	68	11
Fair	30	63
Poorly arranged	2	26
Qualifications of managers:		
Education:		
Grade school or less	2	12
Some high school	28	44
High school graduate	56	42
Some college	14	2
Experience:		
Less than 1 year	0	11
1 to 5 years	52	41
6 to 10 years	36	38
Over 10 years	12	20
Marital status:		
Married	6	24
Single	6	24
Age:		
Under 21	—	3
21–25	4	12
26–30	10	19
31–40	51	36
41–50	19	20
Over 50	16	10
Grades on Mufti's Manager's Aptitude Test:		
Below 40 (not qualified)	0	9
40–59 (acceptable)	17	43
60–79 (good)	42	30
80–100 (outstanding)	41	18
Attended Mufti Manager's School (two weeks' duration)	43	21
Qualifications of service workers:		
Education:		
Grade school or less	18	27
Some high school	43	57
High school graduate	39	16
Experience (similar work):		
Less than 1 year	9	19
1 to 5 years	36	44
6 to 10 years	27	22
Over 10 years	28	15
Grade on Mufti's Aptitude Test:		
Below 40 (not qualified)	10	34
40–59 (acceptable)	47	57
60–79 (good)	36	7
80–100 (outstanding)	7	2
Marital status:		
Married	62	65
Single	38	35
Age:		
Under 21	13	14
21–30	66	33
31–40	17	31
41–50	4	20
Over 50	—	2
Attended Mufti's Service School (one week's duration)	59	27

	S	U
Pricing policy in area:		
Higher than standard	9	23
Equal to standard	74	47
Lower than standard	17	30
Promotion efforts:		
Trading stamps	32	14
Discounts (quantity purchase, special group, etc.)	11	10
Participated in recent company-sponsored contest	93	61
Average hourly wages paid relative to local average:		
$0.76 or more below	0	6
$0.26 to $0.75 below	19	41
$0.25 below to $0.25 above	27	33
$0.26 above to $0.75 above	45	17
$0.76 or more above	9	3
Promotion efforts:		
Participated in Mufti's special quarterly promotions	94	51
Participated in Mufti-sponsored contest	93	54
Conducted own special promotion in past year	19	3
Fringe benefits paid service workers:		
Group life insurance	31	9
Group hospitalization insurance	68	42
Paid vacations	88	52
Bonus, incentive pay, profit sharing, etc.	19	4
Accessories handled:		
Antifreeze	100	100
Oil additives	100	100
Radiator chemicals	100	99
Seat covers	84	21
Tires and tubes	100	100
Floor mats	84	22
Waxes, polishes	96	82
Wiper blades	99	81
Valves and caps	90	78
Car radios	6	0
Car heaters	21	1
Jacks	37	9
Tire chains	84	11
Touch-up paint	18	2
Mirrors	97	30
Spot lights	34	4
Batteries	100	100

	None		$1–$600		$601–$1,200		Over $1,200	
	S	U	S	U	S	U	S	U
Advertising expenditures:								
Annual, by media:								
Newspaper	0	13	7	45	32	31	61	11
Handbills	76	70	14	10	10	19	0	1
Radio–TV	98	89	2	0	0	5	0	6
Novelty (calendars, pens, etc.)	36	47	28	34	29	14	7	5
Direct mail	32	52	28	27	31	19	9	2

	Under $600	$601–$1,200	$1,201–$1,800	$1,801–$2,400	$2,401–$3,000	Over $3,000
Annual, total amount:						
Successful stations	12	14	21	25	18	10
Unsuccessful stations	31	36	22	3	5	3

Unless otherwise specified, the numbers are percentages. S—Successful stations; U—Unsuccessful stations.

36. A search for the permanent grocery clerk. At first you were somewhat disappointed in your new job as an assistant to Hans A. Kuhl, industrial relations director, Thrifty Food Stores, Inc. You didn't know just why. Thrifty is a good company to work for. Completion of its tremendous expansion program affords proof that there is opportunity for advancement. Maybe your disappointment was a result of Mr. Kuhl's choosing Johnny Rollins, an Oklahoma graduate and your rival for promotion, to help him conduct a survey of working conditions in the stores.

You wanted to get your teeth into that survey. You were interested in learning just what is behind the chain's number one personnel problem— the alarmingly fast turnover of grocery clerks. In fact, you were even a little happy when Kuhl came back from the survey with the report that he had found no disturbing conditions that could account for the turnover.

The job really got interesting, though, when Mr. Kuhl called Johnny and you into his office and assigned each of you an important part of his next step toward solving the turnover problem. The boss hurriedly explained his theory to you. He believes that, since working conditions and wages in Thrifty stores are comparable to those of competitors, the large turnover is a result of the stores' hiring the wrong type of employees—the type least likely to become permanent.

So Mr. Kuhl asked you to survey the personnel records with an eye out for any facts that are significant to the turnover problem. Specifically, he wants to know whether there are any factors (such as age, education, and marital status) that point to the grocery clerks most likely to stay on. Since the problem differs for men and women employees, Mr. Kuhl divided the assignment—the women for Johnny and the men for you.

So your first job was to go through the inactive files and pull out all records of men who have worked in the stores since September of 19X5. Because many of their newest employees have not had a chance to prove their permanence, you eliminated from the active files all records of employees who have been with the Company for less than one year. Then you reasoned that the sample's validity would not be changed if you used only every third card from each of the two groups.

Now, with all the preliminary work done and the records before you in two neat stacks (Tables 47 and 48), you are ready to begin tabulating and organizing. A logical comparison of the data from each group, with conclusions and recommendations, should be just what Mr. Kuhl wants, and, of course, you will present your findings to him in a clear and meaningful report.

You want to impress the boss with your superiority over Johnny; so you have decided to write the report from an impersonal viewpoint, and to support your conclusions with some good graphic aids. Also, you plan to dress up the report by including the following parts: a cover (with report title); a title fly; a title page; your letter of transmittal to Mr. Kuhl; a table of contents; a table of illustrations; an epitome; and, of course, the report proper.

Table 47

A Random Sample of Personnel Records of Present Thrifty Food Stores'
Employees

	A	B	C	D	E	F
Abram, Joe T.	29	12	M	1	7	87
Adams, Henry A.	18	8	S	1	0	18
Allen, J. J.	42	11	S	6	4	28
Anderson, A. A.	33	12	M	2	0	20
Antonio, Bernard	34	8	M	5	6	223
Applin, W. R.	20	12	S	1	0	85
Aycock, M. O.	32	12	S	4	0	31
Barker, James D.	45	8	M	5	26	19
Barnett, Anthony	23	12	M	1	5	118
Barr, Burl A.	43	9	M	5	12	17
Bastian, Earl	34	9	M	6	3	13
Baylor, Dan F.	24	7	M	3	2	15
Beaver, Tom W.	26	8	M	2	4	22
Beck, Herbert A.	41	12	M	2	15	43
Bell, Robert E.	19	12	M	1	1	83
Bell, Wm. A.	20	9	S	2	2	26
Broad, E. D.	25	12	S	3	0	78
Buckley, R. V.	19	12	S	1	0	91
Cabanis, Nelson	39	12	M	4	16	40
Cedar, Rex	30	12	M	3	0	25
Champ, Will D.	27	12	S	3	2	18
Clark, Boyce	40	12	M	3	0	45
Cluck, Travis	23	12	S	2	1	98
Coffey, C. E.	36	12	M	3	0	49
Connally, R. P.	29	12	M	2	5	17
Crump, Hal	18	10	S	0	0	95
Darby, T. E.	30	12	S	5	11	31
Davis, Samuel	42	12	M	3	0	13
Deirman, Geo. D.	19	9	M	2	2	17
DePew, Peter T.	32	12	M	4	7	29
Dickerson, Wm. T.	37	12	M	2	0	69
Dixon, Stanley	20	10	S	3	2	24
Eckhardt, B. E.	23	11	S	1	0	30
Ellis, Chas. T.	31	12	M	1	0	68
Erzkus, Ralph	40	12	M	4	0	35
Fischer, Thomas	28	10	M	2	3	21
Fogle, Richard E.	44	9	S	7	6	20
Fredrickson, Von E.	30	12	M	3	4	29
Garner, James T.	24	12	M	2	5	109
Gault, Raleigh Lee	35	9	M	4	11	33
Glaser, Conrad	33	12	M	4	6	27
Gustafson, V. A.	18	10	S	1	2	15
Guyger, Lorenzo M.	29	12	M	3	5	107
Hargrave, Edison E.	25	12	S	2	0	84
Hartkopf, Archie D.	38	10	M	7	4	38
Hess, Nathan D.	29	12	M	2	3	99
Hipple, Buddy	17	12	S	0	0	111
Hooper, Berkeley	36	12	S	6	9	38
Hubener, Chas. T.	21	12	S	3	1	25
Hutchinson, Elwood	34	8	M	3	7	18
Hyltin, Joe Bill	32	12	M	2	0	71
Innes, Bobby I.	18	12	S	1	0	22
Isbell, Floyd M.	41	9	M	4	18	20
Jackson, Michael	19	12	S	2	0	47
Jackson, T. J.	26	12	M	1	0	93
Johnson, Richard A.	21	12	M	1	3	77

Table **47** *(continued)*

	A	B	C	D	E	F
Jordan, Bernard M.	43	12	M	4	9	35
Joslin, Murray V.	33	12	M	2	0	95
Junkin, Humphry T.	20	12	S	1	0	74
Juul, Dalton Lee	36	12	M	3	2	12
Kavanaugh, James J.	31	12	S	4	0	59
Kendall, Morris E.	35	10	M	3	6	31
King, Dexter W.	23	12	S	2	4	73
Koenig, Harold H.	34	12	M	3	4	73
Lawrence, Vincent	32	12	M	2	0	25
Leath, T. Allen	26	11	M	4	6	13
Legge, Woodrow	31	12	M	3	5	30
Lewis, John A.	27	12	M	1	0	109
Lowther, Lester L.	38	10	M	5	5	39
Lundberg, Raymond	27	12	M	2	0	31
Lyons, Eugene W.	45	12	M	4	13	43
Madison, R. R., Jr.	18	12	S	0	0	19
Mancili, Tony T.	46	11	M	4	9	14
McCarty, Casey	37	12	M	4	12	57
McDonald, Albert A.	21	12	S	2	1	67
McMillan, Chester	39	9	M	3	22	36
Miller, Lloyd B.	30	12	M	2	0	13
Motsenbocker, Hugh	20	12	S	1	0	90
Murphy, Grady D.	18	12	S	0	0	79
Mussett, C. E.	35	10	M	3	8	21
Myers, Cecil H.	29	11	M	2	4	70
Myler, Stuart L.	23	11	M	4	3	19
Nason, Hubert G.	32	12	M	4	6	116
Nicholson, Bob E.	19	12	S	1	2	33
Nordlander, Wm. A.	34	12	M	3	0	12
Nunley, Benjamin T.	24	10	M	3	2	17
Nusom, Oscar A.	22	13	S	1	0	89
O'Connel, David	18	12	S	0	0	58
Owens, P. W.	48	10	M	3	21	14
Page, Owen S.	26	12	S	1	0	29
Patton, Kenny T.	32	12	M	4	6	51
Perrenolt, George A.	19	12	S	1	1	30
Powell, Maurice	30	13	M	2	7	91
Purnell, Clarence E.	37	12	M	6	16	38
Quist, Parker G.	25	11	S	4	7	27
Ratchford, E. G.	44	12	S	7	0	23
Reilly, Seth P.	22	12	S	2	3	16
Richardson, William	40	12	M	2	0	46
Richter, H. Lee	33	12	S	4	2	39
Ritter, Roger B.	27	11	M	2	4	83
Robinson, Hatton C.	45	9	M	5	7	22
Rylander, Bennett	31	12	M	2	3	29
Sachs, Jordan E.	25	12	M	1	0	82
Sandall, Othal	27	12	M	2	0	81
Schell, Aaron B.	19	10	M	1	2	25
Schmidt, David	36	8	M	3	10	35
Schreiber, Richard	40	12	M	3	18	33
Seaholm, Anthony C.	20	12	S	1	0	101
Shafer, Roland	35	13	S	3	0	28
Shaw, Andrew V.	44	11	M	3	12	61
Shelton, Russell	25	12	M	2	3	30
Smith, Odis Lee	21	12	M	2	0	118
Tanner, Paul W.	31	12	M	3	0	20
Taylor, Herbert G.	43	12	M	3	7	12

Table 47 *(concluded)* 459

	A	B	C	D	E	F
Thompson, Ernest E.	23	9	S	3	1	19
Todd, Waverly	33	11	M	3	0	24
Tuttle, Claude P.	46	10	M	4	5	17
Underwood, Owen S.	19	12	S	1	2	92
Urbanke, Mack	30	12	M	2	5	77
Varnell, Lester C.	28	12	S	3	2	103
Vinson, T. E.	41	12	M	2	0	39
Vosburg, Amos A.	39	9	M	3	14	26
Ward, Dan C.	20	12	S	1	0	100
Weir, James	35	10	M	3	7	14
Whitten, Lloyd D.	19	11	S	2	1	17
Williams, Oxsheer	43	11	M	4	9	15
Wilson, Walter S.	22	12	M	2	0	96
Wruble, James D.	51	10	M	4	27	24
Wynn, Horace W.	32	10	M	3	9	22
Yarrington, Alden	30	12	M	3	0	24
York, Thomas M.	19	10	M	3	2	22
Young, Leonard	24	12	S	2	0	82
Young, Patrick W.	43	12	M	3	13	37
Zauskey, Kenneth P.	24	10	S	4	2	18
Zietz, Horatio A.	37	9	M	5	4	38
Zissman, Robert Lee	25	12	M	2	4	15

Note: Explanation of column heads: A. Age at time of employment.
    B. Education in years.
    C. Marital status (Divorced counted as single).
    D. Number of jobs held before.
    E. Years of related experience.
    F. Months of employment with Thrifty Food Stores.

Table 48
A Random Sample of Personnel Records of Thrifty Food Stores' Former Employees

	A	B	C	D	E	F	G
Abney, J. B.	27	6	M	6	0	2	D–g
Acock, Thomas	35	8	M	5	0	1	D–g
Adams, William E.	33	12	S	7	1	7	Q–j
Aderholdt, E. D.	37	12	S	7	1	7	Q–e
Agnew, Harold	19	6	M	3	2	2	D–g
Akinson, Wayne E.	30	10	M	4	0	7	D–g
Albright, F. E.	40	8	S	7	0	2	D–g
Alexander, Geo. F.	31	12	M	4	9	10	Q–j
Allen, Tom M.	29	11	M	4	4	7	Q–j
Allman, John D.	38	12	M	3	0	14	Q–m
Amsley, David	46	9	M	3	2	17	D–h
Amundson, Chas. W.	27	10	M	2	3	19	Q–k
Anderson, Paul A.	36	7	M	5	6	6	Q–d
Andrewerka, R. H.	42	8	M	4	3	20	Q–j
Ansohn, Eric W.	30	9	M	5	0	1	D–g
Ashworth, P. T.	44	10	S	5	0	5	D–g
Austin, James T.	31	12	M	4	0	4	D–h
Babcock, R. L.	26	7	S	5	0	3	D–c
Badger, L. E.	41	9	M	3	0	9	D–g
Baggett, Mike	33	10	M	7	0	3	D–i
Bailey, Andrew A.	45	4	M	5	0	4	D–g
Baker, K. T.	35	8	S	5	4	17	Q–d

Table 48 *(continued)*

	A	B	C	D	E	F	G
Balagia, Chas. E.	18	9	S	3	1	9	D–i
Bantel, Fred S.	40	12	M	3	0	2	D–h
Barona, August E.	21	7	S	2	0	5	D–g
Bartholomew, T. E.	38	12	M	4	0	11	Q–e
Baugh, Jeff T.	26	10	S	3	2	47	Q–k
Bedighaus, C. E.	25	9	S	7	1	3	D–h
Bennett, H. A.	38	8	M	4	0	1	D–g
Biggs, Theo. E.	35	9	M	4	0	1	D–g
Boone, David D.	31	10	M	5	0	5	Q–j
Bowden, Arthur M.	40	8	M	5	0	3	D–g
Briscoe, Clyde C.	44	7	S	7	0	1	D–g
Brown, Ed W.	19	8	S	4	0	4	D–g
Bryant, Joe M.	22	8	S	3	0	4	D–g
Bryson, Frank, Jr.	41	4	S	9	0	2	D–g
Byrd, John Milton	45	8	M	6	2	17	Q–m
Bytendorp, Chester	19	8	S	2	1	10	Q–e
Cadwallader, E. A.	38	12	M	3	0	14	Q–m
Caffey, Courtney	46	9	M	3	2	17	D–h
Calhoun, James B.	27	10	M	2	3	19	Q–k
Calvert, Morgan	42	8	M	4	3	22	Q–j
Cameron, Arthur M.	36	9	M	5	6	6	Q–d
Canion, Ralph E.	30	9	M	5	0	1	D–g
Cantwell, Paul D.	35	10	S	5	4	17	Q–d
Cesar, Rudolph	18	9	S	3	1	9	D–i
Chandler, Orville	40	12	M	3	0	2	D–h
Chappell, Wm. O.	21	7	S	2	0	5	D–g
Cheaves, LeRoy, Jr.	44	6	M	8	1	10	D–i
Christianson, W. D.	36	7	M	3	14	9	Q–l
Cloud, Ross S.	25	12	S	4	1	7	Q–e
Conkle, Scott M.	43	7	M	6	0	14	Q–e
Crenshaw, Dennis W.	27	9	M	4	0	15	Q–j
Crews, Adrian	47	11	M	3	4	19	Q–m
Curry, Norman E.	34	9	S	6	0	12	Q–j
Cyrus, Richard E.	45	8	M	4	0	12	Q–j
Darnell, G. G.	19	9	S	3	0	1	D–f
DeLong, Geo. G.	41	6	M	6	0	6	D–g
Dismukes, Ray H.	32	11	M	4	6	16	Q–j
Distler, Tony	21	10	M	1	0	11	Q–e
Douglas, Will L.	44	12	M	5	0	13	Q–m
Drishka, Marvin	37	11	M	3	4	8	Q–e
Dubois, Wm. A.	43	9	M	4	7	4	D–c
Duffy, Floyd D.	34	10	S	8	5	21	D–b
Duval, Harold E.	22	9	S	3	0	4	D–g
Dyer, Neil E.	30	12	M	3	3	6	Q–j
Dykes, H. B.	48	7	M	6	0	1	D–i
Echols, Leland M.	36	8	S	8	0	7	D–a
Edmiston, Matt W.	37	7	M	4	12	11	Q–j
Edwin, Geo. T.	19	12	S	1	0	14	Q–j
Eichelberger, F. A.	43	11	M	5	6	13	Q–m
Ekstrom, Bruce I.	39	6	S	8	0	5	D–a
Elmore, Alfred E.	36	9	M	5	0	23	Q–m
Engbloom, Hans E.	32	8	S	8	0	1	D–g
Estes, Peter T.	34	9	M	5	6	47	Q–k
Ettlinger, Melvin	28	8	S	5	0	9	D–h
Evans, Allan D.	35	6	M	4	0	4	D–g
Evans, Robert E.	28	8	S	5	0	9	D–h
Ezelle, Guy D.	32	10	M	3	0	51	Q–j
Fahrenkamp, G. F.	43	12	M	4	9	17	Q–m
Faris, W. Frank	20	9	M	2	1	10	Q–j

Table 48 *(continued)*

461

Report Problems

	A	B	C	D	E	F	G
Feurbacher, R. S.	43	11	M	5	12	25	Q–i
Floyd, Pat M.	24	11	M	2	0	17	Q–e
Francis, Victor A.	34	12	S	6	0	5	D–g
Franklin, Aubrey	43	10	S	8	3	7	D–a
Frazetti, Antonio	20	12	S	1	0	2	D–b
Friedrich, Chester	32	12	M	5	0	11	D–b
Frost, Edgar E.	38	10	S	7	0	7	D–f
Frymire, Raymond A.	31	11	M	3	0	12	Q–j
Fulbright, E. D.	40	5	M	6	0	5	D–g
Fulcock, Edward	50	4	M	8	1	3	D–g
Fusser, Rodney	35	8	M	6	0	2	D–g
Garner, C. G.	24	9	M	5	1	8	D–g
Goode, Thomas	37	11	M	5	0	10	D–b
Gregory, A. V.	45	8	M	6	2	17	Q–m
Grimes, Carl	31	12	M	3	0	9	Q–e
Gunn, Lloyd, Jr.	38	7	M	6	15	23	Q–j
Hakins, Raymond	49	8	S	9	0	4	D–g
Hancock, Paul V.	28	12	S	5	0	4	D–b
Harrison, Edwin	54	7	M	7	24	18	D–c
Hause, Milton	35	8	M	4	3	9	D–c
Herwig, A. H.	20	8	S	3	0	14	D–a
Hinton, Will D.	19	12	S	2	0	13	Q–e
Hruska, Emil	31	8	M	3	9	5	D–b
Hyltin, Alvin	29	5	M	4	3	17	Q–d
Ischy, Mac	18	12	S	0	0	4	Q–e
Jabour, Clifford	27	9	S	4	0	4	Q–e
Johnson, Arthur	30	10	M	5	0	14	Q–j
Johnson, W. H.	37	6	M	4	0	2	D–g
Jones, Wilfred	41	6	M	4	0	4	D–g
Jordan, Milam B.	19	9	M	2	2	5	D–b
Joslin, A. L.	43	8	M	5	12	25	Q–m
Junkin, Ralph W.	20	10	S	1	0	2	D–h
Jurecka, Leo J.	32	12	M	5	0	11	D–b
Kelly, Patrick	38	5	M	4	2	3	D–g
Key, Theodore	35	12	S	7	7	9	D–h
Kunze, August M.	50	10	M	5	0	11	D–b
Kyle, Sidney	33	9	M	3	0	20	Q–e
Lawrence, W. W.	42	8	M	5	0	5	D–c
Lee, Vernon A.	25	9	S	3	0	10	D–g
Lewis, Fred M.	44	4	M	6	0	3	D–g
Liesman, Wm. A.	31	11	M	5	0	13	Q–e
Lincoln, Walter A.	36	8	M	4	0	8	Q–e
Lloyd, Roy, Jr.	30	8	M	5	4	2	D–i
Lockhart, Marvin	38	10	S	6	0	7	D–g
Lunceford, T. R.	31	11	M	3	0	12	Q–j
Lund, Wm. B.	32	8	S	8	0	1	D–g
Lupton, A. J.	19	12	S	1	0	14	Q–j
Lyckman, Philip	28	9	S	5	0	9	D–g
Lyckman, Tom G.	34	9	M	5	6	27	Q–x
Lyle, Lanier M.	35	6	M	4	0	4	D–g
Lynch, Everett	40	6	M	4	0	3	D–g
Lytton, Earl, Jr.	20	12	S	1	0	41	Q–j
MacDonald, Wm. R.	26	9	S	4	3	11	D–c
Mackey, M. T.	46	12	M	3	0	11	Q–m
Maddox, Calvin C.	33	9	S	6	5	19	D–b
Magoon, Wilson	47	10	M	3	0	8	D–c
Mallett, August	35	8	M	5	0	3	D–i
Marcum, H. H.	41	7	S	7	11	29	Q–j
Martin, Edgar B.	19	6	S	3	0	7	D–g

Table 48 *(continued)*

	A	B	C	D	E	F	G
Martin, Ellis	27	11	M	3	0	9	Q–e
McAngus, Howard	32	8	S	8	0	1	D–g
McCaleb, Clarence	19	12	S	1	0	14	Q–j
McClellan, J. T.	34	9	M	5	6	37	Q–x
McKown, Jack	28	8	S	5	0	9	D–h
McRill, Sam S.	35	6	M	4	0	4	D–g
Mears, I. D.	40	6	M	4	0	3	D–g
Middlebrook, S. S.	20	12	S	1	0	21	Q–j
Miller, Adrian	26	9	S	4	3	11	D–c
Mosley, Willis T.	46	12	M	3	0	11	Q–m
Mosteller, Curtis	33	9	S	6	5	19	D–b
Mueller, Kenneth	47	10	M	3	0	8	D–c
Murphy, Pat J.	35	8	M	5	0	3	D–i
Muston, M. R.	41	7	S	7	11	29	Q–j
Nafcieger, P. T.	27	11	M	3	0	9	Q–e
Nalle, Walter, Jr.	19	6	S	3	0	7	D–g
Nance, Audry	40	9	M	4	0	4	D–g
Nauert, W. H.	30	12	M	4	0	11	Q–x
Nevens, Robert T.	39	4	M	9	0	4	D–g
Newman, Hugh W.	44	12	S	3	0	7	D–b
Nicholas, Alvin A.	29	12	S	5	0	14	D–h
Nichols, Calvin	32	10	M	3	0	57	Q–j
Nicholson, W. W.	43	8	S	4	9	17	Q–m
Norman, Chas. T.	20	11	M	2	1	10	Q–j
Nusom, Burl L.	18	8	S	1	0	5	Q–e
Oates, D. D.	34	12	M	4	11	6	D–c
O'Dea, Dean	33	9	S	6	0	4	D–g
Odell, Francis	34	8	M	5	0	4	D–g
Oertli, Frank	19	8	S	2	0	3	D–g
Olle, E. D.	30	9	M	4	0	11	Q–d
Olson, Olaf, Jr.	22	12	S	2	0	7	Q–j
Owens, Thornton	45	8	S	8	9	15	D–a
Pafenbach, Fritz	31	9	S	6	8	13	D–h
Pafford, Wm. J.	22	12	S	2	0	7	Q–j
Page, Ellis T.	22	10	S	3	0	4	D–g
Page, Morris W.	30	9	M	3	3	6	Q–j
Pannell, G. T., Jr.	48	7	S	6	0	1	D–i
Paralta, Amos	36	9	S	8	0	7	D–a
Park, Gene E.	37	9	M	4	12	11	Q*
Peirce, Preston	43	11	M	5	6	13	Q–m
Peschka, Bernard	28	12	M	2	2	16	Q–j
Porter, Wm. A.	49	9	M	4	0	2	D–g
Prince, A. T.	26	11	M	4	1	8	D–b
Purdy, Donald T.	21	8	S	5	2	4	D–g
Pyles, John L.	39	5	S	8	0	5	D–a
Quaker, P. A.	36	9	M	5	0	23	Q–m
Quante, R. M., Jr.	45	7	S	7	0	6	D–g
Querro, Hortence	24	6	F	6	1	2	D–g
Quick, Dan T.	17	8	M	2	0	4	D–g
Quick, Sam A.	44	12	M	3	0	16	Q–g
Raatz, Frank	42	11	S	5	4	21	D–c
Ragsdale, Buford	31	9	M	4	3	13	Q–d
Railer, W. T.	48	8	M	5	17	12	D–h
Rainbolt, Carrol	35	7	S	9	0	2	D–i
Raisch, Milton D.	36	11	S	3	0	16	Q–j
Ramirez, Joe A.	38	5	M	5	0	9	D–g
Ramsey, Rufe	19	12	S	1	0	29	Q–j
Rawlings, G. G.	19	9	S	3	0	1	D–g
Reed, James T.	41	6	M	6	0	6	D–g

Table 48 *(continued)*

463

	A	B	C	D	E	F	G
Reed, Maxie	32	11	M	4	6	16	D–c
Reeves, Buck	21	10	M	1	0	11	Q–e
Reilly, L. O.	39	8	S	6	0	7	D–c
Renz, C. K.	40	7	M	5	5	14	Q–j
Richardson, Gus	18	11	S	1	1	11	Q–j
Rike, Barney	46	9	M	6	3	31	Q–m
Rucker, Harry	36	9	S	5	0	5	D–b
Sandel, Leonard	39	10	M	3	0	17	Q–m
Sanders, Eugene	27	10	M	3	0	12	Q–e
Saxon, Sam B.	38	6	M	4	0	2	D–g
Scales, T. G.	42	12	M	5	0	13	Q–m
Schaefer, Chas. E.	27	9	S	6	0	2	D–i
Scherbarth, Ben R.	44	12	M	5	0	13	Q–m
Schleuter, Karl H.	37	11	M	4	4	8	Q–e
Schmidt, Richard A.	43	9	M	4	7	4	D–c
Scoffield, Lewis	34	10	S	8	5	21	D–f
Scott, Noel B.	47	5	M	5	0	1	D–g
Sellers, T. M., Jr.	43	12	M	4	0	19	Q–m
Shamrock, Wm. P.	35	8	M	6	0	2	D–g
Sheet, I. A.	48	9	M	6	16	36	Q–j
Sherron, Grover C.	29	9	M	3	1	5	D–g
Shuberg, Geo. T.	25	8	S	3	0	2	D–g
Siek, Mavin T.	21	8	S	1	0	3	D–g
Sifuentes, Fred	34	10	M	3	0	1	D–g
Smith, Geo. A.	18	9	S	2	0	7	D–b
Smith, Leroy	19	11	S	2	0	19	Q–e
Smith, Steve, Jr.	23	12	S	2	1	13	D–b
Stanley, L. V.	30	9	M	3	0	7	Q–e
Sullivan, Pat	44	6	M	8	1	10	D–i
Swenson, Ollie, Jr.	33	9	S	7	0	5	D–h
Swift, Weldon E.	30	11	M	2	7	11	Q–j
Taber, A. H.	47	11	M	4	5	19	Q–m
Tannehill, Geo. H.	34	8	M	4	0	2	D–g
Taylor, Bob A.	31	9	S	5	0	1	D–g
Taylor, O. L.	45	8	M	5	0	12	Q–j
Teaguri, Vincent	19	11	S	1	0	6	Q–e
Terby, Alton	31	10	M	3	0	1	D–g
Thompson, Joe J.	32	9	M	7	2	19	D–h
Thrasher, Wallace	40	7	S	8	0	9	D–i
Travis, John E.	25	10	S	2	0	4	D–a
Tyler, Stanton	33	8	M	4	0	5	Q–e
Ulit, Amos B.	54	5	M	7	24	18	D–c
Umscheid, B. V.	37	11	M	2	0	14	Q–e
Underwood, Tom A.	19	6	M	3	2	2	D–g
Urban, Elmer	26	7	S	5	0	3	D–g
Uzzell, Marshall	41	10	M	3	0	9	D–g
Van Cleave, Homer	34	9	M	3	0	1	D–g
Veteto, Manuel	18	8	S	2	0	7	D–b
Wade, Dennis E.	50	7	S	8	0	9	D–i
Walberg, Eugene	25	11	S	2	0	4	D–a
Walker, Chas. T.	18	11	S	1	1	11	Q–j
Walters, Leo R.	46	10	M	6	3	31	Q–m
Webb, Roy A.	35	12	M	6	0	2	D–g
Weide, James T.	48	8	M	6	16	36	Q–j
Wendlandt, R. M.	34	10	S	5	0	4	D–g
Wheatley, Gordon	19	8	S	2	0	3	D–g
Whisenant, L. D.	42	12	M	5	4	21	Q–j
Wilson, Oscar	31	9	M	4	3	13	Q–d
Yager, Wm. E.	46	12	M	3	0	11	Q–m

Table 48 *(concluded)*

	A	B	C	D	E	F	G
Yeates, John J.	33	10	S	6	5	19	D–b
Young, Melvin	47	11	M	3	0	8	D–c
Zapalac, Ted E.	35	8	M	5	0	3	D–i
Zilker, John R.	33	10	M	3	0	20	Q–e
Zuehel, Gilbert	42	8	M	5	0	5	D–c
Zwiener, A. M.	25	8	S	3	0	10	D–g

Note: Explanation of column heads: A. Age at time of employment.
B. Schooling in years.
C. Marital status (Divorced counted as single).
D. Number of jobs previously held.
E. Years of related experience.
F. Months of employment with Thrifty Food Stores.
G. Nature and reason for termination of employment:
    D—Discharged
    Q—Quit
    a—Absenteeism
    b—Discourtesy
    c—Dishonesty
    d—Dislike of manager
    e—Dislike of work
    f—Drinking on job
    g—Incapacity
    h—Insubordination
    i—Laziness
    j—More pay elsewhere
    k—No promotion
    l—No salary increase
    m—Poor health
    x—No reason

* Purchase of own store

37. **Selecting the right magazine for Moroccan Craft.** For this assignment, assume that you are director of research for Wycliff-Briggs Advertising Agency. Wycliff-Briggs is a comparatively small but rapidly expanding agency which is just now moving up into the big-account class. The new account responsible for the agency's latest move up the success ladder is that of Moroccan Craft, Inc., manufacturers of a line of quality luggage.

Moroccan Craft's current advertising plan calls for more than the usual dealer cooperative campaigns used in the past. This time, a nationwide campaign is to be run in a major periodical. Which periodical will carry the Moroccan Craft story to the people hasn't as yet been determined, but here is where you come in.

At the oral request of Ms. Wanda Dodd, account executive for the Moroccan Craft account, you are to make the analysis which will point the way to the decision. Your analysis is limited to two periodicals—*Newsweek* and *People*—the others having been eliminated by Ms. Dodd for one reason or other. More specifically stated, it is your assignment to get a picture of the advertising characteristics of the two magazines which will show where the Moroccan Craft advertising would be most at home.

Normally, such studies involve extensive survey-type investigations. At the moment, however, Wycliff-Briggs cannot afford a costly study; so you set out to do the next best thing. Working on the assumption that the bigger agencies have long ago made similar studies, you conclude that analysis of the advertisements they place in a magazine reveals their findings concerning that magazine. Thus, your objective is to obtain a summary picture of the advertisements in *People* and *Newsweek*. Your study will get all of the facts which will help make the decision—such information as classes and price levels of goods and services, the buying motives the advertisements appeal to, and the techniques used to present these appeals. These facts can be made to portray the readers they are written for. That is, they'll have a good indication of such things as the typical reader's age, sex, family status, and economic and intellectual status.

You begin your investigation by getting two copies of each of the two magazines in question. Then, based on what you believe to be the major points which reveal the magazines' readers, you construct a tally sheet. Next, you make an ad-by-ad check of the magazines, summarizing your findings after all ads have been checked. Now you are ready for the analysis which will point the way to the best decision. This analysis and the data upon which it is based will be written up in an easy-to-read and eye-pleasing report.

When you are at last ready to write up your report, you face the decision on scope, tone, and form. You decide to use the impersonal tone (no *I, we,* or *you,* but consistent third person), to include enough identification to make the report readily understandable to somebody up the line from Ms. Dodd and to set up the report with adequate prefatory parts. Although you will break your data into smaller units and present lots of graphic illustrations, you will nevertheless translate the whole story into words and not shift the burden to your tables and charts. In so doing, you will seek out the concrete word and the specific instance to keep away from statistical jargon and big generalities of talk. You will, in short, work to make the report a readable thing in an eye-attracting setup.

Specifically, the formal report you plan to write will include these parts: a binding cover, a title fly, a title page, your personal letter of transmittal to Ms. Dodd, a table of contents (in organized-outline form), a table of illustrations, an epitome (in direct style, beginning with a distilled digest of your main findings and then shifting back to its real job of compressing each part in order and in proportion), the report body (arranged in logical order), supporting illustrations, and possibly an appendix.

38. **Finding the problems at Midway's Aton store.** For the past four years, the home office advertising department of Midway Department Stores, Inc., has planned and prepared advertising for all major promotions (January white sales, mid-summer clearances, harvest sales, and the like) for the chain's 27 branch stores. Only the day-to-day advertising and a few of the less important promotions were handled by each store's own advertising managers. In general, the success of this plan has been quite plain to the company.

Particularly was the Midway management pleased when it reviewed the store-by-store sales summaries for the major promotions. For the past few years, sales from promotions have been exceeding quotas at the individual stores—with only limited exceptions. One of these exceptions, the store at Aton, is your concern at the moment.

You, a marketing research specialist of some repute, have been retained by Ms. Rita A. Conn, president of Midway, to make a special study of the problem store. Specifically, Ms. Conn wants to know why the Aton store has failed to keep up with other Midway outlets. If possible, she'd like you to pinpoint the sources of difficulty.

She and others of the Midway hierarchy feel that the trouble lies in a general failure of the Aton store to coordinate its display and personal selling efforts with the promotional advertising which comes from the central office. It's your job to test their theory and to shed whatever light you can on the Company's problem.

So you plan your research efforts to test management's thinking. During the following weeks, you and a crew of assistants shop extensively in all departments of the problem store and of three of the Company's more successful outlets, observing and recording all information which you believe might shed light on the problem. If, you reason, the Aton store summaries show less coordination between advertising on the one hand and the display of advertised material and personal sales efforts on the other, then management's theory is substantiated. But, if the opposite, or no relation is apparent, then other causes need to be investigated. Should management's theory be correct, a department-by-department analysis would be needed to pinpoint the sources of difficulty.

Today, after long weeks of careful record-keeping, you have the data which should point to the answer. You have but to pore over them, weigh them carefully, and then proceed to the obvious conclusions. In keeping with the formality of the situation and the size of the problem, you will do well to present your analysis in formal-report form.

Your summary data are in Tables 49–65. (Note that the data are expressed in percentages.)

Table 49
Displayed Advertised Merchandise in Street Window

	Aton	Bell	Cody	Delta
Sporting goods	0	8	8	8
Automotive	4	2	3	6
Hardware	2	2	4	6
Household furnishings	3	6	5	0
Ready-to-wear:				
Men's	1	8	7	2
Women's	0	12	9	0
Children's	0	8	6	9
Appliances	0	4	0	2

Table 50
Displayed Advertised Merchandise in Other Departments

	Aton	Bell	Cody	Delta
Sporting goods	2	12	15	5
Automotive	0	7	8	6
Hardware	0	7	2	4
Household furnishings	0	8	6	2
Ready-to-wear:				
Men's	4	6	2	0
Women's	0	6	9	0
Children's	2	5	8	0
Appliances	0	0	0	0

Table 51
Displayed Advertised Merchandise in Department Where Sold

	Aton	Bell	Cody	Delta
Sporting goods	82	100	100	100
Automotive	99	96	96	100
Hardware	92	98	94	100
Household furnishings	100	100	100	91
Ready-to-wear:				
Men's	89	100	100	94
Women's	91	100	100	95
Children's	86	100	100	99
Appliances	93	100	99	100

Table 52
Advertised Items Displayed in Selling Department Carried Informative Signs

	Aton	Bell	Cody	Delta
Sporting goods	33	100	100	100
Automotive	92	98	97	100
Hardware	79	89	94	98
Household furnishings	95	100	100	86
Ready-to-wear:				
Men's	62	97	100	90
Women's	69	99	100	89
Children's	66	100	98	100
Appliances	77	100	89	100

Table 53
Informative Signs Included Prices of Advertised Items

	Aton	Bell	Cody	Delta
Sporting goods	100	100	94	100
Automotive	100	98	92	98
Hardware	96	94	100	96
Household furnishings	98	92	100	100
Ready-to-wear:				
Men's	94	100	98	96
Women's	92	96	90	94
Children's	100	94	100	90
Appliances	100	100	100	100

Table 54
Failed to Back Advertised Items with Adequate Merchandise Offerings

	Aton				Bell				Cody				Delta			
	(1)	(2)	(3)	(4)	(1)	(2)	(3)	(4)	(1)	(2)	(3)	(4)	(1)	(2)	(3)	(4)
Sporting goods.......	24	16	19	41	4	4	6	86	0	3	5	92	3	5	6	86
Automotive	4	6	9	81	6	6	9	79	5	7	8	80	1	5	2	92
Hardware	20	13	20	47	6	7	10	77	8	11	5	76	1	3	3	93
Household furnishings	2	6	4	88	4	2	2	92	2	2	3	93	9	11	9	71
Ready-to-wear:																
Men's	16	14	12	58	6	4	9	81	3	5	8	84	12	10	12	66
Women's	33	13	18	36	9	7	4	80	7	6	6	81	13	13	16	58
Children's	8	2	19	71	3	5	4	88	4	4	3	89	3	5	5	87
Appliances	18	12	17	53	1	3	5	91	6	2	12	80	2	7	2	89

1. Sold out first day.
2. Sold out second day.
3. Sold out third day.
4. Adequate stock for sale.

Table 55
Instances in Which Available Salespersons Waited on Customers Immediately

	Aton	Bell	Cody	Delta
Sporting goods	65	94	93	95
Automotive	94	·90	91	94
Hardware...............................	85	85	84	93
Household furnishings	92	91	92	85
Ready-to-wear:				
Men's	74	88	86	80
Women's..............................	67	89	88	81
Children's	79	90	91	93
Appliances.............................	70	89	96	94

Table 56
Greeting Extended Customer by Salesperson

	Aton					Bell					Cody					Delta				
	(1)	(2)	(3)	(4)	(5)	(1)	(2)	(3)	(4)	(5)	(1)	(2)	(3)	(4)	(5)	(1)	(2)	(3)	(4)	(5)
Sporting goods	44	16	6	28	6	6	78	3	2	11	4	60	19	9	8	3	71	7	17	2
Automotive	4	68	14	4	10	12	60	3	3	22	11	54	16	12	7	3	73	16	7	1
Hardware	15	54	5	0	26	13	59	7	1	20	10	66	6	9	9	2	61	17	8	12
Household furnishings	12	70	0	0	18	4	81	6	1	8	3	68	9	1	19	14	57	19	0	10
Ready-to-wear:																				
Men's	30	44	6	12	18	7	70	18	0	5	5	54	11	10	20	12	60	9	14	5
Women's	10	67	19	0	4	4	56	20	11	9	3	69	19	0	9	16	49	21	0	14
Children's	24	53	3	0	20	3	62	14	0	21	3	61	23	0	13	4	58	23	0	15
Appliances	40	36	4	4	16	6	66	6	9	13	12	49	20	3	16	2	71	19	2	6

1. No greeting.
2. "May I help you?"
3. "Are you being waited on?"
4. "Yes, sir?"
5. Other.

Table 57
Courtesy of Salespersons

	Aton				Bell				Cody				Delta			
	(1)	(2)	(3)	(4)	(1)	(2)	(3)	(4)	(1)	(2)	(3)	(4)	(1)	(2)	(3)	(4)
Sporting goods.......	0	36	58	6	39	58	3	0	44	54	2	0	64	32	4	0
Automotive	16	78	6	0	12	79	9	0	10	81	9	0	33	61	6	0
Hardware	6	76	16	0	6	87	7	0	12	79	9	0	44	52	4	0
Household furnishings	68	22	10	0	41	57	2	0	51	47	2	0	7	84	9	0
Ready-to-wear:																
Men's............	2	71	27	0	36	58	6	0	28	69	3	0	2	80	16	2
Women's	16	68	13	0	44	49	7	0	36	62	2	0	2	80	18	0
Children's	8	66	26	0	31	65	4	0	19	77	4	0	33	62	5	0
Appliances	0	51	42	7	60	40	0	0	4	87	9	0	21	76	3	0

1. Very courteous.
2. Courteous.
3. Slightly discourteous or indifferent.
4. Discourteous.

Table 58
Instances when Salespersons Were Informed about Advertised Merchandise

	Aton	Bell	Cody	Delta
Sporting goods	86	100	100	100
Automotive	100	99	90	100
Hardware	96	98	98	100
Household furnishings	100	100	100	92
Ready-to-wear:				
Men's	74	100	100	89
Women's	91	100	100	94
Children's...........................	90	99	100	100
Appliances	100	100	97	100

Table 59
Instances when Salespersons Knew Location of Advertised Merchandise

	Aton	Bell	Cody	Delta
Sporting goods	90	100	100	100
Automotive	98	98	93	100
Hardware................................	92	94	95	99
Household furnishings	99	100	100	93
Ready-to-wear:				
Men's	89	99	99	92
Women's.............................	91	99	98	90
Children's	91	99	94	97
Appliances.............................	96	100	94	100

Table 60

Instances when Salespersons Encouraged Customers to Handle Merchandise

	Aton	Bell	Cody	Delta
Sporting goods	12	67	61	72
Automotive	33	19	21	34
Hardware	17	23	26	33
Household furnishings	11	44	46	19
Ready-to-wear:				
Men's	21	41	71	29
Women's	23	64	57	41
Children's	9	33	37	38
Appliances	16	37	24	34

Table 61

Knowledge of Merchandise Displayed by Salesperson's Presentation

	Aton				Bell				Cody				Delta			
	(1)	(2)	(3)	(4)	(1)	(2)	(3)	(4)	(1)	(2)	(3)	(4)	(1)	(2)	(3)	(4)
Sporting goods	6	20	71	3	32	66	2	0	31	60	9	0	27	71	2	0
Automotive	31	63	6	0	17	61	22	0	13	70	15	2	30	69	1	0
Hardware	22	59	17	2	16	55	21	8	14	61	21	4	29	66	3	2
Household furnishings	28	69	3	0	37	63	0	0	33	67	0	0	17	69	12	2
Ready-to-wear:																
Men's	7	66	20	7	14	81	5	0	20	79	1	0	6	69	25	0
Women's	9	60	24	7	21	78	1	0	31	69	0	0	11	66	21	2
Children's	8	54	21	17	31	67	2	0	23	76	1	0	19	80	1	0
Appliances	2	46	50	2	51	49	0	0	17	69	14	0	47	49	4	0

1. Knew merchandise very well.
2. Knew merchandise adequately.
3. Insufficient knowledge of merchandise.
4. Little or no knowledge of merchandise.

Table 62

Salesperson Suggested Additional Merchandise

	Aton	Bell	Cody	Delta
Sporting goods	2	37	41	41
Automotive	31	19	22	30
Hardware	11	21	24	36
Household furnishings	27	26	29	17
Ready-to-wear:				
Men's	19	46	51	33
Women's	18	56	52	35
Children's	13	31	36	34
Appliances	4	13	13	16

Table 63
Salesperson Attempted to Trade Up

	Aton	Bell	Cody	Delta
Sporting goods	0	16	19	21
Automotive	17	14	13	20
Hardware	9	11	13	21
Household furnishings	21	23	19	13
Ready-to-wear:				
Men's	23	39	37	26
Women's	11	33	30	22
Children's	9	16	18	19
Appliances	67	33	22	36

Table 64
Salesperson's Closing Remark

	Aton			Bell			Cody			Delta		
	(1)	(2)	(3)	(1)	(2)	(3)	(1)	(2)	(3)	(1)	(2)	(3)
Sporting goods	61	33	6	88	0	12	91	0	9	84	1	15
Automotive	87	2	11	81	5	14	79	6	15	89	0	11
Hardware	67	9	24	74	6	20	76	3	21	93	0	7
Household furnishings	91	0	9	88	0	12	87	2	11	81	14	5
Ready-to-wear:												
Men's	86	6	8	91	1	8	92	0	8	87	5	8
Women's	83	7	10	90	0	10	93	0	7	84	6	10
Children's	81	9	10	91	0	9	87	1	12	82	0	18
Appliances	62	29	9	94	0	6	89	2	9	93	0	7

1. "Thank you."
2. None.
3. Other.

Table 65
Average Percent of Promotion Sales Quotas* Achieved during Past Three Years

	Aton	Bell	Cody	Delta
Sporting goods	61	114	119	111
Automotive	107	88	91	109
Hardware	81	87	94	113
Household furnishings	103	116	118	84
Ready-to-wear:				
Men's	69	107	113	87
Women's	74	111	108	91
Children's	72	119	103	116
Appliances	59	122	92	103
Store average	79	108	105	103

* Quotas are based on Midway's own formula, which takes into account such factors as population, past sales records, and competition.

39. Which of three magazines should carry McSwain pipes' advertising? As director of research for the Malcolm, Thames, and Wardlowe Advertising Agency you are working on an assignment for Edward Karnes, account executive for McSwain pipes. As you understand them, the facts of your problem are as follows.

The McSwain Pipe Company, Ltd., of Edinburgh, Scotland, is just now introducing its century-old line of pipes to the U.S. market. The McSwain people can truly say that their pipes are among the world's finest. Made of only top-grade briar, McSwain pipes are built to exacting specifications. And every one of the company's 11 basic models is handsomely designed. Because McSwain pipes are high in quality they must sell for more than most pipes; but they are not out of the reach of discerning pipe fanciers of moderate means. Retail prices in the United States will start at $20 and will range upward to $75.

In spite of the good qualities of McSwain pipes, they are not known in the United States. If they are to sell, they must be promoted. And it is in this regard that Malcolm, Thames, and Wardlowe came on the scene. They were awarded the McSwain account, and now they are planning their initial campaign with Mr. Karnes serving as account executive.

Mr. Karnes plans to publicize McSwain pipes in full-page color advertisements which will be seen in one of the nation's leading magazines for men. Determining which magazine should carry the message, however, is no small problem for Mr. Karnes. It is on this matter that you, the agency's director of research, have been asked to help. Mr. Karnes has narrowed his selection to three men's magazines—*Sportsman, Male,* and *Mechanix Illustrated. Sportsman* is a magazine for those who like hunting, fishing, and the out-of-doors. *Male,* with its nude photographs and risqué writing, caters to swingers. *Mechanix Illustrated* is just what its name suggests—a magazine for those interested in mechanics. Mr. Karnes cannot decide on the best of the three. So he asks you for help. Specifically, he wants you to compare all pertinent information on the three magazines and to recommend the one that should carry the McSwain message.

The magazine you choose should be the one whose readers are most likely to be potential users of McSwain pipes. As Mr. Karnes points out, they should be the kind who appreciate quality and who can afford to pay for it. Although men of all ages buy McSwain pipes, they are especially appealing to the young sophisticate. In addition, older men of means and those with less responsibility are likely purchasers of fine pipes.

As you have done many times before in similar problems, you consult the latest consumer magazines' reports—for information on readership characteristics. Then you consult the latest *Standard Rate and Data Service*— for cost information. From these two sources you find the information which will point the way to your conclusion (see Tables 66–67).

As usual, you will write the information in a concise yet thorough report. Because it may well be reviewed by McSwain management personnel, you will present your material in the form of a formal, long report. You will use graphic aids wherever they will be helpful in supplementing your words.

Table 66
Readership Characteristics

	Sportsman	Male	Mechanix Illustrated
Readers per copy of circulation:			
Males	1.39	1.18	1.31
Females	.38	.61	.32
Total	1.77	1.79	1.63
Projected circulation, numbers:			
Males	1,668,000	1,574,000	1,640,000
Females	456,000	814,000	401,000
Total	2,124,000	2,388,000	2,041,000
Ages of male readers:			
10–17 yrs.	21.6%	5.9%	22.2%
18–24 yrs.	12.9	27.1	12.6
25–34 yrs.	15.1	40.7	14.8
35–44 yrs.	19.4	11.0	19.3
45–54 yrs.	18.0	11.9	17.0
55 & older	12.9	3.4	14.1
Median age	35.4 years	29.3 years	35.4 years
Education of male adult readers (last school attended by adults):			
Grade school or less	14.3%	4.6%	12.6%
High school	55.1	45.6	62.1
College	30.6	49.8	25.3
Married readers 18 years and older: Percent married:			
Men	81.7%	70.3%	81.4%
Women	90.9	90.7	96.3
Percent men by age-groups:			
18–24 yrs.	5.6%	16.7%	6.0%
25–34 yrs.	20.2	48.7	25.3
35–44 yrs.	29.2	12.8	30.1
45–54 yrs.	27.0	16.7	22.9
55 and older	18.0	5.1	15.7
Occupation of adult male readers by percentage:			
Professional and technical workers	12.9%	19.9%	14.3%
Officials	8.4	9.8	5.2
Business owners	6.2	6.1	10.1
Farmers and farm laborers	7.2	—	4.7
Clerical	7.9	5.9	5.5
Sales	4.9	7.1	3.1
Craftsmen	21.9	10.0	24.7
Operatives	16.1	11.8	15.6
Service workers	2.9	2.7	3.6
All others	11.6	26.7	13.2
Total family income of readers, percent of total:			
Under 5,000	1.4%	0.7%	1.3%
5,000– 9,999	1.4	2.4	2.4
10,000–14,999	3.8	3.1	3.4
15,000–19,999	7.1	9.3	6.3
20,000–24,999	20.7	17.4	28.1
25,000–29,999	28.4	28.3	29.8
30,000–34,999	20.2	19.9	15.7
35,000 and over	17.0	18.7	12.9
Stage of life, male head of household, percentage of total:			
Single, under 45	1.8%	12.2%	1.9%
Married, under 45, no children under 18	7.1	15.8	7.7

Table 66 *(continued)*

	Sportsman	Male	Mechanix Illustrated
Married, under 45, youngest child under 6	27.4	36.5	30.0
Married, under 45, youngest child over 6	17.6	9.5	16.1
Married, over 45, children under 18	17.6	8.2	16.4
Married, over 45, no children under 18	23.2	11.7	22.2
Single, over 45	4.0	3.4	3.5
Other	1.3	2.7	2.1

Table 67
Selected Information on Advertising Rates

Sportsman

Rates:

1 page (429 lines)	$ 9,375.00
2 columns (286 lines)	6,250.00
½ page (107 lines on 2 columns)	4,700.00
1 column (143 lines or 2 cols. × 71 lines)	3,125.00
1 inch (single column)	311.50
Agate line	22.25

Colors (Two-color—black and 1 color):

1 page	$10,375.00
2 columns	7,175.00
½ page	5,450.00
1 column	3,750.00

4-color page (3 process colors and black):

1 page	13,125.00

Bleed:

Full pages, extra	10%
⅔, ½ and ⅓ page, extra	15%

No bleed accepted on back cover.
Either 2nd or 3rd cover bleed but not both.

Male

Rates:

1 page	$11,500.00
⅔ page	8,250.00
½ page	6,500.00
⅓ page	4,125.00
⅙ page	2,050.00
1 inch	425.00

Colors:

2 colors:

1 page	$14,500.00
⅔ page	10,375.00
½ page (horizontal)	8,185.00
⅓ page	5,175.00

4 colors:

1 page	17,250.00
⅔ page	12,375.00
½ page (horizontal)	9,750.00

Bleed:

Extra	10%

Table 67 *(continued)*

475

Report Problems

Mechanix Illustrated

Rates:

1 page	$ 7,500.00
½ page	3,750.00
¼ page	1,875.00
⅛ page	925.00
1 inch	468.50
Agate line	33.50

      Line rate applies to that portion of ad in excess of standard unit, but less than next larger unit.

Colors:

1 page (black and 1 color), extra	$	675.00
½ page (black and 1 color), extra		437.50
¼ page (black and 1 color), extra		325.00

    ¼ page minimum space unit. Check availabilities on ¼ page units.

Bleed:

Available in page and ½ page units, extra.....................	15%

      No extra charge for bleed into gutter only, or for bleed on 4-color covers, pages or inserts.

40. Advising the Downtown Merchants Association how to compete with shopping centers. (Requires additional research.) Members of the Downtown Merchants Association of _____ (your city or some other city selected by your instructor) are alarmed about the sales they are losing to suburban shopping centers. For the past few years, the merchants have watched the shopping centers develop around them. At first, they were only annoyed at their new competition. Then, as the centers grew and a trend away from downtown shopping developed, the merchants' annoyance changed to concern. As the trend continued, their concern changed to alarm. Their alarm led them to form a Downtown Merchants Association. They had one objective in mind when they formed the association—to fight back against the inroads made by the shopping centers.

The merchants' plight is understandable. Most have heavy investments in buildings or long-term leases. In fact, most of those who were not heavily invested have already pulled out—many moving to the shopping centers. Thus, those who remain are locked in. Their only chance for survival is to fight back.

At their initial meeting, some of the merchants reported what they had heard other towns were doing; and a few made suggestions on what the group might do. It soon became obvious, however, that a group such as theirs could not develop a coordinated plan of action. They agreed that they needed outside help. Thus, you, a marketing consultant, were called in.

As you understand it, your assignment is first to study all aspects of the shopping situation in the city. Then you will search the literature to find out what has been done in other cities or what the experts say can be done. From this analysis, you will develop a plausible plan for the merchants to follow. In drawing up your plan, keep in mind that the merchants are willing and expect to pay something. But they must be convinced that what they pay for is likely to produce profits.

Of course, you will present your work in formal-report form.

41. Are your store's prices in line with its competitors'? Assume that you, an independent research specialist, are employed by one of your local grocery stores (you choose one) to compare the store's prices with the prices of its two main competitors. For some time now, the management has been hearing comments about how much lower the prices of this and that product are at other stores in town. Much of this talk, of course, could be the result of advertised loss leaders—that is, goods advertised at low prices merely to attract customers. But one can't be too sure. Anyway, the fact that sales have dropped recently makes the manager want to investigate the question. And he wants you to make this investigation for him.

To get the information you need, you plan to construct a diversified shopping basket of grocery items and then to check the prices of each item at each of the three stores. Specifically, you will first select a group of items from each department (meats, canned goods, vegetables, etc.). You will take care to select items which can be checked easily—that is, your selections will be carefully specified by grade, quantity, and brand. Too, the items you select will adequately represent the goods in each department. Once you have selected the items, you will visit each of the stores and record the prices of each item. Because you are concerned primarily with normal prices, you will take care to note any prices that are "specials." Also, you will want to note any possible price effects of trading stamps.

With these data collected, your next chore will be to evaluate them and then to write your results in good report form (as specified by your instructor). Because the management wants to be able to pinpoint the departments and commodities that may be in or out of line, your report will present your findings in some detail.

Subjects for library research reports

The following topic suggestions may be used for library research reports. With most of the topics, the specific facts of the case must be created through the student's (or perhaps the instructor's) imagination before a business-type problem exists.

Accounting

1. Report on the need for and availability of accounting graduates in the years ahead.
2. Design an inventory control system for X Company (your choice).
3. How should X Company (lessee) treat lease transactions on its books?
4. Evaluate the alternative accounting methods available to X Company, which is committed to a policy of tax allocation.

5. Evaluate the use of statistical sampling to determine whether a company's internal control system prevents material errors from finding their way into financial statements. Make a recommendation to Company X.

6. As accountant for X Company, justify your treatment of the assets acquired by the takeover of Y Company.

7. Advise X Company management on the question of uniformity of accounting procedures between X Company and its nearest competitor.

8. Recommend to X Company a policy on the translation of foreign currency in the consolidation of overseas subsidiaries.

9. Advise the chief accountant of X Company on the maintenance of capital in company accounts.

10. Advise X Company management on the accounting problems that will come about if it begins overseas operations.

11. Advise X Company management on the problems of departmentalization of factory overhead.

12. Develop a policy for X Company on the costing of joint products and by-products.

13. Advise the management of X Manufacturing Company on the question of whether to use process-costing or job-costing procedures.

14. Analyze break-even analysis as a decision-making tool for X Company.

15. Evaluate for X Company management the validity of the traditional matching process in determining corporate net income.

16. Analyze the relative effects upon income of the FIFO and LIFO methods of inventory valuation during a prolonged period of inflation.

17. Write a report for the American Accounting Association on the effects of computers on the demand for accountants.

18. Evaluate the utility of traditional variance analysis as a means of cost control.

19. Develop a proposal for the accounting treatment of the costs of a research program in X Oil Company.

20. Justify your progressive accounting treatment of revenues received under a four-year construction contract.

21. Establish a bad-debts policy and design a collection system for X Company.

22. Determine the feasibility of a consolidated delivery service for City Y.

23. How should X Company handle the state sales tax on its books?

24. Design an inventory control plan for X Company.

25. Advise X Company management on the validity of return on investment as a measure of performance.

26. What are the methods X Company can use in handling errors which affected net income in prior years?

27. How should X Company handle its patents and copyrights on its books?

28. Report on the status of the use of operations research as a decision-making tool for accountants and managers.

29. How should X Company use cash-flow analysis as a guide in and for profit planning?

30. Evaluate alternative methods of measuring return on investments for X Company.

31. Report to X Company management on the trends in content and design of corporate annual reports.
32. Report to the American Accounting Association on the status of professional ethics in public accounting.
33. Summarize for the accounting department of X Company the most recent trends and developments in accounting theory.
34. Advise partners X and Y of the XY Company how priorities should be determined for cash distribution in the liquidation of their partnership.
35. Advise X Company management on income tax considerations in the selection of a form of business organization.
36. Report to X Company management on the advantages and disadvantages of the uniform cost accounting system.
37. Should X Company use an accelerated method of depreciation?
38. Recommend to X Company the proper disclosure of long-term leases in its financial statements.
39. Recommend to X Company management how it can make better use of the accounting department and accounting information.
40. How should X Company account for pension costs?
41. Develop for Company X a procedure for human resource accounting.
42. Review the pros and cons of installing a time-sharing computer system for Company X.
43. Prepare a report for Company X management on the diversity of factors and practices in transfer pricing.
44. Report on the need and value of a social audit for Company X.

Business education

1. Evaluate the effectiveness of closed-circuit television instruction.
2. How effective is programmed instruction in business education?
3. What should be the content of the business communication (or other subject) course?
4. How should teaching ability be measured?
5. What should be the role of the student in course and curriculum planning?
6. What should be the role of business leaders in developing courses and curricula for business education?
7. Should business teachers be unionized?
8. Examine the present status of business education teaching as a true profession.
9. Outline historical developments in business education.
10. Recommend an ideal certification program for business teachers.
11. Assess placement responsibilities of business education in secondary schools.
12. How effective is career guidance in business education?
13. What is the ideal education for careers in business?
14. Evaluate the use of student evaluations of teachers.
15. Are programs for exceptional youths desirable in business education?
16. Describe the emerging role of the junior college in business education.

17. How should the standards of achievement in the business education curriculum be set?
18. What is the role of economics education at the secondary level?
19. How should student achievement be measured?
20. What are the proper uses of audiovisual aids in teaching business subjects?
21. What are the relations of theories of learning to the teaching of business subjects?
22. What is the place of student opinions and evaluations in curriculum revisions?
23. Develop a plan for work measurements in the office.
24. Develop an ideal testing procedure for business subjects.
25. What is the place of business education in the public secondary school? (Or in technical vocational schools?)
26. Should the business curriculum be specialized or should it provide a generalized, well-rounded education?
27. Evaluate the development of federal aid to business education.

Labor

1. For X Union investigate the impact technological evolution has had on unionism in the past decade.
2. Develop a new compensation plan for X Company that will best motivate employees.
3. Design a plan of employee discipline for X Company.
4. Evaluate the potential labor problems of X Company in _____ (country) where it is planning a new factory.
5. Advise X Company management on the use of the lockout as a means of dealing with its union.
6. For a specific national union make an objective report on union leadership in the nation during the past decade.
7. Evaluate the effects of a particular strike (your choice) on the union, the company, the stockholder, and the public. Write the report for a federal investigating committee.
8. Advise management of X Company on how to deal with Y Union, which is attempting to organize X's employees.
9. For a national union write a report on the trend of corruption in unions over the past 25 years.
10. How have union contracts limited the area of decision making?
11. Explore the relationships of the union and the white-collar worker.
12. Show trends and implications of teachers organizing.
13. Examine recent trends relative to the older worker and the stand taken by unions in this area.
14. Analyze the problem of automation and the unions' reactions to it.
15. Study the status and effects of "right-to-work" laws.
16. Is it proper for unions to be in business for themselves?
17. Set up plans for unionizing Company X.
18. Recommend a grievance system for Company X.

19. Should antitrust laws apply to unions?
20. Examine and report on discrimination in unions.
21. Should government employees be unionized?
22. Outline the power structure of unions and its implications.
23. Evaluate the future of process unionism.
24. Discuss unionism in retail stores and its effects on prices.
25. What is the status of labor regulations in your state?
26. Are unions monopolistic?
27. How should Company X prepare for upcoming contract negotiations with the union?
28. What are the causes of industrial war and peace?
29. Report on what personnel executives look for in application letters and data sheets.

Finance

1. Advise overcapitalized X Company on the possibility of repurchasing shares.
2. Justify the use of ratio analysis to a major client of your brokerage firm.
3. Evaluate the advantages and disadvantages of issuing "no par" stock for X Company.
4. Advise the medical doctors at X Clinic as to whether they should incorporate their operation.
5. Should X Company lease or buy capital equipment?
6. Advise rapidly growing X Manufacturing Company on the form of organization it should take.
7. Advise faltering X Company on whether it would be more valuable as a going concern than it would be in liquidation.
8. Should X Company establish a holding company in its corporate organizational structure?
9. Should X Company amend its policy of paying dividends at a constant proportion of earnings to one of paying on a constant per-share basis?
10. Examine the possibilities of factoring accounts receivable for X Company, which is experiencing a liquidity crisis.
11. Advise X Company as to whether it should seek to get its stock listed on a major stock exchange.
12. Develop a fundamental inventory control model for X Company.
13. Advise X Company on the policy it should follow in determining dividend payments.
14. Evaluate the utility of the payback method of investment analysis.
15. Recommend and justify a plan for financing expansion of X Company.
16. How will the present state of the market affect the success of the proposed rights offering of X Company?
17. Advise X Company on whether it should select a capital structure that will serve to minimize the cost of capital and so promote maximum share prices.
18. Advise X Company management on how the prevailing condition of

capital rationing in the company should affect its investment decision analysis.

19. What should be the role of the controllership function in cost control at X Company?
20. What is the most feasible way to finance newly formed X Company?
21. Recommend for Company X some compensations and proprietary mechanisms that may serve as an alternative to stock options.
22. Should Investment Group X invest in mutual funds?
23. Should Investment Group X invest in gold?
24. Examine the merits of proposed legislation to regulate the price of consumer credit.
25. Should Company X join an employers' association?
26. Recommend a formal salary scale for X Company.
27. For a national union, evaluate the effectiveness of the Occupational Safety and Health Act (OSHA) on workers' health and safety. Recommend union action based on your findings.
28. For a special committee of Congress, review the question of "fairness" in labor contracts with management. Make recommendations for correcting through legislation.
29. What should be the role of National Union X in helping to reduce inflation?
30. For the National Association of Manufacturers, evaluate the prospects for labor-management relations in the year ahead.
31. What should be the role of Labor Union X (or Company X) in politics?
32. Layoffs based on seniority are causing a disproportionate reduction in women and minority workers at Company X. Investigate alternatives which the company can present to the union.
33. What should be the role of Union X in the matter of environmental protection?

Management

1. Advise Company X management on what it should do to overcome resistance to _____ (some basic change, such as a change in compensation plan).
2. Design an employee-selection procedure for X Company.
3. Recommend and justify to the board of directors of X Company a plan for exercising the firm's social responsibility.
4. Design a control system for preventing individual espionage at X Company.
5. Evaluate for X Oil Company the application of statistical decision theory in overcoming the problems of uncertainty in oil exploration.
6. Evaluate for X Company the possibility of using brainstorming sessions in strategic policy making.
7. Evaluate for X Manufacturing Company the use of the informal grapevine as a means of improving communication within the organization.
8. Using the best authoritative ideas available, design a management information system for X Company.

9. Design a public relations campaign for X Company.
10. Recommend an executive evaluation plan for X Company.
11. Develop for X Company a guide to ethics in its highly competitive business situation.
12. Analyze break-even analysis as a decision-making tool for X Company.
13. Evaluate the various methods of determining corporate performance, and select the one most appropriate for Company X.
14. Design a program for evaluating a business, taking account of nonprofit measures of performance as well as profitability.
15. Determine the business outlook for the _____ industry.
16. Determine the effects of recent labor–management court rulings on X Company.
17. Recommend a suggestion system for X Company.
18. Recommend to X Company the feasibility of using a community computer center.
19. Report on the civil and criminal liabilities of corporate executives.
20. Advise X Company on the procedures for incorporating in _____ (state).
21. Recommend a profit-sharing plan for X Company personnel.
22. Can X Company profitably use a computer?
23. Would hiring handicapped workers be charity or good business for X Company?
24. Can creativity be taught to X Company executives?
25. Design a program for achieving optimum discipline in X Company.
26. Determine for X Company its policy toward aid to education.
27. Assess the extent of pollution control in _____ industry for an association of firms in the industry.
28. Determine the extent of minority recruiting, hiring, and training in the _____ industry for a legislative committee.
29. Determine the extent of discrimination against women in business for an association of businesspeople.
30. For a national association of professional people (your choice) report on the effects of government efforts and plans to regulate professional behavior (minimum fee schedules, ban on advertising, and so on).
31. Evaluate the value of union–management consultation (getting the views of union leadership on employee matters prior to taking action on these matters).
32. Advise Company X on what is the systems approach to planning and how the company can use it.
33. Recommend a plan for using management by objectives at Company X.
34. Review the information available on job stresses related to the social and physical environment. Recommend to Company X what it should do concerning this matter.
35. What should be the role of social responsibility in Company X's operations?
36. Evaluate and determine the effectiveness of the organization design of a company of your choice.

37. Company X is organized by region (or by product or process technology). Evaluate the possibilities of organizing by its major markets.
38. Company X is in the process of becoming a multinational organization. Evaluate the effects this development will have on its internal and external communications.
39. Working for an organization advancing women's rights in business, develop a plan for educating the public to accept the organization's objectives.
40. Advise a manager on how to deal with the informal cliques that develop in his organization.

Personnel administration

1. Interpret for X Company the effects of court decisions on testing and hiring employees.
2. Develop and justify a program of fringe benefits for a large industrial company.
3. Recommend an equitable compensation program for the sales personnel for X Company.
4. Design a program for breaking down line–staff barriers in X Company.
5. Analyze for X Company the problems of hiring under- and overqualified staff.
6. Recommend a retirement plan for X Company.
7. Devise an operational safety program for X Company.
8. Design a workable program for controlling activities of scientific and professional employees of X Company.
9. Survey the literature to find meaningful guides for selecting executives for foreign service for X Company.
10. Design a safety training program for X Company.
11. Develop a method to test morale in X Company.
12. Should X Company use a lie detector test to screen prospective employees?
13. Set up a secretary (or other position) selection plan for X Company.
14. Report to a major labor union the progress of women in the job market.
15. Evaluate the use of teaching machines (or some other innovative teaching technique) for the training programs of X Company.
16. Report to the management of X Company what information the employees need to know about the Company and its operation.
17. Report to the safety director of X Company on the validity of the accident-proneness concept.
18. Report to the safety director of X Company about the effect of age and experience on accidents.
19. Develop a personnel testing program for X Company.
20. Report to X Company management on recent trends and developments in employee remuneration.
21. Advise X Company management on the merits and demerits of the guaranteed annual wage.

22. Evaluate the use of sensitivity training for X Company.
23. Evaluate transactional analysis for the training of X Company executives.
24. Evaluate the effects of an early retirement plan, and recommend what Company X should do about the matter.
25. Evaluate the effectiveness of telephone information programs for Company X (these are programs in which employees can get current, pertinent information on company affairs by dialing a number).

Marketing

1. Determine the major opportunities in the environment for the marketing strategy of X National Bank.
2. Develop a plan for measuring the effectiveness of Company X advertising.
3. Design a PERT/CPM network for the marketing aspect of product management in Company X.
4. Develop a compensation plan for the salespeople of X Company.
5. Assuming a budget of $——, develop an advertising plan for X Company.
6. For a major shopping center in your area, construct a plan for setting the advertising budget.
7. Develop a global advertising policy for the X Company, a multinational retail organization.
8. Determine the future for trading stamps for X Company, a major chain of department stores.
9. What problems will Company X encounter in trading with countries behind the iron curtain?
10. Set up and defend a multistage approach to pricing decisions for X Company.
11. Determine the problems X Company will encounter in introducing a new product to its line.
12. What is the importance of fixed ratios in setting pricing strategy for X Company?
13. Select the optimal channel of distribution for new product Y in your area, and justify your choice.
14. Design a marketing strategy for your professional cleaning service.
15. Develop a segmented profile of the target market for product Y, and analyze the utility of this information in Company X's marketing management.
16. Explore the possibilities of trade with _____ (a foreign country) for X Company.
17. Determine changes in successful sales techniques for X Sales Company.
18. Report on the future of drive-in grocery stores for X Investment Company.
19. Determine the value of a college education in marketing work.
20. Should X Department Stores use credit cards?
21. Will pallet warehousing reduce costs for X Company?
22. Determine for Company X the social and ethical aspects of pricing for the market.

23. Determine for the American Consumer League whether advertising should be regulated.
24. Design a promotion campaign for the opening of Bank X.
25. Explore the possibilities of door-to-door selling for X Company.
26. Determine the best method to sell a new issue of common stock for well-established Company X.
27. Should X Company use contests to increase efforts of its salespeople?
28. Determine for a national department store chain the changing trends in service offered in the field.
29. Answer for the X Manufacturing Company the question of whether it should engage in "lease" sales.
30. Should Company X, a regional automotive supply chain, use centralized or decentralized warehousing?
31. Should Company X rent or lease trucks for distribution of its products?
32. How should X Company determine the amount of its advertising budget?
33. Should X Company use its own advertising department or an agency?
34. Design a promotional program for introducing new Product Y.
35. Where should X Company locate its next supermarket (or drugstore, service station, and so on) in your area?
36. Determine the influences of fashion in the _____ industry.
37. How can downtown merchants in _____ (city) cope with the trend toward suburban shopping centers?
38. Determine the trends in packaging in the _____ industry.
39. Make a market study of _____ (a city) to determine whether it is a suitable location for _____ (a type of business).
40. Should X Company establish its own sales force, use manufacturers' agents (manufacturers' representatives), or use selling agents?
41. Should X Petroleum Company attempt to increase its share of the market by engaging in active price competition?
42. Determine for X Company the best channel of distribution for _____ product line.
43. How should X Company evaluate the performance of its sales personnel?
44. Should X Company enter the _____ market?
45. What price policy should X Company use on entering the _____ market?
46. How should Company X evaluate the performance of its salespeople?
47. Determine for Company X the best procedure for evaluating the effectiveness of its advertising.
48. Should Company X, a canner of citrus and vegetable products, change from its policy of brand marketing to product-line marketing?

17 Oral communication

AS YOU KNOW, your work in business will involve oral as well as written communication. Probably, the written communication will give you more problems; but the oral communication will take up more of your time. In fact, you are likely to spend more time in oral communication than in any other work activity.

You're aware, of course, that much of the oral communication that goes on in business is informal. Primarily, it is the person-to-person communication that takes place whenever people get together. Obviously, this is a form of communication in which we all have experience. And most of us do a reasonably good job of it.

In addition to the informal talking that goes on in business, various kinds of more formal oral communication take place. Sometimes business people have to make formal presentations—speeches, lectures, oral reports, and such. Sometimes they conduct and participate in committee meetings, conferences, and group discussions. From time to time they have oral interviews with job applicants, with departing workers, and with workers being evaluated. Even when they write letters and reports, they often begin these messages orally as spoken dictation. All these more formal kinds of oral communication are a part of the work that business people do.

In the following pages you will find a review of the techniques of these more formal kinds of oral communication. In addition, you will find a review of techniques of the other side of oral communicating, listening. As you will see, good listening is every bit as important to successful communication as good talking.

Making formal presentations

The most difficult kind of oral communication for most of us is a formal presentation before a group. Most of us do not feel comfortable speaking before others, and generally we do a poor job of it. But it need not be this way. With effort, we can improve our public speaking. We can do this by first learning what good speaking techniques are. Then we can put these techniques into practice.

Consideration of personal aspects

A preliminary step to good speech making is to analyze yourself as a speaker. In oral presentations you, the speaker, are in a very real sense a part of the message. Your audience takes in not only the words you communicate but also what they see in you. And what they see in you can have a most significant effect on the meanings that develop in their minds. Thus, you should carefully evaluate your personal effect on the message you present. You should do whatever you can to detect and overcome shortcomings, and to sharpen any strengths you might have.

Although the following summary of such characteristics may prove to be useful, probably you know them from experience. The chances are you can easily recognize the good qualities and the bad. The problem is to some extent recognizing these characteristics, or the lack of them, in yourself. To a greater extent, it is doing something about improving your bad characteristics when you recognize them. The following review should help you to pinpoint these problem areas and should give you some practical suggestions of how to overcome them.

Confidence. A primary characteristic of effective speaking is confidence. Included are your confidence in yourself as well as the confidence of the audience in you, the speaker. Actually, the two are complementary, for your confidence in yourself tends to produce an image that gives your audience confidence in you. Similarly, your audience's confidence in you can give you a sense of security, thereby making you more confident in your ability.

Confidence of your audience in you typically is earned over periods of association. But there are things you can do to project an image which invites confidence. For example, you can prepare your presentation diligently, and you can practice it thoroughly. Such careful preliminary work gives you confidence in yourself. Having confidence leads to more effective communication, which in turn builds confidence in your listener's mind. Another thing you can do to gain confidence is to check carefully your physical appearance. Unfair and illogical as it may be, certain manners of dress and certain hair styles create strong images in people's minds ranging from one extreme to the other. Thus, if you want to communicate effectively, you should analyze the audience you seek to reach. And you should work to develop the physical appearance which projects an image in which your audience can have confidence. Yet another suggestion for being confident is simply to talk in strong, clear tones. Such tones do much to project an image of confidence. Although most people can do little to change their natural voices, they can try to add sufficient volume.

Sincerity. Your listeners are quick to detect insincerity in you. And when they detect it, they are likely to give little weight to what you say.

On the other hand, sincerity is a valuable aid to conviction, especially if the audience has confidence in your ability. About what you can do to project an image of sincerity, the answer is clear and simple: You must *be* sincere. Rarely is pretense of sincerity successful.

Thoroughness. When you are thorough in your presentation, generally your message is better received than when your coverage is scant or hurried. Thorough coverage gives the impression that time and care have been taken, and such an impression tends to make the message believable. But you can overdo thoroughness. If you present the information in too much detail, your listeners may become lost in a sea of information. The secret is to select the important information and to leave out the unimportant. To do this, of course, requires that you use good judgment. You must place yourself in your listeners' shoes and ask yourself just what the listeners need to know and what they do not need to know.

Friendliness. A speaker who projects an image of friendliness has a significant advantage in communicating. People simply like people who are friendly, and they are more receptive to what friendly people say. Like sincerity, friendliness is difficult to feign. It must be honest if it is to be effective. But with most people, friendliness is honest, for most people want to be friendly. Some just are not able to project the friendly image they would like to project. With a little self-analysis, a little mirror-watching as you speak, you can find ways of improving the friendliness of your image.

These are but some of the characteristics that should aid you as a speaker. There are others, such as interest, enthusiasm, originality, and flexibility. But the ones mentioned are the most significant and the ones most speakers need to work on. Through self-analysis and dedicated effort to improve the personal aspects of oral reporting, you can improve your speaking ability.

Audience analysis

A requirement of good speech making is to know your audience. You should study your audience before the presentation, and you should study your audience during the presentation.

Preliminary analysis. Analyzing your audience before the speech requires that you size up the group—that you search for any characteristics that could have some effect on how you should present your speech.

For example, size of audience is likely to influence how formal or informal you make your speech. (As a rule, large audiences require more formality.) The personal characteristics of the audience also can affect how you make your speech. Such characteristics as age, sex, education, experience, and knowledge of subject matter can determine how you present your message. They determine the words you use, the need for illustration, and the detail of information required. Just as in writing, you should adapt your speeches to your audiences. And knowing your audience is a first step in adaptation.

Analysis during presentation. Your audience analysis should continue as you make the speech. Called *feedback*, this phase of audience analysis gives you information about how your listeners are receiving your words. With this information you can adjust your presentation to improve the communication result.

Your eyes and ears will give feedback information. For example, facial expressions will tell you how your listeners are reacting to your message. From smiles, blank stares, and movements you get an indication of whether they understand, agree with, or accept your message. You can detect from sounds coming (or not coming) from the audience whether they are listening. If questions are in order, you can learn directly how your message is coming across. In general, by being alert you can learn much from your audience; and what you learn can help you make a better speech.

Appearance and bodily actions

As your listeners hear your words, they are looking at you. What they see is a part of the message; and it can have a very real effect on the success of your speech. What your audience sees, of course, is you. And they see that which surrounds you. Thus, in your efforts to improve the effects of your oral presentations, you should understand thoroughly the communication effects of what your listeners see.

The communication environment. Much of what your audience sees is all that surrounds you as you speak—all that tends to form a general impression. This would include the physical things—the stage, lighting, background, and such. Although not visual, a related influence here would be outside noises. All such factors as these should not detract from your message. Rather, they should contribute to good communication. Your own experience as a listener will tell you what is important.

Personal appearance. Your personal appearance is a part of the message your audience receives. Of course, you have to accept the physical properties you have; but no one need be at a disadvantage in appearance. All that is necessary is that you use what you have appropriately. Specifically, you should dress appropriately in whatever is right for the audience and the occasion. You should be clean and well groomed. You should use your facial expressions and bodily movements to your advantage. Just how you go about using your facial expressions and bodily movements is described in following paragraphs.

Posture. Posture is likely to be the most obvious of the things your audience sees in you. Even if listeners cannot be close enough to detect such things as facial expressions and eye movements, they can see the general form the body makes.

Probably no one needs to tell you what good posture is. You know it when you see it. The trouble is that you are not likely to see it in yourself. One solution is to have others tell you whether your posture needs improvement. Another is to practice speaking before a mirror.

In your efforts to improve your posture, keep in mind what must go on within your body to form a good posture. Your body weight must be distributed in a comfortable and poised way consistent with the impression you want to make. You should keep the body erect without appearing stiff, and comfortable without appearing limp. Your bearing should be self-poised, alert, and communicative. You should do all this naturally. The great danger with posture is that of appearing artificial.

Walking. The way you walk before your audience also makes impressions on your listeners. A strong, sure walk to the speaker's position gives an impression of confidence. Hesitant, awkward steps give the opposite impression. Walking during the presentation can be good or bad, depending on how you do it. Some speakers use steps forward and to the side as a form of bodily gesture, especially to emphasize points. Too much walking, however, attracts attention and detracts from the message. You would be wise to hold your walking to a minimum, and then only when you are reasonably sure of its effect.

Facial expression. Probably the most apparent and communicative bodily movements are facial expressions. The problem is, however, that you may unconsciously use facial expressions which convey meanings not intended. For example, a frightened speaker may tighten his jaw unconsciously and begin to grin. The effect may be an ambiguous image that detracts from the entire communication effort. A smile, a grimace, a puzzled frown all convey clear messages. Without question, they are effective communication devices, and you should use them.

Equally important in considering facial expressions is the matter of eye contact. The eyes have long been considered "mirrors of the soul" and provide most observers with information about your sincerity, goodwill, and flexibility. Some listeners tend to shun speakers who refuse to look at them. On the other hand, discriminate eye contact tends to show that you have a genuine interest in your audience.

Gestures. As does posture, gestures add to the message you communicate. Just what they add, however, is hard to say, for they have no definite or clear-cut meanings. A clinched fist, for example, certainly adds emphasis to a strong point. But it also can be used to show defiance, to make a threat, or to signify respect for a cause. And so it is with other gestures. They register vague meanings.

Even though they have vague meanings, gestures are strong. They are natural aids to speaking. It appears natural, for example, to emphasize a plea with palms up and to show disagreement with palms down. Raising first one hand and then the other reinforces a division of points. Slicing the air with the hand shows several divisions. Although such gestures as these generally are clear, we do not all use them exactly alike.

In summary, it should be clear that you can use bodily movements effectively to aid in speaking. Just which movements you should use, however, is hard to say. They are related to personality, physical makeup, and the size and nature of the audience. A speaker appearing before a formal group generally should use relatively few bodily actions. A speaker appearing before an informal audience should use more. What you should use on a given occasion is a matter for your best judgment.

Use of voice

Good voice is an obvious requirement of good speaking. Like bodily movements, the voice should not hinder the listener's concentration on the message. More specifically, the voice should not call attention away from the message. Voices that cause such difficulties fall generally into four areas of fault: (1) lack of pitch, (2) lack of variety in speaking speed, (3) lack of emphasis by variation in volume, and (4) unpleasantness in voice quality.

Lack of pitch variation. Speakers who talk in monotones are not likely to hold the interest of their listeners for long. Because most voices are capable of wide variations in pitch, usually the problem can be corrected. Most often the failure to vary pitch is a matter of habit—of voice patterns developed over years of talking without being aware of effect.

Lack of variation in speaking speed. Determining how fast to talk is a major problem. As a general rule, you should present the easy parts of the message at a fairly fast rate. You should present hard-to-understand information at a slower rate. The reason for varying the speed of presentation should be apparent: Easy information presented slowly is irritating; hard information presented fast may be difficult to understand.

A problem related to the pace of speaking is the incorrect use of pauses. Of course, pauses used at the appropriate time and place are effective. When properly used, they emphasize the upcoming subject matter; and they are effective means of gaining attention. But frequent pauses for no reason are irritating and break the listener's concentration. The error becomes worse when the speaker fills in the pauses with *uhs* and meaningless *you knows* and *OKs.*

Lack of vocal emphasis. A secret of good speaking is to give the words the emphasis due them by varying the manner of speaking. You can do this by (1) varying the pitch of the voice, (2) varying the pace of your presentation, and (3) varying the volume of your voice. As the first two techniques have been discussed, only the use of voice volume requires comment.

You must talk loudly enough for all of your audience to hear, but not too loudly. [Thus, the loudness (voice force) for a large group should be more than that for a small group.] Regardless of group size, however, variety in force is good for interest and emphasis. It produces contrast, which is one way of emphasizing the subject matter. Some speakers incorrectly believe that the only way to gain emphasis is to get louder and louder. But you can show emphasis also by going from loud to soft. The contrast with what has preceded provides the emphasis. Again, variety is the key to making the voice more effective.

Unpleasant voice quality. It is a hard fact of communication that some voices are more pleasing than others. Fortunately, most voices are reasonably pleasant. But some are raspy, nasal, or in some other way unpleasant. Although therapy often can improve such voices, some speakers must live with what they have. But by concentrating on variations in pitch, speed of delivery, and volume, one can make even the most unpleasant voice effective.

Improvement through self-analysis. You can overcome any of the foregoing voice problems through self-analysis. In this day of tape recorders, it is easy to hear yourself talk. Since you know good speaking when you hear it, you should be able to improve your presentation.

Use of visual aids

The spoken word is severely limited in communicating. Sound is here a brief moment and is gone. If the listener misses the message, there may be no chance to hear it again. Because of this limitation, speeches often need strong visual support—charts, tables, blackboards, film, and such. Visual aids may be as vital to the success of a speech as the words themselves.

Proper selection. Effective visual aids are those drawn from the message. They should fit the one speech and the one audience.

In selecting visual aids, you should search through the presentation for topics that appear vague or confusing. Whenever a picture or other form of visual aid will help to clear up vagueness, you should use one. Visual aids are truly a part of your message, and you should look upon them as such.

After you have decided that a topic deserves visual help, you determine the form the help should take. That is, should it be a chart, a diagram, a picture, or what? You should base your decision primarily on the question of which form communicates best. As simple and obvious as this point may appear, all too often people violate it. They select visual aids more for appearance and dramatic effect than for communication effect.

Forms to consider. Because no one form is best for all occasions, you should have a flexible attitude toward visual aids. You should know the good and bad qualities of each, and you should know how to use each effectively.

In selecting visual aids, you should keep in mind the types available. Primarily, you will consider the various forms of photographed or drawn illustrations—charts, graphs, tables, diagrams, and pictures. Each of these forms has its special strengths and weaknesses, as described in Chapter 16. Each may be displayed in various ways—by slide, overhead, or opaque projector; by flip chart, by easel display; on a blackboard; on a felt board; or in other ways. And each of these display forms has its strengths and weaknesses. In addition, visual aids may take the form of motion pictures, models, samples, demonstrations, and the like.

Techniques in using visual aids. Visual aids usually carry key parts of the message. Thus they are points of emphasis in your presentation. You blend them in with your words to communicate the message. How you do this is to some extent an individual matter, for techniques vary. They vary so much, in fact, that it would be hard to present a meaningful summary of them. It is more meaningful to present a list of do's and don't's. Such a list follows:

1. Make certain everyone in the audience can see the visual aids. Too many or too light lines on a chart, for example, can be hard to see. Too small an illustration can be meaningless to people far from the speaker.
2. Explain the visual aid if there is any likelihood that it will be misunderstood.
3. Organize the visual aids as a part of the presentation. Fit them into the plan.
4. Emphasize the visual aids. Point to them with bodily action and with words.

5. Talk to the audience—not to the visual aids. Look at the visual aids only when the audience should look at them.
6. Avoid blocking the listener's view of the visual aids. Make certain that lecterns, pillars, chairs, and such do not block anyone's view. Take care not to stand in anyone's line of vision.

A summary list of speaking practices

The foregoing review of business speaking is selective, for the subject is broad. In fact, entire books are devoted to the subject. But this review has covered the high points, especially those that you can transfer into practice easily. Perhaps even more practical is the following list of what to do and not to do in speaking.

1. Organize the speech so it leads the hearer's thoughts logically to the conclusion.
2. Move surely and quickly to the conclusion. Do not leave a conclusion dangling, repeat unnecessarily, or appear unable to close.
3. Use language specifically adapted to the audience.
4. Articulate clearly, pleasantly, and with proper emphasis. Avoid mumbling and the overuse of *ah, er, uh,* and so forth.
5. Speak correctly, using accepted grammar and pronunciation.
6. Maintain an attitude of alertness, displaying appropriate enthusiasm and confidence.
7. Employ bodily language to best advantage. Use it to emphasize points and to assist in communicating concepts and ideas.
8. Avoid stiffness or rigidity of bodily action.
9. Look the audience in the eye and talk directly to your listeners.
10. Avoid excessive movements, fidgeting, and signs of nervousness.
11. Punctuate the presentation with reference to visual aids. Make them a part of the report story.
12. Keep your temper, even when faced with unfair opposition. To lose your temper is to lose control of the presentation.

Reporting orally

A special form of speech is the oral report. You are more likely to make oral reports than speeches in business; and the oral reports you make are likely to be important to you. Unfortunately, oral reporting is a subject in which most of us have had little experience and even less instruction. Thus, the following review should be valuable to you.

A definition of oral reports

In its broadest sense, an oral report is any presentation of factual information using the spoken word. A business oral report logically would limit coverage to factual business information. By this definition, an oral business report covers much of the information exchanged daily in the conduct of business. It varies widely in formality. At one extreme, it covers the most routine and informal reporting situations. At the other, it includes highly formal and proper presentations. Because the more informal exchanges are little more than routine conversations, the emphasis in following pages is on the more formal ones. Clearly, these are the reports which require the most care and skill. They are the ones most deserving of study.

Differences between oral and written reports

Because written reports have been covered thoroughly in preceding chapters, a logical next step in studying oral reports is to note differences between written and oral reports. Differences do exist, and they are significant. Three in particular stand out.

Visual advantages of the written word. The first major difference between oral and written reports is that writing permits greater use of visual aids to communication than does speaking. With writing, you can use paragraphing to show the reader the structure of the message and to make the thought units stand out. In addition, by writing your message, you can use punctuation to show relationships, subordination, and qualification of the information. The result of these techniques is to improve the communication effect of the entire message.

However, when you make an oral presentation, you can use none of these techniques. Of course, you can use others—techniques peculiar to oral communication. For example, you can use inflection, pauses, volume emphasis, and changes in rate of delivery. Depending on the situation, both oral and written techniques are effective in aiding communication. But the point is, they are different.

Reader control of written presentation. A second difference in oral and written reporting is that, in a written report, your readers control the pace of the communication. They can pause, reread, change their rate of reading, or stop as they choose. Since the readers set the pace, your writing can be difficult and still communicate. When receiving an oral report, listeners cannot control the pace of the presentation. They must grasp the meaning intended as the speaker chooses to present the words. Because of this limiting factor, good oral reporting must be relatively simple.

Emphasis on correctness in writing. A third difference in oral reporting is in the degree of correctness permitted in each. On the one hand, because your written words are likely to be looked at carefully, you are likely to work for a high degree of correctness. That is, you are likely to follow carefully the recognized rules of grammar, punctuation, sentence structure, and so on. When you present an oral report, on the other hand, you may be more lax in following these recognized rules. For one reason, your work is not recorded for others to inspect at their leisure. For another, oral communication standards of correctness are less rigid.

Other differences exist, of course; but these are the ones which are most significant. They should serve as foundations from which to explain the techniques of oral reporting.

Planning the oral report

As in written reports, planning is a logical first step in your work on oral reports. For the short, informal report, of course, planning may be minimal. But for the more formal presentations, particularly those involving audiences of more than one, proper planning is likely to be as involved as that for a comparable written report.

Determination of report objective. Logically, your first step in planning an oral report is to determine your objective. Just as it was described for the written report in Chapter 13, in this step you should clearly state the report goal in clear, concise language. Then you should clearly state the factors involved in achieving this goal. These steps give you a clear guide to the information you must gather, and to the framework around which you will build your presentation.

In the process of determining your goal, you must be aware of your general objective. That is, you must decide on your general purpose in making the presentation. Is it to persuade? To inform? To recommend? Your conclusion here will have a major influence on your development of the material for presentation and, perhaps, even on the presentation itself.

Organization of content. Your procedure for organizing oral reports is similar to that for written reports. You have the choice of using either direct or indirect order. Even so, the same information presented orally and in writing is not necessarily presented in the same way. Time pressure, for example, may justify direct presentation for an oral report. The same report problem presented in writing might be best arranged in indirect order. A reader in a hurry can always skip to the conclusion or ending of the report. The listener does not have this choice.

Although oral reports may use either direct or indirect order, the indirect is by far the more widely used order—as well as the more logical. Because your audience is not likely to know the problem well, some introductory comments are needed to prepare them to receive the message. In addition, you may need introductory words to arouse interest, stimulate curiosity, or to impress the audience with the importance of the subject. The main goal of the introductory remarks is to state the purpose, define unfamiliar terms, explain limitations, describe scope, and generally cover all the necessary introductory subjects (see discussion of introduction, Chapter 14).

In the body of the oral report, you should develop the goals you have set. Here, also, there is much similarity with the written report. Division of subject matter into comparable parts, logical order, introductory paragraphs, concluding paragraphs, and such are equally important to both forms.

The major difference in organization of the written and oral report is in the ending. Both forms may end with a conclusion, a recommendation, a summary, or a combination of the three. But the oral report is likely to have a final summary tacked on, regardless of whether it has a conclusion or a recommendation. In a sense, this final summary serves the purpose of a synopsis—by bringing together all the really important information, analyses, conclusions, and recommendations in the report. It serves also to assist the memory by placing added emphasis on the points that should stand out.

Conducting and participating in meetings

From time to time in business you will participate in meetings. They will range from one extreme of formality to the other. On the formal end will be conferences and committee meetings. On the informal end will be discussions with groups of fellow workers. Whatever form the meeting takes, it will involve communication. In fact, the quality of the communication involved will determine the success of the meeting.

Your role in a meeting will be either that of leader or participant. Of course, the leader's role is the primary one; but good participation also is vital. The following paragraphs review the techniques of performing well in either role.

Techniques of conducting meetings

How one conducts a meeting is related to the formality of the occasion. Meetings of groups, such as formal committees, boards of directors, and professional organizations, usually follow generally accepted rules of conduct called "parliamentary procedure." These rules are quite specific and are too detailed for review here. When you are involved in formal meetings, you would do well to study any of the many books covering parliamentary procedure before the meeting. In addition, you should know and practice the following techniques. For less-formal meetings, you can depart somewhat from these procedures and techniques. But you should keep in mind that every meeting has goals and that your departures from procedure and technique never should hinder reaching the goals.

Plan the meeting. A key to conducting a meeting is to plan it thoroughly. That is, you should develop an agenda: a list of topics to be covered. In developing the agenda, you should select the topics that need to be covered to achieve the goals of the meeting. You should arrange these items in the most logical order. Items that explain or lead to other items should come before the items they explain or lead to. After you have prepared the agenda, you should make it available to those who will attend, if the meeting is formal. For informal meetings, you may find keeping the agenda in mind to be satisfactory.

Follow the plan. You should follow the plan for the meeting, item by item. In most meetings, the discussion tends to stray and new items tend to come up. As leader, you should keep the discussion on track. If new items come up during the meeting, you can take them up at the end—or perhaps plan them for a future meeting.

Move the discussion along. As leader, you should control the agenda. When one item has been covered, you should bring up the next item. When the discussion moves off subject, you should move it back on subject. In general, you should do what is needed to proceed efficiently through the items. But, in your efforts, you should not cut off discussion before all important points have been made. Thus, you will have to use your good judgment. Your goal is to permit complete discussion on the one hand and to avoid repetition, excessive details, and useless comments on the other.

Control those who talk too much. One of your harder tasks is likely to be that of keeping certain members from talking too much. In most groups, a few people tend to dominate the discussion. Your task as leader is to control these people. Of course, you want the meeting to be democratic; so you will need to let these people talk as long as they are contributing to the goal. When they begin to stray, to duplicate, or to bring in useless matter, you should step in. You can step in tactfully by asking for other viewpoints or by summarizing the discussion and moving on to the next topic.

Encourage participation from those who talk too little. Just as some people talk too much, some talk too little. In business groups, frequently those who say little are in positions lower than other members of the group. Your job as leader is to bring these people into the discussion. You can do this by asking them for their viewpoints. Also, you can encourage them to participate by showing respect for the comments they make, regardless of how illogical they may be.

Control time. When your meeting time is limited, you have the additional job of controlling time. On such occasions, you need to determine in advance how much time will be needed to cover each item. Then, at the appropriate time intervals, you should end discussion of the items. You may find it helpful to announce the time goals at the beginning of the meeting, and to remind the group members of the time status throughout the meeting.

Summarize at appropriate places. After a key item has been discussed, you should summarize what the group has covered and concluded. In cases in which a group decision is needed, the group's vote will be the conclusion. In any event, you should formally conclude each point and then move to the next one. At the end of the meeting, you could give a summary of the total progress made. You should do this whenever such a review will help the group members understand their accomplishments during the meeting. For some formal meetings, minutes kept by a secretary will provide this summary.

Techniques for participating in a meeting

From the preceding discussion of the techniques a leader should use, you know something about what participants should do. The following review emphasizes them for you.

Follow the agenda. When an agenda exists, you should follow it. Specifically, you should not bring up items not on the agenda; nor should you comment on such items brought up by others. When there is no agenda, you should stay within the general limits of the goal for the meeting.

Participate. The purpose of meetings is to get the input of everybody concerned. Thus, you should do your part. You should participate. Your participation, however, should be meaningful. You should talk only when you have something to contribute, and you should talk every time you have something to contribute.

Do not talk too much. As you participate in the meeting, be aware that other people are attending. You should speak up whenever you have something to say, but do not get carried away. Always respect the rights of others. As you speak, ask yourself whether what you are saying really contributes to the discussion.

Cooperate. A meeting by its very nature requires cooperation from all the participants. So keep this in mind as you participate. You should respect the leader and his or her efforts to make progress. You should respect the other participants, and you should work with them in every practical way.

Be courteous. Perhaps being courteous is a part of being cooperative. In any event, you should be courteous to other group members. Specifically, you should respect the rights and opinions of others. You should permit them to speak.

Interviewing people

In your work in business you may need to participate in an interview for a variety of reasons. Perhaps the best known is the employment interview (when an applicant is being considered for a job). But there are others. In the periodic evaluations some companies make of their workers, interviews frequently are involved. Primarily, these are a means of communicating the evaluations. When workers leave a company, they may be interviewed to determine their reasons for leaving. Sometimes interviews are conducted to gather information on such matters as worker attitudes, working conditions, managerial effectiveness, and worker plans.

Because interviewing is a form of personal communication, usually between two people, it is not a precise activity. That is, no hard and fast set of rules exists for one to follow. Rather, interviewing is a flexible activity that must follow the good judgment of the people involved. Nevertheless, well-established guidelines exist, and you should follow them. In following pages, they are presented from the side of the interviewer and from the side of the interviewee.

Guidelines for the interviewer

Because the interviewer is in charge, success of the interview is in his or her hands. Thus, it is especially important that the interviewer know and follow these general guidelines.

Plan the interview. You conduct interviews because you need information. So, as a starting point, you should determine what information you need. Usually, you can write your needs in a series of specific questions. You should make such a list and use it as the outline for the interview.

Put the interviewee at ease. The chances are that the interviewee will be nervous. Because nervous people are not good subjects for interviewing, you should try to put the interviewee at ease. How you should do this varies with the person involved and with your social skills. You could, for example, begin with some friendly talk on a point of common interest. Or you could begin with comments or questions about the interviewee—hometown, sports interests, hobbies, and the like.

Make the purpose clear. Your interviewee should know the purpose of the interview from the beginning. Of course, sometimes the interviewee knows from the nature of the interview, as in an employment situation. But if he or she does not know, you should explain the purpose clearly and honestly.

Let the interviewee do most of the talking. You can get the information you seek only when the interviewee talks. Therefore, you should let the interviewee do most of the talking. You should talk only to guide the course of the interview—to carry the discussion through the specific questions you want to cover. Because some interviewees are reluctant to talk, sometimes you will need to work to get them to talk. But never should you attempt to put words in their mouths. Rather, you should try to put them at ease: to get them in an informal, relaxed mood.

Guide the interview. Even though the interviewee does the talking, your task is to guide the interview through the information needed. That is, you follow the plan you set up in the beginning. You ask specific questions, and you end the answers when you have the information you need. In guiding the interview, you will need to handle moments of silence. Brief periods of silence may be all right, for sometimes additional information comes after some silence. But too much silence can be awkward for all concerned.

Listen. You should listen carefully to all that the interviewee says. The purpose of an interview is to get certain information, and you get this information by listening. As you will see in a following section of this chapter, most of us do not listen well.

In addition to listening, you should give the appearance of listening. Your interviewees will be more relaxed and will talk more if they feel they have your individed attention.

Keep a record. As you conduct interviews to get information, you will need to make a record of the information. How you record information may vary with the situation. When you need much detailed information, you may need to take notes during the interview. Because your writing may be disturbing to the interviewee, at the beginning of the interview you should explain why you must take notes. Even after explaining, you should write as quickly and briefly as possible.

When you can remember the information you seek after the interview, you need not write during the interview. But you should record the information soon after the interview is over. As you know, not many of us can remember such information for very long.

End the interview. Since you are in charge of the interview, you should end it. If the situation justifies it, some friendly talk can follow the questioning.

But you should avoid letting the conversation trail off to meaningless talk. One good way of ending interviews is to ask a final-type question—one that tells that the interview is over. This one does the job well: "Is there anything else you would like to tell me? If not, thanks for giving me your time."

Guidelines for the interviewee

When you are the one interviewed, you have little control over the situation. Nevertheless, you can help to make the interview successful. The following guidelines tell you how.

Prepare for the interview. When you know the nature of the interview, you should prepare for it. Mainly, your preparation should consist of thinking of the questions you are likely to be asked and forming answers to them. It also may include gathering additional information. In a job interview, for example, you would be wise to learn what you can about the company— its history, what it does, its plans, its current activities. By showing your knowledge during the interview, you can impress the interviewer with your interest in the company. Even if you prepare diligently, you are not likely to cover all that will be asked. So be prepared mentally for the unexpected.

Make an appropriate appearance. What the interviewer sees is a part of the message received—so you should do what you can to make an appropriate appearance. Because what is appropriate varies with the situation, you should consider the situation. In most cases, you will find the conventional standards of neatness and dress to be desirable. In addition, you usually will want your posture, facial expressions, and bodily movements to give favorable impressions. Especially will you want to avoid the appearance of nervousness.

Show interest. You can improve the impression you make in most interview situations by showing interest. How you should show interest varies with the occasion. But always you help your case by looking at the interviewer and by giving her or him your undivided attention.

Answer correctly and completely. If the interview serves a good purpose, it deserves correct and complete answers. You should give them. Dishonest answers benefit no one.

Practice courtesy. Probably you know very well the value of courtesy in business. You know that it is a major part of the impression you make in every human contact. The interview is no exception.

Dictating letters and reports

The odds are you will dictate most of the letters you will write in business. You may even dictate reports—especially the shorter, more informal ones. Thus, the following review of the techniques and procedures of dictating should be useful to you.

Gather the facts. Your first logical step in dictating is to get all the information you need for the message. This step involves such activities as getting previous correspondence from the files, consulting with other employees about the situation, and determining company policy. The important point is to get all that you need so you can work without interruption.

Plan the message. With the facts of the case before you, you next plan the message. Perhaps you may prefer to do this step in your mind. Or perhaps you may prefer to jot down a few notes or an outline. Whatever your preference, your goal in this step is to decide what your message will be and how you will present it. In this step, you apply the procedures covered in our earlier review of letter and report writing.

Give preliminary information and instructions. Your first step in the actual process of dictating is to give the stenographer specific instructions. Included here are instructions about special handling, enclosures, form, and page layout. Also included is all the additional information about the message—such as mailing address, subject line, attention line, and salutation. When this information is easily available, you need only refer to the source (for example, "Get their address from their letter").

Make the words flow. Your next step is to talk through the message. As simple as this step appears, you are likely to have problems doing it. Thinking out loud to a stenographer or to a dictating machine frightens most of us at first. The result is likely to be slow and awkward dictation.

Overcoming this problem requires self-discipline. You should force yourself to concentrate and to make the words flow. Your goal should be to get the words out—to talk through the message. You need not be concerned with producing polished work on the first effort. Probably, you will need to revise, perhaps many times. In time, after you have forced your way through enough messages, your need to revise will decrease. Your speed and quality of dictation will improve.

Speak in a strong, clear voice. Because your dictation must be heard, you should dictate in a strong, clear voice. You should speak at a speed slow enough to clearly separate the words. Words that do not stand out clearly can cause delays in work as well as error in the message. Especially should you be careful when using dictating machines, for usually they do not reproduce voices well.

Give paragraphing, punctuation, and other mechanics as needed. How much of the paragraphing, spelling, punctuation, and other mechanics you should include in your dictation depends on the ability of the person who will type the message. If this person is competent in writing correctness and form, you may leave these matters to her or him. On most occasions, however, you are wise to dictate most such information. Your dictation might well sound like this: "Dear Mrs. Mott *colon paragraph* On Friday *comma* November 12 *comma* your order for 18 cases Bug *hyphen* Nix *comma* 12 *hyphen* ounce packages *comma* should reach your loading docks *period.* (The instructions are indicated by italics.)

Avoid using asides. Asides (side comments not intended to be a part of the message) are better not used. They tend to confuse the stenographer, who must determine which words are a part of the message and which are not. As proof, imagine the stenographer's difficulty in handling the following dictation (asides in italics):

> Dear Mr. Dobbs: *Well, let's see. How about this?* The attached check for $19.45 . . . *Is that the right figure?* . . . is our way of showing you that your good faith in us is appreciated. *That should make him happy.* Our satisfaction-or-money-back policy means much to us. . . .

Read back intelligently. Although you should try to talk through the message without interruption, sometimes you will need to stop and get a read-back of what you have dictated. But do this only when necessary. More than likely, a read-back results from confused thinking. When you are learning to dictate, however, some confused thinking is normal. Until you gain experience, you may profit by getting read-backs. Especially will you find read-backs helpful at the end of the message to give you a check on the overall effect of your words.

Letter dictation illustrated

Many of the foregoing techniques are illustrated in the following example of dictation of a routine letter. This example shows all the dictator's words, with instructions and asides in italics. Note that the dictator does not give some of the more obvious punctuation (such as a colon after the salutation). Also note that the dictation gives unusual spellings.

> *Let's acknowledge the Key Grocery Company order next. Get the address from the order. It's No. 9* Dear Mr. Key: Three crates of orchard *hyphen* fresh Texacates should be in your store sometime Wednesday morning as they were shipped today by Greene *that's G-R-E-E-N-E* Motor Freight *period.* As you requested in your August 29 order *comma* the $61.60 *parenthesis* Invoice 14721 *parenthesis* was credited to your account *period paragraph* Your customers will go for these large *comma* tasty avocados *comma* I am sure *period* They are the best we have handled in months *period paragraph* Thanks *comma* Mr. Key *comma* for another opportunity to serve you *period* Sincerely *Type it for my signature.*

Listening

To this point, our review of oral communication has been about sending information (talking). Certainly, this is a subject in which business people need help. But evidence shows that the receiving side (listening) causes more problems.

The inefficiency of listening

Just how inefficient people are as listeners is hard to say. Most evidence shows that we miss much that is said, and that we forget much that we hear. Authorities tell us that we retain only about a fourth of what we hear after two days. Generally, the authorities agree that listening is the weakest link in oral communication.

Improving your listening ability

Improving your ability to listen is largely a matter of mental conditioning. That is, you have to want to do it first. Listening is a willful act. If you are like most of us, frequently you are tempted not to listen, for it is easier this way. As we all know, we human beings tend to be lazy. We tend to avoid work; and listening requires work.

After you have decided that you want to listen better, you must work to pay attention. What you do, specifically, will depend on your mental makeup, for this effort requires disciplining the mind. You must make yourself be alert. You must force yourself to pay attention to the words spoken. The following Ten Commandments of Listening should serve you as a general guide.[1]

1. *Stop talking.* Unfortunately, most of us prefer talking to listening. Even when we are not talking, we are inclined to concentrate on what to say next, rather than on listening to others. So you must stop talking before you can listen.

2. *Put the talker at ease.* If you make the talker feel at ease, she or he will do a better job of talking. Then you will have a better input to work with.

3. *Show the talker you want to listen.* If you can convince the talker that you are listening to understand rather than oppose, you will help to create a climate for information exchange. Specifically, you should look and act interested. Doing things like reading, looking at your watch, and looking away distract the talker.

4. *Remove distractions.* Things you do can also distract the talker. So don't doodle, tap with your pencil, shuffle papers, or the like.

5. *Empathize with the talker.* If you will place yourself in the talker's position and look at things from his or her point of view, you will help to create a climate of understanding. With such a climate established, a true exchange of information can result.

6. *Be patient.* You will need to allow the talker plenty of time. Remember that not everyone can get to the point as quickly and clearly as you. And do not interrupt the speaker. Interruptions merely serve as barriers to information exchange.

7. *Hold your temper.* From our review of the workings of our mental filters, we know that angry minds do not contribute to communication.

---

[1] To some anonymous author goes a debt of gratitude for these often quoted and classic comments about listening.

Angry people build walls between themselves. They harden their positions and block their minds to the words of others.

8. *Go easy on argument and criticism.* Argument and criticism tend to put the talker on the defensive. Thus, he or she tends to "clam up" or get angry. Even if you win the argument, you lose. Rarely does either party benefit from such controversy.

9. *Ask questions.* By frequently asking questions, you display an open mind. You show that you are listening. And you assist in developing the message and in improving correctness of meaning.

10. *Stop talking!* The last commandment is to stop talking. It was also the first. All other commandments depend on it.

In summary, it should be clear that to improve your listening ability you have to set your mind to the task. Poor listening habits are ingrained in our living patterns. We can alter these habits only through conscious efforts.

Questions & Problems

1. Explain how a speaker's personal aspects influence the meanings of his or her spoken words.
2. An employee presented an oral report to an audience of 27 middle- and upper-level administrators. Then she presented the same information to an audience made up of three top executives of the company. Note some of the differences that probably took place in these two presentations.
3. Explain the role of feedback in making a speech.
4. One's manner of dress, choice of hair style, physical characteristics, and the like are personal. They should have no influence in any form of oral communication. Discuss.
5. By description (or perhaps by example) identify good and bad postures and walking practices for speaking in a public or in a business setting.
6. Explain how facial expressions can miscommunicate.
7. Give some illustrations of gestures that can be used for more than one meaning. Demonstrate them.
8. "We are born with voices—some good, some bad, and some in between. We have no choice but to accept what we have been given." Comment.

9. What should be the determining factor in the use of visual aids?
10. Discuss (or demonstrate) some good and bad techniques of using visual aids.
11. In presenting an oral report to a group of co-workers as well as some bosses, a worker is harassed by the questions of one of his co-workers. Apparently, this person is trying to embarrass the reporter. What advice would you give the worker? Would your advice be different if the critic were one of the bosses? What if the speaker were the boss and the critic the worker? Discuss.
12. Explain the principal differences between written and oral reports.
13. Compare the typical organization plans of oral and written reports. Note the major differences between the two plans.
14. The people attending a meeting should determine the agenda—not the leader. Discuss.
15. Because meetings should be democratic, everyone present should be permitted to talk as much as he or she wants without interference from the leader. Discuss.
16. Assume that you are being interviewed for the job of _____ (your choice) with _____ (company of your choice). What questions

would you anticipate? How would you answer them?

17. Assume that you are the interviewer for the interview in Question 16. Discuss specific ways you would use to put the interviewee at ease.

18. Justify each of the dictating techniques suggested in the chapter.
19. Discuss why we have difficulty listening.
20. What can you do to improve your listening?

Oral communication problems

Speeches

Since one can make a speech on almost any topic, it is not practical to list topics for speeches. You or your instructor can generate any number of interesting and timely topics in a short time. Whatever you select, you will need to determine the goals clearly, to work out the facts of the situation, and to set a time limit.

Oral reports

Most of the written report problems presented in the problem section following Chapter 16 can also serve as oral report problems. The following problems, however, are especially suitable for oral presentation.

1. Survey the major business publications for information about the outlook for the national (or world) economy for the coming year. Then present a summary report to the directors of Allied Department Stores, Inc.

2. As a student leader on your campus, you have been asked by the Faculty Senate (or comparable faculty group) to report to its members on the status of faculty–student relations. You will include recommendations on what can be done to improve relations.

3. Report to a meeting of a wildlife protection organization on the status of an endangered species in your area. You will need to gather the facts through research, probably in wildlife publications.

4. A national chain of _____ (your choice) is opening an outlet in your city. You have been assigned the task of reviewing site possibilities. Gather the pertinent information and make an oral recommendation to the board of directors.

5. You have been asked by the Future Business Leaders Club at your old high school to report to it on the nature and quality of business study at your college. You will cover all factors that you feel high school students need to know.

6. As representative of a travel agency, present a travel package to _____ (place or places of your choice) to the members of Adventurer Travel Club. You will describe places to be visited; and you will cover all the essential details, such as dates, hotels, guide service, meals, costs, and manner of travel.

7. Report to a meeting of Consumers Alliance (a consumer-protection organization) on the economics of renting telephones from the telephone company versus owning the telephones. You will need to gather the facts through research.

8. Look through current newspapers, magazines, and so on, and get the best available information on the job outlook for this year's college graduates. You will want to look at each major field separately. You also may want to show variations by geographic area, by degree, and by schools. Present your findings in a well-organized and illustrated oral report.

9. Present a plan for improving some phase of operation on your campus (registration, scholastic honesty, housing, grade appeals, library, cafeteria, traffic, curricula, athletic events, and such).

10. Present an objective report on some legislation of importance to business (right-to-work laws, environmental controls, taxes, and the like). Take care to present evidence and reasoning from all major viewpoints. Support your presentation with facts, figures, and so on whenever they will help.

11. Assume that you are being considered by a company of your choice for a job of your choice. Your prospective employer has asked you to make a _____-minute (your instructor will specify) report on your qualifications. You may project your education to the date you will be in the job market and may make assumptions that are consistent with your record to date.

12. Prepare and present an informative report on how individuals may reduce their income tax payments (federal or state). Probably you will want to emphasize the most likely sources of tax savings—such as tax-sheltering and avoiding common errors.

13. Make a presentation to a hypothetical group of investors which will get you the investment money you need for a purpose of your choice. Your purpose could be to begin a new business, to construct a building, to develop land—whatever interests you. Make your presentation as real (or realistic) as you can. And support your appeal with visual aids.

14. As chairman of the site selection committee for the National Federation of Business Executives, present a report on your committee's recommendation. The committee has selected a city and a convention hotel (you may choose each). Your report will give your recommendation as well as the reason supporting your choice. For class purposes, you may make up whatever facts you may need about the organization and its convention requirements and about the hotel. But use real facts about the city.

15. As a buyer of men's (or women's, boy's, and such) clothing, report to the sales personnel of your store on the fashions for the coming season. (You may get the necessary information from publications in the field.)

16. The top administrators of your company have asked you to look into the question of whether the company should own automobiles, rent automobiles, or pay mileage costs on employee-owned automobiles. (Autos are used by sales personnel.) Gather the best available information on the matter and report it to the group. You may make up any company facts you may need; but make them realistic.

Meetings

Because group meetings are meaningful only when they concern problems the participants know and understand, the following topics for meetings involve campus situations. For one of these topics, develop a specific problem that would warrant a group meeting. (Example: For student government, one might come up with "To determine the weaknesses of student government on this campus and what should be done to correct them.") Then lead the class (or participate) in a meeting on the topic. Class discussion following the meeting should bring out the good and bad of the meeting and should reinforce the text material.

A. Student discipline.
B. Scholastic dishonesty.
C. Housing regulations.
D. Student-faculty relations.
E. Student government.
F. Library.
G. Grading standards.
H. Attendance policies.
I. Varsity athletics.
J. Intramural athletics.
K. Degree requirements.
L. Parking.
M. Examination scheduling.
N. Administrative policies.
O. University calendar.
P. Homework requirements.
Q. Tuition and fees.
R. Student evaluation of faculty.
S. Community-college relations.

Dictation

Working with a classmate, select a letter problem from the Problem sections following Chapters 10, 11, and 12. Then dictate the letter to your classmate. Because your classmate probably must write your dictation in longhand, you may need to dictate slowly.

After you have finished, reverse the roles.

A listening exercise

Divide the class into two (or more) teams. The instructor then reads some factual information (newspaper article, short story, or such) to only one member of each team. Each of these team members tells what he or she has heard to a second team member. The second team member tells the information to a third member—and so on until the last member of each team has heard the information. The last person receiving the information reports what he or she has heard to the instructor, who checks it for accuracy with the original message. The team which is able to report the information with the greatest accuracy wins.

Appendix A

Physical presentation of reports

When your readers look at your report, they see not only the message you have formed; they also see the overall appearance of your work. As with the words and illustrations, the appearance of your report becomes a part of the communication they receive and has an effect on the messages formed in their minds.

If, for example, they look at your work and see a neat, well-arranged document, a favorable impression is likely to form in their minds. Such favorable impressions probably will make them more receptive to the information in your message. At the other extreme, if they see an untidy, poorly arranged paper, they are likely to form a negative impression. And this impression will negatively affect their receptiveness to the information you seek to communicate. In other words, the impression of appearance of your work formed in your readers' minds becomes a part of their filter content. Thus, it serves to affect the meanings they give to the information communicated.

You can do much to ensure the communication success of your report by giving it the typing care and arrangement which will help in your communication effort. Hence, you should make good use of the following guide to the physical arrangement of reports.

General information on physical preparation

Because your reports are most likely to be typed, you should have a general knowledge of the mechanics involved in manuscript typing. Even if you do not have to type your own reports, you should know enough about report form to make certain that justice is done to your work. You cannot be certain that your report is presented in good form unless you know good form.

Conventional page layout. For the typical text page in the report, a conventional layout is one that appears to fit the page like a picture in a frame (see Figure A–1). This eye-pleasing layout, however, is arranged to fit the page space not covered by the binding of the report. Thus, you

Figure A–1
Recommended Layout for Normal Double-spaced Page

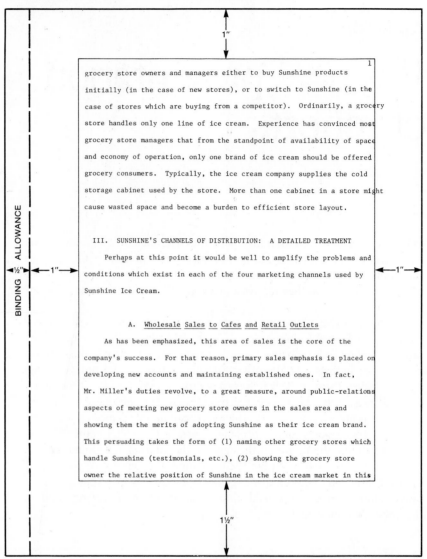

1"

1

grocery store owners and managers either to buy Sunshine products
initially (in the case of new stores), or to switch to Sunshine (in the
case of stores which are buying from a competitor). Ordinarily, a grocery
store handles only one line of ice cream. Experience has convinced most
grocery store managers that from the standpoint of availability of space
and economy of operation, only one brand of ice cream should be offered
grocery consumers. Typically, the ice cream company supplies the cold
storage cabinet used by the store. More than one cabinet in a store might
cause wasted space and become a burden to efficient store layout.

III. SUNSHINE'S CHANNELS OF DISTRIBUTION: A DETAILED TREATMENT

Perhaps at this point it would be well to amplify the problems and
conditions which exist in each of the four marketing channels used by
Sunshine Ice Cream.

A. <u>Wholesale Sales to Cafes and Retail Outlets</u>

As has been emphasized, this area of sales is the core of the
company's success. For that reason, primary sales emphasis is placed on
developing new accounts and maintaining established ones. In fact,
Mr. Miller's duties revolve, to a great measure, around public-relations
aspects of meeting new grocery store owners in the sales area and
showing them the merits of adopting Sunshine as their ice cream brand.
This persuading takes the form of (1) naming other grocery stores which
handle Sunshine (testimonials, etc.), (2) showing the grocery store
owner the relative position of Sunshine in the ice cream market in this

BINDING   ALLOWANCE

½" 1" 1"

1½"

must allow an extra half inch or so on the left margins of the pages of a
left-bound report and at the top of the pages of a top-bound report.

As a general rule, top, left, and right margins should be equal and uniform.
For double-spaced manuscripts, about 1 inch is recommended. From 1¼
to 1½ inches is ideal for single-spaced work (see Figure A–2). Bottom margins
are customarily slightly larger than those at the top—about half again as
much. The left margin, of course, is easily marked by the characters which
begin the lines. The right margin is formed by the average lengths of the

Figure A–2
Recommended Layout for a Normal Single-spaced Page

511

Appendix A
Physical
Presentation
of Reports

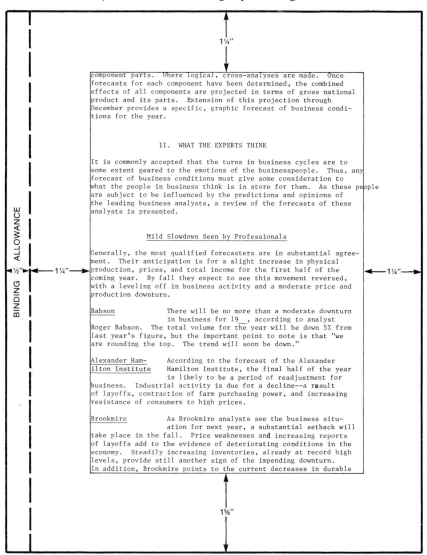

full lines. As nearly as possible, this right margin should be kept straight—that is, without dips or bulges.

You may find it advisable to mark off in black ink a rectangle of the size of the layout you are using. Then you may place the rectangle beneath each page as you type, so you can see the dimensions you are using and can end your typed lines appropriately.

Special page layouts. Certain pages in the text may have individual layouts. Pages displaying major titles (first pages of chapters, tables of contents,

Figure A–3
Recommended Layout for Double-spaced Page with Title Displayed

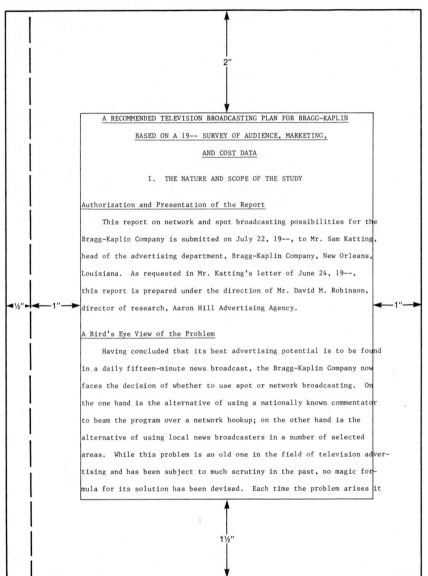

synopses, and the like) conventionally have an extra half inch or so of space at the top (see Figure A–3). This technique has long been followed by publishers and is illustrated in almost all published books.

Letters of transmittal and authorization also may have individual layouts. They are typed in any conventional letter form. In more formal reports, they may be carefully arranged to have the same general outline or shape as the space upon which they appear (see Figure A–7).

Choice of typing form. It is conventional to double-space the typed report. This procedure stems from the old practice of double spacing to make typed manuscripts more easily read by the proofreader and printer. The practice has been carried over into typed work that is not to be further reproduced. Advocates of double spacing claim that it is easy to read—the reader is not likely to lose his or her line place.

In recent years, the use of single spacing has gained in popularity. The general practice is to single-space the paragraphs, double-space between paragraphs, and triple-space above all centered heads. Supporters of this form of presentation contend that it saves space and facilitates fast reading, because it approximates the printing most people are accustomed to reading.

Patterns of indentation. You should indent double-spaced typing to show the paragraph beginnings. On the other hand, because its paragraphs are clearly marked by extra line spacing, you should block single-spaced typing.

There is no generally accepted pattern of indentation. Some sources advocate a distance of four spaces; some prefer five; some like eight; and others like ten and more. Any decision about the best distance to use is purely arbitrary and left up to you, although you would do well to follow the practice established in the office, group, or school for which you write the report. Whatever the selection, the important rule to follow is that of consistency.

Neatness in typed work. Even with the best typewriter available, the finished work is no better than the efforts of the typist. But this statement does not imply that only the most skilled typist can turn out good work. Even the inexperienced typist can produce acceptable manuscripts simply by exercising care.

You should take care in correcting your typing mistakes, for obvious corrections (strikeovers, erasure holes in the page, and the like) stand out in the manuscript like a sore thumb. With a little bit of care, this operation can be done so well that the casual reader doesn't detect the error.

Numbering of pages. Two systems of numbers are used in numbering the pages of the written report. Arabic numerals are conventional for the text portion, normally beginning with the first page of the introduction and continuing through the appendix. Small roman numerals are standard for the pages preceding the text. Although all of these prefatory pages are counted in the numbering sequence, the numbers generally do not appear on the pages preceding the table of contents.

Placement of the numbers on the page varies with the binding used for the report. In reports which are bound at the top of the page, you should center all page numbers at the bottom of the page, a double or triple space below the layout used in the typing.

For the more widely used left-side binding, you should place the numbers in the upper right corner of the page, a double space above the top line of the layout and in line with the right margin. Exception to this placement is customarily made for special-layout pages which have major titles and an additional amount of space displayed at the top. Included in this group may be the first page of the report text; the synopsis; the table of contents;

and, in very long and formal works, the first page of each major division or chapter. Numbers for such pages as these are centered a double or triple space below the imaginary line marking the bottom of the layout.

Display of captions. Captions—or headings, as they are sometimes called—are titles to the various divisions of the report. They represent the organization steps worked out previously and are designed to help the reader find her or his way through this organization plan. Thus, it is important that the captions show the reader at a glance the importance of their part in the report.

You may emphasize this importance of captions in two ways—by type and by position. You may use any logical combination of type and position to show differences in the importance of captions. In actual practice, however, a few standard orders of captions have become widely used.

There are four major positions of captions, as shown in Figure A–4. Highest of these four in order of rank is the centered caption. This caption is on a line by itself and is centered between left and right margins. Next in order is the marginal caption. Beginning on the left margin, this caption is also on a line by itself. The box caption is third in this ranking, but it normally is used only in single-spaced copy. It begins on the left margin and is surrounded by a box of space formed by indenting the first few lines of the text. The box indentations are kept of equal width throughout the report, although the heights of the boxes will vary with the number of words in the captions enclosed. Fourth in importance is the run-in caption. This caption simply runs into the first line of the text it covers and is distinguished from the text only by underscoring.

Were your report to be printed, there would be a wide variety of typefaces and sizes that you could use to show different degrees of importance in the captions. But most reports are typed and thereby limited by what type variations can be made with an ordinary typewriter. Except when unusual typefaces are available, you can show type distinctions in only two ways— by the use of capitals and by the underscore. Spacing between letters is sometimes used, although the space requirements of this technique normally eliminate it from consideration. But even though you are limited to two means of showing importance by type selection, you are able to construct four distinct ranks of type:

SOLID CAPITALS UNDERSCORED

SOLID CAPITALS

Capitals and Lowercase Underscored Capitals and Lowercase

In theory, any combination of type and position which shows the relative importance of the captions at a glance is acceptable. The one governing rule to follow in considering types and positions of captions is that no caption may have a higher ranking type or position than any of the captions of a higher level. It is permissible, however, that two successive steps of captions appear in the same type, if their difference is shown by position, or in the same position, if their difference is shown by type selection. Also, there is no objection to skipping over any of the steps in the progression of type or position.

Figure A–4
Caption Positions in Order of Importance

Although the possibilities of variation are great, some practices have become almost conventional, possibly because they excel in showing each caption's importance at a glance. Also, these practices are no doubt widely accepted because of their simplicity of construction. One such scheme of captioning is the following, which is recommended for use in reports with three orders of division.

The first order of captions in this scheme appears on a separate line, centered, and typed in solid capital letters. Although solid capitals underscored may be used, this high type normally is reserved for the report title, which is the highest caption in the report. Second-order captions are also on separate lines, beginning with the left margin and typed with capitals and lowercase underscored. Third-degree captions are run into the paragraph they cover. To distinguish the line from the text, underscoring is used, and the caption ends with a strong mark of punctuation, usually the period.

Other acceptable schemes include the following:

1. Centered; solid capitals.
2. Centered; capitals and lowercase underscored.
3. Marginal; capitals and lowercase underscored.
4. Run-in; capitals and lowercase underscored.

1. Centered; solid capitals.
2. Marginal; capitals and lowercase underscored.
3. Box cut-in; capitals and lowercase underscored.
4. Run-in; capitals and lowercase underscored.

1. Centered; solid capitals.
2. Centered; capitals and lowercase underscored.
3. Box cut-in; capitals and lowercase.

1. Centered; solid capitals.
2. Marginal; capitals and lowercase underscored.
3. Box cut-in; capitals and lowercase underscored.

Mechanics and format of the report parts

The foregoing notes on physical appearance apply generally to all parts of the report. But for the individual construction of the specific report pages, additional special notes are needed. So you may be able to get and follow these special notes, a part-by-part review of the physical construction of the formal report follows. Much of this presentation is left to illustration, for volumes could be written about the minute details of construction. Major points, however, are indicated.

Title fly. Primarily used in the most formal reports, the title fly contains only the report title. In constructing the page, place the title slightly above the vertical center of the page in an eye-pleasing arrangement. Center all lines with regard to left and right margins. And type it in the highest ranking type used in the report (usually solid capitals underscored); and double-space it if you need more than one line.

Title page. The title page normally contains three main areas of identification (Figure A–5), although some forms present the same information in

Figure A–5
Good Layout for the Three-spot Title Page

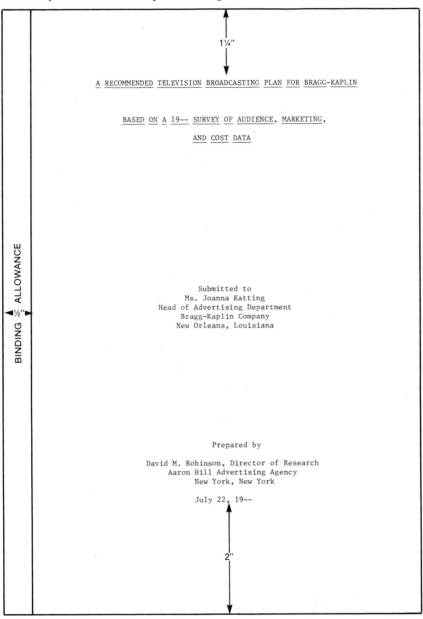

four or five spots on the page (Figure A–6). In the typical three-spot title page, the first item covered is the report title. Preferably, type it in the highest ranking type used in the report, usually solid capitals underscored. Center it; and if more than one line is required, break the lines between thought units and center both lines. Double-space the lines.

Figure A–6
Good Layout for the Four-spot Title Page

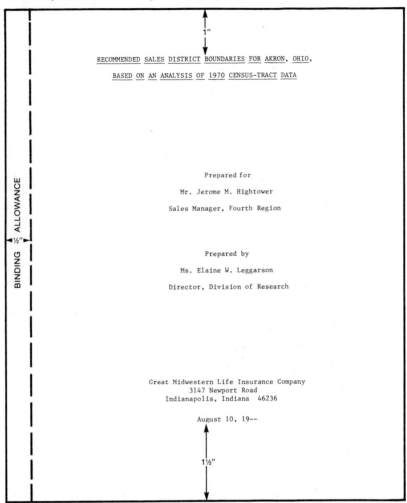

The second area of identification names the individual or group for whom the report is prepared. Precede it with an identifying phrase, such as "Prepared for" or "Submitted to"—words which indicate the individual's role in the report. In addition to the name, include identification by title or role, company, and address, particularly if you and your recipient are from different companies. If the information below the identifying phrase requires three or more lines of type, single-space the lines. If you have fewer than three lines, double-space them. But regardless of how you space this information, the identifying phrase appears best set off from the facts below it by a double-space.

The third area of information identifies you, the writer of the report.

It, also, is preceded by an identifying phrase. You may use "Prepared by," "Written by," or any such wording which describes your role in the report. You, also, may give your title or role, company, and address. As a final part of this group of information, you may include the date of publication. You should single-space this identification information if four lines are required. Double-space it if three lines or less are required. Likewise, set off the identifying phrase with a double space. Preferably double-space the date line from the information preceding it, regardless of previous spacing. Placement of the three spots of information on the page should conform to an eye-pleasing arrangement.

One such arrangement begins the title about 1¼ inches from the top of the page. The final spot of information ends about 2 inches from the page bottom. The center spot of information appears so as to split the space between the top and bottom units in a 2-to-3 ratio, the bottom space being the larger. Line lengths of the information units, of course, are largely governed by the data contained; yet you will have some opportunity to combine or split units. Preferably, the lines will have sufficient length to keep the units from having an overall "skinny" appearance.

Letters of transmittal and authorization. As their names imply, the letters of transmittal and authorization are actual letters. Therefore, they should appear as letters. You should type them in any acceptable letter form—pure block, modified block, or indented. A layout plan recommended for at least the more formal reports is what fits the letter into a rectangle of the same shape as the space on which it is typed (see Figure A–7). This rectangle is marked by the dateline at the top, the initial characters of type at the left, the average of the line lengths at the right, and the last line in the signature at the bottom. For the best optical effect, the rectangle should ride a little high on the page, with a ratio of top margin to bottom margin of about two to three.

Acknowledgments. When you are indebted to the assistance of others, it is fitting that you acknowledge the indebtedness somewhere in the report. If the number of individuals is small, you may acknowledge them in the introduction of the report or in the letter of transmittal. In the rare event that you need to make numerous acknowledgments, you may construct a special section for this purpose. This section is headed with the simple title "Acknowledgments" and is typed with the same layout as any other text page which has a title displayed.

Table of contents. The table of contents is the report outline in its polished, finished form. It lists the major report captions with the page numbers on which these captions appear. Although not all reports require a table of contents, one should be a part of any report long enough for a guide to be helpful to the readers.

The page is appropriately headed by the caption "Contents" or "Table of Contents," as shown in Figure A–8. The page layout is that used for any report page with a title displayed. Below the title you should set up two columns. One contains the caption, generally beginning with the first report part following the table of contents. You have the option of including

Figure A–7

Letter of Transmittal Fitted to the Shape of the Space in which Typed

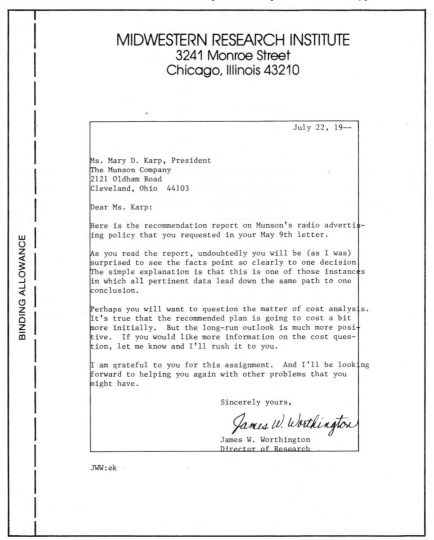

BINDING ALLOWANCE

MIDWESTERN RESEARCH INSTITUTE
3241 Monroe Street
Chicago, Illinois 43210

July 22, 19--

Ms. Mary D. Karp, President
The Munson Company
2121 Oldham Road
Cleveland, Ohio 44103

Dear Ms. Karp:

Here is the recommendation report on Munson's radio advertising policy that you requested in your May 9th letter.

As you read the report, undoubtedly you will be (as I was) surprised to see the facts point so clearly to one decision. The simple explanation is that this is one of those instances in which all pertinent data lead down the same path to one conclusion.

Perhaps you will want to question the matter of cost analysis. It's true that the recommended plan is going to cost a bit more initially. But the long-run outlook is much more positive. If you would like more information on the cost question, let me know and I'll rush it to you.

I am grateful to you for this assignment. And I'll be looking forward to helping you again with other problems that you might have.

Sincerely yours,

James W. Worthington

James W. Worthington
Director of Research

JWW:ek

or leaving out the outline letters and numbers. If you use numbers, so arrange them that their last digits are aligned. In the other column, which is brought over to the right margin and headed by the caption "Page," place the page numbers on which the captions may be found. Align these numbers on their right digits. Connect the two columns by leader lines of periods, preferably with spaces intervening.

As a rule, you should type all captions of the highest level of division with line spaces above and below them. Captions below this level you should uniformly single-space or double-space, depending on the overall lengths of

Good Layout and Mechanics in the First Page of the Table of Contents

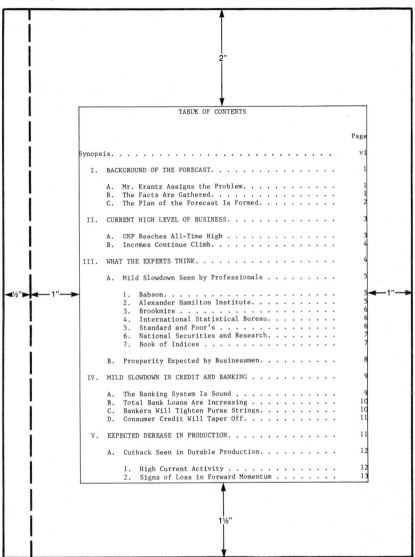

the captions. If the captions are long, covering most of the line or extending to a second line, uniform double spacing between captions is recommended. Short captions appear bulky in consistent single-spaced form. Some authorities, however, prefer double spacing all of the content entries when double spacing is used in the text.

In the table of contents, as in the body of the report, you may vary the type to distinguish different levels of captions. But the type variations of the table of contents need not be the same as those used in the text of the report. Usually, the highest level of captions is distinguished from the other levels; and sometimes second-level captions are distinguished from lower captions by type differences. It is not wrong to show no distinction at all by using plain capitals and lowercase throughout.

Table of illustrations. The table of illustrations either may be a continuation of the table of contents or a separate table. This table, as shown in Figure A–9, lists the graphic aids presented in the report in much the same way as the report parts are listed in the table of contents.

In constructing this table, head it with an appropriately descriptive title, such as "Table of Charts and Illustrations," or "List of Tables and Charts," or "Table of Figures." If you place the table on a separate page, this page layout is the same as that for any other text page with title displayed. And if you place it as a continued part of the table of contents, you should begin the table of illustrations after spacing four or more lines from the last contents entry.

The table is made up of two columns—one for the graphic-aid title and the second for the page on which the aid appears. Head the second column with the caption "Page." And connect the two columns by leader lines of spaced periods. Line spacing in the table is optional, again depending on the line length of the entries. Preceding each entry title, place that entry's number; and, should these numbers be roman or otherwise require more than one digit, align the digits appropriately on their right members. If your report contains two or more illustration types (tables, charts, maps, etc.) and you have given each its own numbering sequence, you may list the entries successively by types.

Variations in forms of reports

Much of the discussion to this point has been about the long, formal report form—the form containing numerous prefatory and appended parts in addition to a complete text. But not all reports need be of this type. In fact, most reports are not of this arrangement. Yet most reports employ much the same writing, organization, and layout principles—so much so, in fact, that a knowledge of how to prepare the longer report forms is usually adequate for the preparation of shorter types. That is, there is a close relationship in all reports, and an understanding of this relationship will allow the writer to apply the same layout, writing, and organization principles to all reports.

Format of letter and memorandum reports. All the stages discussed in the progression of report types discussed in Chapter 14, with the exception of the last two named, involve similar problems and instructions of physical presentation. But there is little similarity in the physical structure of the various letter-type reports.

The physical layout requirements of the letter report are the same as those for any other letter. Any conventional letter form may be used; and, as was explained in the discussion of layout of the transmittal and authorization letters, the letter report might well approximate the shape of the space in which it is typed.

Figure A–9

523

Appendix A
Physical
Presentation
of Reports

Good Layout and Mechanics in the Last Page of the Table of Contents
Showing the Table of Illustrations Attached

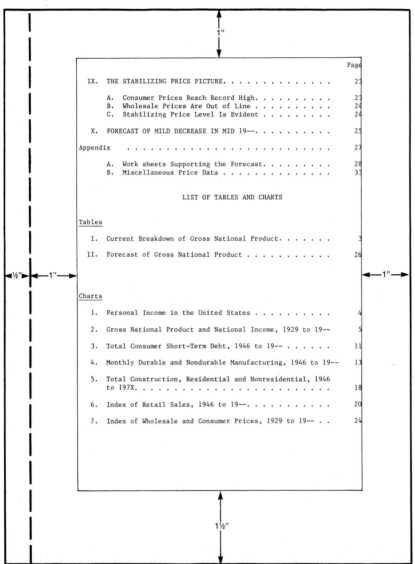

Memorandum reports, although they are a type of informal letter, do not necessarily follow conventional letter format. The most popular form (see Figure A–10) uses the military arrangement of introductory information: *To, From, Subject.* Generally, this information is followed by informal presentation of facts in organized fashion. Other forms of the memorandum vary widely. Some resemble questionnaires, in that they are comprised of lists of topics or questions with spaces provided for the written answers. Others are simply handwritten notes on standard interoffice communication forms.

Figure A–10
Good Form for a Memorandum Report

CAMPUS CORRESPONDENCE

LOUISIANA STATE UNIVERSITY

FROM: Committee on Courses and Curricula
           J. William Hughes, Chairperson

TO: Faculty, College of   DATE: December 15, 19--
           Business Administration

SUBJECT: Report of progress and plans on the study of the
           business administration curricula

<u>Progress for the Period October 1 to December 15</u>

On October 10 the Committee mailed questionnaires (copy attached) to the deans of 24 selected colleges of business administration. To date, 21 of the deans have returned questionnaires.

Professors Byrd, Calhoun, and Creznik have tabulated the replies received and are now analyzing the findings.

<u>Future Plans</u>

Professors Byrd, Calhoun, and Creznik will present their analyses to the Committee at its February 4th meeting. At this time, the Committee expects to study these analyses and to make final recommendations.

Professor Byrd will record the Committee's recommendations in a written report. The Committee will distribute copies of this report to all voting members of the faculty at least one week before the faculty meeting scheduled for May 9.

Appendix B .

Form of the business letter

When we apply communication theory to the business letter situation, it becomes apparent that the appearance of the letter is a part of the message. The readers judge the writer by what they see as they look at the typed page. And their judgments of the writer become a part of their filtering process through which they give meaning to the message. Thus, for the very best communication result, you should make certain that your letter looks good—that it gives a good impression of you. For your guidance in this effort, the following brief review of letter form is presented.

The ideal layout

Ideally, the best letter layout is one which has the same shape as the space in which it is typed. It fits the space much like a picture in a frame. That is, a rectangle drawn around the typing that makes up the letter would have the same shape and be in proportion to the space under the letterhead of the page. This layout would be marked at the top by the dateline, on the left by the line beginnings, on the right by the average line length, and at the bottom by the last line of the typed signature. Because it looks better to the eye, the layout is best placed a little high on the page (see Figure B–1). Side margins should be equal and no less than an inch.

Model layouts are used in business primarily for the really important letters. Sales letters, for example, almost always are arranged this way. So are application letters. Most offices, however, find it impractical to make individual layouts for letters. In the future it is likely that ideal layouts will become more widely used, for improved word-processing equipment will make them easier to construct.

Fixed margins

Offices which use a fixed margin for all letters (usually about six-inch lines are used) vary the heights of the letters by using more or less space, as

Figure B–1
Modified Block, Blocked Paragraphs, Margins Adjusted to Make Ideal Layout

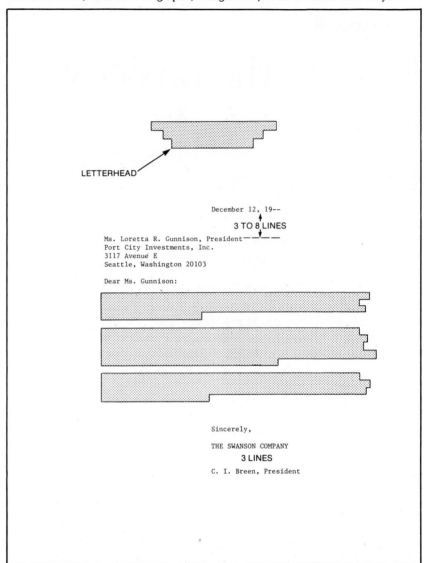

needed, between date and inside address. The arrangements in Figures B–2 and B–3 are typical of this practice.

Style preferences

A variety of styles is available, and any generally recognized one is acceptable. The two most popular ones are the block and the modified block. They are the ones illustrated.

Figure B–2
Block Style, Fixed Margins, Using Subject Line

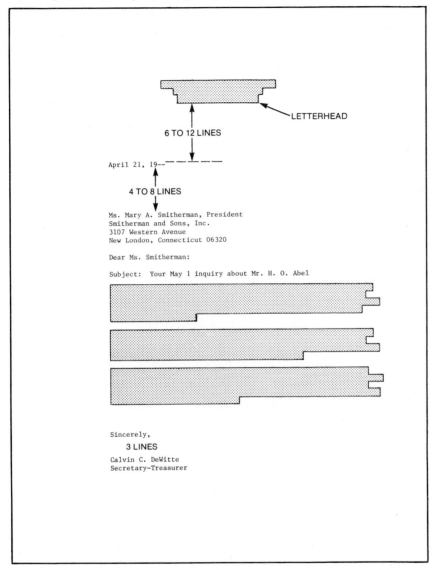

The exact practices to follow in setting up the parts of the letter are not all agreed upon. The suggestions which appear below, however, follow the bulk of authoritative opinion—at least, in most instances.

Dateline. The conventional form (December 9, 1984) should be used, with day, month, and year. Abbreviated forms, such as 12–9–84 or Dec. 9, '84, are informal and do not leave the best impression on some people.

Inside address. The mailing address, complete with title of the person addressed, makes up the inside address. Preferably, it is typed without abbreviations, except for those words commonly abbreviated (Dr., Mr., Ms., etc.).

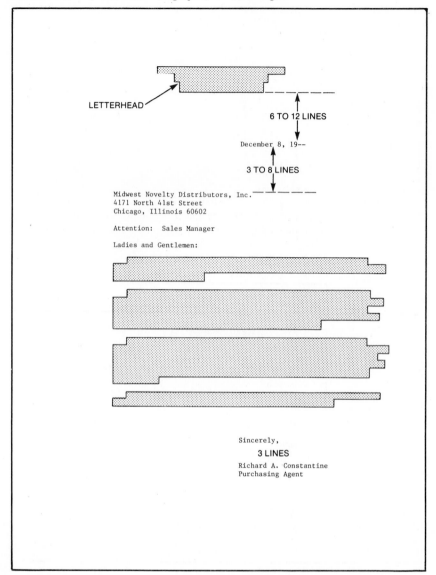

Salutation. The choice of salutation should be determined by the degree of familiarity between reader and writer and the formality of the situation. If they know each other well, the address may be by first name (Dear Joan). An address by last name (Dear Mr. Baskin) is appropriate in most cases, but especially is it appropriate when the people involved are to some extent acquainted. In situations that are formal or impersonal, the forms Dear Sir and Madam are in order.

A movement to eliminate the salutation and the complimentary close is gaining some support. Leading this movement is the Administrative Management Association. Although these groups should be encouraged for promoting a logical change, their letter styles have not yet gained the support of a major section of business.

The women's rights movement has sharply reduced the use of Mrs. and Miss. Why distinguish between married and single women, the group argues, when we make no such distinction between married and single men? The group's solution is to use Ms. for all women, just as we use Mr. for all men.

Although some people (including women) oppose using Ms., the term is gaining widespread acceptance. As you may have noticed, it appears throughout this book. Unless you know that your reader has other preferences, you would be wise to use it.

The impersonal plural greetings *Gentlemen* and *Dear Sirs* are in a similar status. Clearly, they greet the readers as males when in fact females may be among them. One suggested solution is the salutation *Ladies and Gentlemen.* One cannot quarrel with the logic of the term; but it has not yet become popular. For the time being, at least, you will have to use your best judgment in selecting plural greetings.

Subject block. So that sender and receiver may quickly identify the subject of the correspondence, many offices use the subject block on their letters. As illustrated in Figure B–2, it tells what the correspondence is about. In addition, it contains any specific identifying material that may be helpful—date of previous correspondence, invoice number, order number, and the like. Usually, it is placed on a line below the salutation, although some companies prefer to place it higher—often in the upper right corner of the letter layout. The block may be headed in a number of ways, of which the following forms are representative:

Subject: Your July 2 inquiry about . . .
In reply please refer to File H-320
Reference your October 17 order for . . .
About your order No. 712-A dated . . .

Attention line. Some companies prefer to emphasize the company address, rather than the individual offices. Thus, they address the correspondence to the company in the inside address. Then they use an attention line (Figure B–3) to direct the letter to a specific officer or department. Typical forms of this reference are as follows:

Attention of Mr. Clayton E. Haney, Office Manager
For Mr. Charles E. Blake, Director
Attention: William O'Brien, Vice President
Attention Abraham E. Rubbicon, Sales Manager

Second page heading. When a letter must go beyond one page, the following pages should be set up for quick identification. Following pages always are typed on plain paper (no letterhead). Of the various forms used to identify these pages, the following three are the most common:

Ms. Helen E. Mann
May 7, 1984
Page 2

Ms. Helen E. Mann, May 7, 1984, page 2

After each, the letter continues following a triple or quadruple space.

Complimentary close. By far the most commonly used complimentary close is *Sincerely. Sincerely yours* also is used; but in recent years the *yours* has been fading away. *Truly* (with and without the *yours)* also is used; but it also has lost popularity. Closes, such as *Cordially* and *Respectfully,* are appropriate when their meanings fit the writer-reader relationship involved.

Signature block. The typed signature conventionally appears on the fourth line below the complimentary close, beginning directly under the first letter for the block form. A short name and title may be typed on the same line and separated by the comma. If either is long, the title is typed on the following line and blocked under it. Of course, the writer's signature appears in the space between complimentary close and typed signature.

Some firms prefer that their name appear in the signature for strict legal responsibility. The conventional form for this arrangement places the firm name in solid capitals and blocked on the second line below the closing phrase. The typed name of the person signing the letter is on the fourth line below the firm name.

Information notations. In the lower left corner of the letter may appear abbreviated notations of enclosures (Enc., Enc.—3, etc.) and initials of dictator and stenographer (WEH:ga). Indications of carbon prepared for other readers also may be included (cc: William E. Sutton; Copy to William E. Sutton; etc.). Originally, initials of the person who dictated the letter were useful in helping readers decipher illegible signatures. Now with typed signatures, these initials are not so useful. But many firms use them. Stenographers' initials are useful for office checking.

Folding. The carelessly folded letter is off to a bad start with the reader. Neat folding will complete the planned effect by (1) making the letter fit snugly in its cover, (2) making it easy and handy for the recipient to remove, and (3) making it appear neat when opened out.

The two-fold pattern is easiest. It fits the standard sheet for the No. 10 envelope, the monarch sheet for its special envelope, and the note sheet (or "hotel" size) for the No. 6¾ envelope.

First fold of the two-fold pattern is from the bottom up, taking $\frac{1}{12}$ inch less than a third of the sheet. Second fold goes from the top down, taking exactly the same panel as the bottom segment. (This measurement will leave the recipient a quarter-inch thumbhold for easy unfolding of the letter.) Folded thus, the letter should be slipped into its envelope with the second crease toward the bottom and the center panel at the front of the envelope (see Figure B–4).

The three-fold pattern is necessary to fit the standard sheet into the

Figure B–4
Two Ways of Folding and Inserting Letters

Two-fold way (for long envelopes)

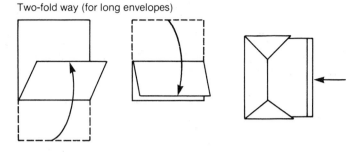

Three-fold way (for short envelopes)

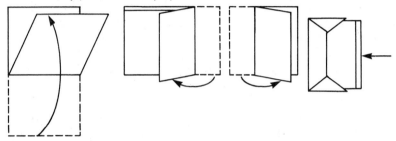

Note: See text descriptions for dimensions

commonly used No. 6¾ envelope. Its first fold is from the bottom up, with the bottom edge of the sheet riding about a quarter inch under the top edge—to allow the thumbhold. (If the edges are exactly even, they are harder to separate.) The second fold is from the right-hand side of the sheet toward the left, taking $\frac{1}{12}$ inch less than a third of the width. The third fold matches the second: from the left-hand side toward the right, with a panel of exactly the same width. (This fold will leave a quarter-inch thumbhold at the right, for user's convenience.) So that the letter will appear neat when unfolded, the creases should be neatly parallel with top and sides—not at angles that produce "dog ears" and irregular shapes. In the three-fold form it is especially important for the side panels (produced by second and third folds) to be exactly the same width; otherwise, the vertical creases are off-centered and tend to throw the whole carefully planned layout off center.

The three-fold letter is inserted into its cover with the third crease toward the bottom of the envelope and the loose edges toward the stamp end of the envelope. (From habit, most recipients of business letters slit envelopes at their top and turn them face down to extract the letter. The three-fold letter inserted as described thus gives its reader an easy thumbhold at the top of the envelope to pull it out by, and a second one at the top of the sheet for easy unfolding of the whole.)

Figure B–5
Illustration of Proper Envelope Address Using Number 6¾ Envelope

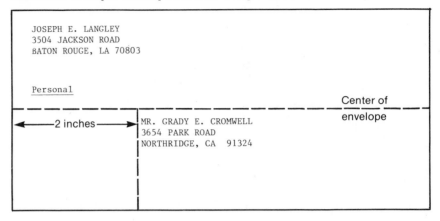

Envelope address. So that the optical character reader may be used in sorting mail, the Post Office requests that all envelopes be typed as follows (see Figure B–5):

1. On the No. 10 envelope (large), start the address four inches from the left edge. On the No. 6¾ (small) envelope, start two inches from the left edge.
2. Use a block address format.
3. Single space.
4. Use all uppercase letters (capitals).
5. Do not use punctuation.
6. Use these two-letter abbreviations for states:

AL	(Alabama)	KY	(Kentucky)	OH	(Ohio)
AK	(Alaska)	LA	(Louisiana)	OK	(Oklahoma)
AZ	(Arizona)	ME	(Maine)	OR	(Oregon)
AR	(Arkansas)	MD	(Maryland)	PA	(Pennsylvania)
CA	(California)	MA	(Massachusetts)	PR	(Puerto Rico)
CO	(Colorado)	MI	(Michigan)	RI	(Rhode Island)
CT	(Connecticut)	MN	(Minnesota)	SC	(South Carolina)
DE	(Delaware)	MS	(Mississippi)	SD	(South Dakota)
DC	(D.C.)	MO	(Missouri)	TN	(Tennessee)
FL	(Florida)	MT	(Montana)	TX	(Texas)
GA	(Georgia)	NE	(Nebraska)	UT	(Utah)
GU	(Guam)	NV	(Nevada)	VT	(Vermont)
HI	(Hawaii)	NH	(New Hampshire)	VI	(Virgin Islands)
ID	(Idaho)	NJ	(New Jersey)	VA	(Virginia)
IL	(Illinois)	NM	(New Mexico)	WA	(Washington)
IN	(Indiana)	NY	(New York)	WV	(West Virginia)
IA	(Iowa)	NC	(North Carolina)	WI	(Wisconsin)
KS	(Kansas)	ND	(North Dakota)	WY	(Wyoming)

Appendix C .

Documentation, footnotes, and the bibliography

Documentation

In writing reports, you will frequently use information from other sources. Because this material is not your own, you may need to acknowledge it. Whether and how you should acknowledge such data is the subject of this brief review.

When and how to acknowledge sources

Two methods are most commonly used in business to acknowledge sources: (1) parenthetic author-date references within the text, and (2) footnote references. A third method, endnote references, sometimes is used. This method is losing favor, however, primarily because the typing advantage it provides has been reduced by the advent of word-processing equipment. Only the first two methods are discussed in the following pages.

The parenthetic author-date method. In recent years the author-date method has become the most popular reference method for business. It involves placing the author's last name and the year of publication in parentheses immediately following the material to be cited:

(Calahan 1981)

The reference is keyed to a list of all publications cited (a bibliography), which appears at the end of the paper (see discussion of the bibliography in a following section). If specific page numbers are needed, they follow the date:

(DeVillier 1983, 117–18)

If multiple authorships are cited, the last names may be listed:

(Smith, Corley, and Doran 1980, 31)

If there are more than three authors, the conventional *"et al."* or "and others" is used:

(Clovis *et al.* 1979)
(Francis and others 1984)

When no author is listed, as in unsigned publications issued by a company, government agency, labor union, or such, the author's name is the organization name:

(U.S. Department of Labor 1983)
(American Federation of Labor 1977, 31)

As noted earlier, these references are keyed to a bibliography which appears at the end of the paper. To find the details of the reference, the reader turns to the bibliography and traces the reference through the alphabetical listing. For the reference "(Sanders 1983)," for example, the reader would find Sanders in the alphabetical arrangement of the bibliography. If more than one publication by Sanders appears, the reader would know to refer to the one written in 1983.

The footnote method. The traditional method of acknowledging sources is by footnotes; that is, the references are placed at the bottom of the page and are keyed with the text material by superscripts (raised arabic numbers). The numbering sequence of the superscripts is consecutive, by page, by chapter, or by the whole work. The footnotes are placed inside the page layout, are single-spaced, and are indented or blocked just as the text is typed.

The short form. Although footnote form varies from one source to another, one generally accepted procedure is presented here. It permits two structures: the short form, which may be used when a bibliography is present, and the complete form. In the short form, the footnote contains only these parts: (1) author's surname; (2) title of the article, bulletin, or book; and (3) page number:

[3] Wilson, *The Report Writer's Guide*, p. 44 (book reference).
[4] Allison, "Making Routine Reports Talk," p. 71 (periodical reference).

The complete form. For the complete reference, the descriptive parts are listed in the proper order below. Commas separate the parts, and the entry ends with a period. Capitals need to be used only with proper nouns, and abbreviations are acceptable if consistently used.

In these lists, all of the items that could possibly be placed in each type of entry are named in the order of arrangement. Those items not available or not pertinent in a given source should be passed over. In other words, the following lists are intended to give the maximum contents in the order of arrangement of the footnote parts. Only as much of the list should be used as fits the source involved.

Book entry:

1. *Superscript.* Arabic numeral keyed with the text reference and placed before the first part of the entry without spacing.
2. *Name of the author, in normal order.* If two or more authors are involved,

all may be presented. If the number of authors is too great to list, the first author followed by the Latin *et al.* or its English equivalent "and others" may be used.

3. *Capacity of the author.* Needed only when contribution to the publication is not truly that of the author, such as *editor* or *compiler.*
4. *Chapter name.* Necessary only in rare instances when the chapter name helps the reader to find the source, as in references to encyclopedias.
5. *Book name.* Book names are placed in italics. In typewritten work, italics are indicated by underscoring or by solid caps.
6. *Publishing company.*
7. *Location of publisher.* If more than one office, the one nearest the writer should be used. United States cities alone are sufficient if population exceeds half a million; city and state are best given for smaller places.
8. *Date.* Year of publication. If revised, year of latest revision.
9. *Page or pages.* Specific page or inclusive pages on which the cited material is found.
10. *Copyright.* The publishers may request that the copyright symbol ⓒ be added to the citations given in the footnotes.

The following are examples of book entries.
A typical book:

¹ Walter W. Perlick and Raymond V. Lesikar, *Introduction to Business: A Societal Approach,* 3d ed., Business Publications, Dallas, Tex., 1979, pp. 317–18. Copyright ⓒ 1979, by Business Publications, Inc.

A book written by a staff of writers under the direction of an editor (chapter title is considered helpful):

² W. C. Butte and Ann Buchannan, editors, "Direct Mail Advertising," *An Encyclopedia of Advertising,* Binton Publishing Company, New York, 1983, p. 99.

A book written by a number of coauthors:

³ E. Butler Cannais and others, *Anthology of Public Relations,* Warner-Bragg, Inc., New York, 1983, p. 137.

Periodical entry:

1. *Superscript.*
2. *Author's name.* Frequently, no author is given. In such cases the entry may be skipped, or if it is definitely known to be anonymous, the word *anonymous* may be placed in the entry.
3. *Article name.* Typed in quotation marks.
4. *Periodical name.* Placed in italics, which are indicated by underscoring in typed work.
5. *Publication identification.* Volume number lowercased and in arabic numerals followed by specific date of publication in parentheses.
6. *Page or pages.*

Examples of periodical entries are shown below:

¹ Mildred C. Kinnig, "A New Look at Retirement," *Modern Business,* vol. 37 (July 31, 1984), pp. 31–32.
² William O. Schultz, "How One Company Improved Morale," *Business Leader,* vol. 17 (August 31, 1982), p. 17.
³ Mary Mitchell, "Report Writing Aids," *ABCA Bulletin,* October, 1983, p. 13.

Newspaper article:

1. *Superscript.*
2. *Source description.* If article is signed, give author's name. Otherwise, give description of article such as "United Press dispatch" or "editorial."
3. *Main head of article.* Subheads not needed.
4. *Newspaper name.* City and state names inserted in brackets if place names do not appear in newspaper title. State names not needed in case of very large cities, such as New York, Chicago, and Los Angeles.
5. *Date of publication.*
6. *Page.* May even include column number.

The following are typical newspaper article entries:

[1] United Press dispatch, "Rival Unions Sign Pact," *Morning Advocate* [Baton Rouge, Louisiana], September 3, 1984, p. 1–A.
[2] Editorial, "The North Moves South," *Austin* [Texas] *American*, October 3, 1983, p. 2–A.

Letters or documents:

1. *Nature of Communication.*
2. *Name of writer.* ⎡ With identification by title and
3. *Name of recipient.* ⎣ organization where helpful.
4. *Date of writing.*
5. *Where filed.*

An example of an entry citing a letter is given below:

[1] Letter from J. W. Wells, president, Wells Equipment Co., to James Mattoch, secretary-treasurer, Southern Industrialists, Inc., June 10, 1984, filed among Mr. Mattoch's personal records.

The types of entries discussed in the preceding paragraphs are those most likely to be used. Yet, many unusual types of publications (not clearly books or periodicals) are likely to come up. When they do, you should classify the source by the form it most nearly resembles—a book or a periodical. Then you should attempt to construct the entry which most correctly describes the one source. Frequently, you will need to improvise—to use your best judgment in determining the source description.

Repeated references to a source. In scholarly writing, repeated references to a source traditionally have been made through the use of the Latin words *ibid.* (in the same place), *op. cit.* (in the work cited), and *loc. cit.* (in the place cited). As indicated by their definitions, each of these forms indicates a specific preceding reference. Scholarly writers of the past considered these forms to be useful because the forms eliminated the need to repeat an entire footnote.

Perhaps for good reason, in recent years these Latin forms have grown out of favor in business writing. Obviously, the short form of footnote needs no such devices to save time. And repeated references in the long form can be shortened by using short-form structure for the repeated reference in this way:

[1] Janice Smith, *Business Writing*, Small-Boch, Inc., Chicago, 1984, pp. 173–74.
[2] Smith, *Business Writing*, p. 181.

Abbreviations in footnotes. As is obvious from the illustrations in this review, abbreviations are acceptable in footnotes. When they are used, they must be used consistently. Abbreviations most commonly used in footnotes are the following:

Abbreviation	*Meaning*
cf.	Compare (directs reader's attention to another passage)
cf. ante	Compare above
cf. post	Compare below
ed.	Edition
e.g.	For example
et al.	And others
et passim	And at intervals throughout the work
et seq.	And the following
i.e.	That is
infra	Below
l., ll.	Line, lines
MS, MSS	Manuscript, manuscripts
n.d.	No date
n.n.	No name
n.p.	No place
p., pp.	Page, pages
f., ff.	Following page, following pages
supra	Above
vol., vols.	Volume, volumes

Discussion footnotes

In sharp contrast with source footnotes are the discussion footnotes. Through the use of discussion footnotes the writer strives to explain a part of the text, to amplify discussion on a phase of the presentation, to make cross-references to other parts of the paper, and the like. The following examples illustrate some possibilities of this footnote type.
Cross-reference:

[1] See the principle of focal points on page 72.

Amplification of discussion and cross-reference:

[2] Lyman Bryson says the same thing: "Every communication is different for every receiver even in the same context. No one can estimate the variation of understanding that there may be among receivers of the same message conveyed in the same vehicle when the receivers are separated in either space or time." See *Communication of Ideas*, p. 5.

Comparison:

[3] Compare with the principle of the objective: Before starting any activity, one should make a clear, complete statement of the objective in view.

Placement of quoted and paraphrased information

You may use data obtained from secondary sources in two ways: You may paraphrase the information (cast it in your own words), or you may use it verbatim (exactly as the original author worded it). In typing paraphrased material, you need not distinguish it from the remainder of the report text. Information which you use verbatim, however, must be distinguished clearly from the other material.

The conventional rule for marking this difference is simple. If the quoted passage is four lines or less in length, it is typed with the report text and is distinguished from the normal text by quotation marks. But if a longer quotation (five lines or more) is used, the conventional practice is to set it in from both left and right margins (about five spaces) but without quotation marks. If the text is typed with double spacing, the quoted passage is further distinguished from the report writer's work by single spacing, as illustrated in Figure C–1.

Frequently, you will find it best to break up or use only fragments of the quoted author's work. Because omissions may distort the meaning of a passage, you must clearly show them. You make these omissions clear by use of the ellipsis (a series of three periods typed with intervening spaces) at the points where material is left out. If it appears at the end of a sentence, you must use four periods—one for final punctuation plus the ellipsis. A passage with such omissions is the following:

> . . . many companies have undertaken to centralize in the hands of specially trained correspondents the handling of the outgoing mail. Usually, centralization has been accomplished by the firm's employment of a correspondence supervisor. . . . The supervisor may guide the work of correspondents . . . , or the company may employ a second technique.

In long quotations, it is conventional to show omissions of a paragraph or more by a full line of periods, usually typed with intervening spaces.

The bibliography

A bibliography is an orderly list of published material on a particular subject. As noted previously, it gives detailed information on footnote references.

Figure C–1
Segment of a Report Showing Mechanics of Typing a Quoted Passage

```
        of those opposing the issue, Logan Wilson makes this penetrating ob-

    servation:

                It is a curious paradox that academicians display a
                scientific attitude toward every universe of inquiry
                except that which comprises their own professions. . . .
                Lacking precise qualitative criteria, administrators
                are prone to fall back upon rather crude quantitative
                measures as a partial substitute.[5]

        These logical, straightforward, and simple arguments of the pro-

    ponents of teacher evaluation appear to be irrefutable.
```

In a formal paper, the list covers references on the subject of the paper. The entries in this list very closely resemble complete source footnotes, but the two must not be confused.

The bibliography normally appears as an appended part of a formal paper and follows the appendix. Typically, a fly page containing the one word *Bibliography* precedes it, usually typed in solid capital letters. Below this title, the publications are presented by broad categories and in alphabetical order within the categories. Such groupings as "Books," "Periodicals," and "Bulletins" may be used. But the determination of groups should be based solely on the types of publications collected in each bibliography. If, for example, a bibliography includes a large number of periodicals and government publications plus a wide assortment of diverse publication types, the bibliography could be divided into three parts: "Periodicals," "Government Publications," and "Miscellaneous Publications."

As with footnotes, variations in bibliographical style are numerous. A simplified form recommended for business use follows the same procedure as that described above for source footnotes, with four major exceptions:

1. The author's name is listed in reverse order—surname first—for the purpose of alphabetizing. If coauthors are involved, however, only the first author's name is reversed.
2. The entry is generally typed in hanging-indention form. That is, the second and all following lines of an entry begin some uniform distance (usually about five spaces) to the right of the beginning point of the first line. The purpose of this indented pattern is to make the alphabetized first line stand out.
3. The bibliography entry gives the inclusive pages of the publication and does not refer to any one page or passage.
4. Second and subsequent references to publications of the same author are indicated by a uniform line (see bibliography illustration). In typed manuscripts this line might be formed by the underscore struck ten consecutive times. But this line may be used only if the entire authorship is the same in the consecutive publications. For example, the line could not be used in a situation in which consecutive entries have one common author but different coauthors.

Bibliography

Books

Burton, Helen, *The City Fights Back*, Citadel Press, New York, 1983, 318 pp.

Converse, Paul D., Harvey W. Huegy, and Robert V. Mitchell, *The Elements of Marketing*, 5th ed., Prentice-Hall, Inc., New York, 1952, 968 pp.

Kiernan, Gladys M., *Retailers Manual of Taxes and Regulations*, 12th ed., Institute of Distribution, Inc., New York, 1984, 340 pp.

Loomis, David A., *Government Control of Business*, Stanton Publishing Company, Boston, 1982, 937 pp.

Surrey, N. M. M., *The Commerce of Louisiana during the French Regime, 1699–1763*, Columbia University Press, New York, 1916, 476 pp.

Government publications

United States Bureau of the Census, "Characteristics of the Population,"
    Nineteenth Census of the United States: Census of Population, vol. II, part
    18, United States Government Printing Office, Washington, D.C., 1971,
    248 pp.
——, *Statistical Abstract of the United States,* United States Government
    Printing Office, Washington, D.C., 1984, 1056 pp.
United States Department of Commerce, *Business Statistics: 1979,* United States
    Government Printing Office, Washington, D.C., 1971, 309 pp.
——, *Survey of Current Business: 1980 Supplement,* United States Government
    Printing Office, Washington, D.C., 1983, 271 pp.

Periodicals

Montgomery, Donald E., "Consumer Standards and Marketing," *The Annals
    of the American Academy of Political and Social Science,* vol. 7 (May, 1984),
    pp. 141–49.
Phillips, Emily F., "Some Studies Needed in Marketing," *The Journal of Marketing,*
    vol. 5 (July, 1940), pp. 16–25.
——, "Major Areas of Marketing Research," *The Journal of Marketing,* vol.
    21 (July, 1984), pp. 21–26.

Miscellaneous publications

Bradford, Ernest S., *Survey and Directory, Marketing Research Agencies in the
    United States,* Bureau of Business Research, College of the City of New
    York, 1984, 137 pp.
Reference Sources on Chain Stores, Institute of Distribution, Inc., New York,
    1983, 116 pp.
Smith, T. Lynn, *Farm Trade Centers in Louisiana, 1901 to 1975,* Louisiana Bulletin
    No. 234, Louisiana State University, Baton Rouge, 1978, 56 pp.

The annotated bibliography

Frequently, in scholarly writing each bibliography entry is followed by a
brief comment on the value and content of the entry. That is, the bibliography
is annotated. Form and content of annotated bibliographies are shown in
these entries:

Donald, W. T., editor, *Handbook of Business Administration,* McGraw-Hill Book
    Co., Inc., New York, 1983, 731 pp.
    Contains a summary of the activities in each major area of business.
    Written by foremost authorities in each field. Particularly useful to the
    business specialist who wants a quick review of the whole of business.
Brown, Stanley M., and Lillian Doris, editors, *Business Executive's Handbook,*
    3d ed., Macmillan Co., New York, 1984, 644 pp.
    Provides answers to most routine executive problems in explicit manner
    and with good examples. Contains good material on correspondence and
    sales letters.

A guide to correctness in writing

In the following pages you will find a review of the punctuation and grammar standards that should be most helpful to you in your efforts to communicate clearly. This review is not complete, so you should not look at it as a thorough English handbook. For the finer points you may need to consult a current handbook on the subject. For your convenience in finding them, and for use as grading marks on your papers, the standards are coded with letters and numbers.

Standards for correctness in punctuation

Apos (Apostrophe)

Apos 1   Use the apostrophe to show the possessive case of nouns and indefinite pronouns. If the word does not end in *s*, add an apostrophe and an *s*. If the word ends in *s*, add only an apostrophe.

Nominative Form	*Possessive Form*
company	company's
employee	employee's
companies	companies'
employees	employees'

Proper names and singular nouns which end in *s* sounds are exceptions. To such words, you may either add the apostrophe and the *s* or just the apostrophe. To the nominative plural, add only an apostrophe.

Nominative Form	*Possessive Form*
Texas (singular)	Texas', Texas's
Jones (singular)	Jones', Jones's
Joneses (plural)	Joneses'
countess (singular)	countess', countess's

Apos 2   Use an apostrophe to mark the place in a contraction where letters are omitted.

> has not = hasn't
> cannot = can't
> it is = it's

Bkts (Brackets)

Set off in brackets words which the author wishes to insert in a quotation.

"Possibly the use of this type of supervisor [the trained correspondence expert] is still on the increase."

"At least direct supervision has gained in importance in the past decade [the report was written in 1970], during which time 43 percent of the reporting business firms that started programs have used this technique."

Cln (Colon)

Cln 1   Use the colon to introduce a statement of explanation, an enumeration, or a formal quotation.

Statement of explanation: At this time the company was pioneering a new marketing idea: it was attempting to sell its products direct to consumers by means of vending machines.

Enumeration: There are four classes of machinists working in this department: apprentice machinist, journeyman machinist, machinist, and first-class machinist.

Formal quotation: President Hartung had this to say about the proposal: "Any such movement which fails to have the support of the rank-and-file worker in this plant fails to get my support."

Cln 2   Do not use the colon when the thought of the sentence should continue without interruption. If it is a list that is being introduced by a colon, the list should be in apposition to a preceding word.

Below standard: Cities in which new sales offices are in operation are: Fort Smith, Texarkana, Lake Charles, Jackson, and Biloxi.

Acceptable: Cities in which new sales offices are in operation are Fort Smith, Texarkana, Lake Charles, Jackson, and Biloxi.

Acceptable: Cities in which new sales offices are in operation are as follows: Fort Smith, Texarkana, Lake Charles, Jackson, and Biloxi.

Cma (Comma)

Cma 1   Use a comma to separate principal clauses connected by a coordinating conjunction. The coordinating conjunctions are *and, but, or, nor,* and *for.* (A principal clause has subject and verb, and it stands by itself.)

Only two of the components of the index declined, and these two account for only 12 percent of the total weight of the index.

New automobiles are moving at record volumes, but used car sales are lagging well behind the record pace set two years ago.

Exceptions may be made to this rule, however, in the case of compound sentences consisting of short and closely connected clauses.

> We sold and the price dropped.
> Sometimes we profit and sometimes we lose.

Cma 2.1   Separate the elements listed in series by commas. To avoid misinterpretation in rare instances when some of the elements listed have compound constructions, it is best to place the comma between the last two items (before the final conjunction).

> Good copy must cover facts with accuracy, sincerity, honesty, and conviction.
>
> Direct advertising can be used to introduce salespeople, fill in between salespeople's calls, cover territory where salespeople cannot be maintained, and keep pertinent reference material in the hands of prospects.
>
> A survey conducted at the 1980 automobile show indicated that black and cream, blue and gray, dark maroon, and black cars were favored by the public. [Note how this example illustrates the need for a comma before the final conjunction.]

Cma 2.2   Separate coordinate adjectives in series by commas when they modify the same noun and if there is no *and* connecting them. A good test to determine whether adjectives are coordinate is to insert an *and* between the words. If the *and* does not change the meaning of the expression, the words are coordinate.

> Miss Pratt has been a reliable, faithful, efficient employee for 20 years.
>
> We guarantee that this is a good, clean car.
>
> Light green office furniture is Mr. Orr's recommendation for the stenographic pool. [If *and* were placed between *light* and *green*, the word meaning would be changed.]
>
> A big Dawson wrench proved to be best for the task. [The *and* won't fit between *big* and *Dawson*.]

Cma 3   Set off nonrestrictive modifiers from the sentence by commas. By a nonrestrictive modifier is meant a modifier which could be omitted from the sentence without changing the meaning of the sentence. Restrictive modifiers (those which restrict the words they modify to one particular object) are not set off by commas. A restrictive modifier cannot be left out of the sentence without changing the sentence meaning.

> *Restrictive:* The salesperson who sells the most will get a bonus. [*Who sells the most* restricts the meaning to one particular salesperson.]
>
> *Nonrestrictive:* James Smithers, who was the company's top salesperson for the year, was awarded a bonus. [If the clause *who was the company's top salesperson for the year* is omitted, the statement is not changed.]
>
> *Restrictive:* The firm which employs most of the physically handicapped in this area has gained the admiration of the community.
>
> *Nonrestrictive:* J. Ward & Company, the firm which employs most of the physically handicapped in this area, has gained the admiration of the community.

Notice how some modifiers could be either restrictive or nonrestrictive, depending on the meaning intended by the writer:

> *Restrictive:* All of the suits which were damaged in the fire were sold at a discount. [Implies that a part of the stock was not damaged.]
>
> *Nonrestrictive:* All of the suits, which were damaged by the fire, were sold at a discount. [Implies that all the stock was damaged.]

Cma 4.1 Use commas to set off parenthetic expressions. A parenthetic expression consists of words which interrupt the normal flow of the sentence. In a sense, they appear to be "stuck in." In many instances, they are simply words out of normal order. For example, the sentence "A full-page, black-and-white advertisement was run in the *Daily Bulletin*" contains a parenthetic expression when the word order is altered: "An advertisement, full-page and in black and white, was run in the *Daily Bulletin.*"

> This practice, it is believed, will lead to ruin.
>
> The Johnston Oil Company, so the rumor goes, has cut back sharply its exploration activity.

Although you may use the dash or parentheses for similar reasons, the three marks differ as to the degree to which they separate the enclosed words from the rest of the sentence. The comma is the weakest of the three, and it is best used when the material set off is closely related to the surrounding words. Dashes are stronger marks than commas and are used when the words set off tend to be long or contain internal punctuation marks. Parentheses, the strongest of the three, are primarily used to enclose material which helps to explain or supplement the main words of the sentence.

Cma 4.2 Use commas to set off an appositive (a noun or a noun and its modifiers inserted to explain another noun) from the rest of the sentence. In a sense, appositives are forms of parenthetic expressions, for they interrupt the normal flow of the sentence.

> The Baron Corporation, our machine-parts supplier, is negotiating a new contract.
>
> St. Louis, home office of our midwest district, will be the permanent site of our annual sales meeting.
>
> President Carthwright, a self-educated woman, is the leading advocate of our night school for employees.

But appositives which identify very closely are not set off by commas.

> The word *liabilities* is not understood by most laboring people.
>
> Our next shipment will come on the steamship *Alberta.*

Cma 4.3 Set off parenthetic words, such as *therefore, however, in fact, of course, for example,* and *consequently,* with commas.

> It is apparent, therefore, that the buyers' resistance has been brought about by an overvigorous sales campaign.

After the first experiment, for example, the traffic flow increased 10 percent.
The company, however, will be forced to abandon the old pricing system.

Included in this group of introductory words may be interjections *(oh, alas)* and responsive expressions *(yes, no, surely, indeed, well,* etc.). But if the words are strongly exclamatory or are not closely connected with the rest of the sentence, they may be punctuated as a sentence. *(No. Yes. Indeed.)*

Yes, the decision to increase production has been made.
Oh, contribute whatever you think is adequate.

Cma 4.4 When more than one unit appears in a date or an address, set off the units by commas.

One unit: December 30 is the date of our annual inventory.
One unit: The company has one outlet in Ohio.
More than one unit: December 30, 1906, is the date the Johnston Company first opened its doors.
More than one unit: Richmond, Virginia, is the headquarters of the new sales district.

Cma 5.1 Use commas to separate subordinate clauses preceding main clauses.

Although it is durable, this package does not have eye appeal.
Since there was little store traffic on Aisle 13, the area was converted into office space.

Cma 5.2 Place commas after introductory verbal phrases. A verbal phrase is one which contains some verb derivative, a gerund, a participle, or an infinitive.

Participle phrase: Realizing his mistake, the supervisor instructed the workers to keep a record of all salvaged equipment.
Gerund phrase: After gaining the advantage, we failed to press on to victory.
Infinitive phrase: To increase our turnover of automobile accessories, we must first improve our display area.

Cma 6.1 Use the comma only for good reason. It is not a mark to be inserted indiscriminately at the whim of the writer. As a rule, use of commas should always be justified by one of the standard practices previously noted.

Cma 6.1.1 Do not be tripped into putting a comma between subject and verb.

The thought that he could not afford to fail spurred him on. [No comma after *fail.*]

Cma 6.1.2 Take exception to the preceding standards whenever insertion of a comma will help clarity of expression.

Not clear: From the beginning inventory methods of Hill Company have been haphazard.

Clear: From the beginning, inventory methods of Hill Company have been haphazard.

Not clear: When eating your hands should be clean.

Clear: When eating, your hands should be clean.

Dsh (Dash)

Use the dash to set off an element for emphasis or to show interrupted thought. Particularly use it with long parenthetic expressions or those containing internal punctuation. With the typewriter, make the dash by striking the hyphen twice, without spacing before or after.

Budgets for some past years—1974, for example—were prepared without consulting the department heads.

The test proved that the new process is simple, effective, accurate—and more expensive.

Only one person—the supervisor in charge—has authority to issue such an order.

If you want a voice in the government—vote.

Ex (Exclamation mark)

Use the exclamation point at the end of a sentence or at the end of an exclamatory fragment to show strong emotion. But use this mark sparingly; never use it with trivial ideas.

We've done it again!

No! It can't be!

Hpn (Hyphen)

Hpn 1   Indicate division of a word at the end of a line by the hyphen. You must divide between syllables. It generally is impractical to leave a one-letter syllable at the end of a line *(a-bove)* or to carry over a two-letter syllable to the next line *(expens-es)*.

Hpn 2   Place hyphens between the parts of some compound words. Generally, the hyphen is used whenever its absence would confuse the meaning of the words.

Compound nouns: *brother-in-law, cure-all, city-state*

Compound numbers under 100 and above 20: *thirty-one, fifty-five, seventy-seven*

Compound adjectives (two or more words used before a noun as a single adjective): *long-term* contract, *50-gallon* drum, *door-to-door* selling, *end-of-month* clearance.

Prefixes [most have been absorbed into the word]: *de-emphasize, ex-chairman, vice-chairman, anti-labor*

Hpn 2.1 A proper name used as a compound adjective needs no hyphen or hyphens to hold it together as a visual unit for the reader: The capitals perform that function.

> *Correct:* A Lamar High School student
> *Correct:* A United Airlines pilot

Hpn 2.2 Two or more modifiers in normal grammatical form and order need no hyphens. Particularly, a phrase consisting of an unmistakable adverb (one ending in *ly)* modifying an adjective or participle which in turn modifies a noun shows normal grammatical order and is readily grasped by the reader without the aid of the hyphen. But an adverb not ending in *ly* had better be joined to its adjectives or participle by the hyphen.

> *No hyphen needed:* A poorly drawn chart
> *Use the hyphen:* A well-prepared chart

Ital (Italic)

Ital 1 For the use of italics for book titles, see QM 4. Note that italics also are used for names of periodicals, of works of art or music, and of naval vessels and aircraft.

Ital 2 Italicize rarely used foreign words—if you must use them *(pro bono publico, raison d'État, ich dien)*. After a foreign word is widely accepted, however, it does not need to be italicized (bon voyage, pizza, rancho). A current dictionary is a good source for this information.

Ital 3 Italicize a word, letter, or figure used as its own name. Without this device, we could not write this set of rules. Note the use of italics all through to label name words.

> The little word *sell* is still in the dictionary.
> The pronoun *which* should always have a noun as a clear antecedent. [Try reading that one without the italics: it becomes a fragment ending in mid air!]

Paren (Parentheses)

Use the parentheses to set off words which are parenthetic or which are inserted to explain or to supplement the principal message (see Cma 4.1).

> Dr. Samuel Goppard's phenomenal prediction *(Business Week,* June 20, 1980) has made some business forecasters revise their techniques.
> Smith was elected chairman (the vote was almost 2 to 1), and immediately he introduced his plan for reorganization.

Pd (Period)

Pd 1 Use the period to indicate the end of a declarative sentence.

Pd 2 Use periods after abbreviations or initials.

Ph.D., Co., Inc., A.M.,A.D., etc.

Pd 3 Use the ellipsis (a series of periods) to indicate the omission of words from a quoted passage. If the omitted part consists of something less than a paragraph, three periods are customarily placed at the point of omission (a fourth period is added if the omission comes at the sentence end). If the omitted part is a paragraph or more, however, a full line of periods is used. In either case the periods are appropriately typed with intervening spaces.

Logical explanations, however, have been given by authorities in the field. Some attribute the decline . . . to the changing economy in the state during recent years. . . .

. . . .

Added to the labor factor is the high cost of raw material, which has tended to eliminate many marginal producers. Also, the rising cost of electric power in recent years may have shifted many of the industry leaders' attention to other forms of production.

Q (Question mark)

Place question marks at the ends of sentences which are direct questions.

What are the latest quotations on Ewing-Bell common stock?
Will this campaign help to sell Dunnco products?

But do not use the question mark with indirect questions.

The president was asked whether this campaign will help to sell Dunnco products.
He asked me what the latest quotations on Ewing-Bell common stock were.

QM (Quotation mark)

QM 1 Use quotation marks to enclose the exact words of a speaker or, if the quotation is short, the exact words of a writer.

By short written quotations is meant something four lines or less. Longer quoted passages are best displayed without quotation marks and with additional right and left margins (see Appendix C).

Short written passage: H. G. McVoy sums up his presentation with this statement: "All signs indicate that automation will be evolutionary, not revolutionary."

Verbal quotation: "This really should bring on a production slowdown," said Ms. Kuntz.

If the quoted words are broken by explanation or reference words, each quoted part is enclosed in quotation marks.

"Will you be specific," he asked, "in recommending a course of action?"

QM 2 Enclose a quotation within a quotation with single quotation marks.

President Carver said, "It has been a long time since I have heard an employee say, 'Boss, I'm going to beat my quota today.'"

QM 3 Always place periods and commas inside quotation marks. Place semicolons and colons outside the marks. Place question marks and exclamation points inside if they apply to the quoted passage and outside if they apply to the whole sentence.

"If we are patient," he said, "prosperity will some day arrive." [The comma is within the quotes; the period is also within the quotes.]

"Is there a quorum?" he asked. [The question mark belongs to the quoted passage.]

Which of you said, "I know where the error lies"? [The question mark applies to the entire sentence.]

I conclude only this from the union's promise to "force the hand of management": Violence will be their trump card. [Here the colon is not a part of the quotation.]

QM 4 Enclose in quotation marks the titles of the parts of a publication (articles in a magazine, chapters in a book). Place the title of a whole publication, however, in italics. Use underscoring to show italics in typewritten material.

The third chapter of the book *Elementary Statistical Procedure* is entitled "Concepts of Sampling."

Joan Glasgow's most recent article, "A Union Boss Views Automation," appears in the current issue of *Fortune*.

SC (Semicolon)

SC 1 Separate by a semicolon independent clauses that are not connected by a conjunction.

Cork or asbestos sheeting must be hand-cut; polyurethane may be poured into a mold.

The new contract provides substantial wage increases; the original contract emphasized shorter hours.

Covered by this standard are clauses connected by *however, nevertheless, therefore, then, moreover, besides* (conjunctive adverbs, not conjunctions).

The survey findings indicated a need to revise the policy; nevertheless the president vetoed the amendment.

Small-town buyers favor the old models; therefore the board concluded that both models should be manufactured.

SC 2 You may separate by a semicolon independent clauses joined by *and, but, or, for, nor* (coordinating conjunctions) if the clauses are long or if they have other punctuation in them. You also may use the semicolon in this situation for special emphasis.

The FTU and the IFL, rivals from the beginning of the new industry, have shared almost equally in the growth of membership; but the FTU predominates among workers in the petroleum-products crafts, including pipeline construction and operation, and the IFL leads in memberships of chemical workers.

The market price was $4; but we paid $7.

SC 3   Separate by semicolons the parts in a list when the parts have commas in them.

The following gains were made in the February year-to-year comparison: Fort Worth, 7,300; Dallas, 4,705; Lubbock, 2,610; San Antonio, 2,350; Waco, 2,240; Port Arthur, 2,170; and Corpus Christi, 1,420.

Elected for the new term were Anna T. Zelnak, attorney from Cincinnati; Wilbur T. Hoffmeister, stockbroker and president of Hoffmeister Associates of Baltimore; and William P. Peabody, a member of the faculty of the University of Georgia.

SC 4   Use the semicolon between equal (coordinate) units only. Do not use it to separate a dependent clause or phrase and an independent clause.

Below standard: The flood damaged much of the equipment in Building 113; making it necessary for management to stop production and lay off all production workers.

Acceptable: The flood damaged much of the equipment in Building 113, making it necessary for management to stop production and lay off all production workers.

Acceptable: The flood damaged much of the equipment in Building 113; thus, it was necessary for management to stop production and lay off all production workers.

Standards for correctness in grammar

Maintaining high standards of grammar is vital to the business writer who desires to excel at her or his work. Although it is not always necessary that high standards of grammar be followed to communicate, little can be said in favor of abandoning these standards. To illustrate, the statement "He ain't never done nothing to nobody" has little chance of not communicating its message. But doesn't it communicate more than the message intended? Doesn't it also communicate some idea about the intellectual level of the writer? Certainly, such impressions would not help the communication of a typical report or letter.

As with the review of punctuation standards, the following summary of grammar standards is not intended to be a complete handbook on the subject. Rather, it is a summary of the major trouble spots encountered by most business writers. Mastery of these grammar principles would almost assure the business writer of achieving the high standards which are vital to the communication of reports and letters.

AA (Adjective-adverb confusion)

Do not use adjectives for adverbs, nor adverbs for adjectives. Adjectives modify only nouns and pronouns; and adverbs modify verbs, adjectives, or other adverbs.

Possibly the chief source of this confusion is in statements where the modifier follows the verb. If the modifier refers to the subject, an adjective should be used. If it limits the verb, an adverb is needed.

> *Below standard:* She filed the records *quick.*
> *Acceptable:* She filed the records *quickly.* [Refers to the verb.]
> *Below standard:* John doesn't feel *badly.*
> *Acceptable:* John doesn't feel *bad.* [Refers to the noun.]
> *Below standard:* The new cars look *beautifully.*
> *Acceptable:* The new cars look *beautiful.* [Refers to the noun.]

It should be noted that many words are both adjective and adverb *(little, well, fast, much).* And some adverbs have two forms: One form is the same as the adjective, and the other adds the *ly (slow* and *slowly, cheap* and *cheaply, quick* and *quickly).*

> *Acceptable:* All of our drivers are instructed to drive *slow.*
> *Acceptable:* All of our drivers are instructed to drive *slowly.*

Agmt SV (Agreement of subject and verb)

Nouns and their verbs must agree in number. A plural noun must have a plural verb form; a singular noun must have a singular verb.

> *Below standard: Expenditures* for miscellaneous equipment *was* expected to decline. [*Expenditures* is plural, so its verb must be plural.]
> *Acceptable: Expenditures* for miscellaneous equipment *were* expected to decline.
> *Below standard:* The *president,* as well as his staff, *were* not able to attend. [*President* is the subject, and the number is not changed by the modifying phrase.]
> *Acceptable:* The *president,* as well as his staff, *was* not able to attend.

Compound subjects (two or more nouns joined by *and*) require plural verbs.

> *Below standard:* The *welders* and their *foreman is* in favor of the proposal. [*Welders* and *foreman* are compound subjects of the verb, but *is* is singular.]
> *Acceptable:* The *welders* and their *foreman are* in favor of the proposal.
> *Below standard: Received* in the morning delivery *was* a *typewriter and* two *reams* of letterhead paper. [*Reams* and *typewriter* are the subjects; the verb must be plural.]
> *Acceptable: Received* in the morning delivery *were* a *typewriter and* two *reams* of letterhead paper.

Collective nouns may be either singular or plural, depending on the meaning intended.

> *Acceptable:* The *committee have* carefully *studied* the proposal. [*Committee* is thought of as separate individuals.]
> *Acceptable:* The *committee has* carefully *studied* the proposal. [The *committee* is considered as a unit.]

As a rule, the pronouns *anybody, anyone, each, either, everyone, everybody, neither, nobody, somebody,* and *someone* take a singular verb. The word *none* may be either singular or plural, depending on whether it is used to refer to a unit or to more than a unit.

> *Acceptable: Either* of the advertising campaigns *is* costly.
> *Acceptable: Nobody* who watches the clock *is* successful.
> *Acceptable: None* of the boys *understands* his assignment.
> *Acceptable: None* of the boys *understand* their assignments.

AN (Adverbial noun clause)

Do not use an adverbial clause as a noun clause. Clauses beginning with *because, when, where, if,* and similar adverbial connectives are not properly used as subjects, objects, or complements of verbs.

> *Not this:* He did not know *if* he could go or not.
> *But this:* He did not know *whether* he could go or not.
> *Not this:* The reason was *because* he did not submit a report.
> *But this:* The reason was *that* he did not submit a report.
> *Not this:* A time-series graph is *where* [or *when*] changes in an index such as wholesale prices are indicated.
> *But this:* A time-series graph is the picturing of. . . .

Awk (Awkward)

Avoid awkward writing. Writing is awkward when its word arrangement is unconventional or uneconomical, or simply not the best for quick understanding.

Dng (Dangling modifiers)

Avoid the use of modifiers which do not logically modify a word in the sentence. Such modifiers are said to dangle. They are both illogical and confusing. Usually, you can correct sentences containing dangling constructions in either of two ways: You can insert the noun or pronoun which the modifier describes, or you can change the dangling part to a complete clause.

> *Below standard:* Believing that credit customers should have advance notice of the sale, special letters were mailed to them.
> *Acceptable:* Believing that credit customers should have advance notice of the sale, we mailed special letters to them. [Improvement is made by inserting the noun modified.]
> *Acceptable:* Because we believed that credit customers should have advance notice of the sale, we mailed special letters to them. [Improvement is made by changing the dangling element to a complete clause.]

Dangling modifiers are of four principal types: participial phrases, elliptical clauses, gerund phrases, and infinitive phrases.

> *Below standard:* Believing that District 7 was not being thoroughly covered, an additional salesperson was assigned to the area. [Dangling participial phrase.]

Acceptable: Believing that District 7 was not being thoroughly covered, the sales manager assigned an additional salesperson to the area.

Below standard: By working hard, your goal can be reached. [Dangling gerund phrase.]

Acceptable: By working hard, you can reach your goal.

Below standard: To succeed at this job, long hours and hard work must not be shunned. [Dangling infinitive phrase.]

Acceptable: To succeed at this job, one must not shun long hours and hard work.

Below standard: While waiting on a customer, the radio was stolen. [Dangling elliptical clause—a clause without noun or verb.]

Acceptable: While the salesperson was waiting on a customer, the radio was stolen.

There are, however, a few generally accepted introductory phrases which are permitted to dangle. Included in this group are *generally speaking, confidentially speaking, taking all things into consideration,* and such expressions as *in boxing, in welding,* and *in farming.*

Acceptable: Generally speaking, business activity is at an all-time high.

Acceptable: In farming, the land must be prepared long before planting time.

Acceptable: Taking all things into consideration, this applicant is the best for the job.

Frag (Sentence fragment)

Avoid the sentence fragment. Although the sentence fragment sometimes may be used for effect, as in sales writing, it is best omitted by all but the most skilled writers. The sentence fragment consists of any group of words which cannot stand alone as a complete and independent statement. Probably the most frequent violation of this rule results from the use of a subordinate clause as a sentence.

Below standard: Believing that you will want an analysis of sales for November. We have sent you the figures.

Acceptable: Believing that you will want an analysis of sales for November, we have sent you the figures.

Below standard: He declared that such a procedure would not be practical. And that it would be too expensive in the long run.

Acceptable: He declared that such a procedure would not be practical and that it would be too expensive in the long run.

Pn (Pronouns)

Pn 1 Make certain that the word to which each pronoun refers (its antecedent) is clear. Failure to conform to this standard causes confusion, particularly in sentences where two or more nouns are possible antecedents or where the antecedent is far away from the pronoun.

Below standard: When the president objected to Mr. Carter, he told him to mind his own business. [Who told whom?]

Acceptable: When the president objected to Mr. Carter, Mr. Carter told him to mind his own business.

Below standard: The mixture should not be allowed to boil; so when you do it, watch the temperature gauge. [*It* doesn't have an antecedent.]

Acceptable: The mixture should not be allowed to boil; so when conducting the experiment, watch the temperature gauge.

Below standard: The model V is being introduced this year. Ads in *Time, The Saturday Evening Post,* and big-city newspapers over the country are designed to get sales off to a good start. It is especially designed for the novice boatman who is not willing to pay a big price.

Acceptable: The model V is being introduced this year. Ads in *Time, The Saturday Evening Post,* and big-city newspapers over the country are designed to get sales off to a good start. The new model is especially designed for the novice boatman who is not willing to pay a big price.

Confusion may sometimes result from using a pronoun with an implied antecedent.

Below standard: Because of the disastrous freeze in the citrus belt, it is necessary that most of them be replanted.

Acceptable: Because of the disastrous freeze in the citrus belt, it is necessary that most of the citrus orchards be replanted.

Except when their reference is perfectly clear, it is best to avoid using the pronouns *which, that,* and *this* to refer to a whole idea of a preceding clause. Many times you can make the sentence clear by using a clarifying noun following the pronoun.

Below standard [following a detailed presentation of the writer's suggestion for improving the company suggestion-box plan]: This should be put into effect without delay.

Acceptable: This suggestion-box plan should be put into effect right away.

Pn 2 The number of the pronoun should agree with the number of its antecedent. If the antecedent is singular, its pronoun must be singular. If the antecedent is plural, its pronoun must be plural.

Below standard: Taxes and insurance are necessary evils in any business, and it must be considered carefully in anticipating profits.

Acceptable: Taxes and insurance are necessary evils in any business, and they must be considered carefully in anticipating profits.

Below standard: Everybody should make plans for their retirement. [Words like *everyone, everybody, anybody* are singular.]

Acceptable: Everybody should make plans for his or her retirement.

Pn 3 Take care to use the correct case of the pronoun. If the pronoun serves as the subject of the verb, or if it follows a form of the infinitive *to be,* use a nominative case pronoun. (Nominative case of the personal pronouns is *I, you, he, she, it, we, they.*)

Acceptable: He will record the minutes of the meeting.
Acceptable: I think it will be he.

If the pronoun is the object of a preposition or a verb, or if it is the subject of an infinitive, use the objective case. (Objective case for the personal pronouns is *me, you, him, her, us, them.*)

Below standard: This transaction is between you and he. [*He* is nominative and cannot be the object of the preposition *between.*]

Acceptable: This transaction is between you and *him*.

Below standard: Because the investigator praised Ms. Smith and *I*, we were promoted.

Acceptable: Because the investigator praised Ms. Smith and *me*, we were promoted.

The case of relative pronouns *(who, whom)* is determined by the pronoun's use in the clause it introduces. One good way of determining which case to use is to substitute the personal pronoun for the relative pronoun. If the case of the personal pronoun which fits is nominative, use *who*. If it is objective, use *whom*.

Acceptable: George Cutler is the salesperson who won the award. [*He* (nominative) could be substituted for the relative pronoun; therefore, nominative *who* should be used.]

Acceptable: George Cutler is the salesperson *whom* you recommended. [Objective case *him* would substitute. Thus, objective case *whom* is used.]

Usually, the possessive case is used with substantives which immediately precede a gerund (verbal noun ending in *ing*).

Acceptable: Our selling of the stock frightened some of the conservative members of the board.

Acceptable: Her accepting the money ended her legal claim to the property.

Prl (Parallelism)

Parts of a sentence that express equal thoughts should be parallel (the same) in grammatical form. Parallel constructions are logically connected by the coordinating conjunctions *and, but,* and *or.* Care should be taken to see that the sentence elements connected by these conjunctions are of the same grammatical type. That is, if one of the parts is a noun, so should the other parts be nouns. If one of the parts is an infinitive phrase, so should the other parts be infinitive phrases.

Below standard: The company objectives for the coming year are to match last year's production, higher sales, and improving consumer relations.

Acceptable: The company objectives for the coming year are to match last year's production, to increase sales, and to improve consumer relations.

Below standard: Writing copy may be more valuable experience than to make layouts.

Acceptable: Writing copy may be more valuable experience than making layouts.

Below standard: The questionnaire asks for this information: number of employees, what is our union status, and how much do we pay.

Acceptable: The questionnaire asks for this information: number of employees, union affiliation, and pay scale.

Tns (Tense)

The tense of each verb, infinitive, and participle used should reflect the logical time of happening of the statement: Every statement has its place in time. If this place in time is to be exactly communicated, you must be careful of your selection of tense.

Tns 1 Use present tense for statements of fact that are true at the time of writing.

> *Below standard:* Boston was not selected as a site for the aircraft plant because it *was* too near the coast. [Boston still is near the coast, isn't it?]
>
> *Acceptable:* Boston was not selected as a site for the aircraft plant because it *is* too near the coast.

Tns 2 Use past tense in statements covering a definite past event or action.

> *Below standard:* Mr. Burns *says* to me, "Bill, you'll never make an auditor."
> *Acceptable:* Mr. Burns *said* to me, "Bill, you'll never make an auditor."

Tns 3 The time period reflected by the past participle *(having been . . .)* is earlier than that of its governing verb. For the present participle *(being . . .)*, the time period reflected is the same as that of the governing verb.

> *Below standard:* These debentures are among the oldest on record, *being* issued in early 1937.
>
> *Acceptable:* These debentures are among the oldest on record, *having been* issued in early 1937.
>
> *Below standard:* Ms. Sloan, *having been* the top salesperson on the force, was made sales manager. [Possible but illogical.]
>
> *Acceptable:* Ms. Sloan, *being* the top salesperson on the force, was made sales manager.

Verbs in subordinate clauses are governed by the verb in the principal clause. When the main verb is in the past tense, you usually should place the subordinate verb also in a past tense (past, present perfect, or past perfect). Thus, if the time of the subordinate clause is the same as that of the main verb, use past tense.

> *Acceptable:* I *noticed* [past tense] the discrepancy, and then I *remembered* [same time as main verb] the incidents which caused it.

If the time of the subordinate clause is previous to that of the main verb in past tense, use past perfect tense for the subordinate verb.

> *Below standard:* In early July we *noticed* [past] that he *exceeded* [logically should be previous to main verb] his quota three times.
>
> *Acceptable:* In early July we *noticed* that he *had exceeded* his quota three times.

The present perfect tense is used for the subordinate clause when the time of this clause is subsequent to the time of the main verb.

> *Below standard:* Before the war we *contributed* [past] generously, but lately we *forget* [should be time subsequent to the time of main verb] our duties.
>
> *Acceptable:* Before the war we *contributed* generously, but lately we *have forgotten* our duties.

Tns 4 The present perfect tense does not logically refer to a definite time in the past. Instead, it indicates time somewhere in the indefinite past.

> *Below standard:* We *have audited* your records on July 31 of 1980 and 1981.

Acceptable: We *audited* your records on July 31 of 1980 and 1981.
Acceptable: We *have audited* your records twice in the past.

WU (Word use)

Misused words call attention to themselves and detract from the writing. Although the possibilities of error in word use are infinite, the following list contains a few of the most common ones:

Don't Use	*Use*
a long ways	a long way
and etc.	etc.
anywheres	anywhere
different than	different from
have got to	must
in back of	behind
in hopes of	in hope of
in regards to	in regard to
inside of	within
kind of satisfied	somewhat satisfied
nowhere near	not nearly
nowheres	nowhere
off of	off
over with	over
seldom ever	seldom
try and come	try to come

Standards for the use of numbers

Quantities may be spelled out or they may be expressed in numeral form. Whether to use one form or the other is often a perplexing question. Especially is it perplexing to business writers, for much of their work is with quantitative subjects. Because the means of expressing quantities is so vital to business writers, the following notes on the use of numbers are presented.

No (Numbers)

No 1 Although authorities do not agree on number usage, business writers would do well to follow the rule of ten. By this rule, you spell out numbers ten and below. You use figures for numbers above ten.

> *Correct:* The auditor found 13 discrepancies in the stock records.
> *Correct:* The auditor found nine discrepancies in the stock records.

No 2 Make an exception to the rule of ten when a number begins a sentence. Spell out all numbers in this position.

> *Correct:* Seventy-three bonds were destroyed.
> *Correct:* Eighty-nine men picketed the north entrance.

No 3 In comparisons, keep all numbers in the same form. The form should be the one that, according to the rule of ten, occurs most often in the series.

> *Correct:* We managed to salvage three lathes, one drill, and thirteen welding machines.
> *Correct:* Sales increases over last year were 9 percent on automotive parts, 14 percent on hardware, and 23 percent on appliances.

No 4 When two series of numbers appear in one sentence, spell out one (preferably the smaller) and present the other in numeral form.

> *Correct:* Three salespersons exceeded $1,500, fourteen exceeded $1,000, and thirty-one exceeded $500.

No 5 Present the days of the month in figure form when the month precedes the day.

> *Correct:* July 3, 19x5.

When they appear alone, or when they precede the month, the days of the month may be either spelled out or put in numeral form according to the rule of ten.

> *Correct:* I shall be there on the 13th.
> *Correct:* The union scheduled the strike vote for the eighth.
> *Correct:* Ms. Millican signed the contract on the seventh of July.
> *Correct:* Sales have declined since the 14th of August.

Other common errors

Sp (Spelling)

Spell words correctly. Consult your dictionary whenever you are in doubt.

Cap (Capitalization)

Capitalize all proper nouns and the beginning words of sentences.

Appendix E

A general checklist for letter grading

The opening

O Ind   *Indirectness needed.* This opening gets to the goal too fast.

O Dir   *Directness needed.* This opening is too slow in getting to the goal.

O Qual   *Quality.* This opening could be improved by making it more (1) on subject, (2) logical, or (3) interesting.

Coverage

C Inc   *Incomplete.* You have not covered all the important information.

C Ex   *Excess information.* You have included more information than is needed.

C Exp   *Explanation.* More or better explanation is needed here.

C Id   *Identification.* Completely identify the situation, either in the letter or in a subject line.

Ending

E AC   *Action close.* A drive for action is appropriate in this situation.

E AC S   *Action strong.* This action drive is too strong.

E AC W   *Action weak.* This action drive is too weak.

E IT   *Individually tailored.* Make your close fit the one case.

E OS   *Off subject.* An off-subject close is best for this case. These words recall unpleasant things to the reader's mind.

Technique

Adp *Adaptation.* Your words should be adapted to the one reader. Here yours are (1) above or (2) below your reader.

Awk *Awkward word arrangement.*

Bky *Bulky arrangement.* Make your paragraphs more inviting by breaking them into shorter units of thought.

Chop *Choppy writing.* A succession of short sentences produces an irritating effect.

Dl *Dull writing.* Bring your writing to life with vivid, concrete words.

Emp+ *Emphasis, too much.*

Emp− *Emphasis, too little.* Here you have given too much or too little (as marked) emphasis by (1) placement, (2) volume, or (3) words or mechanical means.

Intp *Interpretation.* Do more than just present facts. In this situation, something more is needed. Make the data meaningful in terms of the reader's situation.

Los *Loose writing.* Take more care to use words economically. Write concisely.

Ord *Order of presentation.* This information does not fall in a logical order. The information is mixed up and confusing.

RS *Rubber-stamp expression.* Timeworn words from the past have no place in modern business writing.

Trans *Transition.* Abrupt shift of thought here.

Effect

Conv *Conviction.* This is not as convincing as it should be. More fact or a more skillful use of words is needed.

GW *Goodwill.* The letter needs more goodwill. Try to make your words convey friendliness. Here you tend to be too dull and matter-of-fact.

Hur *Hurried treatment.* Your coverage of the problem appears to be hurried. Thus, it tends to leave an effect of routine or brusque treatment. Conciseness is wanted, of course; but you must not sacrifice your letter's objectives for it.

Log *Logic.* Is this really logical? Would you do it this way in business?

Neg *Negative effect.* By word or implication, this part tends to be more negative than it should be.

Pers+ *Too persuasive.* Your words are too high-pressure for this situation.

Pers− *Not persuasive enough.* More persuasion, by either words or facts, would help your letter.

Ton *Tone of the words.* Your words create a bad impression on the reader. Words that talk down, lecture, argue, accuse, and the like work against the success of your letter.

YVP *You-viewpoint.* More you-viewpoint wording and adaptation would help the overall effect of your letter.

A grading checklist for reports

The following checklist should serve two purposes. First, it should serve as a guide to preparing reports. Second, it should serve as an aid to grading reports. (Your instructor can use the symbols to mark errors.) The checklist covers all types of reports—from the simple memorandums to the long, analytical reports. For each report type, you need only to use the items that apply.

Title (T)

T 1 Complete? The title should tell what one may expect to find in the report. Use the five Ws as a check for completeness *(who, what, where, when, why—sometimes how).*

T 2 Too long. This title is longer than it needs to be. Check it for uneconomical wording or unnecessary information.

Letter of transmittal (LT)

LT 1 More directness needed in the opening. The letter should present the report right away.

LT 2 Content of the letter needs improvement. Comments which help the reader to understand or appreciate the report are appropriate.

LT 3 Do not include findings unless the report has no synopsis.

LT 4 A warm statement of your attitude toward the assignment is appropriate—often expected. You either do not make one, or the one you make is weak.

LT 5 A friendlier, more conversational style would improve the letter.

Synopsis (S)

S 1 (If direct order was assigned.) Begin directly—with a statement of finding, conclusion, or recommendation.

S 2 (If indirect order was assigned.) Begin with a brief review of introductory information.

S 3 The summary of highlights should be in proportion and should include major findings, analyses, and conclusions. Your coverage here is *(a)* scant or *(b)* too detailed.

S 4 Work for a more interesting and concise summary.

Organization—Outline (O)

O 1 This organization plan is not the best for this problem. The main sections should form a logical solution of the problem.

O 2 The order of the parts of this outline is not logical. The parts should form a step-by-step route to the goal.

O 3 These parts overlap. Each part should be independent of other parts. Although some repetition and relating of parts may be desirable, outright overlap is a sign of bad organization.

O 4 More subparts are needed here. The subparts should cover all the information covered by the major part.

O 5 This subpart does not fit logically under this major part.

O 6 These parts are not equal in importance. Do not give them equal status in the outline.

O 7 (If talking captions were assigned.) These captions do not talk well.

O 8 Coordinate captions should be parallel in grammatical structure.

O 9 This (these) caption(s) is (are) too long.

O 10 Vary the wording of the captions to avoid monotonous repetition.

Introduction (I)

I 1 This introduction does not cover exactly what the reader needs to know. Although the needs vary by problem, these topics usually are important: *(a)* origin of the problem, *(b)* statement of the problem, *(c)* methods used in researching the problem, and *(d)* preview of the presentation.

I 2 Coverage of this part is *(a)* scant or *(b)* too detailed.

I 3 Important information has been left out.

I 4 Findings, conclusions, and other items of information are not a part of the introduction.

Coverage (C)

C 1 The coverage here is *(a)* scant or *(b)* too detailed.

C 2 More analysis is needed here.

C 3 Here you rely too heavily on a graphic aid. The text should cover the important information.

C 4 Do not lose sight of the goal of the report. Relate the information to the problem.

C 5 Clearly distinguish between fact and opinion. Label opinion as opinion.

C 6 Your analyses and conclusions need the support of more fact and authoritative opinion.

Writing (W)

W 1 This writing should be better adapted to your readers. It appears to be *(a)* too heavy or *(b)* too light for your readers.

W 2 Avoid the overuse of passive voice.

W 3 Work for more conciseness. Try to cut down on words without sacrificing meaning.

W 4 For this report more formal writing is appropriate. You should write consistently in impersonal (third-person) style.

W 5 A more personal style is appropriate for this report. That is, you should use more personal pronouns (I's, we's, you's).

W 6 The change in thought is abrupt here.
  a. Between major parts, use introductions, summaries, and conclusions to guide the reader's thinking.
  b. Use transitional words, phrases, or sentences to relate minor parts.

W 7 Your paragraphing is questionable. Check the paragraphs for unity. Look for topic sentences.

Graphic aids (GA)

GA 1 You have *(a)* not used enough graphic aids or *(b)* used too many graphic aids.

GA 2   For the information presented this graphic aid is *(a)* too large or *(b)* too small.

GA 3   This type of graphic aid is not the best for presenting the information.

GA 4   Place the graphic aid as near as practical to the place where its contents are discussed.

GA 5   The appearance of this graphic aid needs improvement. Possibly this is your best work, but it does not make a good impression on the reader.

GA 6   Refer the readers to the graphic aids at the times they should look at them.

GA 7   Preferably make the reference to the graphic aids incidental, as subordinate parts of sentences which comment on the content of the graphic aids (for example ". . . , as shown in Chart 5," or "(see Chart 5)."

Layout and Mechanics (LM)

LM 1   The layout of this page is *(a)* too fat, *(b)* too skinny, or *(c)* too low, high, or off center (as marked).

LM 2   Neat typing? Strikeovers, smudges, and erasures detract from the message.

LM 3   Make the margins straighter. The roughness here offends the eye.

LM 4   The spacing here needs improvement. *(a)* Too much space here. *(b)* Not enough space here.

LM 5   Your page numbering is not the best. See the text for specific instructions.

LM 6   This page appears *(a)* choppy, or *(b)* heavy.

LM 7   Your selection of type and position for the captions is not the best.

LM 8   This item of form is not generally acceptable.

Appendix G

Readability measurement

The instructions for readable writing presented in Chapter 7 are supported by the findings of communication scientists over the past half century. These studies show conclusively that different levels of readability exist. More specifically, they show that for each general level of education there is a level of writing easily read and understood. Writing that is readable to one educational level can be difficult for those below that level. To illustrate, the general level of writing that is easy reading for the college graduate is difficult for those below this educational level. A level that is easy reading for the high school senior is difficult for those at lower grade levels. Readable levels exist for each general level of education.

Development of readability formulas

In addition to generally supporting the basic need for adaptation, these studies have produced formulas for measuring readability. These formulas are based on the qualities of writing that show the highest correlation with ease of readability. In general, these qualities are two—sentence length and word difficulty.

Measuring sentence length is relatively easy, on the one hand, and a few complexities here and there do not meet the eye. Determining word difficulty, on the other hand, is somewhat complex. The studies show that word difficulty is traceable to many things—to historical origin, extent of usage, and such. But because normally the longer a word is the more difficult it is, word length is used in the formulas as a convenient gauge of word difficulty.

Of the various readability formulas used in business today, the Gunning Fog Index probably is the most popular. Other formulas are just as accurate in measuring readability, but this one is among the easiest to use.

The Gunning Fog Index

The ease with which the Gunning Fog Index can be used is obvious from a review of the simple steps listed below. Its ease of interpretation is also obvious in that the index computed from these simple steps is in grade level of education. For example, an index of seven means that the material tested is easy reading for one at the seventh grade level. An index of 12 indicates high school graduate level of readability. And an index of 16 indicates the level of the college graduate.

The simple steps for computing the index are as follows:

1. *Select a sample.* For long pieces of writing use at least 100 words. As in all sampling procedure, the larger the sample, the more reliable the results can be. So, in measuring readability for a long manuscript one would be wise to select a number of samples at random throughout the work.

2. *Determine the average number of words per sentence.* That is, first count words. Then count sentences, treating as sentences all independent clauses. Divide the total number of words by the total of sentences.

3. *Determine the percentage of hard words in the sample.* Words of three syllables or longer are considered to be hard words. But do not count as hard words (a) words that are capitalized, (b) combinations of short, easy words (grasshopper, dishwasher, bookkeeper), or (c) verb forms made into three-syllable words by adding ed or es (repeated, caresses).

4. *Add the two factors computed above and multiply by 0.4.* The product is the minimum grade level at which the writing is easily read.

Application of the Gunning Fog Index is illustrated with the following paragraph:

In *general, construction* of *pictograms* follows the *general procedure* used in constructing bar charts. But two special rules should be followed. First, all of the picture units used must be of equal size. The *comparisons* must be made only on the basis of the number of *illustrations* used and never by *varying* the areas of the *individual* pictures used. The reason for this rule is *obvious:* the human eye is grossly *inadequate* in *comparing areas* of *geometric* designs. Second, the pictures or symbols used must *appropriately* depict the *quantity* to be illustrated. A *comparison* of the navies of the world, for *example*, might make use of *miniature* ship drawings. Cotton *production* might be shown by bales of cotton. *Obviously*, the drawings used must be *immediately interpreted* by the reader.

Inspection of the paragraph reveals these facts. It has ten sentences and 129 words for an average sentence length of 13. Of the total of 129 words, 26 are considered to be hard words. Thus, the percentage of hard words is 20. From these data, the Gunning Fog Index is computed as follows:

Average sentence length	13
Percentage of hard words	20
Total	33
Multiply by	.4
Grade level of readership	13.2

Readability formulas are widely used in business today. Perhaps the reason for their popularity is the glitter of their apparent mathematical exactness. Or perhaps they are popular because they reduce to simple and workable formulas the most complex work of writing. Whatever the reason, the wise writer will look at the formulas objectively.

Unquestionably, these formulas have been a boon to improving clarity in business writing. They emphasize the main causes of failure in written communication. And they provide a convenient check and measure of the level of one's writing. But they also have some limitations.

The most serious limitation of the formulas is the primer style of writing that can result from a slavish use of them. Overly simple words and a monotonous succession of short sentences make dull reading. Dull reading doesn't hold the reader's attention. And without the reader's attention, there can be little communication.

Perhaps the formulas are most useful to unskilled writers. By intelligent use of the formulas, unskilled writers may at least be able to improve the communication quality of their work. Their writing style, which was poor to begin with, does not suffer. Skilled writers, on the other hand, can violate the formulas and still communicate. Charles Dickens, for example, was a master in communicating in clear yet long sentences. So was Pope. And so are some business writers. Because most business writers fall somewhere between these extreme quality groups, the wisest course for them is to use the formulas as general guides. But never will a formula replace the clear and logical thinking that is the underpinning of all clear writing.

Index

This book has been set VideoComp in 10 and 9 point Electra, leaded 2 points for text, 1 point for extracts. Part titles are 18 point Franklin Gothic italic; chapter numbers and titles are 36 point Franklin Gothic and Electra respectively. The overall size of the type page is 36½ by 47 picas.

PUNCTUATION

APOSTROPHE: Use the apostrophe to
Apos 1   show possession
Apos 2   mark omissions in contractions

BRACKETS: Use Brackets to
Bkts   set off author's words in quotations

COLON: Use the colon to
Cln 1   introduce formal statements
          Do not use the colon
Cln 2   when it breaks thought flow

COMMA: Use the comma
Cma 1   to separate clauses connected by and, but,
          or, not, for
Cma 2.1   to separate items in series
Cma 2.2   to separate adjectives in series
Cma 3   to set off nonrestrictive modifiers
Cma 4.1   to set off parenthetic expressions
Cma 4.2   to set off apposition words
Cma 4.3   to set off parenthetic words
Cma 4.4   to set off units in a date
Cma 5.1   to set off a subordinate clause preceding a
          main clause
Cma 5.2   after introductory verbal phrases
Cma 6.1   only for good reason
Cma 6.1.1 not between subject and verb
Cma 6.1.2 not before second part of a compound
          predicate

DASH: Use the dash
Dsh   to show interruption or emphasis

EXCLAMATION MARK: Use the exclamation mark to
Ex   show strong feeling

HYPHEN: Use the hyphen
Hpn 1   to show word division
Hpn 2   between compound words
Hpn 2.1   not between proper names used as com-
          pound adjectives
Hpn 2.2   not between words that just follow each
          other

ITALICS: Use italics for
Ital 1   book titles
Ital 2   foreign words and phrases
Ital 3   a word, letter, or figure used as its own name

PARENTHESES: Use parentheses to
Paren   set off parenthetic words

PERIOD: Use the period
Pd 1   at ends of declarative sentences
Pd 2   after abbreviations or initials
Pd 3   in a series (ellipsis) to show omissions

QUESTION MARK: Use the question mark
Q   at the end of a question

QUOTATION MARK: Use quotation marks
QM 1   to enclose someone's exact words
QM 2   enclose a quotation within a quotation with
          single marks
QM 3   Commas and periods go inside quotation
          marks. Other marks go outside, except
          when they apply to the quoted part
QM 4   Enclose titles of parts of a publication in
          quotation marks. Type book titles in italics

SEMICOLON: Use the semicolon
SC 1   to separate independent clauses not joined
          by a conjunction
SC 2   to separate other long independent clauses
SC 3   to separate items in a list whose items con-
          tain commas
SC 4   only between equal units

GRAMMAR

AA   Do not use adjectives for adverbs
Agmt SV   Nouns must agree with their verbs in
          number
AN   Do not use adverbial clauses as noun
          clauses
Awk   Avoid awkward writing
Dng   Avoid dangling modifiers
Frag   Avoid sentence fragments
Pn 1   Pronouns should refer clearly to an antece-
          dent
Pn 2   Pronoun and antecedent should agree in
          number
Pn 3   Use the correct case of pronouns
Prl   Express equal thoughts in parallel (equal)
          grammatical form
Tns 1   Use present tense for happenings now
Tns 2   Use past tense for past happenings
Tns 3   Use the past participle (having been) to
          show happening earlier than governing
          verb. Use present participle (being) to show
          happenings later than governing verb
Tns 4   Verbs in main clauses govern verbs in
          subordinate clauses
WU   Use words correctly

NUMBERS

No 1   Generally, spell out numbers ten and under;
          use figures for others
No 2   Spell out numbers that begin a sentence
No 3   In comparisons, keep numbers in same form
No 4   When two series appear in one sentence,
          spell out one and use numerals for the other
No 5   Use figures for days of the month when the
          month precedes the day

SPELLING AND CAPITALIZATION

Sp   Spell correctly. Consult a dictionary
Cap   Capitalize proper names, words beginning
          sentences